CW01203320

Kharkov 1942

**Anatomy of a Military Disaster
Through Soviet Eyes**

*In memory of an able historian and fine friend,
Colonel Paul Adair, British Army Retired,
who worked so hard to reveal the human dimension of
the war on the Eastern Front.*

Kharkov 1942

**Anatomy of a Military Disaster
Through Soviet Eyes**

David M. Glantz

IAN ALLAN
Publishing

First published 1998

ISBN 0 7110 2562 2

All rights reserved. No part of this book
may be reproduced or transmitted in any
form or by any means, electronic or
mechanical, including photocopying,
recording or by any information storage and
retrieval system, without permission from
Publisher in writing.

© 1998 David M. Glantz

The right of David M. Glantz to be identified
as author of this work has been asserted
by him in accordance with the Copyright,
Designs and Patents Act 1988.

Published by Ian Allan Publishing

an imprint of Ian Allan Publishing Ltd, Terminal House,
Station Approach, Shepperton, Surrey TW17 8AS.
Printed by Ian Allan Printing Ltd at its works at
Riverdene, Molesey Road, Hersham, England.

Code: 9805/A3

Picture credits

All pictures in this book are from the author's collection unless credited otherwise.

Front cover: **Soviet tank assault in the Kharkov region.**

Back cover, top: **Soviet troops erecting anti-tank obstacles.**

Back cover, bottom: **German armoured units break through Soviet lines.** *IWM HU40225*

CONTENTS

List of Appendicies	6
List of Maps	7
Glossary and Abbreviations	8
Preface	11
Introduction	15
1 Prelude	17
2 Planning	21
Overview: The Strategic Debate	21
Overview: The Soviet Assessment	37
3 Area of Operations	59
Strategic Aspects	59
Operational and Tactical Aspects	61
4 Opposing Forces	65
Soviet Order of Battle	65
Soviet Force Structure	69
The Southwestern Direction Leaders	75
The Southwestern Direction Forces	80
German Order of Battle	104
German Force Structure	106
Correlation of Forces	111
5 The Course of Combat Operations	114
First Stage: Southwestern Front Offensive	114
Second Stage: Southwestern and Southern Front Defensive Battles in the Barvenkovo Salient	164
6 Costs and Consequences	218
The Price of Combat	218
The Consequences	219
Brief Results and Conclusions	226
7 Conclusions	239
Notes to Chapters	248
Appendices	252
Select Bibliography	280
Index	283

LIST OF APPENDICIES

1	Report No 00137/op of the Southwestern Direction High Command, 22 March	252
2	Report of the Southwestern Direction High Command to the Supreme High Command, 30 March	255
3	Operational Plan of Southwestern Direction Forces for the occupation of the Kharkov Region, 10 April	256
4	From Operational Directive No 00275 of the Southwestern Direction High Command to Southwestern Front Forces, 28 April	258
5	From Operational Directive No 00177 of the Southern Front Command concerning right flank defence, 6 April	261
6	Report of the Southwestern Direction High Command to the Stavka VGK concerning the offensive, 15 May	262
7	Combat Order No 0140/op of the Southwestern Direction Headquarters to the Commander, Southern Front, 17 May	264
8	Report of the Southwestern Direction High Command to the Stavka VGK concerning the enemy offensive, 17 May	264
9	Combat Report No 0119 of the Southwestern Front Commander to the Stavka VGK concerning combat operations, 19 May	265
10	Report of the Military Council of the Southwestern Direction to the Stavka VGK concerning combat operations, 19 May	266
11	Notes of a conversation between the Chief of the Red Army General Staff and the Commander-in-Chief, Southwestern Direction, 19 May	267
12	Notes of a conversation between the Chief of the Red Army General Staff and the Commander-in-Chief, Southwestern Direction, 19 May	268
13	Combat Order No 00320 of the Southwestern Direction High Command to the Commander of 6th Army forces, and the Commander of the Army Group, 19 May	268
14	Combat Order No 0143/op of the Southwestern Direction High Command to the commander of Southern Front and 57th Army forces, 19 May	269
15	Combat Report No 00323/op of the Southwestern Direction High Command to the Stavka VGK concerning the offensive since 12 May and the plan for subsequent operations, 21 May	270
16	Extract from a Southwestern Front Military Council Order to 38th Army, 22 May	271
17	Information concerning the losses of Southwestern Direction forces during the period of battle on the Kharkov Axis, 10–31 May	272
18	Soviet order of battle (participating formations) and abbreviated German order of battle (initial)	273
19	Postscript: The Fate of the Survivors	275

LIST OF MAPS

1	The Barvenkovo-Lozovaia Operation, 18–31 January 1942	19
2	Plan 'Blau'	23
3	Situation on the Eastern Front, April 1942	39
4	Operational Plan	45
5	Strategic axes in the Soviet Union	60
6	The Kharkov region: the Northern Sector	62
7	The Kharkov region: the Southern Sector	63
8	Force dispositions north of Kharkov, 11 May	67
9	Force dispositions south of Kharkov, 11 May	68
10	Combat on 12 May in the Northern Sector	115
11	Combat on 13 May in the Northern Sector	125
12	Combat on 14 May in the Northern Sector	131
13	Combat on 12 May in the Southern Sector	133
14	Combat on 13 May in the Southern Sector	135
15	Combat on 14 May in the Southern Sector	138
16	Combat on 15 May in the Northern Sector	144
17	Combat on 16 May in the Northern Sector	157
18	Combat on 15 May in the Southern Sector	159
19	Combat on 16 May in the Southern Sector	162
20	Combat on 17 May in the Southern Sector	170
21	Combat on 17 May in the Northern Sector	176
22	Combat on 18 May in the Southern Sector	182
23	Combat on 18 May in the Northern Sector	186
24	Combat on 19 May in the Southern Sector	189
25	Combat on 19 May in the Northern Sector	193
26	Combat on 20 May in the Northern Sector	195
27	The situation 21–24 May in the Northern Sector	196
28	Combat on 20 May in the Southern Sector	199
29	Combat on 21 May in the Southern Sector	200
30	Combat on 22 May in the Southern Sector	203
31	Combat on 23 May in the Southern Sector	206
32	Combat on 24 May in the Southern Sector	208
33	Combat on 25 May in the Southern Sector	211
34	Combat on 26 May in the Southern Sector	213
35	Combat on 27 May in the Southern Sector	215
36	Summary map of the Kharkov Operation (12–29 May 1942)	229
37	The Summer-Autumn Campaign, 1942	243

GLOSSARY AND ABBREVIATIONS

A	Army
AAR	Army artillery regiment/Assault aviation regiment/Anti-aircraft artillery regiment
ATAR	Anti-tank artillery regiment
ATBn	Anti-tank battalion
B	Brigade
Bde	Brigade
Bn	Battalion
CAR	Corps artillery regiment
CC	Cavalry corps
CD	Cavalry division
CR	Cavalry regiment
D	Division
Direction	Strategic headquarters of forces operating on a given axis
Excluding	Not included in a force's sector
FAR	Fighter-aviation regiment
FBAR	Fighter-bomber aviation regiment
Front	Operational strategic formation
GA	Guards army
GAR	Gun artillery regiment
GCC	Guards cavalry corps
GCD	Guards cavalry division
Gds	Guards
GdsMBn	Guards mortar battalion
GdsMR	Guards mortar regiment
GKO	State Defence Committee
GMC	Guards mechanised corps
GMRB	Guards motorised rifle brigade
GRD	Guards rifle division
GTA	Guards tank army
GTB	Guards tank brigade
GTC	Guards tank corps
HAR	Howitzer artillery regiment
ID	Infantry division
IR	Infantry regiment
JD	Jaeger (light) division
Kampfgruppe	(plural Kampfgruppen) lit: 'Battle Group'. Used to cover platoon, company and battalion-level task forces

KP	command post
LAR	Light artillery regiment
MC	Mechanised corps
MD	Motorised division
MOT	Motorised
MRB	Motorised rifle brigade
Pz	Panzer
PzA	Panzer army
PzD	Panzer division
PzR	Panzer regiment
RAG	Reconnaissance aviation group
RB	Rifle brigade
RC	Rifle corps
RD	Rifle division
RGK	Reserve of the High Command
RVGK	Stavka reserve
SA	Shock army
SecD	Security division
SRBA	Short range bomber aviation regiment
Stavka	Lit: staff. Shorthand for Headquarters of the Soviet Supreme High Command
Stavka GK	High Command
Stavka VK	Supreme Command
Stavka VGK	Supreme High Command
TB	Tank brigade
TBn	Tank battalion
TC	Tank corps

Notes

Maps: Numerals with no abbreviations attached are divisions (German and Soviet).

Force designations: Force designations adhere to national military standards. For example: Arabic numerals are used to designate Soviet armies and corps, German army numerical designations are spelled out, and German corps are designated by Roman numerals (including the interesting use of XXXX for fortieth), as is standard in German unit records.

Transliteration note: In general, this volume employs the Library of Congress transliteration system. In some maps and quotations, other transliteration systems will be encountered. Place names containing ia, iu or ie may be written ya, yu and ye (or in German style).

Style note: The Soviet General Staff Study and all Soviet archival documents are differentiated in the text by use of a background tint. These have been translated as precisely as possible, but in order to keep them readable some editing has been necessary.

PREFACE

Historians and laymen alike are familiar with many of the great battles on the Eastern Front. The names Moscow, Stalingrad, Kursk, Belorussia (Belarus today) and Berlin evoke vivid images of the fierce four-year struggle between the vaunted Wehrmacht (German Army) and the massive Red Army. In their memoirs famous German generals, such as Guderian, Mellenthin, Balck and von Manstein, recounted and extolled the exploits of bold commanders, daring tank leaders and tactically skilled soldiers struggling simultaneously against a numerous foe and a meddling political leader — Hitler. Their counterparts in the Red Army, such as Zhukov, Vasilevsky, Katukov, Batov and countless others, related their wartime experiences as well. In a view from the foxhole, private soldiers such as Guy Sajer and numerous Russians described the grandeur, brutalities and unmitigated horrors of the war. Finally, legions of historians and military 'buffs' on both sides wrote volumes on wartime campaigns, battles and operations.

Despite this wealth of war literature and the immense amount of fact it contains, a certain mythology continues to envelop the history of the war. In the West, until recently and with few exceptions, historical accounts have been almost exclusively German in their orientation, focus and perception. As a result, most authors and readers alike have accepted as truth German arguments that German military defeat ultimately occurred in spite of military skill and prowess, solely because Hitler harboured excessively grandiose aims and perpetually meddled in operational and tactical military decision-making. Quite naturally, therefore, most German war histories focused on events to mid-1943 and dismissed subsequent military operations as the inevitable disastrous products of Hitler's flawed personality and faulty military policy and strategy.

Soviet military accounts reek of their own mythology. Harsh and restrictive political and ideological constraints stifled Soviet research and writing on the war. The Marxist interpretation of history in general, and Soviet belief in the inevitable victory of socialism in particular, infused all operational history and reflected Communist ideology and the Soviet world view. Consequently, all military memoirs, operational accounts and unit histories of the 'Great Patriotic War' underlined the inevitability of Soviet (socialist) victory. Only the most skilled or privileged writer could hope to escape the stifling embrace of this mythology to any extent. Like their German counterparts, what they wrote was not necessarily incorrect. Dates, chronology, the general course of events, many operational details and the ultimate outcome of individual and collective operations were usually accurate. Despite these factual truths, the facts they included were highly selective; they often twisted their interpretations and they constantly obscured the catastrophic costs of Soviet victories and defeats. Most important, they routinely concealed the most painful and unpleasant aspects of the war; in particular the political blunders and numerous military defeats which punctuated the agonisingly slow wartime education of the Red Army and its subsequent march to victory.

Over time, Soviet war histories tended to become more candid as both the political leadership and everyday circumstances in the Soviet Union evolved. Internal political disputes and concurrent reshuffling of internal military commands, which characterised the period after Stalin's death in 1953, strongly affected the wartime reputa-

Kharkov, 1942

tions of many military leaders, including Zhukov and Konev. After 1958, during Communist Party First Secretary N. S. Khrushchev's de-Stalinisation programme, a new wave of disclosures enhanced the reputation of Khrushchev and his circle of supporters at the expense of Stalin and many of his former cronies. Again, in the 1970s and 1980s, a new spate of revelations had a similar effect on the reputations of Brezhnev and his wartime associates.

In some instances, Soviet leaders themselves judged it in the national interest to expose wartime problems. For example, beginning in 1957, Soviet military scholars began detailed study of the role of strategic surprise during the initial period of war. This study produced the first candid revelations concerning the Soviet Union's lack of readiness for war in June 1941. At the time, the issue of strategic surprise was particularly relevant to current and future Soviet national security in the new nuclear age. Throughout this entire period, military educators argued for more accurate historical accounts so that present and future generations of Soviet military leaders could be educated more effectively. In addition to these cynical and practical reasons for fostering historical candour, honest historians made periodic, but often futile, attempts to improve the overall credibility of Soviet military history.

The most visible aspect of this general Soviet lack of historical candour was the penchant for ignoring (at least in public) the most important negative aspects of war; in particular, planning failures, major military defeats and catastrophic wartime manpower losses. Although it is rather easy to conceal manpower losses by simply ignoring them entirely, as the Soviets have done until very recently, it is more difficult to conceal defeat. One army's notorious defeat is another army's glorious victory, and the victor will inevitably publicise his victory. To avoid complete loss of credibility, the loser must inevitably 'come clean' and at least rationalise his defeat. This imperative has impelled Soviet historians to address only their most obvious military defeats.

Other significant features of combat on the German-Soviet Front, however, made it possible for the Soviets to conceal many of their defeats in the Great Patriotic War. The immense scale, intensity and ferocity of the war conditioned the Germans to expect combat with overwhelming numbers of Soviet soldiers at all times and in virtually every front sector. At the same time, the sheer quantity and savage intensity of Soviet offensive actions, coupled with countless Soviet military failures, made it exceedingly difficult, if not impossible, for the Germans to determine ultimate Soviet intent and to judge which operations were most significant. The context of already famous or infamous large-scale Soviet military successes, such as Moscow and Stalingrad, often masked equally large-scale Soviet military failures.

Through study of massive quantities of German archival materials and extensive, newly released Soviet war archives it is now feasible to identify and fill in many of the existing gaps in the history of the war and to reconstruct painstakingly a more accurate mosaic. The most significant of these gaps are Soviet wartime offensive failures. This study addresses one of the first catastrophic defeats the Soviets attempted to conceal: the defeat at Kharkov in May 1942.

Although the Kharkov operation is a fascinating military case study in its own right, it also provides, in microcosm, a classic example of how the Soviets have approached their major military defeats while writing their military history. Until the early 1960s, Soviet military historians wrote virtually nothing about the operation. Before 1960 their war histories mentioned defeat at Kharkov in May 1942, but provided little detail and treated the defeat as a minor but unpleasant prelude to the more famous German march toward Stalingrad. In the early 1960s, however, a variety of conditions arose

Preface

demanding that they pay greater attention to the operation. First, so many Germans had written about the operation that it was no longer prudent for Soviet historians to maintain complete silence about it. Second, in the interests of de-Stalinisation and his own political career, Party First Secretary N. S. Khrushchev considered it expedient to speak more candidly about Stalin's failures. Khrushchev himself had served as Military Commissar for the Southwestern Front, which had suffered such a grievous defeat at Kharkov, and the earliest accounts of the operations blamed Khrushchev for the defeat. Given Khrushchev's new political position, he deemed it essential to expose Stalin's key role in the operation and, coincidentally, to exonerate himself and his military colleagues from blame. Consequently, a reassessment of the Kharkov operation became one facet of Khrushchev's 1960s de-Stalinisation programme.

When the new Soviet eight-volume History of the Great Patriotic War appeared in the early 1960s, the Kharkov defeat became historical fact. Henceforth, the Kharkov operation became a legitimate topic for treatment in general histories, personal memoirs and unit histories. Not coincidentally, the Kharkov operation became the 'Potemkin Village' of Soviet military wartime failures. Soon, Soviet military works included more detailed information on the operation.

Marshal of the Soviet Union, K. S. Moskalenko, former commander of 38th Army during the Kharkov operation, an associate of Khrushchev, and former commander of the Moscow Military District, was the first to publish an expanded account of the operation. In 1953, during the tense days immediately following the death of Stalin, Moskalenko, while Moscow Air Defence commander, had foiled attempts by NKVD chief Beria to launch a pro-Stalinist (and anti-Khrushchev) coup. In the 1960s Moskalenko was rewarded for his previous loyal service by being permitted to write a memoir marked by its candour regarding hitherto prohibited military aspects of the war. His chapter on the Kharkov operation represented a major step forward in coverage and laid much of the blame for failure at Stalin's feet. Several years later, in 1973, Marshal I. Kh. Bagramian, former Southwestern Direction Chief of Staff and close associate of Khrushchev during the operation, published his memoirs. Stalin had identified Bagramian as one of the primary scapegoats for the Kharkov defeat. Like Moskalenko, Bagramian disclosed many new aspects of the operation and tended to blame Stalin and the Stavka for the defeat.

Thereafter, numerous articles on the Kharkov operation appeared in Soviet military journals. Despite the increased attention paid to this military failure, no full-length and exhaustive military analysis of the operation has yet appeared. The Kharkov operation remains a monument to Soviet historical candour, held up to Westerners as evidence of Soviet willingness to deal frankly with defeat as well as victory. By emphasising this single case, Soviet historians continue to conceal major aspects of their military history without fear of challenge.

During the latter years of the Soviet state and just prior to its fall, Soviet President and Communist Party First Secretary M. S. Gorbachev resumed the policy of *glasnost* (openness) inaugurated over 20 years before by his reforming predecessor, Khrushchev. Gorbachev again loosened the shackles which fettered Soviet military history. He permitted the unearthing and release of extensive archival materials on the war and once again encouraged historians to address more unpleasant aspects of their military history. Among the newly released materials were formerly classified studies prepared by the Soviet Army General Staff during and after the war. These studies have expanded our wealth of knowledge about some, but not all, operations because the release of materials was, as has always been the case, selective. It did include, how-

Kharkov, 1942

ever, the first exhaustive and candid account of the May 1942 Kharkov operation. Ironically, this last great release of archival materials took place during the dying days of the Soviet state. Since the fall of the Soviet Empire, however, release of archival materials has measurably slowed. One hopes the light of candour lit by Gorbachev will not be extinguished in a modern and more democratic Russian Federation.

The formerly classified 1951 Soviet General Staff study of the Kharkov operation serves as the nucleus of this book.[1] Around this nucleus are arrayed a wide variety of Soviet and German sources that fill out the General Staff account and give it greater meaning and character. These sources include formerly classified documentation related to the operation, including intelligence assessments, key operational assessments, periodic combat orders and private official correspondence between key figures at those headquarters which planned and conducted the operation. Finally, the intelligence and operational summary maps which accompanied the study, and which incorporate German archival materials, have been converted into new, clearer maps detailing the overall strategic situation and the daily situation in main operational sectors.

To preserve the authenticity of the original General Staff study, I have incorporated its text into this volume (with a background tint), but have interspersed into it appropriate additional materials from German and other sources. The translation is as close as is practicable — to make the text readable and intelligible, it has been closely edited. The Soviet Army General Staff prepared these studies in strict military format with obligatory references to political context and the decisive role of the Communist Party. As stilted as these seem to Western readers, I have left many of these references in the text as the harmless digressions which they actually were. They in no way detract from the seriousness and accuracy of the analysis. Another fault of these staff studies is that they are depersonalised. No commanders' names appear, and the various units and formations involved in the operation, manoeuvre and fight in seemingly headless and impersonal fashion. To add personality to this otherwise faceless military machine, I have added the commanders' names where appropriate.

Virtually all Soviet classified operational accounts of the German-Soviet War inevitably depersonalise combat to preserve officers' reputations. This reinforces the perception of most German veterans and postwar Westerners that the Red Army was an immense faceless mass of expendable manpower. Although Soviet soldiers did seem expendable and millions died, they undoubtedly endured war in the same fashion as their German counterparts and deserve recognition for their courage and unparalleled suffering. Therefore, I have included extensive new materials about the men involved in this fateful operation — from those at the top who planned and conducted it, to those who fought and died in it, and those who survived.

This is primarily a Soviet-oriented account of the Kharkov operation. Countless German officers and historians have documented the battle. I have incorporated that work together with extensive new materials from the German archives. To improve the work's credibility and satisfy the curiosity of the expert and professional military scholar, I have included daily maps of the operation and appendices which contain complete translations of all key operational documents, a thorough Soviet order of battle and a brief word about the fates of those who survived the operation.

Besides my personal dedication in this volume, history requires that the work be appropriately dedicated to those soldiers, in particular Soviet, who died in combat or subsequent captivity. It serves as a memorial to those tens of thousands whose government until very recently forgot both them and their sacrifice.

INTRODUCTION

DESCRIPTION OF SOUTHWESTERN FRONT FORCE OPERATIONS ON THE KHARKOV AXIS (DIRECTION) IN MAY 1942

This study clarifies the Southwestern Front offensive operation from 12 to 20 May 1942 along the Kharkov axis and the defensive battle of Southwestern and Southern Front forces to repel German Army Group South's counter-stroke against the flank of Southwestern Front's main shock grouping in the Barvenkovo bridgehead from 17 to 28 May.

The Southwestern Front operation being examined is an example of an unsuccessful operation. Despite having everything necessary to destroy the Germans' large Kharkov grouping, the Front did not execute the missions assigned by the Supreme High Command.

Comrade Stalin teaches us that:

'In the history of states, in the history of countries and in the history of armies there have been times when success and victory were possible, but went unnoticed by leaders who therefore were not able to take advantage of them, and so the armies suffered defeat.'[1]

Unwarranted deviations from the plan of operation, poor organisation of Front co-operation, poor reconnaissance and a number of operational errors on the part of the command resulted in Soviet forces suffering a serious defeat in the south in May 1942, and their being forced back beyond the Northern Donets [River].

The unsuccessful outcome of the Southwestern Front's offensive operation and the defensive battle of Southwestern and Southern Front forces in the Barvenkovo bridgehead had a negative effect on the course of combat events in 1942.

This study represents the first attempt to systematise historical data about this operation; it does not claim to be an exhaustive analysis. Factual material cited in the description makes it possible for the reader to judge the particulars of planning, organising and conducting an offensive operation under complex conditions of fighting for the initiative, understand the operation's concept and draw instructive conclusions from it.

The following issues are of particular interest for research:
- organisation of co-operation among large formations in a Front operation in the offence and defence
- operational security of a Front offensive operation
- co-operation between contiguous Fronts
- use of combat arms and large mobile formations in a Front offensive operation
- matériel-technical support of forces during offensives from bridgeheads

1
PRELUDE

To military planners in the Stavka (the headquarters of the Soviet Supreme High Command) mid-May 1942 seemed to be a propitious time to launch their new series of spring offensives. The Kharkov region seemed the best place to strike. Precisely one year before, on 15 May 1941, when Soviet intelligence organs had detected a menacing German force buildup along the Soviet Union's western borders, Gen G. K. Zhukov, then Chief of the Red Army General Staff, had presented Party First Secretary I. V. Stalin with a proposed plan of operations designed to pre-empt the anticipated German attack.[1] Zhukov's warning of war went unheeded, Stalin rejected his proposal for commencing a preventive war and just over one month later the devastating German offensive commenced.

The ensuing year was fraught with disaster for the Soviet Union and the Red Army. The German armies, which struck on 22 June, achieved total surprise. Spearheaded by the armoured forces of four finely-trained Panzer groups, they smashed Soviet forces in the border regions and penetrated rapidly into the depths of the Soviet Union. By December 1941 immense deep mobile operations propelled German forces to the outskirts of Leningrad, Moscow and Rostov. The unprecedented fury and success of the German onslaught inflicted catastrophic losses on the Red Army, destroying or capturing a large proportion of its peacetime forces and grievously damaging Soviet military and civilian morale. By Herculean efforts the Soviet Union was able to mobilise the vast military potential of her large population and commit it to battle against the more tactically skilled German Army. Only this massive mobilisation and over-ambition on the part of the German High Command enabled the Soviet High Command to reverse the fortune of war before disaster became complete.

In November and December 1941, the Stavka marshalled and committed to combat massive numbers of strategic reserves, halted the German advance at the gates of Leningrad, Moscow and Rostov, and launched desperate counter-offensives in all threatened sectors. The famous Moscow counter-offensive, begun in December 1941 and expanded in January 1942, revealed how overextended and vulnerable the conquering German hosts had become. In harsh winter fighting, German forces grudgingly gave ground in the face of the unexpectedly fierce Soviet onslaught. Only by the greatest exertions, after heavy losses and a severe blow to their inflated pride and excessive expectations, were the Germans finally able to bring the Soviet counter-offensive to a halt in late February 1942. Although the Soviets sought in vain to reinvigorate their offensive throughout the remainder of the winter, the exhortations of Hitler to hold fast and the stubborn tenacity of the hard-pressed German soldiers stemmed the Soviet tide. German forces, huddled in a bastion of salients and overlapping defensive positions west of Moscow and struggling with Soviet forces to their front and in their rear, watched anxiously as the Soviet offensive ebbed and flowed; they weathered the rigours of a paralysingly cold winter, while their commanders mentally conditioned themselves to complete Operation 'Barbarossa' in the spring.

In the southern Soviet Union, Soviet forces also achieved unexpected offensive suc-

Kharkov, 1942

cess. In November 1941 Soviet strategic reserves struck back at the advancing armour of von Kleist's First Panzer Group, then driving fast and hard on Rostov. Heavy attacks against von Kleist's northern flank forced the Germans to recoil and then conduct a fighting withdrawal to more secure defensive positions along the Mius River, west of Rostov. Emboldened by their success, the reinvigorated Soviet Southwestern and Southern Fronts tested von Kleist's defences along the Mius and then, in late January, shifted forces northward and struck the German flank along the Northern Donets River south of Kharkov in an attempt to penetrate into the Donbas region, pin down German forces in southern Russia against the shores of the Sea of Azov, and destroy them.

Exploiting the German crisis in the Moscow region, on 18 January the Soviet 6th, 57th, and 9th Armies struck German positions near Izium along the Northern Donets River south of Kharkov (see Map 1).[2] After tearing a gaping hole in German defences, Soviet infantry, ski troops and three exploiting cavalry corps raced deep into the German rear area. Although the Soviets were able to seize the key rail junctions of Lozovaia and Barvenkovo (after which the operation was named) and stretch the German defenders considerably, the Germans were able to exploit their forces' superior mobility to block and contain the Soviet advance short of its ultimate objectives. By 31 January defending German forces had contained the frustrated Soviets within the confines of the Barvenkovo bridgehead, a sizeable salient carved into German defensive positions on the west bank of the Northern Donets River, which jutted threateningly both toward Kharkov to the north and the Donbas in the south.

The Stavka learned important lessons from its winter experiences and resolved to exploit these lessons during renewed offensive action in the spring. Stalin and most of the Soviet senior military leadership were convinced that they had come close to producing total German military collapse. Just as the German High Command had believed in early December that the Soviets were down to literally their 'last battalions', in late winter so the Soviet High Command also believed that the commitment to battle of just a few more fresh divisions in January 1942 would have produced utter German defeat. The Soviet High Command also realised that its woeful lack of mobile armoured forces had contributed to the failure to destroy the Germans in the Moscow region and in the south. During counter-offensive action in both regions, the Soviets had committed to combat handfuls of individual tank brigades, several cavalry corps and lightly-armed airborne troops dropped in the German rear both to assist the Soviet infantry in penetrating German defences and to exploit offensive success into the German tactical and operational rear area. Experience clearly demonstrated that these light mobile forces were simply too fragile to accomplish these challenging missions, even against the battered remnants of German Panzer and motorised forces. Time after time Soviet brigades, regiments and even divisions (corps) of cavalry and airborne troops were frustrated by German platoon, company and battalion task forces (Kampfgruppen).

The Soviets were also aware that German ambition, whetted by recent high expectations and subsequent frustration, would prompt German renewal of offensive action. Vanity and over-optimism, however, drove the Soviets to assume that the damage inflicted by Soviet attacks in the winter would require massive German force refitting and preclude renewed German offensive action before early summer. Further, the Stavka was convinced that the renewed German assault would undoubtedly take place along the Moscow axis to seize what it perceived as the ultimate German objective, the Soviet capital.[3] Accordingly, the Soviets prepared deep and strong defences along the

1 Prelude

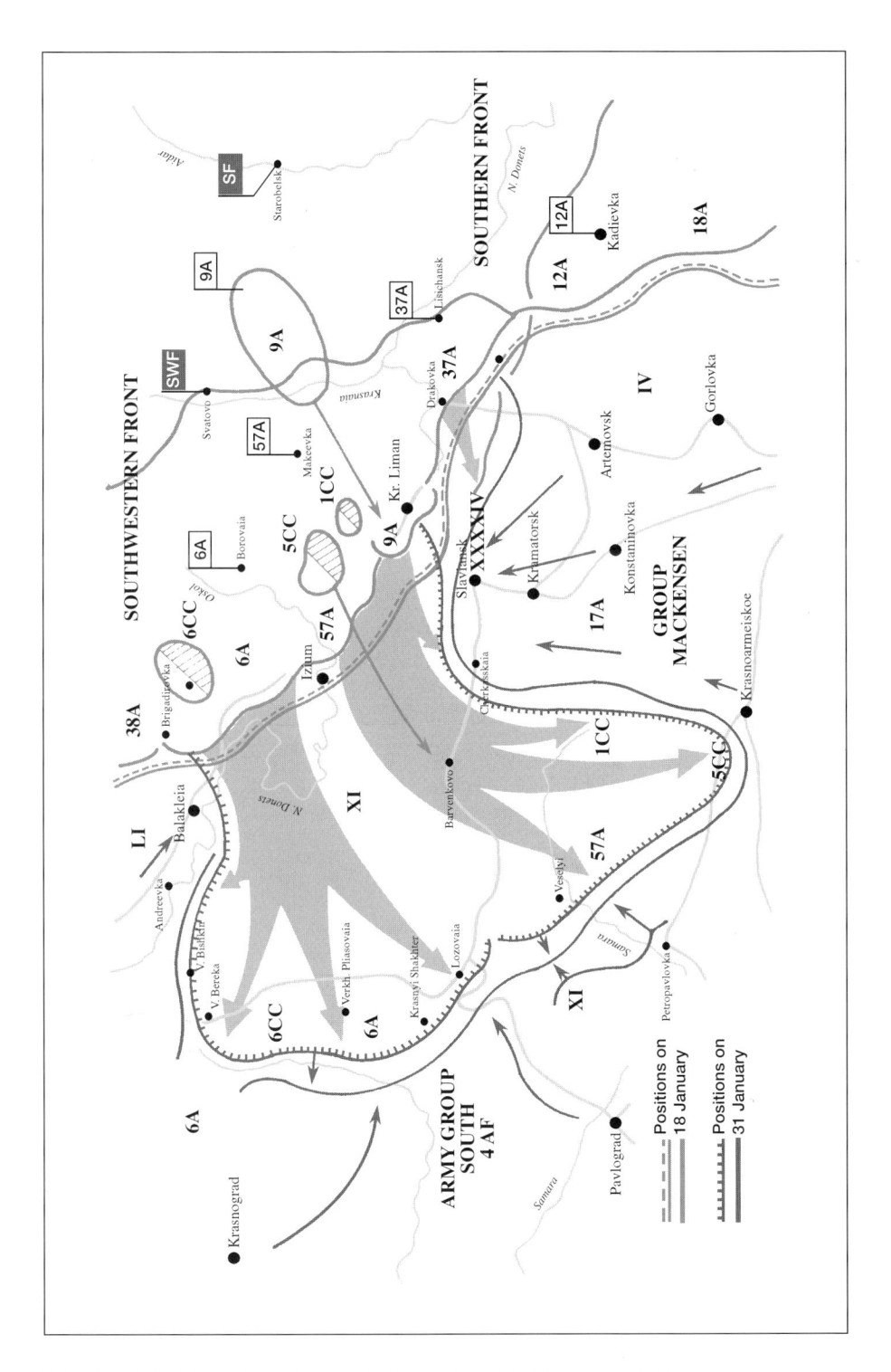

Map 1 — The Barvenkovo-Lozovaia Operation, 18–31 January 1942

Kharkov, 1942

approaches to Moscow and planned to do all in their power to exploit German weaknesses elsewhere to increase German vulnerabilities in the Moscow region.

All the while, the Stavka requested, collected and studied detailed reports from all command levels concerning the nature of recent combat; in particular, on the nature and causes of the many Soviet defeats. Based on General Staff analysis of these war experiences, the Stavka began remedying many of the causes of their winter failures. Most important was the task of equipping Soviet forces with an armoured capability which could cope successfully with German tank forces on the field of battle. Based on initial analysis of combat in 1941, it was abundantly clear to the General Staff that the fragile tank brigades created in autumn 1941 and the few tank divisions which remained from the once proud Soviet prewar mechanised corps, most of which the Germans had destroyed during the first few weeks of war, could not contend with German Panzer formations. Accordingly, in March 1942 the Stavka ordered the formation of new experimental armoured formations, which they first termed mechanised corps and then, in April 1942, renamed tank corps.[4] Unlike their prewar predecessors, which had been large, unwieldy and impossible to employ effectively in combat, these new tank corps were streamlined armoured formations, which the Soviets thought would be capable of countering German Panzer forces and sustaining deeper offensive action, either individually or in combination.

While the Red Army strove to remedy its structural weaknesses, Stalin, the Stavka and field force commanders and their staffs debated the proper course of action for Soviet forces in spring 1942. An air of unreality permeated these planning discussions as the Soviets stubbornly held to the simplistic view that German capabilities had been reduced significantly during the winter and that future German offensive action would inevitably be focused on Moscow. Few recalled the seemingly desperate plight of Soviet arms and fortunes which had prevailed just four months before.

2
PLANNING

Overview: The Strategic Debate

In early spring 1942, both the German High Command and the Stavka sought to regain the initiative and achieve strategic aims which had gone unfulfilled in 1941 and early 1942. Undeterred by their winter defeats, which many, including Hitler, explained away as the fruits of over-ambition, force over-extension and the rigours of an extraordinarily harsh winter, the Germans examined their strategic options and strove to define achievable strategic ends for their 1942 campaign. Inexorably, they reached the same conclusions that they had reached before the launch of Operation 'Barbarossa' in 1941. The Soviet Union, they believed, could be defeated militarily, but to do so they had to destroy the Red Army and seize key Soviet economic and political objectives. As had been the case in 1941, Hitler was convinced these objectives could best be achieved by focusing German efforts in southern Russia.

Ultimately, but after extensive and often heated debate within the German military hierarchy, Hitler defined German strategic objectives, operational priorities and the sequencing of future operations. He decided that Germany would resume the offensive in early summer, once her forces had been refitted following the heavy and costly winter fighting. Unlike 1941, when German armies had advanced along three strategic axes toward Leningrad, Moscow and Rostov, in 1942 German forces would concentrate in the south for an advance through the economically critical Donets Basin into the bend of the Don River west of Stalingrad and, then, south into the oil-rich Caucasus. A concerted advance into such an extensive region across relatively flat terrain, which seemed well suited to armoured operations, would permit the wholesale encirclement of numerous, less mobile Soviet forces in a large-scale repeat of the spectacular encirclements of summer 1941. Thereafter, with Soviet defensive strength weakened and her economic base undermined, German armies would loosen the tenuous Soviet grip on Leningrad and, perhaps, swing northward to seize the elusive prize of Moscow as well.

This was the genesis of Operation 'Blau' (Blue), the German strategic thrust which transfixed German planners' attention in spring 1942 and fuelled renewed over-optimism in the German High Command. It was also the plan that would ultimately produce even greater disasters for German forces than they had experienced during the waning days of Operation 'Barbarossa'. Hitler approved Plan 'Blau' on 5 April (see Map 2). The implementing document for 'Blau', Directive 41, established two objectives for the summer campaign: to destroy the Soviet's defensive strength 'conclusively' and, in so far as possible, to deprive it of the resources necessary to continue the war.[1] Specifically, Hitler sought to seize Leningrad and penetrate through the Donbas into the Don River bend and Caucasus region to gain access to precious raw materials, especially oil. The Germans accorded priority to the southern thrust.

Subsequently, while agonising over how they would achieve these ambitious ends, German planners prepared a series of planning variations — named 'Blau I, II, III, and IV' — based on the campaign's phasing.

Kharkov, 1942

Stalin and the Stavka, transfixed by the traumatic ebb and flow of combat in the Moscow region in late 1941 and early 1942, allowed the Moscow strategic axis to dominate their attention while planning for operations in the spring and summer of 1942. Stavka member Army Gen G. K. Zhukov recalled Stalin's strategic thinking:

'Stalin believed that in summer 1942 the Germans would be able to carry out large-scale offensive operations simultaneously along two strategic axes — most likely at Moscow and in the south of the country . . . he was above all concerned about the Moscow axis where over 70 German divisions operated.'[2]

The Chief of the Red Army General Staff, Gen B. M. Shaposhnikov, who understood the keen operational and tactical skill of the German Army and the danger it still posed to less skilled Soviet forces, argued for the cautious conduct of a strategic defence along the Moscow axis to wear down German forces before Soviet forces undertook an offensive of their own. Zhukov agreed with Shaposhnikov, but, being more impetuous as he had been in May 1941, argued for pre-emptive Soviet offensive action against German forces still locked in salient positions west of Moscow.

Chief of the Operations Department of the General Staff, Army Gen A. M. Vasilevsky agreed with his mentor Shaposhnikov and recognised that the most realistic mission for the Red Army in spring 1942 was to 'conduct a temporary strategic defence to wear the enemy down by defensive battles against prepared defences, disrupt German offensive plans, and create necessary conditions for a Red Army counter-offensive'.[3]

Despite the entreaties for caution of Zhukov, Shaposhnikov and Vasilevsky — his three principal strategic advisors — and egged on periodically by more bellicose commanders at lower echelons, Stalin permitted over-optimism to rule his final decision.

In his memoirs, Vasilevsky later explained the rationale for the ultimate Stavka decision as to how to conduct the summer campaign. All senior Soviet planners recognised that, although the Germans had been repulsed at Moscow during the winter, their 70 divisions deployed along the approaches to the city posed a deadly threat to the Soviet capital. Moreover, all Stavka members and most subordinate Front commanders firmly believed that the main German attack in late spring or summer would be against Moscow. The question, however, was how best to defeat this German thrust and regain the offensive momentum lost by the Red Army during the depths of winter. Stalin's principal advisors, particularly the General Staff officers, feared that premature Soviet action would only play into German hands by offering vulnerable Soviet military shock groups up for sacrifice against skilled, rested and refitted German mobile forces. Then, once Soviet shock power had been dissipated in costly offensive action, the Germans could repeat their performance of summer 1941 — but in 1942 from positions far forward of those they occupied during the previous year.

Stalin, however, turned many of these arguments on their heads. His argument was that early offensive action could catch German forces by surprise, capitalise on German apprehensions still lingering in the wake of their winter defeat and strike German forces before they had time to complete their spring rest and refitting. In the event that the Germans planned strategic action along the Moscow axis, Stalin argued that successful Soviet action there or elsewhere would inevitably weaken the German main effort. Zhukov had promoted pre-emptive action in May 1941. Now, emboldened by the positive results of the recent winter offensive, Stalin accepted Zhukov's general premise that some sort of pre-emptive action would be beneficial. However, he

2 Planning

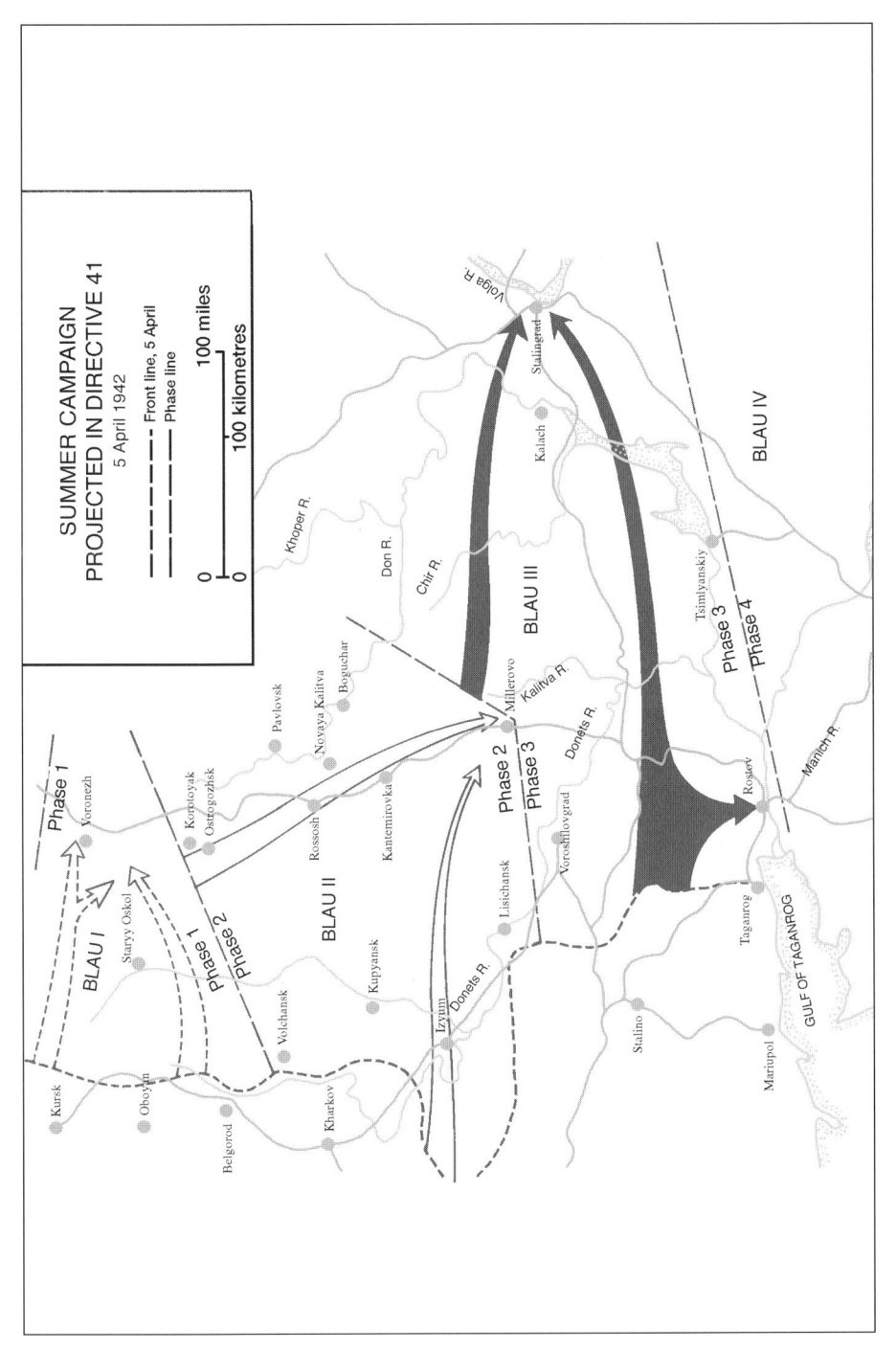

Map 2 — Plan 'Blau'.
Note: Based on a map from *Moscow to Stalingrad: Decision in the East*,
Earl F. Ziemke and Magna E. Bauer

Kharkov, 1942

rejected Zhukov's choice of the Moscow region as the suitable place to conduct these operations.

After listening to and accepting many of the fundamental arguments of his principal political and military advisors, Stalin's initial guidance to the Stavka and General Staff was to prepare the Red Army to conduct an 'active strategic defence.'[4] Disregarding the advice of Shaposhnikov, Vasilevsky and other General Staff members, however, he ordered the General Staff and Front commands to plan and conduct 'local' offensives in seven other Front sectors stretching from the Baltic Sea to the Black Sea, specifically in the Crimea, and the regions around Kharkov, Lgov-Kursk, Smolensk, Leningrad and Demiansk, where he perceived the Germans to be weakest. Expanded offensive operations in southern Russia appealed to Stalin because during the winter Soviet forces there had achieved striking successes, in particular near Rostov and Kharkov. So transfixed was Stalin by prospects for success in the Kharkov region that he ordered renewed offensive action in the region in early March, as a prelude to future, more extensive activity.

In early March the Stavka issued attack orders to Southwestern Direction headquarters, whose forces had defeated the Germans at Rostov in November 1941 and had penetrated into the Donbas in January 1942. Carrying out these orders, on 7 March Lt-Gen K. S. Moskalenko's 38th Army of Marshal S. K. Timoshenko's Southwestern Front struck German defensive positions between Staryi Saltov and Pechenegi along the Northern Donets River east of Kharkov. In heavy fighting, Moskalenko's forces gained a foothold across the river. Subsequently, after four days of combat, 38th Army troops expanded the bridgehead to a depth of up to 8km but, although fighting lasted until early April, that was as far as Moskalenko's troops could advance. Meanwhile, to the south, Southwestern Front's 6th Army attacked German forces defending Balakleia on the eastern bank of the Northern Donets River, but with less success. The Germans held on to Balakleia and continued to defend a bridgehead on the east bank of the Northern Donets between Chuguev and Balakleia. This offensive success, while local in nature and clearly limited, captured Stalin's attention and reinforced his preconceived notions about what could be achieved in the future by an even stronger Soviet force in the Kharkov region.[5] It also indicated to Timoshenko how he might conduct future large-scale operations. Timoshenko and his staff were fascinated by offensive possibilities from the Staryi Saltov and Barvenkovo bridgeheads north and south of Kharkov, but because of the earlier difficulties they had encountered trying to collapse the German Chuguev bridgehead, they avoided that key salient in their offensive plans, to their ultimate discomfiture.

In early March 1942, Stalin ordered the Directions' headquarters to prepare reports based on Stavka strategic guidance, which would provide Direction perspectives on the strategic and operational situation in their respective Front sectors and Direction commanders' recommendations for action during the spring-summer campaign. Soon after Stalin's order, the Southwestern Direction's Military Council (Soviet) met at Direction headquarters in Voronezh to prepare their report to Stalin and the Stavka.[6] It consisted of the Direction (and also Southwestern Front) Commander Marshal Timoshenko, Chief of the Direction's Operational Group Lt-Gen I. Kh. Bagramian and Direction Military Commissar N. S. Khrushchev, joined by Lt-Gen P. I. Bodin, the Southwestern Front Chief of Staff. The assembled council heard an initial appraisal by Timoshenko and then discussed thoroughly the strategic and operational situation, the condition of Direction forces and what should be done to support the Stavka strategy in the spring and summer. Based on these discussions, Timoshenko

2 Planning

ordered Bagramian to prepare a report to Stalin containing the Direction's proposed operational concept, specific Direction missions, attacking force organisation and requirements for reserves, and manpower and matériel reinforcements. Bagramian and Bodin worked jointly on the report, taking into consideration detailed assessments provided by the Direction's intelligence directorate.

Meanwhile, by 15 March, based on Stalin's initial guidance, the General Staff had completed its preliminary concept for the upcoming campaign. It envisioned the conduct of an active strategic defence, a build up of reserves, and then the resumption of a decisive offensive along the Moscow-Smolensk axis. Shaposhnikov and Vasilevsky presented the plan to Stalin, who approved it.[7] Meanwhile, Direction commanders — including the over-optimistic and bellicose Timoshenko — presented Stalin with their general proposals for offensive operations in the spring. Stalin considered his subordinates' recommendations and then prepared his final strategic decision which, according to Vasilevsky, read:

'Simultaneously with the shift to a strategic defence, I foresee the conduct of local offensive operations along a number of axes to fortify the success of the winter campaign, to improve the operational situation, to seize the strategic initiative and to disrupt German preparations for a new summer offensive.'[8]

Stalin judged that these preliminary actions would better prepare the Red Army to launch its main summer counter-offensive along the entire front from the Baltic to the Black Sea. Vasilevsky wryly added that Stalin's decision 'to defend and attack simultaneously turned out to be the most vulnerable aspect of the plan'.[9]

During the remainder of March, the Stavka studied detailed operational proposals from Direction and Front commanders. Although the officers involved have since debated the origins of and the responsibility for all ensuing operations in their memoirs, more often than not attempting to exonerate themselves or blame others for the resulting problems, it is now possible to reconstruct the sequence of decision-making which launched Soviet forces into the Kharkov abyss.

Timoshenko, the most ardent supporter of offensive action, held a second planning conference at his forward headquarters in Kupiansk on 20 March to discuss details of the forthcoming offensive with his staff and key subordinates, and to acquaint them with the assessment, prepared by Bagramian and Bodin, which he was about to dispatch to Moscow. The conference was attended by all Southwestern Front army commanders and their commissars. Timoshenko launched the session by describing his perception of strategic and operational realities facing the Southwestern Direction and by providing his rationale for future operations. He then announced that Stalin had approved his general offensive concept and that more detailed planning could now begin. Chief-of-Staff Bagramian followed Timoshenko and he presented his analysis of current conditions along the front, which he was about to dispatch to the Stavka.[10]

Bagramian's report, according to Moskalenko's memoirs, recounted past Soviet successes in the region and highlighted weaknesses in German defences in southern Russia. He maintained theGerman Sixth Army had been seriously weakened by winter combat, most German divisions now defended in several scattered front sectors, and key German operational reserves had also been fragmented and deployed piecemeal. Specifically, of ten German infantry divisions deployed against Southwestern Front, eight had been 'torn apart' and given defensive duties as separate regiments and

Kharkov, 1942

battalions. Bagramian reached the obvious conclusion that, 'the enemy Kharkov group could not begin active operations before they were refitted with men and equipment, their operational formation had been restored and large operational reserves had been brought up'.[11] In short, Bagramian agreed with Timoshenko that the Germans could not commence active operations before the onset of warmer weather. Bagramian then reported that significant German reserves (with up to 3,500 tanks) were assembling in the Gomel, Kremenchug, Kirovograd and Dnepropetrovsk regions, a clear sign that they intended to initiate 'decisive offensive operations' sometime in the spring, but probably not before mid-May.

However, in his report to the conference of 20 March and in his subsequent report to the Stavka, Bagramian ignored this intelligence appreciation (which he and Timoshenko had approved) and instead argued: 'We consider that the enemy, in spite of the major failure of his autumn offensive on Moscow, in the spring will again strive to seize our capital.'[12] He rationalised the intelligence reports by assuming that the Germans intended to employ forces concentrated east of Gomel and in the Briansk region against the Western Front's left wing. While both Bagramian and Timoshenko acknowledged that other German troop concentrations in the south would be used in a secondary strike against Soviet forces between the Northern Donets River and Taganrog on the Sea of Azov, they apparently felt that Soviet pre-emptive offensive actions could thwart this German threat while also seriously damaging the German effort against Moscow.[13]

In his memoirs Moskalenko claimed that he and other commanders, particularly those involved in March operations, questioned Timoshenko's and Bagramian's decision to conduct such a widespread offensive. They catalogued for Timoshenko the weaknesses of Soviet units, which included an absence of strong mobile forces capable of forming necessary shock groups, shortages of infantry support tanks, inadequate numbers of trained and experienced junior and mid-range officers, and weak second echelons and reserves. In retrospect, Moskalenko explained that, despite his entreaties for caution, Military Council members were carried away by their over-optimism. The council members did admit these deficiencies existed but assured Moskalenko and other worried subordinates they would correct these problems before the offensive began. Moskalenko underscored Khrushchev's remark to the effect that 'the Supreme High Commander, Stalin himself, had assigned the Front that mission and that it was already a guaranteed success'.[14] Moskalenko admitted that his fears finally were assuaged when he and others considered the fact that:

'... their assigned mission was associated with a broad Stavka plan, and it was possible that it (the operation) had special significance for the entire forthcoming Red Army spring-summer campaign. In that event, we understood that Stalin had to take care to strengthen the armies, designated to participate in the offensive in the Kharkov region'.[15]

On 22 March Timoshenko, Khrushchev and Bagramian sent their appreciation and recommendations to the Stavka (see Appendix 1).[16] Bagramian, the principal author of the document, later described the Military Council's rationale for the operation, writing:

'From the point of view of strategy and operational art, the intention of our High Command to undertake the Kharkov operation in May 1942 was correct since it was based on the firmly held Stavka view that, with the beginning of the summer campaign, Hitler's High Command would strike the main blow on the Moscow axis with the aim of capturing the capital of our country — and against the forces of the Southwestern Direction simultaneously as a secondary attack by limited forces ... Personally, I also firmly held that opinion, which turned out to be mistaken.'[17]

Bagramian noted than an operation in the Kharkov region, in addition to securing the important city, would also divert German forces from the critical assault on Moscow.

Bagramian's assessment and proposal to the Stavka surveyed strategic and operational realities along the entire front and in the Southwestern Direction's sector, assessed the impact of the winter campaign on the German Army, found German strength in the south to be wanting and recommended a general offensive by the Briansk, Southwestern and Southern Fronts to smash German defences in southern Russia and clear all German forces from territories east of the Dnepr River line (the line Gomel-Kiev-Cherkassy-Pervomaisk-Nikolaev).

Bagramian argued that the Germans intended to conduct their principal summer operation against Soviet forces defending Moscow, while conducting a secondary assault in the south, a planning assumption which turned out to be false. The intelligence information upon which he based that conclusion was also flawed since the report woefully understated the strength of opposing German forces. Although Bagramian noted the assembly of considerable German reserves in the region opposite the Southwestern Front (at Gomel, Kremenchug, Kirovograd, Dnepropetrovsk and Poltava), he apparently assumed these troops were replacements and did not permit their presence to alter his basic assessment of German strategic intentions. All of these mistakes perverted Soviet assessments of the German forces in the region and underestimated their firepower and superior mobility. Bagramian's report also discounted Southwestern Direction failures during the winter when, on three occasions (at Kursk, Kharkov and in the Donbas), Soviet offensives had fallen far short of achieving their intended ends. Moreover, the human cost of these failures, numbering between 110,000 and 130,000 men, had left Direction forces themselves weakened and in need of reinforcement.

In an addendum to the 22 March report, the Southwestern Direction Military Council asked the Stavka for the sizeable reinforcements necessary to restore Direction strength to levels sufficient to launch an offensive. The request amounted to 32-34 rifle divisions, 27-28 tank brigades, 19-24 artillery regiments, 756 combat aircraft, 250,000 fresh troops and the support of two long-range aviation divisions to strike targets deep in the German rear area.[18]

Recent Soviet accounts have asked why Timoshenko, Khrushchev and Bagramian argued for offensive action in such adverse circumstances. Their answer, supported by the recollections of Moskalenko, is that the recommendation to attack was essentially political. Knowing that Stalin was impatient and inclined to offensive action in the south, all three leaders sought to 'please' him by siding with him against his more prudent Stavka colleagues Shaposhnikov, Zhukov and Vasilevsky, and against the advice of the General Staff.

Having received Stavka agreement in principle to plan and conduct an offensive operation, in late March Bagramian flew to Moscow to meet Stavka members and General Staff officers in order to gain a first-hand appreciation of the strategic situation, to explain the contents of his report, to discuss the upcoming offensive and to receive as much planning guidance as possible. Several days later he was joined by Timoshenko and Khrushchev and together, on 27 March, they met Stalin and

Kharkov, 1942

Shaposhnikov. There, in Stalin's Kremlin office, Bagramian presented the Southwestern Direction's strategic and operational assessment. Stalin questioned Bagramian about the details of his report and technical aspects of proposed combat operations. In the discussion that followed, Shaposhnikov reiterated his opinion that it would be folly to attack in too many front sectors in the spring, thereby dissipating Soviet strength. Bagramian disagreed, arguing that it would be better to strike with the combined two Fronts of the Southwestern Direction, and subsequently Briansk Front forces could act in accordance with the results of that attack or with subsequent action by the Western Front. Stalin interrupted the discussion to support Bagramian's proposal for an offensive, but qualified his support by stating he lacked the resources to reinforce the Direction significantly. While the Stavka had rifle divisions in reserve, Stalin said that many of them were in transit and they were scarcely adequate to satisfy the Direction's request for over 30 rifle divisions and 'huge' amounts of additional tanks and artillery. Therefore, said Stalin, 'Your proposal cannot be accepted.'[19] In light of the likely German drive on Moscow, Stalin argued that the bulk of the reserves would be retained for use there. He added, however, that more limited offensive action in the Kharkov sector would still be useful to weaken the Germans' Moscow blow. With that said, he ordered the Southwestern Direction Military Council to prepare a plan for a more limited operation.

The next day Timoshenko, Bagramian and Khrushchev worked on a plan for the more limited effort. In the evening they again met with Stalin, Shaposhnikov and Vasilevsky and presented the results of their work. Once again there was disagreement over the issue of reinforcements. Stalin refused to approve the full measure of requested reinforcements, rejected resubordination of the Briansk Front to Timoshenko's control during the offensive and impressed upon Timoshenko and his staff the necessity for limiting the scope of the Kharkov offensive for the sake of the situation elsewhere along the front. Intense negotiations continued as the Kremlin meeting continued into the small hours of the morning. Once again Bagramian presented a new Southwestern Direction proposal, and the assembly was joined by representatives of the Southern Front to plan critical flank protection for Timoshenko's forthcoming offensive.[20]

Two days later, on 30 March, the Southwestern Direction Military Council again met Stalin and presented him with a written document which reiterated the intent of the proposed offensive and again asked for the reinforcements necessary to launch it (see Appendix 2).[21] Timoshenko's repeated requests for reinforcements reflected the concerns of Moskalenko and other subordinate commanders about the inadequacies of Southwestern Direction forces for such a massive undertaking. This time Timoshenko's request amounted to 37 infantry formations, 29 mobile brigades and 25 artillery regiments, totalling 1,200 tanks, 1,200-1,300 artillery pieces and 620 aircraft. This staggered even Stalin and forced him to listen more closely to the call for caution by his other Stavka colleagues.[22] Since Stalin did not possess the necessary reserves to satisfy Timoshenko's request, while again agreeing with his Stavka colleagues' proposal for adopting an active strategic defence, he nevertheless characteristically left the door open to 'local' offensive action by permitting Timoshenko to plan an offensive against German forces around Kharkov and by continuing to mandate local offensives elsewhere along the front.

Near the end of the Moscow meetings, Timoshenko presented the Stavka with yet another revised request for reserves, this time prudently reduced to 10 rifle divisions, 26 tank brigades, 10 artillery regiments and enough men to bring Southwestern

2 Planning

Direction forces up to 80%. Dispatch of these reinforcements by 15 April, Timoshenko argued, would enable the attack to take place in late April, in time to disrupt German spring offensive plans. Satisfied with this display of reason, the Stavka finally approved Timoshenko's request and ordered him to complete his offensive planning.[23]

During the ensuing weeks, while Timoshenko prepared and submitted his new plan, the Stavka dispatched orders to other Fronts to plan for limited offensive action elsewhere along the front. On 9 April it ordered the Leningrad and Volkhov Fronts to prepare an operation to rescue the Liuban Group (2nd Shock Army), which had been encircled in the German rear area south of Leningrad since January 1942. On 22 April the Northwestern Front was ordered to prepare yet another operation to eliminate German II Army Corps, nearly encircled since January in the Demiansk region, and the Stavka dispatched Vasilevsky to supervise the operation's planning. Western Front was to reinforce Group Belov, a combined force of cavalry and airborne troops then operating in the German rear area southwest of Viazma, and assist that force in escaping from encirclement. Further south, on 20 April Briansk Front received orders to conduct an operation in the Kursk region to support the Southwestern Direction's thrust on Kharkov, and, a day later, the Stavka ordered the Crimean Front to resume its offensive from its bridgehead on the Kerch Peninsula to relieve the German siege of Sevastopol and clear German forces from the Crimea. Finally, in early May, the Karelian Front received orders to attack Finnish forces and restore the Soviet-Finnish border along the Svir River. All of these operations were designated to begin in late April or early May and, collectively, they would comprise Stalin's package of pre-emptive or diversionary offensives.[24] Of the total number, however, the Kharkov operation was the largest in scale and the most important effort.

While each of these operations was indeed 'local' in nature, the emerging pattern clearly reflected Stalin's impatience with his Stavka associates, and his confidence that renewed offensive action against a weakened German Army would succeed. Stalin's insistence on launching these attacks illustrates clearly the fundamental characteristics of his strategic and operational philosophy that had dominated Soviet military planning in 1941 and 1942 and would continue to impinge on numerous occasions later in the war. Specifically, Stalin believed that the application of force in numerous sectors, successively if not simultaneously, was the best way to defeat an opponent. Zhukov, Vasilevsky and others in the General Staff appreciated the twin military principles of force concentration and economy of force and well understood the logistical realities and problems associated with preparing for, conducting and sustaining major operations. Stalin, however, placed immense faith in his views particularly as applied in this case, against German forces he assumed were overextended. He emphasised the logistical difficulties such a strategy would impose on the Germans, who possessed fewer natural or manpower resources than the Soviets. Although Stalin realised his strategic philosophy often produced embarrassing defeats as well as glorious victories and, moreover, was costly in terms of manpower and equipment losses, he believed these effects were only temporary and transitory. In his view, a skilfully applied strategy of attrition would inevitably exhaust enemy strength and ultimately produce catastrophic enemy collapse. Stalin's view prevailed in spring 1942 and provided the rationale for all subsequent Soviet military action during the spring and summer campaign.

During the days following the March 1942 Moscow meetings, Bagramian and the Southwestern Direction staff worked hard to develop a new and complete operational plan, while the Stavka implemented the decisions of the Moscow meetings. On 1 April

Kharkov, 1942

the Briansk Front was removed from Southwestern Direction control and resubordinated directly to the Stavka, and 40th Army on Southwestern Front's right flank was shifted to Briansk Front control to participate in that Front's anticipated May offensive. A week later Timoshenko was given direct command of Southwestern Front, and the Front's former commander, Lt-Gen F. Ia. Kostenko, was appointed deputy commander of the Southwestern Direction. Bagramian became Southwestern Front Chief of Staff replacing Bodin, who returned to Moscow to become Assistant Chief of the General Staff. In addition, Bagramian retained his job as Chief of the Southwestern Direction's Operational Group.[25] These measures were designed to tighten control over the planning and conduct of the forthcoming Kharkov operation.

In accordance with previous Stavka guidance, on 10 April Timoshenko and the Southwestern Direction Military Council submitted to the Stavka a full-scale, detailed operational plan for the defeat of German forces in the Kharkov region (see Appendix 3). The scope of the operation called for by the plan was far from local. Despite Stavka guidance to the contrary, the plan's opening paragraph, which contained Timoshenko's proposed mission and overall offensive aims, went far beyond what many on the Stavka had expected. It read:

'1. In accordance with directives of the Stavka of the Supreme High Command for forestalling enemy development of offensive operations and preserving the initiative in the hands of our forces on the southwestern axis during the April-May period, I establish for ourselves the following principal aim: to secure the Kharkov region, to conduct a force regrouping, and, by a subsequent attack in the direction of Dnepropetrovsk and Sinelnikovo Station, deprive the enemy of important crossing sites over the Dnepr.'[26]

Rather than simply liberating Kharkov, Timoshenko again proposed an advance to the line of the Dnepr River; in subsequent paragraphs, he specified how he would do so. The Southwestern Front alone would launch two powerful blows along converging axes, a main attack from the Barvenkovo bridgehead south of Kharkov and a secondary assault from the Staryi Saltov bridgehead northeast of Kharkov. The two attacking forces would then link up west of the city to encircle and destroy German forces around Kharkov, seize the city and prepare the way for subsequent operations toward the Dnepr River.

The operation would unfold in three stages. The first stage, which was to take place over a period of more than three weeks, was preparatory; during it Southwestern Front forces would carry out an extensive force regrouping and concentration, all under the cover of an ambitious deception plan. During the second stage, which was to last six to seven days, rifle units would penetrate German defences in both sectors, and then mechanised forces would exploit the breakthrough. In the critical southern sector, Timoshenko planned to mass 200 tanks to support the infantry forces of 6th Army in the initial penetration operation and then employ a mobile group of two mechanised corps (2nd and 3rd with 269 tanks) to exploit success toward German lines of communication west of Kharkov. In the north 300 tanks would support the initial attack by the massed infantry of 21st and 28th Armies and then the three divisions of 3rd Guards Cavalry Corps, reinforced with one tank brigade, would join the race to Kharkov to link up with the mobile force advancing from the south. During the third stage, anticipated to last between seven and eight days, Soviet mechanised and cavalry forces would smash German operational reserves and encircle Kharkov,

2 Planning

while rifle forces would complete the occupation of the city and the destruction of its defenders. Timoshenko left the details of the subsequent advance to the Dnepr to future orders.

Timoshenko's proposed plan met with instant resistance from Stavka members as well as from many of his subordinate commanders. Marshal Shaposhnikov, in particular, was horrified about the prospects for conducting such a risky operation in view of the looming German threat to Moscow and the apparent vulnerability of forces attacking from an operational 'sack', the term which he used to describe the Barvenkovo bridgehead. Despite Shaposhnikov's and, apparently, also Vasilevsky's and Zhukov's reservations, Stalin sided with Timoshenko and the Southwestern Direction Military Council. According to Vasilevsky, Timoshenko lobbied hard for his proposal, 'continuing to insist on his proposal and assuring Stalin of the full success of the operation'. Stalin, in turn, supported his long-time associate, 'gave permission for its conduct, and ordered the General Staff to consider the operation an internal matter of the [Southwestern] Direction and not to interfere on any question concerning it'.[27] With Stalin's guidance and attitude toward the operation clear, it was not prudent for others to criticise it further.

Within the Southwestern Direction Command, however, Moskalenko and perhaps others as well, voiced concern over certain operational and tactical aspects of the plan. To his credit, Timoshenko listened to and acted upon their concerns. Moskalenko was concerned about Timoshenko's decision to employ the newly created 28th Army as the principal Front shock group in the critical Staryi Saltov bridgehead east of Kharkov. Not only was 28th Army's command group and staff 'green' with inexperience; so also were its troops. Moreover, the army was to occupy and launch its attack from the sector which had formerly been seized and was now defended by veteran 38th Army troops. Further, all of 38th Army's reinforcing cavalry, tanks, motorised infantry and artillery were to be transferred to 28th Army control, and 38th Army would be relegated to a defensive role deployed opposite the Chuguev bridgehead between the attacking 28th and 6th Armies. Moskalenko was 'completely bewildered' by the plan. Not only was 38th Army fully acquainted with every square yard of the area of operations and each peculiarity of the German defence, but Moskalenko's command group, staff and men were also among the most combat-experienced in the Southwestern Direction in the organisation and conduct of offensive operations. Even more important, Moskalenko felt the penetration operation involved too broad a front and the forces would be too dispersed throughout the bridgehead.[28]

Fearing that these mistakes would cause the offensive to abort, Moskalenko requested that Timoshenko shift 38th Army's boundary with 28th Army to the right (north) into the Staryi Saltov bridgehead so that Moskalenko could concentrate his forces on the army's right flank and participate in the attack. Moskalenko argued that he could effectively cover the German Chuguev bridgehead with his remaining forces.

To his credit, Timoshenko paid attention to Moskalenko's concerns. On 27 April, during a visit to Moskalenko's forward command post, Timoshenko informed him that, after considerable thought, he had approved his proposal, and 38th Army would join the offensive on the southern most sector of the Staryi Saltov bridgehead. Timoshenko agreed that this would not only measurably increase the force of the attack, but also protect better 28th Army's potentially vulnerable left flank.

Participants in the planned attack from the Barvenkovo bridgehead voiced similar protestations to Timoshenko. Here, too, many felt that 6th Army's shock group was

Kharkov, 1942

too large and cumbersome and occupied too extensive a sector for the army commander to control all his forces effectively. In addition, as was the case in the north, the shock group's left flank seemed vulnerable to German counter-attacks from the Krasnograd region to the southwest and south. Timoshenko again agreed with his subordinates and amended his plan. Accordingly, he formed a new shock group (Army Group Bobkin) consisting of a cavalry corps and reinforcing tanks and infantry from 6th Army and Front forces, and ordered the group to operate on 6th Army's left flank and cover that army's flank throughout the offensive.

On 28 April the Southwestern Direction Military Council issued Directive No 00275, a revised operational plan for the Kharkov offensive, which incorporated the recommendation of subordinate commanders and Stavka suggestions (see Appendix 4).[29] The revised plan still called for a main attack from the Barvenkovo bridgehead and a secondary attack from the Staryi Saltov bridgehead. Both forces would then converge west of Kharkov to encircle and destroy the city's German defenders. Soviet rifle and supporting forces were to penetrate German tactical defences by the third and fourth day of the operations, and mobile forces would complete the envelopment of the city. All units were to be ready to attack on the morning of 4 May, and the operation was to be completed in 15-18 days. The order of 28 April increased the strength and improved the organisation of attacking forces and protected their flanks; on top of this, unlike its 10 April predecessor, it assuaged Stavka reservations by saying virtually nothing about a subsequent advance toward the Dnepr River.

Timoshenko materially strengthened the power of both assaulting shock groups. In the north, all of 28th Army would spearhead the attack from the small Staryi Saltov bridgehead over the Northern Donets River, flanked on the right by the bulk of 21st Army and on the left by the concentrated forces of 38th Army. He reinforced his three attacking armies with seven tank brigades and a separate tank battalion in addition to the three cavalry divisions and motorised rifle brigade of 3rd Guards Cavalry Corps, which were designated to carry out the exploitation. In the critical Barvenkovo bridgehead to the south, two attacking forces would replace the one envisioned in the 10 April plan. 6th Army, reinforced by four tank brigades, would conduct the penetration operation flanked on the left by a specially designated army group consisting of two rifle divisions and a cavalry corps. Thereafter, two tank corps (renamed from the mechanised corps designated in the earlier order) and a cavalry corps would exploit into the region west of Kharkov to encircle German forces defending the city.

Lt-Gen R. Ia. Malinovsky's Southern Front, whose forces occupied defences along the southern face of the Barvenkovo bridgehead, was to play a particularly important role in the operation by providing additional deep flank protection for the advance on Kharkov. In his memoirs, Bagramian claimed that the Southwestern Direction was particularly concerned about the possibility of a German thrust from the Slaviansk region in the south against the flank of its attacking group, especially since the Southwestern Direction lacked the forces necessary to attack in strength in its sector while simultaneously defending in strength along its southern flank.[30] Therefore, both Timoshenko and Bagramian believed adequate protection of the offensive's southern flank by Southern Front forces was absolutely essential for the operation's success.

In early April, Timoshenko summoned Southern Front Commander Lt Gen R. Ia. Malinovsky, Front Commissar L. P. Korniets and Front Chief of Staff, Gen A. I. Antonov to Southwestern Direction headquarters in Voronezh where he briefed them on the concept of operations and informed them of their critical role in protecting the

2 Planning

flank of the operation. Closely co-ordinated planning between the two force staffs produced a Southern Front plan on 6 April that seemingly satisfied Timoshenko's requirements. Southern Front Operational Directive No 00177 (see Appendix 5) specified just how the Front would provide necessary flank protection for the Southwestern Direction while continuing to defend the extensive sector from the Northern Donets River to the Sea of Azov.[31] The order required the Southern Front's armies to dig in along occupied lines, protect the left flank of Southwestern Front's attacking forces, and cover the Rostov and Voroshilovgrad axes in Malinovsky's centre and on his left flank. Specifically, Malinovsky's 57th and 9th Armies, defending along the southern face of the Barvenkovo bridgehead, supported by two cavalry corps and limited reserves, were to provide immediate flank protection for Timoshenko's Barvenkovo shock groups.

Intense debate has ensued over whether the mission Timoshenko assigned to Malinovsky was suitable and whether the forces both he and Timoshenko provided to protect the Southwestern Front's right flank were adequate. Many have criticised Timoshenko for severely limiting the Southern Front's operational capabilities by assigning it a passive mission and also for weakening that Front's right wing armies by taking from them seven artillery regiments, three tank brigades and two rifle brigades to reinforce Southwestern Front's offensive and to strengthen its reserves. In addition, during mid-April Timoshenko shifted another rifle division from 9th Army to strengthen 18th Army defending along the Voroshilovgrad axis. As a result, 'Only 11 weak rifle divisions and one rifle brigade (with average strengths of from 5,000 to 7,000 men) were left in 57th and 9th Armies to cover the Barvenkovo axis, where a German strike was most likely.'[32] The defensive front of these armies was 176km long and, as a result, they had insufficient strength to establish even the strong defence mandated by Timoshenko.

In his memoirs, Bagramian wrote that the Direction Military Council, when considering the flank defence dilemma, concluded that the enemy would have to shift forces from other sectors further south in order to mount an offensive against the southern face of the Barvenkovo bridgehead. Therefore, he wrote, the Southern Front had to 'be ready, if necessary, to reinforce the defences of its two right flank armies in timely fashion with operational reserves concentrated on the left wing of the Front'.[33] Apparently, Bagramian was confident in the ability of the Soviet commands to fulfil that task.

Subsequent difficulties the Soviets encountered while regrouping their forces for the Kharkov offensive, however, vividly demonstrated the futility of Bagramian's planning assumption. It took more than 30 days to effect the necessary regrouping and, in the end, because of those difficulties, the Soviets had to postpone the beginning of the offensive from 4 May to 12 May.[34] The more cynical of Soviet critics accused Bagramian of later blaming the guiltless Southern Front command for the failures of Southwestern Direction planners — the subsequent elevation during the Kharkov operation of Gen A. I. Antonov, Southern Front's chief of staff, to Chief of the Red Army General Staff ultimately validated this criticism.

With all necessary orders issued, final preparations for the Kharkov offensive commenced. At the highest level, on 4 May the Stavka transformed the Southwestern Direction Operational Group into a full Direction staff by concentrating in Direction headquarters all force commanders (artillery, armour, etc) and chiefs of services (logistics, communications, etc), who could co-ordinate the operations of all forces and functions on the two Fronts. Bagramian assumed the task of Direction chief of staff

Kharkov, 1942

as well as chief of staff of the Southwestern Front. Despite this centralisation of authority and the expansion of its responsibilities and functions, however, Direction headquarters received no additional support personnel to handle the increased load of administrative, planning and command and control tasks.[35]

Detailed planning of the Kharkov operation in the subordinate armies began in earnest in early May, in particular in the shock groups of 28th and 6th Armies. Bagramian, other Southwestern Direction Military Council members, chiefs of forces and Southwestern Front staff officers visited these and other army headquarters to supervise implementation of the plan and assist in providing necessary resources for Direction and Front.

Less than two weeks before, on 16 April, Timoshenko had ordered the start of a large-scale regrouping to concentrate forces for the offensive. The elaborate plan called for substantial movement of forces under stringent security and deception measures. The Southwestern Front had to concentrate its three armies and separate army group first into assembly and then into attack positions; it then had to form and deploy forward the new 28th Army and integrate into its structure numerous supporting units from Stavka reserve. In addition, on 17 April the Stavka ordered the Front to form three new tank corps, using tank brigades organic to the Front (the 10 April order had presumed these new corps would be called mechanised). This difficult task of creating command and control and logistical structures for the tank corps was especially critical since these corps were to spearhead the Soviet exploitation operation. In addition, the Southern Front was to form a fourth tank corps and had to shift forces from its centre and left flank to its right flank and to the Southwestern Front in order to fulfil its mission of covering the southern flank of the Southwestern Front against possible German counter-attack. The short planning and preparation time imparted a sense of urgency, if not haste, to those performing these difficult preparatory tasks. Already force regrouping was behind schedule, and the timing of the attack had to be altered accordingly.

The regrouping effort itself was severely hindered by the spring *razputitsa* (thaw), which began in mid-April and which turned the soil into mud of a considerable depth. Bagramian later wrote, 'Flooded rivers and the absence of hard surface roads and railroad lines along corresponding axes hindered the movement and transfer of troops and their timely arrival in designated regions.'[36] Other senior Soviet participants in the Kharkov operation have severely criticised the regrouping process and the efficiency of deception measures, which were to have concealed Soviet attack preparations and the points of Soviet main effort. Because much of the regrouping force had to traverse the front laterally, the Germans detected some Soviet movement. The limited preparation time exacerbated the problem further by forcing hasty and often careless movement; control over regrouping forces was frequently lax. Moskalenko, commander of 38th Army, noted the problem, later writing:

'But the Front staff and we also, in the command and staffs of the armies, did not take matters into our own hands. We did not create a single regrouping plan and did not give clear orders regarding the order and priority of crossing bridges, the conduct of road marches, the organisation of air defence on the march and in concentration areas, and, finally, about the observation of *maskirovka* (deception).'[37]

Consequently, movement was slowed, the secrecy of Soviet regrouping was compromised, and many planned preparations were not completed in time. As a result,

2 Planning

according to Moskalenko:

'. . . the regrouping of large masses of forces to their appointed penetration sectors occurred without required organisation and secrecy. Therefore, no one was surprised that the German-Fascist command divined our plans. Having divined them, he hurriedly undertook measures to strengthen the defences in threatened sectors . . . Thus, the prepared operation was not unexpected, nor was it a surprise for the enemy.'[38]

In his memoirs, Bagramian defended the effectiveness of his planning and that of other Southwestern Direction staff officers and downplayed the significance of the operation within the overall context of German intentions, stating:

'Comparing the plans of both sides it is necessary to underscore one very important factor in order to understand that, during the summer campaign, the Soviet High Command intended to limit its offensive operations on the southern wing to missions of an operational nature; that is, to improve somewhat the position of its forces along the southwestern strategic axis. [On the other hand] Hitler's High Command decided to accomplish there a large-scale mission with long-range aims.'[39]

This disingenuous after-the-fact claim by Bagramian was a feeble attempt to absolve himself, his associates in the Southwestern Direction headquarters and those in the Stavka who supported the operation, of blame for the disaster which ensued. The principal roots of that disaster, of which Bagramian was unaware at the time, were the nature of German plans for their 1942 campaign.

Unknown to Bagramian and other Soviet leaders, the German High Command had completed additional planning to supplement their original Plan 'Blau'. Most important in a strategic sense was the plan code-named Operation 'Kreml', which, although formally approved on 28 May, accurately reflected German intelligence operations throughout the spring. Prepared by German Army Group Centre, 'Kreml' was an elaborate deception plan designed to reinforce Soviet perceptions that Moscow was the German's principal strategic target in the summer campaign. Although in his memoirs Bagramian provides a detailed account of the general intent and specific features of Operation 'Kreml', he concluded that the plan 'did not receive the desired results'.[40] Other historians have treated the German deception plan with similar disrespect. Despite these views, the plan in all probability achieved its ends. Weeks after the Kharkov battle had ended, and when German forces were commencing Operation 'Blau', Stalin's attentions were still riveted to the German threat along the western approaches to Moscow, and he continued stubbornly to claim that the main German summer target was Moscow. Only subsequent wholesale Soviet defeat in the south ultimately disabused him of that view.

Other German operational plans had even greater significance for the success or failure of Soviet forces in the Kharkov operation. Army Group South, disturbed over Soviet seizure of bridgeheads at Barvenkovo and east of Kharkov during the winter and early spring and fearing that these bridgeheads would impede its summer offensive, developed plans to eradicate the salients before the planned commencement of 'Blau'. On 25 March Army Group South issued a directive for Operation 'Friderikus', a simple two-pronged drive from the north and south against Izium to cut off and destroy Soviet forces in the Barvenkovo bridgehead. Originally German planners considered delivering the northern thrust by Sixth Army along the eastern bank of the

Kharkov, 1942

Northern Donets River. However, because this would have exposed the army's flank to a Soviet attack from the east, the final plan, tentatively scheduled for 22 April, had Sixth Army attacking in a circuitous manner along the west bank of the river when it was in full flood and would therefore protect the army's left flank. When Hitler and Halder reviewed the plan, they insisted a second version ('Friderikus II') be developed to commit Sixth Army east of the Northern Donets. While debates raged over which plan would be implemented, difficulties in the forward transport of necessary German reinforcements forced delay of the operation well past its original planned starting date of 22 April. Finally, on 30 April Field Marshal Fedor von Bock, commander of Army Group South, issued his final directive for 'Friderikus II', with a probable start date of 18 May.[41]

On 12 May, when Soviet forces struck north and south of Kharkov, German armoured forces under the control of Sixth Army and Army Group von Kleist had already completed their concentration in the Kharkov region and south of the Barvenkovo bridgehead. Although Soviet intelligence had detected some German troop activity north of Kharkov, it failed to notice the German concentration in the south, with catastrophic consequences.

Ironically for the Soviets, the deception plan for the Kharkov operation, although considered by Moskalenko to have been compromised, achieved considerable success. German intelligence picked up some indicators of Soviet troop movements as early as mid-April. In his diary entry of 17 April, Chief of the German General Staff Franz Halder noted, 'In south, opposite Kleist's front, confused movement and radio silence.'[42] On 22 April he wrote, 'The movements opposite Kleist's Group continue. Opposite Sixth Army the enemy is shifting forces southward,' he presumed into the Izium (Barvenkovo) bridgehead; he repeated that judgement on 24 and 26 April.[43]

On 4 May Halder reported Soviet forces concentrating in the northwestern corner of the Izium salient as well as attack preparations in the Volchansk sector. Bock's diary also reflected German concerns over a future Soviet attack in the Kharkov area. He noted on 8 May that 'the Russians may forestall us with their own attack' and that Sixth Army projected such an attack both at Volchansk and Kharkov. He was uncertain, however, whether Soviet troop movements near Izium were indicative of Soviet attack intentions. On 10 May Bock again noted Soviet reconnaissance — probing attacks in the Volchansk and Slaviansk sectors — but again it was not enough activity to warrant undue concern.[44]

In sum, set within the context of German intelligence reports from the vast expanse of the Eastern Front, neither Halder's nor Bock's notations were remarkable. They were certainly in no way indicative of the strength of the forthcoming Soviet attack at Kharkov, nor did they reflect adequately the surprise of lower level German commanders when the Soviet bombardment began early on 12 May. As the dean of German military historians, Earle Ziemke, has recorded:

'... [although] the Russians were stirring ominously in the northwest corner of the Izyum [sic] bulge and in the Volchansk sector ... Hitler and Halder, who had done the same with earlier reports of similar Russian activity, dismissed the idea of an attack toward Kharkov, although, as the weather and condition of the ground improved, Halder did so "with less conviction than before".'[45]

Despite these fragmentary intelligence indicators, to most German participants in the

2 Planning

Kharkov operation the attack came as a distinct surprise; in particular in its timing and ferocity. Soviet achievement of operational surprise would, however, become irrelevant as a well-thought-out Soviet operational concept would fall victim to more sophisticated German strategic and operational planning. In short, Bagramian, his associates and over a quarter million Soviet troops were marching confidently into a killing ground.

As the attack date approached and the Southwestern Direction began experiencing difficulties in meeting its offensive timetables, the Stavka itself showed signs of either prudence or cold feet about its ambitious spring offensive plans. At the least its actions demonstrated a wave of last-minute caution. After several inept attempts by the Crimean Front to resume the offensive towards Sevastopol in the Crimea, on 6 May the Stavka ordered the Front to defend in place along the narrow neck of the Kerch Peninsula. Only days later, on 8 and 9 May, the Stavka ordered the Kalinin, Western, Briansk, Southwestern and Southern Fronts to adopt economy of force measures in all sectors of the front to assist forces with penetration missions, to create reserves necessary to defeat enemy counter-attacks and to prepare defences in depth along all possible enemy avenues of approach into their sectors. The Stavka cancelled the projected Briansk Front offensive toward Orel and Kursk pending the outcome of the Kharkov operation, and ordered the Karelian Front and associated 7th Separate Army to halt their offensive preparations and resume the defence.[46] After early May, the Stavka planned offensive operations only in the Liuban (Leningrad Front), Demiansk (Northwestern Front) and Kharkov (Southwestern Front) sectors. Of the three, the Kharkov attack was still the most critical and would turn out to be the most fateful.

Overview: The Soviet Assessment
Overall Situation on the Soviet-German Front up to April 1942, Soviet Force Commands and Enemy Plans

As a result of the dynamic defence by Soviet forces along the entire Soviet-German front and the counter-offensive at Moscow in 1941–1942, German-Fascist forces suffered heavy losses. Main enemy shock groupings, which had advanced against Moscow, suffered a serious defeat.

To fortify their position on the Soviet-German Front, from January through March 1942, the German-Fascist command was compelled to transfer more than 30 divisions from Western Europe.

The defeat of German-Fascist forces at Moscow had exceptionally important military and political significance. This was the first major German defeat in World War II, exploding forever the myth of the German-Fascist army's invincibility.

It became obvious that the Soviet Army, having become tempered and stronger in battle, had accumulated rich combat experience and was capable of defeating the enemy hordes and driving them from the confines of our Motherland. The Germans had lost their temporary superiority, which they had gained as a result of their perfidious and sudden attack against the Soviet Union. Initiative shifted into the hands of the Soviet command.

Comrade Stalin spoke of the further prospects of the war in his historic Order No 55 dated 23 February 1942:

'The element of surprise gained by the German-Fascist forces has been completely expended, eliminating the unequal conditions of war under which we have been fight-

Kharkov, 1942

ing. Now the fate of the war will be decided not by the element of surprise, but by factors constantly in force: rear stability, the army's morale, the quantity and quality of divisions, armaments, and the organisational capabilities of the army's leadership.'[47]

As a result of our Party's and the Soviet government's enormous organisational work and of the Soviet people's self-sacrificing labour, in 1942 our country's military-economic situation improved.

Industrial enterprises, relocated in the country's eastern regions, had already improved production. Output of military products in March 1942 had reached their prewar level.

The Soviet Army began to receive a significant quantity of first-class combat equipment, which exceeded the enemy's in quality.

Comrade Stalin, the Supreme Commander-in-Chief, tasked the Soviet Army with the goals of mastering completely the first-class equipment and new weapons which the Motherland provided, and of learning how to defeat the enemy and liberate the Soviet Union from the Fascist invaders within the shortest period of time.

During early April, after the Soviet Army's winter offensive battles were basically completed, the Soviet-German Front ran along the line Leningrad, Novgorod and Demiansk, where our forces had encircled German Sixteenth Army; further the front line ran through Rzhev, Viazma, east of Orel, Kursk and Kharkov, and along the Northern Donets and Mius Rivers.

To fulfil the mission assigned by the Supreme High Command, it was necessary to conduct a series of operations, which were designed to consolidate the winter offensive's success and improve our forces' overall operational situation in separate Front sectors.

It was necessary to break the Leningrad blockade, eliminate the Demiansk and Rzhev-Viazma groupings, continue the offensive operation in Crimea, and prepare and conduct an offensive on the southwestern axis to destroy the enemy's Kharkov grouping.

The Stavka of the Supreme High Command focused considerable attention on the offensive operation along the southwestern axis. The Stavka charged the Southwestern Front with conducting the offensive and allocated a considerable number of artillery units from the Stavka reserve. The new 28th Army was added to the Front's composition in accordance with Stavka instructions.

At the same time as it prepared for offensive operations, the Stavka also undertook a series of defensive measures. It ordered Front commanders to create an echeloned defence to a depth of 100km.

The overall situation on the Soviet-German Front as of May 1942, however, had worsened sharply because the Anglo-Americans had refused to fulfil their obligation to open a second front in Europe in 1942. Moreover, since autumn 1941 they had been conducting talks with Hitler's representatives about concluding a separate peace behind the USSR's back.

Consequently, in its 1942 planning, the German command proceeded on the basis that no danger would threaten Germany in the West; therefore, all of its forces could be used in the war against the Soviet Union.

Directive No 41 of German Armed Forces High Command, dated 5 April 1942, stated the following:

2 Planning

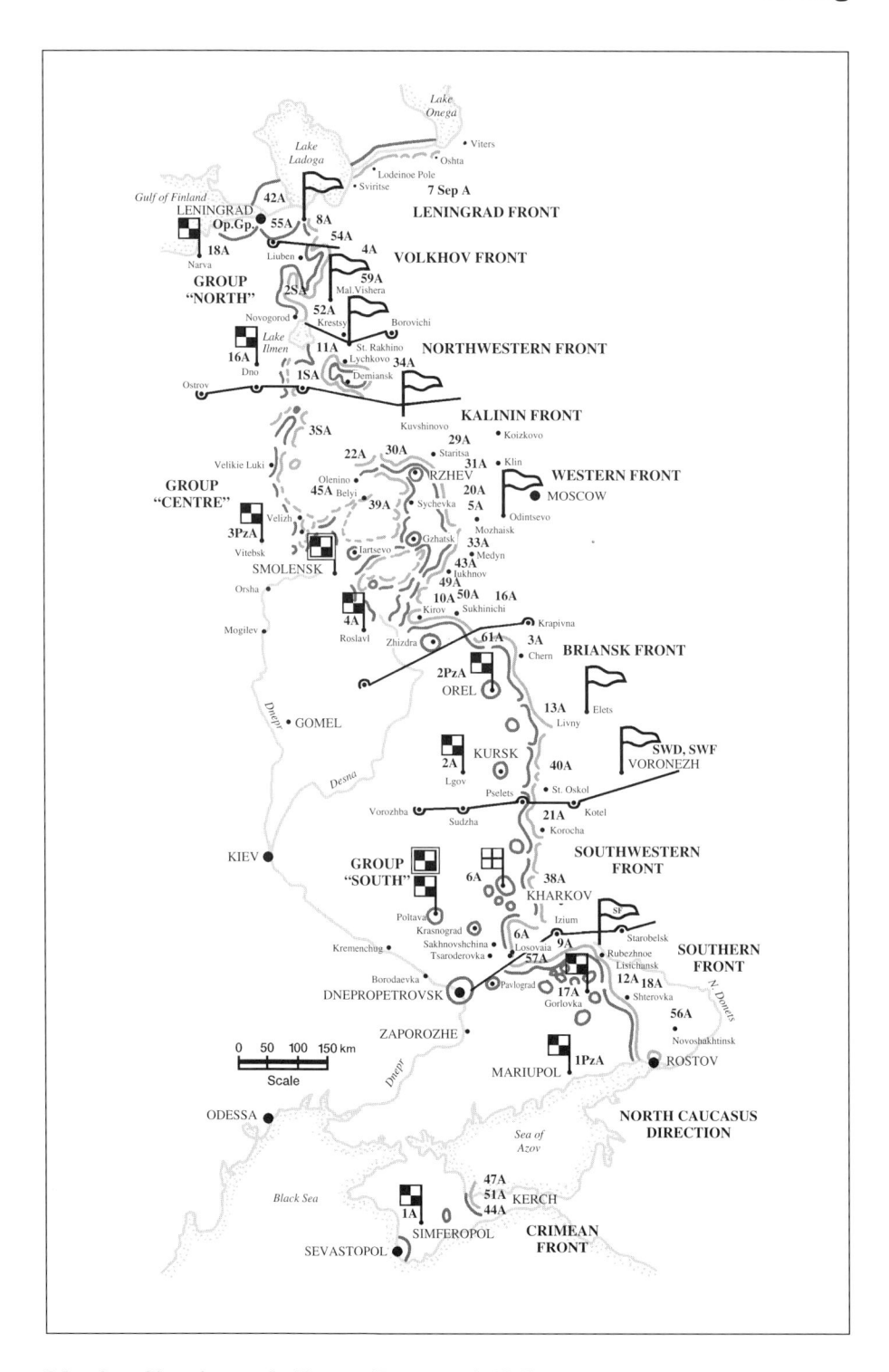

Map 3 — Situation on the Eastern Front, April 1942

Kharkov, 1942

'Winter operations in Russia are coming to an end . . . As soon as weather conditions and the nature of the terrain create favourable opportunities, the German command and forces, making use of their superiority, should seize the initiative to bend the enemy to their will. Here, the following goal should be pursued: to destroy decisively the armed forces of the Soviet Union and deprive the country of its most important military-economic centres by capturing or destroying them.'

The content of this directive demonstrated that Hitler's command was completely unconcerned about its rear area in the West, and that it had decided to focus all its efforts in summer 1942 against the Soviet Union.

Having presented itself with this ambitious goal of destroying the Soviet armed forces, Hitler's command still did not have at its disposal the forces and means necessary to develop offensive operations along the entire Soviet-German Front as was done in 1941. In 1942 the Germans were forced to plan offensive operations only in the Front's southern sector. During this offensive the German command counted on breaking through to the Volga, rending the Soviet Army's front into two parts, and severing communication lines joining the central regions of the Soviet Union with the Caucasus. Subsequently, it proposed to direct its main attack northward to cut Moscow off from the Volga and Urals, and, by a combined strike from the east and west, to defeat the Soviet Army's main forces and capture the capital.

To implement this plan, the Germans planned to conduct a series of operations in spring and early summer 1942 to improve the overall operational situation of their forces, free up the maximum quantity of forces and means to participate in the main strike, and inflict maximum losses on Soviet forces. By conducting these separate operations, German forces in April and May intended to liquidate the Kerch bridgehead and break the resistance of the Coastal Army in Sevastopol' in order to support the right flank of their own forces, free up Eleventh Army's main forces, and use the Black Sea as a communications line for subsequent operations.

In May 1942, the enemy planned an offensive operation to liquidate the Soviet forces' bridgehead in the Barvenkovo and Lozovaia regions and seize a favourable line to develop the offensive further along the left bank of the Northern Donets.

The German command proposed to conduct this operation, code-named 'Friderikus I', with an offensive by two shock groups in the general direction of Izium. The first (southern grouping), consisting of Army Group Kleist, was to strike Izium from the Slaviansk and Aleksandrovka region. The second group, consisting of 44th and 71st Infantry Divisions, 23rd Panzer Division and units of 305th Infantry Division, was to strike Izium from the north from the Balakleia region.

Thus, both sides planned their most dynamic missions of the 1942 summer campaign in the southern sector of the Soviet-German front.

Position of Forces on the Southwestern Axis as of 1 April 1942
GROUPING OF SOUTHWESTERN AND SOUTHERN FRONT FORCES
During the offensive battles in February and March 1942, Southwestern and Southern Front forces had improved and consolidated their positions and by 1 April assumed the following posture:
Southwestern Front
Consisting of 21st, 38th and 6th Armies, Southwestern Front defended the northern

sector of the front along the southwestern axis, with 20 rifle, one motorised rifle and four cavalry divisions, and one motorised rifle and two tank brigades. These forces were deployed on a 370km front. The average operational density was one division every 14km.[48]

21st Army, consisting of three rifle divisions (293rd, 297th and 76th), one motorised rifle division (8th) and one motorised rifle brigade, defended the front from Marino, through Shakhovo and Shebekino to Volchansk, which extended 125km. The army's main forces were located on the left flank, in a sector up to 25km wide.

38th Army, consisting of 10 rifle divisions (1st and 13th Guards, 169th, 81st, 226th, 124th, 227th, 300th, 199th and 304th) and three cavalry divisions (5th and 6th Guards, and 32nd), defended the front from Volchansk to Balakleia, with an overall length of 110km. The army's main forces were concentrated on the right flank in a sector 25km wide.

6th Army, consisting of seven rifle divisions (337th, 47th, 343rd, 411th, 393rd, 270th and 253rd), one cavalry division (28th) and two tank brigades (13th and 133rd), defended the northern part of the Barvenkovo bridgehead along a 135km front from Balakleia through Nizhne-Ruskii Bishkin, Alekseevskoe and Novo-Vladmirovka to Samoilovka. The army's main forces were located on the right flank.

310th, 175th, 162nd and 38th Rifle Divisions, which had arrived from the Stavka reserve of the Supreme High Command, and 28th Army headquarters were concentrated in the Krasnaia Poliana, Shalaevo, Kupiansk and Kantemirovka regions in the operational depth of the Southwestern Front. 41st, 248th and 103rd Rifle Divisions, transferred from Southern Front, were in reserve in Svatovo, Kabane and Starobelsk.

In addition to these formations, two tank brigades (198th and 199th) and 18 artillery regiments, which had begun to arrive at their designated concentration regions at the beginning of April from the Stavka reserve and from Southern Front, were at the disposal of the Southwestern Front Commander.

Southern Front
This Front had 31 rifle, nine cavalry and one motorised rifle divisions, seven rifle and nine tank brigades, defending the southern sector of the Southwestern Direction's front. These forces were made up of six armies, which were deployed on a front of 415km. One division was responsible for around 8km.

Southern Front's 57th and 9th Armies, and 2nd, 5th and 6th Cavalry Corps defended the southern sector of the Barvenkovo bridgehead on a front of 170km. There were 13 rifle divisions (14th Guards, 255th, 216th, 351st, 106th, 341st, 349th, 335th, 333rd, 99th, 51st, 150th and 317th), nine cavalry divisions (38th, 49th, 26th, 62nd, 70th, 60th, 34th, 64th and 30th), one motorised rifle, one rifle and six tank brigades (6th, 7th, 12th, 121st, 130th and 131st) in the bridgehead.

The average operational density here was one division for 7km of front.

The remaining front
A distance of 245km from Krasnyi Liman to the Gulf of Taganrog, the remaining front was defended by 37th, 12th, 18th and 56th Armies, which by this time had 18 rifle divisions, 6 rifle brigades and 3 tank brigades.

The average operational density in the zone of these armies was one division for 10.8km of front.

102nd, 73rd, 242nd and 228th Rifle Divisions, which had arrived from the Stavka reserve of the Supreme High Command, were concentrated in Southern Front's oper-

Kharkov, 1942

ational depth along the Voroshilovgrad axis. 266th and 244th Rifle Divisions, sent into the Stavka reserve from Southern Front, were concentrated on the Rostov axis in the towns of Shakhty and Novocherkassk. 277th Rifle Division, which was in the reserve of the Southwestern Direction commander-in-chief, was deployed in Sverdlovsk (60km southeast of Voroshilovgrad).

Thus, the greatest force density of both Fronts was in the Barvenkovo bridgehead. Three of nine armies making up Southwestern and Southern Fronts, three of four cavalry corps, and the principal mass of tanks were concentrated here.

THE ENEMY FORCE GROUPING OPPOSING SOUTHWESTERN AND SOUTHERN FRONTS ON 1 APRIL 1942

Prior to 1 April 1942 and after the winter defensive battles, the German command reordered its forces and concentrated the reserves, which were arriving on the Soviet-German front from the West, in regions east of the line Gomel', Kiev, Poltava and Dnepropetrovsk.

In front of the Southwestern Front

Here the enemy consisted of forces from German Sixth Army (XXIX, XVII, LI and VIII Army Corps) and units from Romanian VI Army Corps of German Seventeenth Army.

Units of the Hungarian 108th Light Infantry Division, German 62nd, 113th and 298th Infantry Divisions and Romanian 1st Infantry Division were deployed against Soviet forces located in the Barvenkovo bridgehead of the Southwestern Front's sector. In addition to these formations, three combat groups were operating in this sector: Group Witte (whose size was slightly less than that of an infantry regiment) covered Zmiev, Group Koch (up to two infantry regiments in size) covered the junction of Sixth and Seventeenth Armies, and Group Friedrich was defending along the Berestovaia River in the Zmiev, Taranovka, Petrovka sector.

Corps reserves — the main forces of Hungarian 108th Light Infantry Division and German captured equipment [trophy] and construction battalions — were deployed in the region east of Krasnograd, and in the town of Zmiev on the rear defensive line.

Units of the 297th and 44th Infantry Divisions defended in the Chuguev bridgehead, and units of 57th, 168th, 75th, 79th and 294th Infantry Divisions defended to the north of the bridgehead.

In addition to all these formations, the German command had at its disposal large operational reserves in this sector of the front. 23rd Panzer Division and 454th Security Division were located in Kharkov, as were 71st Infantry Division units. 3rd Panzer Division units, brought into the reserve, were concentrated in the Liptsy and Russkie Tishki region. One regiment of Romanian 2nd Infantry Division was concentrated east of Shandrovka, and German 305th Infantry Division was *en route* from France. Thus on the Kharkov axis the Germans had in all 16 infantry divisions, two Panzer divisions and two combat groups with a total of 856 guns of 75-210mm calibre, 1,024 mortars and 370 tanks. The average operational density was one division per 18.5km.

Southwestern Front headquarters did not have data on the arriving infantry divisions, and thought that the German grouping on their front consisted of 12 infantry and one tank division; ie, an underestimation of three to four infantry divisions and one panzer division.

In front of the Southern Front

Here the enemy consisted of 26 divisions and 5 combat groups. The numerical size of

2 Planning

each combat group did not exceed two infantry regiments. All these forces were organisationally part of Kleist's Army Group (First Panzer and Seventeenth Armies). The group consisted of around 350 tanks and 1,600 guns.

Units of Romanian 5th Cavalry Division, serving as security, were deployed on the northern coast of the Sea of Azov. 73rd and 125th Infantry Divisions, 13th and 16th Panzer Divisions, and the 'Adolf Hitler' and 'Viking' SS Motorised Divisions, which were part of XIV Motorised Corps, defended the right bank of the Mius River, from the Taganrog Estuary to Kuibyshevo. An Italian expeditionary corps consisting of three divisions (Pasubio, Torino and Celere), and the German XXXXIX Mountain-Rifle Corps, consisting of 198th Infantry Division, 4th Mountain-Rifle Division and one Slovak motorised division, were deployed in defences from Kuibyshevo to Debaltsevo. 111th, 9th, 94th, 76th, 295th, 257th and 68th Infantry Divisions, 97th and 101st Light Infantry Divisions, which were part of LII, IV and XXXXIV Army Corps of Seventeenth Army, were deployed on the front from Debaltsevo to Slaviansk. Five combat groups, 1st Mountain-Rifle, 100th Light Infantry, 60th Motorised and 14th Tank Divisions (both part of III Motorised Corps) and Romanian 2nd Infantry Division, which belonged to Romanian VI Army Corps of Seventeenth Army, operated in the remaining sector against the Barvenkovo salient and Southern Front forces. 384th and 389th Infantry Divisions arrived by rail from Germany and served as the Seventeenth Army commander's reserves in the Gorlovka region.

The average operational force density was one division per 14.5km.

The strongest enemy grouping was located on the Voroshilovgrad and Rostov axes, where the operational density was one division per 10-11km, and the weakest grouping was against the southern face of the Barvenkovo bridgehead. Here the German force grouping consisted primarily of combat groups created from the remnants of German divisions which had been beaten and driven here by Southern Front forces during the winter and spring 1942 offensive battles, and of First Panzer Army units, which had been transferred to fortify Seventeenth Army's front from the less active sectors of the front in the south (III Motorised Corps units).

While preparing its forces for an offensive, in April the German command began organisational-organic reinforcement of cadre formations using arriving replacements and personnel from improvised combat groups. At the same time, it created strong second echelons and reserves from mobile forces and infantry divisions arriving from the West.

A BRIEF SKETCH OF THE GERMAN DEFENCE

While re-forming and refitting its forces, the German command required that they improve their defence. Strongpoints and centres of resistance remained the basis for the defence, and engineer obstacles and fire points were set up in the gaps between them. Continuous trenches were outfitted along important axes.

The main defensive belt, consisting of 2-3 positions, with an overall depth of 8-12km, had primary significance in the German defensive system. Regimental reserves were deployed in the second position and divisional reserves in the third.

The forward edge of Sixth Army's main defensive belt ran east of Pokrovskoe, and then along a line through the populated areas of Mironovka, Grushino and Cherkasskii Bishkin and further along the left bank of the Northern Donets River to Balakleia. Further north the enemy's forward edge ran east of the populated areas of Balakleia, Volkhov Iar, Gavrilovka, Pechenegi, Peschanoe, Ternovaia and Izbitskoe, east of Staritsa and Grafovka, and further north along the right bank of the Northern

Kharkov, 1942

Donets River through Maslova Pristan and Sabinino. While forming a bridgehead on the left bank of the Northern Donets River in the region east of Belgorod, the enemy's forward edge continued further north, west of the populated areas of Malo-Iablonovo, Vikhrovka and Spartak.

The enemy used all populated areas located in the main defensive belt as strongpoints and centres of resistance, and they prepared these for all-round defence.

The enemy had his best developed system of fortifications facing the centre of the Southwestern Front, and, in addition to the main defensive belt, here he had alternate positions, and second and third defensive belts.

The Krasnograd axis was covered by the second and third defensive belts, which were not fully prepared. The second defensive belt was constructed along the right bank of the Orel River from Pavlovka to Velikaia Bereka, and the third (rear) defensive belt was formed along the right bank of the Bogataia River (to Medvedovka) and Berestovaia River (to Taranovka), where they joined the Zmiev defensive system.

The Germans prepared anti-tank defences in the Taranovka and Zmiev sectors most strongly; anti-tank ditches were located there.

The enemy had been preparing the defences of the Chuguev bridgehead and the sector north of it since November 1941, and it was well developed in depth. The second defensive belt ran 10-15km from the forward edge of the main belt, north of Balakleia to Korobochkino and further, intersecting the Northern Donets River along a line through the populated areas of Zarozhnoe, Nepokrytaia, Petrovskoe, Veseloe, Murom and Grafovka.

The third (rear) defensive belt extended to a depth of 20-25km from the main belt along the line of the populated areas of Zmiev, Chuguev, Liptsy and Cheremoshnoe and was based on large populated areas prepared for defence, dominating heights and water obstacles.

In structuring the defence, the enemy envisioned extensive manoeuvre of personnel, fire assets and equipment, both along the front and from the depth.

Preparation of the Operation:
THE DECISIONS OF THE SOUTHWESTERN DIRECTION COMMANDER-IN-CHIEF AND THE SOUTHWESTERN FRONT COMMANDER

On the basis of the Supreme High Command's overall concept and instructions, the Southwestern Direction Commander-in-Chief, Marshal Timoshenko, developed an operational plan, and on 10 April 1942 issued Operational Directive No 00251, which required Southwestern Direction forces to begin to regroup and concentrate on the axes of the Southwestern Front's offensive. [ed. This study refers to the original plan and does not specifically mention the 28 April amended order No 00275.[49]]

The operational plan assigned Southwestern Front the mission of preparing and conducting an offensive operation to defeat the German Kharkov grouping and capture the Kharkov region. Southern Front's mission was to create a solid, deeply echeloned defence along the Voroshilovgrad and Rostov axes. With the start of the offensive by Southwestern Front forces, Southern Front was to begin active operations using part of its forces to pin down opposing enemy forces.

In accordance with the directive's mission, the Southwestern Front commander decided to penetrate the enemy defence in two sectors: the first — from Volchansk to Bolshaia Babka — using forces of the newly organised 28th Army and formations of 21st and 38th Armies; and the second, the main thrust, from Verkhnii Bishkin to Mironovka, using 6th Army forces and an army group detached on 29 April 1942

2 Planning

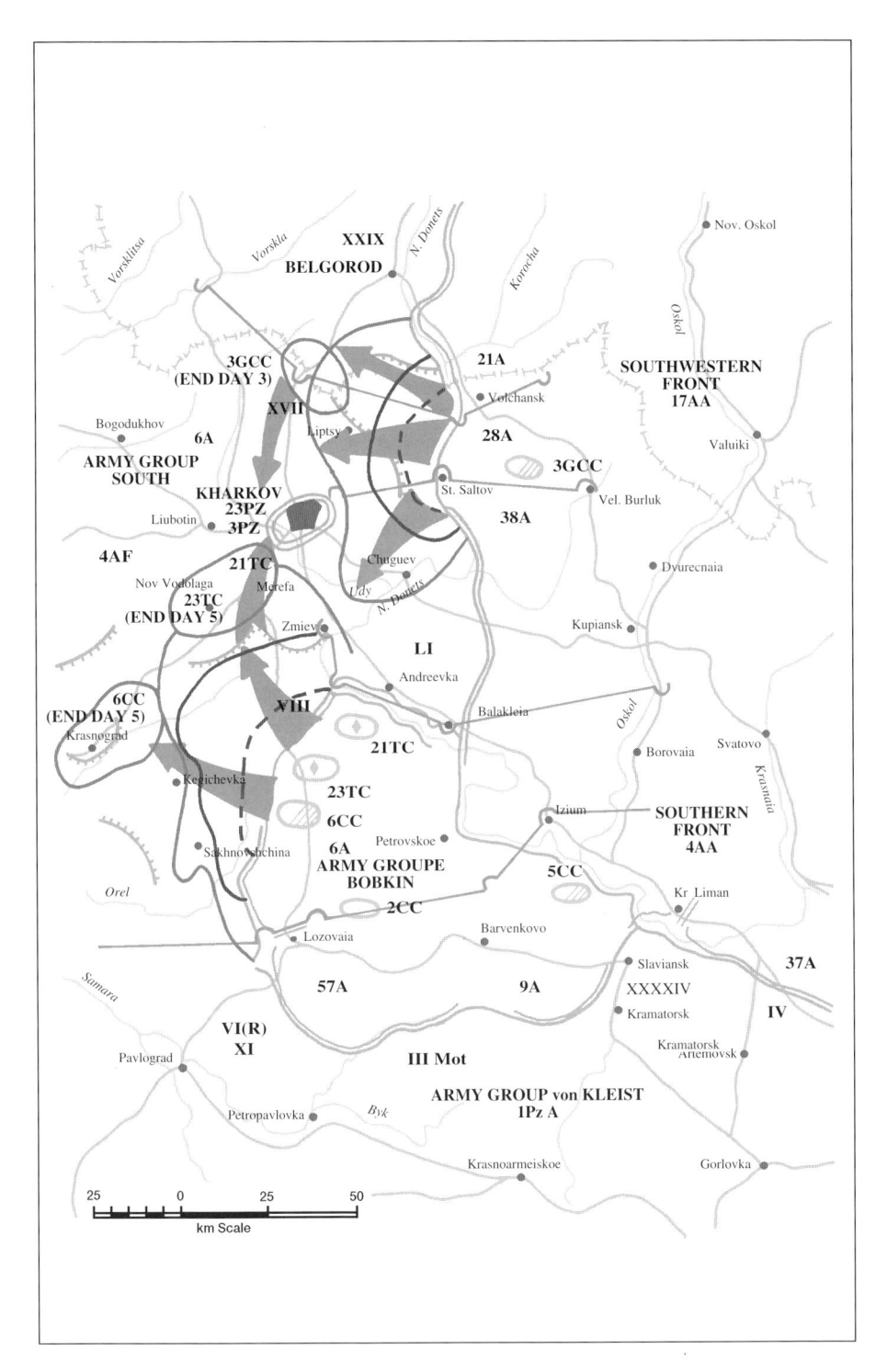

Map 4 — Operational plan

Kharkov, 1942

from 6th Army. After the combined-arms' armies had completed their immediate missions, strong mobile groups would be committed into the penetration to develop success along converging axes toward Kharkov.

One cavalry corps was to attack in 28th Army's sector; two tank corps, consisting of six tank and two motorised rifle brigades, were to attack in 6th Army's sector; and one cavalry corps with one tank brigade was to attack in the Army Group's sector. Front forces were to encircle and destroy the German Kharkov grouping and simultaneously wipe out enemy bridgeheads on the eastern bank of the Northern Donets River in the Zmiev, Balakleia and Pechenegi regions.

The operational plan envisioned two stages.

The first stage of the operation was to continue for three days to a depth of 20-30km. During this stage forces would penetrate the first and second defensive belts, rout the enemy's reserves, and introduce mobile groups into the penetration.

The second stage was to continue for three or four days to a depth of 25-35km. During this stage the enemy's operational reserves would be routed, the immediate approaches to Kharkov would be reached, and mobile forces were to complete the encirclement of the German Kharkov grouping. During this stage, 38th Army would direct its main efforts toward Ternovoe with the mission, in co-operation with 6th Army forces, of encircling and destroying the enemy grouping east of Kharkov.

Forces were assigned the missions outlined below.

21st Army

Consisting of 8th Motorised Rifle, 297th, 301st, 76th, 293rd and 227th Rifle Divisions, 1st Motorised Rifle and 10th Tank Brigades, and 8th Separate Tank Battalion with four RGK artillery regiments, which occupied defences along the front Spartak, Shliakhovo, Titovka and Oktiabrskoe, 21st Army was to penetrate the enemy defence south of Nezhegol in a 14km sector on its left flank, using forces of 76th, 293rd and 297th Rifle Divisions and 10th Tank Brigade, and develop success to Cheremoshnoe. By the end of the third day, the army was to secure the line from Murom to Vysokii, and, when it arrived on a front running from Pristen through Nedostupovka to Petrovka, it was to consolidate and protect 28th Army's right flank against possible enemy counter-attacks from the north and northwest.

The army demarcation line (boundary) on the left flank ran through Poserednoe, Volokonovka, Efremovka, Pervoe Krasnoarmeiskoe, Izbitskoe, Kazachia Lopan and Graivoron (all points, except for Poserednoe, Efremovka and Pervoe Krasnoarmeiskoe, were exclusively for 21st Army).

28th Army

Consisting of 13th Guards, 244th, 175th, 169th, 162nd and 38th Rifle Divisions, 3rd Guards Cavalry Corps (5th and 6th Guards and 32nd Cavalry Divisions and 34th Motorised Rifle Brigade), 6th Guards, 84th, 90th and 57th Tank Brigades, reinforced by nine RGK artillery regiments and six engineer pontoon battalions, 28th Army was to penetrate the enemy defences in the 15km Izbitskoe sector, excluding Dragunovka, and, while developing the attack along the Borshchevoe axis, by the close of the third day, it was to reach the line from Sereda through Veseloe to Petrovskoe and support the introduction of 3rd Guards Cavalry Corps into the penetration.

On the sixth day of the operation, the army was to capture a line running from Zhuravlevka through Cherkasskoe-Lozovoe to Bolshaia Danilovka and support cavalry corps' operations toward Dergachi and Gavrilovka. 3rd Guards Cavalry Corps,

2 Planning

consisting of three cavalry divisions and one motorised rifle brigade, was to enter the penetration in 28th Army's sector from the line of Sereda to Veseloe, capture the Kazachia Lopan, Dementevka and Vysokaia Iaruga regions, support the advance of army forces to the line of Cherkasskoe-Lozovoe through Bolshaia to Danilovka, and be prepared for operations toward Dergachi and Gavrilovka to link up with 6th Army's mobile forces.

The demarcation line on the left flank ran through Velikii Burluk, Seredovka, Staryi Saltov, Gordienko, Mikhailovka Pervaia and Shevchenki (all points, except for Seredovka, Staryi Saltov and Mikhailovka Pervaia, were inclusively for 28th Army).

38th Army
Consisting of 226th, 300th, 199th, 304th, 81st and 124th Rifle Divisions, and 133rd, 36th and 13th Tank Brigades, reinforced by six artillery regiments of the Reserve of the Supreme High Command and six engineer battalions, which defended the 74km front from Martovaia, Bazaleevka, Bogodarovka to Olkhovatka, 38th Army was to strike using forces of four divisions and three tank brigades in the 25km Dragunovka, Bolshaia Babka sector and, by the close of the third day, secure the line Lebedinka through Zarozhnoe to Piatnitskoe, while supporting 28th Army forces against enemy counter-attacks from the south and southwest.

Subsequently, when the offensive developed toward Rogan and Ternovoe and the shock grouping arrived in the Vvedenskoe and Chuguev region, 38th Army, in co-operation with 6th Army units, was to complete the encirclement and rout the German grouping east of Kharkov and prepare for an offensive against Kharkov from the east.

The demarcation line on 38th Army's left flank was Mankovka, Zagryzova, Balakleia, Cherkasskii Bishkin, Zmiev (all points, except for Zmiev, were inclusive for 38th Army).

6th Army
Consisting of 337th, 47th, 253rd, 41st, 411th, 266th, 103rd, and 248th Rifle Divisions, 5th Guards, 37th, 38th, and 48th Tank Brigades, and 21st and 23rd Tank Corps, reinforced with 14 artillery regiments of the Reserve of the Supreme High Command and five engineer battalions, 6th Army was to strike from its left flank, penetrate enemy defences in the 26km sector from (excluding) Verkhnii Bishkin to Grushino, capture the line from Velikaia Bereka to Efremovka, secure the introduction of the tank corps from this line into the penetration and, by the close of the fourth day of the operation, capture Zmiev, Taranovka and Berestovaia.[50] Subsequently, co-operating with mobile formations, the army was to develop the attack in the general direction of Merefa and Kharkov. When forces reached a front running from Butovka through Merefa to Rakitnoe, three reinforced regiments were to strike from the Zmiev region against Ternovoe into the rear of the German grouping operating southeast of Kharkov, in order to destroy it quickly in co-operation with 38th Army and eliminate bridgeheads on the left bank of the Northern Donets River in the Zmiev, Balakleia and Pechengi regions.

21st and 23rd Tank Corps, after their commitment into the penetration, were to reach the Komarovka, Rakitnoe, Novaia Vodolaga and Ostroverkhovka regions by the close of the fifth day of the operation and cut off all routes from Kharkov to the west. Subsequently, these corps, after linking up with 3rd Guards Cavalry Corps forces, were to complete the encirclement of the German Kharkov grouping.

The army demarcation line on the left flank ran from Gorokhovka through

Kharkov, 1942

Grushino to Kirillovka (all points were inclusive for 6th Army).

Army Group Bobkin
Consisting of 393rd and 270th Rifle Divisions, 7th Tank Brigade, and 6th Cavalry Corps (49th, 26th and 28th Cavalry Divisions), Army Group Bobkin was to penetrate the German defence in the 10km Koshparovak to Kiptivka sector, with the immediate mission of capturing the line from Dmitrovka to Seredovka and protecting the introduction of 6th Cavalry Corps into the penetration. Developing success to the west and southwest, Army Group forces were to capture the line Sofievka through Tarasovka to Andreevka by the close of the fourth day of the operation, and reach the front extending from Kegichevka, Dar Nadezhdy and Sakhnovshchina to Lukashevka by the close of the seventh day of the operation.

6th Cavalry Corps, by entering the penetration and developing the attack toward Kazachii Maidan, was to capture Krasnograd and protect 6th Army forces against counter-attacks from the west by the close of the fifth day.

Other Forces
According to Combat Order No 00241 of the Southwestern Direction Commander-in-Chief, dated 6 April 1942, the demarcation line between the Southwestern and Southern Fronts as of 16 April was established to be Veshenskaia, Starobelsk, Izium, Velikaia Kamishevakha, Tsaredarovka, Pavlovka, Borodaevka (all points, except for Veshenskaia, were inclusive for Southern Front).

Two rifle divisions (277th and 343rd), one cavalry corps, and three separate tank battalions (96 tanks) were located in the Southwestern Front commander's reserve. 277th Rifle Division, then preparing defensive positions along the line of Arkadievka, Ivanovka and Hill 182.4, was to be in constant readiness to repel enemy counter-attacks along the axes Pechenegi, Arkadievka and Balakleia, Poltava.

343rd Rifle Division was to prepare a defence along the line of Nurovo, Hill 191.0 and Kune, and be constantly ready to repel possible enemy attacks along the Bogodarovka, Nurov; Balakleia, Aleksandrovka; and Izium, Kune axes.

2nd Cavalry Corps, consisting of 3 cavalry divisions deployed in the Privole, Rozhdestvenskoe and Mechebilovka region, was to prepare counter-attacks against Gorokhovka, Shebelinka; Rozhdestvenskoe, Lozovaia; and Mechebilovka, Barvenkovo.

71st Separate Tank Battalion was deployed in Savintsy, and 132nd and 92nd Tank Battalions were in Voronezh.

On 6 April 1942 the Southwestern Direction Commander-in-Chief assigned Southern Front the mission of organising a solid defence and supporting Southwestern Front's offensive operations. Directive No 00241 and Directive No 00177 from the Southern Front commander envisaged no dynamic actions for this Front's forces.

PREPARATION OF FORCES AND STAFFS
According to High Command instructions, Southwestern Direction's forces and staffs were to prepare for combat in the forthcoming offensive between 1 and 15 April. During this period, units and formations were brought up to required personnel strength. The combat preparation plan allocated 70% of the time for tactical training of forces. Forces conducted exercises on the terrain in conditions close to actual combat. Each developed training theme was concluded by battalion and regimental exercises.

2 Planning

Artillery units focused primary attention on fire training, study of matériel (logistic) units, and full combat readiness of units.

The primary mission for combat training in tank forces was crew co-ordination and the study of procedures for fighting against enemy tanks.

However, during the preparatory period a significant portion of force and staff combat training measures were not completed because a large amount of time was lost while regrouping forces.

ORGANISATION OF CONTROL AND COMMUNICATIONS

Control of Southwestern Direction forces was [complicated by] the combining of the function of the Direction's command and operational group with the functions of the Southwestern Front's command and staff. This took place because the Direction's Commander-in-Chief and his chief of staff at that time were also the Southwestern Front commander and the Front's chief of staff respectively.

Readying the staff to control troops during the forthcoming offensive operation took place while force regrouping was under way and was combined with continuing work on troop leadership. During the preparatory period, combined-arms command posts executed troop control measures. These made extensive use of signals officers, who of all available means of communications, relied most on wire.

The distance of division, army and front headquarters from first-echelon forces, and the distance from the army control apparatus to the front line was as follows:

Unit	KP* distance from front	VPU** distance from front
21st Army	60km	20km
28th Army	30km	30km
38th Army	70km	30km
6th Army	40km	22km
Army Group	20km	none

* Command post
** Auxiliary field control post

The distance from division headquarters to army headquarters was as follows: 21st Army — 18-40km; 28th Army — 23-28km; 38th Army — 20-60km; and 6th Army — 16-32km.

Division command posts were, as a rule, 4km and sometimes 8-10km from the forward edge of the defence. The axis of deployment of command posts, as indicated in combat orders, did not go beyond the limits of the front line. Further deployment of command posts was left to the discretion of divisional commanders.

PLANNING AND PREPARATION OF THE ARTILLERY OFFENSIVE

Southwestern Front forces in the forthcoming operation were to penetrate a deeply echeloned, prepared enemy defence. The use of a considerable quantity of artillery and mortars was necessary to ensure successful ground force operations.

During the offensive, the Stavka reserve of the Supreme High Command reinforced the Southwestern Front with 18 artillery regiments. In addition, 14 artillery regiments were transferred to the Front from Southern Front. Thus, forces delivering the main attack were reinforced by 32 artillery regiments.

Kharkov, 1942

There were 13 artillery regiments concentrated in 6th Army's penetration sector, and 19 regiments in 28th Army's sector and on the flanks of adjacent 21st and 38th Armies.

Front headquarters developed the overall plan for the artillery offensive and provided armies with instructions on the use of artillery.

Directive No 03 from the Supreme High Command, dated 10 January 1942, established the basis for planning the artillery offensive. It required that artillery support not be limited to artillery preparation, but include, as well, preparation and accompaniment of infantry to the entire tactical depth of the enemy defence.

During the entire period of the artillery preparation, the German defence was to be subjected to fire power to a depth of 5-6km. Artillery fire raids were to ensure reliable suppression of enemy strongpoints. Artillery fire was to accompany the infantry until the entire tactical depth of the German defence had been overcome.

In planning the offensive, artillery staffs focused special attention on the organisation of continuous, well-co-ordinated co-operation with infantry and tanks, precise knowledge of missions being executed by infantry and tanks, reconnaissance of enemy fire assets and firm mastery of fire control signals.

Twelve days before the commencement of the offensive, armies held brief assemblies for the divisional artillery chiefs. During these meetings, operational missions were worked out on the terrain.

Artillery control was basically assigned to chiefs of division artillery. The chief of army artillery organised his forward observation post along the main axis, and communicated with the chiefs of division artillery and the army artillery group.

Artillery regimental and battalion commanders observation posts were to be co-located with those of combined-arms commanders.

By 5 May 1942, armies had basically completed planning for the artillery offensive. By this time army and division staffs had compiled a fire planning table, plans for shifting regiments of the Reserve of the High Command, army artillery group force tables and signal tables for co-operation with infantry and tanks.

The artillery offensive included artillery preparation of the enemy defence and successive concentrations of artillery fire against specific lines and objectives to accompany the infantry and tanks.

According to the operational plan, all armies conducted artillery target ranging (registration) from 05.00 to 06.30 on 12 May. Artillery preparation was to be conducted from 06.30 to 07.30. Table 1 shows the planning for army artillery preparation:

Table 1 Period of artillery preparations for each army

	21st	28th	38th	6th	Army Group
1. Initial fire raid	5min	5min	none	5min	5min
2. Destruction of enemy defensive structures and suppression of enemy personnel	45min	45min	40min	35min	35min
3. Fire raid by all artillery at the end of the artillery preparation	10min	10min	20min	20min	20min

During the final minutes, artillery was to fire at a depth of up to 6km subjecting the first 1.5km of the enemy defence to the greatest action.

Army artillery groups were created from army reinforcement artillery assets. 6th Army's artillery group consisted of 4 artillery and 2 Guards mortar regiments and 1 Guards mortar battalion and 28th Army's consisted of three artillery regiments. The

2 Planning

groups were at the disposal of army commanders and had the following missions:

- fighting against enemy artillery
- supporting infantry during the offensive in the depth of the enemy defence
- protecting the flanks of shock groupings
- fighting against enemy reserves in concentration regions and on approaches
- supporting the commitment of mobile formations and the rout of withdrawing enemy units

As illustrated above, the complexity of force regrouping was a primary feature of Southwestern Front's preparatory period for the offensive. In this case, it was necessary to consider especially carefully the transfer of artillery assets to new regions. However, Southwestern Front staff failed to do so.

The transfer of artillery from the southern part of the Barvenkovo salient to Southwestern Front's northern penetration sector and from Southern Front's left flank to the Barvenkovo salient (to Southwestern Front's offensive sector) was conducted on the basis of personal (verbal) instructions and orders of each artillery units in isolation, in the absence of a general regrouping plan. This disrupted rather than assisted the normal course of regrouping.

Of the 32 artillery regiments allocated to reinforce troops participating in the penetration operation, only 17 were in their firing positions by 11 May. 11 regiments were still in concentration areas, 12-15km from firing positions, and 4 artillery regiments had not arrived at the penetration sector by the commencement of the operation. Thus, taking into consideration mortars as well, around 34% of artillery and mortar assets were unable to participate in the artillery offensive on the first day of the operation. The planned grouping and sequence of employing artillery units had already changed at the very beginning of the operation. Table 2 shows the actual number of guns and mortars concentrated in penetration sectors by the time the operation commenced:

Table 2 Gun and mortar concentrations by sector

Army	Sector width	Guns 152mm	122mm	76mm	Total	Mortars 120mm	82mm	Total	Total guns /mortars	Density per km of front
21st	14km	18	23	80	121	20	190	210	331	23.6
28th	15km	41	61	191	293	76	524	600	893	59.5
38th	26km	38	52	165	255	40	190	230	485	18.7
6th and Army Group	36km	127	117	241	485	70	596	666	1151	32.0

PLANNING AND PREPARATION FOR USING ARMOURED FORCES

The Southwestern Front concentrated 19 tank brigades and 4 separate tank battalions to break through the main enemy defensive belt. Of these, 5 tank brigades (6th, 7th, 64th, 139th and 131st) were resubordinated from Southern Front to the Southwestern Front commander. Two tank brigades (198th and 199th) and three separate tank battalions (96 tanks) were transferred from the Stavka reserve of the Supreme High Command and transported from the Voronezh region. The primary tank mass (560 of 925) was allocated to the first echelon for direct infantry support in the offensive sector of the Front's shock groupings.

• 21st Army was reinforced by 10th Tank Brigade and 8th Separate Tank Battalion (48 tanks).

Kharkov, 1942

- 28th Army was reinforced by 84th, 90th, 57th and 6th Guards Tank Brigades (181 tanks).
- 38th Army was reinforced by 36th, 13th and 133rd Tank Brigades (125 tanks).

In all, 354 tanks were concentrated in the northern sector. 6th Army was reinforced by 38th, 48th, 37th and 5th Guards Tank Brigades, and the army group by 7th Tank Brigade. 206 direct infantry support tanks were concentrated in the southern sector of the penetration.

The distribution of direct infantry support tanks by armies, and the average density in the sectors is shown in Table 3.

Table 3 Distribution of infantry support tanks by sector

Army	Sector length	Tanks in 1st echelon	Tanks in 2nd echelon	Total	Tank density per km of front
21st	14km	48	—	48	3.5
28th	15km	138	43	181	12.0
38th	26km	125	—	125	4.8
6th	26km	124	42	166	6.4
Army Group	10km	40	—	40	4.0

The missions for direct infantry support tanks were to support the infantry attack and swiftly penetrate the enemy defence to create conditions for commitment of tank and cavalry corps into the penetration.

Six tank brigades (6th, 130th, 131st, 64th, 198th and 199th) and two motorised rifle brigades were combined into 23rd and 21st Tank Corps (269 tanks), and were to be used as mobile groups in the southern offensive sector.[51]

After the infantry reached the line of Verkhniaia Bereka, Efremovka, the tank corps were to enter into the penetration, defeat the enemy's operational reserves, reach the Komarovka, Rakitnoe and Ostroverkhovka region, and protect the southern shock group against enemy strikes from the west. The tank corps' subsequent mission was to link up with 3rd Guards Cavalry Corps west of Kharkov and assist in the encirclement and destruction of the German grouping.

The Southwestern Front commander assigned missions to the tank corps. The 6th Army Commander determined the time for introducing tank corps into the penetration and specified the line of commitment.

PLANNING AND PREPARATION FOR USING AVIATION

Preparation of Front air forces for the operation began in April 1942, and took place in complex conditions. Unfavourable meteorological conditions during the preparatory period of the operation made it impossible for aviation to act effectively against the enemy's operational reserves and defence objectives. This weakened the protection of the ongoing regrouping.

In addition, work on preparing and outfitting the large number of temporary field airstrips and landing areas required a large quantity of forces and equipment.

During the period of the offensive operation, Southwestern Front air forces were reinforced by 233 aircraft at the expense of Southern Front. These aircraft, while remaining subordinate to the Southern Front commander, were to support the offensive of Southwestern Front's southern shock group.

Table 4 shows the distribution by armies of Front aviation and aviation of the reserve of the Supreme High Command, according to the decision of the

2 Planning

Southwestern Front commander:

Table 4 Distribution by army of aviation assets[A]

Army	Fighters	Bombers Night	Bombers Day	Ground attack	Recce	Total aircraft	Aviation regiment Fighter	Aviation regiment Bomber	Aviation regiment Other
21st	13	15	6	—	—	34	43	135	596 (FB)
28th	35	18	31	14	—	98	2/254/ 148/273	52	431 (Ass) 709 (FB)/ 99 (M)
38th	49	19	18	10	4	100	164/282/ 248/168/ 512/6		598 (FB)/ 10(M)/ 91 (R)
6th	41	51	19	34	—	145	23/296/ 181/789/ 146/581	13 Guards/ 818	623/633/ 714 (FB)/ 92/245/ 211 (Ass)
Army Group	4	22	11	9	—	46	8/149/494[B]/?		

[A] Abbreviations used: FB= Fighter-bomber, Ass= Assault, M= Mixed, R= Recce, Sqn= Squadron
[B] RAG-5

Because all aviation was distributed by army, its control was decentralised. At the same time, not only army commanders, but also the front commander, assigned aviation missions.

Aviation was to perform the following missions:

- Assist ground forces in penetrating the enemy defence and committing mobile groups into the penetration by means of bomber and ground attack strikes against enemy artillery, tanks and personnel.
- Prevent the approach of enemy reserves from the Belgorod, Gotnia, Akhtyrka, Poltava and Krasnograd direction.
- Assist mobile formations in developing success by means of continuous strikes against withdrawing German forces, enemy force assembly regions and enemy communications junctions
- Reconnoitre the enemy.
- Destroy [river] crossings in the Kremenchug and Dnepropetrovsk regions.
- Support force operations by fighting against enemy aviation at airfields and in the air.

During the preparatory period, aviation was to cover the concentration of ground forces at bridgeheads and continuously reconnoitre the enemy.

On the night before the commencement of the offensive, night bomber aviation forces were to conduct air strikes against enemy rear objectives, strongpoints, headquarters and communications centres to disrupt command and control and supply.

From the commencement of the artillery preparation, all aviation would be employed in army penetration sectors. Aviation's primary missions during this period were to demolish strongpoints, destroy personnel, suppress artillery and mortar batteries, and demolish communications centres.

When the attack commenced, aviation was to shift to suppressing enemy reserves, disrupting enemy movement through primary road junctions in the immediate rear

Kharkov, 1942

and supporting operations of tank and cavalry corps comprising the mobile groups.

During the second and subsequent days of the operation, aviation was to support the infantry battle in the depth of the German defence and accompany mobile formations.

Detailed planning of aviation actions was accomplished for the first six days of the operation.

MATÉRIEL SUPPORT AND PREPARATION OF REAR SERVICES

The preparation of Southwestern Front forces' rear services for the offensive operation began during the first days of March 1942.

Directive No 0188 from the Front commander, dated 27 February, specified the volume of rear preparatory work. Forces were to receive one outfitted route for each rifle division and two for each army, bring all available transport into order, lay in lumber to outfit routes and crossings, and organise traffic regulation and provost service on crossings and routes.

On 10 April 1942, the Southwestern Direction Commander-in-Chief established norms for assembling all kinds of reserves for the forces by 25 April, while placing special emphasis on material for 28th and 6th Armies' formations. It suggested stockage in deployment regions of 4-5 ammunition loads per man, 7-8 POL fuellings and a 15-day ration of food and forage.

By the end of April, in Operational Directive No 00275, the Southwestern Front commander specified the reserve norms in armies with respect to various types of weapons, and obligated the chief of the Front's rear service to prepare two army roads each for 28th and 6th Armies' shock group, to support the tank and cavalry corps with delivery means and to establish a precise sequence for route movement. This directive required that supplies be assembled before 5–6 May.

The expenditure of material for the conduct of an operation was as follows: 5.5 loads of artillery shells, 4.5 loads of mines and rifle cartridges and 7-8 POL refuellings (reckoning on 0.2 refuellings per day per vehicle).

Table 5 shows matériel reserves gathered during the preparatory period of the operation in Southwestern Front's armies (by 12 May 1942):

Table 5a Matériel reserves — ammunition (in firing loads)

Ammunition	Reserves [a]	Armies			
		21st	28th	38th	6th
Mines — 120mm	0.47				
in Forces		0.6	0.75	1.2	0.7
in Army Warehouses		1.0	0.61	0.2	0.5
Shell — 45mm	1.07				
in Forces		2.4	2.1	2.0	1.8
in Army Warehouses		3.5	3.1	2.8	1.3
Shell — 76mm Regimental	0.29				
in Forces		1.5	1.1	1.1	1.3
in Army Warehouses		0.4	1.54	0.2	0.8
Shell — 76mm Divisional	0.28				
in Forces		1.9	0.4	1.0	0.9
in Army Warehouses		0.6	0.32	0.3	0.4

2 Planning

Ammunition	Reserves[a]	Armies			
		21st	28th	38th	6th
Shell — 122mm How (1931)	4.25				
in Forces		0.7	2.0	2.2	0.5
in Army Warehouses		0.5	2.75	0.4	0.8
Shell — 122mm Gun (1938)	—				
in Forces		3.1	—	0.4	—
in Army Warehouses		3.6	0.58	—	0.6
Shell — 152mm How (1909/30)	1.29				
in Forces		—	—	1.2	—
in Army Warehouses		—	4.1	—	1.7
Shell — 152mm How-Gun (1938)	0.11				
in Forces		—	2.5	2.0	1.2
in Army Warehouses		—	2.4	1.3	2.1
Shell — 152mm Gun (1937)	0.4				
in Forces		1.5	2.1	1.1	1.5
in Army Warehouses		2.1	1.5	2.0	1.2

Table 5b Matériel reserves — POL (in fuellings)

POL	Reserves[a]	Armies			
		21st	28th	38th	6th
Aviation Gasoline	10.0				
in Forces		—	—	—	—
in Army Warehouses		—	—	—	—
Motor Vehicle Gasoline	4.2				
in Forces		3.0	3.9	1.4	2.2
in Army Warehouses		1.5	0.6	1.2	0.5

[a] Reserves in Front warehouses

The actual presence of ammunition in first-echelon division artillery units and reinforcing units with respect to principal types of weaponry did not exceed an average of 1.5 loads, and 0.3 loads were in reserve at front depots. By the time the operation commenced, shock groups still had not amassed the quantity of ammunition envisioned by the operational plan.

Reserves of food and forage in front forces were distributed very unequally, and amounted to from 1-12 daily rations.

By the time the operation commenced, forward supply bases in 28th Army's offensive sector were deployed on the left bank of the Northern Donets River, and in 6th Army all rear installations were located in the Barvenkovo bridgehead.

The gathering of material for the forces necessary to conduct battle encountered a series of difficulties during the preparatory period because of the poor outfitting of rear regions. Railroads and Northern Donets River crossings were continually under pressure from enemy aviation and were unable to support the required traffic capacity.

The Staryi Oskol, Valuiki, Kupiansk and Rubezhnoe railroad, which had branches in the Kupiansk region toward Volchansk, Shevchenkovo and Izium supported Southwestern Front forces and units of Southern Front forces located in the Barvenkovo bridgehead. The traffic capacity of this road was up to 10-12 trains every 24 hours, and the railroad branches were in a state of reconstruction. The railroad outside the Barvenkovo bridgehead was not used because of massive destruction of the roadbed and the absence of rolling stock.

Given these conditions and the fact that the distance from the active railroad sta-

Kharkov, 1942

tions to the front line in several places reached 100-150km, the primary weight of transport lay on motor vehicles.

The Staryi Saltov bridgehead was connected to the left bank of the Northern Donets by two high bridges, with a cargo capacity of 30 tons (one in the Pisarevka region and the other in the Staryi Saltov region).

The Barvenkovo bridgehead in the Southwestern Front sector was connected with the left bank only by a single high bridge in the Savintsy region, with a cargo capacity of 60 tons. A second bridge also with a cargo capacity of 60 tons, was in the Southern Front sector in the Izium region.

Available bridges were often put out of action because of demolition carried out by German aviation. Thus, the bridge in the Pisarevka region was demolished three times, and the bridge in the Staryi Saltov region five times. The bridge in the Izium region was also demolished, and, by the commencement of the Southwestern Front offensive, had not been fully reconstructed.

PARTY-POLITICAL WORK
Events on the Soviet-German front, which took place from December 1941 until April 1942, sharply changed the military and political situation to the Soviet Union's advantage and favourably affected our forces' morale.

The Southwestern Front's Military Council, when determining the missions for party-political work among the forces, proceeded from Comrade Stalin's instructions that 1942 should be a decisive year in the war, with respect to defeating the Fascist armies.

Stalin provided exhaustive instructions on the direction and content of party-political work in the entire Soviet Army for 1942 in Orders No 55, dated 23 February, and No 130, dated 1 May 1942.

The Soviet Army was assigned the great mission of liberating Soviet land from the German-Fascist invaders, and the mission of liberating our brothers — the Ukrainians, Moldavians, Belorussians, Lithuanians, Latvians, Estonians and Karelians — from the shame and humiliation to which the German-Fascist villains had subjected them. The execution of this exalted mission required great intensity of physical and moral strength on the part of all Soviet Army personnel.

During the preparatory period for the offensive, Front and army political organs directed all their work toward imparting high offensive spirit, strengthening the political-morale condition of all units and formation personnel, strengthening combat discipline and inculcating a righteous hatred for the Fascist invaders.

Extensively developed party-political work in the forces introduced Stalin's instructions into the deep consciousness of each soldier.

Rallies, meetings and lectures publicised issues concerning the Soviet Union's international position, the Soviet Army's successes and the labour exploits of the Soviet people in the rear and told about the Fascist barbarians' atrocities on temporarily occupied Soviet land.

The consciousness of each soldier and officer was indoctrinated with confidence that the Soviet Army and Soviet people would defeat the Fascist army, and that the day of Fascist Germany's perfidious invasion of the USSR was the beginning of the end of Hitler's Germany.

Political organs and party organisations focused considerable attention on clarifying the problems of strengthening the Soviet Union's defence capabilities, reinforcing the friendship of the entire world's freedom-loving nations and creating conditions for

2 Planning

the ultimate defeat of Hitler's army. By their work, political organs introduced confidence that the might of the Soviet Union was indestructible.

As a result of all-encompassing party-political work, the political-morale condition of forces increased considerably. Personnel were inspired to devote all their efforts, skill and experience to preparing for the decisive battles. Troop combat training was elevated.

The increased inclination of enlisted men, sergeants and officers toward the Komsomol and the Party was a clear indicator of improved political-morale condition of the forces. A month and a half before the offensive the Front's armies received as many as 12,000 applications for acceptance as party candidates and members.

As a result, the number of Communists in some units reached 52%. Komsomol and Party organisations in companies and battalions were strengthened. The best and most progressive enlisted; sergeant and officer personnel entered the Komsomol and Party.

REGROUPING OF SOUTHWESTERN FRONT FORCES
The Southwestern Front began regrouping its forces at the end of March 1942. The regrouping encountered great difficulties, and its execution was particularly complex. The regrouping complexity resulted from the fact that a large number of formations had to be shifted along the front. All reserves of the Southwestern Direction Commander-in-Chief deployed in Southern Front's sector were located a great distance from the penetration sectors. Simultaneously with the regrouping, it was necessary to accommodate newly arrived formations from the Stavka reserve of the Supreme High Command and continue the formation of the new 28th Army.

On 13 April the directorate of this Stavka reserve army arrived in Belyi Kolodez. In accordance with the Commander-in-Chief's decision, 28th Army consisted of six rifle divisions. Two of these (13th Guards and 169th Rifle Divisions) had to shift from 38th Army northward to the sector allocated for 28th Army and transfer their sectors to 38th Army's remaining right-flank units. The combat sector between them was given to 244th Rifle Division, which was arriving from Novocherkassk. The remaining three rifle divisions (175th, 162nd and 38th) were transferred to 28th Army from the Stavka reserve. 175th Rifle Division was to occupy a staging area for the offensive as part of the first echelon of 28th Army's operational formation on its right flank, while 38th and 162nd Rifle Divisions were to be part of the army's second echelon.

21st Army's shock group, contiguous with 28th Army's right flank, consisted of three rifle divisions. Of them, one (227th) was transferred from the Piatnitskoe region, where it had earlier occupied the defence as part of 38th Army; the second (293rd) was being transferred from 21st Army's right flank.

38th Army, two of whose divisions occupied a defence along a wide front on its left flank, concentrated its main forces (226th, 124th, 81st and 300th Rifle Divisions) in a 26km front contiguous with 28th Army's left flank. 1st Guards Rifle Division was transferred to the Stavka of the Supreme High Command and was moved out of 38th Army's sector.

Along the southern axis, 6th Army's shock group was created out of four rifle divisions and two tank corps, which had recently arrived from Southwestern Direction Commander-in-Chief's reserve. Three rifle divisions (41st, 248th and 103rd) were transferred from the Svatovo, Kabane and Starobelsk region, and a fourth rifle division (266th) was moved forward from the Shakhty region, where it had earlier been in Stavka reserve.

Kharkov, 1942

The limited number of Northern Donets River crossings and the transfer over great distances of 41st and, in particular, 266th Rifle Divisions increased the complexity of 6th Army's regrouping. These divisions were part of the army shock group's first echelon. The distances from the regions where these divisions were located to the front lines were 150 and 350km respectively.

The force regrouping in the Army Group's sector was less complicated. Here, the shock group was formed, using primarily 6th Army units which had been released from defensive sectors, and units of 6th Cavalry Corps and 7th Tank Brigade, which were transferred into the Army Group from Southern Front forces located in the Barvenkovo bridgehead.

During the offensive, as mentioned above, a large number of tank units and 32 artillery regiments from the Reserve of the Supreme High Command reinforced the Southwestern Front. The bulk of these assets were to concentrate in the Staryi Saltov bridgehead and in the Barvenkovo salient. Arriving artillery concentrated a distance of 10-15km from their firing position regions.

The regrouping and concentration of Southwestern Front forces ensued during the spring thaw. River floods and the absence of good, outfitted roads (routes) made the timely arrival of units and formations at their assigned regions difficult.

Given the limited preparation time for the operation, the formation of two shock groups and their concentration in penetration sectors, the transport of forces over large distances required highly intense physical efforts on the part of the forces and intense staff work to organise continuous control over the course of the regroupings.

The absence of a sufficient number of highways and dirt roads, the presence of only one lateral railroad line with a traffic capacity of 10-12 trains every 24 hours, and the limited number of crossings over the Oskol and Northern Donets Rivers required army staffs to plan precisely for the arrival of forces in their regions, exploit correctly all routes, regulate traffic precisely on crossings and organise reliable air cover over crossing sites and concentration areas. It was also necessary to expend a large quantity of matériel and employ a considerable number of people for repair, road construction and road maintenance to keep roads in readiness for exploitation.

Front and army staffs worked very fervently, but did not achieve necessary precision in troop control.

Front and army staffs had no unified plan for regrouping forces. Forces were moved on the basis of separate instructions, which specified only the concentration areas and time of movement. Staffs provided no instructions on the sequence and order of movement along routes, observation of *maskirovka* [deception] or establishment of the order for crossing bridges. There were no instructions for organising air defence on the march or in concentration areas.

3
AREA OF OPERATIONS

Strategic Aspects

The Kharkov area was indeed a pivotal region on the German-Soviet front. Located almost midway between Moscow and the Black Sea, the city lay at the junction of two strategic axes heading eastward across the Soviet Union (see Map 5).[1] North of the Pripiat River, two well-defined (and often used) axes led to Leningrad via the Baltic States and to Moscow via Minsk and Smolensk. South of the Pripiat, a clear axis traversed the Soviet Union emanating from the Lvov region, across the Dnepr River at Kiev and eastward across northern Ukraine through Konotop and Kursk to the Volga River at Voronezh. Kharkov was situated on the right flank of this axis. Further to the south, yet another strategic axis stretched across the southern Ukraine from the Romanian border to Dnepropetrovsk on the Dnepr, through the Donbas region, across the Northern Donets River into the 'Great Bend' of the Don River and on to the banks of the Volga River at Stalingrad. Kharkov lay just north of this strategic axis. Finally, a fifth strategic axis digressed from the third (Stalingrad) axis southward into the vast Caucasus region.

German strategic planners faced a dilemma once their forces had reached the Kharkov region as to the direction of advance. At the start of the Russian campaign the German High Command had attacked with single army groups — north towards Leningrad, centre towards Moscow and south towards Kiev and the Ukraine. Once their forces had reached, roughly, the line Leningrad-Moscow-Kharkov, they found that they lacked sufficient strength to attack with entire army groups simultaneously along each of the axes towards the next three critical strategic points — Moscow, Voronezh and Rostov. So, Guderian's 2nd Panzer Army — which had been deployed adjacent to Army Group South along the Konotop-Kursk axis after completion of the Kiev encirclement — had turned northward towards the southern approaches to Moscow to give Army Group Centre what was felt to be sufficient forces to seize the Soviet capital. Von Kleist's 1st Panzer Group, with the remainder of Army Group South, had swept southward along the Donbas axis to seize Rostov. As a result, the two panzer groups diverged, leaving the Voronezh axis uncovered, and, in so doing, exposed their respective flanks. Soviet counter-offensives against Guderian's right flank south of Moscow and von Kleist's left flank north of Rostov had played a major role in the German winter defeat.

A similar dilemma faced German strategic planners in spring 1942. The campaign proposed in Operation 'Blau' saw Army Groups North and Centre holding along the Leningrad and Moscow axes and Army Group South conducting offensive action along the two axes in the southern Soviet Union, towards Voronezh and into the Don bend. Once their advance spread east from Kharkov, the mistakes of 1941 were not repeated and full army groups operated along the strategic axes — 'B' towards Voronezh and 'A' towards Stalingrad. However, when German planners optimistically chose to operate into the Caucasus along a third strategic axis, a third army group was unavailable. When they tried to strengthen their lines with non-German troops, the

59

Kharkov, 1942

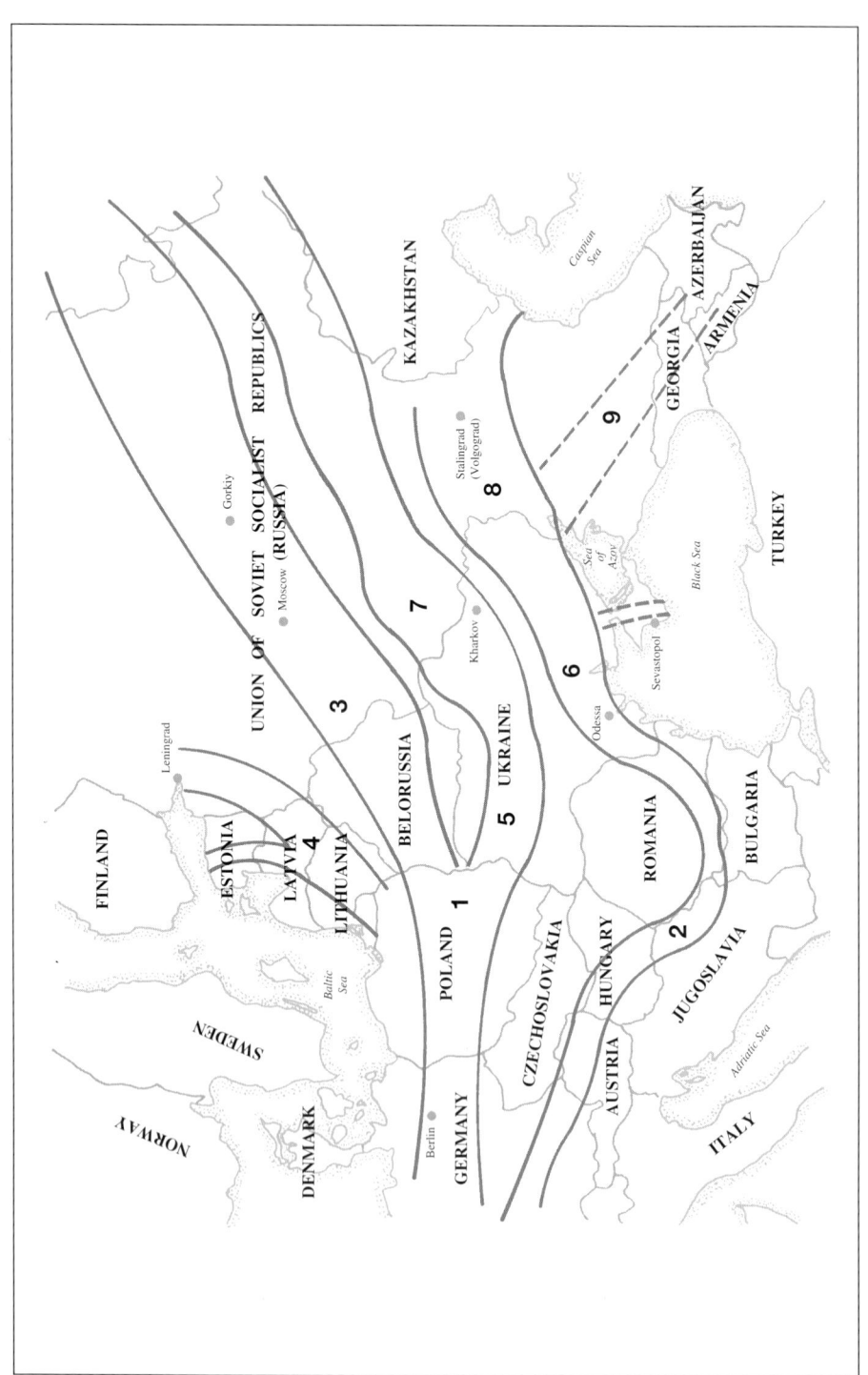

Map 5 — Strategic axes in the Soviet Union.
Note: Political boundaries as of 1991.

3 Area of Operations

result was similar to that of autumn 1941: German force over extension, resultant flank vulnerability and, ultimately, catastrophic defeat.

Early in the 1942 campaign, Soviet strategic planners well understood the geographical realities and the importance of the two strategic axes flanking the Kharkov region. Presuming that the German main strategic thrust would be towards Moscow and detecting German operational reserves concentrating north and south of Gomel (along the Konotop-Kursk axis) and at Kremenchug and Dnepropetrovsk (along the Donbas axis), Soviet planners envisioned a near repeat of the German autumn 1941 offensive when Guderian's southern thrust on Moscow had come so close to achieving its aims. They reasoned that a major drive through Kursk north of Kharkov would converge on Moscow to join Army Group Centre's thrust on the city. A second German advance, south of Kharkov, would threaten Rostov and the Don bend.

Therefore, both Timoshenko's and Stalin's plan presumed that the Kharkov region, because of its vital strategic location, was the suitable location to launch an offensive to thwart German summer strategic aims. Timoshenko felt that, by attacking at Kharkov, his forces could defeat and destroy German forces east of the Dnepr River, thereby defeating the Germans' secondary thrust and weakening the German main attack on Moscow. Stalin's plan, although less ambitious than Timoshenko's, sought to achieve the same aim, only on a lesser scale. Both of their assessments regarding the importance of the Kharkov region were correct. Unfortunately for the Soviets, in light of true German strategic intentions, the assessments were also irrelevant.

OPERATIONAL AND TACTICAL ASPECTS

Military-geographic characteristics of the region of combat operations

The region where Southwestern and Southern Front combat operations developed in May 1942 is located in the northeast part of the Ukraine... The entire region, and especially the territory of the Donets Basin, has a large number of populated areas... [the towns of] Kharkov, Dnepropetrovsk, Poltava and Dneprodzerzhinsk. Populated areas are connected to one another by a broad network of railroads, highways and dirt roads.

From north to south the region is traversed by the Northern Donets River, along whose banks ran the forward edge of both sides' defences, in the northern sector from Maslova Pristan to Staritsa and in the sector from Nizhne-Ruskii Bishkin to Balakleia. In its northern reaches to Staritsa and in its middle course from Chervonyi Shakhter to Maiaki, the Northern Donets River has a large number of shallows and fords, which are accessible for tanks (on the average, one ford every 10km). In the upper course, the width of the river is varied. In narrow places during May, it does not exceed 10-20m; in the middle course it reaches 100m. Soviet forces in the Staryi Saltov and Barvenkovo regions occupied large bridgeheads on the right bank of the Northern Donets River; these had operational significance. The depth of the Staryi Saltov bridgehead was 9km, its width was around 40km, and the overall area was 200sq km. The Barvenkovo bridgehead had a depth of up to 80km, extended along a front of up to 300km, and had an overall area of 6,800sq km.

The presence of these bridgeheads created favourable conditions for conducting an offensive operation to surround and destroy the German Kharkov grouping.

An enemy bridgehead was located between those of Soviet forces, at the bend of the Northern Donets in the Chuguev region. The depth of this bridgehead was around 52km, its width up to 100km, and its overall area 1,400sq km. East of Belgorod, the enemy had a bridgehead in the Miasoedovo and Maslova Pristan' region. Its depth

Kharkov, 1942

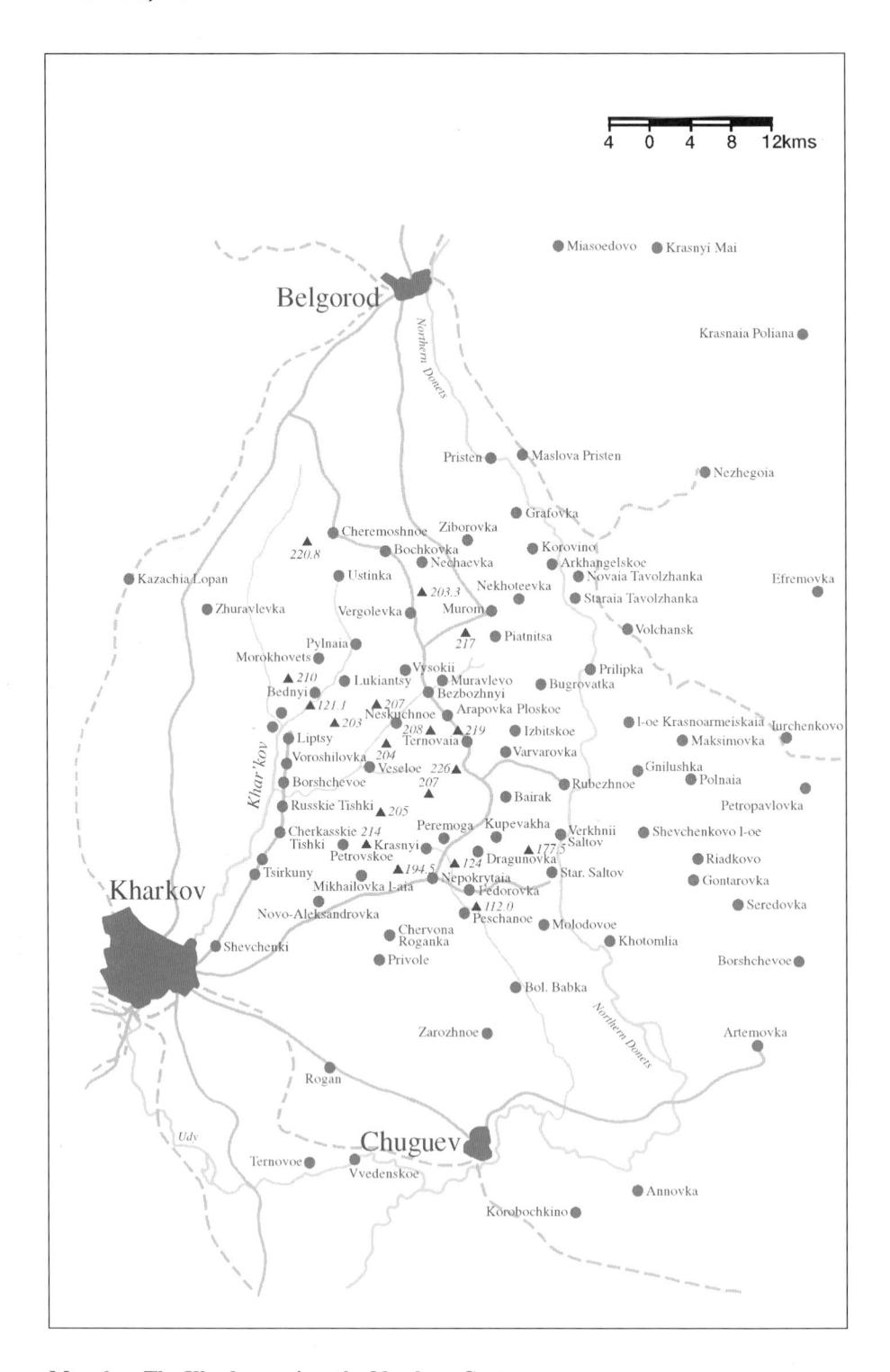

Map 6 — The Kharkov region: the Northern Sector

3 Area of Operations

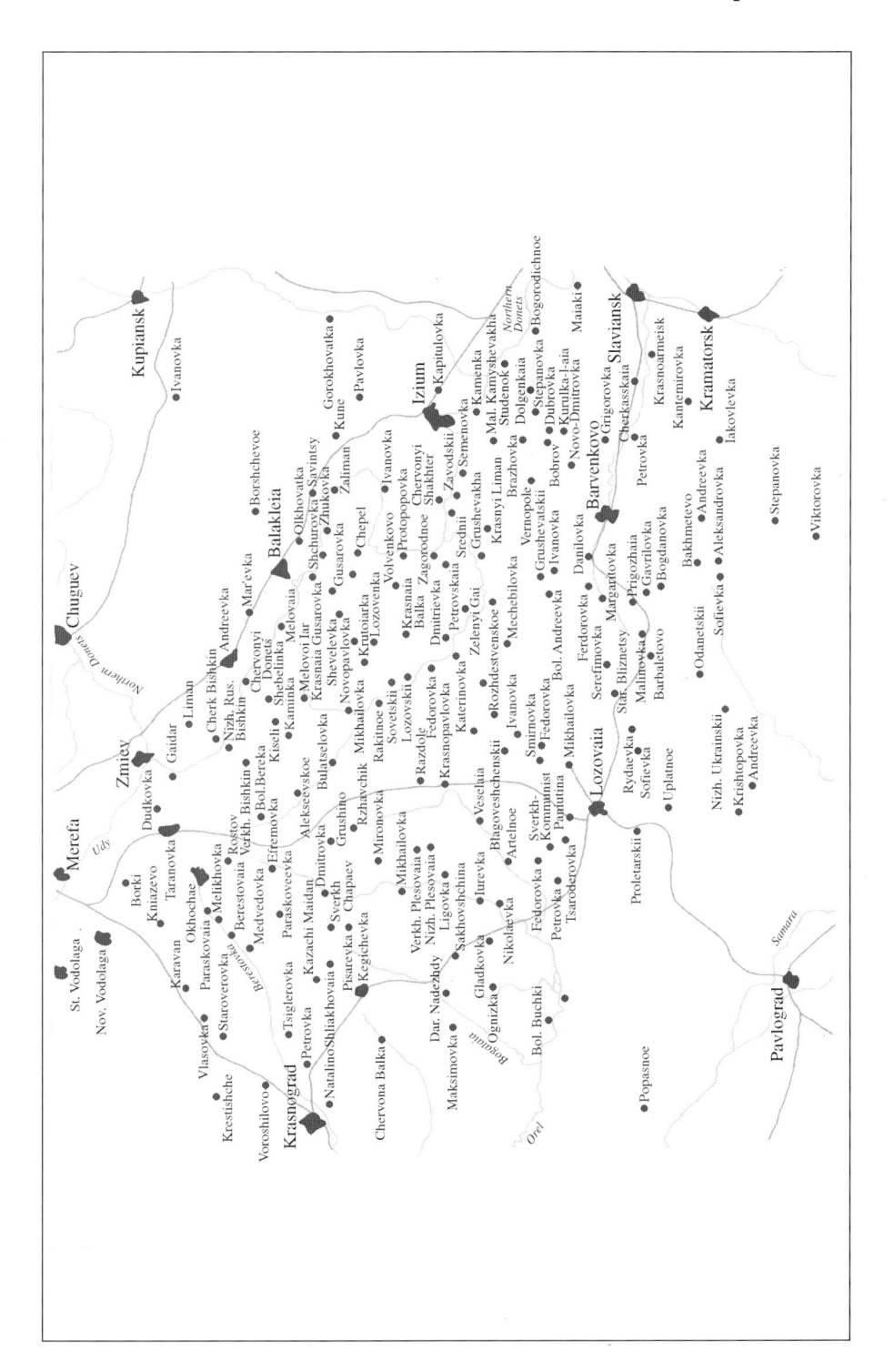

Map 7 — The Kharkov region: the Southern Sector

Kharkov, 1942

was up to 12km, the front extended 37km, and its overall area was 200sq km.

Operationally speaking, the Chuguev bridgehead had the greatest significance for the enemy. This bridgehead made it possible for him to attack to the northeast in co-operation with the grouping operating in the Belgorod region and to the southeast in co-operation with the grouping located in the Slaviansk region.

The terrain in the region of our bridgeheads and further west permitted free use of all combat arms in all directions. Some of the difficulties for the forces were the numerous small rivers (Bolshaia Babka, Kharkov, Lopan, Udy) and streams—the tributaries of the Northern Donets (on the Kharkov axis) and those of the Dnepr on the Krasnograd axis. The late spring floods and the swampy floodlands which formed forced attacking forces to create crossings to surmount the rivers and streams.

The western banks of the rivers and streams, with rare exception, are dominant over the eastern banks.

Terrain in the Barvenkovo bridgehead region and along the entire Krasnograd axis has a predominantly open, flat character. The small quantities of natural camouflage require reliable cover of ground forces by aviation and AA artillery. Most difficult for combat operations is the axis extending to Taranovka and Merefa, where attacking forces must surmount the Berestovaia and Mzha Rivers, as well as a forested tract located south of Zmiev. The terrain along this axis is more rugged than on other axes.

The terrain in the bridgehead in the Staryi Saltov region and along the Kharkov axis is hilly. Forests on the right bank of the Northern Donets River and in the environs of Kharkov ensure secrecy of manoeuvre by forces deployed in this region.

Ground cover in the area of operations is varied; black earth basically predominates. Sandy and loamy soils predominate along the banks of the Northern Donets, Bolshaia Babka, Orel, Berestovaia, Bogataia and Samara Rivers.

Here, during the period of spring rains, dirt roads quickly soak through and become difficult to traverse.

Meteorological conditions in May 1942 were unfavourable for ground forces, and frequent rains during the first half of the month and low clouds sharply restricted aviation operations. Airfields, which did not have outfitted take-off and landing strips, were put out of action. Their exploitation became possible only during the second half of May.

On the whole, the region of combat operations was suitable for conducting offensive and defensive operations with extensive use of all combat arms.

4
OPPOSING FORCES

SOVIET ORDER OF BATTLE
Grouping of Southwestern Front Forces on 11 May 1942

By the close of 11 May, Southwestern Front forces had basically occupied jumping-off positions for the offensive. By this time Front forces numbered 29 rifle divisions, nine cavalry divisions, one motorised rifle division, four motorised rifle brigades, 19 tank brigades and four separate tank battalions (925 tanks).

21st Army
While continuing to defend the Spartak, Miasoedovo and (excluding) Pristen sector with forces of 8th Motorised Rifle and 297th Rifle Divisions and one regiment of 301st Rifle Division, 21st Army concentrated 76th, 293rd and 227th Rifle Divisions, reinforced by 10th Tank Brigade, to penetrate the enemy defence south of Bezliudovka.

Two regiments of 301st Division were in the army reserve in the Krasnaia Poliana region, and 1st Motorised Rifle Brigade with 8th Separate Tank Battalion was in the Chuevo, Krivye Balki and Kholodnoe region.

28th Army
This army deployed 175th, 169th, 244th and 13th Guards Rifle Divisions, reinforced by 84th, 57th and 90th Tank Brigades, and all artillery in the first echelon on a front from Izbitskoe up to but excluding Dragunovka. 38th and 162nd Rifle Divisions with 6th Guards Tank Brigade were deployed in second echelon. 3rd Guards Cavalry Corps, consisting of 5th and 6th Guards and 32nd Cavalry Divisions and 34th Motorised Rifle Brigade, which were deployed in the Efremovka, Volokhovka and Zakharovka region, comprised the mobile group.

38th Army
While defending in the centre and on the left flank with the forces of 199th and 304th Rifle Divisions, 38th Army deployed three rifle divisions (226th, 124th and 300th) and one regiment of 81st Rifle Division in the penetration sector of Dragunovka, Peschanoe, Piatnitskoe, and reinforced them with 36th and 13th Tank Brigades and almost all army artillery assets. Two regiments of 81st Rifle Division and 133rd Tank Brigade were in army reserve in the Molodovoe region.

6th Army
This army, using two rifle divisions (47th and 337th), defended the right bank of the Northern Donets River in the Shchurovka, Nizhne-Ruskii Bishkin sector. The main forces of six rifle divisions with four tank brigades attached were concentrated along the front from Verkhnii Bishkin to Grushino. Here, 253rd, 41st, 411th and 266th Rifle Divisions, reinforced by 5th Guards, 38th and 48th Tank Brigades and all army

Kharkov, 1942

artillery assets, were deployed in the first echelon. 103rd and 248th Rifle Divisions and 37th Tank Brigade were in the second echelon.

Other Units
By the close of 11 May 1942, 21st Tank Corps was in the Krutoiarka, Novopavlovka region and 23rd Tank Corps in the Aleshki, Bunakovo region — a total of 269 tanks.

393rd Rifle Division and one regiment of 270th Rifle Division were concentrated in the first echelon in the Koshparovka, Kiptivka sector, where the Army Group was to prepare the penetration. The two remaining regiments of 270th Rifle Division occupied a defence along the front from Nizhniaia Plesovaia to Petrovka. 6th Cavalry Corps and 7th Tank Brigade were concentrated in the Beliaevka, Petrovskii region in the second echelon of the Army Group to exploit success.

277th Rifle Division in the Novo-Nikolaevka, Volosskaia Balakleika, Blagodatnoe region; 343rd Rifle Division in the Sukhoi Iar, Kune, Bugaevka sector; 2nd Cavalry Corps in the Bogdanovka, Rozhdestvenskoe, Mechebilovka region; and three separate tank battalions were in the reserve of Southwestern Direction Commander-in-Chief.

The Grouping of Southern Front Forces on 11 May 1942

Southern Front regrouped in April 1942, under instructions from the Southwestern Direction Commander-in-Chief [Timoshenko], as a result of the change in the demarcation line between Fronts in the Barvenkovo bridgehead and the acquisition by [Timoshenko] of reinforcing artillery units from the High Command's reserve and a significant portion of Southern Front reserves.

On 7 May, Southern Front began a local operation in the Maiaki region to improve the position of 9th Army forces and create favourable conditions for further combat to capture the town of Slaviansk. Accordingly, on 11 May the Front commander's reserves and 9th Army forces had an operational formation which corresponded to the interests of an offensive battle, but did not provide for firm defence of the Barvenkovo bridgehead.

The positions of Southern Front forces by the close of 11 May was as follows:

57th Army
This consisted of 150th, 317th, 99th, 351st and 14th Guards Rifle Divisions and defended on the line from Tsaredarovka, Krishtopovka, Novo-Pavlovka, to (excluding) Sofievka, with 14th Guards Division in second echelon, one regiment deployed in the Lozovaia region, and two regiments in the Starye Bliznetsy region. The army was reinforced by three artillery regiments. The average operational density in the army defensive sector, whose front was 80km, was one division per 16km, with 4.6 guns and mortars per kilometre of front.

9th Army
Consisting of 341st, 106th, 349th, 335th, 51st and 333rd Rifle Divisions, 78th Rifle Brigade, 121st and 15th Tank Brigades, and five artillery regiments, 9th Army occupied a defence on a 96km front from Sofievka through Alisovka, north of Maiaki, to Brusovka. The 341st, 106th, 349th and 335th Rifle Divisions were deployed inclusively in the defence in the right flank and in the army centre to Krasnoarmeisk. Units of 51st and 333rd (minus one regiment) Rifle Divisions and one battalion of 78th Rifle Brigade, reinforced by 15th and 121st Tank Brigades and two cavalry divisions of 5th

4 Opposing Forces

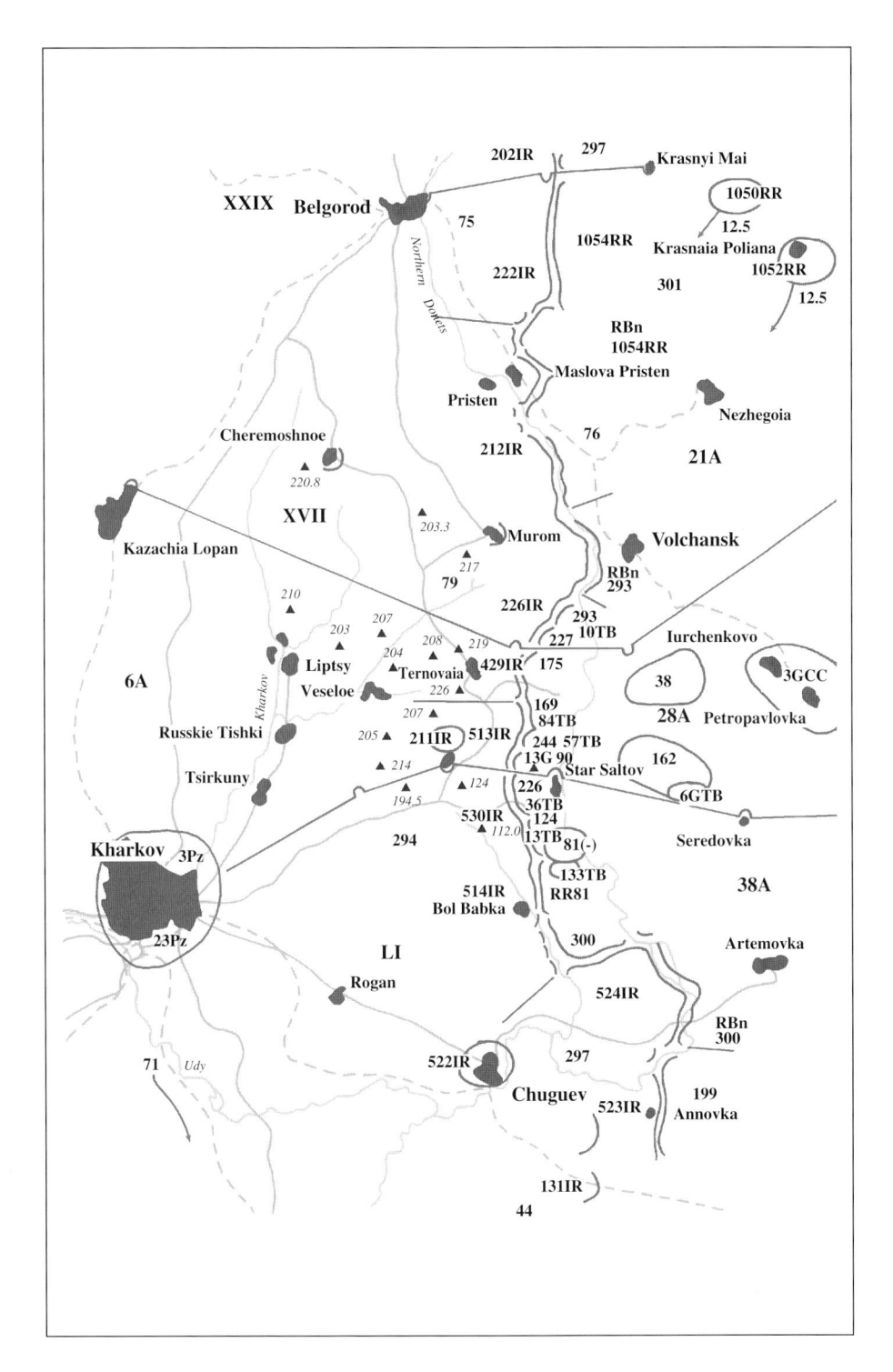

Map 8 — Force dispositions north of Kharkov, 11 May

Kharkov, 1942

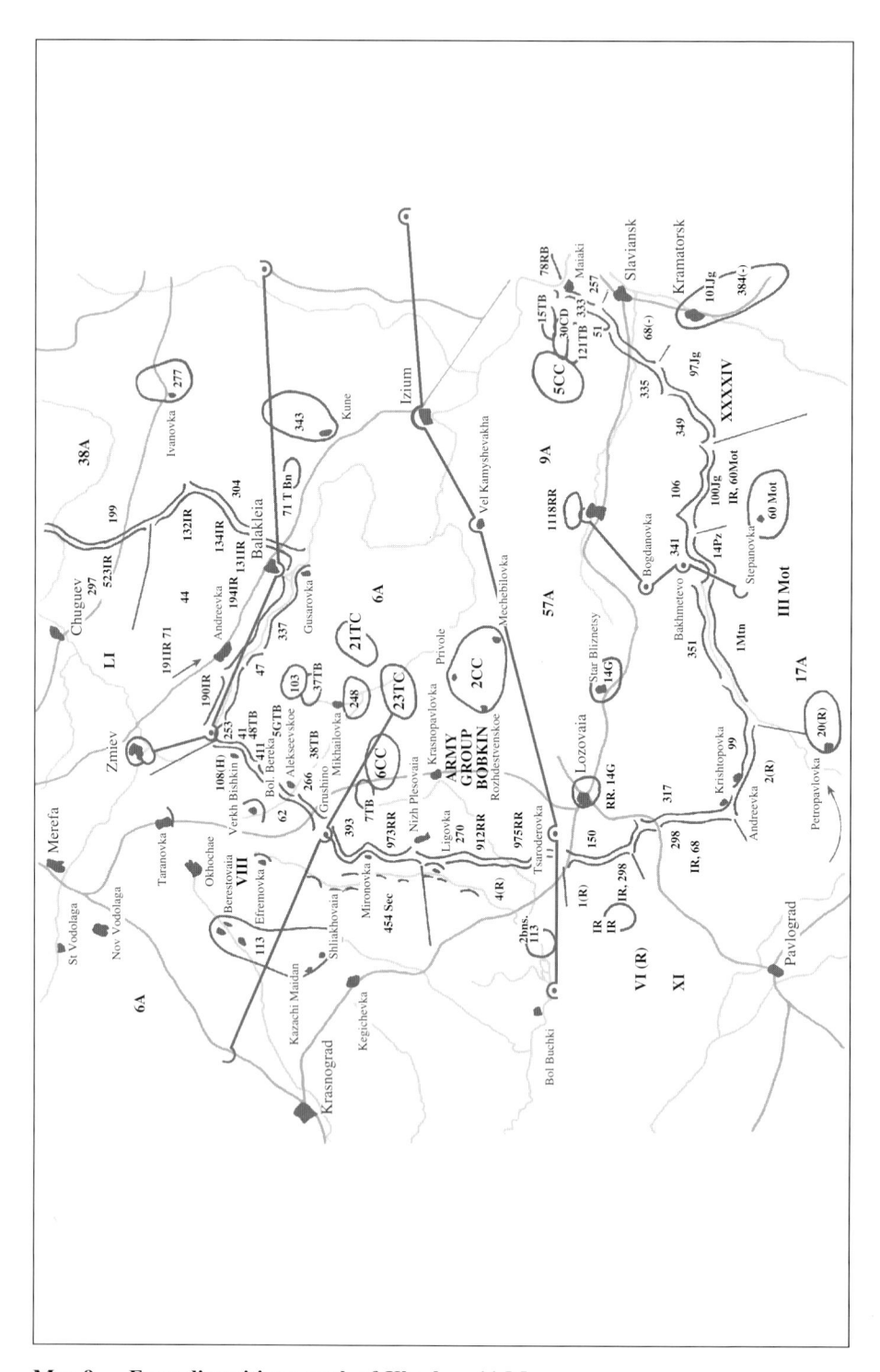

Map 9 — Force dispositions south of Kharkov, 11 May

4 Opposing Forces

Cavalry Corps with 12th Tank Brigade (the Front commander's reserve), were conducting offensive operations in the Bylbasovka, Maiaki sector to capture the Maiaki region.

One regiment of 333rd Rifle Division was in the 9th Army commander's reserve, in the Barvenkovo region.

The operational density in 9th Army's sector, taking into account all forces operating there, was one division per 10km, with an average of 11-12 guns and mortars per kilometre of front.

Other Units

As a result of the regrouping, 30 rifle divisions and one rifle brigade were left in the remaining Southern Front sectors, in the defensive sectors of 37th, 12th, 18th and 56th Armies. The 296th, 176th and 216th Rifle Divisions, respectively, were brought into the reserves of these armies' commanders. 3rd Guards Rifle Corps (2nd Guards Rifle Division, 76th, 81st and 68th Guards Rifle Brigades, and 63rd Tank Brigade) was in the 56th Army commander's reserve.

24th Tank Corps (24th Motorised Rifle, 4th Guards, 2nd and 54th Tank Brigades), 5th Cavalry Corps (60th, 34th and 30th Cavalry Divisions and 12th Tank Brigade), 347th, 255th and 15th Guards Rifle Divisions, and the 102nd, 73rd, 242nd and 282nd Rifle Divisions, sent by the Stavka of the Supreme High Command, were in the Southern Front commander's reserve.

According to Order No 13986 of the Stavka of the Supreme High Command, the cited reserves, except for 24th Tank Corps and 5th Cavalry Corps, could be used only with the Stavka's permission.

102nd Rifle Brigade, located in Rostov, and 6th Rifle Brigade, deployed in Starobelsk, became part of the Southwestern Direction Commander-in-Chief's reserves.

On the entire front of 57th and 9th Armies, which were occupying the southern face of the Barvenkovo salient, the defence was structured around a system of strongpoints and centres of resistance. Divisional combat formations were not echeloned. There were no second echelons or reserves in divisions and armies. Therefore, the depth of the tactical defence did not exceed 3-4km. Despite having been on the defence for a month and a half, work on creating defensive structures and engineer obstacles was unsatisfactory.

Thus, in 57th and 9th Armies' defensive sector, the density of structures and obstacles per kilometre of front was as follows: earth-and-timber pillboxes — around 3; anti-personnel mines — 25-30; and anti-tank mines — around 80.

In all, 11km of wire obstacles were built on the entire 180km front of the armies. Thus, neither the operational formation of Southern Front's 57th and 9th Armies in the defence, nor the engineer preparation of the terrain, which was everywhere accessible to tanks, supported a strong defence of the southern face of the Barvenkovo salient.

SOVIET FORCE STRUCTURE

The trials of almost a full year of combat had exacted a harsh toll on the Red Army's force structure. The excessive size of its 1941 combat formations and the imposing array of armaments available to it had, at least in theory, covered up the grim reality that both the huge force and its leadership were sorely wanting. Consequently, it failed

Kharkov, 1942

the test of combat. The more experienced and streamlined German Army smashed the Red Army's force structure and embarrassed those in the Red Army military leadership that it did not kill. Within a month the Red Army's massive prewar rifle armies, corps and divisions and its menacing mechanised corps were a shambles. Throughout summer 1941 and into the autumn, the Stavka made do with the remnants of its once proud force and threw into the field armies and lesser formations, which were seldom more than *ad hoc* collections of unseasoned infantry supported by whatever artillery and armour remained undestroyed after the first months of combat carnage.

By late autumn 1941, however, attrition had taken its toll on the Germans, and the sheer quantity of hastily mobilised Red Army troops took on a quality of its own. This seemingly limitless mobilisation capability, combined with Soviet offensive ferocity born of a mixture of frustration and desperation, were instrumental in the Red Army's winter victories at Rostov, Moscow and in the Donbas. However emboldened it was by its victories, the Stavka well understood that a new Red Army force structure was required if victory were to be achieved. The new structure had to be one that commanders could effectively control and one with the requisite firepower and mobility to contend successfully with the more experienced German Army.

The Soviets had begun reforming their force structure in autumn 1941, when they augmented their existing threadbare armies with an array of new units and formations. Almost 100 new rifle brigades, smaller and more manageable on the battlefield, supplemented the many existing, cumbersome and often weakened, rifle divisions. Over 80 tank brigades and a host of simple artillery regiments of various types appeared to provide the infantrymen struggling in field armies with a modicum of tank and artillery support. Finally, the Stavka formed almost 100 light cavalry divisions and, in December, grouped these smaller formations into cavalry corps to strengthen the flagging mobile arm of the Red Army. Most important, perhaps, was the Stavka's decision in March 1942 to create new mechanised formations which could spearhead offensive action and challenge the German panzer divisions. First called mechanised corps, in late April these mobile formations were formally renamed tank corps.[1]

The Stavka understood that these steps were only the beginning of what would be a long process of force structure reform. They were confident, however, that implementation of these reforms would produce future battlefield success. The spring campaign was the first test of this new force structure.

In spring 1942 the highest level strategic headquarters in the Red Army was the Strategic Direction headquarters, which controlled multiple Fronts operating along a specific strategic axis. Since Strategic Directions lacked full staffs, they co-ordinated rather than controlled operations and received most of their strategic guidance directly from the Stavka.[2] Subordinate to the direction headquarters were Fronts, which before the war had been strategic high-level formations of multiple armies considered capable of performing strategic (war-winning) missions. By early 1942 the Stavka realised from unpleasant combat experiences that Fronts were less capable than previously thought in coping with the rigours of modern mobile warfare. Therefore, it redesignated Fronts as operational-strategic formations; that is, formations capable of operating along an operational axis and partially contributing to the achievement of a strategic aim. Front headquarters had their own planning staff but no combat or support forces other than small reserves and combat forces found in armies assigned to them by the Stavka. The primary function of a Front was to plan and control operations by its subordinate armies.[3]

4 Opposing Forces

In spring 1942 the basic operational level building block of the Red Army was the rifle army, which normally fought under a Soviet Front but occasionally operated by itself in a separate sector. The rifle army controlled 5-6 rifle divisions and rifle brigades, 2-3 tank brigades, sometimes 2-3 cavalry divisions, and artillery regiments and battalions attached to the army from the Stavka reserve (RVGK). The army's strength, depending on whether it was operating in a defensive or offensive mode, ranged from 50,000 to 100,000 men, 385-990 guns and mortars, and 24-150 tanks.[4]

The basic tactical formations in the Red Army were the rifle (strelkovyi) divisions. As organised under their 18 March 1942 establishment, rifle divisions were considerably smaller than their nearly 15,000-man June 1941 predecessors. The organisation table of the new divisions is shown in the accompanying table 6.

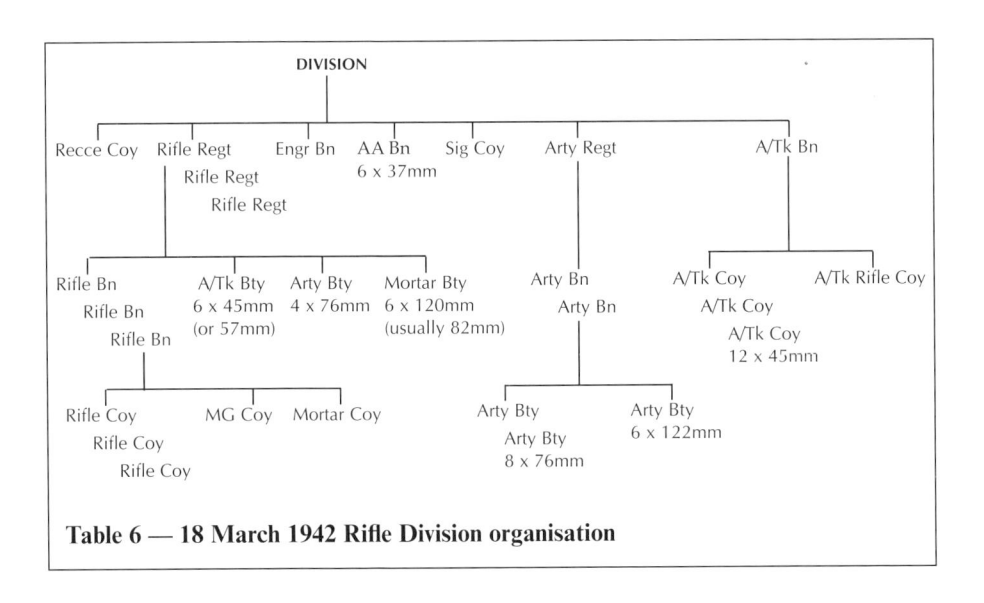

```
                              DIVISION
    ┌──────┬─────────┬────────┬───────┬────────┬──────────┬───────────┐
 Recce Coy Rifle Regt Engr Bn AA Bn  Sig Coy Arty Regt              A/Tk Bn
          Rifle Regt         6 x 37mm
          Rifle Regt

 Rifle Bn  A/Tk Bty  Arty Bty  Mortar Bty   Arty Bn    A/Tk Coy   A/Tk Rifle Coy
 Rifle Bn  6 x 45mm  4 x 76mm  6 x 120mm    Arty Bn    A/Tk Coy
 Rifle Bn  (or 57mm)           (usually 82mm)          A/Tk Coy
                                                       12 x 45mm

 Rifle Coy  MG Coy  Mortar Coy   Arty Bty   Arty Bty
 Rifle Coy                       Arty Bty   6 x 122mm
 Rifle Coy                       8 x 76mm
```

Table 6 — 18 March 1942 Rifle Division organisation

By 1942 infantrymen in rifle companies were increasingly equipped with submachine guns as well as their rifles to improve their firepower. In addition, some divisions fielded a training battalion and, although not listed in the formal establishment, a penal battalion assigned by army to spearhead infantry assaults against prepared enemy defences. This practice was formalised in a July 1942 Stavka order.[5] In total, full-strength rifle divisions numbered 12,795 men, 44 artillery pieces (32 x 76mm and 12 x 122mm), 170 mortars (76 x 50mm, 76 x 82mm and 18 x 120mm), 6 anti-aircraft guns, 30 anti-tank guns and 279 x 12.7cm anti-tank rifles. In reality, however, most divisions were not maintained at full strength and, instead, ranged between 7,000 and 10,000 men with reduced supporting armaments.[6]

Rifle brigades were truncated rifle divisions, stripped of their intermediate regimental headquarters. The organisation table of the 17 April 1942 rifle brigade establishment is shown in Table 7.

Kharkov, 1942

Brigades numbered 4,197 to 4,997 men, with 12 x 76mm guns, 56 mortars (8 x 120mm, 24 x 82mm and 24 x 50mm), 12 x 45mm anti-tank guns and 72 x 80 anti-tank rifles.[7]

The new Soviet tank corps formed in late April 1942 replaced the three-brigade experimental mechanised and tank corps of March and early April with a four-brigade corps. The organisation table of the new corps establishment is shown in Table 8.

It had no logistical support structure whatsoever (logistical support was to be provided by cooperating army). In essence, the corps consisted of co-operating mobile brigades — three tank and one motorised rifle — operating under a single command headquarters. Organisation tables for the new tank brigade, organised under an April 1942 establishment, and motorised rifle brigade are shown in Tables 9 and 10.

The tank brigade totalled 1,471 men, 46 tanks, 8 mortars (82mm) and 4 anti-aircraft guns (37mm).[8] The motorised rifle brigade totalled 3,152 men, 12 x 76mm guns, 34 mortars (4 x 120mm and 30 x 82mm), 12 x 37mm anti-aircraft guns, 12 x 45mm anti-tank guns and 54 x 12.7cm anti-tank rifles.[9] Since the Red Army had no armoured personnel carriers, motorised infantry rode on trucks — which were scarce — or, more

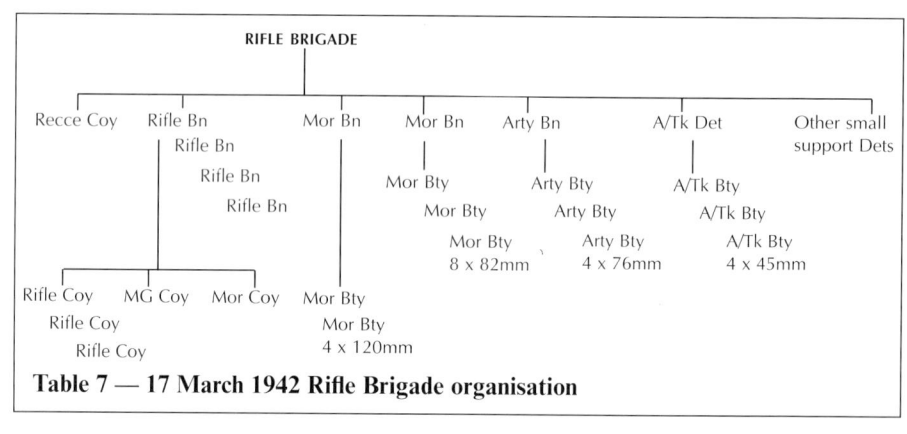

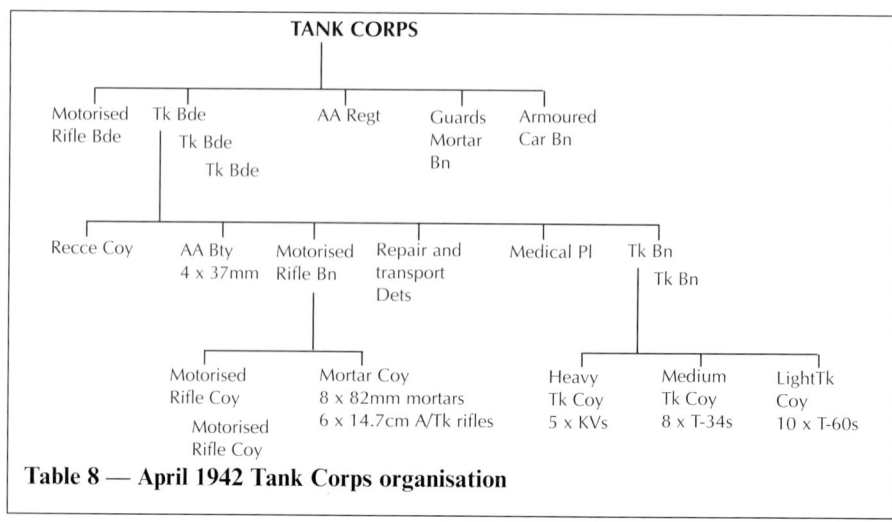

Table 7 — 17 March 1942 Rifle Brigade organisation

Table 8 — April 1942 Tank Corps organisation

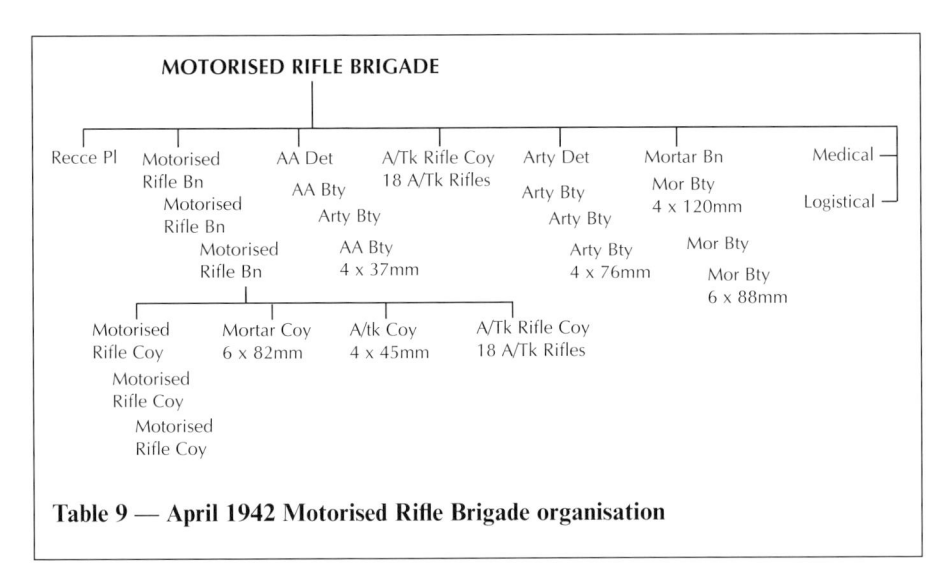

4 Opposing Forces

```
                        MOTORISED RIFLE BRIGADE
                                 |
  ┌──────┬──────────┬────────┬──────────────┬─────────┬─────────┬─────────┐
Recce Pl  Motorised  AA Det   A/Tk Rifle Coy  Arty Det  Mortar Bn  Medical
          Rifle Bn            18 A/Tk Rifles                       
                    AA Bty                   Arty Bty   Mor Bty   Logistical
          Motorised Arty Bty                            4 x 120mm
          Rifle Bn
                    AA Bty                   Arty Bty   Mor Bty
          Motorised 4 x 37mm
          Rifle Bn                            Arty Bty   Mor Bty
                                              4 x 76mm   6 x 88mm
     ┌────────┬──────────┬──────────┬─────────────┐
   Motorised  Mortar Coy  A/tk Coy   A/Tk Rifle Coy
   Rifle Coy  6 x 82mm    4 x 45mm   18 A/Tk Rifles
   Motorised
   Rifle Coy
   Motorised
   Rifle Coy
```

Table 9 — April 1942 Motorised Rifle Brigade organisation

often, on the backs of accompanying tank brigade tanks; otherwise, they functioned as simple infantry.

In sum, the new tank corps numbered over 7,500 men, 138 tanks (30 x KV, 48 x T-34, and 60 x T-60), and 106 guns and mortars. Despite the corps' impressive armoured strength, as subsequent operations would reveal, they lacked the logistical support necessary to sustain operations at any depth.

Supplementing the mobile power of the new tank corps were older cavalry corps and divisions, which had been thoroughly reorganised in December 1942. The February 1942 cavalry corps (see Table 6) consisted of three cavalry divisions (primarily light), a co-operating tank or motorised rifle brigade (sometimes regiments), and reconnaissance, signal and engineer battalions. Often, cavalry corps also possessed a cavalry artillery battalion, a mortar regiment, anti-aircraft, anti-tank and signal battalions, and, occasionally, a guards mortar (katiusha) multiple-rocket launcher battalion. Cavalry corps ranged in strength from 10,000-12,000 men and 40-60 tanks.[10]

Each light cavalry division (see Table 10) contained three cavalry regiments, but no divisional combat or logistical support elements. Each light regiment included four sabre squadrons and one machine gun squadron, and a regimental artillery battery consisting of 7 x 76mm field guns and 2 x 45mm anti-tank guns. The squadron troopers were equipped with light and heavy machine guns, rifles and explosive charges. The light cavalry paper strength was 3,447 men, 12 x 76mm guns, and 6 x 45mm anti-tank guns.[11]

The few remaining heavy cavalry divisions (such as the guards divisions in 3rd Guards Cavalry Corps — see Table 11) included reconnaissance, engineer and signal elements, an anti-aircraft (machine gun) battery and a cavalry artillery battalion of 8 x 76mm guns and 8 x 120mm mortars. The heavy regiments each included 4 x 76mm infantry, 4 x 45mm anti-tank guns and 16 x 50mm mortars (four in support of each sabre squadron). The heavy cavalry division numbered almost 4,500 men, 20 x 76mm guns, 8 x 120mm mortars, 12 x 45mm anti-tank guns and 48 x 50mm mortars.[12] Cavalry rode into battle on horseback, but normally fought on foot.

Red Army infantry, tank and cavalry forces serving in field armies received artillery fire support from a wide array of artillery regiments maintained under Stavka control

Kharkov, 1942

in the Reserve of the High Command (RVGK). The Stavka provided each field army with artillery support necessary to perform only its specific offensive or defensive mission. RVGK artillery consisted of a dizzying array of regiments and battalions, including artillery, light artillery, howitzer artillery, gun artillery, canon artillery, anti-tank artillery and guards mortar artillery regiments, and separate guards mortar battalions. Initially, during summer 1941, Soviet artillery regiments included from 24 to 48 artillery tubes; by December 1942 the Soviets had been forced to reduce this number to 16-24 tubes in order to create more numerous regiments and tailor regimental size to match the size of the smaller armies and divisions.

The standard artillery regiments assigned to the RVGK were, in essence, artillery regiments which had been assigned to rifle corps before the corps' abolition in summer 1941. They generally resembled those artillery regiments organic to rifle divisions.

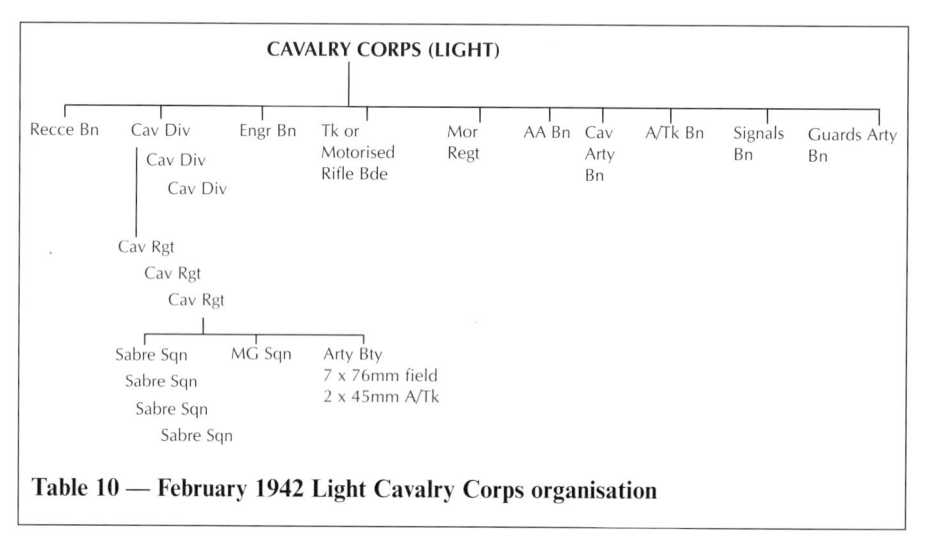

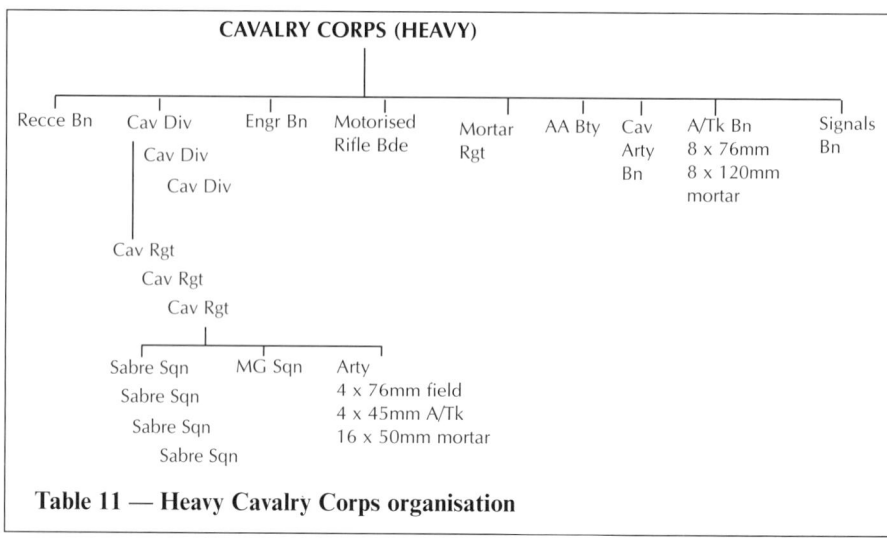

```
                        CAVALRY CORPS (LIGHT)
                                |
 ┌──────┬────────┬────────┬────────────┬────────┬──────┬──────┬────────┬───────────┐
Recce   Cav Div  Engr Bn  Tk or        Mor      AA Bn  Cav    A/Tk Bn  Signals  Guards Arty
Bn      Cav Div           Motorised    Regt            Arty            Bn       Bn
        Cav Div           Rifle Bde                    Bn

        Cav Rgt
         Cav Rgt
          Cav Rgt
            |
     ┌──────┬────────┐
    Sabre Sqn  MG Sqn   Arty Bty
    Sabre Sqn           7 x 76mm field
    Sabre Sqn           2 x 45mm A/Tk
    Sabre Sqn
```

Table 10 — February 1942 Light Cavalry Corps organisation

```
                        CAVALRY CORPS (HEAVY)
                                |
 ┌──────┬────────┬────────┬────────────┬────────┬──────┬──────┬────────┬────────┐
Recce   Cav Div  Engr Bn  Motorised    Mortar   AA Bty Cav    A/Tk Bn  Signals
Bn      Cav Div           Rifle Bde    Rgt             Arty   8 x 76mm Bn
        Cav Div                                        Bn     8 x 120mm
                                                              mortar

        Cav Rgt
         Cav Rgt
          Cav Rgt
            |
     ┌──────┬────────┐
    Sabre Sqn  MG Sqn   Arty
    Sabre Sqn           4 x 76mm field
    Sabre Sqn           4 x 45mm A/Tk
    Sabre Sqn           16 x 50mm mortar
```

Table 11 — Heavy Cavalry Corps organisation

4 Opposing Forces

Each had a combined total of between 24 and 28 x 76mm guns and 122mm howitzers organised into two composite battalions. Light artillery regiments were equipped with 24 x 76mm guns, heavy artillery regiments with 28 x 122mm howitzers, and gun artillery regiments with 18 x 152mm guns. Regiments usually consisted of two battalions and batteries of two tubes. In May 1942 the anti-tank artillery regiment consisted of four or five anti-tank batteries, each equipped with 4 x 45mm and 76mm anti-tank guns, for a total of 16-20 guns.[13]

The rocket artillery regiments, with which the Stavka first experimented during autumn 1942, contained three rocket artillery battalions, each with 8 x BM-13 (or BM-8) multiple-rocket launchers (katiushas) organised into two 4-launcher batteries. The regiment's 24 launchers could fire a single devastating volley of 384 M-13 or 864 M-8 rockets at an area target, but with limited accuracy. They, and the separate guards mortar battalions also assigned to support armies, were superb terror weapons, and useful as well against massed enemy tanks and infantry.[14]

All of this artillery operated in accordance with the provisions of Stavka Order No 03, issued on 10 January 1942, which was specifically designed to improve the combat employment of artillery during offensive operations.[15] Noting the frequent absence of massed artillery during the Moscow offensive and the tendency of armies to fire artillery preparations and, then, to organise supporting fires separately, the Stavka ordered attacking forces to concentrate artillery resources and conduct an 'artillery offensive' which would persist throughout the penetration and exploitation phases of the operation. In theory, the order sought to provide 'seamless' artillery fire support for infantry and mobile forces throughout the entire duration of the operation. The Kharkov operation would become one of the first combat tests of this new fire support concept.

THE SOUTHWESTERN DIRECTION LEADERS

The Southwestern Direction headquarters, which proposed, planned and conducted the Kharkov offensive, had been controlling operations by Soviet forces in southern Russia since a few days after the German invasion. Soviet prewar military theory required Front headquarters to control wartime operations along strategic axes. Accordingly, when the Germans launched Operation 'Barbarossa', the Baltic, Western Special, and Kiev Special Military Districts immediately transformed themselves into the Northwestern, Western and Southwestern (and, later, the Southern) Fronts, and their armies attempted to contain and repel the German advance. The disastrous initial two weeks of combat quickly and vividly indicated that these Fronts could not effectively control their hard-pressed forces. Fronts had neither the experienced personnel, the communications, nor the forces to conduct operations effectively over so large an expanse and against so experienced an enemy. In addition, the total breakdown in Moscow's ability to control, or even properly monitor, force operations required immediate formation of an entirely new strategic command system.

Immediately after hostilities had commenced, on 23 June 1941, Stalin and the Communist Party Politburo formed the Stavka (staff) of the High Command (Stavka GK) under the titular direction of Commissar of Defence S. K. Timoshenko, to provide 'uninterrupted and qualified command and control'.[16] On 10 July, as the situation at the front deteriorated further, the Stavka created Strategic Direction headquarters

Kharkov, 1942

and, dispensing with its military figurehead, Stalin renamed the strategic organ the Stavka Supreme Command (Stavka VK), with himself as chairman. Once again, on 8 August, the Stavka reorganised, this time into the Stavka of the Supreme High Command (Stavka VGK) with Stalin as Supreme High Commander or, in more common terms, 'Generalissimo'. The Stavka VGK had 'full authority for strategic leadership of the Red Army, Navy, border and internal forces, and partisan forces. It was fully responsible to the Party Central Committee and the GKO (State Defence Committee) for the conduct of operations and the combat readiness of forces.'[17] In 1941 the Stavka consisted of Stalin, the Chief of the Soviet General Staff (B. M. Shaposhnikov), Politburo members and other key military figures such as Zhukov.

The Northwestern, Western and Southwestern Direction headquarters, which were formed on 10 July 1941, were supposed to provide a firm and continuous link and foster close co-ordination between Stavka planners and decision-makers and Fronts and naval forces operating along their respective strategic axes. In reality, the direction headquarters performed their assigned functions quite poorly and, as defeats mounted, the Stavka increasingly interceded directly through its special representatives, which it dispatched to direction headquarters to see to it that its plans and orders were carried out.

The Southwestern Direction had experienced catastrophic defeats during the summer of 1941, when, under Marshal S. M. Budenny's command, its two subordinate Fronts suffered losses exceeding the scale of the Russian Army's 1914 Tannenberg disaster. The Germans encircled and destroyed the bulk of Southwestern Front forces around Kiev and Uman in the Ukraine and besieged large elements of its Southern Front in Odessa. Surviving direction forces withdrew in disorder across the Ukraine and Donbas region to the line of the Northern Donets and Mius Rivers. Only sizeable reinforcements dispatched by the Stavka from its strategic reserves and German preoccupation with the seizure of Moscow enabled the direction to regain its equilibrium. Under a new commander, Marshal S. K. Timoshenko, former commander of the Western Direction who replaced Budenny in September 1941, the Southwestern Direction's Southern Front mounted the successful November counter-attack against General von Kleist's First Panzer Group at the gates of Rostov and forced the Germans to withdraw to defences along the Mius River line. In January 1942 the direction's reinvigorated Southwestern Front achieved limited success south of Kharkov by seizing the Barvenkovo bridgehead across the Northern Donets River. Now, in May 1942, Stalin assigned Timoshenko the mission of completing the defeat of German forces in the Kharkov region. Timoshenko hoped to achieve even more.

MARSHAL SEMEN KONSTANTINOVICH TIMOSHENKO

Born in 1895 and a World War 1 and Civil War veteran, Timoshenko was a member of Stalin's 'inner circle' of 1st Cavalry Army cronies, who had fought with Stalin in the defence of Tsaritsyn (later renamed Stalingrad). Thereafter, his personal and professional reputation and military career were closely associated with Stalin's political career. Although Timoshenko's career was strictly military, and he was never a 'political' officer, as so many of Stalin's other military cronies were, when Stalin consolidated his political power in the late 1920s and early 1930s, Timoshenko's fortunes also soared. During the 1920s Timoshenko commanded a variety of cavalry units, including the 4th Cavalry Division (later commanded by Zhukov) and 3rd Cavalry Corps (in which Rokossovsky was a division commander and Zhukov a regimental commander). After twin two-year tours as deputy commander of the Belorussian and Kiev

4 Opposing Forces

Military Districts, he benefited from the wholesale purges of the military in and after 1937 by rising to military district command, first of the North Caucasus Military District and, later, the Special Kiev Military District. As he himself later admitted:

'I commanded practically every military district as a trusted agent of Stalin and Voroshilov. I would just manage to install a little order and then they'd telephone and ask, "Everything all right? We've sent a plane for you, fly straightaway to Rostov because there's no one in charge there and the local Cossacks are dangerous; from there go straight on to Kharkov, which has been stripped bare." I'd be making these trips from place to place the whole time.'[18]

That Timoshenko participated in the purges there is no doubt, but participation was the price of his personal survival. As a reliable and competent officer, when war approached Timoshenko was accorded ever greater responsibility. He commanded Kiev Special Military District forces during the occupation of eastern Poland in September 1939, and, after the Red Army suffered embarrassing defeats at the hands of the Finns in autumn 1939, in January 1940 Stalin appointed Timoshenko to command the Northwestern Front against Finnish forces. He planned and conducted the successful 1940 winter campaign against the Finns and, for his success, on 8 May 1940 was rewarded with the rank of Marshal of the Soviet Union, the job of Defence Commissar, and the difficult task of reforming the Red Army, which had performed so dismally in Poland and Finland. Timoshenko's subsequent attempts at reform sought to restructure, re-equip and retrain the Red Army, a formidable task since the army's command cadre had been emasculated by the purges. As it turned out, it was also a dangerous task, for although positive in its intent, its timing was appalling, and the partially effected reforms left Soviet forces particularly vulnerable on the eve of German invasion in summer 1941.

When the German invasion did occur, Timoshenko shared with Stalin, fairly or unfairly, responsibility for the Red Army's initial catastrophic defeats. He served briefly as Stavka head, and, when replaced by Stalin himself on 30 June, the next day Timoshenko assumed command of the Western Front, replacing his just-executed predecessor, D. G. Pavlov, with orders from Stalin to halt the German advance at the Dnepr River. Within days, as German forces poured over the Dnepr, Stalin appointed Timoshenko Supreme Commander of the Western Direction. In July and August 1941, while a complex struggle raged around Smolensk, Timoshenko attempted to orchestrate a series of Soviet counter-attacks. Although his offensives ultimately failed, the Germans experienced their first limited setbacks in the war, and their high losses in the ferocious fighting around Smolensk prompted them to postpone an immediate advance on Moscow.

Ironically, Timoshenko's limited success at Smolensk led to his presiding over one of the Red Army's most disastrous defeats during the first year of war. As a reward for his performance at Smolensk, Stalin assigned Timoshenko to command the Southwestern Direction in place of Marshal Budenny. He arrived at his new headquarters in Poltava just as German forces, thwarted in their advance on Moscow, instead struck south against Southwestern Direction forces in the Kiev region. Despite Timoshenko's efforts, most of the Southwestern Front, together with its commander, Gen M. P. Kirponis, perished in the Kiev encirclement. Timoshenko, serving both as Southwestern Direction and Southwestern Front commander, then presided over the precipitous eastward withdrawal of Southwestern Direction forces through the east-

Kharkov, 1942

ern Ukraine and Donbas region in autumn 1941. Then, in November, as the Germans reached the gates of Rostov, and with considerable help from the Stavka, which provided him with fresh reserves, Timoshenko orchestrated Soviet victories at Rostov and along the Northern Donets River in November 1941 and January 1942.

Timoshenko, in Zhukov's words, was 'an old and experienced war leader, stubborn, strong-willed and well-versed in tactical and operational terms'.[19] A strict disciplinarian and excellent organiser, he was also a creature of Stalin. In good times this meant promotion and increased responsibility. In bad times, as Timoshenko would learn, it would mean less prominence rather than full disgrace or death.

At Timoshenko's side in the Southwestern Direction's Military Council were his political commissar, N. S. Khrushchev; his chief of staff, Lt-Gen I. Kh. Bagramian and his deputy, Lt-Gen F. Ia. Kostenko.

NIKITA SERGEEVICH KHRUSHCHEV

Born of Ukrainian peasant stock in Kurks *oblast* (province) in 1894, Khrushchev participated in the Civil War and rose to political prominence through 'grass roots' work in the Communist Party apparatus as a supporter of Stalin.[20] During the initial stages of the 1930s political purges, he served as Second and then First Secretary of the Moscow City Soviet and First Secretary of the Moscow Party Committee. For his service, in January 1938 Stalin appointed him First Secretary of the Ukrainian Party, a post which he occupied until the outbreak of war in June 1941. While serving in the Kiev Special Military District, Khrushchev worked closely with many leading military figures in the district, such as Zhukov and Kirponis. After the outbreak of war, he became Military Commissar of the Southwestern Direction and Stalin's personal representative in the theatre. While sharing in the direction defeats and victories during the first year of war, he formed lasting relationships which would endure during the war years and assist his political fortunes after the war had ended. Khrushchev's 'earthy' and peasant-like personal demeanour concealed his keen skills as a politician and able henchman of Stalin.

LT-GEN IVAN KHRISTOFOROVICH BAGRAMIAN

An Armenian born in Azerbaijan in 1897, Bagramian represented a sizeable minority of Armenians who reached high rank in the Soviet Army.[21] An enlisted man during World War 1, he joined the Red Army in 1920 and helped restore Soviet power in Armenia and Georgia. After the war he served in a wide variety of cavalry assignments, ultimately commanding a regiment in the Transcaucasus for seven years and becoming divisional chief of staff in 1936. Although he graduated from the Frunze and Voroshilov General Staff Academies in 1934 and 1938 respectively and thereafter joined the faculty of the Voroshilov General Staff Academy, unlike most of his contemporaries, he did not join the Communist Party until 1939. It is likely he owed his subsequent advancement to the effects of the purges, his experience as a cavalry officer and his personal relationship with Zhukov, to whom he turned in 1940 to obtain a troop posting in the Kiev Special Military District, which Zhukov then commanded. After serving briefly as Chief of Operations for 12th Army in occupied Poland, in December 1940 Col Bagramian became Kiev Special Military District Deputy Chief of Staff, a post which he occupied up to the German invasion.

4 Opposing Forces

During the difficult days following the German attack, Bagramian, while serving in the joint capacity as Southwestern Front's Chief of the Operations and Deputy Chief of Staff, became enmeshed in the key strategic and operational decisions affecting the Front's fate during the withdrawal to Kiev and the subsequent Kiev encirclement. In September 1941 it was Maj-Gen Bagramian who carried Timoshenko's oral order to Front commander Kirponis to withdraw from the threatened encirclement. Kirponis, however, demanded a written order from Stalin before ordering a withdrawal; in the subsequent encirclement, Kirponis perished, and over half a million Soviet soldiers died or were taken captive. Bagramian made a harrowing escape from the Kiev encirclement with his operations staff and finally reached the safety of Soviet lines. Timoshenko, now commanding the Southwestern Direction, kept Bagramian on as Front Chief of Operations through the ensuing winter campaign. Described by Zhukov as 'an extremely profound, coolheaded, diligent and competent officer,' during December 1941, Bagramian was instrumental in orchestrating the successful offensive by the Southwestern Front's right flank against German forces in the Elets sector south of Moscow.[22] Bagramian played an important part in that Soviet victory while serving as Chief of Staff for Gen Kostenko's special operational group and, for his accomplishments, was promoted to lieutenant-general. Now, in early 1942, the Stavka and his patron Timoshenko called upon Bagramian to repeat his planning feat of December 1941, only this time at Kharkov.

LT-GEN FEDOR IAKOVLEVICH KOSTENKO

The Southwestern Direction Deputy Commander, Kostenko, also a cavalry officer, was born near Rostov in 1896, served in the Tsarist Army, participated in the Petrograd February Revolution and fought with the Red Guards during the October Revolution. Kostenko joined the Red Army in 1918, served for four years in Budenny's cavalry corps and 1st Cavalry Army, and was wounded four times while participating in all of the important campaigns in the Ukraine, Poland and Crimea. During the interwar years, he rose through cavalry channels to command (in 1933) the 19th Manych Cavalry Regiment in Zhukov's 4th Cavalry Division and an army cavalry group of the Kiev Military District during the 1939 invasion of Poland. After graduating from the Voroshilov General Staff Academy in May 1941, Kostenko was posted to the Kiev Special Military District where, as lieutenant-general, he commanded 26th Army defending west of Lvov.[23]

Subsequently, Kostenko's army defended the southern approaches to Kiev and was trapped by the Germans in the Kiev encirclement. Like Bagramian, Kostenko and elements of his staff fought their way out of the trap, and Kostenko was then appointed Deputy Southwestern Front commander by Timoshenko. In December 1941 he commanded the special operational group formed around the nucleus of 5th Cavalry Corps and 13th Army forces which defeated the Germans at Elets. For his superb performance Kostenko received the Order of Lenin and was appointed Southwestern Front commander. Subsequently, he planned and conducted the Front's January 1942 Barvenkovo-Lozovaia operation, during which Soviet forces seized the Barvenkovo bridgehead. In April 1942 this rising star in Soviet command circles was appointed Deputy Southwestern Direction commander, and he and his commander, Timoshenko, planned to complete the destruction of German forces in the Kharkov region.

Kharkov, 1942

THE SOUTHWESTERN DIRECTION FORCES

Southwestern Front Forces

28TH ARMY

As we have seen, to accomplish this task the Stavka allocated the Southwestern Front four armies and a specially designated Army Group, all commanded by experienced and distinguished combat veterans. The newest of these armies, the 28th, commanded by Lt-Gen D. I. Riabyshev, already had a difficult history in the war. Activated in the Arkhangel'sk Military District in June 1941, in July it deployed forward to the Roslavl region south of Smolensk as part of a new Reserve Front, which was formed to counter the German advance on Smolensk. During August, while it was launching heavy counter-attacks south of Smolensk, Guderian's Second Panzer Group encircled and destroyed 28th Army and killed its first commander, Lt-Gen V. Ia. Kachalov. After its headquarters was deactivated in August 1941, in November 1941 the Stavka formed a second 28th Army and positioned it in reserve, first along the Moscow axis and then, in early spring 1942, along the Stalingrad axis. In May Timoshenko and the Stavka assigned 28th Army the critical mission of spearheading the Southwestern Direction's main offensive effort northeast of Kharkov.[24]

Lt-Gen Dmitri Ivanovich Riabyshev, 28th Army's commander, was an experienced combat officer.[25] Born near Rostov in 1894, he too was a cavalry officer who had risen through the Civil War and 1920s to command, in succession, a cavalry squadron, regiment, brigade and a division. In the 1930s he attended the Frunze Academy and commanded, in succession, the 1st and 4th Cavalry Corps and the 8th Mechanised Corps. These assignments, in particular the command of one of the Red Army's prized mechanised corps, placed him among the foremost Soviet commanders. When war began it was his 8th Mechanised Corps, which, although ultimately destroyed, launched fierce, but futile, counter-attacks near Dubno in the Ukraine against the flanks of von Kleist's advancing First Panzer Group. Subsequently, Riabyshev commanded 38th Army during the period of the Kiev encirclement (and escaped with much of his army), the Southern Front from August into October 1941, and 57th Army from October 1941 into early May 1942. Riabyshev's 57th Army participated with distinction in the series of Soviet winter counter-attacks and, in particular, during the Barvenkovo-Lozovaia operation, when his army spearheaded the Southern Front assault. During the pause before the spring offensive, Timoshenko assigned Riabyshev the task of preparing 28th Army for its decisive role in the Kharkov operation.

Riabyshev's 28th Army consisted of six rifle divisions (13th Guards, 38th, 162nd, 169th, 175th and the 244th) and four supporting tank brigades (6th Guards, 57th, 84th and 90th), all under experienced commanders.

13th Guards Rifle Division

The most distinguished of 28th Army's divisional commanders was Maj-Gen Aleksandr Ilich Rodimtsev of the 13th Guards. Born in 1905 near Orenburg in the southern Urals, Rodimtsev had earned the award of Hero of the Soviet Union for service in the Spanish Civil War of the late 1930s, participated in the 1939 invasion of Poland as a cavalry division commander and had begun his wartime service as commander of 5th Airborne Brigade (3rd Airborne Corps).[26] A defender of Kiev and an

4 Opposing Forces

escapee from the encirclement, after the airborne corps' remnants were re-formed into the 87th Rifle Division, Rodimtsev assumed command of the division and fought under 40th Army control during its eastward withdrawal. For its skilful performance during this period, the division earned the designation of 13th Guards. It was Rodimtsev's division which, in March 1942, had spearheaded 38th Army's seizure of the Staryi Saltov bridgehead northeast of Kharkov.

38th Rifle Division
The second formation of the 38th Rifle Division was raised at Alma Ata in Kazakhstan in January 1942 and had a heavy Kazakh representation in its ranks.[27] The earlier 38th had been destroyed at Viazma in October 1941. Under its new commander, Col N. P. Dotsenko, himself a hardened combat veteran, the new division would see its first combat at Kharkov.

162nd Rifle Division
Like the 38th, the 162nd Rifle Division's predecessor had also been destroyed at Viazma. The second 162nd was formed in Cheliabinsk in the Urals in January 1942 and consisted of 70% Russians, 20% Ukrainians and 10% other nationalities, some of whom had returned from convalescence or served in penal units. Commanded by Col M. I. Matveev, it would also see its first combat at Kharkov.

169th Rifle Division
Commanded by the experienced Maj-Gen S. M. Rogachevsky, the 169th Rifle Division had emerged intact, but heavily damaged, from its baptism of fire in 1941. Raised in the Kherson and Nikolaev region of the Ukraine Military District in August and September 1939, it participated in the invasion of eastern Poland in September and the invasion of Romanian Bessarabia in June 1940. When Operation 'Barbarossa' began, the 169th was serving as part of the Kiev Special Military District's reserve 55th Rifle Corps and had been moved to the border near Kamenets-Podolsk on the eve of the German attack. During July and August 1941, it lost over half its strength serving as 'fire brigade' (used in a series of critical sectors) for 18th Army in the fighting withdrawal across southern Ukraine. Thereafter, it retreated eastward and joined 6th Army's defence of the Dnepr River line and, then, 38th and 21st Armies defending the Kharkov sector. On 3 October, during heavy fighting on the approaches to Kharkov, S. M. Rogachevsky was appointed division commander. In March the veteran division was reinforced from its depleted strength of 2,500 men and was assigned to 28th Army to provide a leavening of experienced troops for the Kharkov operation.[28]

175th Rifle Division
Commanded by Maj-Gen A. D. Kuleshchev, the 175th was also a second formation division, its predecessor having been destroyed in the Kiev pocket. The new division was formed in December 1941 at Tiuman in the Ural Military District. The division was composed of Siberians, Bashkirs and Tartars, most between 33 and 42 years, many of whom had been just released from prison camp. After initial combat training at Staritsa, in March the division was assigned to 28th Army for the Kharkov operation.[29]

244th Rifle Division
The final division in 28th Army was Col Afansiev's 244th Rifle Division, whose name-

Kharkov, 1942

sake had been destroyed in the Viazma pocket in December 1941. The new 244th was raised in Stalingrad in December 1941 on the base of the Transcaucasian Military District's 469th Rifle Division. 10% of the division's troops were experienced veterans, and 90% were 42-year-old conscripts.[30] The 244th also joined 28th Army in March 1942.

28th Army tank brigades
Only one of 28th Army's four tank brigades was combat-tested. The 6th Guards, under the command of Lt-Col M. K. Skuba, was the most experienced. Formed in the Moscow Military District in August 1941 as the 1st Tank Brigade, it was awarded its 'guards' designation on 16 February 1942 after participating in Southwestern Front's autumn and winter battles. Lt-Col M. I. Malyshev's 90th Tank Brigade, Maj-Gen V. M. Alekseev's 57th Tank Brigade and the 84th Tank Brigade (commander unknown) were newer formations. The 57th was formed in April 1942 at Staryi Oskol in the Orel Military District and the 84th and 90th also in April at Stalingrad in the North Caucasus Military District.[31] All three would see their first combat at Kharkov.

3rd Guards Cavalry Corps
Supporting 28th Army was Maj-Gen V. D. Kriuchenkin's crack 3rd Guards Cavalry Corps, consisting of the 5th and 6th Guards Cavalry Divisions, the 32nd Cavalry Division and the 34th Motorised Rifle Brigade. Formed as 5th Cavalry Corps in May 1936, K. K. Rokossovsky commanded the corps in 1936 and again in 1940. As one of the Red Army's élite corps, it formed the nucleus of one of the Ukrainian Front's cavalry-mechanised groups that spearheaded the Soviet invasion of eastern Poland in September 1939 and took part in the July 1940 Soviet invasion into Romanian Bessarabia. Later in 1940 it served as a nucleus for the newly-formed 9th Mechanised Corps. Shortly before the outbreak of war in 1941 and during the Soviet partial mobilisation, a new 5th Cavalry Corps was formed from units taken from other cavalry corps. After war began, the new 5th Cavalry Corps fought near Dubno against the First Panzer Group and was later involved in the abortive attempt to rescue Soviet 6th and 12th Armies from the Uman encirclement south of Kiev. Throughout autumn 1941 the corps defended north of Kharkov and east of Kursk and, in December, it formed the nucleus of Gen Kostenko's operational group in its successful counterstroke at Elets. After the operation, on 26 December 1941, the corps received the honorary title '3rd Guards' for its remarkable performance at Elets.[32]

The corps' commander, Vasili Dmitrievich Kriuchenkin, born in 1894, had joined the Red Army in 1918 and participated in the Civil War as a cavalryman. After the Civil War, he led cavalry forces at all levels, rising to command the 14th Cavalry Division in 1938. In 1941 he graduated from the Frunze Academy. After the outbreak of war, he commanded a cavalry regiment and division and led 5th Cavalry Corps in the Elets operation.[33] After the corps' successful performance at Elets, it regrouped and refitted throughout the winter and then spearheaded and supported 38th Army's seizure of the Staryi Saltov bridgehead east of Kharkov in March 1942.

5th Guards Cavalry Division
Maj-Gen M. F. Maleev's 5th Guards Cavalry Division began its history during the Civil War as the 4th Cavalry Division. In 1919 and 1920, it fought as part of the Turkistan Army and on the eastern (Ural) front against Admiral Kolchak's White forces. After the war ended, in January 1923 it was redesignated the 3rd 'Bessarabian'

4 Opposing Forces

Cavalry Division, and in 1939 it participated in the Polish invasion under the Ukrainian Front's 2nd Cavalry Corps. Returning to Ukraine in 1940 with Kostenko's 2nd Cavalry Corps, it helped form the new 5th Cavalry Corps in spring 1941, when the High Command converted the original 5th Cavalry Corps into a mechanised corps. When war began, the 3rd Cavalry Division served with 5th Cavalry Corps during the difficult campaigns of 1941 and earned its guards' designation in December 1941 for its role in the Elets operations.[34]

6th Guards Cavalry Division
Commanded by Col A. I. Belogorsky, 6th Guards also had an illustrious history. It served during the Civil War as the 14th Cavalry Division, with 10th Army and with Budenny's 1st Cavalry Army in the northern Caucasus, Ukrainian and Crimean operations. After the war, in 1928 14th Cavalry earned the honorific 'International Communist Youth *imeni* (named after) Gen Parkhemenko'. During the late 1930s, it served under 2nd Cavalry Corps during the 1939 invasion of eastern Poland. Thereafter, its history paralleled that of the 5th Guards. It also earned its honorific '6th Guards' for service during the Elets operations.[35]

32nd Cavalry Division
The 'late arriver' to the 3rd Guards Cavalry Corps was the 32nd Cavalry Division, which was created in January 1937 at Donskoi in the Odessa Military District from elements of 1st Cavalry Division. In 1938 it participated in the mobilisation accompanying the Czech crisis, under control of 4th Cavalry Corps of the Ukrainian Front's Vinnitsa Army Group. The following year it was stationed in Proskurov, Ukraine, as part of Rokossovsky's 5th Cavalry Corps. When this corps was mechanised, it became part of the new 5th Corps. Its subsequent combat record was the same as its counterpart cavalry division in 5th Corps, although it did not earn a 'guards' designation in December 1941.

34th Motorised Rifle Brigade
This unit was formed in November 1941 at Ostrogoshzk in the Orel Military District.[36] Creation of the new motorised rifle brigades was an attempt by the Stavka to form mobile units with a greater proportion of motorised infantry to accompany tank brigades and cavalry formations in field operations. After initial training the brigade joined 5th Cavalry Corps in time to prove its worth by playing a critical role in the December Elets operations.

28th Army Supporting Artillery Units
Several of 28th Army's supporting artillery regiments had performed illustrious service in earlier operations. The 764th Anti-tank Artillery Regiment and 266th Gun Artillery Regiment had supported 37th Army in the Rostov operation and had supported the Southwestern Front in the Barvenkovo-Lozovaia operation. The 870th Howitzer Artillery Regiment also fought in the latter operation. The records of the other seven artillery regiments and the separate guards mortar battalions cannot yet be traced, but they certainly had some prior combat experience.

38TH ARMY
Commanded by Lt-Gen K. S. Moskalenko, 38th Army had already received its baptism of fire in heavy fighting in the Ukraine and the Kharkov region in 1941 and early

Kharkov, 1942

1942.[37] The army was activated in early August 1941 just after the encirclement of Soviet 6th and 12th Armies at Uman. The remnants of 8th Mechanised Corps, escapees from the Uman pocket, and newly raised Ukrainian divisions formed its nucleus, and under its new commander, Gen D. I. Riabyshev, it initially took up defensive positions along the Dnepr River south of Kiev. After being nearly destroyed in fighting near Kremenchug, the remnants of the army escaped the Kiev encirclement, withdrew east and were reinforced to participate in the defence of Kharkov. Forced to abandon the city in October 1941, 38th Army later joined the Southwestern Front's January 1942 offensive toward Kharkov and, in March 1942, seized the Staryi Saltov bridgehead just east of the city.

Lt-Gen Kirill Semenovich Moskalenko was an experienced commander who had survived harrowing combat during the first eight months of war.[38] He was born in 1902 at Grishino in the Donbas and joined the Red Army in 1920, first fighting as an enlisted man in Budenny's 1st Cavalry Army against the Whites and Makhno's partisans in the Ukraine and, later, fighting under Budenny in the Crimea and Caucasus. As a cavalry artilleryman during the 1920s and early 1930s, Moskalenko commanded at battery, battalion and regimental level in the 6th Chongar Cavalry Division. He also attended the School for Red Army Commanders (in 1922) and, much later, the Dzherzhinsky (NKVD) Academy (in 1939). In the mid-1930s, as the Red Army embarked on its large-scale motor-mechanisation programme, Moskalenko transferred from cavalry to mechanised forces, commanding in 1935 the 23rd Mechanised Brigade in the Far East and, in 1936, the 133rd Mechanised Brigade of the Kiev Special Military District. He served during the Finnish War as the élite 51st (Perekop) Rifle Division's chief of artillery and, after the war, in June 1940 he commanded the 35th Rifle Corps during the invasion of Romanian Bessarabia. After the incursion, in August 1940 he took command of a tank division in the Odessa Military District's 2nd Mechanised Corps. In May 1941, when the Red Army formed new motorised anti-tank brigades to accompany and protect the mechanised corps, Moskalenko organised and commanded the 1st Anti-tank Brigade of the Kiev Special Military District.

When World War 2 began, Moskalenko led his brigade in fierce battles against German First Panzer Group, and, when his brigade was destroyed, he commanded, in succession, 15th Rifle Corps, 6th Cavalry Corps and a cavalry-mechanised group in combat near Kiev, Chernigov and, during the Southwestern Front's offensive, at Elets in December 1941. For his exemplary service at Elets, in late December 1941 the Stavka appointed Moskalenko Deputy Commander of 6th Army, then attacking toward Kharkov. In that capacity he was instrumental in planning 6th Army's role in the January 1942 Barvenkovo-Lozovaia operation. For his excellent performance he was given command of 38th Army in March 1942. Moskalenko was known as a superb organiser and a skilled and courageous combat commander.

Moskalenko's army consisted of six rifle divisions (81st, 124th, 199th, 226th, 300th and 304th) and three tank brigades (13th, 36th and 133rd).

81st Rifle Division
Col F. A. Pimenov's 81st Rifle Division, formed in January 1936 in Lubny, Kharkov Military District, soon reorganised into the 81st Motorised Rifle Division. As one of the Red Army's first four motorised divisions, it possessed a powerful armour complement of 275 tanks. The 81st Division participated in the famous 1936 Belorussian Manoeuvres and took part in the September 1939 invasion of eastern Poland as part of the Ukrainian Front's Zhitomir Army Group. After the outbreak of war in 1941,

4 Opposing Forces

it fought in the Lvov region as part of 6th Army's 4th Mechanised Corps. Although it was heavily damaged in the fighting, it successfully withdrew and later escaped encirclement at Kiev. Thereafter the 81st, now redesignated as a rifle division, defended under 21st Army in the sector north of Kharkov throughout the autumn and fought with 21st Army during the winter offensive on the approaches to Kharkov. In February, during heavy fighting outside Kharkov, the division's commander, Col V. S. Smirnov, was killed, and Col Pimenov became its commander. The division joined 38th Army on 25 February 1942, and, at a cost of heavy casualties, it helped Moskalenko's army secure the Staryi Saltov bridgehead.[39]

124th Rifle Division
Commanded by Col A. K. Berestov, the 124th Rifles was a second formation division whose predecessor had been destroyed in the Kiev pocket. The new 124th was raised at Voronezh in the Orel Military District in December 1941 from wounded veterans and conscripts, and it was joined by an artillery regiment from the experienced 100th Rifle Division in January.[40] Serving under 21st Army, it fought during the first offensive against Kharkov in January 1942 and was transferred to 38th Army control on 25 February. Like the 81st, it then fought for possession of the Staryi Saltov bridgehead in March.

226th Rifle Division
Unlike the 124th, the 226th Rifle Division, under commander of Maj-Gen A. V. Gorbatov, was a veteran division. Formed at Zaporozhe in the Odessa Military District in July 1941, it fought first under 6th Army and escaped from the Uman pocket in August to fight first near Dnepropetrovsk and then in the October defence of Kharkov by 38th Army. After abandoning the city, throughout the winter the 226th fought with 21st Army and participated in the January 1942 Kharkov offensive. In February it was transferred with its sister 81st and 124th Division to 38th Army and in March joined the battle for the Staryi Saltov bridgehead, also suffering heavy casualties in the process.

The commander of 226th Rifles, Aleksandr Vasilevich Gorbatov, was the senior and most experienced commander in Moskalenko's army. Born in 1891, he had served in the Tsarist Army during World War 1 and the Red Army from 1919. Also a cavalry officer, he rose through cavalry ranks to command a regiment, brigade and division during the Civil War and postwar years. A 1930 graduate of the Frunze Academy, when war broke out in 1941 he was assistant commander of 25th Rifle Corps stationed in Kharkov. Transferred to the Western Front in late June, the corps fought under Konev's 19th Army in the defence of Vitebsk and Iartsevo where Gorbatov was wounded and evacuated to Viazma and later Moscow for convalescence. Meanwhile, Gorbatov's corps was encircled and destroyed in the Smolensk pocket. After recuperating from his wounds, in late September Gorbatov was personally selected by Timoshenko for command in the Southwestern Front. He assumed command of the 226th Rifle Division on 1 October and led it with distinction throughout the winter campaign.[41]

300th and 304th Rifle Divisions
These were two veteran formations. The 300th was raised in July 1941 at Krasnograd, south of Kharkov, and was first deployed as part of the Western Strategic Direction's reserve. In August it regrouped to Poltava and soon joined 38th Army's defence of the

Kharkov, 1942

Dnepr River line south of Kiev. Thereafter, it fought with 38th Army in the defence of Kharkov in October and during the winter offensive battles which followed. The 304th Rifle Division was formed at Solotnoshcha, near Kharkov in July and August 1941. It was made up of reservists and veterans of the disbanded 109th Motorised Division of 5th Mechanised Corps, which had just been heavily damaged in battles at Lepel and around Smolensk. Thereafter, the division's record of assignments and combat paralleled that of the 300th. Both divisions were severely weakened during the autumn operations. (In November 1941 the divisions numbered 2,684 and less than 1,000 men, respectively.)[42] Perhaps because of their earlier heavy losses, in the Kharkov operation both divisions were assigned peripheral missions covering German forces, defending in the Chuguev bridgehead.

22nd Tank Corps
Prior to the Kharkov operation, the Stavka directed 38th Army's three supporting tank brigades to form a new tank corps, the 22nd, which was to be similar in structure to the two such corps supporting 6th Army (21st and 23rd). However, because of the short time available to reorganise and the army's acute requirement for infantry support armour, the three brigades remained separate.

13th Tank Brigade
The most experienced of the three brigades, the 13th Tank Brigade was commanded by Lt-Col I. T. Klimenchuk. It was formed in the Stalingrad region in August 1941 and saw action during the autumn and winter, providing armour support to the Southwestern Front.

36th Tank Brigade
Commanded by Col T. I. Tanaschishin, the 36th Tank Brigade was formed in November 1941 at Gorki in the Moscow Military District and joined 38th Army soon after its formation.

133rd Tank Brigade
Commanded by Lt-Col N. M. Bubnov, the 133rd Tank Brigade was also an experienced unit. Formed at Mitschurinsk in the Orel Military District in September 1941, in October it fought under the control of 13th Army defending along the Kursk axis against Guderian's advancing Second Panzer Group. After refitting, throughout the winter it and the 13th Brigade supported Southwestern Front armies.[43]

Artillery
The six artillery regiments (738th Anti-tank, 468th and 507th Light, 574th Heavy, and 51st and 648th) and two battalions of guards mortars (katiushas) (3rd Battalion, 5th Guards Mortar and 3rd Battalion, 4th Guards Mortar) all had prior service. The 738th Anti-tank Regiment fought in the Barvenkovo-Lozovaia operation under 6th Army control, and the 648th Artillery Regiment supported 37th Army in both the Rostov and the Barvenkovo-Lozovaia operations.

21ST ARMY
Lt-Gen V. N. Gordov's 21st Army, which was designated to launch a supporting attack on the Southwestern Front's right flank, was also a battled-hardened, although battle-scarred, formation. The army was formed at Kuibyshev in the Volga Military

4 Opposing Forces

District in April and May 1941 during the prewar partial force mobilisation. It then regrouped in mid-May to the Chernigov-Konotop region southeast of Gomel', where it soon joined the Group of Reserve Armies under Stavka control. In July 1941, when German forces were approaching the Dnepr River, it deployed forward to the Rogachev area where, over a period of three weeks, it launched a series of desperate counter-attacks against Guderian's Second Panzer Group (the infamous 'Timoshenko counter-offensive'). During subsequent fighting in September, it was annihilated in the Kiev pocket but reformed in the Kharkov region from remnants of the encircled force and Stavka reserves. It then took part in the Southwestern Front's January offensive toward Kharkov and drove German forces to the banks of the Northern Donets River.[44]

Its commander, Vasili Nikolaevich Gordov, was one of the Red Army's senior army commanders. Born in 1896 at Matveevka in the Tartar Autonomous Republic, he joined the Tsarist Army in 1915 as an enlisted man and rose to junior officer rank during World War 1. In 1917 he joined the Red Guard and, in 1918, the Red Army, subsequently serving during the Civil War as a commander at all levels from platoon to regiment on the Eastern and Western Fronts, and against Makhno's Ukrainian partisans. After the war he served in a variety of staff and command positions, including advisory duty with the Mongolian Army, chief of staff of the Moscow Military District Infantry School and as a rifle division chief of staff. As was the case with many other mid-grade officers, the purges quickly propelled him to ever greater prominence. In 1937 he rose to division command, and two years later he became chief of staff of, first, the Kalinin and, then, the Volga Military District. After war began, from July to September 1941 he served as 21st Army Chief of Staff and then as 21st Army commander.[45] Gordov combined broad military experience with unquestioned political reliability.

Three of 21st Army's Rifle Divisions (76th, 227th and 293rd) and one of its tank brigades (10th) took an active part in the Kharkov operation.

76th Rifle Division
Col G. G. Voronin's 76th Rifle Division, originally a mountain division, was formed in 1938 at Nakichevan in Armenia and consisted primarily of Armenian troops. Up to July 1941 it served in the Transcaucasus Military District, ultimately under the newly mobilised 47th Army. After being withdrawn into Stavka reserve, in September 1941 it was assigned to 38th Army. The 76th Division participated in the Poltava defensive operation in September and the subsequent defence of Kharkov under 38th Army control in October. In November 1941 it was the strongest of 38th Army's divisions with a strength of 6,000 men.[46] Shortly after the turn of the year, as the Southwestern Front regrouped for the January offensive, the Front commander transferred the 76th Rifle Division to 21st Army, where it remained until May 1942.

227th Rifle Division
Commanded by Col G. A. Ter-Gasparian, the 227th Rifle Division was raised at Slaviansk in the Kharkov Military District during the June 1941 mobilisation. After a short period in Stavka reserve, in July it was assigned to 26th Army, then operating in the Zhitomir region of Ukraine. The division escaped across the Dnepr River after 26th Army's unsuccessful defensive battles south of Kiev and avoided the grizzly fate of its encircled sister divisions in 26th Army; subsequently during early autumn the 227th defended in the Konotop and Belgorod regions north of Kharkov under 40th

Kharkov, 1942

Army control. In late autumn it was transferred to 21st Army, under which it fought through to February. On 25 February it was again transferred, this time to 38th Army, and it participated in the Staryi Saltov operation in March 1942. Heavily damaged in the operation, in April the division was reassigned to 21st Army and rested and refitted before the Kharkov operation.[47]

293rd Rifle Division
Gordov's third shock division was the 293rd Rifle, commanded by Maj-Gen P. F. Lagutin. This division's combat record was similar to the 227th's. It was formed at Sumy north of Kharkov in July 1941 and was assigned almost immediately to 40th Army, then forming east of Kiev. The predominantly Ukrainian and Russian division defended around Konotop and Kursk in August and September, attempting to restore the front after the Kiev disaster. Thereafter, throughout the autumn it defended along the Kursk-Staryi Oskol axis, and combat attrition reduced the division's strength by November to under 1,000 men.[48] During December 1941 and again in January and February 1942 it took part in limited offensive action under 40th Army in the Kursk sector. In March the 293rd was transferred to 21st Army to prepare for spring operations.

10th Tank Brigade
21st Army's supporting 10th Tank Brigade was raised at Saratov in the Volga Military District in September 1941 and had a long, arduous and distinguished combat record. It defended alongside the 169th, 300th and 304th Rifle Divisions of 38th Army during the bitter fighting around Poltava and Kharkov in September and October 1941, losing all of its tanks in September and, after refitting, returning to a strength of 20 tanks in early October.[49] After again refitting during the winter under 21st Army control, on 25 February the brigade returned to 38th Army, and in March 1942 it supported 38th Army's attack at Staryi Saltov. During the planning for the Kharkov operation the brigade was reassigned to support 21st Army in the new offensive.

Artillery
The exact combat record of 21st Army's three supporting artillery regiments (338th Light, 538th Heavy and 135th and 156th Artillery) cannot be precisely determined, but they certainly participated in earlier operations.

6TH ARMY
The veteran 6th Army, commanded by Lt-Gen A. M. Gorodniansky, had the honour of spearheading the Southwestern Front's main effort at Kharkov along with Army Group Bobkin. The 6th Army's history had embraced operations during the Civil War in the Arkhangel'sk and Murmansk regions; after the war ended, the army staff formed the headquarters first for the White Sea Military District and then the Kharkov Military District. The army was reactivated in August 1939 in the Kiev Special Military District. After it took part in the invasion of eastern Poland in September 1939, it occupied defences along the Lvov axis as a premier military district 'covering army'. The 6th absorbed the main German attack in June 1941, falling back under pressure to Uman south of Kiev where it was encircled and destroyed in August 1939; its commander, Lt-Gen I. N. Muzychenko, was captured. Deactivated on 10 August, in September it was reactivated around the nucleus of 48th Rifle Corps and deployed as a reserve army in the Kharkov sector. After defending the Northern

4 Opposing Forces

Donets River line near Izium throughout the autumn, it spearheaded the Barvenkovo-Lozovaia operation in January 1942 and occupied the northern half of the Barvenkovo salient carved deep into German defences.[50]

Lt-Gen Avksentii Mikhailovich Gorodniansky had a long and illustrious war record. Born in 1896, he served in the Tsarist Army during World War 1, joined the Red Army in 1918 and fought with it through the Civil War. After the war, in 1924 he attended the 'Vystrel' School and later commanded a rifle regiment and rifle division. When war began in 1941, Gorodniansky commanded 19th Army's 129th Rifle Division, and when the Stavka transferred the army northward in July, Gorodniansky's division participated in first 19th and then 16th Army's defence of Smolensk. Having escaped with elements of his division from the Smolensk pocket, in late August 1941 the Stavka appointed him commander of 13th Army.

Gorodniansky commanded 13th Army in September 1941 during the abortive Soviet counter-attack against Guderian's Second Panzer Group and then during the battles around Briansk in October. There he again escaped from encirclement with the bulk of his army and took part in the ensuing Soviet withdrawal during the German advance on Moscow in November. In December 1941 he was instrumental in planning and conducting the Soviet counter-attack by 13th Army and Group Kostenko against over extended German forces at Elets and Livny. On 3 January 1942 Lt-Gen N. P. Pukhov replaced him as 13th Army commander, and Gorodniansky assumed command of 6th Army, subsequently leading it in its battles throughout the winter.[51]

Gorodniansky's 6th Army was the most powerful of Southwestern Direction and Front armies. It consisted of eight rifle divisions (41st, 47th, 103rd, 248th, 253rd, 266th, 337th and 411th) and four separate tank brigades (5th Guards, 37th, 38th and 48th) and was supported by two new tank corps, the 21st and 23rd.

41st Rifle Division
Commanded by Col V. G. Baersky, the 41st Rifle Division was a new, second formation division whose namesake had been destroyed in the September Kiev encirclement. The new division was raised at Chapaevsk in the Volga Military District in December 1941 and joined 6th Army shortly thereafter.[52]

47th (Mountain) Rifle Division
Commanded by Maj-Gen F. P. Matykin, the 47th was an older division which had served in the Civil War. After its deactivation in 1920, in 1932 it had been re-formed at Kutaisi in the Transcaucasus Military District, where it was stationed until the end of 1939. Upon the outbreak of war it was subordinate to 3rd Rifle Corps, 46th Army, and in September the Stavka assigned it to reinforce 38th Army. The division fought with that army through the autumn of 1941 in the defence of Kharkov and the subsequent withdrawal to Kupiansk. After conversion to a standard rifle division, the 47th joined 6th Army for the Kharkov offensive.[53]

103rd Rifle Division
Commanded by Col Ia. D. Chanyshev, the 103rd Rifle Division was a second formation division whose predecessor had been destroyed in the October 1941 Viazma pocket. The new division was raised at Samarkand, Central Asian Military District, in December 1941. Half of its soldiers were ethnic Russians and the other half Kirghiz and Uzbek. Typical of many divisions raised during this period, it was manned by both the young and old: 90% of its soldiers were between the ages of 39 and 40; the

Kharkov, 1942

rest were 19 to 21 years old.[54] Assigned initially to 28th Army, in late April the division was reassigned to 6th Army.

248th Rifle Division
Col A. A. Mishchenko's division was also a second generation force, replacing the original 248th, which had also been destroyed in the Viazma pocket. Raised at Astrakhan in the Stalingrad Military District in December 1941, its composition was 60% Russian and 40% Kirghiz and Kalmuk, and the age range of its soldiers approximated to that of the 103rd.[55] Originally assigned to 28th Army, it was resubordinated in April to 6th Army.

253rd Rifle Division
Commanded by Lt-Col M. G. Grigorev, the 253rd Rifle Division was a first generation division raised at Volchansk in the Kharkov Military District in July 1941 and manned by former NKVD troops.[56] Apparently an elite division, it first operated during July, August and September 1941 as a Southern Front 'fire brigade' unit, deploying in succession to Nikopol, the Krivoi Rog region and into defences along the Dnepr River south of Dnepropetrovsk. After the division was withdrawn from the front in late September, it was used to form the nucleus of newly created 37th Army and spearheaded that army's successful counter-attack at Rostov in November 1941. In January 1942 the 253rd joined 6th Army and took part in the Barvenkovo-Lozovaia operation, attacking the key German strongpoint of Balakleia on the army's right flank. It remained with 6th Army, and as the May offensive approached, characteristically the division was assigned the mission of seizing the strongest German defensive position at Verkhnii Bishkin, on the western edge of the Barvenkovo bridgehead.

266th Rifle Division
Col A. A. Tavantsev's 266th Rifle Division was a second formation division. Its predecessor 266th had been destroyed at Kiev during the September encirclement. The new division was formed in December 1941 at Stalingrad in the Stalingrad Military District around the nucleus of the already partially formed 477th Rifle Division.[57] The division joined 6th Army shortly after the winter offensive ended.

337th Rifle Division
Commanded by Col I. V. Vasilev, the 337th was a veteran formation raised at Astrakhan in the North Caucasus Military District in August 1941. It first served in October with 57th Army in the Stavka reserve. In January 1942 it was reassigned to 6th Army and participated in the Barvenkovo-Lozovaia operation, fighting alongside the 253rd Rifle Division for possession of German strongpoints along the Northern Donets River.

411th Rifle Division
The last of 6th Army's rifle divisions, the 411th was commanded by Colonel M. A. Pesochin and raised locally at Chuguev, south of Kharkov, in August 1941. In September the division joined 10th Army, a newly formed Stavka reserve army designated to reinforce the Southern Front. When 10th Army was dissolved in October 1941, the 411th was transferred to reinforce the Southern Front's 6th Army.[58] Under 6th Army, the 411th participated in the January 1942 offensive, occupying the centre sector of 6th Army's attack.

4 Opposing Forces

5th Guards Tank Brigade
The most experienced of Gorodniansky's tank brigades was the 5th Guards Tank Brigade, formerly the 142nd, which had been formed in August 1941 and received its 'guards' designation for services rendered in support of 6th Cavalry Corps during the January Barvenkovo-Lozovaia operation.

The remaining three tank brigades were newly formed, and all three would experience their baptism of fire in the Kharkov operation. The 37th and 38th Tank Brigades were formed at Dzherzhinsk and Gorki in the Moscow Military District in November 1941, and Col A. P. Sil'nov's 48th formed at Katchalinskaia in the North Caucasus Military District in December.[59]

Gorodniansky's designated exploitation forces for the Kharkov operation were the 21st and 23rd Tank Corps, both formed on the eve of the operation from tank brigades already assigned to Southwestern Front.

21st Tank Corps
Maj-Gen G. I. Kuzmin's 21st Tank Corps consisted of the 64th, 198th and 199th Tank Brigades and the 4th Motorised Rifle Brigade, all of which were raised in the Moscow Military District in March and April 1942. The 64th Tank Brigade was formed at Gorki, the 198th and 199th at Dzherzhinsk, and the 4th Motorised at Moscow proper.[60]

23rd Tank Corps
Commanded by Maj-Gen E. G. Pushkin, the 23rd Tank Corps contained the 6th, 130th and 131st Tank Brigades, and the 23rd Motorised Rifle Brigade. The 6th Tank Brigade was formed in the North Caucasus Military District in September 1941 and supported 57th Army during the Barvenkovo-Lozovaia operation in the winter. Both the 130th and 131st were formed in September 1941 at Stalingrad in the North Caucasus Military District. The former saw combat in support of 57th Army during the Barvenkovo-Lozovaia operation, while the latter's combat record is unclear. The 23rd Motorised Rifle Brigade was formed in April on the eve of the Kharkov operation.[61] Both the 21st and 23rd were the first of the new Soviet 1942 tank corps, and each was equipped with its full armour complement of 138 tanks.

Artillery
The Stavka and Timoshenko provided 6th Army with a great number of experienced artillery units to support the army's assault. The two anti-tank artillery regiments designated to accompany and support the two tank corps, the 582nd and 591st Anti-tank Regiments, fought with distinction with 6th Army throughout the Barvenkovo-Lozovaia operation. The 8th and 269th Gun Artillery Regiments supported 37th Army in both the Rostov and the Barvenkovo-Lozovaia operations, and the 116th Gun Artillery Regiment supported 57th Army in the January operation. The 671st Howitzer Artillery Regiment and the 1st and 2nd Battalions, 5th Guards Mortar Regiment, fought under Front control at Barvenkovo-Lozovaia. The other regiments (375th, 209th, 399th, 435th Gun, 3rd Guards and the 206th Separate Guards Mortar Battalion) all had prior service, although their precise combat records cannot be determined.

Kharkov, 1942

ARMY GROUP BOBKIN

In early April, on the advice of his subordinates, Marshal Timoshenko created a special army group formation to operate alongside and protect the left flank of Gorodniansky's 6th Army. Army Group Bobkin was named after its commander, Maj-Gen L. V. Bobkin, and it consisted of 6th Cavalry Corps and the 270th and 393rd Rifle Divisions. The army group's rifle divisions were to conduct the initial penetration operation and, thereafter, protect the cavalry corps' flanks while it conducted the exploitation in tandem with 6th Army's two tank corps. Maj-Gen Leonid Vasilevich Bobkin was typical of the many 'faceless' Soviet commanders who fought and died on the Soviet-German front. Although referred to on countless occasions in accounts of the Kharkov battle, little official biographical information about him exists. Bagramian relates that:

'Maj-Gen Leonid Vasilevich Bobkin (birthplace unknown) joined the Red Guard in 1917 and later served during the Civil War, where he earned the Order of the Red Banner. A cavalry officer, during 1924 and 1925 he studied with G. K. Zhukov, K. K. Rokossovsky, A. I. Eremenko and Bagramian at the Higher Cavalry School in Leningrad. There, and subsequently, he proved to be a skilled commander and expert in cavalry tactics. In May 1942 he was Assistant Commander of Southwestern Front forces for cavalry. In this capacity Timoshenko tasked him with organising and leading the specially formed Army Group.'[62]

Moskalenko identifies Bobkin as one of two operational group commanders he appointed in March 1942 to control 38th Army operations in the Staryi Saltov bridgehead. Moskalenko described him as an extremely capable, skilful and energetic commander. Presumably these talents plus his cavalry experience earned him command of the special army group on 6th Army's flank. Curiously, with him at his headquarters as he prepared for and conducted the operation, was his 13-year-old son.[63]

Timoshenko assigned two experienced rifle divisions (the 270th and 383rd) to Bobkin to assist him in performing his critical mission.

270th Rifle Division

Maj-Gen Z. Iu. Kutlin's 270th Rifle Division was the senior division. Raised at Melitopol in the Odessa Military District in July 1941, it fought throughout the summer with 12th Army in the Zaporozhe, Krasnograd and Izium sectors. In January 1942 the 270th led 6th Army's offensive in the Izium sector of the Barvenkovo-Lozovaia operation and seized the key rail junction at Lozovaia late in the month.[64]

393rd Rifle Division

Formed at Sviatogorsk in the Kharkov Military District in August 1941, the 393rd Rifle Division was originally assigned to 10th Army in Stavka reserve. Like the 411th Rifle Division, it left 10th Army when it disbanded in October 1941 and moved to join 6th Army the following month. It was a first echelon division during 6th Army's attack in January 1942.[65]

6th Cavalry Corps

The critical shock force in Bobkin's Army Group was Maj-Gen A. A. Noskov's 6th Cavalry Corps, which consisted of three cavalry divisions (the 26th, 28th and 49th) and the 7th Tank Brigade. The 6th Cavalry Corps had an illustrious history.[66] During

4 Opposing Forces

World War 1, it had been commanded by Finland's future Marshal Mannerheim, and during the Civil War it fought in the Ukraine, Poland and Crimea as part of Budenny's 1st Cavalry Army. Assigned to the Belorussian Military District in the interwar years, Zhukov command it in 1937–38, and later, while under the command of A. I. Eremenko, it participated in the 1939 invasion of eastern Poland as part of the Belorussian Front's cavalry-mechanised group. In June 1941 the corps occupied a critical position at Lomza in the Bialystok bulge. The corps was destroyed during early wartime operations south of Grodno as part of a special cavalry-mechanised force organised under command of the assistant Western Front commander I. V. Boldin.

In September and October 1941, the new corps re-emerged as a cavalry group (made up of the 26th, 28th and 49th Cavalry Divisions), which fought on the southern sector of the front in the Pavlograd and Slaviansk regions. In late December 1941 the Stavka reformed the 6th Cavalry Corps under Southwestern Front control, and it soon participated in the Barvenkovo-Lozovaia operation as 6th Army's deep exploitation force. Maj-Gen A. A. Noskov, the veteran commander of 26th Cavalry Division, became the corps commander in late January 1942.

Noskov's 26th Cavalry Division, formed in the Odessa Military District in July 1941, fought on the southern front during autumn 1941 before joining 6th Cavalry Corps. Col L. N. Sakovich's 28th Cavalry Division served alongside the 26th, and Col T. V. Dedeogly's 49th, which was formed at Omsk in Siberia in July 1941 and was initially assigned to 10th Army, fought under 12th Army control until it joined its sister 6th Corps' divisions in late December.[67] Col I. A. Iurchenko's 7th Tank Brigade added a veteran armoured element to the cavalry corps. Formed at Moscow in August 1941, the brigade moved south in the autumn and subsequently supported 38th Army in the defence of Kharkov in October and 6th Army in the January 1942 Barvenkovo-Lozovaia operation.[68]

Artillery
The three artillery regiments supporting Group Bobkin (872nd Cannon, and 29th and 236th Heavy) all came from the Stavka reserve. Their prior combat experience cannot be determined.

RESERVES
Timoshenko kept a cavalry corps (2nd), two rifle divisions (277th and 343rd) and three separate tank battalions (71st, 92nd and 132nd) in Southwestern Front reserve.

2nd Cavalry Corps
The most powerful reserve force was Col G. A. Kovalev's 2nd Cavalry Corps, which Timoshenko positioned in the Barvenkovo bridgehead in Army Group Bobkin's rear area. 2nd Corps was a second generation cavalry formation, only distantly related to the older 2nd Cavalry Corps, a venerable force whose roots dated back to the Civil War years. The original 2nd Cavalry Corps fought during the Civil War as 2nd Cavalry Army until truncated into corps size in December 1920. In 1921 the corps campaigned in the Transcaucasus, extending Bolshevik power to the region. After the Civil War, 2nd Cavalry Corps was stationed in the Ukrainian and Kiev Military District, and in 1938 it formed part of the Ukrainian Front's Zhitomir Army Group, which was mobilised during the Czech crisis. A year later it participated in the invasion of eastern Poland under 6th Army command. In the wholesale Soviet force reorganisation of 1940, 2nd Cavalry Corps was moved to Lvov and soon took part in the

Kharkov, 1942

invasion and annexation of Bessarabia. Thereafter, and until the outbreak of war in June 1941, the corps remained in the Odessa Military District with its 5th and 9th Divisions. During the initial six months of war 2nd Corps fought across southern Russia, ultimately ending up in 1941 in the Moscow area, where it was converted into 1st Guards Cavalry Corps.[69]

The new 2nd Cavalry Corps was raised in the Rostov region in January 1942 at a time when the Soviets were drastically expanding their cavalry force structure. Originally, the corps consisted of the 62nd, 64th and 70th Cavalry Divisions, and its initial mission was to support 56th Army, fighting east of Rostov. After refitting, in February 1942 the corps completed a forced march to join the Southwestern Front, then struggling south of Kharkov, and to reinforce the three cavalry corps already involved in the operations (1st, 5th and 6th). By this time the 38th Cavalry Division had replaced the corps' 64th Cavalry Division.[70] Kovalev's corps would see its first combat in the Barvenkovo bridgehead in May. All three 2nd Corps divisions had been blooded during the winter campaign. The 38th Cavalry Division was raised at Rostov in July 1941 as part of 10th Army, and it fought with 18th Army on its withdrawal across the southern Ukraine and Donbas, and during the December Rostov offensive. For its heroic performance during the October battles defending the Donbas with 18th Army, Maj-Gen N. A. Kirichenko's 38th Cavalry Division was awarded the Order of the Red Banner.[71] Col N. P. Smirnov's 62nd and Col N. M. Iurchenko's 70th Cavalry Divisions were formed at Tichoresk and Voroshilovsk in the North Caucasus Military District in September 1941, and both played a major role in support of 56th Army during the December 1941 Rostov counter-offensive.[72]

Timoshenko's two reserve divisions had also seen considerable action during the winter.

277th Rifle Division
Col V. G. Chernov's 277th Rifle was a second generation division formed at Frolov in the Stalingrad Military District in December 1941. Its predecessor had been destroyed in the Kiev pocket. The new 277th consisted primarily of Ukrainians from the partially formed 468th Rifle Division.[73] In February the division moved into Southwestern Direction reserve south of Voroshilovgrad and after 26 April to new reserve positions near 38th Army headquarters at Kupiansk.

343rd Rifle Division
Commanded by Maj-Gen Iu. A. Naumenko, the 343rd Rifles was a battle-hardened division, which had been formed at Stavropol in the North Caucasus Military District in August and September 1941. Initially it served in Stavka reserve under 56th Army, and in November while spearheading 56th Army's offensive against the Germans in the Rostov region, it led the assault into the city. Thereafter, it drove German forces back to the Mius River and in January joined 9th Army. During the Barvenkovo-Lozovaia operation, it was initially in Southwestern Front's reserve in 6th Army's sector, but late in the operation it joined battle to seize the village of Nizhne Bishkin, the furthest point of 6th Army's advance into the bridgehead. On 22 April 1942, the 343rd turned over its defensive sector in the Barvenkovo bridgehead to another division and withdrew into Southwestern Front reserve southeast of Kharkov.[74]

Southern Front Forces
Although the Kharkov offensive was not his idea, and he is likely to have harboured

4 Opposing Forces

some reservations about its conduct, the Southern Front commander, Col-Gen R. Ia. Malinovsky, and his forces were to play a critical role in the operation. In existence since the first month of war, the Southern Front, like so many others, had suffered bitter hardship punctuated by occasional successes during the initial 10 months of war. Originally formed on 25 June 1941, three days after the outbreak of war, by headquarters personnel from the Moscow Military District and the forces of the Odessa Military District, the Southern Front defended the Soviet Union's southern borders with Romania. Although elements of its 9th Army were encircled in Odessa, as a whole its two armies (9th and 18th) were able to withdraw in good order across the southern Ukraine in July, August and September 1941, while its neighbour to the north, the Southwestern Front, lost most it its forces in the Kiev and Uman encirclements. During October 1941 the Southern Front conducted a fighting withdrawal across the Donbas but, reinforced by the Stavka, in November it struck back at its German tormentors at Rostov and drove von Kleist's First Panzer Army back to the line of the Mius River. Thereafter, Malinovsky's armies joined in the Barvenkovo-Lozovaia operation in January and ended up occupying the southern half of the fateful Barvenkovo bridgehead.

THE LEADERS
Col-Gen Rodion Iakovlevich Malinovsky

Malinovsky's service stretched back into World War 1.[75] Born in Odessa in 1898, he joined the Tsarist Army as a private and for two years (1916–18) fought with a Russian expeditionary force in France. Although he was awarded for bravery with a Russian St George's Cross and a French Croix de Guerre, in 1917 Malinovsky and his unit became infected with the same mutinous spirit that tore apart the French Army. After the expeditionary force copied its Russian counterparts by electing a Revolutionary Committee, the French government dispatched it to North Africa. Malinovsky, however, made his way back to Russia via Vladivostok, and in autumn 1919 he joined the Red Army as a machine gunner in the 27th Rifle Division's 240th Tver Regiment. During the ensuing two years he served with the 27th through the campaigns against Kolchak's White Army on the Eastern Front. After the war ended he attended a junior officer command school and later commanded at platoon, company and battalion level in the 246th Rifle Regiment. He joined the Communist Party in 1927 and graduated from the Frunze Academy in 1930.

Thereafter, he rose through cavalry ranks as a regimental chief of staff in the 10th Cavalry Division, a staff officer in the North Caucasus and Kiev Military Districts, and in 1936 as the chief of staff of the Belorussian Military District's élite 3rd Cavalry Corps. In 1936, like many other Soviet officers, Malinovsky 'volunteered' for service in Spain, where he fought with the International Brigade in the defence of Madrid under the name 'Colonel Malino'. Summoned back to Moscow in 1938, he miraculously avoided the purges, which decimated the ranks of his Spanish War colleagues, was awarded with the Orders of Lenin and Red Banner for his service in Spain and assumed a teaching position at the Frunze Academy. With war approaching, in March 1941 Malinovsky took command of the Odessa Military District's 48th Rifle Corps. There he began his wartime service defending along the Prut River on 22 June. In August 1941, during the harrowing Soviet retreat across the Ukraine, Malinovsky assumed command of 6th Army. He then orchestrated 6th Army's unsuccessful defence of the Dnepr River line and the Donbas. In mid-December Malinovsky's army joined in the Southwestern Direction's advance to the Northern Donets and

Kharkov, 1942

Mius Rivers; for his performance Timoshenko appointed him to command the Southern Front in late December. He subsequently helped plan and carry out the Barvenkovo-Lozovaia operation, but would now, in the spring, play only a secondary role in the upcoming Kharkov offensive.

Lt-Gen A. I. Antonov

At Malinovsky's side during the planning for the Kharkov operation was his chief of staff and one of the Red Army's most promising staff officers, Lt-Gen A. I. Antonov.[76] Born in 1896, Aleksei Innokentevich Antonov joined the Tsarist Army in 1917 and served during the famous 1917 Brusilov offensive, where he was wounded. After recuperating in Petrograd, he served briefly in the forces of the Kerensky Provisional government as it put down the Tsarist forces of General Kornilov. In mid-1919 he joined the Red Army and served in staff assignments in the Ukraine, the Kuban region and the Transcaucasus. After the war he served in staff assignments during the 1920s and graduated from the Frunze Academy in 1931. Thereafter, he combined staff assignments in the 46th Rifle Division (Ukraine) and as head of the Kharkov Military District's Operations Department, with periodic teaching assignments at the Frunze Academy. In 1935 he was instrumental in organising the famous Kiev Manoeuvres, and as a result in 1936 he attended the Voroshilov General Staff Academy where his work was singled out for its excellence. Benefiting along with his classmates from the ongoing purges, Antonov was appointed chief of staff of Budenny's Moscow Military District in summer 1937. Soon, however, he returned to the Frunze Faculty, where he reformed the curriculum based on Spanish Civil War combat experiences.

In January 1941 Antonov became deputy chief of staff for the Kiev Special Military District, where he worked closely with Bagramian on prewar operational and mobilisation planning. After the German invasion Antonov served briefly as Southwestern Front Chief of Staff and was then, in August 1941, made Southern Front Chief of Staff. In that post he organised the defence of the Dnepr River line and, later, the Southern Front's successful Rostov and Barvenkovo-Lozovaia offensives. After his success in the Rostov operation, Antonov was promoted to lieutenant-general. After their successful offensive efforts in December 1941 and January 1942, Malinovsky and Antonov had to look on almost passively as their Southwestern Front colleagues planned to reap new offensive successes in the spring of 1942.

Two armies of Col-Gen R. Ia. Malinovsky's Southern Front, the 57th and 9th, were assigned the mission of protecting the attacking Southwestern Front's left flank in the Barvenkovo bridgehead. Because of their critical location and subsequent German actions, they were inexorably drawn into the Kharkov operation and shared the same fate as the Southwestern Front's left wing.

57TH ARMY

Lt-Gen K. P. Podlas's 57th Army was deployed on Army Group Bobkin's immediate left flank. The 57th Army, one of the wave of reserve armies created in autumn 1942, was formed at Stalingrad, North Caucasus Military District, in October. After training under Stavka control, the army was committed to combat as the spearhead of the Southern Front attack in the Barvenkovo-Lozovaia operation of January 1942. After over a month of heavy fighting, it erected and manned defences along the Barvenkovo salient's southwestern flank.

Lt-Gen Kuzma Petrovich Podlas was one of the Red Army's most experienced com-

4 Opposing Forces

manders.[77] Born in 1893 at Dushatino in Briansk *oblast'*, he served as a junior officer in the Russian Army during World War 1. When the Civil War began he joined the Red Army and fought as a company, detachment and brigade commander on the Eastern, Southern and Western Fronts, and as a brigade commander during the Polish War (1920). After the war he served as a regimental and division commander, punctuated by attendance at the 'Vystrel' and Frunze Academies in 1925 and 1930. In the mid-1930s, he commanded a rifle corps and, in 1940, became Deputy Commander of the Kiev Special Military District. During the hectic days after the German invasion, Podlas served as Southwestern Front Deputy commander until August 1941, when he took command of 40th Army defending the Korosten and Kiev fortified regions. Podlas and his army were fortunate to escape the subsequent German encirclement of Kiev and, thereafter, struggled against the German advance along the Sumy-Kharkov axis in October, and in the Voronezh region until the end of the year. Podlas commanded 40th Army throughout the Soviet winter campaign, until he replaced Lt-Gen Riabyshev as 57th Army commander in February 1942 after the Barvenkovo-Lozovaia operation (Riabyshev received command of the new 28th Army).

Podlas's army contained five rifle divisions (14th Guards, 99th, 150th, 317th and 351st) backed up by a separate tank battalion (92nd).

14th Guards Rifle Division
Commanded by Maj-Gen I. M. Shepetov, the 14th Guards Rifle Division was an experienced and battle-scarred formation.[78] Formed originally as the 96th Division (Territorial) in 1923 at Vinnitsa in the Kiev Special Military District, it converted to a cadre (regular) division in 1931 and was stationed at Zhmerinka, in the Ukraine, under 17th Rifle Corps. In September 1939 it took part in the invasion of eastern Poland under 5th Army control. In April 1940 the 96th Division returned to the Kiev Military District and was converted into a mountain division, with its garrison at Chernovtsy in southern Ukraine. After the war began, the 96th fought under 17th Rifle Corps (12th Army) through the bitter initial days and into the Uman pocket in August, where its commander was killed, but the division escaped destruction. The fortunate division also barely escaped the Kiev encirclement and was subsequently refitted as a rifle division (in October) and then defended the Soviet lower Dnepr River defence line near Nikopol. When, in November, the Germans broke through Soviet defences and lunged toward Rostov, the 96th formed the nucleus of the newly raised 37th Army which subsequently launched the November 1941 counter-thrust north of Rostov, halted the German advance and drove German forces back to the Mius River. In January 1942 the 96th participated in 37th Army's offensive during the Barvenkovo-Lozovaia operation by attacking but failing to seize German strongpoints east of Slaviansk. In January 1942 the division received the designation of 14th Guards for its exemplary combat performance, and, shortly after, it was reassigned to 57th Army.

99th Rifle Division
The history of the 99th Rifle Division, commanded by Col V. Ia. Vladimirov, paralleled that of the 96th. Originally, in 1923, the 99th was a territorial division of 17th Rifle Corps stationed at Cherkassy in the Ukraine. In the 1930s it converted into a regular division and transferred to Uman. In August 1940 the division was reorganised and manned with Siberian troops. With its new commander, A. A. Vlasov, it participated in the 1940 Kiev Manoeuvres and was designated by Timoshenko as the best

division in the Red Army. When war broke out in 1941 the 99th defended the Peremysl sector under 26th Army's 8th Rifle Corps. Its valorous defence of Peremysl, which included one of the few successful Soviet counter-attacks early in the war, earned the plaudits of the Germans, and it was christened by them as the 'Communist' division.[79] The 99th survived the first few months of war, but only barely, by escaping from the Uman encirclement after suffering heavy losses. In October 1941 Timoshenko withdrew the 99th into Southwestern Front reserve for refitting. Thereafter, it joined 37th Army and fought with that army during the Rostov counter-offensive and throughout the winter campaign. During the Barvenkovo-Lozovaia operation, it operated alongside the 96th Division. In early February it regrouped to occupy positions in the Barvenkovo bridgehead under 57th Army control.

150th Rifle Division
Commanded by Maj-Gen D. G. Egorov, a former regimental commander in the 99th Rifle Division, the 150th Rifle Division had been raised at Viazma in the Western Military District during the September 1939 mobilisation.[80] After service with 50th Rifle Corps of 7th Army and 3rd Rifle Corps of 13th Army during the Finnish War, where it fought its way through the Mannerheim Line, the division redeployed in 1940 to the Odessa Military District. In June 1941 it defended along the Prut River and at Tiraspol under 9th Army's 14th Rifle Corps. When the Germans broke through Soviet defences in the south, during the period August to October, it and its parent corps withdrew along the Black Sea coast through Nikolaev and Melitopol to Taganrog. The 150th served under 9th Army during the November 1941 Rostov defensive and counter-offensive operations and with 37th Army during the January 1942 Barvenkovo-Lozovaia offensive. In early May it reinforced 57th Army positions in the Barvenkovo bridgehead.

317th Rifle Division
Commanded by Col D. I. Iakovlev, the 317th Rifle Division was a new division. Formed at Baku, Transcaucasus Military District, in August 1941, it consisted of 30% regular troops (22-24 years old) and 70% reservists (25-37 years old). Many of its troops were Azerbaijanis.[81] In October the division was assigned to the Stavka reserve 56th Army in the North Caucasus, and it fought under that army during the November and December Rostov operations. The 317th was then transferred to 9th Army and, under that army's control, it participated in the Barvenkovo-Lozovaia operation.

351st Rifle Division
Commanded by Col N. U. Gursky, 351st Rifle Division was formed in September at Stalingrad in the North Caucasus Military District; it too had a large non-Russian component.[82] It joined 57th Army in October and thereafter served with that army through the Barvenkovo-Lozovaia operation.

9TH ARMY
Maj-Gen F. M. Kharitonov's 9th Army defended on 57th Army's left flank along the southern face of the Barvenkovo bridgehead opposite Slaviansk, the sector most threatened by potential German counter-action. 9th Army was a veteran unit whose service stretched back to Civil War years. In its most recent configuration, it had been formed in the Odessa Military District on 22 June as the 9th Separate Army with the

4 Opposing Forces

mission of defending the Soviet border along the Prut River. After the collapse of Soviet defences in the region, from July to October it conducted an arduous withdrawal eastward through Nikolaev and across the Dnepr to the Mariupol' region. Thereafter, it fought in the Rostov and Barvenkovo-Lozovaia operations before occupying positions in the Barvenkovo bridgehead.[83]

The 9th Army commander, Maj-Gen Fedor Mikhailovich Kharitonov, was as experienced as his army. Born in 1899 at Vasilevskoe in Iaroslavl region, he joined the Red Army in 1919 and served throughout the Civil War, fighting on the Eastern and Southern Fronts.[84] After performing military administrative work in the 1920s, in 1931 he attended the 'Vystrel' course and then assumed command of a rifle regiment. From 1937 to 1941, Kharitonov was chief of staff of 17th Rifle Division of 57th Rifle Corps in the Moscow Military District. In 1941, on the eve of war, he attended the Voroshilov General Staff Academy and in June was appointed chief of staff of the Southern Front. He assumed command of 9th Army and led it during the winter campaign, distinguishing himself during the army's defence of Rostov, for which he received the Order of the Red Banner. Subsequently, he commanded 9th Army during the Barvenkovo-Lozovaia operation.

Kharitonov's army contained seven rifle divisions (51st, 106th, 216th, 333rd, 335th, 341st and 349th), one rifle brigade (78th) and two tank brigades (51st and 121st).

51st Rifle Division
Lt-Col B. K. Aliev's 51st Rifle Division began service with Odessa Military District's 9th Army and fought throughout the summer and autumn under that army's command.[85] It served under 37th Army during the Rostov operation and again joined 9th Army during the Barvenkovo-Lozovaia operation.

106th Rifle Division
This division had two predecessors with the same number. The first, a motorised division, was destroyed in the Viazma pocket, and the second was destroyed at Kerch in November 1941. The new 106th was formed at Krasnodar in the North Caucasus Military District in December 1941 from remnants of the Kerch division.[86] In late January 1942, it was transferred to 9th Army control for defence in the Barvenkovo bridgehead.

216th Rifle Division
Raised in May 1941 at Staro Konstantinov in the Kiev Special Military District as a motorised division in 24th Mechanised Corps, the 216th Rifle Division was stationed at Proskurov south of Kiev when war began. It defended with 24th Corps in the Vinnitsa region in July and August and was encircled with 26th Army at Uman in late August and destroyed. Re-formed in September around a nucleus of survivors of the Uman encirclement, the 216th served as a rifle division under 38th Army during the army's October and November defensive battles on the approaches to Kharkov and Kupiansk.[87] In November the division joined 37th Army and participated in the Rostov offensive throughout December. After refitting, in February the division joined 9th Army's defences in the Barvenkovo bridgehead.

333rd Rifle Division
Maj-Gen Ia. S. Dashevsky's 333rd Rifle Division was formed at Kamyshin in the North Caucasus Military District in September 1941 as a part of newly formed 57th

Kharkov, 1942

Separate Army. 10% of its troops were older veterans, and half were young recruits; many were non-Russian.[88] Initially earmarked for service with 10th Army, instead the division was retained by 57th Army, and it participated in the Barvenkovo-Lozovaia offensive operation. At the end of the operation, the 333rd occupied defences in the Slaviansk sector, where it remained until May when it was turned over to 9th Army control.

335th, 341st and 349th Rifle Divisions
The 335th Rifle Division was raised at Stalingrad in the North Caucasus Military District in September 1941; the 341st was formed at the same location in December and the 349th formed at Astrakhan in the North Caucasus District in September. All three contained a significant number of non-Russians and served alongside the 333rd in 57th Army throughout the winter operations, including participation in the Barvenkovo-Lozovaia offensive.[89] In early spring the defensive sectors of all three divisions were turned over to 9th Army.

78th Rifle Brigade
Rounding out 9th Army's rifle forces, the 78th Rifle Brigade was formed at Novorossiisk in the North Caucasus in October 1941 and served under 9th Army throughout the January operations.[90]

51st and 121st Tank Brigades
The small tank complement of 9th Army consisted of the 51st and 121st Tank Brigades, both relatively fresh units. The former was formed at Saratov in the Moscow Military District in December 1941 and the latter at an unknown location in early 1942. Neither had combat experience prior to May 1942.[91]

RESERVES
The Southern Front's principal reserve force in the Barvenkovo bridgehead was Lt-Gen I. A. Pliev's 5th Cavalry Corps, consisting of the 30th, 34th and 60th Cavalry Divisions and the 12th Tank Brigade.

5th Cavalry Corps
The 5th Cavalry was a relatively new formation created in late December 1941 when the first 5th Cavalry Corps was redesignated as 3rd Guards Cavalry Corps.[92] Commanded initially by Maj-Gen (and future Marshal) A. A. Grechko, the corps saw initial combat supporting 57th Army during the Barvenkovo-Lozovaia operation in January 1942. As the mobile group of 57th Army, it operated skilfully and penetrated deep into the German defences south of Barvenkovo, but it was too fragile to contend with the small German armoured task forces fielded against it and fell short of achieving its ultimate objectives. After the operation 5th Cavalry regrouped, served as Front reserve and supported local operations by 9th Army.

Lt-Gen Issa Aleksandrovich Pliev, commander of 5th Cavalry Corps, was an Ossetian by birth.[93] Born in 1903 at Staryi Batakoiurt in Northern Ossetia (on the northern slopes of the Caucasus Mountains), Pliev joined the Red Army in 1922 as a cavalryman. For four years following his graduation from the Leningrad Cavalry School in 1926, he headed the Red Army Cavalry School in Krasnodar, North Caucasus. In 1933 he graduated from the Frunze Academy and for three years was 5th Cavalry Division's Chief of Operations in the 2nd Cavalry Corps based in the Kiev

4 Opposing Forces

Special Military District. While there his division took part in the famous 1935 Kiev Manoeuvres. In June of the following year, Pliev was assigned to Ulan Bator, Mongolia, as an advisor to the Mongolian Army to help it cope with increasing Japanese military pressure. After returning to Moscow from Mongolia in July 1938, he worked for several months in the General Staff's Main Intelligence Directorate, probably sharing his perceptions of the Japanese Army, then threatening Soviet forces from Manchuria. In early 1939 he was given field command of a regiment in the 6th Cavalry Division in the invasion of eastern Poland.

Pliev graduated from the Voroshilov General Staff Academy in 1941 and, upon the outbreak of war with Germany, was sent to the North Caucasus to organise the 50th Separate Cavalry Division. After initial training, in early July Pliev travelled by rail with his division to join the hard-pressed 22nd Army, then struggling against the German advance near Velikie Luki, northwest of Moscow. There his division went into action with only 3,500 men in a futile effort to relieve the German pressure on Soviet forces defending Vitebsk and Smolensk. In late July Pliev's division (with the 53rd Cavalry Division) formed a mobile group under Gen V. A. Khomenko, which was ordered to attack the German spearhead at Smolensk. Although the attack failed, Pliev earned the plaudits of his fellow commanders for his audacity.[94] During subsequent action throughout the autumn, Pliev's division, renamed 3rd Guards Cavalry in November, continued to be noted for its audacious raids. In December 1941 Pliev received command of the newly designated 2nd Guards Cavalry Corps and led it with distinction throughout the Moscow counter-offensive. In April 1942 he was given command of the newly blooded 5th Cavalry Corps, then supporting the Southern Front. Pliev was, and would remain, one of the finest cavalry commanders in the Red Army.

30th Cavalry Division
The 30th Cavalry Division, Pliev's most experienced formation, was formed in mid-1939 at Tashkent in the Central Asian Military District and joined 5th Cavalry Corps in Poland in time to participate in the Polish invasion.[95] When war broke out in June 1941 the 30th Cavalry, then a cadre formation, mobilised in the Odessa Military District and fought with 18th and 12th Armies in the Ukraine and Donbas region. In the Rostov offensive that November, it fought under 18th Army command and joined 6th Cavalry Corps in 1941.

34th Cavalry Division
Formed at Priluki in the Kharkov Military District in July 1941, the 34th Cavalry Division joined 5th Cavalry Corps in the arduous battles around Uman.[96] Escaping the Uman encirclement, throughout September it defended with 38th Army on the approaches to Kharkov and then defended with other Southwestern Front armies until late October, when it was withdrawn from combat for refitting.

60th Cavalry Division
The 60th was formed in September 1941 at Stalingrad in the North Caucasus Military District as part of 57th Army.[97] Both the 34th and the 60th played minor roles in the Rostov operation before joining the new 5th Cavalry Corps in late December.

12th Tank Brigade
This brigade was formed at Kharkov in August 1941 and supported 6th Army during

Kharkov, 1942

defensive battles south of Kharkov during the autumn. In December it provided a critical armoured capability to 5th Cavalry Corps.[98]

The Soviet soldier
The force the Stavka assembled to conduct the Kharkov operation reflected the composition of the Red Army as a whole in spring 1942. Senior commanders at Direction, Front, and army level had extensive combat experience, but that experience had been largely defensive and, on the whole, unsuccessful. Their recent offensive successes during the winter had been against weakened German forces, which had lost much of their accustomed mobile capability. In the spring the Stavka called upon their forces to contend with a reinvigorated German force, which was anxious to prove its military prowess once more. At the divisional and regimental levels, while most Soviet commanders were likewise experienced and adequately trained to their tasks, many had recently commanded either under-strength divisions or units at one level below their present command.

The Red Army soldier in May 1942 was either a survivor of the intense combat of 1941 or a newly mobilised and hastily trained replacement. The cream of experienced Russian soldiery had been sacrificed to the slaughter of 1941. The Red Army began the war with a personnel strength of approximately 5.5 million men. In 1941 the army suffered roughly 6.1 million casualties, a figure encompassing well over half of the pre-war Red Army's combat strength. By March 1942 the Red Army counted approximately 9.2 million soldiers. This meant that a sizeable percentage of the 10 million personnel who were mobilised in the first nine months of war also fell victim to the harsh combat. Such unprecedented carnage had an inescapably adverse impact on the combat readiness of Soviet military formations and the individual combat skills of surviving and fresh Red Army soldiers.

While some Soviet military formations and their men survived the first nine months of war intact, nevertheless they suffered frightful losses, and their depleted ranks were refilled with raw and partially trained conscripts. A host of new formations was mobilised to replace those that had been destroyed and to form an imposing array of new armies. Within these newly fielded rifle armies, however, divisions were manned at ever-reduced combat strength. The conscripts that replaced the fallen and manned these new units cannot be stereotyped according to age or social, economic or ethnic origin, since the demands on manpower forced Soviet conscription authorities to abandon the rigid criteria to which they had previously adhered. The sons of intellectuals and former *Kulaks* (small private farmers), as well as those of Soviet officialdom (the *nomenclatura*) and Soviet bureaucrats, shared the rigours and hazards of combat service with economically, politically and socially correct workers and peasants. Kazaks, Uzbeks, Tartars, Chechens, Armenians, Jews and a host of ethnic minorities fought side by side with ethnic Russians, Ukrainians and Belorussians. As specific unit compositions indicate, entire Red Army rifle divisions and brigades were formed from specific minority groups, although many but not all of these formations were at first commanded by Slavic senior officers. To an increasing extent, the Red Army was becoming ethnically diverse. Its ranks included a growing array of divisions and brigades manned by soldiers from the Transcaucasus, Central Asia and other non-Slavic ethnic regions. While ethnic Slavs were still mobilised by the hundreds of thousands, German seizure of Belorussia and huge areas of Russia and Ukraine deprived the Red Army of a large segment of its traditional Slavic mobilization base. In essence, the Red Army was becoming a multinational Soviet Army.

4 Opposing Forces

Necessity prompted other departures from the traditional Soviet mobilization system. NKVD border guards from across the expanse of the Soviet Union helped form the nucleus of some new rifle divisions and brigades, while inmates of penal institutions and 'politicals' (political prisoners) suddenly found themselves suitable candidates for combat duties. Officers and some senior commanders emerged from the *Gulag* to command Red Army formations in combat. All the while, age restrictions on military service were gradually lifted and an increasing flow of 18–22-year-olds and 37–42-year olds swelled the ranks of the Red Army. Although the Soviets have routinely obscured their contribution, even women joined the ranks in increasing numbers, particularly as snipers and flyers, but in other combat functions as well.

Generally speaking, these new troops and the formations in which they served shared one common characteristic — they were less well trained than their prewar predecessors. Hastily recruited soldiers received only rudimentary individual training. Most received their training on the job in their new formations, either in training battalions formed in rifle divisions or in combat itself. Newly mobilised units and formations also received only limited training, although Soviet authorities attempted, whenever possible, to assign to these forces both an experienced command cadre and a nucleus of combat veterans. Often this leavening of experienced officers and men came directly from the ranks of convalescents who had been wounded in earlier battles or from the remnants of units destroyed or shattered in previous combat.

At least in part, these realities help explain why Soviet commanders consciously limited the initiative accorded to their less experienced subordinates and soldiers, primarily in line rifle units and formations and to a lesser extent in the fledgling armoured forces. Sadly, but correctly, Soviet authorities believed their partially and poorly trained massed infantry (rifle) armies could function effectively only if they did precisely what they were ordered to do. The trade-off for whatever effectiveness the High Command derived from this draconian insistence on order in the ranks was a appalling casualty toll which would continue to remain high. In 1942 this was a price Soviet military authorities consciously paid for whatever battlefield successes they could achieve over a battle-hardened foe whose combat effectiveness they recognised, respected and ultimately sought to negate. In 1942 they would do so with mass. They hoped that finesse would follow later.

In 1942 these gruesome realities tended to affect operations by Soviet armoured forces as well. The tragic fate of their large and numerous mobilised forces in 1941 clearly demonstrated to the Soviets that their mobile capability fell far short of matching the performance of the more experienced German panzer and motorised forces. The Soviets well understood the fact that flexible mobile operations by well-structured and skilfully led armoured and motorised forces would be the key to future combat success. The sordid tale of their earlier attempts to create such a structure and the ignominious fate of those earlier mobile formations indicated how difficult was the task of forming new tank and other mobile corps which could operate more effectively on an operational scale. However, the perceived necessity of launching the new round of spring offensives cut short the Soviet's studied approach and careful experimentation with the combat employment of these new armoured formations. Therefore, the new Soviet tank corps which appeared in combat in May 1942 were but a pale reflection of what was actually required and not surprisingly the Soviets knew it. The new corps were made up of brigades which, while better trained in their own right, had no experience operating as part of a larger corps. Nor did the corps commanders and staffs have the requisite experience in commanding and controlling such large

Kharkov, 1942

armoured formations. The tanks corps too were no match for the more experienced German panzer and motorised divisions — as the grim results would clearly indicate.

Finally, by spring 1942 the Soviet High Command had not yet formed that imposing array of supporting forces which in future years would so often both compensate for and mask deficiencies in other combat arms. Most tellingly, the Soviets lacked the overwhelming superiority in field, anti-tank and rocket artillery, which would later accord the Soviets that crushing fire superiority on the battlefield. Air forces were in the midst of restructuring. There were insufficient numbers of modern aircraft with day and night combat capability available, Soviet pilots were relatively inexperienced and Soviet air tactics lacked flexibility and imagination. Engineer forces were weak, anti-aircraft weapons and their users were largely ineffective and logistical support was still unreliable.

In short, the Soviet Army was not ready to conduct a large-scale offensive in spring 1942 against so accomplished a foe. Sadly for the Soviet soldier and many senior officers, the Soviet High Command and the Southwestern Direction Command did not know it.

GERMAN ORDER OF BATTLE

Grouping of Enemy Forces on 11 May 1942

The Southwestern and Southern Fronts staffs and the Southwestern Direction's operational group assessed the enemy force groupings opposite the two Fronts based on data received at the beginning of May.

Southwestern Front headquarters thought that German Sixth Army, which consisted of 12 infantry and 1 panzer division, reinforced by 10 medium-calibre artillery regiments and 2 high-powered (heavy calibre) regiments, would continue to operate against Front forces. Thus, according to staff calculations, at the beginning of the offensive, Southwestern Front forces might encounter resistance from an approximate total of 105 infantry battalions equipped with 650-700 guns (75mm-210mm calibre) and 350-400 tanks.

Southern Front headquarters also based its assessment of enemy strength on the situation which existed at the beginning of May. The staff thought that 24 infantry, 3 panzer and 2 motorised enemy divisions with 200 tanks would be operating in the first line against Southern Front forces.

Southern Front headquarters assumed that the German command would have 6 or 7 infantry, 1 panzer and 1 motorised division (250-300 tanks) in operational reserve and, moreover, was confident that the primary German grouping was located on the Rostov and Voroshilovgrad axes. Thus, the Front staff thought that a German grouping consisting of 31 infantry, 4 panzer and 3 motorised divisions with 400 tanks in all would be operating against Southern Front forces.

However, by 11 May these conclusions by Southwestern and Southern Front headquarters did not correspond to reality.

As a result of our headquarters' failure to maintain secrecy in command and control and its poor operational *maskirovka* (deception) when concentrating forces in planned penetration sectors, the German command surmised our command's plan and swiftly carried out a number of measures to fortify their defences on the threatened axes. To this end, the Germans used forces of Sixth and Seventeenth Armies and reserves, which had arrived in accordance with the plan for preparing the May offensive.

As a result of the enemy regrouping, basically conducted 1–11 May, the density of

4 Opposing Forces

German forces in the main defensive belt of Southwestern Front's shock group sectors and along the entire front opposite Southern Front's 57th and 9th Armies had sharply increased, and strong reserves were deployed in the operational depth.

In fact, on 11 May, German Sixth Army, consisting of XXIX, XVII, LI and VIII Army Corps, and 4th Infantry Division of Romanian VI Army Corps, which was part of Seventeenth Army, were operating against Southwestern Front.

XXIX Army Corps occupied a front from Pselets to Belgorod with units of 57th, 168th and 75th Infantry Divisions. Replenished by the disbanding of Hungarian 102nd Infantry Brigade, it was defending on the left flank of Sixth Army.

XVII Army Corps, with its two infantry divisions (79th and 294th), was defending the sector from Maslova Pristan' to Peschanoe. 3rd Panzer Division units, which had been operating earlier in this region, were withdrawn by the Germans into operational reserve, and by 11 May were concentrating in Kharkov.

LI Army Corps (297th and 44th Infantry Divisions) defended the Chuguev bridgehead, using its main forces, along the front from Pechenegi through Balakleia to Cherkasskii Bishkin.

VIII Army Corps, consisting of Hungarian 108th Light Infantry Division and the German 62nd Infantry Division and 454th Security Division, which had occupied a defence along the front from Verkhnii Bishkin through Grushino to Mironovka, was used on the Krasnograd axis. German 113th Infantry Division was withdrawn into the German Sixth Army commander's operational reserve and was deployed in the Berestovaia, Kazachii Maidan and Andreevka region. Units of Romanian 4th Infantry Division were deployed on the front from Mironovka to Pokrovskoe.

By 11 May, 3rd and 23rd Panzer Divisions and units of 71st Infantry Division had completely concentrated in Kharkov. The 211th Regiment of this latter division was moved to the Peremoga region to reinforce 294th Infantry Division, and two regiments were on the march to the Balakleia region.

The forward units of German 305th Infantry Division, transferred from Western Europe, were approaching Kharkov. Thus, by 11 May up to 15 infantry divisions and 2 panzer divisions were operating in front of the Southwestern Front, instead of the 12 infantry and 1 panzer division assumed by Southwestern Front headquarters. The enemy could use all of these 17 divisions during the first 3-4 days of our offensive.

The German command had increased its grouping to six divisions in front of Southern Front. All combat groups and mixed units which had been occupying the defence in April were consolidated into infantry and light infantry divisions, and by 12 May had become part of Seventeenth Army and Panzer Group Kleist, and had occupied the following position:

On the northern coast of the Sea of Azov, from Osipenko to Taganrog, Romanian 5th and 6th Cavalry Divisions were performing security service. The German XIV Motorised and XXXXIX Mountain-Rifle Corps, consisting of 73rd, 125th and 198th Infantry Divisions, 4th Mountain-Rifle Division, the 'Adolf Hitler' and 'Viking' SS Motorised Divisions, 13th Tank Division, a Slovak motorised division and a three-division motorised Italian corps, occupied defences along the western bank of the Mius River, from Taganrog Estuary to Debaltsevo. LII Army Corps, consisting of 111th and 9th Infantry Divisions and IV Army Corps, consisting of 94th and 76th Infantry Divisions, occupied defences along a front from Debaltsevo to Bondari. 295th and 257th Infantry and 97th Light Infantry Divisions, and one regiment of 68th Infantry Division, all of XXXXIV Army Corps, were defending in the sector from Bondari through Maiaki to Varvarovka. 100th Light Infantry, 60th Motorised, 14th

Kharkov, 1942

Panzer and 1st Mountain-Rifle Divisions of III Motorised Corps were deployed in defences along a front from Varvarovka through Aleksandrovka to Vishnevyi. Further, Romanian VI Army Corps units, consisting of units of German 68th and 298th and Romanian 1st, 2nd and 4th Infantry Divisions, were defending in front of the juncture of Southern and Southwestern Fronts in the sector from Vishnevyi through Petrovka to east of Sakhnovshchina. Of these forces, one (4th) division and a regiment of 298th Division were operating in the Southwestern Front sector.

By 12 May the German command had concentrated 389th and 384th Infantry and 101st Light Infantry Divisions (German), 20th Infantry Division (Romanian) and 16th Panzer Division in the operational reserve opposite the southern face of the Barvenkovo salient. One regiment of the 389th Infantry Division reinforced LII Army Corps, and two regiments of the 384th Infantry Division was moved forward into the sector of XXXXIV Army Corps.

In all, the German force grouping facing the Southern Front consisted, in fact, of 34 divisions (24 infantry, 3 panzer, 5 motorised and 2 cavalry).

All enemy divisions were outfitted with equipment and replenished with personnel comprising up to 70-80% of what was authorised. Infantry divisions had 12,000-13,000 men each.

GERMAN FORCE STRUCTURE

German divisional structures varied considerably during wartime.[99] In general, as the war progressed, regular army divisions shrank in size and strength, while SS divisions expanded. The most numerous division was the standard infantry division. Its organisation in May 1942 is shown in Table 12. It consisted of three infantry regiments, each of three-battalion composition, an artillery regiment, and signal, anti-tank, engineer (sapper) and reconnaissance battalions. The infantry regiment consisted of three infantry battalions, an artillery howitzer company and an anti-tank company. The infantry battalion normally contained three infantry companies and either a machine gun or heavy weapons company. The latter included 81mm mortars and heavy machine guns.

Infantry division (and light division) artillery regiments consisted of four battalions, three equipped with towed or horse-drawn 105mm howitzers and the fourth armed with

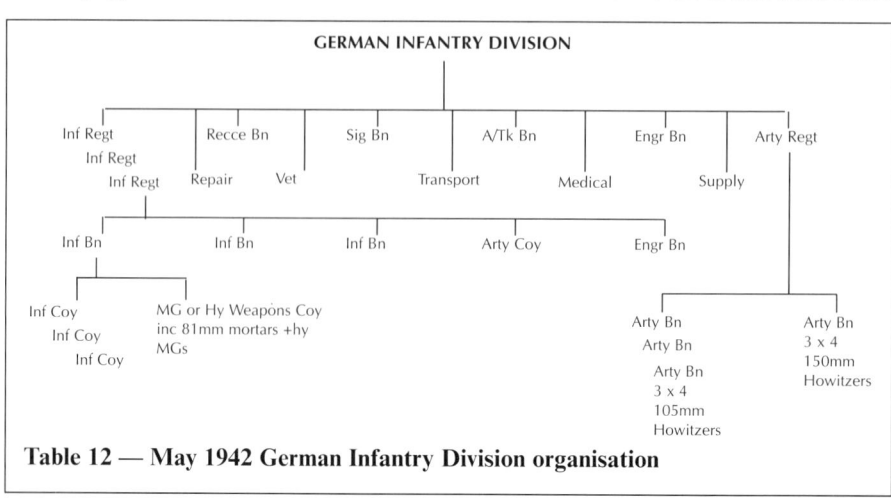

Table 12 — May 1942 German Infantry Division organisation

4 Opposing Forces

150mm howitzers. Artillery battalions contained three batteries of four guns each, for a total of 48 tubes per artillery regiment. The divisional anti-tank battalion normally contained short-range 75mm or 150mm anti-tank guns. Engineer battalions included assault, construction, demolition and bridging troops. The signal battalion included a headquarters detachment, a telephone (wire) company and a radio company.

Finally, the infantry division had a wide range of support units, including supply, transport, repair, veterinary and medical companies, and a divisional train. For transport, the division had between 3,000 to 6,000 horses and as many as 911 motor vehicles. By establishment, the infantry division numbered 17,000 men, but few divisions were at full strength. In terms of combat strength, weaponry and mobility, the German infantry division was over twice as strong as the Soviet rifle division.

German panzer divisions shrank in size considerably during wartime as older divisions were truncated to create new panzer formations. By 1942 the division consisted of a panzer regiment, two motorised regiments, a panzer artillery regiment and had many of the same supporting battalions as an infantry division, although the reconnaissance battalion was motorised and was an effective combat element in its own right. In addition, the division had a motorcycle battalion, which was particularly useful in a reconnaissance role and during pursuit operations. Of course, the division lacked a veterinary company.

The panzer regiment consisted of three battalions and totalled somewhat less than its paper strength of 190 tanks. The motorised infantry regiment (renamed Panzergrenadier in November 1942) had roughly the same composition as an infantry regiment except that it was equipped with armoured personnel carriers and half-tracks, which accorded it a unique advantage over Soviet motorised infantry, which had to ride on accompanying tanks. The panzer artillery regiment usually had three artillery battalions, two equipped with 105mm howitzers and the third with 150mm howitzers. These artillery battalions were more mobile than their infantry division

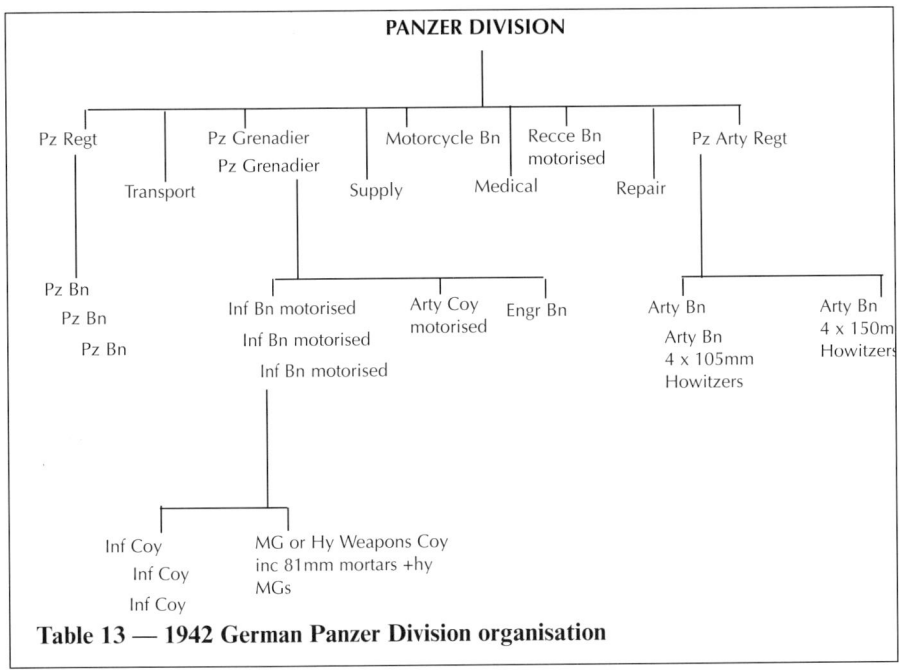

Table 13 — 1942 German Panzer Division organisation

Kharkov, 1942

counterparts and, to an increasing extent, were equipped with self-propelled guns. With its imposing complement of motor vehicles, half-tracks and armoured personnel carriers, the panzer division task organised for combat by forming mixed combat groups (Kampfgruppen) of tanks and armoured infantry. A typical battalion panzer division combat group, with its superior firepower and mobility, could often take on and defeat a full Soviet rifle division.

The German motorised infantry division had a structure similar to that of the standard infantry division except that it was motorised and, hence, more mobile, and it possessed heavier firepower. It consisted of two motorised infantry regiments of three battalions each, or six motorised infantry battalions, and a wide array of supporting battalions and companies similar to those found in panzer divisions. From late 1941 on, the division added a panzer or assault gun battalion of 30 to 50 tanks or guns each, and the line infantry battalions traded in their trucks for half-tracks. The division's artillery regiment resembled that of the panzer division.

German mountain divisions were similar in structure to line infantry divisions except for their training and the fact that their artillery and anti-tank weaponry was generally lighter. On paper, the mountain artillery regiment consisted of three battalions of 75mm howitzers and one of 105mm howitzers, but mountain divisions used in regular combat usually replaced their artillery with heavier calibre models. The division's line regiments consisted of three battalions of five companies each, the last two being heavy weapons and machine gun companies. Light (or Jaeger) divisions were similar in structure to the mountain divisions except that they had only two regiments. Finally, security divisions, formed and designed for local and rear area defence, consisted of two security (infantry) regiments, organised like regular infantry regiments with lighter weaponry. They had no artillery and limited logistical support.

Army Group and army generally fielded a wide array of combat and combat service support units to supplement the power of their organic divisions. For example, reserve artillery at General Headquarters (GHQ) (corps and army) level were often organised into Arko (artillery commands). These contained GHQ observation units, light, medium, heavy or super-heavy artillery battalions of various types, which were combined to support specific operations or front sectors. Other artillery units, such as separate assault gun battalions and Flak (anti-aircraft) battalions often were also attached to corps or divisions.

The Germans assigned their division to motorised (panzer) or army corps. At this stage of the war, army corps contained primarily infantry divisions, and motorised corps a heavier complement of panzer or motorised divisions. Corps structures, however, were exceedingly flexible and could include virtually any type of division, and German army commands routinely shifted divisions from corps to corps.

In May 1942 the more experienced German command cadre could effectively control and employ larger units than its Soviet counterparts. For this reason and greater German experience in structuring forces, German units were vastly more combat capable than their counterpart Soviet formations. As the war progressed, however, this gap would close. Virtually all elements of the German force structure would shrink, and corresponding Soviet formations would increase in firepower and combat capability. Although specific Soviet-type formations and units would decrease in manpower, their increased number would more than compensate for their declining manpower strength.

4 Opposing Forces

KEY GERMAN LEADERS
In May 1942 the German command cadre was far more experienced than its Soviet counterpart. Unlike the latter, German commanders were able to control and employ larger forces effectively in complex fluid combat conditions.

Field Marshal Fedor von Bock
The commander of German Army Group South was a tested veteran of the Polish War who had commanded German Army Group B in the battles for the Low Countries and France in May and June 1940. In recognition of his achievements in the West, he was assigned to command Army Group Centre in Operation 'Barbarossa'. Subsequently, von Bock led his prestigious army group with its powerful Second and Third Panzer Groups during the heady border battles of June and July 1941 and during the bitter fighting in August around Smolensk. After objecting to Hitler's decision to halt his direct drive on Moscow in August 1941 and instead turn south in September to eliminate Soviet forces around Kiev, in October and November von Bock led his army group to the very gates of Moscow in Operation 'Typhoon'. Removed from Army Group Centre command by Hitler in December 1941 as German forces faltered on the very outskirts of Moscow, ostensibly due to poor health but actually because of disputes with Hitler over strategic and operational matters, in January 1942 von Bock was assigned to command Army Group South. After fulfilling Hitler's instructions to 'tidy up' the situation in the south in the wake of the Soviet winter counter-offensive, von Bock was instrumental in drafting German plans for the coming summer offensive across southern Russia.

Von Bock was a professional whose realistic understanding of the complex nature of combat in Russia often prompted him to take issue with Hitler's less informed view of realities in the east. Ultimately, this would again cost von Bock his command in July 1942 in the very midst of the German 1942 summer campaign. He would never return to command.

General of Panzer Troops Friedrich Paulus
The commander of Army Group South's strongest and most prestigious army, the famous Sixth, was a relative newcomer to command. Paulus had been a penultimate General Staff officer before taking command of Sixth Army in January 1942. A protégé of the previous commander of Sixth Army, General Walther Reichenau, Paulus had served as Reichenau's chief of staff when Reichenau had commanded the German Tenth Army in the 1939 Polish campaign and remained in this position after the army was redesignated the Sixth and when it fought successfully in the Low Countries and France in 1940. From September 1940 to January 1942, Paulus served as the senior member of Franz Halder's OKH (General Staff of the Army) Staff. During this period Paulus helped plan Operation 'Barbarossa' and, when 'Barbarossa' had faltered, he received his field command. After helping von Bock to stabilise the southern front in winter 1942, Paulus was instrumental in planning the subsequent German summer campaign. It was indeed ironic that his army, the first to engage in mortal combat with the Soviets during that fateful summer campaign, would itself have its fate determined by the same campaign.

Although recognised as a superb staff officer, many have since questioned Paulus's suitability for army command.

Kharkov, 1942

Field Marshal Ewald von Kleist

The armoured spearhead of von Bock's Army Group South was von Kleist's First Panzer Army. A famed commander of the German XX Panzer Corps in Poland and the German Army's panzer group in the West in 1940, in 'Barbarossa' von Kleist had commanded the vaunted First Panzer Group in its spectacular advance from the Polish border across Ukraine and southern Russia in summer and autumn 1941. In November his group had reached the city of Rostov before recoiling under the blows of Soviet counter-strokes in winter 1941–2. Von Kleist's panzers helped restore stability to the southern front in the winter and, redesignated First Panzer Army, prepared to spearhead the headlong thrust of German forces across southern Russia and into the Caucasus in summer 1942.

Von Kleist was a fighter who had fought against the best the Soviets could offer. He faced the heaviest Soviet resistance during the border battles of 1941 and he felt the full brunt of the ferocious Soviet counter-offensive at Rostov in November and December 1941. Nevertheless, he and his panzer army were fully prepared to play their crucial role in the upcoming summer campaign. In May 1942 he did not realise how soon and how critical that role would be.

THE GERMAN SOLDIER

Unlike their Soviet counterparts, in spring 1942 German combat formations were still led and manned by battle-hardened and experienced combat veterans. For the most part, German corps, division and regimental commanders who commanded in 1942 had fought in Poland, the West and during the initial year of campaigning in the Soviet Union. Most Wehrmacht officers, NCOs and soldiers had not yet fallen victim to the attrition which would so deplete their ranks and reduce their effectiveness later in the war. Although their initial exuberant optimism had by now been tempered by the disappointments of the previous winter, they were still motivated by hope and belief in ultimate German victory. Their units reflected this spirit.

Although by now blooded in a war that scarcely resembled the war in the West, German combat units were near full strength, were effectively trained and knew how to exploit their combat equipment to the fullest extent. German unit cohesion generated by the practice of raising and manning units from distinct geographical regions had not yet broken down and this tight-knit cohesion only added to both morale and unit combat effectiveness. The flexibility and initiative so characteristic of German low-level commanders, coupled with the instinctive response of units in combat situations conditioned by effective battle-drill training, well equipped the Germans to deal effectively with their more numerous opponent. German quality could thus cope with Soviet quantity, at least at this stage of the war.

In short, for these reasons and because of greater German experience in structuring their forces to accommodate both routine and unique combat situations, German units were vastly more capable than their counterpart Soviet formations. As the war progressed, however, this effectiveness gap would narrow, particularly in mobile forces. Virtually all elements of the German force structure would shrink as the Germans struggled in vain to wage a war designed for the western European theatre in the vast and forbidding spaces of the eastern European theatre. The Germans would learn that Soviet quantity had a quality of its own. Corresponding Soviet units would increase in sophistication, firepower and combat capability and, inevitably, Soviet leadership and experience would improve. Although specific Soviet-type formations and units would decrease in manpower, their increased number, firepower and relative combat

4 Opposing Forces

effectiveness would more than compensate for their declining manpower strength. The events at Kharkov proved this would have to occur if the Red Army and the Soviet Union were to survive the war.

CORRELATION OF FORCES

The following tables (14-18) show the correlation of forces and means facing the Southwestern and Southern Fronts and the condition of these Fronts' forces on 12 May 1942.

Table 14 — Correlation of forces in the Southwestern Front sector

Southwestern Front forces		Correlation	German Sixth Army forces
Rifle divisions	32[a]	2.1:1	15 infantry divisions
Cavalry divisions	9	absolute superiority	0 cavalry divisions
Tanks	925	2.5:1	370 tanks (23rd and 3rd Pz Div)[b]
Guns	1,154[c]	1.3:1	872 Guns[d]
Mortars	1,706[e]	1.7:1	1,024 Mortars

Notes
[a] Included in the number of divisions are four brigades calculated as two divisions. A rifle division had 8,000-9,000 men.
[b] The number of tanks is indicated by calculating 200 tanks in a panzer division, with the division at 80% strength.
[c] Artillery and artillery of the RVGK without regimental artillery.
[d] Division Artillery Reserve of High Command, 75-100mm.
[e] 50mm mortars, which numbered more than 1,500, were not included.

As a result of the regroupings, the correlation of forces by 12 May 1942 in the penetration sectors of Southwestern Front's armies was to the Soviet advantage and was characterised by the following data (see Table 7):

Table 15 — Correlation of forces in the Southwestern Front's penetration sector

Penetration Sector	Infantry	Arty and Mortars	Tanks
21st Army Sector	2.3:1	1.5:1	0.7:1
28th Army Sector	2.8:1	2.2:1	2.1:1
38th Army Sector	2.6:1	1.4:1	1.1:3
6th Army and Army Group Bobkin Sector	1.6:1	2.0:1	11.8:1

By 12 May 1942, the correlation of air forces in the Southwestern Front sector is shown in Table 8.

Table 16 — Correlation of air forces in the Southwestern Front's sector

Aircraft Types	Southwestern Front	Correlation	Enemy
Fighters	245	1.4:1	180
Bombers	316	1:1	310
Ground-attack	85	—	—
Reconnaissance	10	1:9	90
Total	656[a]	1:1.1	580

Notes
[a] Of the overall number of Southwestern Direction aircraft shown in the table, 423 were part of the Southwestern Front, and 233 were from Southern Front forces. One must bear in mind that, of the overall number of 316 bombers, only 93 (Pe-2s and SU-2s) could fly during the day, and the remaining aircraft could carry out their combat tasks only at night. Therefore, the factual superiority in daytime bombers was 3.3:1 in the enemy's favour.

Kharkov, 1942

Table 17 — Correlation of forces in the Southern Front sector

Southern Front	Quantity	Correlation	Quantity	German Forces
Rifle Divisions	32[a]	1.2:1	29	Infantry and mechanised divisions
Cavalry Divisions	3	1.5:1	2	Cavalry divisions
Tanks	209	1:2.4	510	Tanks
Guns	2,089	1:1.9	4,090	Guns
Mortars	5,513 2	3.8:1	1,148[b]	Mortars

Notes

[a] The number of divisions includes six brigades, with two brigades equal to one division.

[b] 50 and 51mm mortars are included in the overall totals.

Table 18 — Correlation of forces on the front of 57th and 9th Armies

57th and 9th Armies	Quantity	Correlation	Quantity	German Forces
Rifle divisions	12[a]	1.2:1	10[b]	Infantry divisions
Cavalry divisions	6	—	—	Cavalry divisions
Tanks	52	0.2:1	230	Tanks
Guns	310[c]	0.6:1	520	Guns
Mortars	990[d]	1:1	950	Mortars

Notes

[a] Two brigades are counted as one division in this table.

[b] Three light infantry divisions are included in this figure, calculated that one light infantry division equals 2/3 of a full division.

[c] 76mm guns are not included.

[d] Includes 81 and 120mm mortars.

As a result of all the measures carried out by the Southwestern Direction Commander-in-Chief, Southwestern Front forces were structured to deliver attacks in the following manner (see Map 4, page 45).

The northern shock group, attacking along a 55km front, consisted of 14 rifle and 3 cavalry divisions, and 8 tank and 1 motorised rifle brigade.

The southern shock group, advancing on a 36km front, consisted of 8 rifle and 3 cavalry divisions, and 11 tank and 2 motorised rifle brigades.

Taking into account enemy forces which were opposing our forces' offensive sectors, one can conclude that our shock groups could have completely coped with their assigned missions.

The commencement of the Southwestern Front offensive was first designated for 4 May.[100] However, because forces were unprepared, it was postponed until 12 May 1942.

The course of the combat operations of Southwestern Front forces and, subsequently, Southern Front forces, can be divided into two stages.

The first stage, lasting from 12–16 May, encompasses the Southwestern Front offensive. This stage includes: penetration of the main German defensive belt in the northern and southern offensive sectors from 12–14 May, the development of the offensive, and the struggle against the enemy's operational reserves from 15–16 May.

The second stage (from 17 to 28 May) encompasses the defensive battles of Southwestern and Southern Front forces in the Barvenkovo bridgehead.

The principal content of this stage is as follows:

1. Repulsion of the German counter-attack on the Izium-Barvenkovo axis, associated with the enemy's penetration of Southern Front's 9th and 57th Armies' defences;

4 Opposing Forces

and a continuation of the Southwestern Front's southern shock group's offensive from 17–19 May;

2. Defensive battles of the Southwestern Front's left flank and the Southern Front's right flank in the Barvenkovo bridgehead from 20–24 May;

3. Battles in encirclement by Southern Front's 9th and 57th Armies and the Southwestern Front's 6th Army and Army Group in, and the struggle to break out of encirclement from 25–28 May.

5
THE COURSE OF COMBAT OPERATIONS

FIRST STAGE: THE SOUTHWESTERN FRONT OFFENSIVE (12–16 May 1942)

1 The Penetration of the Enemy Main Defensive Belt (12–14 May)

After receiving combat orders from the Front Military Council, all units and subunits within Front armies held assemblies and Komsomol and party meetings late in the evening on 1 May; these acquainted each soldier with the troop combat missions.

The order to go over to a decisive offensive was greeted with great enthusiasm. In their addresses soldiers and officers assured Comrade Stalin and the Soviet people that they would mercilessly destroy the Fascist villains. Junior Sergeant Larygin announced, 'At the idea alone of the brutality of the Fascist bands, our blood chills and our hands themselves take up arms. We will fight and destroy the Fascist snakes until our land is purged of the Fascist occupiers.'

The results of fruitful party-political work were quickly felt on the first day of the offensive.

THE NORTHERN SHOCK GROUP'S OFFENSIVE
Combat operations on 12 May (see Map 10)
The offensive commenced at 06.30 with an artillery preparation that continued for 60 minutes. At the end of it, a 15-20 minute air raid was conducted against enemy artillery positions and strongpoints in his main defensive belt.

Infantry and direct support tanks went over to the attack at 07.30. First echelon rifle subunits of 21st, 28th and 38th Armies, having advanced during the first half of the day to a depth of 1-3km, encountered fire from a large number of fire points which had not been suppressed, as well as counter-attacks by enemy tactical reserves. The greatest success during penetration of the enemy defence was expected in 28th Army's sector, where the largest number of direct infantry support tanks were operating. However, 28th Army's attack was the least successful. Combat on the first day of the offensive demonstrated that the enemy had great tactical defensive density in this army's offensive sector.

Formations of Lt-Gen V. N. Gordov's 21st and Lt-Gen K. S. Moskalenko's 38th Armies advanced the furthest.

5 The Course of Combat Operations

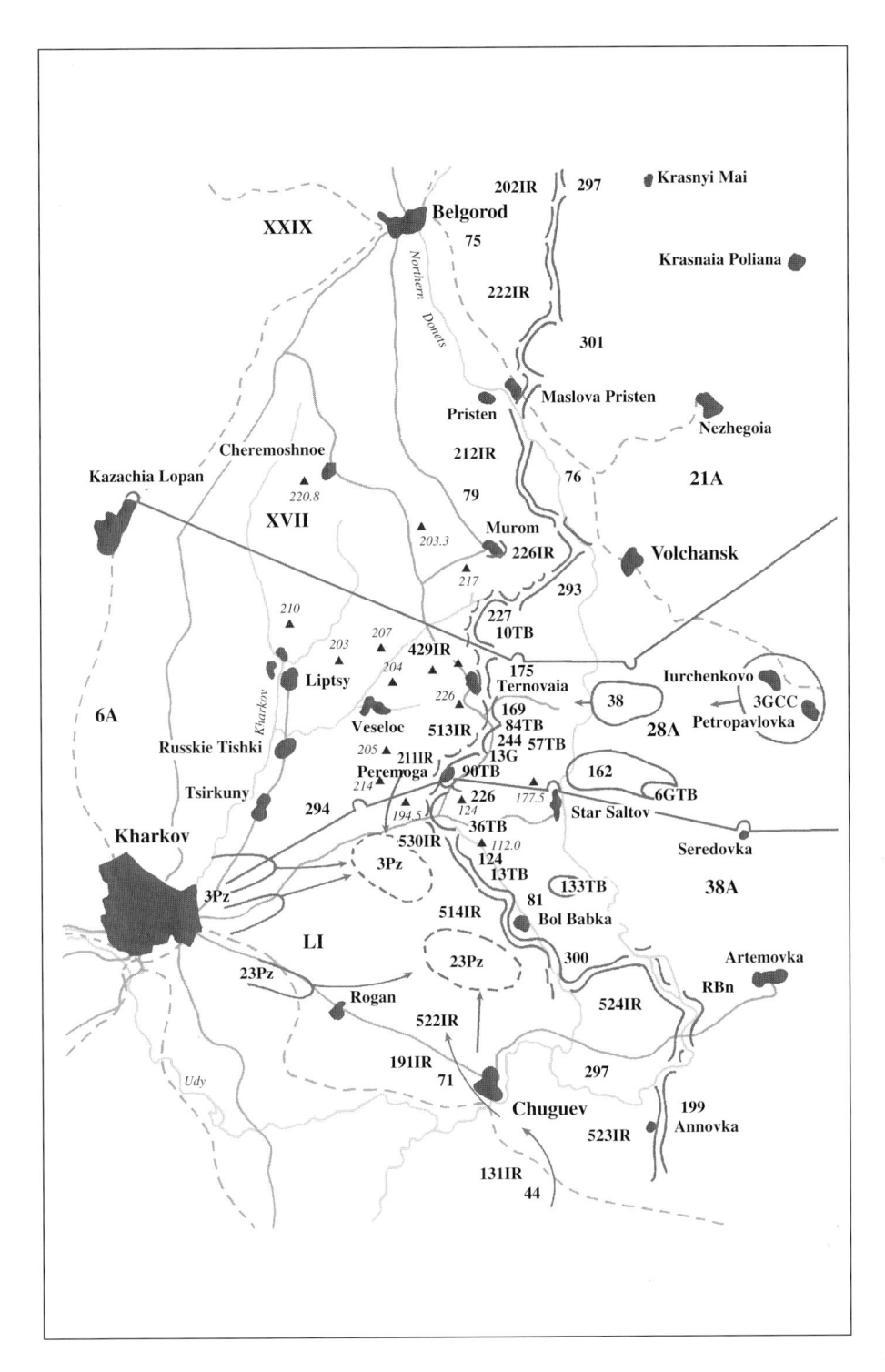

Map 10 — Combat on 12 May in the Northern Sector

Kharkov, 1942

On the night of 11–12 May in 21st Army's sector, specially prepared detachments of Col G. G. Voronin's 76th Rifle Division captured small bridgeheads on the western bank of the Northern Donets River in the Bezliudovka area and northwest of Novaia Tavolzhanka. On the morning of 12 May, divisional main forces began the offensive from these bridgeheads along converging axes. By the close of the day, divisional units had joined together and formed an overall bridgehead with a width of 5km and a depth of up to 4km.

Attacking on Voronin's left flank, Maj-Gen P. F. Lagutin's 293rd and Col G. A. Ter-Gasparian's 227th Rifle Divisions successfully crossed the river, penetrated the enemy's defensive belt and, achieving success, by the close of the day captured the populated areas of Ogurtsovo, Bugrovatka and Staritsa, having advanced 10km to the north and 6-8km to the northwest. However, that day 76th and 293rd Rifle Divisions' forward units were unable to link up and create a general bridgehead.

As a result of intense combat, Lt-Gen D. I. Riabyshev's 28th Army formations captured the German strongpoints of Bairak, Kupevakha and Dragunovka, and encircled the German garrison in Varvarovka. The enemy, however, halted our forces' further advance . . . By the close of the day, Maj-Gen A. I. Rodimtsev's 13th Guards Division units, reinforced by Lt-Col M. I. Malyshev's 90th Tank Brigade tanks, had driven the Germans from Peremoga.

Gen Rodimtsev's experienced 13th Guards Rifle Division, positioned on 28th Army's critical left flank, fought hard on 12 May and came close to achieving its initial objectives. The division's combat order, issued to subordinate units several days before, spelled out the force's mission:

'The 13th Guards Order of Lenin Rifle Division, supported by the 90th Tank Brigade and the 7th Guards Artillery Regiment, must, in co-operation with the 244th and 226th Rifle Divisions, penetrate the defences of the enemy, 126th Motorised Regiment [sic], secure the line Krasnyi-Peremoga-Gordienko-Rogachevka and, by the end of the day, reach the line Hill 214.3-Riaznovka-Hill 212.3. A battalion of the 233rd Artillery Regiment (RGK), the 51st Guards Mortar Regiment and aviation will support in accordance with the army plan.'[1]

Rodimtsev ordered his 39th and 42nd Guards Rifle Regiments to attack in division-first echelon. The 39th was to seize Kupevakha, Peremoga and Krasnyi on the division's right flank by the end of the first day and advance forward detachments to occupy Hill 214.3. It was supported by two platoons from the 2nd Company of the division's 8th Guards Separate Sapper Battalion and tanks of Lt-Col Malyshev's 90th Brigade. The 42nd was to secure Dragunovka, Gordienko, Rogachevka and Riaznovka on the left flank and, co-operating with troops of the neighbouring 226th Rifle Division, push its forward detachments forward to Hill 212.3. It was supported by the 24th Separate Guards Mortar Battalion, a half company of the 8th Guards Sapper Battalion and 90th Brigade tanks. Rodimtsev's 34th Guards Rifle Regiment was in second echelon as the troops of his lead regiments occupied jumping-off positions for the attack after dark on 11 May.

That very evening, opposite Rodimtsev's front line, German troops from the combat-worn and tired 211th Infantry Regiment (71st Infantry Division) were being relieved by troops from the 513th Regiment, 294th Infantry Division. Flares lit up the night skies as the relief took place.

5 The Course of Combat Operations

As dawn broke on 12 May, at 06.30 the Soviet artillery preparation began against German strongpoints and firing positions, while Soviet machine gun fire raked German forward trenches, and aircraft rained bombs on deeper defensive positions. At 07.00 signal flares from division and regimental observation points announced the start of the Soviet ground assault. Taking advantage of the confusion in the German forces opposite as the 513th Regiment relieved the 211th and the losses caused by the subsequent heavy Soviet fire preparation which interrupted it, Rodimtsev's forward regiments quickly seized the German forward positions and, during the course of the day, moved forward towards their final objectives. After Rodimtsev's 39th Regiment had secured the southern outskirts of Peremoga near nightfall, he ordered his second echelon 34th Regiment into combat just south of the village at the juncture of the hard-pressed German 513th and 211th Infantry Regiments' flagging defences.[2]

In 28th Army's centre sector between Bairak and Ternovaia, Maj-Gen S. M. Rogachevsky's 169th Rifle Division faced heavy defences manned by the German 429th Infantry Regiment (294th Infantry Division). Division reconnaissance thoroughly surveyed the minefields, wire obstacles, trench network and strongpoints facing it and passed 43 specific targets to its supporting artillery to engage during the artillery preparation. Among those targets were three artillery and two mortar batteries and two anti-tank guns, a total of 26 guns which faced the 54 guns of the 169th Division's regimental and divisional artillery.

Rogachevsky's division had the immediate mission of penetrating enemy forward defences, destroying German forces defending in Bairak and in the forests southeast of Ternovaia; subsequently the division was to secure Liptsy along the Kharkov River deep in the German rear. On the 169th Division's left flank, Col Afansiev's 244th Rifle Division would advance on Nepokrytoe; on its right flank, Maj-Gen A. D. Kuleshchev's 175th Rifle Division would march on Maloe Prokhody. Rogachevsky deployed his 680th Rifle Regiment in first echelon on his left flank and his 556th Regiment on his right, each with a single tank battalion from the 84th Tank Brigade to support the infantry assault. He left Col I. P. Mishin's 434th Rifle Regiment in second echelon with orders to follow the 556th into battle.

At 06.30 Lt-Col S. M. Bichek's divisional artillery, supported by almost 100 tubes of RVGK artillery, began pounding German forward trench lines. As the hour progressed, the rain of devastation shifted methodically deeper into the German defences. At precisely 07.30, as the last artillery rounds roared from their tubes, signal rockets lit the dawn skies, and the crouched infantry rose from their forward trenches and began their assault. Troops of the 556th Regiment easily overcame the pulverised German advanced positions and occupied the dominant ground (marker 203.4) astride the Ternovoe-Rubezhnoe road just north of Bairak. The regimental commander, however, was careless and neither ordered his troops to dig in nor brought forward his supporting artillery. As a result, alert German troops of the 429th Regiment counter-attacked and drove the 556th back to its starting positions. This exposed the 680th Regiment's right flank and placed the entire army offensive in jeopardy.

Rogachevsky, the division commander, joined his beleaguered regiment and dispatched his chief of staff, Maj V. A. Petrenko, to inform army headquarters of the crisis. However, the army commander, Gen Riabyshev, knew of the problem and was already *en route* to the 169th Division's command post. Without stopping at the divisional CP, he too immediately joined the regiment and personally organised a counter-attack to retake the high ground. In addition to ordering the division to bring concentrated fire to bear on German positions on the heights, he arranged with his head-

Kharkov, 1942

quarters for aviation strikes on the Germans. After an hour of heavy fire, Riabyshev personally led an infantry and tank assault on the German positions. Whether through fear or admiration of Riabyshev the troops followed, and within an hour the heights were again in Soviet hands, thus enabling the 556th Regiment to resume its advance. It did so and drove withdrawing Germans into the woods southeast of Ternovoe. A spirited German counter-attack from the woods failed when it was met and repulsed by direct fire from the 556th Regiment's 76mm gun battery firing over open sights into the attacking mass of German infantry. After repelling a second German counter-attack, the 556th dug in and prepared to renew its attack in the morning.

On the 556th's left flank, once the threat to its right flank had been neutralised, the 680th Rifle Regiment launched a co-ordinated three-battalion assault against the heavily fortified village of Bairak. In vicious house-to-house fighting, 3rd Battalion finally forced its way into the village, followed by 1st and 2nd Battalions. With their exit routes threatened, the German defenders withdrew to new positions dug in along the north-south road just west of the village. Too fatigued to continue the advance, the 680th also halted operations for the night.[3]

Riabyshev's second echelon divisions edged forward during the day, prepared to join their colleagues when necessary. On this first day of combat, elements of these formations were already influencing the action. For example, on the eve of battle, the army command detached Maj A. P. Chamov's 343rd Rifle Regiment and two batteries of the 134th Anti-tank Battalion from Col N. P. Dotsenko's 38th Rifle Division and attached them to Rodimtsev's 13th Guards Rifle Division. Throughout the day on 12 May, Rodimtsev kept the attached regiment in reserve. At the same time, the 38th Division's 214th Artillery Regiment and 160th Separate Mortar Battalion fired throughout the first day of combat in support of Rogachevsky's 169th Rifle Division and provided the added punch necessary for the 169th to overcome the two German counter-attacks.[4]

In 38th Army's sector, Maj-Gen A. V. Gorbatov's 226th Rifle Division achieved the greatest success. The division, reinforced by Col T. I. Tanaschishin's 36th Tank Brigade, penetrated the tactical depth of the German defence, pursued the defeated units of 294th Infantry Division and 71st Infantry Division's 211th Regiment and, after a brief battle, captured Nepokrytaia, a key centre of enemy resistance. During the day the division advanced 10km. Col A. K. Berestov's 124th Rifle Division, the neighbouring unit on the left, exploited the 226th Division's success to develop the offensive. Operating jointly with Lt-Col I. T. Klimenchuk's 13th Tank Brigade, Berestov's 124th Rifle Division crossed the Bolshaia Babka River and drove the Germans out of the strongpoint at Peschanoe by an enveloping attack from the north and east. Col F. A. Pimenov's 81st Rifle Division (on the 124th Rifle Division's left flank) captured the populated area of Bolshaia Babka after a stubborn battle which lasted all day. While executing this mission, Gen Moskalenko, the 38th Army commander, committed his reserves (two regiments of 81st Division) into battle during the day.

Like 28th Army, Moskalenko's 38th Army commenced its action at 06.30 with a heavy one-hour artillery preparation. During the later stages of the preparation, tank and infantry assault groups moved forward through lanes in minefields and barbed-wire obstacles, earlier cut by army and division sappers. At 07.30 the combined infantry

5 The Course of Combat Operations

and tank assault began, led by infantry mounted on tanks; simultaneously, army aviation launched a 15-20 minute aircraft raid on deeper German positions. Very early in the assault, however, it became apparent to Soviet commanders that the artillery had not done its work as effectively as planned, since many German firing positions remained undestroyed: German infantry greeted the Soviet infantry assault with intense counter-fire combined with counter-attacks by local reserves. Infantry tank support for the advancing infantry also proved inadequate. As a result, initial forward progress was agonisingly slow and amounted to only 1-3km during the first several hours of the attack.[5] The pace of the attack, however, accelerated in the afternoon.

Gen Gorbatov's 226th Rifle Division made the most progress, primarily due to the skilful support provided by the division's Chief of Artillery, Maj V. M. Likhachev. Likhachev's fire plan was thorough and, throughout the infantry and tank assault, he suppressed German firing positions covering the key strongpoints near Nepokrytaia and crossings over the Bolshaia Babka River. Of particular importance were German defensive positions on the high ground (marker 199.0), which covered the approaches to Nepokrytaia. Soon after the assault began, divisional infantry, supported by Capt M. D. Shestakov's lead tank battalion from Col Tanaschishin's 36th Tank Brigade, crossed the Bolshaia Babka River without suffering losses, but immediately encountered heavy resistance from German infantry dug in around Marker 199.0 and supported by an estimated 20 field guns and numerous mortars. While Likhachev concentrated artillery fire on German firing positions, Shestakov's tanks worked their way into the German rear near Nepokrytaia and, at a cost of several casualties, engaged and defeated a German 155mm artillery battery in a direct fire duel during which Shestakov and his battalion commissar were killed.[6]

Intense combat continued for hours in the seesaw battle for Nepokrytaia as the Germans launched three local counter-attacks. In his memoirs, General Rodimtsev accorded the 226th Division full credit for his division's success, writing:

'I knew that our neighbour to the left — 226th Rifle Division commanded by General Gorbatov — repulsed the first counter-attacks by enemy tanks. At first the Germans threw eight tanks and accompanying infantry from the south against the heights defended by the division's infantry. Hardly had this attack been repulsed when the enemy struck with 20 tanks from the west. Here the enemy lost 15 machines to the meeting fire of anti-tank guns and rifles.'[7]

As darkness fell on 12 May, infantry from Maj P. F. Osintsev's 985th Rifle Regiment, co-operating with 36th Tank Brigade tanks, finally penetrated into Nepokrytaia, although not without suffering grievous losses. With the added support of the 226th Rifle Division's other first echelon regiments, by nightfall the German strongpoint was in Gen Gorbatov's hands. The advance of nearly 10km by Gorbatov's 226th Rifle Division and Rodimtsev's 13th Guards Rifle Divisions materially assisted the advance of beleaguered Soviet divisions on their left and right flanks.

On Gorbatov's left flank, infantry and tanks from Col Berestov's 124th Rifle Division and Lt-Col Klimenchuk's 13th Tank Brigade attacked across the Bolshaia Babka River against the German fortified village of Peschanoe. After heavy fighting which lasted all day, Maj I. F. Bezugly's 781st Rifle Regiment led an enveloping assault from the north and east that cleared German defenders from the village and the surrounding high ground. Further south, a single regiment of Col Pimenov's 81st Rifle Division struggled all day to overcome the even more formidable German defences

Kharkov, 1942

around the village of Bolshaia Babka on the west bank of the river. By day's end, after Pimenov had received permission to employ his two additional regiments (then in army reserve), this German position also fell, but at high cost to the attackers. As was generally the case, more than 50% of the men in lead assault regiments became casualties. Further south, a multi-battalion task force from the 300th Rifle Division attempted to seize German positions around Piatnitskoe, just east of the Bolshaia Babka River, but was repulsed with heavy losses.[8]

Moskalenko, the 38th Army commander, spent the morning observing the battle from his 124th Rifle Division's forward observation post. By midday he realised that, although the Germans were already employing their divisional reserves to launch counter-attacks, they were retaining corps and higher level reserves for future actions on the approaches to Kharkov. Later in the day, however, it became apparent to Moskalenko that the greater than expected progress of his 38th and Riabyshev's 28th Armies had forced the Germans to begin committing higher level reserves to combat. By the end of the day, army intelligence organs had already detected the northward movement into his army's sector of additional German forces from the Chuguev salient and the possible concentration of fresh German armour east of Kharkov. This was particularly disconcerting, since Moskalenko lacked an army second echelon and had already committed his army's reserves.[9]

By evening the Soviet command knew why the day's difficult fighting had been so costly. Intelligence finally determined that elements of two German divisions (71st and 294th) faced them, rather than one. Even more disquieting for the Soviets was the fact that German documents captured at Peschanoe, including the diary of the German battalion commander who died defending the village, indicated that the Germans may have had advanced warning of the attack and had reinforced their positions accordingly.[10]

In his memoirs Moskalenko later wrote that he had warned Timoshenko of the danger posed by German reserves and had urged him to shift the main axis of the Front's advance into the sector of his 226th and Rodimtsev's 13th Guards Divisions, where progress had been most marked and where reinforced Soviet spearheads could blunt the nose of freshly committed German reserves. Timoshenko, however, rejected Moskalenko's proposal and declared that 6th Army's offensive success to the south would certainly negate the threat posed by reinforcing German armour to the Northern Shock Group. Moreover, the Front Military Council firmly believed that 28th Army's assault would finish off the German opposition the next day and, therefore, dismissed Moskalenko's fears about the threat of a counter-attack by German armour. Nevertheless, to assuage his fears, the Military Council ordered Moskalenko to withdraw his three tank brigades from battle and to concentrate them, by the morning of the following day, on his left flank to protect against possible German counter-attacks. Moskalenko noted bitterly:

'I was only ordered to withdraw [my] tank brigades from battle and concentrate them to protect the Staryi Saltov axis, which could not be considered a sufficiently effective measure. All the more so, since the enemy was completing the concentration in that region of three fresh infantry regiments, which we would learn about the following day.'[11]

Thus, as a result of the first day of the offensive in the northern penetration sector, 28th Army forces and formations of 21st and 38th Armies, which had advanced

5 The Course of Combat Operations

2-4km in the centre of the shock group's offensive sector, and 6-10km on the flanks, by the end of the day fought along a line from Rzhavets through Priiutovka, Bezliudovka, Korovino, Arkhangelskoe, Ogurtsovo, west of Staritsa, western edge Ladytskoe, Izbitskoe, Bairak, Peremoga, Nepokrytaia and Peschanoe to Bolshaia Babka.

The enemy, while holding onto the well-fortified populated areas of Varvarovka and Ternovaia, obstructed the development of 28th Army's offensive.

Col Anton Freiherr von Bechtelzheim, the Chief of Staff of the German XXIX Army Corps, vividly recorded the German command's surprised reaction to the 12 May Soviet offensive. He wrote:

'In the evening of 11 May 1942, there was a small party at Sixth Army Headquarters, now commanded by Gen Paulus, at Kharkov. The army chief of staff, following a strenuous day's conference on various current matters, invited the chiefs of staff of the four subordinate corps to dinner. It was a farewell party, the chief of staff having been assigned the command of a division. I was at that time the senior corps chief of staff. In a short speech, I reviewed the performance of the army during the arduous winter, thanked my superior for his sympathetic appreciation, and expressed the best wishes for the army in the days to come. Well I might! In the early morning hours of 12 May, everybody in Kharkov was aroused by a tremendous rumbling of artillery from the east. While the Germans at Slaviansk and Taranovka were still busy preparing their counter-attack on the Izium pocket, Marshal Timoshenko struck full strength at Kharkov, accompanying his attack with propaganda broadcasts in which he promised the liberation of the Ukraine and the destruction of the German Army's southern wing.'[12]

Bechtelzheim confirmed the early Soviet success north of Kharkov, attributing it to overwhelming Soviet force superiority, and admitted that:

'The German 297th Infantry Division [probably 294th] was virtually annihilated as it bore the brunt of the attack. Ternovaya, however, held out in the midst of the rising Soviet tide, which some days later lashed at the outskirts of Liptsi, dangerously near the great lateral Kharkov-Byelgorod-Kursk highway.'[13]

From the very beginning of Southwestern Front's offensive, the German Sixth Army command directed its principal efforts toward holding its first (main) defensive belt, and used divisional reserves for counter-attacks. It concentrated corps reserves at a depth of 4-8km, ready for counter-attacks and for defence along the immediate approaches to Kharkov, since the Germans considered the northern axis the most threatening. The penetration operations conducted by our forces along the front of 294th and 79th Infantry Divisions, which did not have sufficient forces at their disposal, created a severe crisis for the enemy. The German Sixth Army command was forced to transfer reserves from neighbouring corps and use army reserves to counter our forces. Thus, at the very beginning of the battle, 297th Infantry Division's 522nd Regiment from LIst Army Corps' reserve in the Zarozhnoe region was transferred into 38th Army's penetration sector. In addition, during the day the Germans began to transfer 3rd and 23rd Panzer Division units from Kharkov to the Chervona Roganka, Privole and Zarozhnoe regions. By the close of the day, remnants of 71st Infantry

Kharkov, 1942

Division's 211th Infantry Regiment, which had been operating during the day in the Peremoga region, were also concentrated there.

The Germans also dispatched the 131st Regiment of 44th Infantry Division (LIst Army Corps) and 71st Division's 191st Regiment, which had completed the march to Balakleia from Kharkov, from the Chuguev grouping to the threatened axis. The 131st Regiment had just been replaced in the Balakleia region by 71st Division's 194th Regiment.

Southwestern Front intelligence detected the location of enemy tactical reserves, but knew nothing specific about the advance of operational reserves. Thus, air reconnaissance observed the accumulation of enemy forces in front of the Northern Shock Group's left flank, but incorrectly determined the composition of these forces. Instead of the two panzer divisions and three infantry regiments concentrated here, air reconnaissance established the concentration of only the two panzer divisions.

The results of the first day of the Northern Shock Group's offensive instilled confidence in the Southwestern Front commander, Timoshenko, and his staff that the offensive could be developed subsequently in accordance with earlier decisions and with the existing force grouping. They assumed that more decisive operations by Front forces advancing along the main attack axis would break enemy resistance by the morning of the next day. They also assumed that the appearance of one panzer division in the Zarozhnoe region and another in the Privole region resulted from the successful disorientation of the enemy regarding the axis of Southwestern Front's main attack.

To parry possible counter-strokes by enemy tanks, Timoshenko ordered the 38th Army commander, Moskalenko, to withdraw his 36th, 13th and 133rd Tank Brigades from combat and to concentrate them (as 22nd Tank Corps) by the morning of 13 May behind the left flank of the army shock group with the mission of covering the Staryi Saltov axis. However, no measures at all were undertaken by engineer forces to organise anti-tank protection along this axis.

On this day, all of the 28th Army's second-echelon units were brought up to the eastern bank of the Northern Donets and, on the night of 13 May, 162nd Rifle Division began to cross to the western bank of the river in the Verkhnii Saltov region.

Enemy aviation was not particularly active on 12 May. They used groups of 5-7 aircraft to protect their own forces, conducted reconnaissance and corrected their artillery fire. The bulk of German Fourth Air Fleet was supporting the assault on Soviet defences on the Kerch Peninsula in the Crimea. In all, only 21 overflights were observed over Southwestern Front territory on this day of battle, while, during the same period, Southwestern Front aviation conducted 660 sorties.

At this juncture the Southwestern Direction and Front commands were still optimistic that they would achieve their ambitious objectives. Bagramian later reflected:

'While analysing the consequences of the Northern Shock Group actions on the first day, the High Command and the Front staff reached the conclusion that the overall offensive was developing as planned. The appearance of the two panzer divisions was very troubling for us. As one could see, Paulus and his staff judged that our offensive from the Volchansk region was the most dangerous of the initial operations and probably, therefore, made the decision to introduce their panzer divisions along that axis.

'While giving the 38th Army commander, Gen K. S. Moskalenko, the order to withdraw his 22nd Tank Corps from battle with the intent to prepare to counter the

5 The Course of Combat Operations

expected enemy tank battering ram, Timoshenko hoped that the army commander could skilfully employ the corps with existing artillery and engineer assets to repel successfully the expected blow. After all, he considered Moskalenko to be a great specialist in combat with enemy tanks. That evening, in a conversation with Marshal Timoshenko, Kirill Semenovich [Moskalenko] was full of optimism. That can be seen in his memoirs related to that moment. He then considered that it was necessary to shift the axis of the main attack into 38th Army's offensive sector, supposing that the penetration of enemy defences to their entire depth by the divisions of Gen D. I. Riabyshev's army would considerably ease not only the task of destroying the approaching enemy tank reserves, but also the liquidation of the entire German Kharkov group. Marshal Timoshenko did not agree with the army commander's view. He presumed that an attack by Gen Riabyshev's shock army along that axis, both of whose flanks were covered by neighbouring formations, would, in the coming days, undoubtedly fulfil its assigned main mission of securing Kharkov.'[14]

On the evening of 12 May, the German command faced a serious decision. Should it withdraw forces it had assembled for Operation 'Friderikus' — the attack south of Kharkov — for use north of Kharkov, or should it use them to reinforce the sagging defensive lines of Sixth Army near Taranovka? Paulus reported:

'... being hit by 12 rifle divisions and 300 tanks in the first waves. Veteran troops, who had fought through the winter, were overawed by the masses of armour rolling in on them that morning. Bock [the Army Group commander] told Halder [in the General Staff] Sixth Army was fighting "for its life".'[15]

After convincing Halder that Soviet gains were not mere 'cosmetic flaws', Bock released to Paulus's control the most critical units earmarked for use in Operation 'Friderikus', 23rd Panzer and 71st and 113th Infantry Divisions. Col Bechtelzheim later noted:

'There was nothing else to be done. The remnants of 3rd Armoured Division, the newly arrived but not yet battle-tried 23rd Armoured Division and local infantry reserves were committed in a counter-attack from the area southeast of Kharkov on Ternovaya. Motley units were rushed down from the north through Byelgorod for defence and counter-attacks west of Murom. The army group hurriedly recalled the bulk of the Fourth Air Fleet from the Crimea — where fortunately victory was in the offing — to the battlefields around Kharkov.'[16]

Combat operations on 13 May (see Map 11)
At dawn on 13 May our forces, with strong aviation support which as before achieved air superiority over the battlefield, renewed the offensive along the former axes.
   In the offensive sector of Gen Gordov's 21st Army, units of Col Voronin's 76th and General Lagutin's 293rd Rifle Divisions linked up and secured an overall bridgehead on the western bank of the Northern Donets River, but attempts to develop the offensive deep into the enemy's defences encountered stubborn resistance in the Grafovka and Murom regions; battles were fought during the day, but these points could not be captured.
   Col Ter-Gasparian's left flank 227th Rifle Division achieved the greatest success in 21st Army's offensive sector. Bypassing Murom from the south, units of this division

Kharkov, 1942

advanced 12km and captured the line from Hill 217 to Vysokii.

By the end of the day, army forces were fighting along a front from Maslova Pristan' to Priiutovka, the eastern outskirts of Grafovka, the eastern outskirts of Nekhoteevka, the western edge of the grove east of Murom, Piatnitsa and Hill 217 to Vysokii.

The enemy group defending in Varvarovka on the right flank in 28th Army's offensive sector was liquidated on the morning of 13 May. However, the Germans continued to defend Ternovaia stubbornly.

Taking advantage of the success of neighbouring 38th Army on the left, Gen Riabyshev decided to develop the offensive to the southwest using his left flank units. To accomplish this, he enlisted the main forces of Col Afansiev's 244th and Gen Rodimtsev's 13th Guards Rifle Divisions which, together with Maj-Gen V. M. Alekseev's 57th and Col Malyshev's 90th Tank Brigades, advanced 6km while developing the offensive toward Petrovskoe. By the close of the day, the army's front ran along the line of Hills 219, 226, 205 and 214. The German garrison defending Ternovaia was encircled by our units.

The heaviest and most frustrating fighting in 28th Army's sector occurred when army forces attempted to seize the key German strongpoint at Ternovaia. Both Gen Kuleshchev's 175th and General Rogachevsky's 169th Rifle Divisions attacked the strongpoint from the northeast, east and southeast. In the south, the 169th Division's 680th and 556th Regiments plunged into the woods south of the town, cut the road leading north into Ternovaia and, finally, seized Hill 226 southwest of the town. However, neither the 556th Regiment nor the 175th Rifle Division's left flank regiment could force their way into the town proper. By day's end, the German garrison was encircled but still stubbornly held out. Its presence in the Soviet shallow rear area formed a serious impediment to further Soviet advance. Consequently, late in the evening Gen Riabyshev ordered Col Dotsenko to commit the remaining two regiments of his 38th Rifle Division to relieve the 169th and 175th Divisions so that they could continue their advance while the 38th reduced the encircled German force.[17]

Despite the slow advance in 28th Army's centre and on its right flank, the progress on the army's left flank was encouraging. There, early on 13 May, Gen Rodimtsev's 13th Guards Rifle Division, reinforced by the 38th Rifle Division's 343rd Rifle Regiment, attacked north into Peremoga and westward toward the German fortified villages of Krasnyi and Petrovskoe. Rodimtsev's 39th Guards Rifle Regiment led the Soviet assault on Peremoga, supported by the 42nd Guards Regiment. In heavy fighting the 39th Regiment's 1st Battalion, commanded by Capt Tsuladze, penetrated into Peremoga from the south, and the battalion's chief of staff and a small group of soldiers overcame a German battery and seized its six guns. Almost simultaneously, the regiment's 2nd Battalion pierced German defences along the northern perimeter of the village; within minutes, the village was in Soviet hands. After the fall of Peremoga, the 42nd Regiment advanced west towards Hills 205 and 214, and the 39th reverted to second echelon to rest and refit. Col Afanisev's 244th Rifle Division advancing on Rodimtsev's right flank, took over responsibility for the Peremoga sector, seized Hill 207 several kilometres to the front and set up defences facing north to protect Rodimtsev's right flank as the 13th Guards Rifle Division regiments pushed still further westward.

Meanwhile, Rodimtsev's 34th Rifle Regiment, the attached 343rd Rifle Regiment and 90th Tank Brigade advanced steadily throughout the day, but still fell short of

5 The Course of Combat Operations

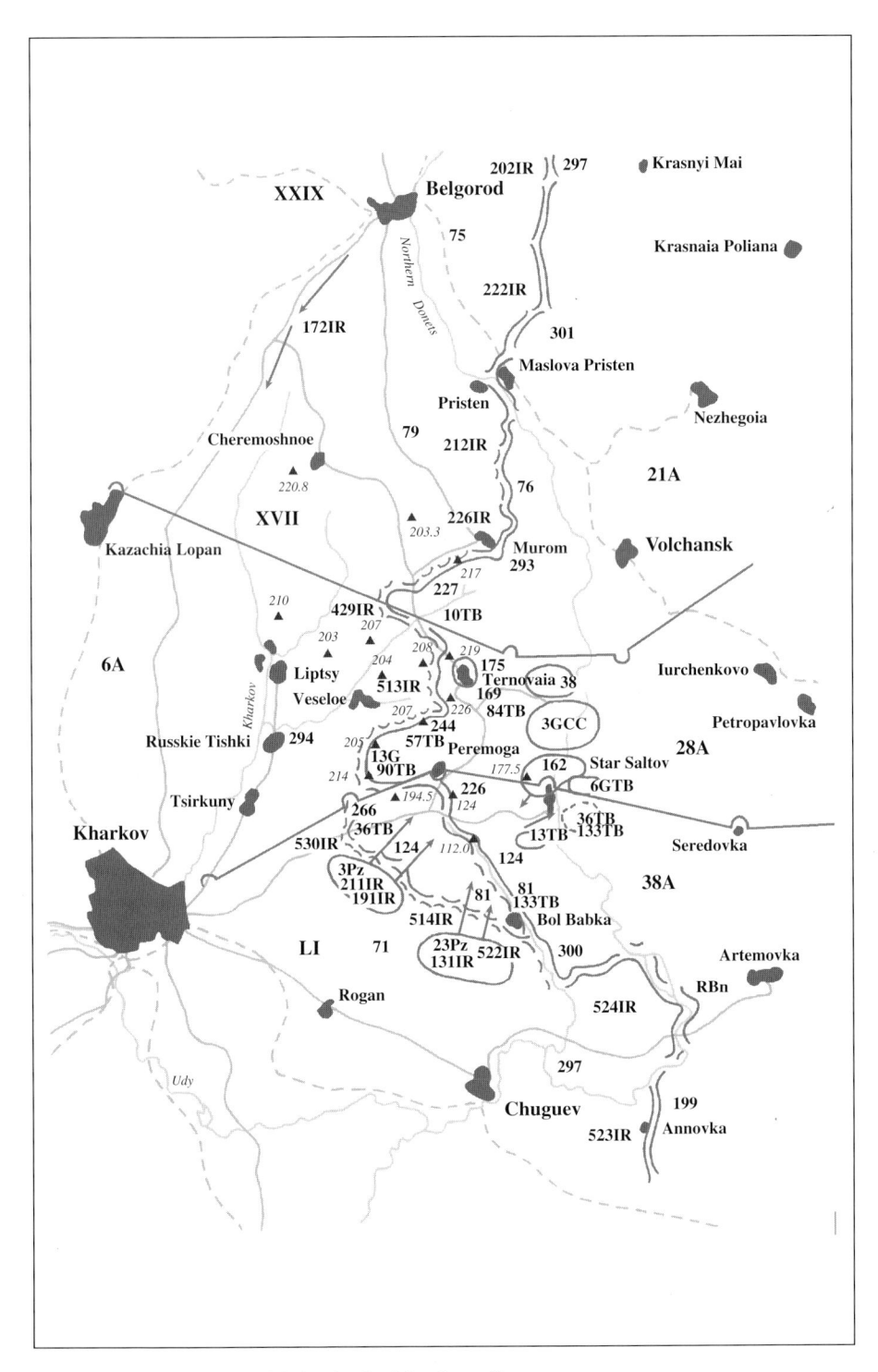

Map 11 — Combat on 13 May in the Northern Sector

Kharkov, 1942

reaching that day's objective. By mid-afternoon they had secured the village of Krasnyi despite heavy German resistance, but when night fell they were halted by persistent heavy German fire on the approaches to the next village, Petrovskoe. By virtue of their performance, the 42nd and 34th Guards Regiments, along with neighbouring 38th Army rifle divisions to the south, had carved a sizeable salient in German defences pointing menacingly toward Kharkov. This gain would soon, however, become a liability.

Disconcerting intelligence reports, received throughout the morning at 28th Army headquarters, identified large concentrations of German armour and infantry massing east of Kharkov, apparently preparing to launch counter-attacks. The reports proved correct, and in the afternoon heavy German attacks threatened to collapse 38th Army's front and threatened the right flank of Rodimtsev's division. Consequently, in the evening Riabyshev ordered Rodimtsev to regroup his forces and form a defensive front facing south. While Rodimtsev's 34th Regiment dug in outside Petrovskoe, his 42nd Regiment turned its sector over to the 244th Rifle Division, moved to the division's left flank and established defensive positions facing south near Krasnyi village. 28th Army took control of Rodimtsev's reserve 39th Regiment and positioned it in new defensive positions between Peremoga and Gordienko, to the rear of the juncture of 28th and 38th Armies.[18]

During the first half of the day, 38th Army formations continued to advance successfully along the entire front and by 13.00 had advanced 6km on the right flank and in the centre, capturing the populated areas of Mikhailovka Pervaia and Novo-Aleksandrovka, and became engaged in a battle for Chervona Roganka. On the left flank, army formations reached the road from Chervona Roganka to Bolshaia Babka. 13th and 133rd Tank Brigades had also advanced to this line.

During the second half of the day, the situation on 38th Army's front changed abruptly. At 13.00 on 13 May the enemy, having completed the concentration of two shock groups without interference (one in the Privole region, consisting of 3rd Division and two regiments — 211th and 191st — of 71st Infantry Division; the second in the Zarozhnoe region, consisting of 23rd Panzer Division and 44th Infantry Division's 131st Regiment), delivered a counter-stroke against the flank of advancing 38th Army forces in the general direction of Staryi Saltov.[19]

Bagramian, in his memoirs, recalled the serious moment:

'At 13.00, while at the Front command post, I received a phone call, and in the receiver I heard the anxious voice of Kirill Semenovich [Moskalenko]. He reported that the enemy, supported by heavy air assaults, was delivering a counter-attack with a heavy tank force against his attacking force flank along the Staryi Saltov axis.'[20]

Bagramian said that this and the second assault, which followed shortly thereafter, were made by between 150-200 German tanks.

Prior to the German counter-attack, Moskalenko's army had made impressive gains. Col A. A. Tavantsev's 266th Rifle Division, supported by a small number of tanks from Col Tanaschishin's 36th Tank Brigade (whose main body was regrouping in accordance with Timoshenko's earlier order), overcame German defences at Gordienko and Nepokrytaia and drove forward against dwindling German resistance to Mikhailovka Pervaia, within 12km of the outskirts of Kharkov. Just to the south,

5 The Course of Combat Operations

Col Berestov's 124th and Col Pimenov's 81st Rifle Divisions kept pace with Col Tavantsev's division and reached the outskirts of Chervona Roga. What the advancing Soviet troops did not know, however, was that the German withdrawal was leading them on to more vulnerable ground and into the teeth of the planned German counter-attack.

The concerted German thrust, delivered shortly after noon by 3rd and 23rd Panzer Divisions and supported by three infantry regiments, struck the 124th and 81st Rifle Divisions directly 'on the nose' and sent them reeling back, exposing the left flank of Col Tavantsev's 266th Rifle Division along the Kharkov-Staryi Saltov road. Col Berestov's 124th Rifle Division was hit particularly hard and suffered heavy casualties. Up to 80 3rd Panzer Division tanks with accompanying infantry struck Maj V. A. Mamontov's 622nd Rifle Regiment as it was approaching Chervona Roga. Although the regiment and a supporting battery of the 46th Artillery Regiment destroyed 12 German tanks, Mamontov's regiment was smashed and recoiled westward toward the Bolshaia Babka River. The 124th Division's 781st Rifle Regiment, on the 622nd's left flank, joined the withdrawal and both were encircled in the village of Pesochnoe by the armoured spearheads. The fighting raged around the village until early evening, when a small force formed by Moskalenko around the nucleus of Lt-Col N. M. Bubnov's 133rd Tank Brigade broke through the German perimeter and rescued the besieged Soviet force.[21]

All along Moskalenko's front, it was the same story. Under strong German pressure, his three shaken rifle divisions withdrew as best they could to new defensive positions along the Bolshaia Babka River, where army artillery laid down heavy concentrations of defensive fire, and Moskalenko's tank brigades, earlier withdrawn into reserve, moved forward to help the shaken infantry halt the German onslaught. With casualties mounting into the thousands, the offensive role of Moskalenko's army in the Kharkov operation had ended. Even more disturbing for Marshal Timoshenko and the Soviet Front command, losses to German 3rd and 23rd Panzer Divisions Divisions had been minimal (an estimated 35-70 tanks out of an initial force of almost 300). This meant that the panzer force could continue to wreak havoc on the northern Soviet shock force.[22]

At the same time as the counter-attack on the Staryi Saltov axis, the German command took measures to bolster 79th and 294th Infantry Divisions' defensive sectors. To this end, it trimmed one infantry regiment (172nd) from 75th Infantry Division and, during 13 May and that night, transferred it by motor vehicle to the rear army boundary in the Liptsy region. It also reinforced its garrison in Veseloe.

As a result of the German counter-stroke and strong air support, 38th Army's right-flank forces were forced to withdraw to the eastern bank of the Bolshaia Babka River, thus exposing the flank of neighbouring 28th Army on the right. Moskalenko had already used up all of his reserves (two regiments of 81st Rifle Division, and 133rd Tank Brigade) by 12 May.

Assessing the existing situation, Timoshenko ordered Moskalenko to go over to the defence with the mission of firmly holding the eastern bank of the Bolshaia Babka River and protecting the Staryi Saltov axis. Col M. I. Matveev's 162nd Rifle Division and Lt-Col M. K. Skuba's 6th Guards Tank Brigade — 28th Army's second echelon — were seconded to 38th Army as reinforcements, moving up on the morning of 14 May.

By the end of 13 May, 38th Army was fighting defensive battles along a line running

Kharkov, 1942

from Gordienko through Fedorovka to Bolshaia Babka. Further south, the front line remained unchanged.

Col V. G. Chernov's 277th Rifle Division, located in Volosskaia Balakleika, was transferred from the Front reserve to 28th Army, to replace 162nd Division — although it was only expected to arrive in the area of combat operations on 17 May at the earliest. Marshal Timoshenko now assigned Riabyshev's 28th Army the mission of continuing the offensive in its previous sector. All army second-echelon forces, with the exception of 34th Motorised Rifle Brigade, crossed to the right bank of the Northern Donets River during the night of 13 and on the morning of 14 May; by 1500 on 14 May they were deployed in the forested areas along the river and in Rubezhnoe, Ku and Verkhnii Saltov.

Combat operations on 14 May (see Map 12,)
On 14 May, the situation in the Northern Shock Group's offensive sector became even more complex. Throughout the day the Germans tried to exploit the success of their tank group at the boundary of 28th and 38th Armies by concentrating their main thrust from around Nepokrytaia against Peremoga. At the same time, up to two enemy battalions began to force the crossing of the Bolshaia Babka River in the region northeast of Peschanoe.

Having gained air superiority over the battlefield, the enemy was able to protect its operations with strong tactical aviation support, concentrating its bombers on 28th and 38th Armies' second echelons, and on roads and river crossings within the area of combat operations.

The enemy increased the number of aircraft on the Kharkov axis by using all of its assets from the front's entire southern sector, specifically the bulk of Gen von Richthofen's Fourth Air Fleet. On 14 May, Timoshenko ordered Front Chief of Aviation Gen F. Ia. Falaleev temporarily to move 6th Army's air assets to counter German aviation.

The commanders of 28th and 38th Armies took measures to strengthen the position at the boundary between their units: and it worked. The enemy captured Nepokrytaia, but advanced no further. At the same time, 28th Army's offensive slowed in those sectors where before there had been success.

During these battles, 28th Army commander Gen Riabyshev reinforced Rodimtsev's 13th Guards Division with 57th Tank Brigade . . . and part of Rodimtsev's left flank forces went over to the defence. On the 14th, while continuing to blockade the German garrison in Ternovaia, remaining army forces advanced 5-6km, defeating a number of small formations which the enemy had successfully formed from rear service units, and, by the end of the day, its right flank reached the Murom River and capturing Bezbozhnyi, Neskuchnoe, Veseloe and Petrovskoe. Thus, 28th Army units, having advanced 6-8km on 14 May, reached the approaches to the German rear defence line, which ran along the right bank of the Kharkov River.

Despite the growing crisis of his left flank, Gen Riabyshev urged his divisions on. Early on 14 May, Gen Rogachevsky's 169th and Gen Kuleshchev's 175th Rifle Divisions fully disengaged from the Ternovaia encirclement, leaving the German garrison contained by elements of Col Dotsenko's 38th Rifle Division. By day's end, the 175th had seized Neskuchnoe and occupied positions along the western bank of the Murom River, which were defended by the threadbare remnants of the German 429th Infantry Regiment. Meanwhile, the 680th Rifle Regiment of Rogachevsky's 169th

5 The Course of Combat Operations

Rifle Division, supported by 84th Tank Brigade tanks, fought a difficult battle to expel German forces from Veseloe. By nightfall, after being reinforced by the adjacent 556th Rifle Regiment, the tired Soviet troops took the town and prepared to resume the advance on Liptsy in the Kharkov river valley the following day. Losses to both divisions had been severe and the continued advance owed a great deal to the weakness of the defending forces — the remnants of German 294th Infantry Division.[23]

Early in the morning, two regiments of Col Dotsenko's 38th Rifle Division prepared to finish off the beleaguered German Ternovaia garrison. At 05.00 the 48th Rifle Regiment took up jumping-off positions east and southeast of the town and the 29th Rifle Regiment deployed south and west of Ternovaia. After a short artillery preparation, the two regiments attacked. German air attacks complicated their task with continuous fighter-bomber strikes against the advancing forces. Dotsenko's troops soon realised that the only protection against the air strikes was to get so close to the defenders that the Germans did not dare call in ground-support missions. This made the fighting that much more severe. However, despite all attempts to seize the town, the German garrison would hold firm for several days more, resupplied by air and at one point reinforced by parachutists.[24]

Further south Col Afansiev's 244th Rifle Division and one regiment (34th Guards) of Rodimtsev's 13th Guards Rifle Division also renewed their advance in the early morning of the 14th, preceded by a brief artillery preparation. Almost immediately the division's advancing troops were struck by waves of up to 50 German bombers. With no anti-aircraft artillery or air cover of their own, the Soviet troops stoically-continued their attack despite growing losses and finally took the village of Petrovskoe. While Rodimtsev's left wing continued to advance, his forces in the centre and on his division's left flank were caught up in the violent and successful German counter-attack against 38th Army positions. They were forced to conduct an increasingly desperate defence against renewed assaults by 3rd Panzer Division Kampfgruppen (combat groups), which were attempting to cut into the Soviet flank, seize Staryi Saltov and expel the Soviet Northern Shock Group from the bridgehead.[25]

The German main attack struck toward Hills 214.3 and 212, which were defended by a battalion of the 34th Guards Rifle Regiment, the 42nd Guards Rifle Regiment and tanks of Col Alekseev's 57th Tank Brigade. A divisional artillery battalion firing over open sights destroyed or damaged nine German tanks during the initial assault, but the Germans rolled forward nevertheless. They overran and destroyed a 34th Guards' 45mm anti-tank battery located on Hill 214.3 and an infantry battalion defending the anti-tank position. A bloody three-hour battle ensued during which the Soviet defenders destroyed five more German tanks before being expelled from the hill. The seizure of Hill 214.3 placed the Germans on a dominant feature in the 42nd Guards Rifle Regiment's rear. The Soviet regimental commander, Col I. P. Elin, assembled his regimental reserve — an anti-tank rifle company commanded by Senior Lt P. D. Kuimov and an automatic weapons group with anti-tank grenades commanded by a battalion commissar I. A. Trofimenko — and threw it into hasty positions blocking the German advance into the regiment's flank and rear. When the force of 25 German tanks, supported by infantry, renewed their advance, a desperate battle ensued. Kuimov's company destroyed nine tanks and Trofimenko's group six more, the latter fighting hand-to-hand in amongst the advancing German armour. Although both Soviet groups were virtually wiped out, their efforts saved the 42nd Regiment from near certain destruction as the German advance finally ground to a halt.

Similar cases of heavy fighting took place in the 13th Guards' sector defended by

Kharkov, 1942

the 39th Guards Rifle Regiment, supported by a few tanks from Lt-Col Malyshev's 90th Tank Brigade. Another German Kampfgruppe of 25 tanks and infantry struck the centre of this regiment. Here the efforts of Maj Kliagin's 32nd Guards Artillery Regiment helped save the day by laying down a curtain of blocking fire in front of the regiment's defences. Despite the intense fire, eight German tanks succeeded in breaking through and were engaged by the regimental reserve, a sapper platoon armed with anti-tank mines. Again, the platoon destroyed all the tanks, but was itself destroyed in the action along with the regimental commissar who was accompanying the reserve.[26]

Despite the determined German assaults and the devastating German air strikes, when the frenzied battle ebbed late on 14 May, Rodimtsev's division still clung to its defensive positions covering Krasnyi, Gordianka and the adjacent rolling terrain. But Rodimtsev's defences were stretched to breaking point and his casualties had been immense, perhaps as much as one third of his force. Clearly the right wing of 28th Army had also lost any capability for further offensive action.

According to the operational plan, a mobile group (Maj-Gen V. D. Kriuchenkin's 3rd Guards Cavalry Corps) and Col Dotsenko's 38th Rifle Division were to be committed into the penetration when our infantry reached the River Murom. However, because of poor 28th Army staff work, these forces completed their concentration northeast of Ternovaia only on the night of 14–15 May. Dotsenko's division had first to disengage from combat between Veseloe and Ternovaia, and Ternovaia itself was still in German hands.

In the offensive sector of Gen Gordov's 21st Army, as before, the enemy struggled hard to hold on to the strongpoints at Grafovka, Sverkh, Shamino and Murom. All 76th and 293rd Rifle Division attempts to capture these areas by frontal attacks were unsuccessful. By the end of the day, by order of Gen Gordov, these forces ceased direct attacks and began to envelop these areas to blockade the garrisons in them and develop the offensive toward the northwest.

Col G. M. Zaitsev's 227th Rifle Division (Col Ter-Gasparian had been wounded) had the greatest success during the day; it penetrated the defence, routed defending enemy units and advanced 6km, capturing Vergelevka and Pylnaia. By the close of the day, army forces fought along a line running from Nizhnii Olshanets through the eastern, southern and western outskirts of Grafovka, the eastern outskirts of Sverkh Shamino, the northern outskirts of Murom and Vergelevka to Pylnaia and attempted to encircle the German garrisons in Grafovka, Sverkh Shamino and at Murom.

Combat operations in the offensive sector of Gen Moskalenko's 38th Army were intense. On the night of 13–14 May, units of Gen Gorbatov's 226th Rifle Division once again drove the enemy out of Nepokrytaia and attempted to develop their success to Mikhailovka Pervaia. The Germans had concentrated the main forces of 3rd Panzer Division in this region, and 23rd Panzer Division in the region west of Peschanoe. At 10.00 on 14 May, these two divisions, supported by strong air forces, attacked simultaneously towards Peremoga. As a result of the tank attack, 226th Rifle Division abandoned Nepokrytaia and withdrew to the Bolshaia Babka River. During the second half of the day, 38th Army forces repelled continuous counter-attacks by German infantry and tanks, which were attempting to break through to Staryi Saltov and Peremoga. By day's end, having withdrawn to the river's eastern bank, they consolidated along a front from Dragunovka through Fedorovka to the eastern outskirts of Bolshaia Babka. The enemy was unable to force the Bolshaia Babka River in the Peschanoe region.

5 The Course of Combat Operations

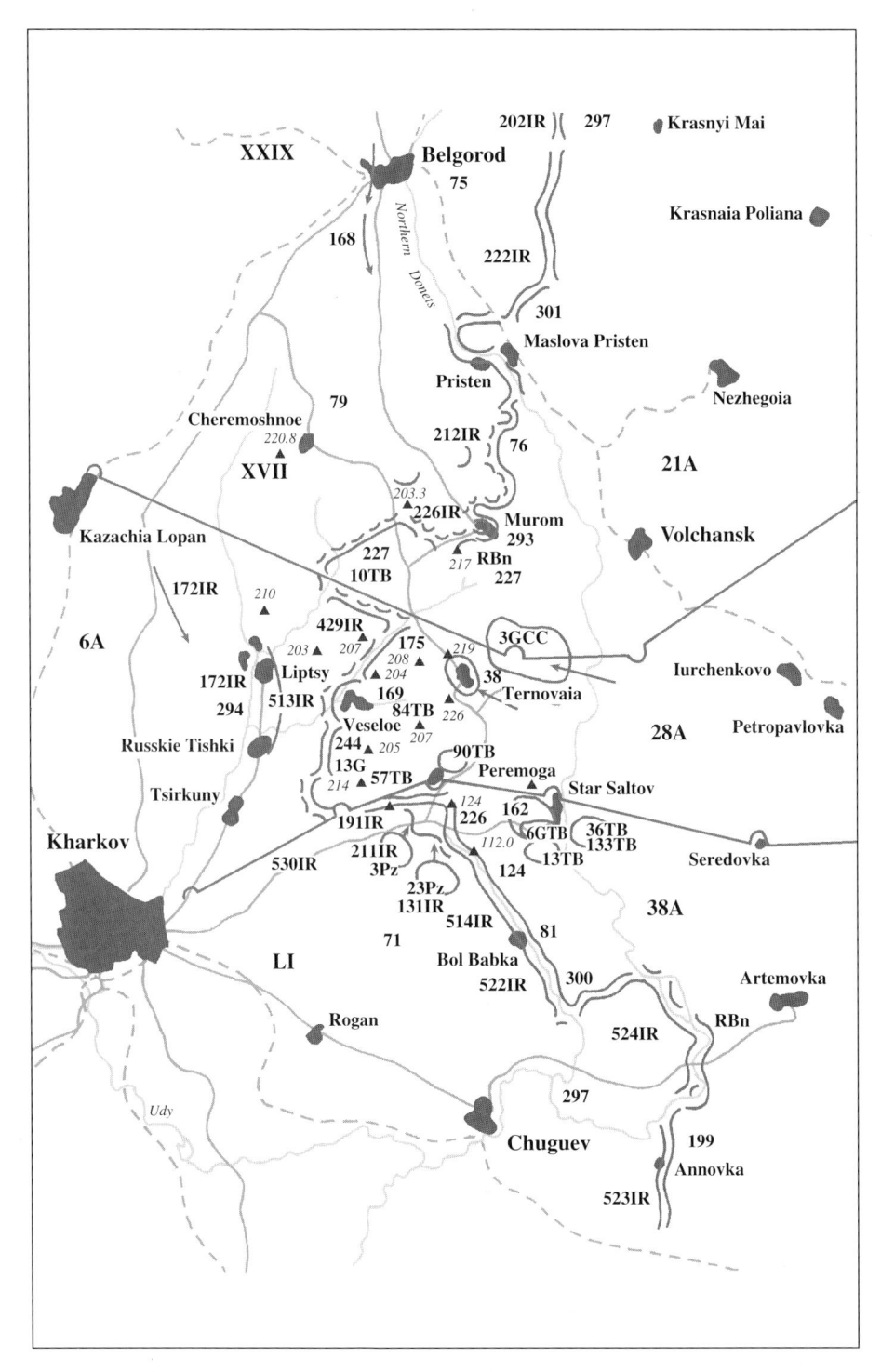

Map 12 — Combat on 14 May in the Northern Sector

Kharkov, 1942

As a result of the battles of 12–14 May, the Northern Shock Group's overall penetration front amounted to 56km. Forces operating in the centre of this group had advanced 20-25km into the depth of the German defence.

The successful advance of forces attacking in the centre created a serious situation for the enemy. Having no large reserves on this axis, the German command was forced to create them by transferring units from other, less active sectors of the front. During the day on 14 May, the German command began to withdraw and transfer 168th Infantry Division units, by means of motor vehicle transport along roads running behind the front, to Belgorod and further south (from XXIX Corps' sector). These units were defending 21st Army's right flank, and this increased the defensive sectors of neighbouring 57th and 75th Infantry Divisions.

Aerial reconnaissance noted this movement and, wishing to impede the enemy regrouping, Marshal Timoshenko ordered the 21st Army commander, Gen Gordov, to begin operations on his right flank. However, these instructions were not carried out because the army could not create an attacking force capable of conducting active operations to pin down the enemy. An offensive by a 301st Rifle Division detachment designated for this purpose was unable to produce any changes in the Miasoedovo region, and the Germans continued to withdraw forces from this sector and transfer them to the region east of Kharkov.

Bagramian later lamented the Soviet inability or unwillingness to undertake expanded operations on the Northern Shock Group's right flank or further north to take advantage of the German transfer of forces from the Kursk and Belgorod sectors. He wrote:

'Our neighbouring Briansk Front could have rendered great assistance to our Front's forces in the Kharkov offensive. It was unfortunate, however, that the offensive by that Front's 48th and 40th Armies along the Kursk-Lgov axis was postponed. One must suppose that the Stavka had a sound basis for doing so. We regretted this very much. It is not difficult to imagine what a great influence the delivery of a strong strike along the Kursk-Lgov axis with two armies of the Briansk Front, which consisted of 10 rifle divisions, 11 separate rifle brigades and more than 300 tanks, would have had on the outcome of the battle for Kharkov and the entire Kharkov operation.'[27]

THE SOUTHERN SHOCK GROUP'S OFFENSIVE
Combat operations on 12 May (see Map 13)
Simultaneously with Northern Shock Group forces, at 07.30 on 12 May, after a 60-minute artillery preparation and air raid, forces of Lt-Gen A. M. Gorodniansky's Southern Shock Group attacked German forces of VIII and LI Army Corps on a front from Verkhnii Bishkin through Alekseevskoe and Grushino to Mironovka. Attacking with part of its left flank forces, 6th Army's 47th Division, commanded by Maj-Gen F. P. Matykin, overcame strong German resistance, advanced up to 2km and by day's end was battling for the eastern outskirts of Verkhnii Bishkin. Delivering the main attack on its left flank, Lt-Col M. G. Grigorev's 253rd Division penetrated the enemy defence, routed units of German 62nd Infantry Division, which were withdrawing to Verkhnii Bishkin and Verkhniaia Bereka, and reached these towns by the close of the day. Units of Col V. G. Baersky's 41st Division, co-operating with Col A. P. Silnov's 48th Tank Brigade, smashed up to an infantry regiment of the 454th Security Division and reached Verkhniaia Bereka from the southeast and south.

The offensive was developed most successfully in the sectors of Col M. A.

5 The Course of Combat Operations

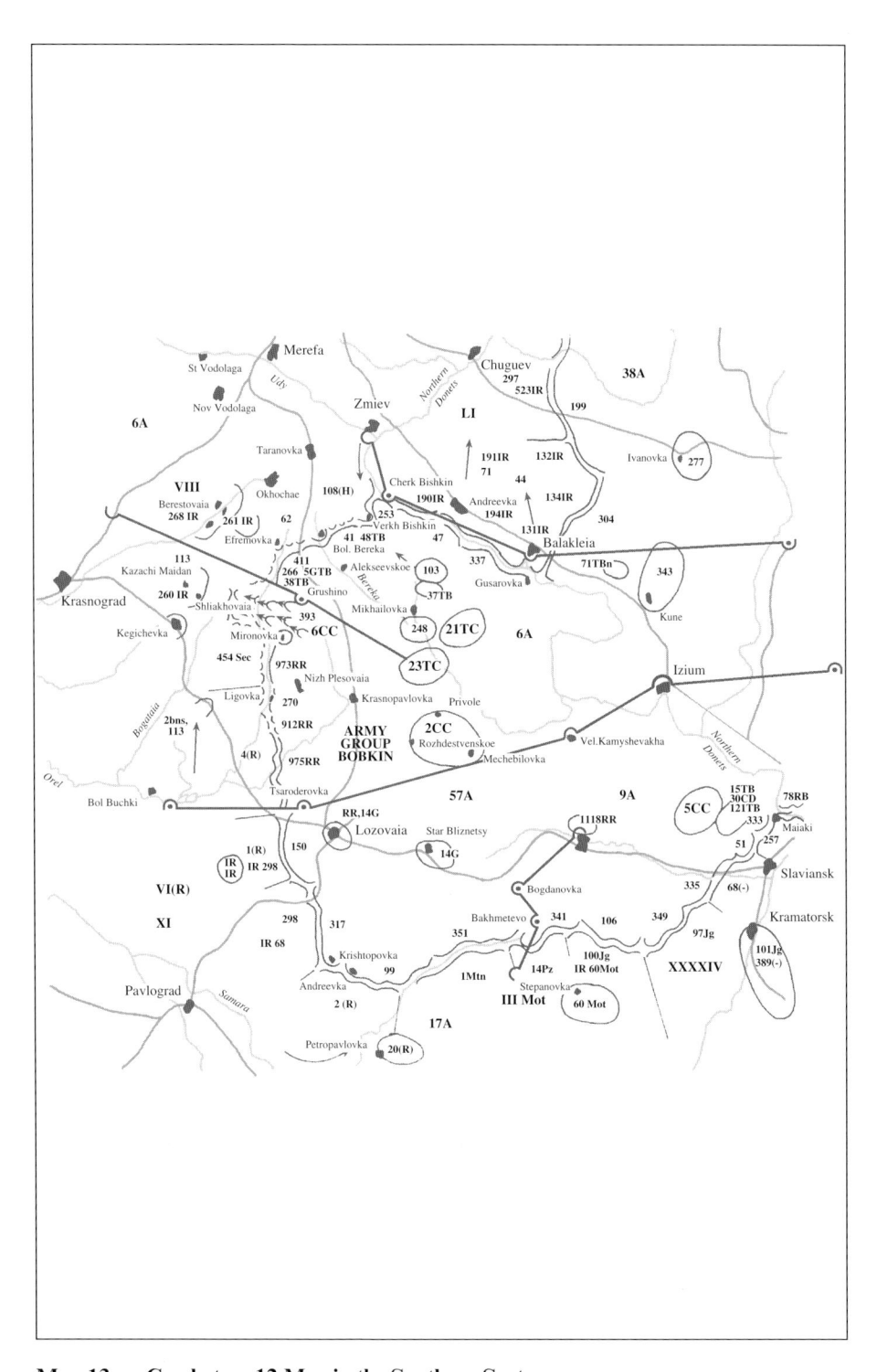

Map 13 — Combat on 12 May in the Southern Sector

Kharkov, 1942

Pesochin's 411th and Col A. A. Tavantsev's 266th Rifle Divisions. They had small penetration sectors (around 4km each) and were outfitted with considerable artillery and tank assets.

During the first half of the day, these divisions smashed the resistance of 454th Security Division's 208th and 375th Infantry Regiments, and by the close of the day reached the bank of the Orel River on a front from Novo-Semenovka to Marevka.

Army Group Bobkin conducted its offensive on 12 May without air support. The reason for this was the lack of co-operation between the Southwestern and Southern Front's headquarters. The Southern Front's aviation command, which was designated to support the Army Group's offensive, participated in neither the development of the plan, nor in support of the Army Group's offensive.[28] Nevertheless, Maj-Gen L. V. Bobkin's Army Group penetrated the enemy defence successfully to a depth of 4-6km on a front from (excluding) Grushino to Mironovka. During the second half of 12 May, Bobkin introduced Maj-Gen A. A. Noskov's 6th Cavalry Corps and Col I. A. Iurchenko's 7th Tank Brigade into the penetration. These forces pursued the defeated fragments of 454th Security Division's 375th and 610th Infantry Regiments and, by day's end, reached the Orel River, captured bridgeheads in the Shevchenko and Nizhnii Orel regions and developed success to Kazachii Maidan. They encircled the enemy in the Mironovka region. Thus, by the end of 12 May, Southern Shock Group forces had shattered German resistance along a 42km front and advanced 12-15km into German lines.

The Southern Shock Group forces reached the Germans' second defensive belt, which ran along the western bank of the Orel River, across a 30km front and, using their advanced units, forced it in the Shevchenko, Nizhnii Orel and Ulianovka regions.

As was the case in the northern penetration sector, forces operating on secondary axes achieved the greatest offensive success. Units advancing in main attack sectors on 6th Army's centre and on its left flank failed to accomplish their missions. They did not capture, as planned, Verkhnii Bishkin or Velikaia Bereka and this created difficulties for the further development of the offensive along the main axis toward Merefa.

The Army Group achieved considerable success thanks to the timely commitment of its mobile group, which prevented the enemy from consolidating along intermediate defensive lines.

The enemy used all reserves of the 454th Security Division (11th and 16th Captured Equipment (trophy) Battalions and a construction battalion) in combat for the main defensive belt against Southern Shock Group forces and began to transfer Hungarian 108th Light Infantry Division's 38th Regiment, which was in the VIII Army Corps' reserve in the Zmiev region. The approach of fresh forces made it possible for the enemy to stabilise his position along the front for some time and hold on to the strongpoints of Verkhnii Bishkin and Velikaia Bereka.

Along the line of the Orel River in the evening of the 12th and the night of 12-13 May, the enemy committed into battle one regiment of 113th Infantry Division from the the Sixth Army commander's reserve in an unsuccessful attempt to eliminate Army Group Bobkin's bridgehead.

On 12 May the first reinforcing elements of 305th Infantry Division began to arrive in Kharkov by train.

Southwestern Front headquarters, as well as 6th Army headquarters, did not have information about this division. They also did not have information about the fact that 113th Infantry Division was in German Sixth Army's operational reserve on the

5 The Course of Combat Operations

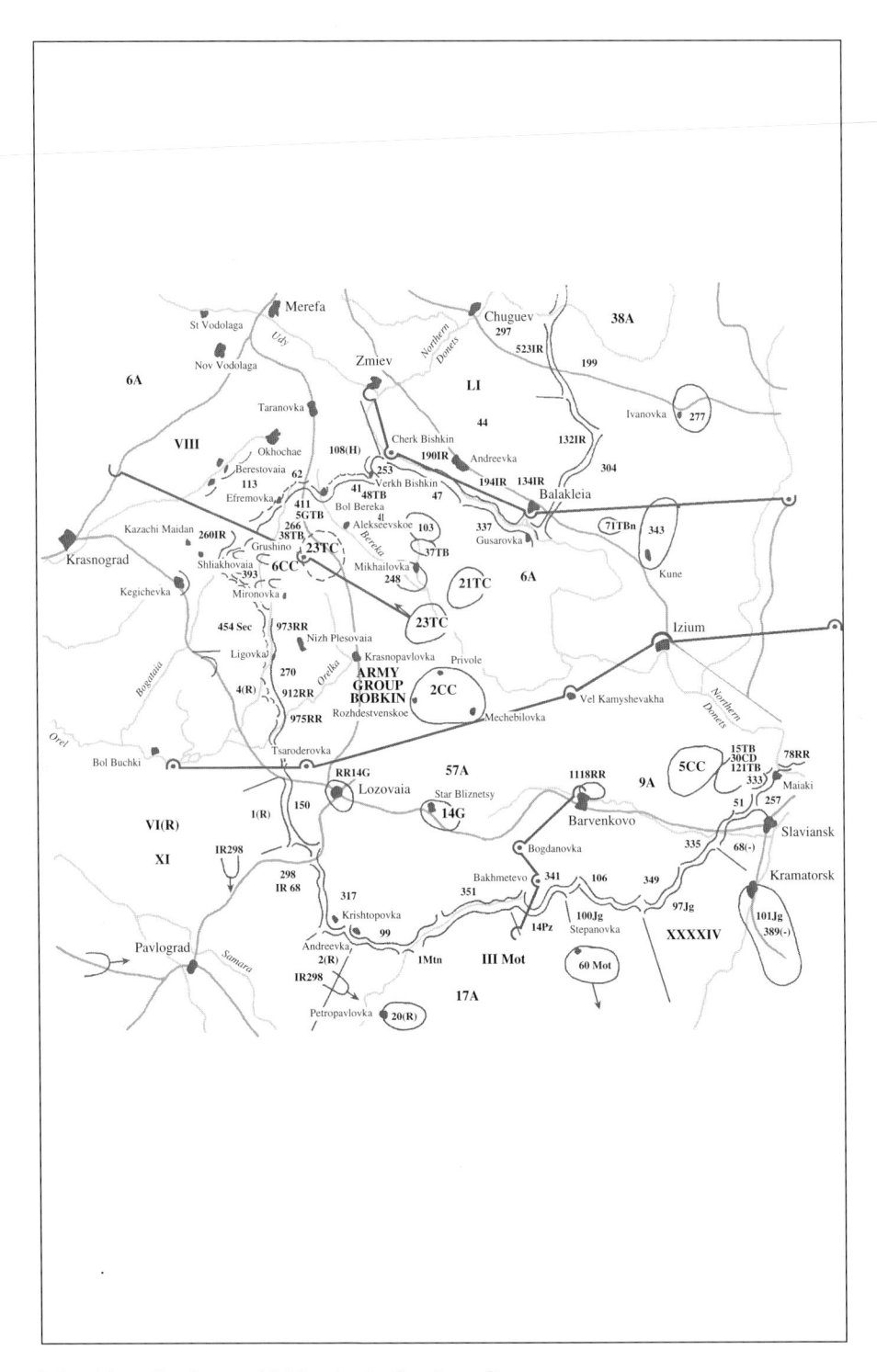

Map 14 — Combat on 13 May in the Southern Sector

Kharkov, 1942

Krasnograd axis.

On the night of 12–13 May, second-echelon units of 6th Army — Col Ia. D. Chanyshev's 103rd Rifle Division in the Kaminka region and Col A. A. Mishchenko's 248th Rifle Division in the Sivash region — began to advance. Formations of the mobile group (Maj-Gen G. I. Kuzmin's 21st and Maj-Gen E. G. Pushkin's 23rd Tank Corps) remained in their previous concentration areas. As a result of our forces' advance, the distance from their assembly area to the front line increased and reached 35km.

In his memoirs Bagramian wrote that the Southwestern Front staff assumed the two tank corps which comprised the Front's mobile group would move forward during the night and, in fact, reported to Front that they would do so. Nevertheless, they did not move.[29]

Combat operations on 13 May (see Map 14)
The Southern Shock Group's offensive continued successfully on 13 May.

The advance of General Noskov's 6th Cavalry Corps formations into the penetration in the Army Group's offensive sector represented the greatest threat for the enemy ... [who] attempted to prevent Soviet forces from widening the penetration and reaching the rear line, which ran along the Berestovaia River to Medvedovka, along the line of Shliakhovaia and Andreevka, and along the Bogataia River.

On the morning of 13 May, while attempting to destroy 6th Cavalry Corps units which had advanced beyond the Orel River, the enemy once again introduced into battle 113th Infantry Division's 260th Regiment, reinforced by a tank company. The 6th Cavalry Corps' forward units successfully repelled this regiment's counter-attacks and continued to develop the offensive.

Throughout the day, stubborn battles continued in 6th Army's sector for Verkhnyi Bishkin to Velikaia Bereka. On the morning of 13 May, the army's left flank formations (Col Pesochin's 411th and Col Tavantsev's 266th Rifle Divisions) overcame enemy resistance along the eastern bank of the Orel River and, after repelling a number of strong counter-attacks, by the close of the day occupied a bridgehead on the right bank of the river. Forward units battled for possession of the enemy strongpoint at Efremovka.

As a result of 6th Army's and Army Group Bobkin's offensive, on 13 May, the tactical depth of the enemy defence was penetrated along the Krasnograd axis. The width of the penetration sector amounted to 50km. Forces advanced 16km on the operational axis of 6th Army's main forces, while 6th Cavalry Corps units advanced 20km.

By the end of the day, Southern Shock Group forces, while enveloping the strongpoints of Verkhnii Bishkin and Velikaia Bereka from the north and south, battled along a line extending from the northwest outskirts of Velikaia Bereka through Trochatyi Station, the eastern outskirts of Efremovka, Par-Shliakhovaia, Pavlovka, Kaliuzhnoe, Mikhailovka and Ligovka to Alekseevka.

In two days of battle the main units of Hungarian 108th Light Infantry and German 62nd Infantry Divisions were routed, and heavy losses were inflicted on 113th Infantry Division's 260th Regiment.

According to the operational plan, Generals Kuzmin's and Pushkin's 21st and 23rd Tank Corps were to be introduced into the penetration on the third day of the offensive, after the infantry had reached a line extending from Verkhniaia Bereka to

5 The Course of Combat Operations

Efremovka. However, on the night of 13–14 May, the Front commander changed the line of commitment for the armour. According to his new decision, the two tank corps were to be committed into the penetration when the infantry had arrived at the line of the Berestovaia River. Army aviation, which had been designated to support the commitment of 6th Army's tank corps into the penetration, was temporarily redirected on 14 May to support the Northern Shock Group, where 28th and 38th Armies were repelling counter-strokes by the enemy's tanks.

In connection with these changes, 6th Army commander, Gen Gorodniansky, ordered the 23rd Tank Corps commander, Gen Pushkin, to transfer his units on the night of 14 May to the Novo-Semenovka, Krasnyi and Grushino region, while the remaining units of the army's second echelon (248th and 103rd Divisions) and Gen Kuzmin's 21st Tank Corps were left in their previous regions.

Combat operations on 14 May (see Map 15)
Intense fighting continued for the whole day in 6th Army's offensive sector for possession of Verkhnii Bishkin and Velikaia Bereka. The enemy only abandoned these areas late in the day, under threat of encirclement. Having driven the enemy out, Gen Gorodniansky's forces continued their offensive in the general direction of Taranovka and by the close of the day were fighting along a line extending from Glinishche through northern outskirts of Verkhnii Bishkin, Zapadenka, Novo-Beretskii and Rostov to Semenovka.

In Army Group Bobkin's offensive sector, the greatest advance was along the axis of Noskov's 6th Cavalry Corps forces.

In an attempt to cover the Krasnograd axis, the German command committed the 113th Infantry Division's 268th Regiment to combat. After repelling the counter-attacks by the enemy's 113th Infantry Division's 268th and the earlier-committed 260th Regiments, cavalry corps units captured the Kazachii Maidan, Rosokhovatoe and Novolvovka regions.

Meanwhile, units of Bobkin's 393rd and 270th Rifle Divisions widened the penetration front to the southwest and by day's end had captured positions from Kokhanovka through Grigorevka, Voroshilovka and Kutso Ganebne to Ulianovka. Defeated German 454th Security Division units withdrew to the southwest.

Thus, by the close of 14 May, the penetration of the enemy defence in the Southern Shock Group's offensive sector had been widened to a front of 55km, while the depth of the penetration reached 25-40km.

Col Bechtelzheim recounted the apparent Soviet successes in the south, noting that German and Hungarian troops defending in the Taranovka sector 'showed signs of crumbling', and, as a consequence, 'The front line west of the Donets bend, to all appearances, seemed on the point of collapse.'[30]

The morale-political condition of the forces was strong. Party-political work, which continued even during the offensive, ensured a high degree of offensive spirit among Southwestern Front forces. Party-political organs indoctrinated Soviet soldiers with the examples of heroic exploits of individual soldiers and officers, and with the heroic traditions of units and formations, intending that these high morale-political qualities became the attribute of all soldiers.

Kharkov, 1942

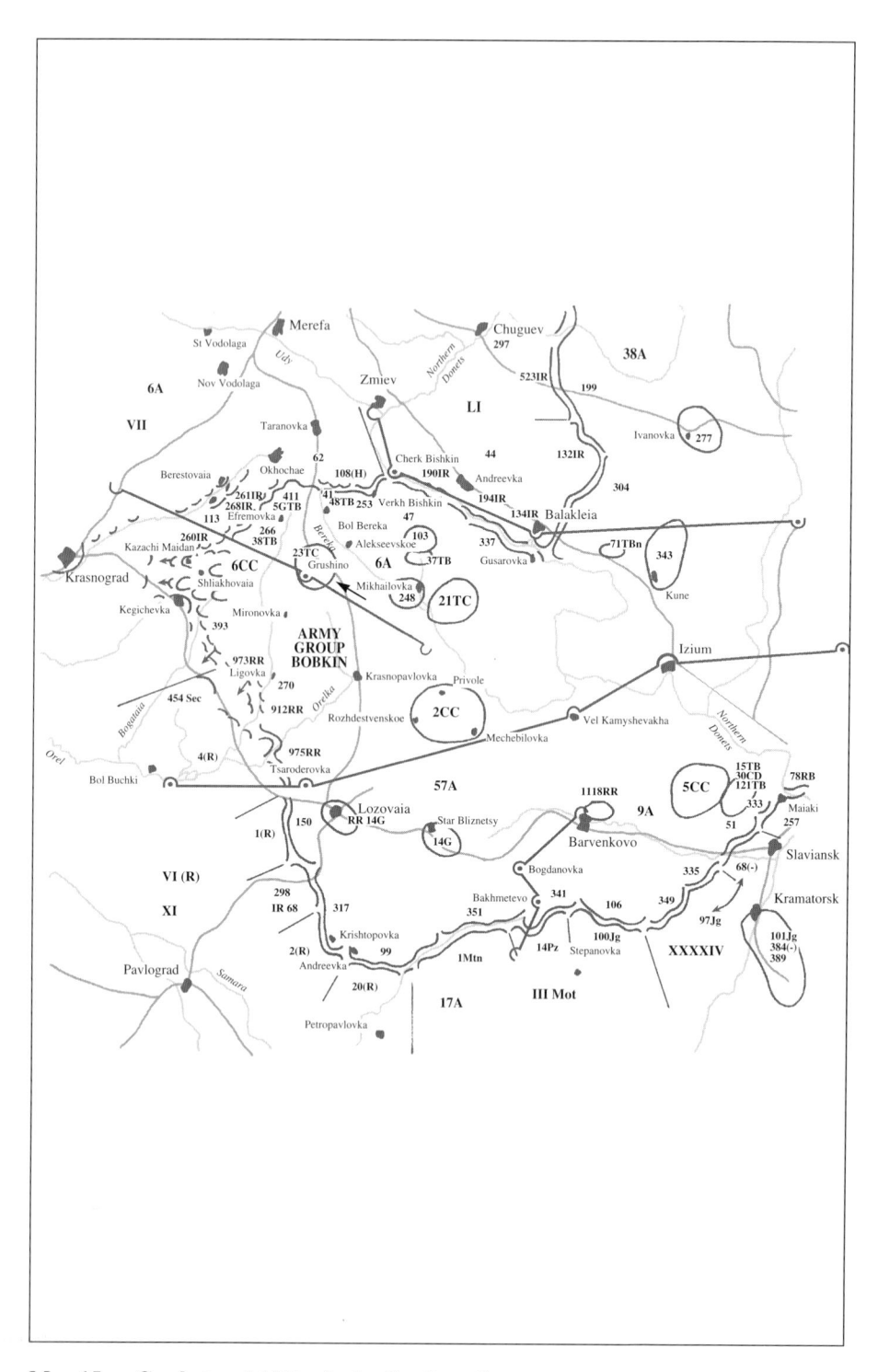

Map 15 — Combat on 14 May in the Southern Sector

5 The Course of Combat Operations

Results of combat operations 12-14 May
In assessing the overall results of the offensive by Southwestern Front forces during the first three days of the operation, Marshal Timoshenko, Commander-in-Chief of the Southwestern Direction, sent a report to the Stavka of the Supreme High Command, in which he verified the success of the first days of the offensive and noted that the enemy's commitment of forces, which were ready for an offensive in the secondary sector of Southwestern Front, would provide freedom of action to the front's shock groups, since the enemy's capabilities were very limited [see Appendix 6].

In its report to the Stavka of the Supreme High Command, dated 15 May 1942, the Military Council of the Southwestern Direction noted:

'It is completely clear to us now that the enemy, having concentrated two full-blooded panzer divisions in Kharkov, was probably ready for an offensive in the direction of Kupiansk, and that we succeeded in thwarting this offensive during its preparation. It is also obvious that the enemy now does not have at his disposal in the Kharkov region forces with which to engage us in a meeting offensive . . .'[31]

While assessing the results of the Front's Northern Shock Group battles against enemy reserves, Timoshenko observed that, despite the great losses suffered by the German armour group, it still continued to be a serious hindrance to our forces' development of the offensive toward Kharkov. He requested that the defeat of this group be accelerated and that the operation to strengthen the Front's right flank with reserves from the Stavka of the Supreme High Command be successfully completed.

Timoshenko's positive report to the Stavka actually reinforced Stalin's preconceived notions and congenital optimism. As Vasilevsky has subsequently written, it provided 'Stalin with grounds for sending a sharp rebuke to the General Staff that, on our insistence, he had nearly cancelled the operation which was developing so successfully'.[32]

The assessment of successes and outlook for the development of the offensive provided in this report resulted, in fact, not from a consideration of the actual forces and capabilities of friendly and enemy forces, but rather from erroneous suppositions about the enemy which had been the basis for planning the operation, and which had already been refuted by reality at the very commencement of the battles. Marshal Timoshenko continued to view the Southwestern Front's offensive operation in isolation from Southern Front's operations. He believed that the latter's position in the Barvenkovo salient was completely protected, and that the enemy was incapable of attacking in any Front sectors whatsoever, except for the Kharkov sector. In fact, the offensive by the Southwestern Front's left flank forces placed only those units which were operating on German Sixth Army's right flank along the Krasnograd axis in a difficult position. The penetration of the German defence on this axis had created such a tense situation for the enemy that the commander of Army Group 'South', Field Marshal von Bock, was close to abandoning the offensive operation planned by the German Supreme Command. On 14 May he requested permission from Germany's ground forces headquarters (OKH) to transfer two or three divisions from the south, from von Kleist's Group, to fill in the breach south of Kharkov.

However, the situation in German Sixth Army's centre along the Kharkov axis was more stable as a result of the commitment to combat of 3rd and 23rd Panzer Divisions. The passivity of Southwestern Front's right flank forces made it possible for

Kharkov, 1942

the German command to withdraw part of its forces from this sector and transfer them to the threatened axis. Moreover, the inaction of the entire Southern Front made it possible on 13 May for German Seventeenth Army and von Kleist's entire Army Group to begin to regroup their forces and prepare for a counter-stroke along the Izium-Barvenkovo axis without any hindrance.

The success of Southwestern Front's operation depended entirely on achieving high offensive tempos. However, Timoshenko underestimated the enemy's ability to manoeuvre forces and made errors of judgement in predicting the likely length of time it would take the enemy's strategic reserves to be brought into battle (according to the operational plan, their involvement was considered possible only on the fifth or sixth day of the offensive). As a result of these errors of judgement by the Front commander, the problem of increasing operational tempos to a maximum was not immediately given necessary attention.

In the Northern Shock Group's offensive sector, at the very beginning of the battle, Timoshenko gave instructions that weakened 28th Army's shock group by removing one rifle division and two tank brigades to repel the enemy counter-stroke in 38th Army's sector, and one rifle division to eliminate the enemy strongpoint in the Ternovaia region.

By the close of 14 May, of the eight tank brigades operating along this axis, six (57th, 90th, 36th, 13th, 133rd and 6th Guards) were tasked with protecting Northern Shock Group's left flank, instead of participating actively in the offensive. 84th Tank Brigade, designated for joint operations with 3rd Guards Cavalry Corps, had suffered heavy losses in the first days of combat, and by this time had a total of only 13 tanks. At the same time, neither all of 38th Army's forces nor all available engineer assets were used in the struggle against the counter-attacking enemy.

All of these mistakes and the unjustified manoeuvring of forces and equipment complicated the Northern Shock Group's offensive which was already slowing.

One way Timoshenko could have increased the offensive tempos of his forces on the main axis in 28th Army's sector was by quickly introducing the mobile group into the planned penetration; but he couldn't do so, because by the close of 14 May this group was 20km from the front line. It should also be added that on 14 May, 28th Army's artillery had only somewhere between 0.2 and 0.6 units (loads) of ammunition.[33] Combat aviation resources on this axis were also very limited, and as a result, aviation was unable to execute missions to support simultaneously the offensive in the centre and the defensive battles on the Northern Shock Group's left flank.

In the Southern Shock Group's offensive sector, intensification of efforts to develop apparent success were conducted more purposefully and, in accordance with the plan, without diverting second echelons to execute secondary missions. By 14 May the offensive initiative along this axis was completely in our forces' hands.

The capture of the line from Velikaia Bereka to Efremovka was the prerequisite for the commitment into the penetration of the echelon for developing success. By the time first-echelon units of Gen Gorodniansky's 6th Army had taken this line, all German operational reserves, with the exception of one infantry regiment, were engaged in battle. At this time German Sixth Army's reserves were being used against Southwestern Front's Northern Shock Group. German aviation's main forces were also operating there. Conditions for committing the mobile group into the penetration were most favourable.

However, by the end of 14 May, the second-echelon tank corps (with 260 tanks) and rifle divisions were a long way from the front line. Gen Kuzmin's 21st Tank Corps was

5 The Course of Combat Operations

42km away from 6th Army's forward units; Gen Pushkin's 23rd Tank Corps was 20km away and the 248th and 103rd Rifle Divisions, which comprised 6th Army's second echelon, were 20-40km away. Such a separation of second-echelon forces and forces of the echelon for developing success made difficult their timely commitment into battle, which was urgently dictated by the situation.

Timoshenko's decision to postpone the commitment of the mobile group into the penetration along this axis was not appropriate for either the actual situation or the overall interests of the operation, and made it possible for the enemy to gain time to consolidate Sixth Army's right flank.

The removal of the entire aviation group supporting Gen Gorodniansky's 6th Army to repel the counter-attack of 3rd and 23rd Panzer Divisions without doing everything possible to compensate for it by using Southern Front aviation complicated conditions even more for the commitment into battle of the mobile groups of the Front's Southern Shock Group.

Thus, despite the fact that the enemy's defence in the northern offensive sector had been penetrated along a front of 50km, and forces had advanced to a depth of 20-25km, by the close of 14 May the Northern Shock Group had, in fact, no prospects for further successful development of the offensive. Its shock force (first-echelon divisions and tank brigades) was too exhausted from the battles to penetrate the main defensive belt and to repel counter-attacks by enemy reserves. The forces designated to intensify the shock effort of the first echelons — Army second echelons, reserves and the echelon for developing success — were used for defence rather than attack.

The Northern Shock Group's successful actions during the first two days of the offensive drew considerable enemy reserves to the penetration sector. This made it easy for the Southern Shock Group to penetrate the entire tactical depth of the enemy defence in a short time and defeat the forces defending along this axis.

By the close of 14 May, the Southern Shock Group had widened the penetration front to 55km and had advanced 25-50km into the German defence.

German forces suffered heavy losses during the battles of 12-14 May. 62nd Infantry Division's 515th and 208th Regiments, 454th Security Division and four separate battalions were completely routed. 79th, 294th and 71st Infantry Divisions, 3rd and 23rd Panzer Divisions, 62nd, 44th and 113th Infantry Divisions and Hungarian 108th Light Infantry Division suffered heavy losses. All of the necessary prerequisites for committing the echelon for developing success into the penetration had been created. In these circumstances, a powerful blow by the two tank corps, supported by Southern Front's aviation, would have been the most effective means for both developing the southern group's offensive and for assisting the Northern Shock Group's forces. Refusal to employ the second echelons and the echelon for developing success in 6th Army's offensive sector on 13 and 14 May prejudiced the future course of operations. The enemy acquired the opportunity partially to regroup his forces and organise a defence along intermediate lines.

On the evening of 14 May the German command was making decisions which would have immense impact on the outcome of the operation and on all subsequent operations on the southern wing of their Eastern Front. On 4 May Gen von Kleist, commander of German First Panzer Army, had been personally briefed by Hitler concerning the conduct of Operation 'Friderikus'. Now, von Kleist was methodically assembling his armoured armada for the blow on Izium at the very time that German positions south of Kharkov were crumbling, and the German salient at Slaviansk was

Kharkov, 1942

still exposed to heavy local counter-attacks (and one was taking place near Maiaki). Clearly, existing circumstances made the planned German thrust impossible to conduct precisely as planned.

Von Bock had two choices. He could become directly involved in the struggle to save Sixth Army by going ahead with Operation 'Friderikus' and hope that its conduct would also save Sixth Army, or he could conduct a lesser attack with Seventeenth Army forces against Soviet defences south of Izium. In either case, Sixth Army's two panzer divisions were tied up in fighting on the eastern approaches to Kharkov and would not be able to participate in the initial counter-attack. Von Bock assessed that a limited attack by Seventeenth Army would not reach Izium and, thus, would not substantially assist Sixth Army. He favoured the addition of several extra First Panzer Army divisions to Seventeenth Army's assault force to enable it to reach Izium, but realised that Hitler would probably prefer a third choice, the 'big solution', which would entail the full commitment of First Panzer Army as called for in the Operation 'Friderikus' plan. Von Bock prudently recommended the latter to Hitler, and Hitler quickly approved. As Earle Ziemke has written, 'As expected, Hitler did promptly order the big solution, which Bock then said he could "approach cheerfully", particularly since Hitler had also undertaken to send out of the Crimea "every aircraft that can possibly be spared".'[34]

Thus, the German command made the daring decision to attack as soon as possible after assembly of its forces with only the southern arm of its 'Friderikus' force. Kleist's panzers were to gain the high ground around Barvenkovo and then push on to Balakleia to link up with Sixth Army and destroy the Soviet Barvenkovo force.

The decision was not taken lightly, and at the last minute, von Bock had second thoughts about the operation's feasibility. Col Bechtelzheim revealed:

'But just before the attack was to begin, a serious crisis developed in the German command echelon. On 14 May, after all the orders for the attack had been released to the troops, Field Marshal von Bock, the commander of the army group, suddenly lost confidence. In the nerve-wracking atmosphere created by the enemy advance on Poltava and the heavy enemy attacks on Slavyansk and Merefa, which pointed to considerable enemy reinforcements west of the Donets, he proposed to call off the attack with its doubtful outcome and to rush Kleist's mobile and armoured forces in a wide, sweeping movement to Dnepropetrovsk and Poltava. There, having contained the enemy's offensive — at least for the time being — they were to attack in an easterly direction, with the hope of gradually squeezing the enemy out of the bulge. Anyone who has not at some time felt sobered and chilled by the burden of superior military command will be unable to fathom the secret of this nervous crisis. To impartial spectators, after a period of more than 10 years, it is obvious that factors of time and space did not allow Kleist's lateral movement to be executed with sufficient speed to attain its objective, and that the only chance to seize the initiative would have been lost. Fortunately, this was also the view not only of Kleist, Paulus and the army group's General Staff, but also of Adolf Hitler, who, in a hurried discussion over the telephone, strongly disapproved of Field Marshal von Bock's view and ordered him to adhere strictly to the plan of attack from the south.'[35]

Once again, as he had been during the preceding winter when he had issued his stand-fast orders in the face of the withering Soviet offensive, Hitler's decision was correct. That fateful decision determined the ultimate fate of the Soviet offensive.

5 The Course of Combat Operations

2 Development of the Offensive and the Fight Against the Enemy's Operational Reserves (15–16 May)

THE BATTLE OF THE NORTHERN SHOCK GROUP
Combat Operations on 15 May (see Map 16)
According to the operational plan of attack, 28th Army forces, in co-operation with 6th Army, were to exploit the offensive and capture Kharkov from the north and northwest, thus setting up the subsequent encirclement and defeat of the enemy's entire Kharkov grouping. By developing offensive success and co-operating with 6th Army forces, 38th Army forces were to reach the Udy River in the Ternovoe region, hence ensuring the encirclement of the Germans in and around Chuguev. Operations by 28th Army were to be supported from the north by 21st Army's advance to a line from Maslova Pristan' to Cheremoshnoe and from the south by the advance of 38th Army's centre and left flank against the Chuguev salient.

Only General Gordov's 21st Army and the two right flank divisions of General Riabyshev's 28th Army received the Southwestern Front commander's instructions to continue the offensive on the morning of 15 May. 28th Army's two left flank divisions and all of Gen Moskalenko's 38th Army were ordered to consolidate along achieved lines, with the mission of supporting the shock group's flank.

On the morning of 15 May, 21st Army forces set about executing their missions; however, after meeting increased enemy resistance, they were unsuccessful. During the day, the operational situation in the northern sector continued to become complicated. No sooner had Bagramian, the Front chief-of-staff, begun his work at Front headquarters than report after report arrived announcing increased German activity.

By 12.00 hours the forward units of German 168th Infantry Division, transferred from the north on trucks and armoured personnel carriers, had reached the Ziborovka, Nechaevka, Bochkovka and Cheremoshnoe regions, and they immediately commenced counter-attacks in the general direction of Murom. Soon, Col S. I. Ivanov, 38th Army chief of staff, called Bagramian and reported that 3rd and 23rd Panzer Divisions, two regiments of 71st Infantry Division and a regiment of 44th Infantry Division had resumed their offensive. An enemy force consisting of an infantry regiment, supported by 80 tanks, began an offensive eastward from the Borshchevoe and Cherkasskie Tishki regions, and advanced 3km to the east of Petrovskoe. Another enemy group consisting of an infantry regiment and 40 tanks delivered a blow from the Nepokrytaia region against the boundary between 28th and 38th Armies, and began to advance northeastward towards Peremoga and Ternovaia; in Ivanov's view, it was trying to link up with the garrison encircled by our forces in Ternovaia.

At this juncture, according to Bagramian, Timoshenko himself took the phone and ordered the 38th Army Chief of Staff to halt all offensive action and to defend along existing lines.[36]

At 15.00, Soviet aerial reconnaissance reported that nine enemy transport aircraft had dropped up to 300 paratroopers into the region northeast of Ternovaia to reinforce the surrounded garrison. At the same time, the enemy activated his units in front of 38th Army's right flank formations, especially against 226th and 124th Rifle Divisions. Up to two infantry battalions supported by tanks attempted to force a crossing of

Kharkov, 1942

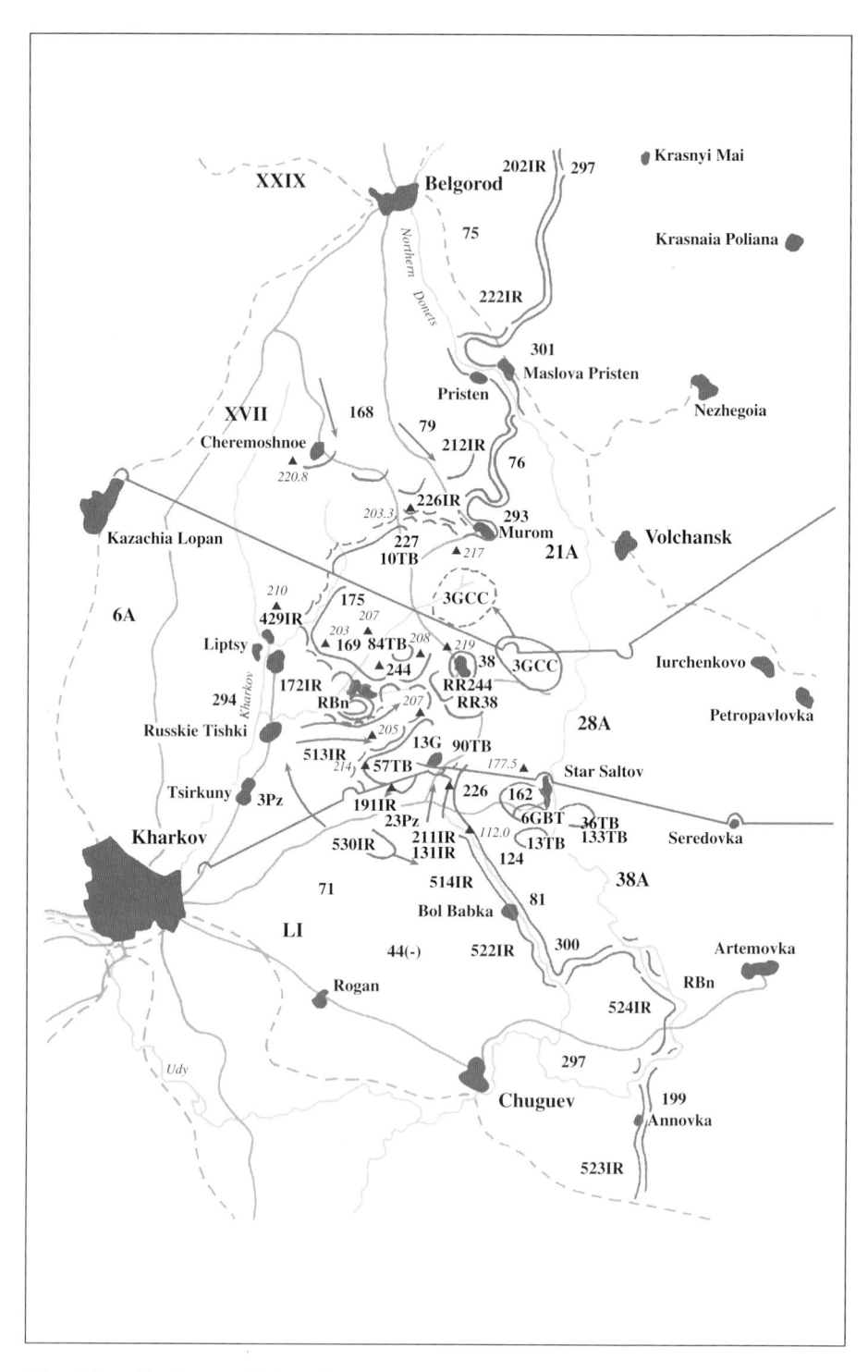

Map 16 — Combat on 15 May in the Northern Sector

Stavka Planners

Above left: **Marshal B. M. Shaposhnikov, Chief of the Red Army General Staff.**

Above centre: **Army Gen A. M. Vasilevsky, Deputy Chief of the Red Army General Staff and Chief of the General Staff's Operational Directorate.**

Above right: **Army Gen G. K. Zhukov, Stavka member.**

Southwestern Direction Command and Southwestern Front Leaders

Right: **Marshal S. K. Timoshenko, Commander, Southwestern Direction and Southwestern Front.**

Below left: **Lt-Gen F. Ia. Kostenko, Deputy Commander, Southwestern Direction.**

Below centre: **Division Commissar K. A. Gurov, Military Council Member (Commissar), Southwestern Front.**

Below right: **Col-Gen I. Kh. Bagramian, Chief-of-Staff, Southwestern Direction and Southwestern Front.**

28th Army Leaders

Above left: **Lt-Gen D. I. Riabyshev, Commander, 28th Army.**

Above centre: **Maj-Gen A. I. Rodimtsev, Commander, 13th Guards Rifle Division.**

Above right: **Maj-Gen S. M. Rogachevsky, Commander, 169th Rifle Division.**

Left: **Maj-Gen V. D. Kriuchenkin, Commander, 3rd Guards Cavalry Corps.**

Below left: **Maj-Gen V. M. Alekseev, Commander, 57th Tank Brigade.**

21st Army Leaders

Below left: **Lt-Gen V. N. Gordov, Commander, 21st Army.**

Below right: **Col G. A. Ter-Gasparian, Commander, 227th Rifle Division.**

38th Army Leaders

Above left: **Lt-Gen K. S. Moskalenko, Commander, 38th Army.**

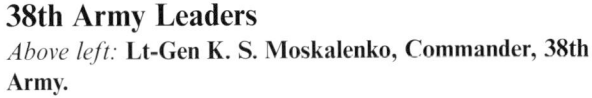

Above centre: **Maj-Gen G. I. Sherstiuk, Deputy Commander, 38th Army.**

Above right: **Col S. I. Ivanov, Chief-of-Staff, 38th Army.**

Right: **Maj-Gen A. V. Gorbatov, Commander, 226th Rifle Division.**

Below right: **Col G. T. I. Tanaschishin, Commander, 36th Tank Brigade.**

Army Group Bobkin Leaders

Below left: **Maj-Gen L. V. Bobkin, Commander, Army Group Bobkin.**

Below right: **Maj-Gen Z. Iu. Kutlin, Commander, 270th Rifle Division.**

6th Army Leaders

Above left: **Lt-Gen A. M. Gorodniansky, Commander, 6th Army.**

Above centre: **Brigade Commissar A. G. Batiunia, Chief-of-Staff, 6th Army.**

Above right: **Maj-Gen A. G. Zusmanovich, Deputy Commander for Rear Services, 6th Army.**

Below: **Maj-Gen F. P. Matykin, Commander, 47th Rifle Division.**

Below left: **Maj-Gen I. V. Vasilev, Commander, 337th Rifle Division.**

Below centre: **Maj-Gen G. I. Kuzmin, Commander, 21st Tank Corps.**

Below right: **Maj-Gen E. G. Pushkin, Commander, 23rd Tank Corps.**

Southwestern Front Reserve Leaders
Above left: **Col V. G. Chernov, Commander, 277th Rifle Division.**

Above centre: **Maj-Gen Iu. A. Naumenko, Commander, 343rd Rifle Division.**

Southern Front Leaders
Above right: **Col-Gen Rokossovsky, Commander, Southern Front.**

Right: **Lt-Gen A. I. Antonov, Chief-of-Staff, Southern Front.**

9th Army Leaders
Below left: **Maj-Gen F. M. Kharitonov, Commander, 9th Army.**

Below centre: **Division Commissar K. V. Krainiukov, Military Council Member (Commissar), 9th Army.**

Southern Front Reserve Leaders
Below right: **Maj-Gen I. A. Pliev, Commander, 5th Cavalry Corps.**

57th Army Leaders

Above left: **Lt-Gen K. P. Podlas, Commander, 57th Army.**

Above centre: **Maj-Gen A. F. Anisov, Chief-of-Staff, 57th Army.**

Above right: **Maj-Gen Shepetov, Commander, 14th Guards Rifle Division.**

Right: **Maj-Gen D. G. Egorov, Commander, 150th Rifle Division.**

German Army Leaders

Below: **Field Marshal F. von Bock inspecting tank crews on the Russian Front, 1942/3.** *IWM MH12829*

Left: **Gen F. Paulus (shown later in the war after his capture).** *IWM HU1797*

Top: **Soviet tank readying for the attack.**

Above: **A German tank destroyed during the Soviet assault.**

Below: **The beginning of the German counter offensive.**

Top: **Luftwaffe dominance was vital in the German counteroffensive.** *IWM HU 40224*

Above: **German infantry in the front line during the battle.** *IWM HU40223*

Below: **The aftermath: some of the hundreds of thousands of Russian soldiers captured by the end of the battle.** *IWM HU40226*

5 The Course of Combat Operations

Bolshaia Babka River south of Peschanoe.

The enemy supported his ground operations with air strikes — 532 sorties throughout the offensive sector on 15 May. A large portion of these were in Northern Shock Group's offensive sector. Southwestern Front aviation also exhibited great activity. While attempting to support its forces, gain air superiority and destroy enemy armoured units, it flew 341 sorties in a single day. Twenty-nine enemy aircraft were brought down in 25 air battles.

Having suffered heavy personnel and tank losses (up to 50), by the end of 15 May the enemy was forced to cease his counter-attacks without having achieved his goals. The situation for 38th Army forces remained as before.

Battles in 28th Army's sector reached their height on 15 May. All tactical reserves were dispatched to contain and destroy the enemy breakthrough, and one regiment of Gen Kuleshchev's 175th Rifle Division was immediately extracted from the front to destroy the paratroops.

The advance of the counter-attacking enemy tanks from the Nepokrytaia region against the boundary between 28th and 38th Armies was halted on a line from Krasnyi to Dragunovka. However, the situation remained tense in the sectors of 28th Army's left flank 244th and 13th Guards Divisions. One regiment of Col Afansiev's 244th Rifle Division had to withdraw 10km northeast and was only able to consolidate its positions in the region 2-3km southwest of Ternovaia; a second regiment abandoned Veseloe and took up positions on the line of hills north of the town; a third regiment was encircled by German forces in the region southwest of Veseloe. On the night of 15–16 May, the 244th Rifle Division consolidated the remnants of its units in defences along the line of hills north, northeast and east of Veseloe.

Rodimtsev's 13th Guards Rifle Division, having turned its right flank to face Hill 207, took up a defence along the line of Hills 207 and 214 and Gordienko.

The day had been particularly difficult for the already tired troopers of the 13th Guards Rifle Division. Only the day before they had had to contend with fierce German assaults against their centre and left flank, and their defences had barely held. Now German 3rd Panzer Division Kampfgruppen had smashed 244th Rifle Division defences on their right flank and driven deep into their rear area. Once again the division's 42nd Regiment had to parry the German blow. An excerpt from the divisional history captured the intensity of the action:

'The command post of the 42nd Guards Rifle Regiment was located in a small thicket. "Special attention must be paid to the junction of the road and the grove of trees," said Senior Battalion Commissar Kokushkin, to the regimental commander, Colonel Elin. "That is correct," he answered, "but they will not pass through there, Krikly has blocked the road against them."

"Krikly's battalion is providing support?" responded Kokushkin, "That's good, it means they will not get through." The firing accuracy and uncommon bravery of Guards Captain Ivan Il'ich Krikly and the men of his artillery battalion were well known throughout the division. The men knew of his battalion's work from the volleys and fall of its shells.'[37]

Krikly's battalion, and the entire 42nd Guards Rifle Regiment, had its work cut out for it on 15 May. While German tanks and infantry fell upon 1st Battalion's artillery battery from three sides, reconnaissance observers announced that about 80 tanks and

Kharkov, 1942

a company of infantry were enveloping the 42nd Regiment's flank. That very morning Krikly had established an elaborate series of firing positions, lines and sectors of fire, and prearranged targets for his guns. An intense fight ensued, which lasted for an hour as the German tanks, ignoring heavy losses, attacked into the centre of the regiment's positions. Soviet artillery fired directly into the advancing Germans, and, in the midst of the fight, a German shell ignited a battery ammunition dump, spectacularly blowing up attackers and defenders alike. When the carnage ended, the German force fell back. Once again the 42nd Regiment had held, but only barely, and at considerable cost. Many in Krikly's battalion fell, and Krikly himself was severely wounded. For his performance, and that of his battalion, in destroying an estimated 32 tanks, he was the first Soviet soldier to receive the Order of the Fatherland War (1st Degree). Similar acts of desperate heroism took place throughout the regiment, and another artilleryman, Senior-Lt Ivan Mikhailovich Bykov, commander of a battery of the 32nd Guards Artillery Regiment, earned a Hero of the Soviet Union for his performance.

The fighting on 15 May took a heavy toll on Rodimtsev's division. Down to well under 50% strength, it would see only sporadic combat over the next three days as the German assaults shifted northwards against neighbouring Soviet divisions. The 13th held on to its positions, while claiming almost 100 destroyed or damaged German tanks. When it finally withdrew from its hard-won terrain, it did so because of events elsewhere along the front and not because direct German pressure forced it to do so.[38]

The withdrawal of 28th Army's left flank affected the results of the offensive by its right flank formations. Despite weak enemy resistance, the 175th and 169th Rifle Divisions advanced only 5km westward and reached the Lipets River, but here the offensive stopped.

The experience of Gen Rogachevsky's 169th Rifle Division typified the seesaw nature of combat east of Kharkov. While Col Afansiev's 244th Rifle Division on Rodimtsev's right flank absorbed the brunt of the German attack and gave way in fragments placing the 13th Guards Division in a tenuous position, Rogachevsky's division continued its westward advance. Early on the morning of 15 May, Maj M. M. Aleksandrov's 556th Rifle Regiment and the 680th Rifle Regiment swept across the Murom valley and, against only light resistance, by noon on the 15th, reached the outskirts of Liptsy. Col I. P. Mishin's 434th Regiment followed closely in second echelon.

Aleksandrov's lead 1st Rifle Battalion, commanded by Senior-Lt I. G. Shchegrenev, penetrated into the town and, in heavy street fighting, drove the German defenders to the town's western edge along the Kharkov River. A German counter-attack, however, killed or wounded almost half of the men in the lead battalion before the 2nd Battalion, 556th, and the 1st Battalion, 680th Regiment, arrived to lend their support. At a terrible cost, the Soviet troopers maintained their tenuous foothold in Liptsy. Wave after wave of German fighter-bombers then struck the 169th Division's positions, supporting the assault by 3rd Panzer Division against the 244th Rifle Division, on the 169th's left flank. Throughout the day, and before the Germans struck back, Col Afansiev's 244th had joined in the Soviet advance and by noon had reached the outskirts of Borshchevoe, south of Liptsy.

The new German assault wreaked havoc on the 244th's advanced regiments and forced them to withdraw in disorder back through Veseloe, where one of its regiments was encircled. The precipitous withdrawal of Afansiev's division exposed the left flank of the 169th Rifle Division and forced it to abandon its hard-won foothold in Liptsy

5 The Course of Combat Operations

and withdraw eastward, although in good order, to new defensive positions anchored on Hill 203. There the fighting ended for the day as the 169th Rifle Division and 28th Army scratched up units to fill the yawning gap in Soviet lines once occupied by the 244th.[39]

Meanwhile, two regiments of Col Dotsenko's 38th Rifle Division continued their bitter struggle to overcome the German garrison in Ternovaia, the target of 3rd Panzer Division's relief effort. Throughout 15 and 16 May, assault teams from the 48th and 29th Rifle Regiments fought to destroy German strongpoints one by one. In intense fighting on 15 May, these assault teams penetrated the initial German perimeter defences but were pushed back with heavy losses by the Germans' secondary line of defence. Lacking the heavy artillery necessary to destroy the German fortified positions frustrated the attackers and German aircraft continued to resupply the German garrison despite the heavy ground fighting. Try as they might to take the German-held town, 38th Rifle Division simply lacked the strength to do so. Meanwhile, the courage and tenacity of the German garrison only impelled 3rd Panzer Division forward.[40]

To counter the German relief force and fill the gap in torn Soviet defences, late on 15 May Col Dotsenko dispatched one of his battle-worn regiments from the Ternovaia perimeter to block the path of 3rd Panzer Division. The German bastion of Ternovaia, however, would continue to stand like a rock in the path of the Soviet advance.

On 15 May Marshal Timoshenko demanded that the Northern Shock Group's formation commanders rapidly defeat enemy tanks and infantry which had penetrated their operational areas.

By order of the Front commander, on 16 May Gen Gordov's 21st Army was to carry out its earlier assigned missions. Gen Riabyshev's 28th Army was to consolidate its right flank positions along existing lines, and its left flank formations (244th and 13th Guards Divisions) were to defeat enemy forces who had penetrated between it and 38th Army and re-establish the position.

Marshal Timoshenko returned Col Matveev's 162nd Rifle Division to the 28th Army commander with the task of reinforcing the army's left flank and defending in the Peremoga, Gordienko sector. Dotsenko's 38th Rifle Division was to continue fighting to destroy the German garrison in Ternovaia, while one regiment defended the line from Hill 207 to the road junction west of Bairak in order to cover the approaches to Ternovaia from the south. By the morning of 16 May, 28th Army's mobile group (3rd Guards Cavalry Corps) was to move forward 10-12km and concentrate behind the contiguous flanks of 21st and 28th Armies in the Novaia Derevnia, Neskuchnoe and Ladytskoe region. General Moskalenko's 38th Army received the mission to defend its occupied positions firmly.

On 15 May and the night of 15–16 May, the German command continued to redeploy and concentrate 168th Infantry Divisions units in front of 21st Army's shock group. In addition, during that night, the enemy removed up to 100-120 tanks with motorised infantry from 38th Army's front and concentrated them in the Veseloe and Petrovskoe region.

Not limiting itself to forces already involved in the fighting, the German command continued to transfer other units to Kharkov. On 14–15 May it began to transfer the 88th Infantry Division (Gollwitzer's understrength combat group) from the Kursk axis. On 16 May, this division's forward units were located in the Oboian region, a distance of 120-150km from 21st Army's area of combat operations.

Kharkov, 1942

Combat Actions on 16 May (see Map 17)
On 16 May Southwestern Front's Northern Shock Group moved from attack to defence. The enemy stoutly resisted attempts by Gen Gordov's 21st Army to continue the offensive and launched several counter-attacks which Gordov's forces beat back. On the army's left flank, the 227th Rifle Division commander, Col Zaitsev, as a result of his forward detachments' operations, realised that the enemy had moved his main forces back to the line of the Kharkov River. Taking advantage of the enemy withdrawal, this division and the neighbouring 175th Rifle Division of 28th Army advanced units to the western shore of the Lipets River into the populated areas of Ustinka, Morokhovets and Bednyi.

In the afternoon of 16 May, the enemy attempted on several occasions to penetrate 28th Army's front using attacks by small numbers of tanks and motorised infantry from the Veseloe region in the direction of Ternovaia, but his counter-attacks were beaten back by means of concentrated artillery and air strikes and by the defenders of 244th Rifle Division and a regiment of the 38th Rifle Division.

Blocked in their direct advance on Ternovaia from the southwest, German 3rd Panzer Division now turned its attacks northward towards the left flank of Gen Rogachevsky's 169th Rifle Division. After liquidating the regiment of the 244th Rifle Division encircled in Ternovaia, the Kampfgruppen struck northwards along the Murom valley toward Neskuchnoe. At first light on 16 May, after a short artillery preparation, a German force of an estimated 100 tanks and assault guns struck the division's left flank, presumably defended by the 434th Rifle Regiment and a large portion of the division's 307th Artillery Regiment, commanded by Maj G. G. Baklaia. Ordered by division to halt the German advance, the regiment's 2nd Gun Battalion, commanded by Senior-Lt V. K. Kharziia, confronted the advancing tanks with direct artillery fire over open sights. In the terrible struggle which followed, Kharziia, his chief of staff and tens of soldiers fell, but the German attack was halted amidst the flaming gun positions. Both Soviet artillerymen received posthumous Orders for their performance, including a Hero of the Soviet Union for Kharziia. Despite their sacrifice, the respite from German attack was brief. During the coming days, the 169th Rifles would once again have to give up the terrain so thoroughly soaked with the blood of its soldiers.[41]

The planned offensive of 244th Rifle and 13th Guards Rifle Divisions was not carried out because the units were not ready. Thus, on 16 May both sides regrouped their forces and conducted no decisive operations.

During the period 14–16 May, the German command transferred units of 3rd Fighter, and 55th and 76th Bomber Squadrons from Crimea to the southwestern axis, mainly to airfields in Artemovsk, Konstantinovka and Zaporozhe. At the same time, the 220th Fighter Division (two LAG regiments and two MiG-3 regiments) bolstered Southwestern Front air forces. This division was given the mission to reinforce the air cover over 28th Army.

On 17 May forces of the northern group continued its attempts to defeat the penetrating German tank group. Timoshenko decided that 28th Army was to play the principal role in the defeat of this group.

In his Combat Order No 00317, dated 16 May, the Southwestern Front commander assigned new missions to 28th Army forces. The order's basic concept was as follows: by means of a concentrated attack and exploiting the favourable configuration of the

5 The Course of Combat Operations

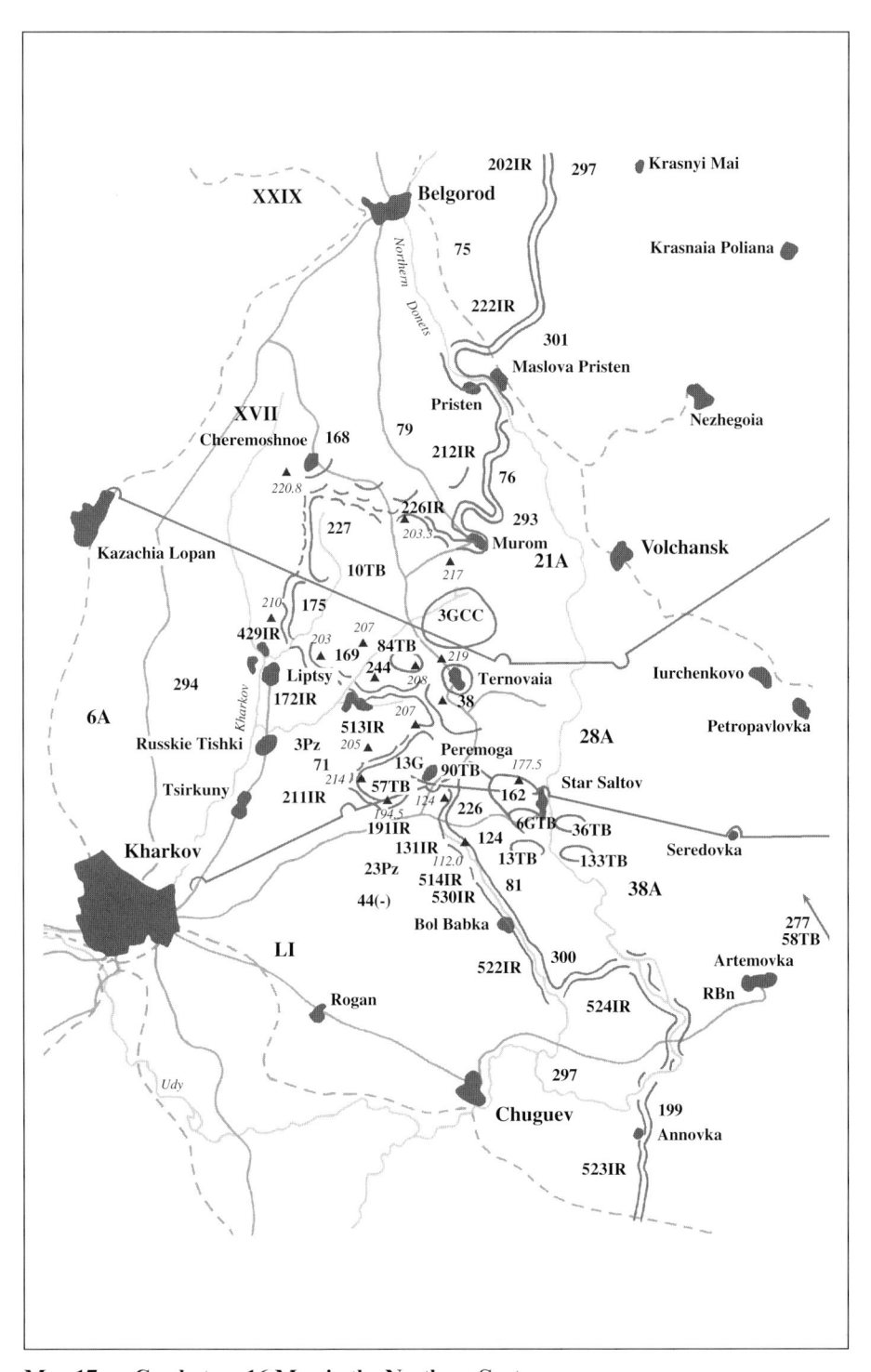

Map 17 — Combat on 16 May in the Northern Sector

Kharkov, 1942

front, the army's three left flank divisions (244th, 162nd and 13th Guards) were to deliver the main thrust in the general direction of Hill 205 in order to rout enemy forces which had penetrated to that point, and then continue the army's general offensive. While under way, the attack would be reinforced with the 277th Rifle Division and 58th Tank Brigade forces, just arriving from the Kupiansk region.

Col Matveev's 162nd Rifle Division was assigned the main role in this offensive, with subordinated units being 6th Guards Tank Brigade, one regiment of 244th Division and one regiment of 38th Division.

At the same time, on the morning of 17 May, Gen Moskalenko's 38th Army was to resume the offensive by delivering its main attack on its left flank against the enemy's Chuguev group, with the mission of capturing a line from Annovka through Nikolaevka and Volkhov Iar to Iakovenkovo by the close of 18 May. Moskalenko's army was to deliver a secondary attack on its right flank to capture the German strongpoints in Nepokrytaia, Peschanoe and Bolshaia Babka, also by the end of the day.

Given the situation existing by the end of 16 May, when German defences in the Chuguev salient had been weakened and only up to 10 German battalions remained in the 60km front opposite 199th and 304th Rifle Divisions, this offensive had good prospects for success. The enemy also had no tank units there, while 38th Army had at its disposal the fresh 114th Tank Brigade, which had arrived in 199th Rifle Division's area from the reserve of the Stavka of the Supreme High Command. The success of the offensive could have been exploited by Maj-Gen Iu. A. Naumenko's 343rd Rifle Division, which was located in Front reserve on the Chuguev axis.

THE OFFENSIVE OF THE SOUTHERN SHOCK GROUP

After penetration of the German defences, the main role in developing the offensive of the Front's Southern Shock Group belonged, as before, to General Gorodniansky's 6th Army. The remaining 15km to the Berestovaia River — the line newly indicated by Timoshenko for the commitment of the tank corps into the penetration — was to have been overcome in a short period, since the slightest delay would enable the enemy to organise a defence along this line using forces of the 113th Infantry Division and the newly arrived 305th Infantry Division.

Combat Actions on 15 May (see Map 18)
On 15 May, when 6th Army and Bobkin's Army Group resumed the offensive, the enemy activated his air operations, taking advantage of the weakening of our units' air cover. For the whole day enemy aviation, operated in large groups of aircraft, inflicting considerable losses on the Southern Shock Group's advancing units and slowing down the advance of the tank corps. This, naturally, reduced 6th Army's offensive tempo and affected the results of its operations.

6th Army's 411th and 266th Rifle Divisions, advancing along the main axis, after great efforts reached the Berestovaia River in the afternoon of the 15th. One regiment of Col Pesochin's 411th Rifle Division captured Okhochae. By this time the right flank 47th Division of Gen Matykin had arrived at the Northern Donets River in the Glinishche and Korobov sector, while Lt-Col Grigorev's 253rd Division had reached the Sukhaia Gomelsha River and fought for possession of the village of Bolshaia Gomelsha.

Army Group Bobkin units also continued to develop their offensive, and, by day's end, General Noskov's 6th Cavalry Corps had arrived at the immediate eastern

5 The Course of Combat Operations

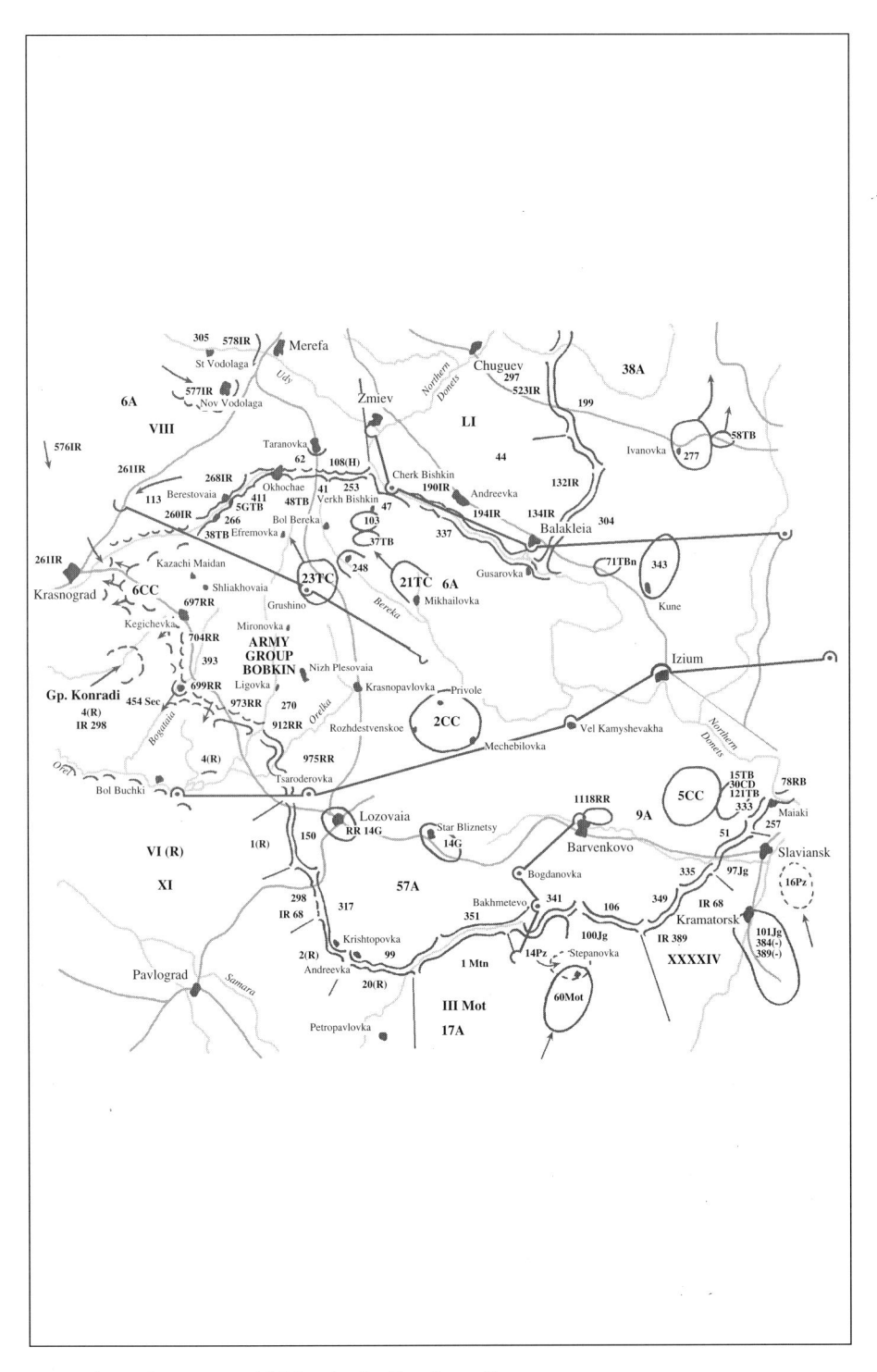

Map 18 — Combat on 15 May in the Southern Sector

Kharkov, 1942

approaches to Krasnograd. 393rd and 270th Rifle Divisions, continuing to pursue beaten units of German 454th Security Division, advanced 10km westward and southwestward, crossed the Krasnograd and Lozovaia railway line, and captured the populated areas of Kegichevka, Dar Nadezhdy and Kasenivka.

Thus, during the second half of 15 May, forces of the Front's Southern Shock Group created all necessary conditions for the mobile group to be committed into the penetration on the main axis and formed a solid front for protecting the flank of the penetration. But at this time, mobile group units were still located 25-35km distant from the area of combat operations. They therefore could not take part in completing the penetration of the enemy's rear defensive line and then, immediately thereafter, achieve operational freedom.

The successful offensive by the Front's Southern Shock Group on 15 May created a very difficult situation for the German command, and German forces did all that was possible to hold their positions along the Berestovaia River at any cost. The 113th Infantry Division's 261st Regiment was sent to the Kegichevka region to reinforce the 454th Security Division's left flank. This regiment withdrew to Krasnograd under heavy attack by 6th Cavalry Corps units. The remaining two regiments of 113th Infantry Division withdrew to the western bank of the Berestovaia River and occupied defensive positions there jointly with the remnants of the shattered 62nd Infantry Division.

Gen Paulus, the commander of German Sixth Army, did not want to concentrate 305th Infantry Division, currently *en route* by train, in Kharkov. He changed the destination of elements of the division, sending one of its regiments from Poltava to Krasnograd, while he immediately dispatched the remaining two regiments piecemeal from Kharkov to Taranovka to reinforce 62nd Infantry Division. The river sector captured by 411th Rifle Division in the Okhochae region was the greatest threat to the enemy. By the close of the day, the Germans organised a strong counter-attack using forces of one of the 113th Infantry Division's regiments and some units of the newly arriving 305th Infantry Division; the attack pushed 411th Division's regiment back to the southern outskirts of Okhochae.

According to the German command's overall plan, von Kleist's Army Group was to play the chief role in eliminating the developing Soviet offensive. This group's counter-stroke from the south against the Barvenkovo group was to decide the success of the entire German defensive operation. Together with this counter-attack, the German command also decided to execute a series of thrusts, the goal of which was to prevent the penetration of Soviet forces westward, behind the rear army line, and to the south, which would have threatened the entire German defence in front of Southern Front's 57th Army.

With the arrival of units of Army Group Bobkin in the Krasnograd region, the Germans lost an important railway line, connecting their Sixth and Seventeenth Armies. The Krasnograd railway junction was especially important, since it controlled the Krasnograd-Poltava and Krasnograd-Dnepropetrovsk rail lines.

Striving to keep the town in its own hands, the German command allocated reserves from Seventeenth Army's left flank units (units of Romanian 4th Infantry Division and one regiment of German 298th Infantry Division) and began to prepare a counter-stroke against Andreevka and Sakhnovshchina on the left flank of the advancing Army Group Bobkin. In addition, the German command made extensive use of local police units, hurriedly forming 'obstacle detachments' to defend on all axes.

5 The Course of Combat Operations

At the same time, the enemy continued the complex regrouping of his forces in front of Southern Front's 57th and 9th Armies. The purpose of the regrouping, which had started on 13 May, was to make the combat formations of first-line units denser in narrow penetration sectors and to allocate strong second echelons and operational reserves to von Kleist's Army Group.

On 15 May, all enemy formations in front of Southern Front's right flank — a distance of 110km — were regrouping. Fragmentary information concerning the movement of enemy forces arrived at our army and division headquarters. However, this information was not given the necessary attention, nor was significance attached to information on German force movements obtained from prisoners and aviation reconnaissance data. Higher headquarters were simply not informed about this. Having no data to presume that the enemy was preparing for an offensive against the southern side of the Barvenkovo salient, the Commander-in-Chief of the Southwestern Direction, Marshal Timoshenko, decided to commit his tank corps into the penetration at dawn on 16 May as follows: Gen Kuzmin's 21st Corps in the sector between Taranovka and Okhochae, and General Pushkin's 23rd Corps from the line of the Berestovaia River in the Okhochae, Berestovaia sector. Bobkin's Army Group was ordered to capture Krasnograd, using forces of General Noskov's 6th Cavalry Corps.

This order from Timoshenko was not executed. During the night, the tank corps were unable to reach their line of commitment and, by the second half of the day, they were concentrated as follows: 21st Tank Corps — in the Bolshaia Gomelsha, Novo-Beretskii and Zapadenka region, a distance of 8-10km from the front line; and 23rd Tank Corps — in the Efremovka, Semenovka and Novo-Semenovka region, a distance of 15km from the front line.

During the night of 15–16 May and throughout the whole of 16 May, the enemy regrouped those units which had been withdrawn across the Berestovaia River and destroyed all the river bridges. In late spring flood conditions, this river had a width of 10-20m in the Okhochae, Medvedovka sector. The boggy bottom and wide, marshy floodlands made it impossible for tank units to cross to the other bank without bridges or crossings.

The German command attempted to exploit the slowing of our offensive tempo to energise its units. Co-operating with units of the 113th Infantry Division, subunits of the 305th Infantry Division, which had now arrived in the Taranovka region, struck the right flank of 411th Rifle Division, thereby improving the position of German 62nd Division. The main forces of 305th Division (minus one regiment) continued to concentrate in the Merefa region.

Combat Operations on 16 May (see Map 19)

For the whole of 16 May, the enemy stubbornly resisted from occupied positions. The Germans supported their ground force operations with a large number of aircraft.

Favourable conditions for committing the tank corps into the penetration were created only by the end of the 16th, when Col Tavantsev's 266th Rifle Division forced the Berestovaia River near Paraskovaia. Even here, however, it was necessary to restore the bridges. This forced the 6th Army commander, Gen Gorodniansky, to postpone the commitment of 23rd Tank Corps until the morning of 17 May. He also postponed the introduction of 21st Tank Corps until morning.

At dawn on 16 May, Army Group Bobkin captured crossings over the Berestovaia River in the Krasnograd region. By the end of the day, General Noskov's 6th Cavalry Corps units half encircled the town and joined battle for its northern, eastern and

Kharkov, 1942

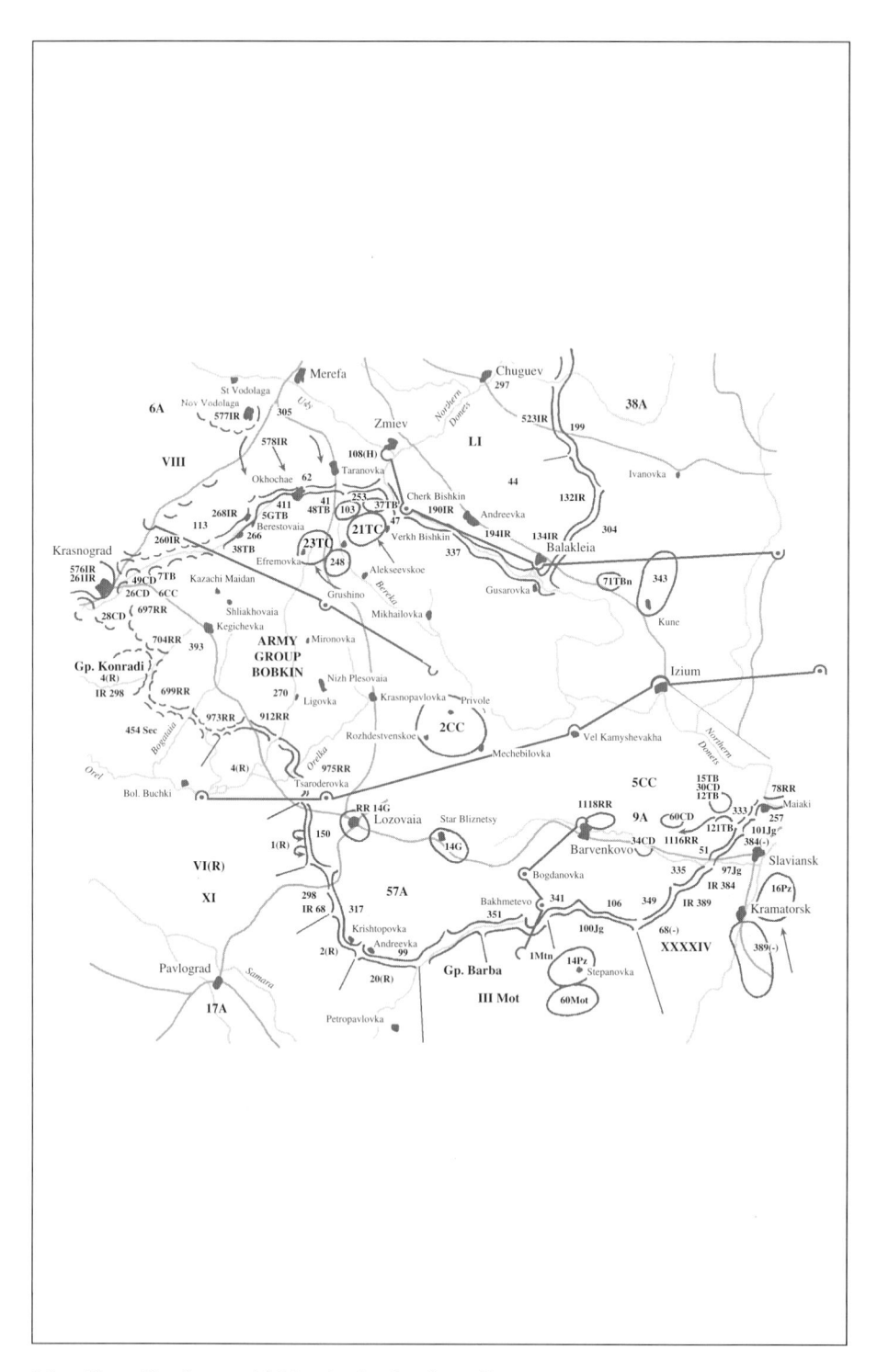

Map 19 — Combat on 16 May in the Southern Sector

5 The Course of Combat Operations

southern outskirts. By the close of 16 May, 393rd Division units had captured a line from Shkavrovoto to Mozharka. By then, Army Group Bobkin's offensive frontage exceeded 50km.

The enemy conducted several counter-attacks against the group's left flank in the Sakhnovshchina region. Units of Col Kutlin's 270th Rifle Division, however, repelled the counter-attacks and captured Garkushino.

On the 16th, the 150th Rifle Division, commanded by Maj-Gen D. G. Egorov, on the right flank of Southern Front's 57th Army and immediately to the left of 270th Rifle Division, went over to the offensive. However, during the day its advance was insignificant (up to 6km).

Thus, during the course of 15 and 16 May, while developing the offensive, the Northern Shock Group's forces were forced to fight fierce battles against enemy operational reserves and were unable to advance. In the offensive sector of the Front's Southern Shock Group, 6th Army's first-echelon forces did not receive timely reinforcement from second echelons, reserves or tank corps; as a result, they were only able to advance 8-12km in two days of battles. The enemy committed to combat along this axis the full force of 113th Infantry Division and a regiment of 305th Infantry Division and was able to stop 6th Army's offensive at the Sukhaia Gomelsha and Berestovaia Rivers.

The offensive developed successfully in Army Group Bobkin's sector, where mobile forces were promptly introduced into battle. 6th Cavalry Corps units deepened the penetration up to 50km, and on 16 May they fought for Krasnograd. Having repelled German counter-attacks, the 393rd and 270th Rifle Divisions advanced 14-22km in two days and threatened the enemy defending in front of the right flank of Southern Front's 57th Army. All attempts by the Germans to stop Army Group Bobkin's offensive failed.

On the whole, with the exception of these successes on the secondary axis, Southwestern Front's five-day offensive failed to produce decisive results, either in the northern or the southern sectors.

By the end of 16 May, both shock groups' rifle formations had advanced 20-35km and were fighting along lines which, according to plans, should have been captured on the third day of the operation. Instead of the planned deep penetration into the operational depth of the enemy defence, mobile forces were still in the front defensive belt: in the northern sector, they were drawn into defensive battles; in the southern sector, they were preparing to be committed into the penetration.

Since both shock groups were drawn into a protracted struggle to overcome the main enemy defensive belt, and the enemy had reinforced his combat formations with operational reserves, the initial correlation of forces changed in his favour.

By committing two reserve panzer and up to two infantry divisions in the northern sector, the German command achieved force superiority on the flanks of Southwestern Front's Northern Shock Group and imposed intense defensive battles upon it. In the southern sector, by committing up to two infantry divisions into battle, the enemy attained a temporary balance of forces with 6th Army and held its rear defensive line along the Berestovaia River.

By committing fresh aviation formations into battle, the enemy was able to provide air cover for his forces' operations in both sectors.

In previous combat, our intelligence had improved its operations and acquired information which made it possible for Southwestern Front's staffs to assess more correctly the enemy's formation and intentions. However, as subsequent events demon-

Kharkov, 1942

strated, this capability was not exploited. The Southwestern Front commander, Marshal Timoshenko, did not alter his erroneous assessment of enemy forces and, as before, he assumed they were at the brink of exhaustion. He demanded that army commanders rout opposing German-Fascist forces using only first-echelon units and underestimated the exhaustion of these forces in an uneven battle against German operational reserves.

During the entire course of the ensuing stage, the commands pursued the principal concept of Southwestern Front's offensive operation — the destruction of the enemy's Kharkov grouping by enveloping it with the main forces of the northern and southern groups — inconsistently and without adequate energy. In fact, from 13 May on, the principal efforts of the Northern Shock Group and all Front aviation were devoted to the destruction of the German panzer group operating against the juncture between 28th and 38th Armies. In neither the northern or southern sectors were successes by separate formations developed.

The command conducted Southwestern Front's offensive as before, in isolation from the Southern Front, which itself undertook no decisive actions to support the operation. The offensive by the 150th Rifle Division of Lt-Gen K. P. Podlas's 57th Army was also not developed and had no effect on the operational situation.

SECOND STAGE: SOUTHWESTERN AND SOUTHERN FRONT'S DEFENSIVE BATTLES IN THE BARVENKOVO SALIENT (17–28 MAY 1942)

1. Repulsion of the Enemy Counter-stroke on the Izium-Barvenkovo Axis and Continuation of the Offensive of Southwestern Front's Southern Grouping (17–19 May)

SOUTHERN FRONT'S GROUPING ON THE BARVENKOVO BRIDGEHEAD ON 17 MAY 1942

During the entire first stage of Southwestern Front's offensive, with the exception of 57th Army's 150th Rifle Division, the Southern Front's right flank forces, located in the Barvenkovo bridgehead, failed to conduct active combat operations which would have assisted this offensive.

From 7–15 May, Maj-Gen F. M. Kharitonov's 9th Army forces conducted local operations to capture the Maiaki region.

Bagramian later bitterly complained about the action at Maiaki and Southern Front's neglect of Southwestern Front's left flank. He wrote:

'The Southern Front staff did not pay requisite attention to reconnaissance and could not correctly evaluate the enemy grouping and his intentions. Finally, and most importantly, on his own initiative and with the approval of the Front commander [Malinovsky], but without the permission of the Direction High Commander, during the period 7–15 May, Gen F. M. Kharitonov conducted a local operation in 9th Army's sector which did not accord with existing conditions, whose aim was to secure the strongly fortified enemy strongpoint of Maiaki. To accomplish this he employed considerable forces, including almost all army reserves and 5th Cavalry Corps, which constituted the Front's reserve. All of these reserves were, above all, designated to repel enemy penetration of 9th Army's defences along the Barvenkovo axis. The operation in the Maiaki region turned out unsuccessfully; the reserves committed

5 The Course of Combat Operations

there suffered heavy losses and, when Kleist's group began its offensive, they were unable to regroup and occupy defensive positions in the army operational formation.'[42]

The operation at Maiaki was unsuccessful and was halted. Thereafter, the army commander planned to regroup his forces on his left flank and form reserves in the depth of the Barvenkovo bridgehead, since this was required in the interests of a stable defence. These measures had not been completed by 17 May, and Southern Front forces were deployed in the following grouping in the southern part of the Barvenkovo bridgehead (see Map 19).

Lt-Gen K. P. Podlas's 57th Army, occupying defences along the front from Tsaredarovka through Krishtopovka and Novopavlovka to (excluding) Sofievka, had the 150th, 317th, 99th and 351st Rifle Divisions in the first echelon, reinforced by three artillery regiments of the Reserve of the VGK. The army reserve consisted of 14th Guards Rifle Division, two regiments of which were deployed in the Starye Bliznetsy, Miroliubovka, Korostovka region, and one regiment of which was in the Lozovaia region.[43] The average operational density of first-echelon forces in 57th Army's defensive sector, whose width was 8km, was one division every 20km, with 4.6 guns and mortars per kilometre of front.[44] The army command post was located in Miroliubovka, 20km from the front line.

Maj-Gen F. M. Kharitonov's 9th Army, continuing to regroup on its left flank, occupied a defence with units of 341st, 106th, 349th and 335th Rifle Divisions on a front from Sofievka through Iakovlevka and Kantemirovka to Krasnoarmeisk. 51st Rifle Division was completing the relief of 30th Cavalry Division and units of 333rd Rifle Division in the Rybkhoz and Maiaki sectors. After its relief by 51st Rifle Division, one regiment (1116th) of 333rd Division was on the march to the Nikolskoe region and its division in the Barvenkovo region. A second regiment (1120th) still had not been relieved, and defended in a sector west of Maiaki. The third regiment (1118th) and the 34th Cavalry Division were deployed on a line from Barvenkovo through Nikopol to Petrovka.

The army command post was located in Kamenka, 30km from the front line, and the auxiliary command post was located in Dolgenkaia, 20km from the front line.

One battalion of 78th Rifle Brigade defended along the right bank of the Northern Donets River in the region north of Maiaki. East of Maiaki the brigade had a small bridgehead. The brigade's main forces occupied defences along the left bank of the Northern Donets River, adjacent to 37th Army's flank in the Brusovka region.

9th Army's overall defensive front was 96km wide. With five rifle divisions, one rifle brigade and five artillery regiments of the Reserves of the Supreme High Command in the make-up of the army's first echelon, the average density of army first-echelon forces was one rifle division every 19km and nine guns and mortars per kilometre of front.

In addition, Maj-Gen I. A. Pliev's 5th Cavalry Corps, consisting of 60th, 34th and 30th Cavalry Divisions and 12th Tank Brigade, which formed the Southern Front commander's reserve, was deployed in the army sector. This corps continued to withdraw its units from forward positions and concentrated its 60th Cavalry Division units in the region south of Dolgenkaia, ready to occupy rear defensive positions along a line from Kurulka Vtoraia through Vysokii to Nikolskoe; units of 30th Division with the 12th Tank Brigade were prepared to march to the Golaia Dolina and Bogorodichnoe region. Taking into account these forces, the operational density in

Kharkov, 1942

9th Army's sector was one division every 10km, while the artillery density was up to 11-12 guns and mortars per kilometre of front.

Col G. A. Kovalev's 2nd Cavalry Corps (38th, 62nd and 70th Cavalry Divisions), which formed the Commander-in-Chief of the Southwestern Direction's reserve, concentrated behind the junction of Southwestern and Southern Fronts in the Nadezhdovka, Mechebilovka and Shatovo regions.

By 05.00 on 17 May, forces on the 9th Army's left flank and in Front reserve had not yet completed their regrouping; part of these forces were moving to new concentration areas and lacked reliable communications with army and Front headquarters.

As indicated above, the defence along the front of 57th and 9th Armies was structured into a system of strongpoints and centres of resistance, poorly equipped with engineering assets and therefore poorly prepared to defend against a concerted tank attack. Divisional combat formations were not echeloned, and regiments occupied defences along the front in single echelon. There were no second echelons or reserves in the divisions. The depth of this prepared defence did not exceed 3-4km.

Thus, the formation of 57th and 9th Army forces in the defence and the poor engineer preparation of the terrain allowed easy access for an attacking tank force and did not ensure a strong defence in this sector of the front.

The commanders of these armies assessed opposing enemy actions as defensive. They excluded the possibility of an enemy offensive against the Barvenkovo bridgehead in the immediate future.

B. GERMAN PLANS AND FORCES ALONG THE SOUTHERN FACE OF THE BARVENKOVO BRIDGEHEAD ON 17 MAY

Since Soviet forces had forestalled the enemy in preparing and initiating an offensive, as indicated above, the German command was forced to send all of its shock group's forces, which were to have concentrated in the Chuguev salient, to fight against the Northern and, in some instances, against the Southern Shock Groups of Southwestern Front. A considerable portion of the enemy forces defending the Chuguev salient was also enlisted to fight against the northern group. In all, these forces amounted to three infantry (71st, 305th and two regiments of 44th) and two armoured (3rd and 23rd Panzer) divisions.

However, these measures did not exhaust the enemy's operational capabilities. In the situation existing on 16 May, the German command was unable to count on the rapid freeing-up of forces from its northern grouping to take part in the offensive against the Barvenkovo bridgehead. However, since it had at its disposal large forces in front of the southern face of the Barvenkovo bridgehead, it decided to thwart the offensive by Southwestern Front's southern group by launching from the south a counter-stroke in the general direction of Izium.

The overall plan for the counter-stroke involved the delivery of two blows along converging axes against the southern face of the Barvenkovo bridgehead, while limited forces defended along the Rostov and Voroshilovgrad axes. One thrust was planned from the Andreevka region against Barvenkovo; the second was to be from the Slaviansk region against Dolgenkaia. Subsequently, the two groups would develop the offensive in the general direction of Izium. The German command was counting on these blows to cut through 9th Army's defence, encircle and destroy units of this army east of Barvenkovo. They would subsequently reach the Northern Donets River, force a crossing in the Izium and Petrovskaia sectors, and, while developing the offensive in the general direction of Barvenkovo, unite with Sixth Army units which were

5 The Course of Combat Operations

defending the Chuguev salient and complete the encirclement of all of Southwestern Direction's forces around Barvenkovo.

The German command began to regroup its forces to form shock groups in the designated penetration sectors on 13 May, after completing rail transport of its reserves into Seventeenth Army's sector — Romanian 20th Infantry Division to the Petropavlovka region and German 384th and 389th Infantry Divisions to the Kramatorsk, Konstantinovka and Gorlovka regions. By this time 16th Panzer Division had been transferred to the Makeevka region from the south.

As a result of this regrouping, from 13–16 May the overall quantity of enemy forces facing Southern Front's 57th and 9th Armies increased by three infantry (20th, 384th and 389th) and one armoured (16th Panzer) division.

All enemy formations in this sector of the front were organisationally combined into two army and one motorised (Panzer) corps.

German III Motorised (Panzer) Corps, consisting of Romanian 20th Infantry, German 1st Mountain-Rifle, 100th Light Infantry, 60th Motorised and 14th Panzer Divisions and Combat Group Barbo (with a total of 170 tanks), was deployed along a front from Vodianoi through Chervonyi and Andreevka to (excluding) Iavlenskaia. The overall corps frontage was 62km. Its main forces were concentrated in the 21km sector from Petrovka through Andreevka to just south of Gromovaia Balka. 60th Motorised Division was concentrated in the corps' second echelon in the Stepanovka, Viktorovka, and Velikoe Pole region, while two regiments of Romanian 20th Infantry Division were concentrated in the Khoroshee, Logovoi and Aleksandropol region.

XXXXIV Army Corps, consisting of 68th, 389th and 384th Infantry, 97th Light Infantry [Jaeger], and 16th Panzer Divisions, was deployed on a front from Iavlenskaia to (excluding) Sobolevka. 68th Infantry Division and one regiment of 389th Division occupied defences on a 2km front from Iavlenskaia through Alisovka to (excluding) Bylbasovka. The corps' main forces (384th Infantry and 97th Light Infantry Divisions) occupied staging areas for the offensive in an 11km sector from Bylbasovka to (excluding) Sobolevka. 16th Panzer Division (170 tanks) concentrated in the second echelon in the Slaviansk, Andreevka region.

The main forces of LII Army Corps (101st Light Infantry Division, two regiments of 257th Infantry Divisions and the 500th Penal Battalion) occupied a staging area for the offensive in the 9km Sobolevka, Maiaki sector. One regiment of 257th Infantry Division took up the defence on a front from (excluding) Maiaki to Raigorodok, and 295th Infantry Division units defended further southeast. III Motorised Corps and XXXXIV and LII Army Corps comprised 'Panzer Group Kleist'. Command of this group was located in the town of Stalino (60km south of Konstantinovka). In all, the group consisted of 11 divisions, which resulted in an average operational density of one division per 10km.[45] Two regiments of 389th Infantry Division were in Group Kleist's reserve in the Konstantinovka and Chasov Iar region.

In all, in the 20km sector from Petrovka to Golubovka, the enemy concentrated in the first line up to five infantry regiments and 170 tanks of 14th Panzer Division against the juncture of 9th Army's 341st and 106th Rifle Divisions. In the 21km Krasnoarmeisk, Maiaki sector, the Germans concentrated up to 12 infantry regiments and more than 170 tanks of 16th Panzer Division against the juncture of 9th Army's 335th and 51st Rifle Divisions.

Having concentrated large forces in narrow front sectors, the German command was able to create a considerable superiority in forces — especially tanks and artillery — in penetration sectors, despite the comparatively small overall density of its forces

Kharkov, 1942

on the southern face of the Barvenkovo bridgehead. This is shown by Table 19:

Table 19 Comparison of Soviet and German Forces

	9th Army's Front (96km)			In German Penetration Sectors (41km)		
	9th Army	Enemy	Ratio	9th Army	Enemy	Ratio
Battalions	58	81	1:1.4	34	59	1:1.7
Guns	408 [a]	826	1:2.0	107 [b]	794	1:7.4
Mortars	568 [c]	768	1:1.3	275 [d]	570	1:2.1
Tanks	52	340	1:6.5	52	340	1:6.5
ATk Guns 5	31 [e]	570	1:18	80	380	1:4.7

[a] Guns by Calibre: 47-152mm, 90-122mm, 236-76mm (Divisional), and 15-85mm
[b] 122mm howitzers and 76mm guns
[c] Mortars by Calibre: 68-120mm and 500-82mm
[d] 120mm and 82mm mortars
[e] 76mm and 45mm

The general underestimation of the threat of an enemy offensive against the southern face of the Barvenkovo bridgehead by the Southwestern Direction and Southern Front commands and the resulting lack of readiness on the part of our troops to repel the offensive of an enemy, who was able to achieve superiority in narrow front sectors, created a situation which was fraught with the most serious operational consequences for our forces occupying the bridgehead.

In his memoirs Gen Bagramian attempted to address this criticism of the Southwestern Direction Command by describing his actions in light of what he considered to be the major mistakes made by Malinovsky's Southern Front. 'Understanding immediately the dangerous consequences of actions along the Maiaki axis,' wrote Bagramian, 'I quickly reported this to the Military Council and requested they make an urgent decision to cease the offensive and return all units and formations to the Barvenkovo region.'[46] Marshal Timoshenko and Southwestern Direction Commissar Khrushchev concluded that, in as much as the operation was over, the action was irrelevant and, besides, it had likely drawn German operational reserves to the region. Moreover, Khrushchev noted that it would be improper to limit the freedom of action of such experienced generals as Malinovsky and his chief of staff, Antonov. Both Timoshenko and Khrushchev told Bagramian to consult with the Southern Front staff and clarify the situation. Bagramian did so through his deputy, Maj-Gen L. V. Vetoshnikov who, at 15.00 on 14 May, telephoned Antonov asking, 'Who gave permission to conduct the local operation at Maiaki?' and 'What is the intent of the operation, and when will it be completed?' Antonov responded that the operation was considered 'important' by the Southern Front Military Council, and, although unsuccessful, it would continue. Moreover, the command believed its conduct would be 'beneficial', since a weakening of enemy reserves in the Barvenkovo region accorded with the desires of the Front commander. Vetoshnikov reiterated Bagramian's concerns to Antonov, and the latter promised to revisit the proposal to halt the action the following evening after a final attempt had been made to achieve victory at Maiaki.[47]

Bagramian cryptically recorded that, on the following day, Antonov notified him of Southern Front's failure to secure Maiaki, and that the sector opposite 9th Army was still quiet. Antonov went on to relate intelligence obtained from a captured German of the 1st Mountain Division to the effect that his regiment had just arrived in sector

5 The Course of Combat Operations

from the Stalino region further south. Since this was the only intelligence regarding enemy movement, and it was not particularly serious, Antonov had shifted 5th Cavalry Corps' 34th Cavalry Division into the Barvenkovo region. Bagramian remarked in disgust:

'The contents of these conversations, taking place only days before General Kleist's army group shifted to the attack on the Barvenkovo axis, clearly showed how mistaken was the position taken by the staff and command of the Southern Front as they neglected the serious necessity of preparing the armies on the Front's right wing to repel the dangerous blow along the Barvenkovo axis, whose preparation we now know was nearing completion.'[48]

C. SOUTHERN FRONT DEFENSIVE BATTLES; CONTINUATION OF OFFENSIVE OPERATIONS BY SOUTHWESTERN FRONT 17–19 MAY 1942

Combat Operations of 9th and 57th Armies on 17 May (see Map 20)
On the night of 17 May, German forces concluded their regrouping and occupied their staging areas, and on the morning of 17 May they went over to the offensive.

The artillery and aviation preparation continued from 04.00 to 05.30, after which enemy infantry and tanks with air support from around 400 aircraft went over to the attack along the Andreevka-Barvenkovo and Slaviansk-Dolgenkaia axes.

A particularly colourful German account of the action captured the drama of the developing surprise German assault:

'At last the moment had come. A roar of thunder filled the air. To the raw soldiers on the battlefield, it was just an unnerving, deafening crash, but the old soldier of the Eastern Front could make out the dull thuds of the howitzers, the sharp crack of the cannon and the whine of the infantry pieces. From the forest in front of them, where the Soviets had their positions, smoke was rising. Fountains of earth spouted into the air, tree branches sailed up above the shell bursts — the usual picture of a concentrated artillery bombardment preceding an offensive. This, then, was the starting line of the "Bear" Division from Berlin — but the picture was the same in the sectors held by the regiments of the 101st Light Division, the grenadiers of 16th Panzer Division and the Jaegers of 1st Mountain Division, the spearhead of the attack of von Mackensen's III Panzer Corps. Along the entire front between Slavyansk and Lozovaya, south of Kharkov, the companies of von Kleist's Army Group were, on that morning of 17 May 1942, standing by to mount their attack under the thunderous roar of the artillery. At last the barrage in front of the German assault formation performed a visible jump to the north. At the same moment, Stukas of IV Air Corps roared over the German lines. "Forward!" called second lieutenant Teuber. And, like him, some 500 lieutenants and second lieutenants were, at that very second, shouting out their command, "Forward!" . . . Thus, von Kleist's Group — now called an Armeegruppe, or an Army-sized combat group — mounted its attack in the morning of 17 May from the area south of Izyum *[sic]* with units of First Panzer and Seventeenth Army. Eight infantry divisions, two panzer divisions and one motorised division constituted Kleist's striking force. Romanian divisions were covering its left wing.'[49]

Kharkov, 1942

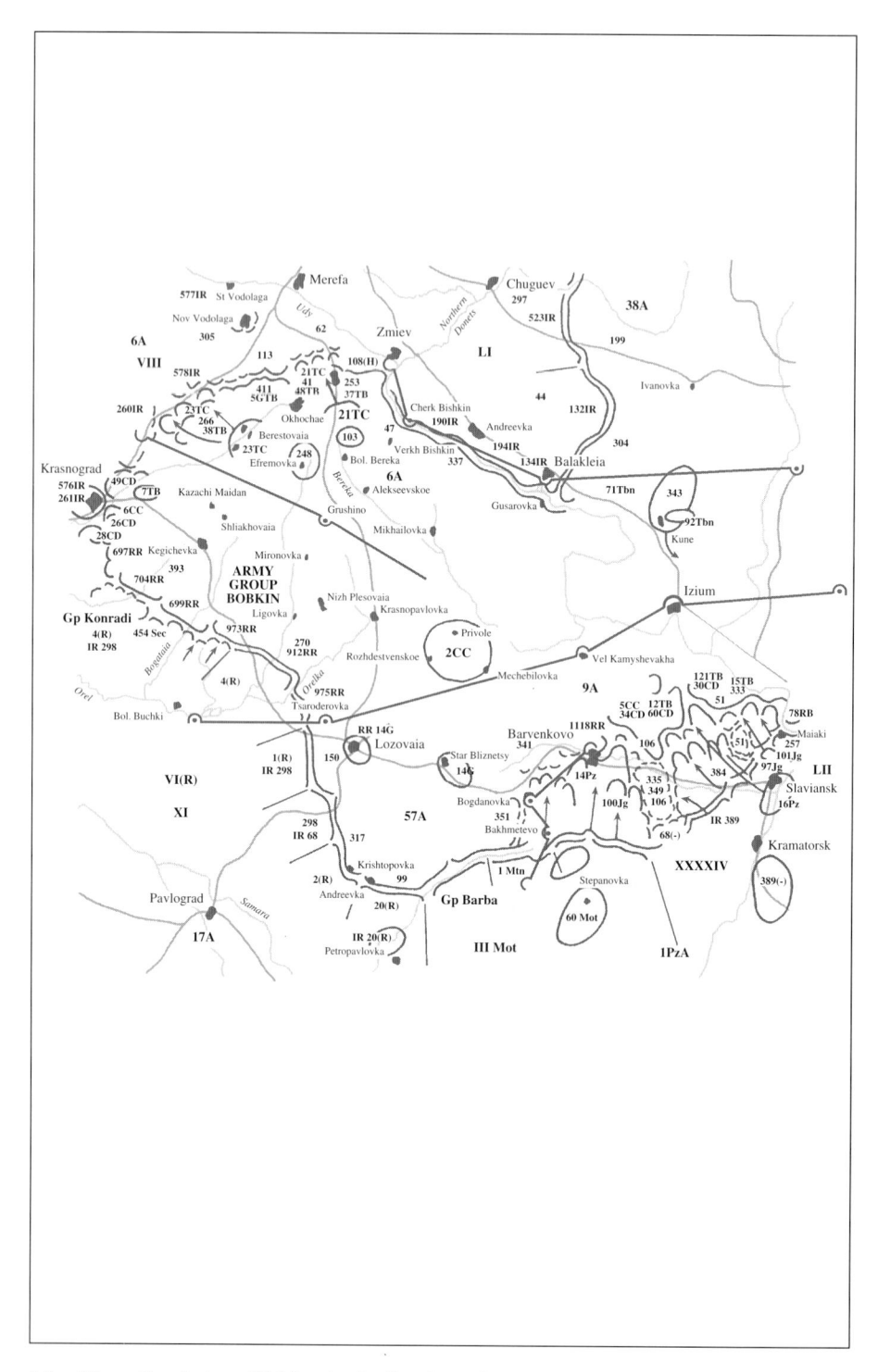

Map 20 — Combat on 17 May in the Southern Sector

5 The Course of Combat Operations

The enemy attack on the Barvenkovo axis occurred against the boundary of 341st and 106th Rifle Divisions, while along the Slaviansk and Dolgenkaia axis an attack was delivered against 51st Rifle Division's front and 335th Rifle Division's left flank.

While enveloping strongpoints and obstacles, enemy mobile groups concentrated on the flanks and rears of our divisions. By 08.00, 9th Army's defensive front had been penetrated along both axes. Enemy forces advanced 6-10km north on the Barvenkovo axis and 4-6km in the direction of Dolgenkaia.

By this time enemy air raids had demolished 9th Army's auxiliary command post and centre of communications in Dolgenkaia. The 9th Army Chief-of-Staff, Maj-Gen E. K. Korzhenevich, was wounded during one of the air raids. The enemy ultimately disorganised 9th Army troop control with subsequent raids. By 1300 the army commander, Gen Kharitonov, together with his staff, had moved to their main command post in Kamenka, and from there to the forest region 2km west of Peski (on the left bank of the Northern Donets River). This shift of the army command post took place without the knowledge or consent of Southern Front headquarters or Front commander, Gen Malinovsky. The enemy's destruction of the wire communications centre in Dolgenkaia, through which 57th Army's lines of communication also passed, and the inability to use radio communications fully, resulted in loss of communications between Southern Front headquarters and the command of both armies, and complete loss of troop control on the part of the 9th Army commander at the most critical moment of the battle.

While rupturing 9th Army's front on its flanks, by midday German forces had already advanced up to 20km into the depth of units defending along the Barvenkovo and Izium axes, and were fighting along the southern outskirts of Barvenkovo and in the Golaia Dolina region.

Given these conditions, 9th Army's formation and unit commanders were fighting in isolation, without co-ordination of their actions with neighbouring and reserve army and Front units.

Also caught up in the initial welter of combat was the headquarters of Lt-Gen K. P. Podlas's 57th Army. While the army's alternate command post was near Starye Bliznetsy, east of Lozovaia, the main command post was at Bolshaia Andreevka, southeast of Izium and astride the main axis of 14th Panzer Division's advance. Within hours of the German attack, Podlas and his staff helped orchestrate the attempt by 5th Cavalry Corps to establish some semblance of a defence east of Barvenkovo. Podlas's action, however, was futile and, early on 18 May, his headquarters was overrun by advanced elements of 14th Panzer Division. Podlas led a fighting withdrawal eastward into the Kopanki region south of Izium, where after being encircled he, his staff and remnants of 5th Cavalry Corps waged a desperate and futile battle.[50]

The Fascists burst through to Barvenkovo. Up to an infantry regiment with 14 tanks attacked the 8th Company of 442nd Regiment (106th Rifle Division). Soviet forces, headed by officer Minaevskii, commander of 8th Company, fought steadfastly, repelling the enemy's fierce attack. The enemy, having lost eight tanks, did not achieve success, and in the afternoon began to envelop 8th Company from the direction of Vikino.

By 17.00, the enemy, having overcome the resistance of the 333rd Rifle Division's 1118th Rifle Regiment and units of 34th Cavalry Division, had captured Barvenkovo,

Kharkov, 1942

with the exception of the northwest part, which was shielded by the Sukhoi Torets River where units of 341st Rifle Division and remnants of the 333rd Rifle Division's 1118th Regiment, which had withdrawn here, continued to defend. After this, the Germans began to advance eastward along both banks of the Sukhoi Torets River. 34th Cavalry Division began to withdraw north of the Sukhoi Torets River, and by the close of the day, together with subunits of the withdrawing 106th Division, occupied a defensive line from Sverkh. Ilichevka through Krasnozorevka to Grigorovka, blocking German forces along the path to Izium.

Artillerymen of the 897th Artillery Regiment of Maj-Gen Ia. S. Dashevsky's 333rd Rifle Division displayed exceptional heroism in defensive battles on the approaches to Barvenkovo and in the city itself. When enemy tanks approached Barvenkovo, Senior Lieutenant Parokhin's battery was the first to open fire. Having destroyed the lead tank, the artillerymen forced the entire column to halt. Then the entire battery opened very heavy fire and put another nine tanks out of action.

When the guns of Parokhin's battery occupied firing positions on the southern outskirts of Barvenkovo, enemy tanks were already in the town and had begun to envelop the battery's fire position.

Sergeant Sukhonos's gun team destroyed four tanks by direct fire and forced the remaining ones to retreat.

On 9th Army's left flank the German shock groups reached the Dolgenkaia, Golaia Dolina region by 14.00. Separate groups of German tanks and infantry on tanks and in automobiles began to spread westward and eastward, attempting to envelop General Pliev's 5th Cavalry Corps units in the Ilichevka, Grigorovka, Kurulka Pervaia and Dubrovka regions, and advance northeast and east from Dolgenkaia to seize crossings over the Northern Donets River in the Bogorodichnoe and Bannovskii regions. However, the enemy did not successfully carry out these intentions.

Joining battle on its own initiative, 5th Cavalry Corps units repelled German attacks from the Dolgenkaia region. 333rd and 51st Rifle Divisions' units repelled enemy attempts to reach the crossings over the Northern Donets River.

Here, as well as at Barvenkovo, our officers and soldiers performed miracles of heroism. Forced to withdraw under pressure by a numerically superior enemy, they inflicted heavy personnel and equipment losses upon him.

The high fighting spirit of our forces under these difficult conditions resulted from unceasing party-political work during the fiercest battles, the direct moral influence of officers on all personnel and the unprecedented bravery and heroism of Communists and Komsomol members.

Only during the second half of the day, after the Germans had already penetrated the tactical depth of the defence, did Southern Front headquarters find out about the enemy offensive. It was reported to Southwestern Direction headquarters only by the end of the day, after the enemy had not only penetrated the tactical depth, but had also broken through into the operational depth of 9th Army's defence and had engaged its reserves in battle.

By this time 9th Army's defensive front had been penetrated everywhere. On the right flank, subunits of Col A. I. Shagin's 341st Rifle Division and 333rd Rifle Division's 1118th Regiment continued to fight in the northwestern part of Barvenkovo. Further, a breach had been formed between Barvenkovo and Ilichevka, where we had no forces; thereafter the front ran along the line from above Ilichevka through Grigorovka, Kurulka Pervaia, Solenyi, Stepanovka, Dolgenkaia, Golaia Dolina, and Bogorodichnoe to Prishib.

5 The Course of Combat Operations

Units on the right flank and in the centre of Gen Podlas's 57th Army remained in their previous positions, while at the boundary with 9th Army they turned their flanks to the north and, by the close of the day, they defended the line extending from Dobrovele through Malyi Razdol to Novo-Prigozhaia. Withdrawn subunits of 9th Army's 341st Rifle Division defended on the left flank of 57th Army's 351st Rifle Division.

Thus, a 20km breach in our defences formed at the juncture of 57th and 9th Armies between Novo-Prigozhaia and Barvenkovo. As indicated above, Col Kovalev's 2nd Cavalry Corps, which constituted the Commander-in-Chief of the Southwestern Direction's reserve, was concentrated west and northwest of Barvenkovo in the Nadezhdovka, Shatovo and Mechebilovka region, in the depth of 57th Army's forces. Two regiments of 14th Guards Rifle Division were in the 57th Army commander's reserve in the Starye Bliznetsy, Miroliubovka and Korostovka region.

These forces received no instructions from the command concerning movement and commitment into battle; they remained in place all day and, therefore, had no influence on the course of events which occurred at the boundary of 57th and 9th Armies. By the end of 17 May, these forces were 18-28km from the front line.

Enemy air forces supporting their ground forces completed around 2,000 sorties, whereas Southern Front aviation demonstrated little activity, completing a total of only 67 sorties.

After receiving reports about the enemy's penetration of 9th Army's defences, Gen Malinovsky, the Southern Front commander, decided to transfer immediately Gen Pliev's 5th Cavalry Corps from his own reserve to 9th Army and ordered that 296th Rifle Division and 3rd Tank Brigade be immediately transported by motor vehicles and railway from the Lisichansk region (50km east of Brusovka) to the Radkovskie Peski region and be subordinated to the 9th Army commander.

According to a report by the Southern Front commander, Marshal Timoshenko transferred his own reserve — Col Kovalev's 2nd Cavalry Corps — to Gen Malinovsky and ordered that he destroy the penetrating enemy with the forces of 2nd and 5th Cavalry Corps, 333rd and 14th Guards Rifle Division (57th Army's reserve), and 12th, 15th and 121st Tank Brigades and restore the situation.[51]

However, none of these instructions, with the exception of those concerning the movement of the deep operational reserves, had been carried out by the close of 17 May, since by this time the Southern Front commander's immediate reserve — Pliev's 5th Cavalry Corps — was already fighting defensive battles and its units were broken up. In addition, the 9th Army commander, Gen Kharitonov, had completely lost troop control and he was unable either to organise co-operation between 57th and 9th Armies or to direct the combat operations of his own reserves. Communications between Front headquarters and the 9th Army command post were re-established only by 24.00 on 17 May.

German progress on 17 May had been spectacular. It had torn Soviet 9th Army defences apart, and it left surviving Soviet forces in an utter state of shock. A German account vividly relates that progress:

'By nightfall on 17 May, the regiments of Colonel Puchler's 257th [Bear] Infantry Division had reached the Donets along the entire width of their front. On 18 May they took their most northerly objective — Bogorodichnoye. Just as First-Lieutenant Gust, commanding 3rd Battalion, 477th Infantry Regiment, reached the edge of the

Kharkov, 1942

village with his foremost platoon, a river ferry crowded with 30 horses [of Soviet 5th Cavalry Corps] was making a desperate effort to cast off from among the blazing barges. On catching sight of the Germans, however, the ferry-man gave up the attempt. Burning boats were drifting down the river like meandering islands of fire. Further to the left, the 101st Light Division also reached the Donets by the evening of 18 May. In a sweltering damp heat of 30° Centigrade, the battalions had to drive through a vast area of woodland, pick their way cautiously past well-camouflaged Soviet forest positions, moving in line abreast, and struggle laboriously through deep minefields. The sappers worked wonders. Engineer Battalion 213, advancing with 101st Light Infantry Division, rendered harmless 1,750 mines of all types on the first day.'[52]

Combat Operations of Southwestern Front's Southern Shock Group on 17 May (see Map 20)
At the time when Southern Front's right flank forces were fighting severe defensive battles, both of Southwestern Front's shock groups were continuing to develop the offensive. On the night of 17 May, Gen Gorodniansky's 6th Army forces repaired three bridges across the Berestovaia River. They had also completed preparations for committing the tank corps into battle. At 05.00 on 17 May, Gen Kuzmin's 21st Tank Corps began to advance in the direction of Taranovka. General Pushkin's 23rd Tank Corps completed crossing the Berestovaia River in the Berestovaia and Paraskovaia region, and at 08.00 went over to the offensive in the general direction of Novaia Vodolaga. On 17 May the German command shifted all aircraft operating on the Krasnograd axis to support Group Kleist's offensive. As a result, the activity of German aviation in the offensive sector of Southwestern Front's Southern Shock Group decreased sharply.

Smashing enemy resistance, Gen Kuzmin's 21st Tank Corps units captured Taranovka and, by the close of the 17th, had reached positions running from Shurino to Zelenyi Ugolok. By this time units of Gen Pushkin's 23rd Tank Corps had advanced 15km to the northwest, reached the Staroverovka region, and severed the Kharkov-Krasnograd railway line at Vlasovka Station.

Thanks to the successful armoured operations, on the 17th all 6th Army formations advanced 6-10km. On the army's right flank, Lt-Col Grigorev's 253rd Rifle Division, with 37th Tank Brigade in support, cleared out the forest tract along the Northern Donets River and reached the immediate vicinity of the town of Zmiev. In the centre and on the left flank, rifle formations broke enemy resistance on the northern bank of the Berestovaia River and, by the end of the day, had secured positions from the southern outskirts of Dudkovka through Shurino, Zelenyi Ugolok and Karavanskaia Vershina to Staroverovka.

As before, Army Group Bobkin spent the whole day attacking Krasnograd. Unable to penetrate into the town on the shirt-tails of the withdrawing enemy, Gen Noskov's 6th Cavalry Corps units were forced to begin a systematic fight to capture the town, but in increasingly unfavourable conditions. On 17 May the distance between Army Group Bobkin's forward units and their rear bases was 190km. Rear service organs could not cope with the task of timely resupply of ammunition; at the same time, the Germans had unlimited quantities of ammunition at their disposal, since Krasnograd was a strong German rear service base. All of this forced Gen Bobkin to decide to halt his assault on the town and begin to gather ammunition. Units along the remainder of the Army Group's front had not advanced significantly. Repelling enemy counter-

5 The Course of Combat Operations

attacks, group forces fought along a front from Bezeka State Farm through Dar Nadezhdy to Sverkh Kommunist.

The 150th Rifle Division of Gen Kharitonov's 57th Army had halted its offensive, and on 17 May remained in its former positions.

Combat Operations of Southwestern Front's Northern Shock Group on 17 May (see Map 21)

These operations developed independent of events unfolding in the south. However, from the very beginning they deviated quite significantly from the decision made by the Southwestern Front commander on 16 May.

On the night of 16–17 May, 38th Army commander Gen Moskalenko, reported that the army's left flank units were not ready for the offensive designated for the morning of 17 May and was given permission to postpone the commencement of the offensive by 24 hours. However, the Southwestern Front commander, Marshal Timoshenko, left in force his order requiring an offensive by 28th Army and right flank units of 38th Army on the morning of 17 May.

The 28th Army commander, Gen Riabyshev, did not fulfil the Front commander's order and instead of concentrating all of his army's efforts on carrying out the limited mission, he dissipated the army's forces.[53] According to Timoshenko's combat order, Gen Rogachevsky's 169th Division was to attack westward along its entire front, and Col Afansiev's 244th Division was to attack southwestward. Co-operation between them and Col Matveev's 162nd Division was lacking. In addition, 162nd Rifle Division received none of the reinforcing assets promised by the Front commander.

The 6th Guards Tank Brigade commander, Lt- Col M. K. Skuba, was appointed commander of a composite tank group, consisting of his tank brigade and the remnants of 57th and 84th Tank Brigades. The entire group numbered 70 tanks. It was to attack at the juncture of 244th and 162nd Divisions rather than along the axis of 162nd Division's attack.

The force regrouping and simultaneous reorganisation of tank units caused the offensive to be postponed. By order of the 28th Army commander, Gen Riabyshev, it was now prescribed for 07.30 on 17 May. The enemy, however, forestalled 28th Army by commencing their offensive at 06.00 and, instead of an offensive, army forces had to fight heavy defensive battles. 3rd and 23rd Panzer and 71st Infantry Division forces delivered the German main attack from the Veseloe, Hill 200.9 and Petrovskoe region in the general direction of Arapovka-Ploskoe and Murom. The 168th Infantry Division delivered a secondary strike from the Ziborovka and Nechaevka region, also in the general direction of Murom. In addition, the enemy began attacks from the Nepokrytaia region, using forces of 71st Infantry Division's 191st Infantry Regiment, reinforced with tanks.

The German offensive against 28th Army surprised the 244th Rifle Division. This division's units were unable to withstand the strong enemy tank attack and began to withdraw to the northeast, thus uncovering both the rear areas of its right flank neighbour and the Murom axis.

Enemy infantry and tanks reached Ternovaia, relieved their surrounded garrison and, having resupplied their tanks with fuel and ammunition, continued to develop the attack eastward. This blow forced Col Dotsenko's 38th Division units to withdraw 2-3km east of Ternovaia.

As a result, Rogachevsky's 169th Rifle Division was also forced to withdraw 5-8km northward and, having joined up with the second echelon combat formations of Maj-

Kharkov, 1942

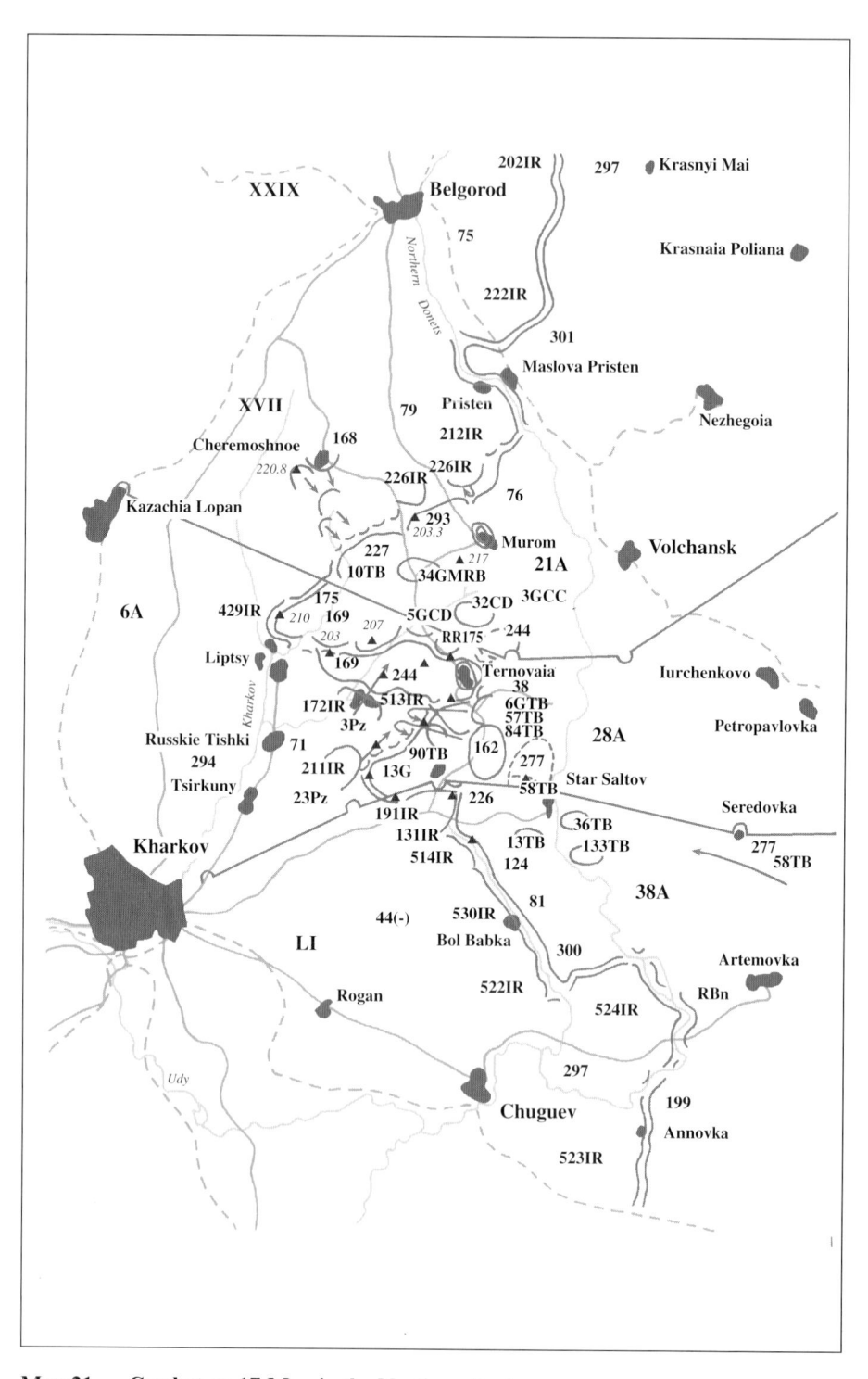

Map 21 — Combat on 17 May in the Northern Sector

5 The Course of Combat Operations

Gen M. F. Maleev's 5th Guards Cavalry Division, it occupied defences in the Hill 207, Kozlov and Bezbozhnyi sector.

Strong resistance by 5th Guards Cavalry Division and a 175th Rifle Division regiment located in Arapovka-Ploskoe halted any further enemy advance toward Murom. While the Germans were pressing their attack against 169th and 244th Rifle Division units, the 162nd Rifle Division went over to the offensive from positions between Hill 218.6 and Peremoga and attacked the flank of the German group, which was developing the offensive toward Murom. The enemy then turned part of his tanks from the Ternovaia region to strike the rear area of the 162nd Rifle Division. However, this tank group, in turn, suffered heavy losses from an attack by a tank group from the region of Hill 218.6 and Veseloe and from anti-tank artillery of Col A. I. Belogorsky's 6th Guards Cavalry Division and was forced to retreat.

On 17 May combat continued in very tense conditions, exacerbated by frequent interruptions in wire and radio communications. Thus, for example, technical communications between Gen Riabyshev, the army commander, and the 169th and 244th Rifle Divisions had already been broken on the morning of 17 May and were not re-established until the end of the day.

The uncertain situation and the absence of necessary tank support affected the offensive tempos of 162nd and 13th Guards Divisions. By the end of the day, having advanced a total of 2-3km, they occupied lines along the commanding heights adjacent to the western bank of the Bolshaia Babka River and halted their offensive.

On the night of 17–18 May, Col Afansiev's 244th Rifle Division units, having suffered heavy losses, were sent to the rear to be reorganised and refitted. The sector between 169th and 162nd Rifle Divisions was, in fact, defended only by 5th Guards Cavalry Division units.

By the close of 17 May, 28th Army's front ran along a line from Morokhovets through Hill 210, Hill 207.0, Kozlov, Arapovka-Ploskoe, Hill 218.6, Hill 207.2, and Hill 189.0 to Krasnyi.

The German offensive by 168th Infantry Division forces from the Ziborovka and Nechaevka region toward Murom against the right flank of 21st Army's shock group was unsuccessful and was stopped by units from Maj-Gen P. F. Lagutin's 293rd Division. However, this German attempt to strike the flank of Gen Gordov's 21st Army shock group prompted Marshal Timoshenko's decision to halt a further offensive by 21st Army forces and redeploy its shock group to new positions running from Krasnaia Alekseevka to Pylnaia. By the close of 17 May, 21st Army's divisions had gone over to the defence along a line running from the eastern outskirts of Grafovka, Sverkh Shamino through Hill 203.3 and Vergelevka to Pylnaia.

Meanwhile, the enemy offensive against the right flank of Gen Moskalenko's 38th Army was unsuccessful, and his army continued to defend its former positions along the western bank of the Bolshaia Babka River.

By the close of 17 May, Southwestern Front headquarters had received information from secret enemy documents captured by 38th Army's intelligence which made it clear that, since 11 May, the German command intended to begin preparing an attack by forces of 3rd and 23rd Panzer and 71st Infantry Divisions southeast from the Balakleia region toward Savintsy and Izium, and that they would begin this offensive between 15 and 20 May.

Although these had been captured on 13 May, they did not reach 38th Army headquarters until 17 May. The army commander, Gen Moskalenko, reported their content to the Southwestern Front chief of staff, Bagramian, by wire at 22.00 on 17 May.

Kharkov, 1942

A comparison of these German documents with the actual fact of a large enemy tank group offensive against the southern face of the Barvenkovo bridgehead led us to conclude that the German command did not intend to limit their offensive to operations against Southern Front forces, but rather intended to thwart the Southwestern Front's offensive and capture the entire Barvenkovo bridgehead. It was also clear that the German command would attempt to support the operations of its Southern Shock Group with a strike from the north in the direction of Savintsy and Izium.

Having reached the appropriate conclusion, Marshal Timoshenko called off the planned offensive on 38th Army's left flank and immediately ordered Gen Moskalenko to prepare a strong defence along the Savintsy axis in the existing army configuration. In addition to strengthening 9th Army with immediate reserves, Marshal Timoshenko decided to defend the approaches to the river crossing sites over the Northern Donets River in the Izium region with units designated to conduct 38th Army's offensive. He also decided to concentrate a strong tank grouping in the depth of the Barvenkovo bridgehead, which could prevent further German advance into the rear areas of Southwestern Front's shock group located in the Barvenkovo bridgehead and, after the penetrating enemy had been defeated, could restore the situation in Southern Front's 9th Army.

For this purpose, he ordered Maj-Gen Iu. A. Naumenko's 343rd Rifle Division, the 92nd Separate Tank Battalion and an anti-tank gun battalion, all in the Commander-in-Chief's reserve positioned behind 38th Army's left flank north of Izium, to concentrate in the Izium region, cross to the right bank of the Northern Donets River and take up defensive positions on the southern approaches to Izium.

He ordered the 6th Army commander, Gen Gorodniansky, to withdraw Gen Pushkin's 23rd Tank Corps from battle and transfer it immediately to the Bereka River line, where it would be resubordinated to Gen Podlas, the 57th Army commander. The tank corps regrouping was to be completed by the close of 18 May. At 00.35 on 18 May, Timoshenko transmitted instructions by radio to the 6th Army commander for the withdrawal of 23rd Tank Corps from battle.

After receiving the report about the commencement of the enemy's offensive, the Stavka of the Supreme High Command authorised Marshal Timoshenko to reinforce Southern Front's right flank by transferring Col A. M. Koshkin's 242nd Rifle Division from the Voroshilovgrad axis and by allocating 278th Rifle Division and 156th and 168th Tank Brigades from his Direction reserve.

Timoshenko expected the tank brigades to arrive in Radkovskie Peski by the morning of 20 May and the rifle divisions to arrive by 21–23 May.

Beginning on 18 May and until the operation ended, Timoshenko or Bagramian assigned missions to forces operating in the northern sector of the offensive by individual instructions, usually orally (by wire), to the army commanders.

Judging by captured documents, the German command was attempting to complete the operation against Northern Shock Group forces as quickly as possible in order to free up 3rd and 23rd Panzer Divisions which were operating there, and to send them to reinforce the Chuguev grouping for a subsequent attack on the Izium axis. Therefore, the measures Timoshenko undertook sought to prevent this manoeuvre and defeat the enemy by means of active operations by the limited forces of 28th and 38th Armies.

Timoshenko ordered these armies to renew their offensive on the morning of 18 May. Gen Riabyshev's 28th Army was to defeat the German group operating in the Veseloe, Arapovka-Ploskoe and Ternovaia region by means of a concentrated attack

5 The Course of Combat Operations

by 169th and 162nd Divisions and reach the Veseloe, Hill 205 and Petrovskoe region.

Col Matveev's 162nd Rifle Division, cooperating with the tank group, was to play the main role at this stage. Gen Riabyshev envisioned completing the destruction of the German group by committing units of Col V. G. Chernov's 277th Rifle Division, which had arrived in the Verkhnii Saltov region, and 58th Tank Brigade into 162nd Division's sector. Riabyshev assigned Col Dotsenko's 38th Rifle Division, reinforced by a 32nd Cavalry Division regiment, the mission of crushing the German garrison in Ternovaia and capturing this town.

The right flank formations of Gen Moskalenko's 38th Army were to go over to the offensive simultaneously with 28th Army's attack, with the mission of capturing Nepokrytaia and Peschanoe. To execute this mission, Moskalenko reinforced Col Tavantsev's 266th and Col Berestov's 124th Divisions with two tank brigades (Lt-Col I. T. Klimenchuk's 13th and Col Tanaschishin's 36th), which were replenished with matériel and had a total of 71 tanks. Units of Col Pimenov's 81st and the 300th Divisions received the mission of delivering a secondary attack against Peschanoe and Bolshaia Babka.

Thus, as a whole, Marshal Timoshenko's decisions resulted from a correct assessment of the operational situation and took the enemy's intentions into account. However, Timoshenko's decision regarding operations by the Northern Shock Group failed to take into account the actual condition of the German Chuguev grouping, which on 17 May was not only unable to deliver a secondary strike southward, but was also itself threatened with defeat by an offensive of part of 38th Army's left-flank forces.

In his memoirs Gen Bagramian recorded the frenzy of messages and telephonic consultations between headquarters, which intensified throughout 17 May and into the 18th as the reality of the German counter-offensive struck home in Red Army headquarters at all levels. After ordering Southwestern Front's 38th and 6th Armies to detach forces to deal with the crisis, at 16.00 Marshal Timoshenko sent Gen Malinovsky Combat Order No 0140/op, which required the Southern Front commander to gather reserves immediately, assigned him 2nd Cavalry Corps and insisted his Front attack 'at first light on 18.5' to repel the Germans and restore the situation in 9th Army's sector (see Appendix 7).[54]

At 17.30 on the same day, Timoshenko dispatched a report to the Stavka, which candidly related the day's unsettling events (see Appendix 8).[55] The report correctly assessed the German's intention 'to secure the Barvenkovo, Izium region and attempt to cut off [our] offensive on Kharkov from the south'. Timoshenko admitted that '9th Army units could not withstand the first enemy attack,' and admitted the Germans had already advanced up to 8km. In light of the situation's seriousness, the direction commander asked for additional reserves needed to repel the German advance. Within hours the Stavka assigned Timoshenko two rifle divisions and several separate tank brigades from RVGK reserve. It would take days, however, for these reinforcements to reach the battlefield.[56]

No sooner had the Stavka ordered this assistance to Southern Front than Gen Bagramian received more frightening news. Gen Moskalenko reported personally by telephone from 38th Army headquarters that operational documents seized from captured German soldiers indicated that, days before, German Sixth Army had been ordered to prepare 3rd Panzer, 23rd Panzer and 71st Infantry Divisions for a strike southward from Balakleia toward Izium to cut off Soviet forces in the Barvenkovo

Kharkov, 1942

bridgehead. Supposedly, the attack was to take place 15-20 May. This news and the day's events led Bagramian to 'the logical conclusion that the enemy intended to encircle all of our forces in the salient'.[57]

Bagramian later recounted his anxiety over the developing situation and his realisation that events were moving so quickly as to require an equally decisive response from direction headquarters. Despite Bagramian's supposed entreaties to act, Timoshenko 'limited himself to ordering the transfer of, first, 21st Tank Corps and, then, 248th Rifle Division from Gen A. M. Gorodniansky's 6th Army.' 'Semen Konstantinovich,' wrote Bagramian, 'thought that this force would be sufficient to restore 9th Army's defensive position. While doing so he repeated his initial order to Southwestern Front forces to continue their assault on Kharkov the next day.'[58]

Early on 18 May, by telephone, Timoshenko reported the actions he had taken to the Stavka. He ended the conversation by declaring that it was simply not possible to change 6th Army's and Army Group Bobkin's direction of attack to deal with von Kleist's thrust toward Izium. When Bagramian learned of Timoshenko's report to Stalin, he claimed he then turned to Direction Commissar Khrushchev for assistance. For a brief period, it seemed as if Khrushchev had succeeded in convincing Stalin to order Timoshenko to cease the Southwestern Front offensive. However, soon these hopes were dashed. According to Bagramian, 'Stalin, believing the personal assurances of Timoshenko that he could liquidate the threat in the Barvenkovo sector without diverting the main strength of 6th Army and Group Bobkin, rejected the suggestion.'[59]

Bagramian recalled that on that very day the new Chief of the General Staff, Col-Gen A. M. Vasilevsky, called him twice, asking anxiously what the chances were for defeating the German thrust. Bagramian answered that, in light of the shortage of reserves, the chances were poor.[60] The day before, just after the German attack had begun, Vasilevsky had already called his old friend, Maj-Gen A. F. Anisov, Chief of Staff of 57th Army, to learn of the situation. Anisov's depressing report prompted Vasilevsky to recommend to Stalin that the Southwestern Front offensive be halted and the Southern Shock Group be redirected southward. Stalin, having just been reassured by Timoshenko, told Vasilevsky that the situation was under control and the Southern Shock Group's offensive would continue.[61]

In his memoirs, Vasilevsky recalled phoning Khrushchev at 18.00 on 18 May for a fresh report. During the conversation Khrushchev told him that both Timoshenko and Stalin refused to halt the offensive and asked that Vasilevsky again intercede with Stalin. He did so, and once again Stalin refused to change his mind. Vasilevsky called Khrushchev back and asked him to speak with Stalin as a member of the Politburo. Khrushchev reached Stalin through Malenkov, another Politburo member, but Stalin's answer was the same.[62]

Despite these retrospective accounts of who was responsible for what, archival documents reveal that, at this time, all three members of the Southwestern Direction Military Council — Timoshenko, Khrushchev and Bagramian — approved and signed a report to the Stavka, which said nothing about abandoning the offensive on Kharkov. The report, No 0119, dated 00.30 19 May recounted the day's events in matter-of-fact fashion, scarcely noting the growing crisis on the Southwestern Front's right flank (see Appendix 9).[63] An hour and a half later, at 02.00 19 May, Commissar Khrushchev dispatched to Stalin a personal encoded radio transmission prepared by his assistant. The transmission related the course of combat in the Direction's sector, but again said nothing about the necessity for undertaking extraordinary measures to

5 The Course of Combat Operations

deal with von Kleist's attack (see Appendix 10).[64] From these reports it is obvious that either all three senior leaders agreed among themselves that the German threat could be dealt with successfully without postponing the Kharkov offensive or both Bagramian and Khrushchev were so intimidated by Stalin and Timoshenko that they did nothing to incur their wrath. In either case, the terrible consequences of their error would soon be apparent to them all.

Combat actions of 9th and 57th Armies on 18 May (see Map 22)
On the morning of 18 May, the enemy renewed his offensive from the Barvenkovo region against Velikaia Kamyshevakha and Malaia Kamyshevakha, and from the Dolgenkaia region against Izium and Studenok. The main forces of the German Panzer divisions (up to 150 tanks) advanced on Izium.

The crisis in Gen Kharitonov's 9th Army sector worsened as the German assaults intensified, and Timoshenko's order of 17 May for 2nd and 5th Cavalry Corps and the 14th Guards Rifle Division to counter-attack could not be carried out. Gen Pliev's cavalry corps was fully engaged, and the Germans had severed all remaining army communications with frontline forces. Therefore, Kharitonov had no control over any of his beleaguered forces.

A German account describes action on 18 May:

'With the Donets line gained, 257th Infantry Division and 101st Light Infantry Division took over the eastern flank cover for the deep thrust by the armoured striking groups, a thrust aimed at the creation of a pocket. The 16th Panzer Division, acting as the spearhead of Lieutenant-General Hube's striking force, drove through the Russian positions with three combat groups [Kampfgruppen] under von Witzleben, Krumpen and Sieckenius. They then drove on, straight through, into the suburbs of Izyum. At 12.30 hours on 18 May, tanks and motorcyclists of the Westphalian 16th Armoured Division were covering the only major east-west road crossing the Donets at Donetskiy. Combat group Sieckenius, the mainstay of which was 2nd Battalion, 2nd Panzer Regiment, turned left and drove on westward, straight into the pocket. The main blow of Operation 'Friderikus', however, was to be dealt by General of Cavalry von Mackensen with his III Panzer Corps. He attacked with 14th Panzer Division from Dresden in the centre and with the Viennese 100th Light Division and the Bavarian 1st Mountain Division on the right and left respectively. The Russians were taken by surprise and routed in the swampy Sukhoy Torets river. Barvenkovo was taken. A bridge was built. The 14th Panzer Division crossed over and pushed on toward the north. Eddying clouds of dust veiled the tanks. The fine black earth made the men look like chimney-sweeps.'[65]

Taking advantage of his superiority in combat equipment over Gen Pliev's 5th Cavalry Corps and Gen Dashevsky's 333rd and Lt-Col B. K. Aliev's 51st Rifle Divisions, the enemy penetrated the defence at the juncture between 60th and 30th Cavalry Divisions in the Dolgenkaia and Stepanovka region, developed the offensive northward and by 10.00 had captured the populated areas of Kamenka, Malaia Kamyshevakha and the southern part of Izium. A very tense situation existed in the Izium region, since Gen Naumenko's 343rd Rifle Division had still not managed to reach the area.

Units of Col V. S. Golovsky's 30th Cavalry Division and remnants of 12th, 15th and 121st Tank Brigades and the 51st Rifle Division withdrew from combat to the

Kharkov, 1942

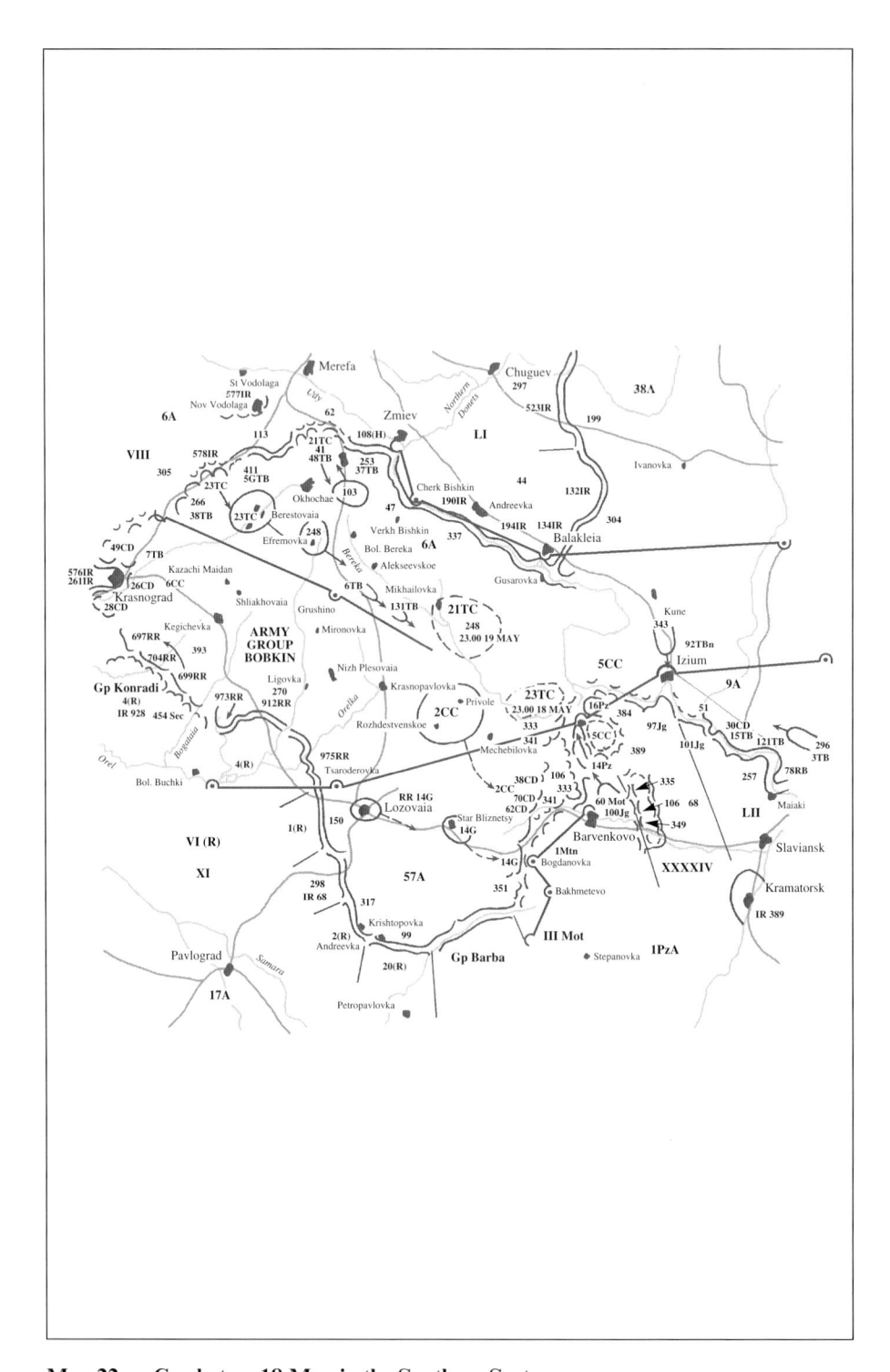

Map 22 — Combat on 18 May in the Southern Sector

5 The Course of Combat Operations

Northern Donets River and fought defensive battles in the Studenok, Bogorodichnoe and Bannovskii regions until the end of the day.

Personnel of 51st Rifle and 30th and 60th Cavalry Division units and the artillery regiments of these divisions displayed enormous heroism in these battles, but suffered heavy losses.

Late on 18 May, German forces completed their destruction of Soviet troops encircled near Malaia Kamyshevakha. The final struggle was personally led by General Podlas, the 57th Army commander, and his remaining staff. Podlas fell dead, along with his chief of artillery, Gen F. G. Mariarov, and the army commissar, Brigade Commissar, A. I. Popenko, near Kopanki Farm [Kholkhoz] and, according to eyewitness testimony, he was buried by the Germans 10 days after the battle in the forests near the farm. Podlas's chief of staff, Vasilevsky's friend Maj-Gen A. F. Anisov also perished, but it is unclear whether he died with his army commander or elsewhere.[66]

Officers and soldiers fought steadfastly for every inch of Soviet land. A company political officer of 51st Rifle Division's 348th Regiment, who was in charge of a 15-man group, held the enemy onslaught in check for 10 hours at the crossings north of Bogorodichnoe. Only after an order on the night of 18–19 May did the soldiers abandon their occupied positions and cross to the left bank of the Northern Donets River, carrying away with them the corpse of the heroic officer.

Subunits of 51st Rifle and 30th Cavalry Divisions held a small bridgehead in the region of Studenok. Fierce attacks by enemy infantry and tanks followed one after the other. Artillerymen in particular distinguished themselves in these battles. During a single day of combat, the Machine Gun Squadron of 30th Cavalry Division's 138th Cavalry Regiment killed 380 German officers and soldiers.

When darkness fell 9th Army forces abandoned the southern portion of Bannovskii and Bogorodichnoe and withdrew to the left bank of the Northern Donets River to protect personnel and equipment and to organise a defence along more advantageous lines.

As a consequence of these units' tenacious resistance, the enemy was unable to force the river in the Studenok and Izium sector. Therefore, his tanks, which had been advancing directly on Izium, changed direction and began to move west, along the right bank of the Northern Donets River.

By turning the main forces of his group from the Izium region to the west, the enemy cut off from the river crossings the remaining units of Gen Pliev's 5th Cavalry Corps and the remnants of 106th, 349th and 335th Rifle Divisions, which had linked up with them.

The German command committed its fresh 389th Infantry Division from second echelon against this group, which was continuing to defend stubbornly on a line from Novokamyshevakha to Kopanki.

The stubbornly resisting units of 5th Cavalry Corps withdrew to the northwest, and by the close of the day fought in the Dmitrievka region.

The swift advance by the enemy's mobile groups into the depth of 9th Army's defences created a threat to this army's airfields, as well as 6th Army's airfields, located in Izium and Petrovskaia. Because of their immediate evacuation, Southern Front's aviation was unable to affect substantively the course of combat operations. During the whole day, 9th Army's aviation flew a total of only 70 sorties.

By the end of 18 May, forces on 57th Army's right flank and in its centre occupied

Kharkov, 1942

their starting positions. Units of 14th Guards Rifle Division and 2nd Cavalry Corps, which had moved into the region of German penetration on the army's left flank, fought containment battles against the enemy along a front from Novo-Prigozhaia through Prigozhaia to Margaritovka.

9th Army forces lacked a continuous front. Isolated units, uncontrolled by army headquarters, waged defensive battles in the Riadnovka, Pavlovka, Kasianovka, Dmitrievka, Kopanki, Studenok, Bogorodichnoe and Bannovskii regions.

Combat Operations of Southwestern Front's Southern Shock Group on 18 May (see Map 22)

Poor staff work by Gen Gorodniansky's 6th Army delayed the receipt and execution of Marshal Timoshenko's order to withdraw 23rd Tank Corps from combat and, therefore, on the morning of 18 May, 6th Army continued its offensive in its existing configuration and in accordance with previous orders. Co-operating with units of Col Tavantsev's 266th Rifle Division, Gen Pushkin's 23rd Tank Corps continued to advance until noon on 18 May.

The enemy strongly resisted 6th Army formations along the entire offensive front, attempted to hold on to the line from Zmiev through Dudkovo, Shurino, Riabukhino, Kniazhnoe and Karavan to Kirillovka and sought to prevent the advance of Soviet forces to the Mzha River.

By noon, Gen Pushkin's 23rd Tank Corps units had captured the populated area of Karavan and halted its offensive, since by this time the order from Timoshenko to transfer the corps to a new axis had finally been received. At 12.00, that is 12 hours after the Commander-in-Chief's order had been sent, Pushkin began to withdraw two tank brigades from battle.

Meanwhile, Gen Kuzmin's 21st Tank Corps spent all day on 18 May penetrating the enemy defence along a line extending from Dzhgun to Krasnyi Gigant [Red Giant] State Farm and, by the end of the day, it had captured these points and was engaged in combat for Borki.

Army Group Bobkin was also unable to achieve decisive results. A forward detachment of Col T. V. Dedeogly's 49th Cavalry Division captured the Kirillovka and Vysokii region north of Krasnograd and fought in this area for the entire day. The remaining units of Gen Noskov's 6th Cavalry Corps with 7th Tank Brigade fully encircled Krasnograd and fought in the town proper. Units of 393rd Rifle Division captured Bogdanovka and Ogievka and, by the close of 18 May, continued to fight along this line. The positions of 270th Division remained unchanged.

On the whole, the situation in the Barvenkovo bridgehead became even more complicated during the battles on 18 May.

As was earlier indicated, after an unsuccessful attempt to force the Northern Donets River from the march, the German command turned the main forces of its shock group westward from the Izium region. This made the task of organising the defence along the left bank of the river easier for our forces. At the same time, it created an extremely hazardous situation on 57th Army's flank and a genuine threat that the enemy would force the Bereka River before the arrival of 23rd Tank Corps units.

In these circumstances, Marshal Timoshenko decided to withdraw Col Mishchenko's 248th Rifle Division and Gen Kuzmin's 21st Tank Corps from 6th Army into his reserve and transfer them to the Mikhailovka, Lozovskii and Lozovenka region. The concentration of two of the corps' tank brigades in this region was to have been completed by the close of 19 May, while the third brigade and the

5 The Course of Combat Operations

rifle division were to arrive 24 hours later.

According to Marshal Timoshenko's earlier order, on the night of 18-19 May Maj-Gen Naumenko's 343rd Rifle Division was to force the enemy out of the southern part of Izium and, while co-operating with Gen Pliev's 5th Cavalry Corps, protect crossings over the Northern Donets River and erect a defence on the southern approaches to the town.

Units of the newly arrived 296th Rifle Division and 3rd Tank Brigade, which were concentrating in Sviatogorskaia, were to cross the river into the bridgehead in the Studenok region and attack the flank of the German group in the direction of Dolgenkaia and Novo-Dmitrovka. At the same time, the 57th Army commander, Gen Podlas [already dead], was to prepare and execute a counter-attack using forces from his reserves (14th Guards Rifle Division and 2nd Cavalry Corps) from the Margaritovka region along the Sukhoi Torets River against Barvenkovo. Co-operating with approaching 23rd Tank Corps units, he was to begin to eradicate the enemy who was then advancing to the line of the Bereka River. Subsequently, when the main forces of 23rd and 21st Tank Corps approached the region, Timoshenko hoped they could defeat the entire German shock group and re-establish 9th Army's position.

Thus, Timoshenko finally decided to transfer the main shock forces of Southwestern Front's southern group to eliminate the enemy penetration opposite the front of 9th and 57th Armies. At the same time, however, he did not halt 6th Army's offensive, and on 19 May he reaffirmed the army commander's mission to continue the offensive in the direction of Merefa and capture the line of the Mzha River. To execute this mission, on 19 May he gave the 6th Army commander, Gen Gorodniansky, permission to commit to battle Col Ia. D. Chanyshev's 103rd Rifle Division from the second echelon.

The state of communications in and command and control of 9th Army forces during all of 18 May continued to be unsatisfactory. Having received information to this effect, the Stavka of the Supreme High Command categorically demanded that the Commander-in-Chief of the Southwestern Direction immediately rectify matters of troop control.

In its directive, the Stavka pointed out the impropriety of underestimating the value of radio communications in formation headquarters when troop control was based only on wire communications.[67]

The Stavka of the Supreme High Command categorically demanded that Front and army Military Councils use radio assets more extensively and that the 'radiophobia' that existed in some headquarters be decisively suppressed.

Combat Operations of Southwestern Front's Northern Shock Group on 18 May (see Map 23)

These combat operations on 18 May were unsuccessful. The offensive of Gen Riabyshev's 28th and Gen Moskalenko's 38th Armies was set to begin at 07.00 on 18 May. As a result of poor organisation of offensive preparations, however, it was not begun simultaneously. Only 38th Army began the offensive at the appointed time. Having successfully begun the attack, units of Gen Gorbatov's 226th and Col Berestov's 124th Divisions advanced 1.5-2km. General Moskalenko then ordered his tank brigades into the battle. Lt- Col Klimenchuk's 13th Tank Brigade reached the approaches to Nepokrytaia, was subjected to strong enemy air strikes and, after losing a large portion of its tanks, withdrew to its initial position.

On the 18th, enemy aviation flew no fewer than 200 sorties in 38th Army's sector.

Kharkov, 1942

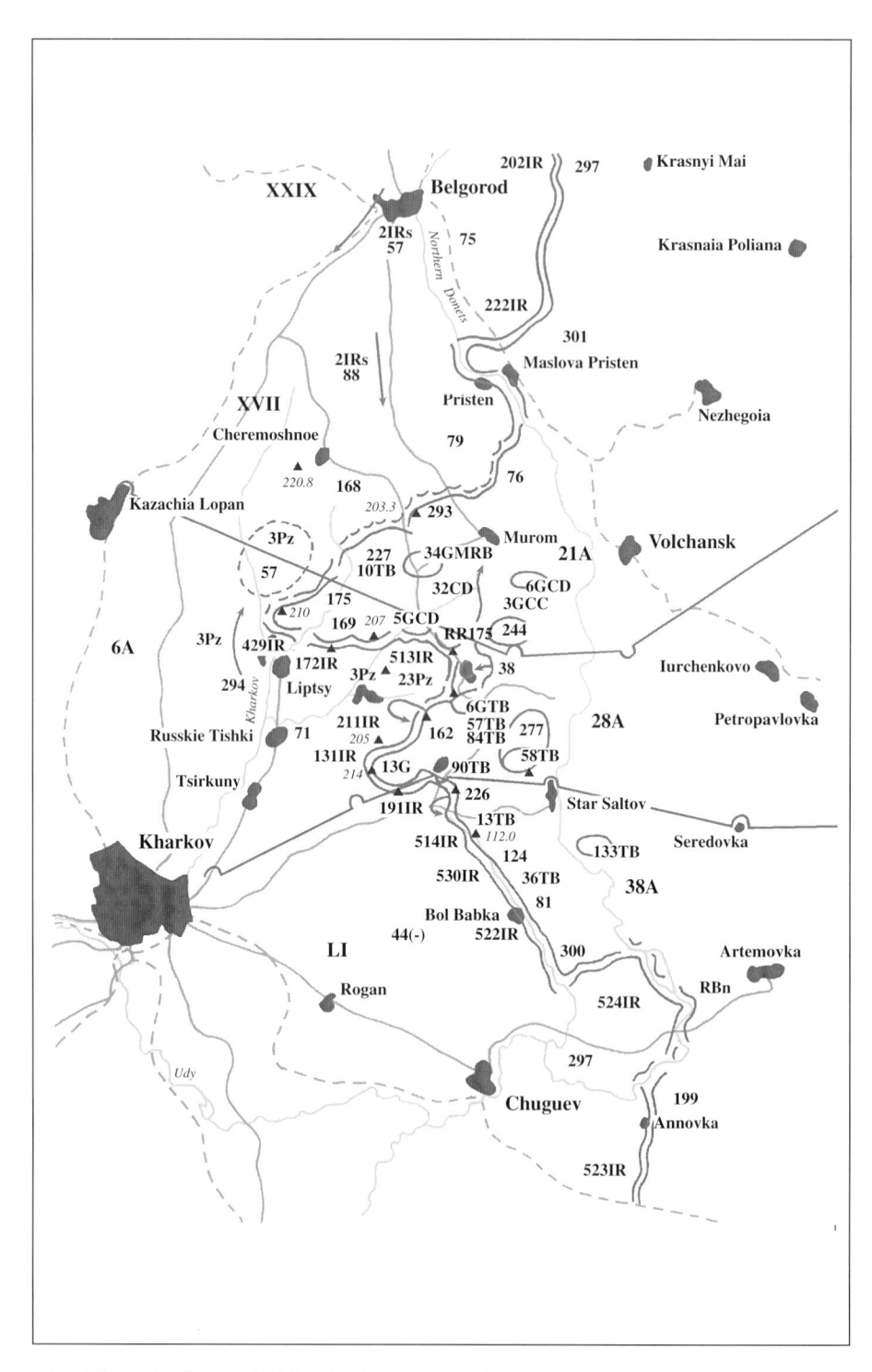

Map 23 — Combat on 18 May in the Northern Sector

5 The Course of Combat Operations

Col Tanaschishin's 36th Tank Brigade reached the area of combat operations only by the close of the day. Attempts by the 226th and 124th Divisions to continue their offensive with this brigade's support and to execute their assigned mission were not crowned with success. Operations by the 81st and 300th Divisions were also unsuccessful.

In his memoirs, Moskalenko vividly described the intent and course of his army's actions on 18 May and recounted the causes of his failure to achieve the mission assigned him by Marshal Timoshenko. 'It was clear,' he wrote, 'that the German-Fascist command was attempting to accelerate the completion of their operation against our northern group in order to free up and transfer the 3rd and 23rd Panzer Divisions to the Izium axis.'[68] Therefore, the renewed attacks by 28th and 38th Armies were essential. To achieve success where his forces had earlier failed, Moskalenko concentrated his 226th, 124th and 81st Rifle Divisions and three supporting tank brigades in a narrower offensive sector than before and ordered his left flank 199th and 300th Rifle Divisions to attack German positions in the Chuguev bridgehead. At a cost of heavy losses, however, these attacks penetrated only 1.5-2km before they ground to a halt. Moskalenko criticised his own operations as follows:

'As regards 38th Army, among the reasons for its lack of success, one must, in the first place, mention our mistakes and miscalculations. The decision to attack in a 26km sector was not well founded. Although we disposed of some information about the enemy in the forward region and in the immediate rear area, we lacked the necessary information about the strength of the enemy defence. We did not study the forces and equipment with which the enemy could reinforce the penetration sector from the depths and other quiet sectors of the front. In essence, we did not create sufficient strength to achieve decisive superiority on the most important axis.'[69]

The offensive of 28th Army's shock group finally began at 11.30. While attempting to go over to the offensive, however, Gen Rogachevsky's 169th Rifle Division was subjected to massed German air strikes and remained in its staging area.
 Co-operating with the special tank group, Col Matveev's 162nd Division advanced more successfully and by 16.00 had captured the region south of Veseloe. However, the enemy, taking advantage of 169th Division's passivity and without interference, concentrated up to an infantry regiment and 45 tanks in the Veseloe region, and at 19.00 delivered a strong attack against the flank and rear of 162nd Division's advancing units, forcing them to return to their initial positions.
 Col Chernov's 277th Division and the 58th Tank Brigade, which were earmarked to exploit a successful attack, did not concentrate on time in their assigned regions and did not take part in the battles.
 Exploiting the fact that the enemy had weakened the southern portion of its Ternovaia defences, on the 18th Col Dotsenko's 38th Rifle Division again encircled the enemy garrison there and began to destroy it.

Combat Operations of 9th and 57th Armies on 19 May (see Map 24)
On 19 May, forces of Gen Kharitonov's 9th Army continued to fight heavy defensive battles. As indicated above, as a result of the westward turn along the Northern Donets River of the enemy group advancing on Izium the remnants of Gen Pliev's 5th Cavalry Corps and other 9th Army formations were cut off from the river crossings.

Kharkov, 1942

Without centralised control, this group of forces broke out of encirclement on their own initiative. At dawn on 19 May, it arrived at the region of Zavodskaia and, with heavy losses, crossed to the left bank of the river.

Gen Naumenko's 343rd Rifle Division, which had approached Izium, was not ready to force the Northern Donets River, so was unable to carry out its mission.

296th Rifle Division with 3rd Tank Brigade, which was to cross to the right bank of the Northern Donets River and reinforce units of 51st Rifle and 30th Cavalry Divisions in the Studenko region, did not carry out this mission on 18 May. By 0900 on 19 May, forces which were occupying the bridgehead on the right bank of the Northern Donets in the Studenok region withdrew under enemy pressure to the left bank of the river in the Malaia Efremovka region.

By the end of 19 May, remnants of Gen Kharitonov's 9th Army had withdrawn to the left bank of the Northern Donets and occupied defences on a front from Protopopovka through Izium, Studenok and Prishib to Brusovka. Units of Col Shagin's 341st and Gen Dashevsky's 333rd Rifle Divisions, supported by the brigades of Gen Pushkin's 23rd Tank Corps, occupied defences at the juncture of 57th and 9th Armies in the Novonikolaevka, Krasnyi Liman, northern part of Grushevakha and Petrovskaia sector.

The enemy did not exhibit particular activity on 57th Army's front, and army forces remained in their former positions. On the morning of 19 May, Col Kovalev's 2nd Cavalry Corps went over to the offensive and, failing to encounter strong enemy resistance, by the end of the day reached a line extending from Zolotivka through Fedorovka to Grushevatskii, where it engaged in battle with the main forces of 60th Motorised Division.

Gen Pushkin's 23rd Tank Corps reached the line of the Bereka River not by the end of 18 May as planned, but during the second half of 19 May, at a time when the enemy had already reached the river and, by using forward detachments, had penetrated to its left bank in the Petrovskaia region.

Now, supplementary instructions from Marshal Timoshenko again changed 23rd Tank Corps' missions. Instead of delivering a counter-stroke against enemy units approaching the line of the Bereka River, by day's end the corps received an order to occupy defences along the left bank with its main forces and to drive the enemy out of the Grushevakha region with forces from one of its brigades.

Taking advantage of the inconsequential dynamism of our forces, on 19 May the German command regrouped its forces. As a result, all of the shock forces of Kleist's group — 16th and 14th Panzer and 60th Motorised Divisions — were brought forward to the line of the Bereka River and two infantry divisions (389th and 384th) were withdrawn into second echelon, deployed behind the panzer divisions. By the close of 19 May, the German shock group's main forces had concentrated north of Barvenkovo in the Velikaia Kamyshevakha, Petropole and Dmitrievka region.

Combat Operations of Southwestern Front's Southern Shock Group on 19 May (see Map 24)

Like 23rd Tank Corps, Gen Kuzmin's 21st Tank Corps received Marshal Timoshenko's instructions to withdraw from battle 8-10 hours late because of inadequate efficiency on the part of Gen Gorodniansky's 6th Army headquarters. Corps units began to withdraw from battle only at 10.00 on 19 May. Having begun their offensive with the tank corps' support, 6th Army's right flank had reached the southern outskirts of Zmiev by 10.00, but was unable to advance further because 21st Tank

5 The Course of Combat Operations

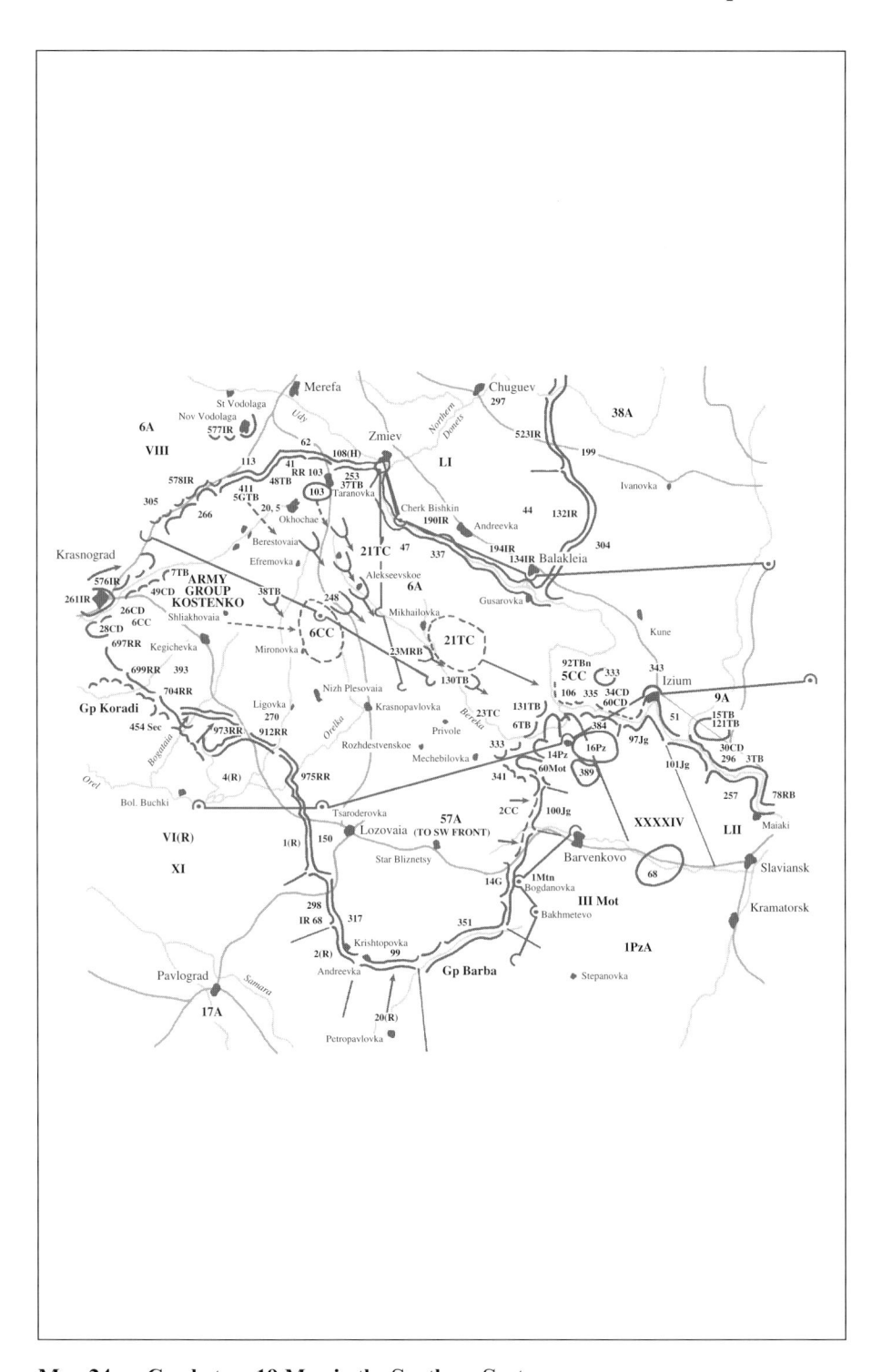

Map 24 — Combat on 19 May in the Southern Sector

Kharkov, 1942

Corps was withdrawn from combat.

6th Army formations were unable to relieve 21st Tank Corps in timely fashion during its withdrawal from battle. Hence, they were forced to enter battle piecemeal against an enemy which was counter-attacking in the sectors where tank corps units were being replaced.

Having been deprived of the greater part of his operational reserves, on 19 May Gorodniansky decided not to commit all of 103rd Division into battle, but committed only one regiment, while he kept this division's main forces in reserve. The commitment of this regiment stabilised the situation on the front, but did not provide for decisive development of the offensive.

From 15 to 19 May, 6th Army forces advanced 15-20km along the main axis. The depth of Army Group Bobkin's advance was 32km on the main axis, and 15-20km along secondary axes. During the entire offensive, the depth of advance of 6th Army forces on the main axis to Merefa and Kharkov was 28km, and that of Army Group Bobkin's forces was 60km. The overall offensive front was 145km, of which 55km were in 6th Army's offensive sector, 35km in 6th Cavalry Corps' offensive sector and 55km in the offensive sector of Army Group Bobkin's two left flank divisions.

After assessing the existing situation on 9th Army's front and 57th Army's left flank, on 19 May Marshal Timoshenko [finally] rejected the idea of continuing the offensive toward Merefa and Krasnograd, and decided to concentrate all forces of Southwestern Front's southern group to defeat the German grouping attacking from the Barvenkovo region.

The stark realities confronting Timoshenko by midday on 19 May finally forced him to admit that not only had his offensive failed, but the entire Southern Shock Group, together with the Southern Front's two armies in the Barvenkovo bridgehead, faced possible catastrophe. Timoshenko now accepted the course he had been rejecting for days — to commit the bulk of 6th Army's shock group in an attack to the south and southeast.

At 15.35 on 19 May, Timoshenko, with commissar Khrushchev at his side for moral support, telephoned Chief of the General Staff, Vasilevsky, in Moscow and, together, they sheepishly sought the Stavka's approval for their change in plans (see Appendix 11).[70] Timoshenko described 'the sharply worsening situation' along 9th Army's front and declared his intention '. . . without wasting time, to assemble all that it is possible, depending on our capabilities, for a blow to destroy the enemy grouping deployed around Izium'.[71] After Timoshenko provided details of the new plan, Vasilevsky asked for the timing of the operation. Satisfied with Timoshenko's assurances that the attack could begin late on 21 May or early on 22 May, Vasilevsky promised to raise the proposal with Stalin. Fifteen minutes later, at 15.50, Vasilevsky called Timoshenko back and gave him the Stavka's blessing to implement the plan 'quickly' (see Appendix 12).[72]

With Stavka approval at hand, at 17.20 on 19 May, Timoshenko transmitted Combat Order No 00320 by wire, which required all 6th Army and Army Group Bobkin formations to go over to the defence along existing lines [positions] and to begin to regroup their forces and carry out new missions (see Appendix 13).[73] A new Army Group was formed under the command of the Southwestern Front deputy commander, Lt-Gen F. Ia. Kostenko, who used the staff of former Army Group Bobkin for troop control, which consisted of all formations of former Army Group Bobkin as

5 The Course of Combat Operations

well as the 253rd, 41st and 266th Rifle Divisions, 5th Guards and 48th Tank Brigades, and part of the artillery assets reinforcing 6th Army. Timoshenko ordered Army Group Kostenko to assume the defence on 20 May along a front running from Zmiev through Karavan and Krasnograd to Sakhnovshchina and to withdraw the main forces of Gen Noskov's 6th Cavalry Corps into the reserve. At the same time, he ordered the new Army Group to employ a strong detachment to capture the Zmiev region and crossings over the Northern Donets River in the Cheremushnaia region.

The 337th, 47th, 103rd, 248th and 411th Rifle Divisions, 21st and 23rd Tank Corps, 37th Tank Brigade and six artillery regiments of the Supreme Command's reserve remained in General Gorodniansky's 6th Army. The army was to use 337th and 47th Rifle Division forces to defend the right bank of the Northern Donets River from Balakleia to Zmiev and, while holding on to crossings over the Bereka River, the army's main forces were to deploy covertly along a line running from Bolshaia Andreevka to Petrovskaia. After defeating the enemy's Barvenkovo group in co-operation with 9th and 57th Armies, the main force was to restore the situation on Southern Front's right flank.

Combat Order No 00320 also mandated that a force of four rifle divisions and two tank brigades on the left flank of General Moskelanko's 38th Army deliver a blow in the direction of Volkhov Iar, Andreevka and Zmiev to link up with forces of Army Group Kostenko, which was to attack toward Cheremoshnoe with part of its forces in the Zmiev region.[74] Marshal Timoshenko was counting on this attack to permit 38th Army's left flank to join up with Army Group Kostenko's right flank in the Zmiev region. Subsequent destruction of the German Chuguev group would thereby free up as many as five rifle divisions for subsequent operations against Kharkov from the south.

Timoshenko ordered Gen Pushkin's 23rd Tank Corps to occupy Petrovskaia and Grushevakha, and Gen Kuzmin's 21st Tank Corps to occupy Protopopovka and Zagorodnoe to protect the deployment of 6th Army's shock group along a front from Bolshaia Andreevka to Petrovskaia.

Combat Orders Nos 0141, 0142 and 0143, issued by the Commander-in-Chief of the Direction on 19 May 1942, specified missions for Southern Front armies (see Appendix 14).[75]

The [now leaderless] 57th Army, consisting of 150th, 317th, 99th, 351st and 341st Rifle Divisions and 2nd Cavalry Corps and reinforced by 38th Tank Brigade, which had been dispatched from 6th Army, was to continue to defend on the right flank and simultaneously prepare an attack from the line Novo-Prigozhaia against Vikino, enveloping Barvenkovo from the south using the forces of three rifle and three cavalry divisions and all reinforcing assets.

Having consolidated its positions on the left bank of the Northern Donets River in the sector from the mouth of the Bereka River through Izium to Studenok, Gen Kharitonov's 9th Army, consisting of 349th, 343rd, 106th, 335th, 51st and 296th Rifle Divisions, two regiments of 333rd Rifle Division, 49th, 34th and 60th Cavalry Divisions and four tank brigades, was to organise an offensive against Dolgenkaia from the Studenok region and, using part of its forces, clear enemy forces from Izium.

The series of orders which Marshal Timoshenko issued on 19 May were not only too late, they also probably hastened the destruction of his entire force in the Barvenkovo bridgehead. By evening, perhaps by intercepted Soviet radio transmissions, the German command seemed to know of Timoshenko's change in plans — in particular,

Kharkov, 1942

about his intent to relieve the pressure on Sixth Army. That night Hitler and von Bock conferred by telephone and:

'. . . quickly agreed it would now be a good idea to accomplish the whole original "Friderikus" by having the Army Group Kleist go the rest of the way from Petrovskoye to the Sixth Army line at Balaklaya. As soon as they had finished, Bock called Kleist's chief of staff, gave him the gist of what he had talked about with Hitler, and said he wanted Protopopovka, the next Donets crossing north of Petrovskoye, taken "under all circumstances and as soon as possible".'[76]

Combat Operations of Southwestern Front's Northern Shock Group on 19–20 May
On 19 May forces of Gen Riabyshev's 28th and Gen Moskalenko's 38th Armies attempted, in a somewhat altered grouping, to continue the offensive with their previous missions (see Map 25).

At 09.00 on 19 May, the Germans once again dropped paratroops and cargo from 11 transport planes in the Ternovaia region, attempting to reinforce their encircled garrison and to spread panic in 28th Army's rear areas. This time units of 38th and 175th Rifle Divisions destroyed a large part of the assault force.

At 09.30, 28th Army units began their offensive, but were unsuccessful as were neighbouring formations of Moskalenko's 38th Army. The enemy counter-attacking, supported by massed air strikes, forced all army units to return to their initial positions.

During the second half of the day, the enemy 168th Infantry Division units went over to the offensive in the sector of 21st Army's 293rd Rifle Division and pressed the division back from its defensive position to the western outskirts of Murom.

This forced the 28th Army commander, Gen Riabyshev, to cover his flank and rear from the direction of Murom with mobile group units, which had not yet been committed into battle. The commanders of 34th Motorised Rifle Brigade and 32nd Cavalry Division were ordered to erect defences in 21st Army's sector along a line from Piatnitsa to Novaia Derevnia. The 277th and 244th Divisions, the latter being re-formed and refitted, remained in the 28th Army commander's reserve.

Because of the increasingly complex situation in the Barvenkovo salient, Marshal Timoshenko categorically demanded that the 28th Army commander, Riabyshev, quickly defeat the German tank group to free up his forces so he could transfer them to reinforce the Southwestern Front's left flank.

Gen Riabyshev received orders from Timoshenko to begin the offensive on the morning of 20 May, but not to commit the 277th Rifle Division or 58th Tank Brigade into battle. Taking into account the experience of previous battles, in which the enemy forestalled army forces at the start of the offensive, Riabyshev ordered the attack to begin at dawn on 20 May. The principal aim was, as before, to defeat the enemy tank group in the Veseloe, Arapovka-Ploskoe and Ternovaia region.

The commanders of 21st and 28th Armies were rather optimistic in their assessment of the overall condition and intentions of enemy forces opposite the front of the Northern Shock Grouping. In their opinion, the enemy had suffered enormous losses in previous battles, and was exhausted and ready to halt his offensive. They reported this conclusion to Timoshenko. The 21st Army commander, Gen Gordov, did not receive instructions about the offensive and decided to use 20 May to bring his forces into order, replace their winter uniforms with summer ones and restricted himself to assigning the forces missions to improve their positions.

5 The Course of Combat Operations

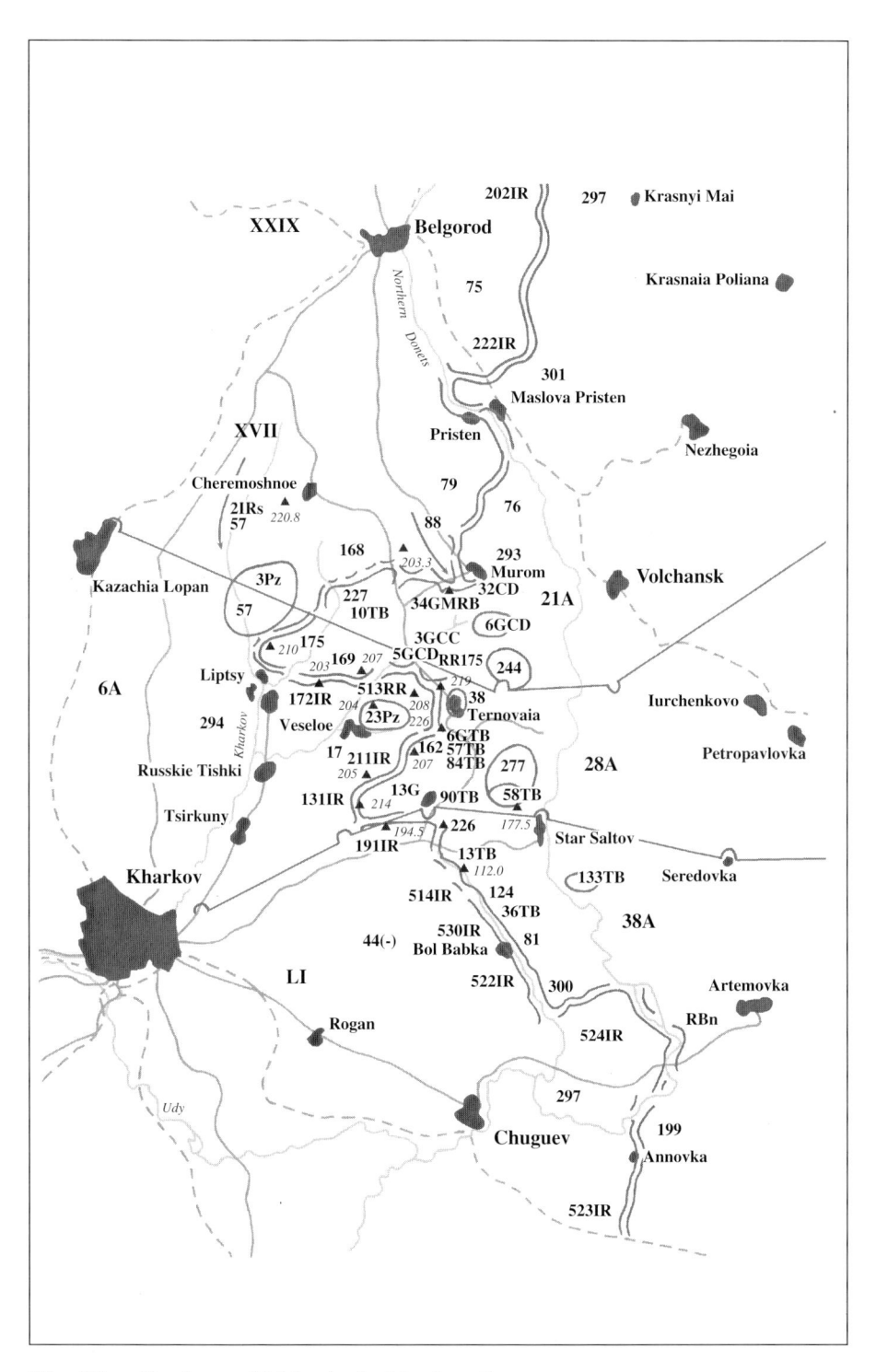

Map 25 — Combat on 19 May in the Northern Sector

Kharkov, 1942

The 21st and 28th Army commanders' perception of the enemy did not, however, correspond to reality. By the end of 19 May, the German command had concentrated Combat Group Gollwitzer (up to two regiments of 88th Infantry Division) in the salient which had been formed on 19 May between Murom and Vergelevka as a result of the withdrawal of 21st Army units, and had regrouped its forces opposite 28th Army's front. The essence of this regrouping was that in the region west of Morokhovets, 3rd Panzer Division (up to 40 tanks) and two regiments of 57th Infantry Divisions were transferred against the juncture of 21st and 28th Armies, while 23rd Panzer Division units (up to 100 tanks) and two regiments of 71st Infantry Division were shifted from the region west of Ternovaia to the Neskuchnoe region.

At first light on 20 May, 28th Army formations, with the exception of 175th Rifle Division, went over to the offensive and began to advance successfully (see Map 26). However, when they reached the region south of Neskuchnoe where the main forces of 23rd Panzer Division were concentrated, the advancing units were stopped by strong artillery, tank fire and air raids. At 12.00, the enemy set about implementing his counter-attack against units of 28th Army's 175th and 169th Rifle Divisions.

Under the pressure of enemy tanks and air attack, the latter operating continuously over the battlefield, these divisions began to withdraw eastward along the entire front, thereby uncovering the rear areas of 21st Army's formation.

At 17.00, Group Gollwitzer commenced its offensive, penetrated 21st Army's defences and captured the northwestern part of Murom.

In this situation Gen Gordov began to withdraw units of 227th Rifle Division and 34th Motorised Rifle Brigade from the pocket which had been formed and attempted to organise a defence along intermediate lines, but the hasty withdrawal of 28th Army's right flank formations thwarted these plans.

By the end of 20 May, all formations along the boundary flanks of 21st and 28th Armies had withdrawn 10-15km eastward with heavy losses. The front line of the Northern Shock Group ran across the central part of Murom to the south, along the western edges of the forests to Ternovaia and along the line of hills on the western bank of the Bolshaia Babka River. Ternovaia remained in enemy hands up to 21 May.

Having pressed 21st and 28th Army units to this line, the German Sixth Army command did not pursue the offensive further along this axis, and on 21 May it began to withdraw 3rd and 23rd Panzer Divisions from battle, sending them to the Liptsy region for subsequent transfer to the Barvenkovo salient.

The operations of 21st, 28th and 38th Armies during the subsequent period were limited to local battles to improve their positions. The 21st and 28th Armies' commanders, by order of Marshal Timoshenko, regrouped these forces in order to withdraw the 175th, 169th and 227th Rifle Divisions from combat and to replenish and refit all tank brigades in the second echelon.

Subsequently, a large part of the reinforcing artillery assets and part of 21st, 28th and 38th Armies' reserves were transferred to the Chuguev axis to reinforce 38th Army's left flank.

Thus, the offensive by Southwestern Front's Northern Shock Group concluded on 20 May (see Map 27). This offensive, which had begun successfully and promised to achieve great operational results, concluded unsuccessfully as a result of a number of mistakes made in the organisation and conduct of the offensive. Forces of the Northern Shock Group, having suffered considerable losses, were forced to withdraw under enemy attacks to their initial positions, having abandoned all territory captured as a result of the first three days of battle.

5 The Course of Combat Operations

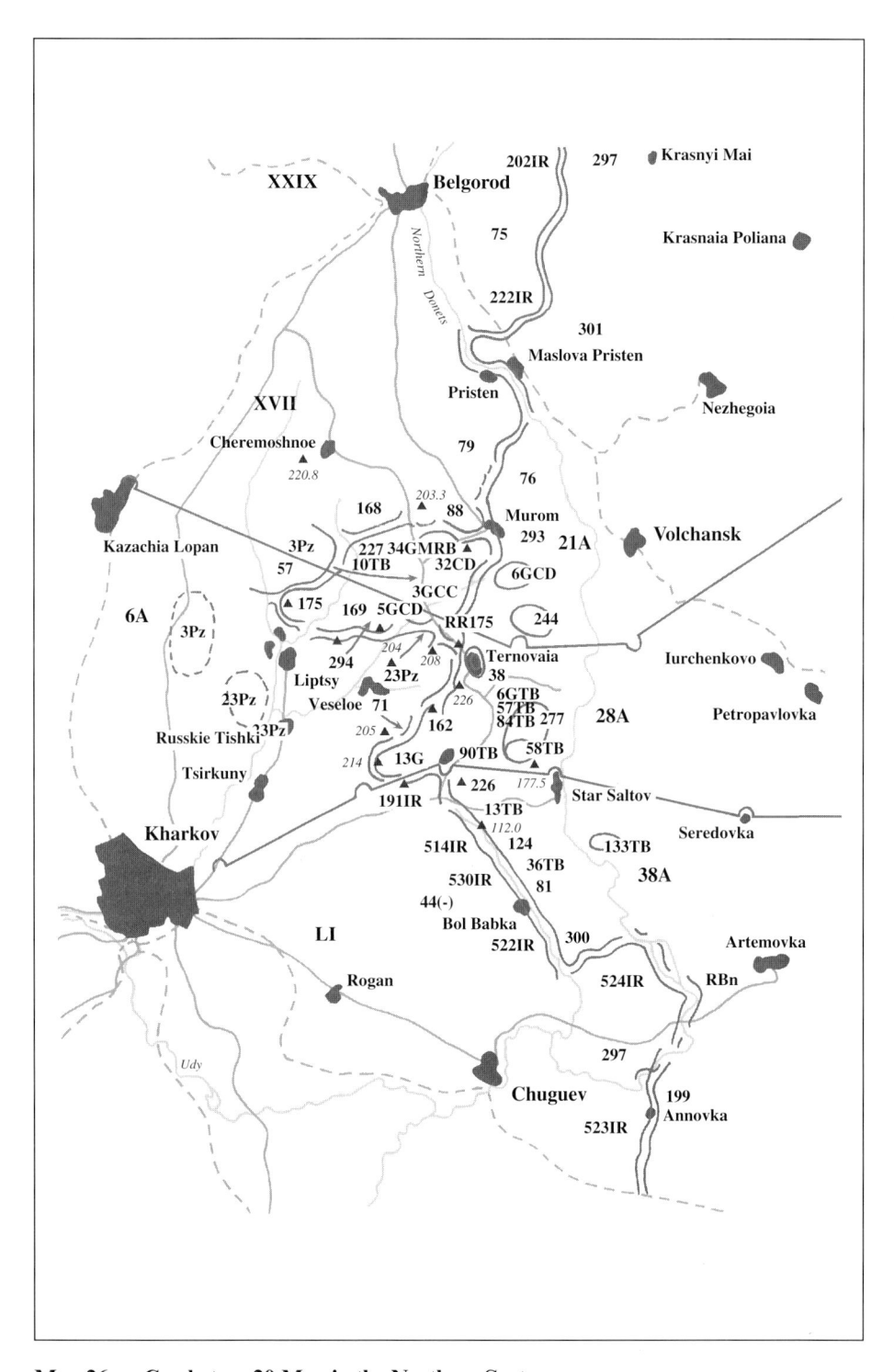

Map 26 — Combat on 20 May in the Northern Sector

Kharkov, 1942

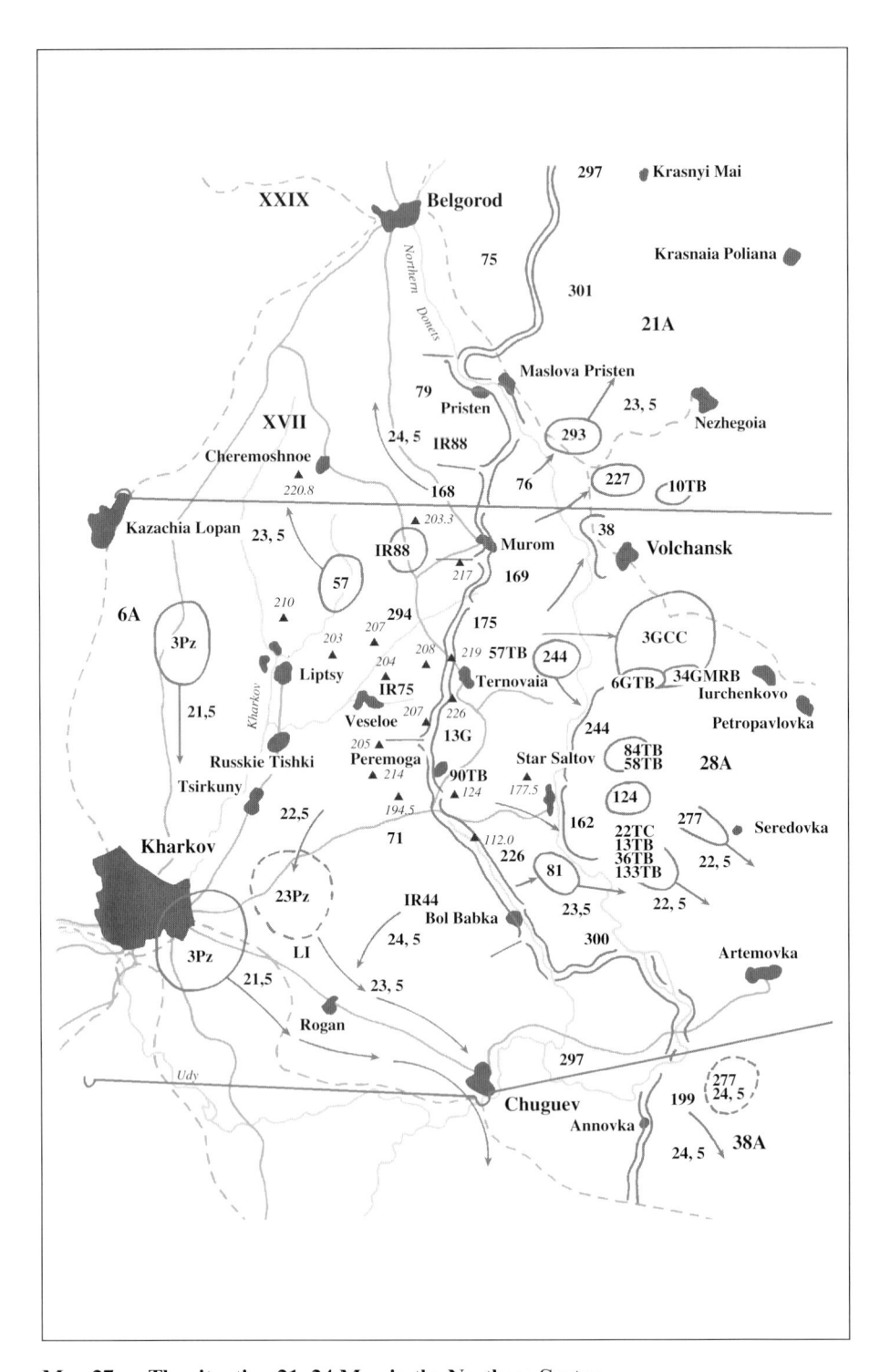

Map 27 — The situation 21–24 May in the Northern Sector

5 The Course of Combat Operations

The failure of the Northern Shock Group forces to execute their missions to destroy the enemy tank group permitted the German command to withdraw this group from battle and transfer it for operations on the Barvenkovo axis, which complicated the situation even more for our forces operating in the Barvenkovo salient.

2 Defensive Battles in the Barvenkovo Salient (20–24 May 1942)
Combat operations on 20 May (see Map 28)
On the night of 19-20 and during the whole of 20 May, forces of Army Group Kostenko and Gen Gorodniansky's 6th Army regrouped. The withdrawal of units from battle and their arrival in concentration areas were complicated by increased enemy activity. Inadequate energy in staff work and imprecise assignment of missions to the forces when organising the march to new areas led to a delay in the deployment of 6th Army forces along the line from Bolshaia Andreevka to Petrovskaia.

Decisive events unfolded on 20 May on the left flank of Gen Kharitonov's 57th Army. Successful operations along this axis on 19 May by Col Kovalev's 2nd Cavalry Corps had filled the German command with apprehension concerning the possible development of a counter-attack by Soviet forces against Barvenkovo, into the rear of the enemy's shock group. Therefore, on the night of 20 May the German command transferred 16th Panzer Division from the Velikaia Kamyshevakha, Petropole and Vernopole region to a line from Molochnyi to Danilovka.

On the morning of 20 May, this division, co-operating with 100th Light Infantry and 1st Mountain-Rifle Division units, went over to the offensive and broke through 2nd Cavalry Corps' front, capturing Bolshaia Andreevka by 12.00.

Developing the attack, the enemy reached the line Malinovka, Bratoliubovka, Fedorovka, Ivanovka, Rozhdestvenskoe, Ianovichivka and Egorovka by the close of 20 May. The enemy penetration to the Lozovaia region posed a threat of encirclement to the divisions which were defending south of Lozovaia. To eliminate this threat, the 57th Army commander took part of his forces from the 99th and 150th Rifle Divisions sectors in the Andreevka and Rybakova regions, and transferred them to Bratoliubovka where, jointly with other defending units, they stopped any further enemy advance.

On the night of 20 May, Gen Kuzmin's 23rd Tank Corps prepared defences in its designated sector along the left bank of the Bereka River, and one of its brigades fought for possession of Petrovskaia, forcing the enemy out. However, 131st Tank Brigade, which had carried out this mission, concentrated in Marevka without having left adequately strong security in Petrovskaia; this made it possible for the Germans to reoccupy the town on the morning of 20 May and, by exploiting the offensive of their tank units, to capture Zagorodnoe.

At 13.00 on 20 May, German 60th Motorised Division captured Mechebilovka, Novosemenovka, Novonikolaevka and Krasnyi Liman; however, its attempts to cross the Bereka River from the march were repelled. 23rd Tank Corps' 6th and 131st Tank Brigades halted the enemy, and battles along a line from Fedorovka through Semenovka to the northern outskirts of Krasnyi Liman continued until the close of 20 May.

On the morning of 20 May, using forces of 257th and 384th Infantry and 97th and 101st Light Infantry Divisions, the enemy went over to the defence in front of 9th Army forces on the front extending from Srednii through Zavodskoi, Donetskii, Studenok, Bogorodichnoe and Prishib to Brusovka.

On the night of 20 May, Gen Naumenko's 343rd Rifle Division, advancing from the

Kharkov, 1942

north, captured crossings over the Northern Donets River in the southern part of Izium, and at 13.00 on 20 May it drove the enemy out of the town toward Donetskii.

At the same time, 296th Rifle Division units seized a small bridgehead in the Studenok region and during the day they fought to widen it.

Soldiers and officers of the 2nd Battalion of this division's 252nd Rifle Regiment distinguished themselves in battles for crossings in the Studenok region.

Forty men from the battalion led by Senior Lieutenant Samokhvalov and Senior Political Officer Bogdanov completely cleared Studenok of the enemy. During the day they repelled more than 10 fierce attacks of superior enemy forces supported by 30 tanks and held on to the bridgehead in this area. These battles meant that 57th Army forces had stopped the enemy offensive on their left flank by the close of 20 May and, while mainly covering the axis toward Lozovaia, they continued to repel enemy attacks on the front from Odanetskii through Barbalatovo, Malinovka, Serefimovka, Nadezhdino, Mikhailovka and Smirnovka to Rozhdestvenskoe; they also continued to defend their existing positions on the right flank and in the centre.

At the juncture of 57th and 9th Armies, 6th Army forces, while repelling attacks by German infantry and tanks, by day's end held the line Nadezhdovka, Fedorovka, southern outskirts of Semenovka, northern outskirts of Krasnyi Liman.

Having withdrawn to the left bank of the Northern Donets River, 9th Army forces went over to an active defence along the entire front, simultaneously attempting to improve their position in the Zagorodnoe, Izium and Studenok regions.

Late on 20 May, based on the day's successes, both von Bock and von Kleist reached a final series of decisions which determined the remaining course of battle and inexorably sealed the fate of Timoshenko's force in the Barvenkovo bridgehead. Succinctly put by the doyens of German military history, Earle Ziemke and Magna E. Bauer:

'The 14th Panzer Division took Protopopovka on the 20th, which reduced the mouth of the bulge between there and Balakleya to twelve miles. The bridgehead was then 8 miles wide but only a mile or two across. The III Panzer Corps main force, still on the westward orientation, gained almost twelve miles, however, with disappointing results. The object was to smash Fifty-seventh Army in the western end of the bulge, but the outer ring of the front there was held by Romanian divisions and they showed little determination and less enthusiasm. One of the Romanian division commanders had sent himself home on leave when he heard the attack was about to start. Having an alternative that he also preferred, Kleist began turning the 16th Panzer Division, 60th Motorised Division and 1st Mountain Division around after dark and sending them into the Bereka bridgehead behind 14th Panzer Division. On Bock's urging, Paulus agreed to shift the 3rd and 23rd Panzer Divisions south from the Volchansk salient and thus partially to reconstitute his former 'Friderikus' force. Bock observes, ". . . tonight, I have given orders aimed at completely sealing off the Izyum bulge. Now everything will turn out well after all!" '[77]

Combat operations on 21 May (see Map 29)
On the night of 20–21 and during the whole of 21 May, 9th and 57th Army forces fought successfully along occupied lines and regrouped. Timoshenko, considering the danger which had been created by enemy penetration of 9th Army's defensive front and his penetration into our dispositions beyond the Bereka River, decided to trun-

5 The Course of Combat Operations

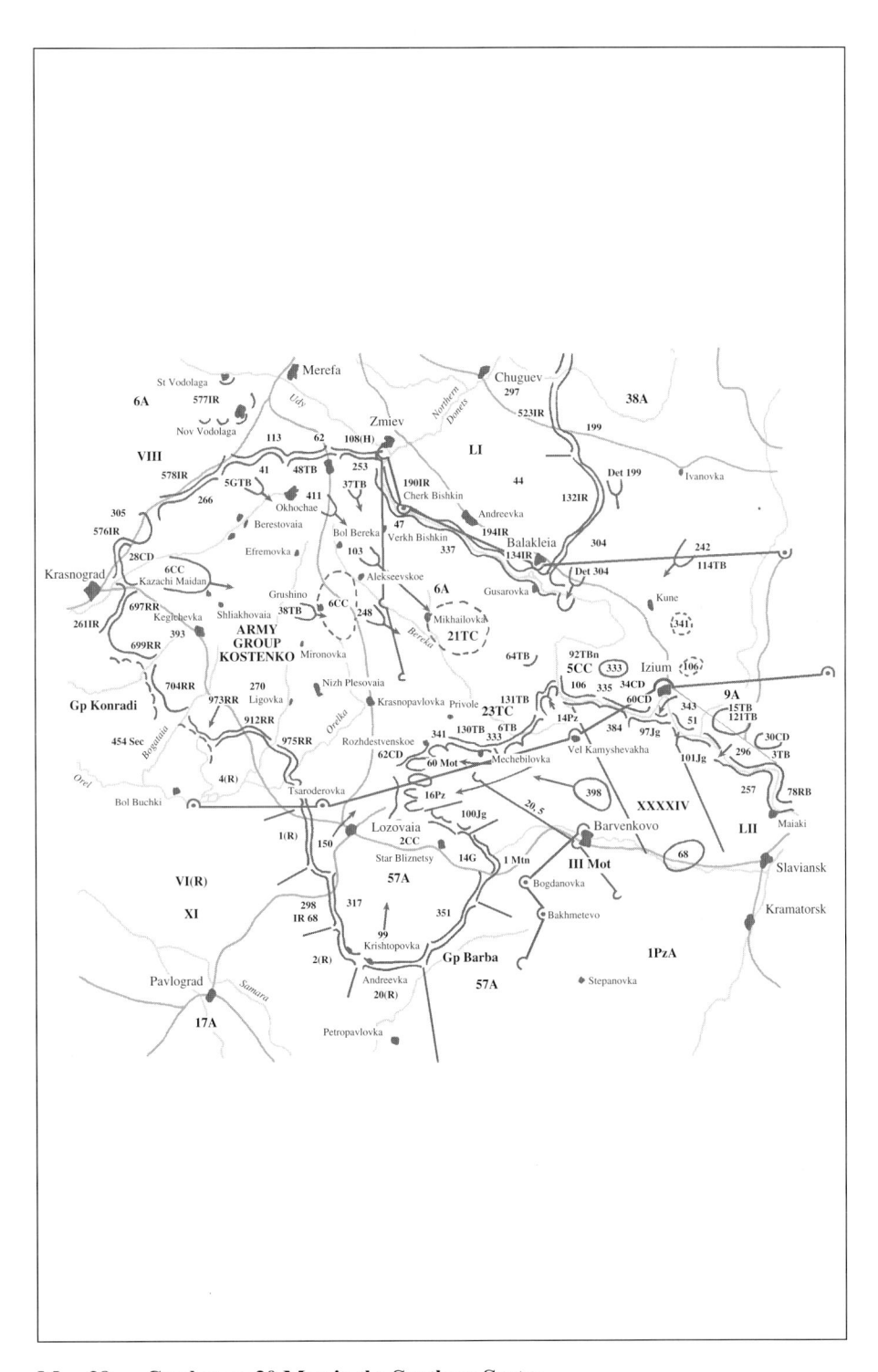

Map 28 — Combat on 20 May in the Southern Sector

Kharkov, 1942

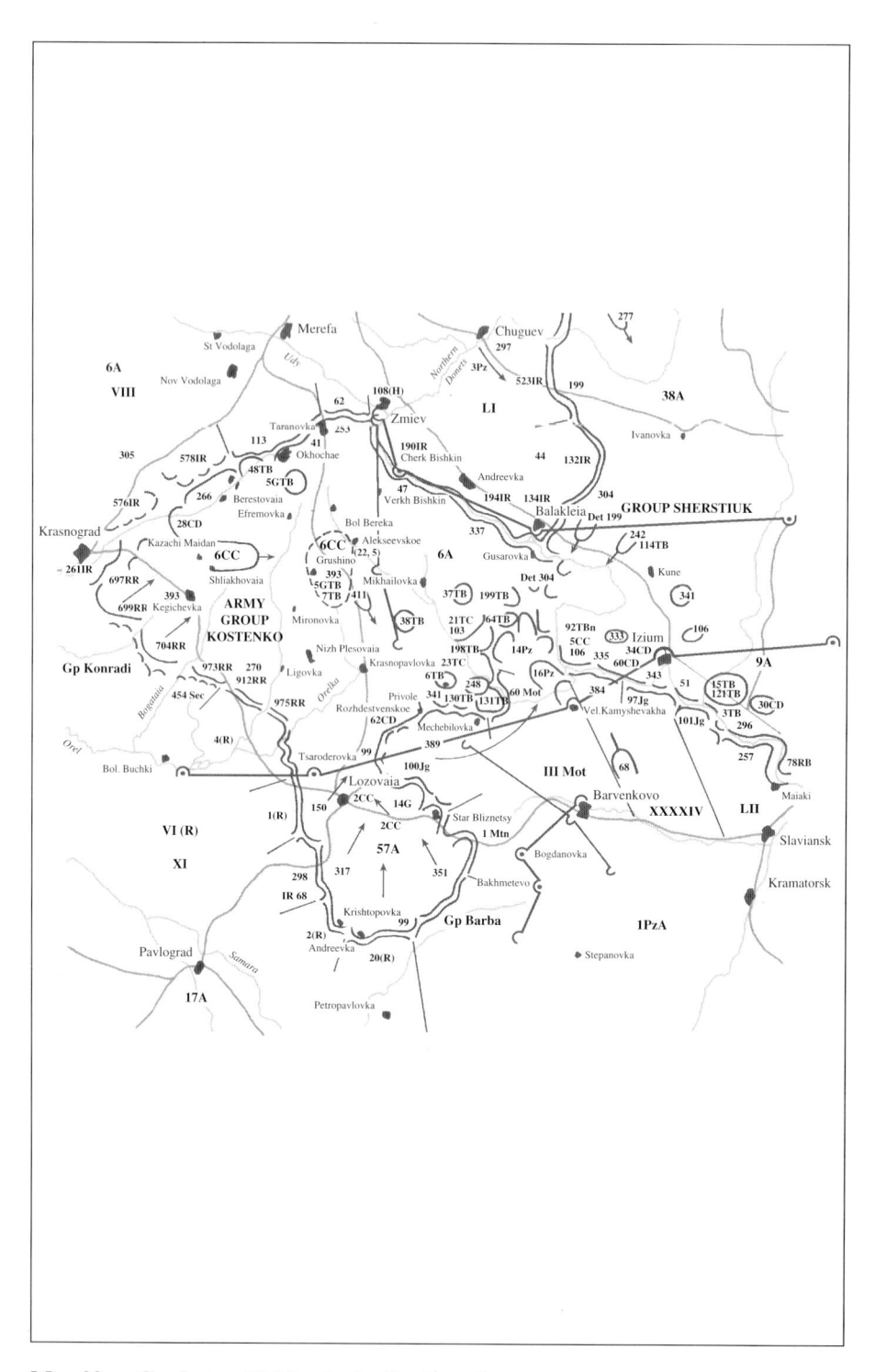

Map 29 — Combat on 21 May in the Southern Sector

5 The Course of Combat Operations

cate the front line of Army Group Kostenko and 57th Army forces to a maximum, thereby creating powerful reserves.

To this end, Army Group Kostenko forces were ordered to withdraw to the line Taranovka, Efremovka, Ligovka and Veselaia by the close of 22 May, and to place 6th Cavalry Corps, 393rd Rifle Division and 5th Guards and 7th Tank Brigades in the group's reserve in the Alekseevskoe region.

Continuing to hold onto their former positions on the right flank, 57th Army forces were to withdraw part of their strength (317th, 99th and 351st Rifle Divisions) to a front running from Uplatnoe through Rudaevka to Smirnovka by the close of 22 May. On 21 May all of these units were moving toward their assigned positions and fighting defensive battles.

At the same time, Marshal Timoshenko took measures to prepare an attack from the line Nadezhdovka to Petrovskaia, planned for the morning of 23 May using 6th Army forces in co-operation with 9th and 57th Armies, to defeat the enemy group which was advancing from the Barvenkovo region.

He ordered the 6th Army commander, Gen Gorodniansky, to start the offensive with his tank corps, clear the enemy from Petrovskaia and Zagorodnoe and protect the deployment of the army's shock group along a line running from Krasnopavlovka to the Bereka River. The 411th, 248th and 103rd Rifle Divisions, earmarked for participation in the offensive from this line, were transferred from the Taranovka and Okhochae region. By the close of 20 May, the forward units of these divisions arrived in the Alekseevskoe region.

On 21 May the Germans began to transfer 23rd and 3rd Panzer Divisions from Kharkov to deliver an attack from the Andreevka region against Chervonyi Donets and link up with Group Kleist.

At the same time, having concentrated two Panzer divisions (14th and 16th), one motorised division (60th) and two infantry divisions (389th and 384th) in the Petrovskaia, Krasnyi Liman and Novonikolaevka region, the Germans attacked powerfully to the north. By the close of the day, German infantry and tanks had succeeded in seizing Marevka and joined battle for Protopopovka. 6th Army units repelled German attempts to penetrate to Dmitrievka and Katerinovka.

In the late afternoon of 21 May, Timoshenko ordered yet another attempt to rescue the beleaguered 6th Army, this time from the left flank of Gen Moskalenko's 38th Army opposite German defences in the Chuguev bridgehead. His order required Moskalenko to concentrate a large force between Pechenegi and Balakleia and attack to clear German forces from the bridgehead and link up with Gorodniansky's 6th Army forces attacking toward the Northern Donets River from the west (see Appendix 15).[78] The air of unreality which permeated Timoshenko's headquarters was apparent as he ordered Moskalenko to use his 22nd Tank Corps to spearhead his attack. The corps had never existed as a single unit, and its component brigades were already weakened from their participation in earlier operations. Obviously, Timoshenko was grasping at straws, and the attack had no chance of success, nor could it even be launched. Moskalenko, noting that the content of the order was preposterous and that it was soon rescinded, added wryly:

'Shortly after issuing the order, the Front staff reached the conclusion that 38th Army forces could not reach the designated region. For that reason it was cancelled. The order and its history should be of definite interest for analysts, since it can help them

Kharkov, 1942

better understand the acuteness and complexity of existing conditions.'[79]

However, Timoshenko believed enough in Moskalenko's chances to include a description of the planned attack in a report he sent late that day to the Stavka (see Appendix 16).[80] Combat Report No 00323/op, dated 19.00 21 May and signed by all three Southwestern Direction Military Council Members, related the day's events and outlined Timoshenko's plans for relieving the German pressure on 'heavily battered units of 6th Army'. His last paragraph described the planned attack by 38th Army, which was to commence on the morning of 23 May.

Almost immediately after dispatching the report of the Stavka, however, Timoshenko realised his folly and rescinded the order. Within hours, on 22 May he would conjure up yet another relief attempt by 38th Army, only this time with a reduced force.

Combat Operations on 22 May (see Map 30)
On 22 May the enemy delivered his main attacks — to the north against Chepel using formations from Group Kleist and to the south from the Chuguev salient employing units of 23rd and 3rd Panzer Divisions — in order to link up with Group Kleist so that both of these groups would reach the lines of communication of our forces operating in the Barvenkovo salient.

Having concentrated up to 230 tanks of 14th and 16th Panzer Divisions in the Protopopovka and Zagorodnoe region on the night of 22 May, the Germans renewed their offensive on the morning of 22 May in the general direction of Chepel and Volobuevka. By the close of the day, having penetrated deeply into our forces, the Germans reached a front running from Chepel through Volobuevka, Gusarovka, Shevelevka, Aseevka, Novopavlovka, Zapolnyi and Krasnaia Balka to Marevka.

A German account cryptically recorded the day's actions and correctly identified the perilous consequences for Timoshenko's command:

'In co-operation with the Panzer companies of Combat Group Sieckenius, the Bereka River was crossed. Soviet armoured thrusts were successfully repulsed. In the afternoon of 22 May, 14th Panzer Division reached Bayrak [south of Balakleia] on the northern Donets bend.

'This was the turning point. For across the river, on the far bank, were the spearheads of Sixth Army — companies of the Viennese 44th Infantry Division, the "Hock-und-Deutschmeister". With this link-up, the Izyum bulge was pierced and Timoshenko's armies, which had driven on far westward, were cut off. The pocket was closed.

'Too late did Timoshenko realise his danger. He had not expected this kind of reply to his offensive. Now he had no choice but to call off his promising advance to the west, turn his divisions about, and attempt to break out of the pocket in an easterly direction, with reversed fronts. Would the thin German sides of the pocket stand up to such an attempt? The decisive phase of the battle was beginning.'[81]

Subsequent action would bear out this peril.

During the second half of 22 May, the Germans, using forces of their Chuguev grouping, forced the Northern Donets River in regions south of Andreevka and Balakleia,

5 The Course of Combat Operations

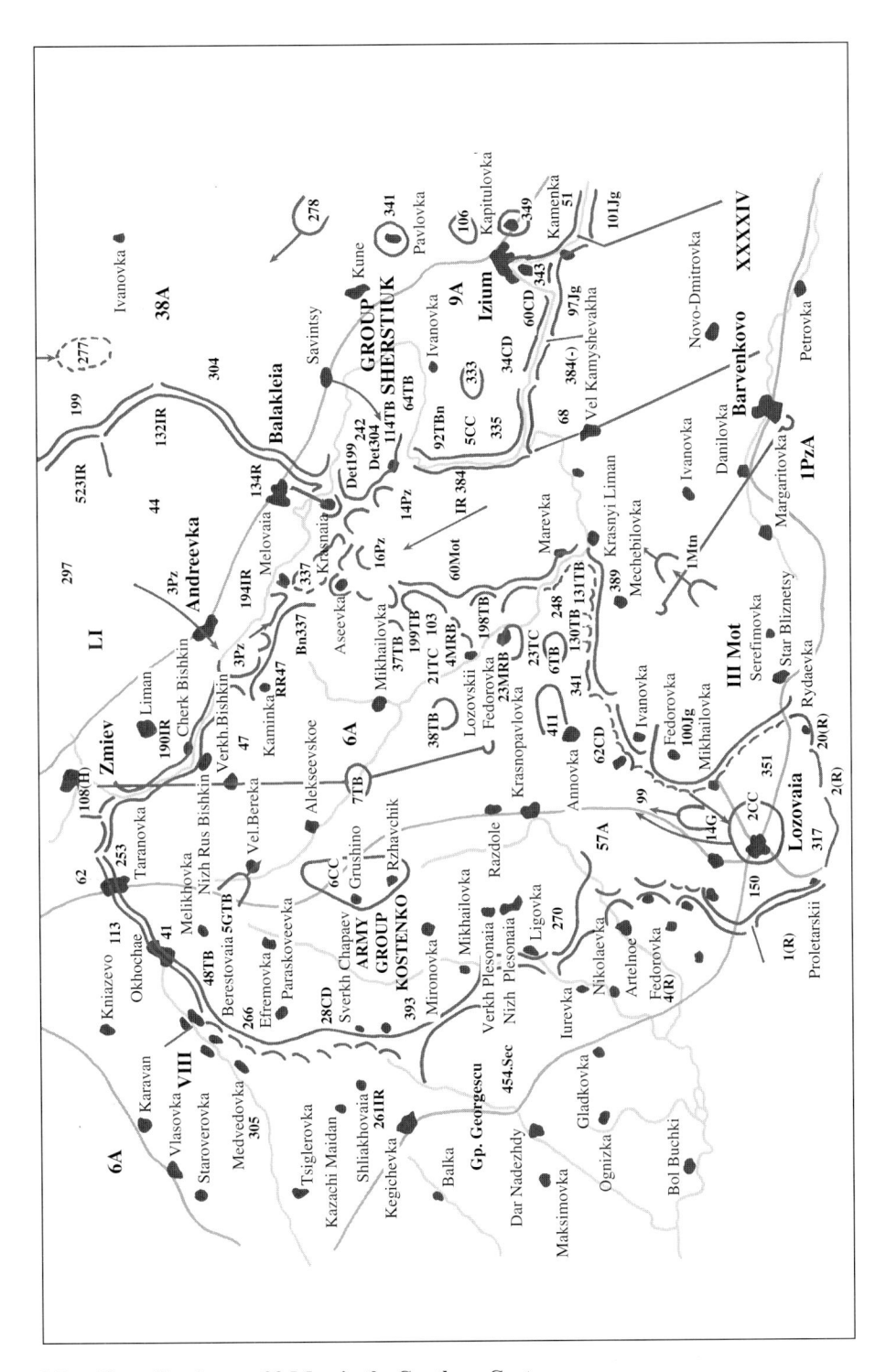

Map 30 — Combat on 22 May in the Southern Sector

Kharkov, 1942

seized the bridgehead and, having crossed the forward units of 3rd and 23rd Panzer Divisions, commenced an offensive to the south.

The defensive front of Col Vasilev's 337th and General Matykin's 47th Rifle Divisions, which were along the right bank of the Northern Donets, were torn to pieces by German tank attacks, and the divisions were forced to fight heavy battles in encirclement. [Both Vasilev and Matykin died in the struggle, along with most of their staffs.]

On the evening of 22 May, the German offensive to the south from the Andreevka region was halted along a line running from Glazunovka to Shebelinka by withdrawn 337th and 47th Division units, and by 47th Division's reserve regiment.

As a result of the German capture of crossings over the Northern Donets in the Chervonyi Donets and Krasnaia Gusarovka sector, all of our forces' lines of communication in the Barvenkovo salient were severed.

Considering the existing situation, in the middle of 22 May, Marshal Timoshenko decided to use 38th Army's shock group, which earlier had been designated for an offensive from the Volkhov Iar region against Andreevka and Zmiev, to defeat the German tank group which was penetrating into the Savintsy region and to restore our forces' lines of communication along this axis.

Marshal Timoshenko's new plan called for a concerted breakout to the west from the Barvenkovo bridgehead by the combined remnants of 6th and 57th Armies, now designated as the 'Southern Group' and commanded by Lt-Gen Kostenko. Timoshenko ordered Gen Moskalenko of 38th Army to organise a relief force to fight its way through German lines west of the Northern Donets River and link up with Kostenko's Southern Group. At midday on 22 May, Moskalenko and his commissar, Brigade Commissar V. M. Laiok, visited the headquarters of the designated commander for the new relief force, Maj-Gen G. I. Sherstiuk, the 38th Army Deputy Commander. He ordered Sherstiuk 'to cross the Northern Donets River near Savintsy and, in co-operation with Front reserves, destroy the enemy tank group in the Chepel region, and re-establish communications with 6th and 57th Armies'.[82] To accomplish the task, Moskalenko subordinated to Sherstiuk's command the 242nd Rifle Division and 114th Tank Brigade, which had assembled in the region as a result of Timoshenko's earlier abortive offensive plans for 38th Army forces. Two other tank brigades (3rd and 15th), which the Stavka promised to provide from its reserves, never did arrive.

General Sherstiuk's shock group, which consisted by this time of Col A. M. Koshkin's 242nd Rifle Division and Lt- Col I. V. Kurilenko's 114th Tank Brigade, in early afternoon crossed to the right bank of the Northern Donets in the Savintsy region, subordinated to itself the remnants of 64th Tank Brigade [of Gen Kuzmin's 21st Tank Corps], which had withdrawn from the Chepel region, and, with an energetic attack, drove the enemy out of Chepel; however, it was unable to develop the offensive further, and went over to the defence along a line from Shchurovka to Chepel.

By the close of 22 May, Army Group forces were carrying out their order to withdraw to the line Paraskoveevka, Pisarevka, Mikhailovka and Ligovka.

As a result of attacks by Romanian units along the front from Novo-Aleksandrovka through Nikolaevka, Sverkh. Kommunist and Tsaredarovka to Udarnik against Army Group Kostenko's 270th Rifle Division and 57th Army's 150th Rifle Division, the enemy captured Artelnoe, Mikhailovka, Sverkh. Kommunist, Udarnik and Novo-

5 The Course of Combat Operations

Uplatnoe. By the close of the day, 270th Rifle Division units had taken up the defence along a line from Zheltye Zori to Veselaia; 57th Army's right flank formations had withdrawn to the line Tsaredarovka, Proletarskii, Uplatnoe, Rudaevka and Mikhailovka. The breech between 270th Division and 57th Army's right flank was covered by separate detachments. By this time, Col Kovalev's 2nd Cavalry Corps units had concentrated in the Lozovaia region.

Right flank formations of Gen Gorodniansky's 6th Army fought defensive battles in the Nadezhdovka, Tikhopole, western outskirts of Marevka, Panteleeva Balka and Lozovenka regions.

Thus, as a result of battles on 22 May, German tanks had reached the lines of communication of our forces occupying the Barvenkovo salient, cut them off from crossings over the Northern Donets River and widened the penetration sector to 25km.

Since forces of General Moskalenko's 38th Army shock group had not succeeded in getting ready, and reserves designated to reinforce this group were late in arriving in the Savintsy region; the enemy tank group which had broken through to the Chepel region from the south was not destroyed, and communications were not re-established.

All subsequent operations by forces on the left bank of the Northern Donets and in the Barvenkovo bridgehead were directed toward penetrating the encirclement front of German forces.

Combat Operations on 23 and 24 May (see Map 31)
On 23 and 24 May, fierce battles continued in the Barvenkovo bridgehead. The German command strove to widen the corridor which cut off Soviet forces operating in the Barvenkovo salient from the crossings over the Northern Donets River.

What the German command had to do was clear. The only question remaining on 23 May was, 'Could they do it?' Again, a German source recounts the German command's challenge:

'Colonel-General von Kleist was faced with the task of making his encircling front strong enough to resist both the Soviet breakout attempts from the west and their relief attempts mounted across the Donets from the east. Once more it was a race against time. With brilliant tactical skill, General von Mackensen grouped all infantry and motorised divisions under his command like a fan around the axis of 14th Panzer Division. The 16th Panzer Division was first wheeled west and then moved north towards Andreyevka on the Donets. The 60th Motorised Infantry Division, the 389th Infantry Division, the 384th Infantry Division and the 100th Light Infantry Division fanned out toward the west and formed the pocket front against Timoshenko's armies as they flooded back east.

'In the centre, like a spider in its web, was Gen Lanz's 1st Mountain Division; it had been detached from the front by von Mackensen to be available as a fire brigade.

'This precaution finally decided the battle. For Timoshenko's army commanders were driving their divisions against the German pocket front with ferocious determination. They concentrated their efforts in an attempt to punch a hole into the German front, regardless of the cost, in order to save themselves by reaching the Donets front only 25 miles away.'[83]

Southwestern and Southern Front forces, in turn, implemented measures to penetrate

Kharkov, 1942

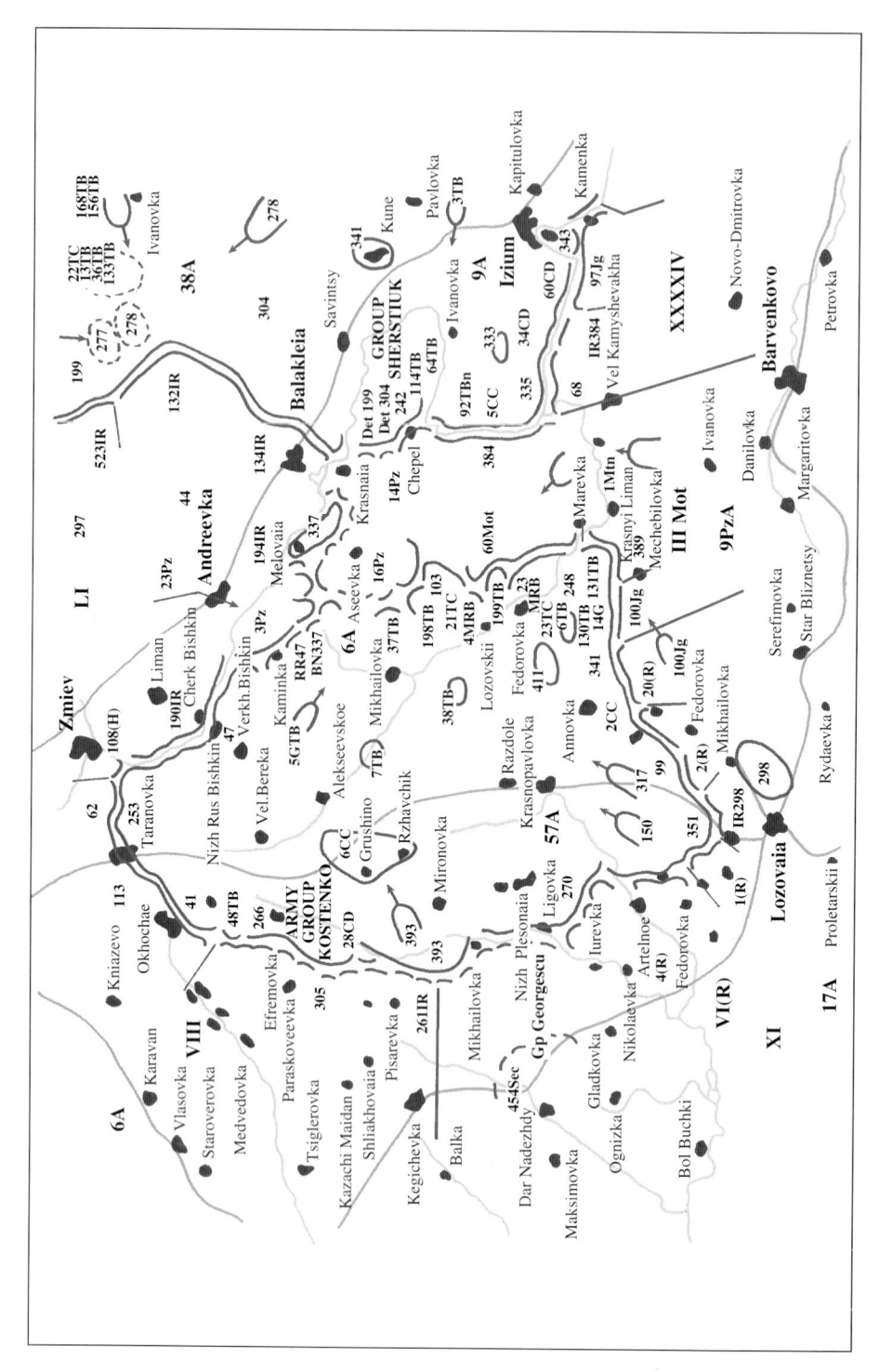

Map 31 — Combat on 23 May in the Southern Sector

5 The Course of Combat Operations

the encirclement ring and withdraw systematically to the left bank of the Northern Donets River.

The most intense battles on 23 May developed in the Lozovenka, Chepel and Shebelinka regions, where Gorodniansky's forces fought desperately to open the way through the German Panzer cordon to the safety of the Northern Donets River.

On the night of 23 May, the German command concentrated the main forces of 3rd and 23rd Panzer Divisions in the bridgehead south of Andreevka, and during the second half of the day developed the offensive toward Shebelinka and Kiseli. Remnants of 337th and 47th Rifle Divisions, which were defending along a line from Glazunovka to Shebelinka, could not withstand the onslaught of enemy tanks and were forced to withdraw to the south. Units of Group Kleist also renewed their offensive, and by the close of the day they had reached the Aseevka, Glazunovka, Krutoiarka and Lozovenka regions. The tank group advancing south from the Andreevka region linked up with tank units from Group Kleist in the Glazunovka region.

On 23 May, Army Group Kostenko continued to withdraw to the line of the Orel River to shorten the front line and free up forces to form a new reserve.

By the close of the day, 57th Army forces had abandoned Lozovaia under presssure of the enemy onslaught, and had withdrawn to the line Vero-Nikolaevka, Blagoveshchenskii.

Combat operations of Gen Kharitonov's 9th Army forces on 23 May were limited to unsuccessful attempts to widen the bridgehead in the Izium and Studenok regions.

On this day, the left flank forces of Gen Moskalenko's 38th Army operated indecisively and were not only unable to achieve any substantial success, but also abandoned Chepel by the close of the day, under pressure of the enemy onslaught.

Thus, as a result of combat on 23 May, German forces completed the encirclement of our Barvenkovo group and began to widen the corridor which separated the forces from the remaining front. Under difficult encirclement conditions, Soviet forces continued to maintain their combat capability and fought stubborn battles against the constant attacks.

Having assessed the situation which had resulted from the battles on 23 May, Marshal Timoshenko decided to penetrate the ring of encirclement and bring his forces to the left bank of the Northern Donets River. For this purpose, Group 'South' [the 'Southern Group'] had been created from the encircled forces of 6th and 57th Armies and Army Group Kostenko.

In accordance with Timoshenko's combat order No 00330, dated 24 May 1942, Group 'South', while covering itself from the southeast, was to employ its main forces to deliver a blow against Savintsy, destroy the enemy, penetrate the ring of encirclement and systematically bring its forces beyond the Northern Donets River in the Savintsy and Protopopovka sector. At the same time, the group operating on 38th Army's left flank (Group Sherstiuk), reinforced by a composite tank corps (3rd, 64th and 114th Tank Brigades), was to advance once again to link up with those units which were breaking out of the encirclement. However, the enemy's renewed offensive on a wide front on the morning of 24 May did not permit the forces of Group 'South' to regroup in timely fashion and begin to execute their intended operation. Striving to dismember the encircled grouping into separate, isolated units, after regrouping at night, the Germans began to develop the offensive on the morning of 24 May simultaneously, along several axes (see Map 32).

The 3rd and 23rd Panzer Divisions and a regiment of 44th Infantry Division con-

Kharkov, 1942

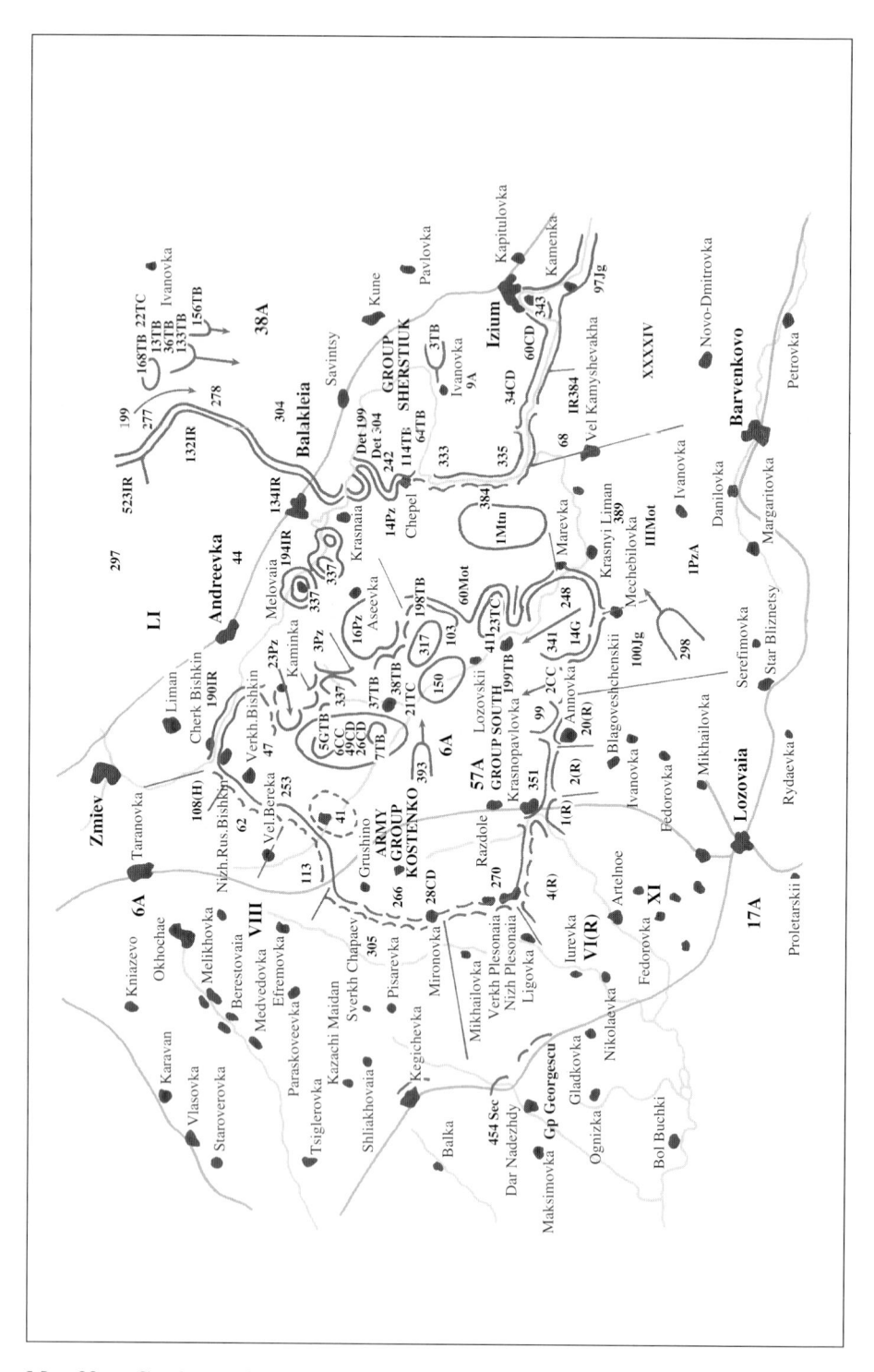

Map 32 — Combat on 24 May in the Southern Sector

5 The Course of Combat Operations

tinued to advance in the direction of Kiseli, captured this point and began to spread out to Verkhnii Bishkin (in the rear areas of 47th and 253rd Rifle Divisions) and to Bukitselovka (in the rear areas of 6th Cavalry Corps). Consequently, Southern Group forces defending along a front from Gaidar to Okhochae began to withdraw to the southeast, and by the close of 24 May had reached the line Glinishche, Verkhnii Bishkin and Vysokii Poselok. Gen Noskov's 6th Cavalry Corps withdrew to the Mikhailovka region. The 113th Infantry, 305th Infantry and 454th Security Divisions, Group Georgescu and Romanian 1st Infantry Division attacked on a front from Paraskoveevka and Pisarevka to Ligovka. These forces delivered their main attack at the boundary of Col Tavantsev's 266th and the 393rd Rifle Divisions. Holding back the German offensive, by the close of the day our forces had withdrawn to new positions along a front from Vysokii Poselok through Mironovka, Verkhniaia and Nizhniaia Plesovaia to Krasnopavlovka. Col Baersky's 41st Rifle Division was brought up into Army Group Kostenko's reserve in the Alekseevskoe region.

During the course of continuous, intense combat operations lasting 13 days, 57th Army forces had exhausted almost all their munitions. Therefore, they were unable to contain the intensified enemy onslaught and withdrew to the line Dobropol, Kamyshevakha and Privole, linking up with the right flank of 6th Army's 248th Rifle Division.

German tanks captured Zelenyi Gai on 6th Army's right flank. Having been cut off from the main forces, Col Pesochin's 411th Rifle Division with the remnants of Gen Pushkin's 23rd Tank Corps fought in encirclement in the Panteleeva Balka region. Units of Col Chanyshev's 103rd Rifle Division, together with 198th, 38th and 37th Tank Brigades, repelled the continuous enemy tank and infantry counter-attacks along the front from Lozovskii to Krutoiarka.

As mentioned above, the enemy offensive, which began on the morning of 24 May, prevented Group 'South' forces from regrouping as planned. By the close of 24 May, only 57th Army's 150th and 317th Rifle Divisions had been concentrated to break through the encirclement ring in the Kartamysh, Rakitnoe and Sovetskii region. The left flank group of 38th Army was still concentrating in the Savintsy region and was unable to resume the offensive in timely fashion.

By the close of the day, the front lines of our forces encircled in the Barvenkovo salient ran along a line from Glinishche through Verkhnii Bishkin, Vysokii Poselok, Mironovka, Verkhniaia and Nizhniaia Plesovaia, Krasnopavlovka, Dobropol, Privole, Lozovskii, Krutoiarka, and Mikhailovka to Kaminka. There were considerable breeches between forces in a number of sectors.

3. Battles of Group 'South' Forces in Encirclement (25–28 May 1942)

Carrying out the order from the Commander-in-Chief of the Southwestern Direction, Marshal Timoshenko, the commander of Group 'South', Gen Kostenko, decided to penetrate the ring of encirclement using forces of Gen Gorodniansky's 6th Army by delivering an attack in the general direction of Chepel from a front extending from Panteleeva Balka through Lozovenka to Krutoiarka. A shock group comprised of 317th, 393rd and 150th Rifle Divisions, 49th and 26th Cavalry Divisions, 5th Guards, 7th and 37th Tank Brigades and remnants of 21st and 23rd Tank Corps was created for the breakthrough.

Army Group Kostenko units (253rd, 41st, 266th and 270th Rifle and 28th Cavalry Divisions), remnants of 351st, 99th, 248th and 14th Rifle Divisions, and 2nd Cavalry Corps were to defend firmly the front from Glinishche through Verkhnii Bishkin,

Kharkov, 1942

Alekseevskoe, Mironovka, Krasnopavlovka and Pavlovka to Fedorovka to protect the shock group from the south and southwest.

The order was given to begin combat operations to penetrate the encirclement at dawn on 25 May; in fact, however, they got under way at 10.00, and were disorganised throughout the day (see Map 33).

A German account captured the flavour of the almost frenzied Soviet attempts to break out of the trap:

'On Whit Monday the encircled armies succeeded in streamrolling their way through the barrier set up by 60th Motorised Infantry Division and 389th Infantry Division and in driving to Lozovenka. It was clear that the Russians were trying to reach the main road to Izyum. It was then that Mackensen's precaution proved decisive. The Soviets encountered the 1st Mountain Division, which had taken up a switchline east of Lozovenka. The cover groups of 384th Infantry Division, supported by IV Air Corps, also flung themselves into the path of the Soviets. The action which followed was among the bloodiest of the whole war in Russia.'[84]

During the first half of the day, when units of the shock group were preparing for the offensive, units of Col Kovalev's 2nd Cavalry Corps, Col Shagin's 341st Rifle Division and 57th Army's rear service units began to withdraw from the line Pavlovka, Egorovka to the Sviatushino, Lozovskii and Baksharovka region. When arriving at their line of deployment, Gen Noskov's 6th Cavalry Corps units were mixed with forces of 337th, 47th and 253rd Rifle Divisions, which were withdrawing southeast without any official control. As a result, there was a disordered massing of men, combat equipment and transport in the Mikhailovka, Krutoiarka and Novo-Ukrainka region. At this very time, units of 393rd Rifle Division, which was being brought up into the Army Group's reserve, had begun to concentrate in Novo-Ukrainka. At the same time only isolated subunits of 41st Rifle Division and units of 28th Cavalry Division remained on the front protecting the shock group. Attacking enemy on the shoulders of the withdrawing units of 341st Rifle Division and 2nd Cavalry Corps, captured Kniazevo, Egorovka, Blagodatnyi and Dmitrievka, and during the second half of the day, having brought up artillery and mortars to this region, opened heavy fire against the Sviatushino, Lozovskii and Baksharovka regions. Simultaneously, air raids intensified against the Mikhailovka and Krutoiarka regions and the combat formations of the deploying shock group.

Soviet troop command and control was completely disrupted. As a result of the disorganised withdrawal and continuous enemy operations, the units suffered heavy losses, were disorganised and did not execute their missions for breaking through the encirclement.

On the evening of 25 May, the Soviet breakout attempt continued unabated, and the horrors of battle intensified. Maj-Gen Lanz, commander of German 1st Mountain Division, recorded the grizzly scene in his divisional records:

'By the light of thousands of white flares, the Russian columns struck at the German lines. Officers and commissars were spurring on their battalions with shrill shouts of command. Arms linked, the Red Army men charged. The hoarse "Urra" ranged eerily through the night.

5 The Course of Combat Operations

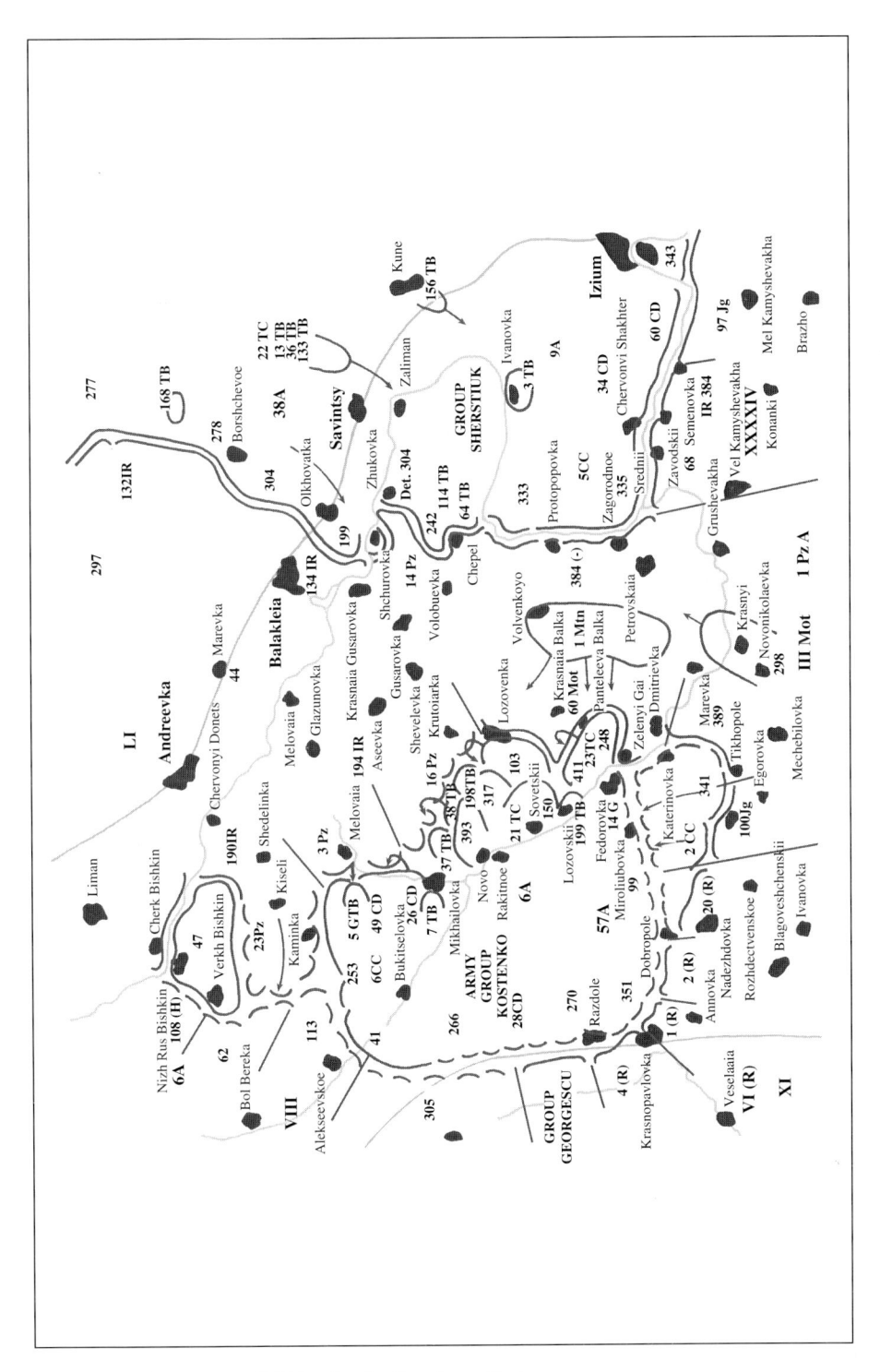

Map 33 — Combat on 25 May in the Southern Sector

Kharkov, 1942

' "Fire," commanded the German corporals at the machine guns and infantry guns. The first wave of attackers collapsed. The earth-brown columns wheeled through the night.

'But there too they encountered the blocking positions of the Mountain Jaegers. They ebbed back and, now, regardless of casualties, came pounding against the German front. They beat down and stabbed whatever opposed them, gained a few more hundred yards, and then sagged and collapsed in the enfilading fire of the German machine-guns. Whoever was not killed staggered, crawled or stumbled back into the ravines of the Bereka River.[85]

By afternoon on 26 May, the remaining Soviets were crowded into a ten-by-two mile pocket along the Bereka River valley (see Map 34).

'From a hill south of Lozovenka, Bock could see over almost the whole of it. "An overpowering picture," he said, as shells exploded in the cloud of smoke hanging over the valley, and 23rd Panzer Division and 1st Mountain Division troops, still on the attack, pushed past crowds of prisoners streaming out of the pocket.'[86]

Units of Gen Noskov's 6th Cavalry Corps, mixing together with forces withdrawing from the front, were subjected to enemy air raids in the Mikhailovka region and lost their combat capability. Under enemy pressure, Army Group Kostenko withdrew to the line Bulatselovka, Razdole and remnants of 351st, 99th and 14th Guards Rifle Divisions, by occupying defences along a front from Razdole through Chernokamenka and Miroliubovka to Fedorovka, joined up to the right flank of 248th and 411th Rifle Divisions. A continuous security front simply did not exist.

Meanwhile, for four days Group Sherstiuk of 38th Army had repeatedly and unsuccessfully attempted to break through German defences covering Chepel to link up with Group South. Those attacks continued on 25 May, but to no avail. German ground resistance was strong, and German aircraft constantly rained bombs on Sherstiuk's troops. Moskalenko related one case illustrating the intensity of the bombing. Early on 25 May, Timoshenko and a small group of staff officers were *en route* to Moskalenko's forward observation post in Gen Shertiuk's sector, when they were struck by German fighter bombers while crossing the Northern Donets River bridge near the town of Savintsy. According to Moskalenko:

'They [Timoshenko and his staff] left the vehicles and sought cover to wait out the aviation bombardment. But how did they wait it out? All day, without interruption, the fascist aircraft bombed and strafed the bridge, the approaches to it, and nearby forces. Only at dusk was the staff vehicle able to leave, and it never reached the 38th Army observation post.'[87]

Moskalenko went on to describe the carnage wrought by the initial futile escape attempts by Group South's lead elements:

'Enemy infantry forces, tanks and aviation furiously opposed the small attempts to penetrate the encirclement from within or without. A considerable number of those in the enemy ring of fire fell in battle. Only separate groups escaped from the "sack". And, as their number gradually grew, all the more still remained in encirclement. They

5 The Course of Combat Operations

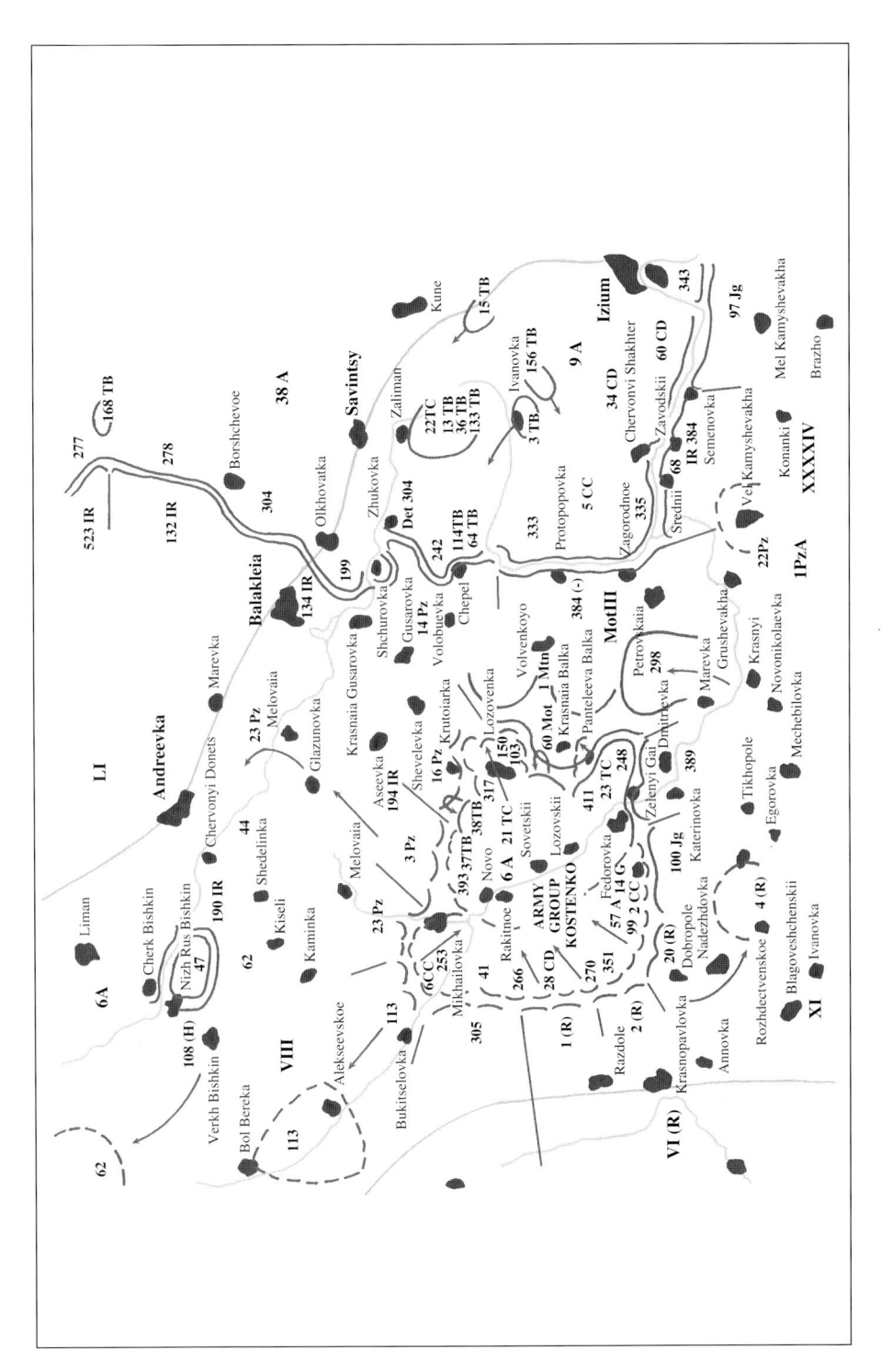

Map 34 — Combat on 26 May in the Southern Sector

Kharkov, 1942

stubbornly and heroically struggled with the enemy, trying to escape from him.'[88]

On the morning of 26 May, our forces renewed their attempts to break out of the encirclement. Col Chanyshev's 103rd Rifle Division and the remnants of Maj-Gen Egorov's 150th and Col Iakovlev's 317th Rifle Divisions with a tank group from Genl Pushkin's 23rd Tank Corps were employed as the first echelon of the shock force. However, these attempts were unsuccessful, and Egorov perished. All day on 26 May the enemy displayed exceptional activity on the ground and in the air. The commander of Group 'South,' Gen Kostenko, his deputy and his staff exerted great efforts toward protecting personnel and combat equipment against enemy air raids and artillery fire, co-ordinating command and control, and preparing for more decisive operations to break out of the encirclement.

The offensive was renewed at 22.00 on 26 May. The shock group of forces which were breaking out drove the enemy out of Lozovenka and advanced 4-6km eastward.

German observers recorded the same carnage as had occurred the night before:

'The following evening the same scene was repeated. But that time several T-34s accompanied the charging infantry. The Russian troops, their arms still linked, were under the influence of vodka. How else could the poor fellows find the courage to charge with shouts of "Urra!" into certain death? Whenever a German strongpoint had been overwhelmed by the Soviets, the bodies of its defenders were found, after a counter-attack had been launched, with their skulls cracked open, bayoneted and trampled into unrecognisability. The fighting was marked by savage fury. It was an appalling highway of death.'[89]

Among the many dead bodies littering the battlefield was that of Lt-Gen Gorodiansky, Soviet 6th Army commander.

At first light on 27 May, the enemy once again occupied Lozovenka (see Map 35). At the same time, the German command brought all its air forces down on the grouping of Soviet soldiers breaking out. During the whole of 27 May, enemy aviation delivered continuous bomber strikes against this group. By the close of 27 May this group of forces had scattered, and on 28 and 29 May, they broke out of encirclement in small groups and detachments.

Forces which had not managed to break through to the east and forces which had withdrawn from the security front were concentrating in the region west of Lozovenka. By the morning of 27 May, Col Tavantsev's 266th Rifle Division, whose units were the most organised and combat-capable, had reached this region. On the night of 28 May, 266th Rifle Division units, which comprised the nucleus of the shock group, penetrated the German encirclement front and, by the morning of 28 May, reached the Volvenkovo and Volobuevka region. Remaining units and subunits which had been concentrating in the region west of Lozovenka arrived with them in this region. On the night of 29 May this group penetrated the enemy front line along the right bank of the Northern Donets River by means of an attack from the rear and arrived at 38th Army's positions in the Chepel region. An attempt to assist the forces breaking out from the encirclement region by means of an offensive by 38th Army's group from the external front was unsuccessful.

5 The Course of Combat Operations

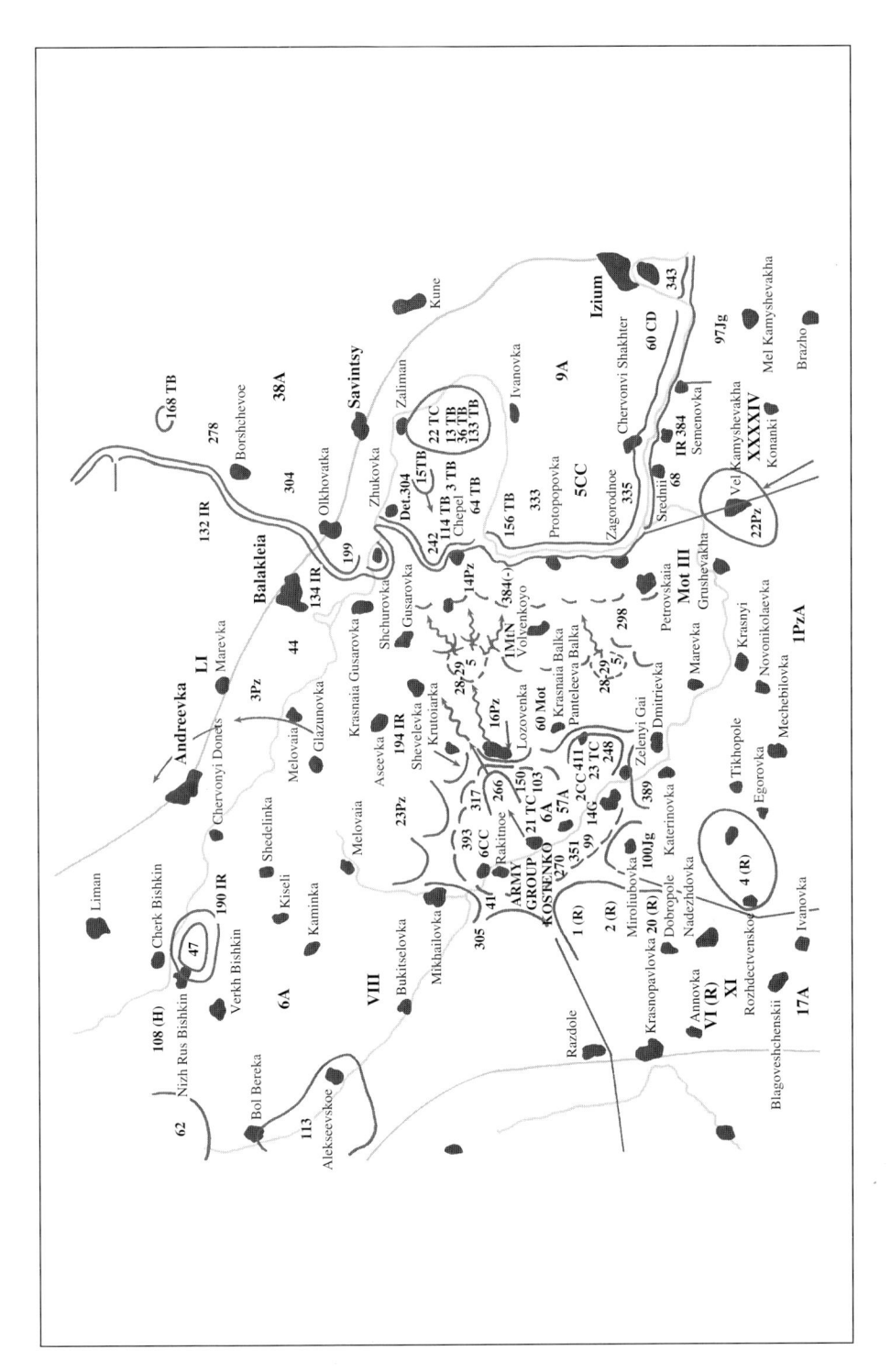

Map 35 — Combat on 27 May in the Southern Sector

Kharkov, 1942

Once again Moskalenko offered a vivid portrait of the tragic battles on 28 May from his vantage point near Chepel. He wrote:

'On the eve of 27 May, the most combat-capable units of encircled forces concentrated in the region west of Lozovenka. They formed the nucleus of the shock group which, on the night of 27-28 May, penetrated the internal encirclement line and by morning reached the Volvenkovo and Volobuevka region. Numerous other units and subunits united with them here and joined in the battle.

'As I already mentioned, before this such groups had made attempts to penetrate, but unsuccessfully. Even if they were able to overcome the internal encirclement front, the external front turned out to be beyond their strength. It was possible that such a fate awaited this group that, on the morning of 28 May, reached the Volvenkovo and Volobuevka region. But, at that time, 38th Army forces made a puncture in the external encirclement of about one kilometre along the Volobuevka axis. The enemy resisted bitterly. While concentrating at the location of the forces' penetration, he began to pour on the narrow corridor massed fire from all types of ground weapons, and his aircraft constantly delivered air strikes from the skies. The Hitlerite command applied great force to liquidate the penetration and prevent the release of the encircled from the deadly ring. But they failed. 38th Army struck from outside at the same time that the encircled did so from within. Thanks to this, we succeeded in releasing from encirclement around 22,000 Red Army soldiers, commanders and political workers.

'I remember that among the first to approach were six T-34 tanks. From one of them emerged the Commissar of the Southwestern Front, Division Commissar K. A. Gurov. Behind his tank came thousands of Soviet soldiers headed by Maj-Gen A. G. Batiunia (Chief of Staff of 6th Army). On their faces the joy of returning to us showed through their heavy pain and combat weariness.'[90]

Moskalenko's poetic description of the heroic escape attempt belied the truth that his army had failed in its mission, and those fortunates who did break through did so largely by their own devices. When all was said and done, as the official staff study of the operation points out, they were few in number. Among those who perished were the cream of the command leadership of the immense encircled forces.

Already, on 24 May, when it had become obvious that a breakthrough by forces encircled in the Barvenkovo salient would meet with increasing difficulty due to the widening of the corridor (amounting to 30km by the close of 24 May) separating them from the crossings over the Northern Donets River, Marshal Timoshenko decided to reinforce 38th Army's group with 3rd and 15th Tank Brigades to break through to the encircled forces from without.

However, it was only on 27 May that these tank brigades arrived in the Savintsy region. Owing to the fact that the crossings over the Northern Donets River had been demolished by the enemy in the Savintsy and Ivanovka regions, the tank brigades were only able to cross to the right bank of the river during the second half of 27 May. With the approach of these brigades, 38th Army's group attempted to go over to the offensive. By this time the Germans had concentrated all the forces of 14th Panzer and 384th Infantry Divisions against the group, and had themselves gone over to the offensive, attempting to liquidate our forces' bridgehead in this region. These enemy attempts were repelled, but the offensive by Moskalenko's group from 38th Army was also unsuccessful. On the morning of 28 May, this group went over to the defence to

5 The Course of Combat Operations

hold onto the bridgehead on the right bank of the Northern Donets in the Zhukovka, Vetrovka and Ivanovka region.

From 27–30 May, separate groups and detachments of Group 'South' forces continued to break out of the encirclement in the Shchurovka, Chepel and Petrovskaia sector.

By order of the Commander-in-Chief of the Direction, Marshal Timoshenko, on 28 May Southwestern Front's left flank forces halted offensive combat and began to regroup to form reserves, reinforce the juncture between Southwestern and Southern Fronts and prepare to repel the expected enemy offensive from the Chuguev bridgehead along the Kupiansk axis.

The front ran along the line from Vikhrovka through Novaia Tavolzhanka, Martovaia, Chepel and Izium to Krasnyi Liman. Further, in Southern Front's sector, the position occupied by our forces remain unchanged.

Ensuing events in the south developed in June–July 1942. Taking advantage of its great superiority in forces and means, the German command developed the initiative which they had seized, conducted a number of separate operations to reach the Oskol River, and began to execute an offensive to the northeast toward Oskol Station and the southeast toward the Don River.

In summer and autumn of 1942, German forces achieved a certain tactical *[sic]* success and reached Stalingrad and the Northern Caucasus. In November of that year, Soviet forces went over to a counter-offensive, defeated the German-Fascist forces at Stalingrad and in the Northern Caucasus, and took the strategic initiative into their own hands until the end of the war.

6
COSTS AND CONSEQUENCES

THE PRICE OF COMBAT

In the wake of the Kharkov operation, neither German nor Soviet failed to appreciate the operation's catastrophic costs for the Red Army. The heaps of bodies, the acres of smashed and abandoned equipment, and the crowds of huddled Soviet prisoners which littered the terrain in the Barvenkovo bridgehead bore mute testimony to the immense scale of the disaster. The scene of death and destruction clashed grotesquely with the verdant signs of advancing spring. The Red Army had suffered greater defeats during summer 1941, but the suddenness and unexpectedness of the Kharkov tragedy stunned Soviet and German observers alike.

In the aftermath of the operation, the German command tallied Soviet losses in men and equipment, and those estimates have been passed down in a variety of German-based accounts. According to those estimates, derived from the records of Army Group Kleist and Sixth Army, the Soviets:

'. . . lost the bulk of twenty-two rifle divisions and seven cavalry divisions. Fourteen armoured and motorised brigades were completely routed. Some 239,000 Red Army men were shuffling into captivity; 1,250 tanks and 2,026 guns had been destroyed or captured.'[1]

The Soviet General Staff Study, while carefully explaining the nature and consequences of the disaster, studiously neglected to mention casualties and losses. In concert with its impersonal approach, it also avoided naming the numerous senior Red Army commanders and staff officers, much less the countless men, who perished or fell into captivity. Recently released Soviet archive materials, however, have now filled in that historiographical gap and provide a definitive, though grisly, tally of Soviet losses.

Loss reports assembled by the Red Army General Staff after the operations, based on official reports from Southwestern Direction headquarters, recorded Soviet losses of 266,927 men, 652 tanks and 4,924 guns and mortars (see Appendix 17).[2] Of the 266,927 men lost in the operation, 46,314 wounded and sick were evacuated to field hospitals and 13,556 dead were buried on German-occupied soil. The remaining 207,057 fell into captivity. These wartime calculations have now been revised upward based on analysis done by postwar commissions and by the work of unofficial groups who have attempted to identify the burial sites of former commanders, soldiers, friends and family members who perished at Kharkov. These revised figures, now officially accepted, set the strength of Red Army in the Kharkov operation at 765,300 men. Of this total, 170,958 soldiers were killed, missing or taken prisoner. Added to the 106,232 wounded, total losses in the operation amounted to 277,190 men.[3]

6 Costs and Consequences

Losses of senior commanders and staff officers were an even better measure of the immense scale of the defeat. While heavy losses occurred throughout the command cadre of all forces in the Barvenkovo bridgehead, the 6th and 57th Army commands were particularly decimated. Lt-Gen F. Ia. Kostenko, Deputy Commander of the Southwestern Front and Southern Group commander perished, together with the commander and senior commissar of 6th Army, Lt-Gen A. M. Gorodniansky and Brigade Commissar I. V. Vlasov. The commanders of the 47th and 337th Rifle Divisions, Maj-Gen F. P. Matykin and Col I. V. Vasilev died and, although complete colonels' losses have not been revealed, many other divisional commanders in 6th Army of that rank probably also perished in the operation. Deputy 6th Army Commander for Rear Services, Maj-Gen G. M. Zusmanovich, was captured and died in captivity in 1944 at the Weissenburg POW Camp in Germany, reportedly from torture and beatings.[4]

Among 57th Army's dead were the army commander, Lt-Gen K. P. Podlas, his chief of staff, Maj-Gen A. F. Anisov, the army commissar, Brigade Commissar A. I. Popenko and the army chief of artillery, Maj-Gen F. G. Mariarov. In addition, the commander of the 150th Rifle Division, Maj-Gen D. G. Egorov, died during the attempted breakout, probably together with several other colonels commanding at divisional level. The commander of 14th Guards Rifle Division, Maj-Gen I. M. Shepetov, was severely wounded and captured near Izium after someone betrayed him. Shepetov survived in the German Flossenburg prison camp until 21 May 1943, when he was executed for anti-fascist agitation.[5]

9th Army's command losses included Maj-Gen E. K. Korzhenevich, the army chief of staff, who was killed in combat along the Northern Donets River and not in the encirclement proper. Losses in Army Group Bobkin included its commander, Maj-Gen L. V. Bobkin, who was killed, along with his young son, during the breakout attempt, Maj-Gen A. V. Borisov, the chief of staff of 6th Cavalry Corps, and Maj-Gen Z. Iu. Kutlin, the commander of 270th Rifle Division. It is likely that Kutlin's unnamed counterpart in 393rd Rifle Division also perished.[6]

Command losses in the Southern Shock Group's tank forces were also high. These included the commander of 21st Tank Corps, Maj-Gen G. I. Kuzmin, and at least four tank and motorised rifle brigade commanders in 21st and 23rd Tank Corps, Cols I. D. Demidov, A. I. Gorshkov, P. D. Drozdov and M. L. Kagarmanov.[7]

To this gruesome list must be added a host of regimental commanders in the line combat forces in the Barvenkovo bridgehead and the many artillery, engineer and logistical units which supported them. The addition of these few names to the faceless mass of Soviet dead and POWs represents a small, if inadequate, attempt to measure the full scope of the human tragedy at Kharkov.

THE CONSEQUENCES

Months after the Kharkov operation had ended, the German command prepared its operational summaries of what had transpired and submitted them to the German Supreme High Command. One of those cryptic reports, prepared by First Panzer Army, read as follows:

Account of the Combat Operations of German First Panzer Army in Spring 1942
Dated: Not earlier than 5 November 1942 (Exact date not available)

... on 28 January, First Panzer Army conducted combat operations in the penetra-

Kharkov, 1942

tion region and along the Mius River front as Army Group von Kleist.

We held on to defensive lines in heavy battles and with heavy losses. Now the supply of two armies, often uninterrupted, is supported by a single road from Dnepropetrovsk to Stalino.

We again expect a counter-offensive by newly refilled divisions before May. We planned to surround and destroy the Russians by two blows immediately to the west of the Donets: the Army Group from the south and Sixth Army from the north.

However, Sixth Army was forced to deviate from its plan, since several days before the beginning of the offensive Russian tank units delivered an attack on Kharkov and thus pinned it down. Conditions turned out to be favourable for the Army Group, since the Russians concentrated their principal efforts in the offensive on Kharkov, and this weakened their front in the Army Group sector. Therefore, the aim of the offensive became not only the dismemberment of the enemy, but also distracting their forces from Sixth Army.

On 17 May the Army Group went over to the offensive. Already by the second day, Seventeenth Army and III Panzer Corps' units had thrown the enemy on the right flank back to Izium.

On the fourth day, the successfully developing offensive to the west to attract enemy forces away from XI Army Corps was halted and a daring, critical decision was made which could affect the outcome of the operation: to deploy III Panzer Corps mobile formations to the north to link up with Sixth Army, and thus destroy the large enemy forces in the region south of Kharkov.

On 22 May, the sixth day of combat operations, after regrouping, 14th and 16th Panzer Divisions, which were attacking northwest of the bend in the Donets, linked up with Sixth Army in the Balakleia region, while 60th Motorised and 1st Mountain Divisions were completing the encirclement of the enemy. Sixth Army pursued the enemy, who withdrew eastward as a result of the successful encirclement.

Then XI Army Corps succeeded in throwing the enemy back to the north. The Russians certainly concentrated all their efforts to penetrate through the narrow corridor of III Panzer Corps. On 24 May Red forces were compressed into a territory of 48 x 27km as a result of the continuous offensive by formations of Sixth Army and Army Group von Kleist. Only insignificant enemy units succeeded during heavy battles in tearing themselves out of encirclement and escaping full destruction.

On 26 May the army announced the destruction of the Red main forces. During the course of the spring battle at Kharkov, the most combat-ready shock grouping of the Southwestern Front was destroyed. The chief prerequisite for the summer operation was created.

The commander-in-chief of the Army Group, General Field Marshal von Bock, noted the army's success in a special order. In special recognition of the successes of mobile forces, commands and formations, which made major contributions to the success of the operations, the Führer awarded oak leaves for the Knights Cross to the commander of III Panzer Corps, Gen von Mackensen.

First Panzer Army alone took 137,355 prisoners, and also seized or destroyed 50 tanks, 641 guns, 195 anti-tank and anti-aircraft guns, and 15 aircraft. In all, 22 rifle divisions, 7 cavalry divisions and 15 tank brigades were destroyed.

Army Group von Kleist and Sixth Army took 215,000 prisoners and also seized or destroyed 1,812 guns and 1,270 tanks. 542 aircraft were destroyed.

During the course of this time, forces on the Mius Front and on the eastern front of Seventeenth Army, weakened in the interests of the offensive, unswervingly held their

6 Costs and Consequences

positions and, thus, also made essential contributions to the destruction of the enemy in the cauldron south of Kharkov.[8]

The Stavka also had reports prepared by its subordinate headquarters which had participated in the operation. After 30 May Marshal Timoshenko, Commissar Khrushchev and General Bagramian dispatched their report, which read, in part, as follows:

FROM THE REPORT OF THE SOUTHWESTERN DIRECTION HIGH COMMAND TO THE STAVKA VGK CONCERNING THE RESULTS OF THE MAY OPERATION OF THE SOUTHWESTERN FRONT AND ARMIES OF THE SOUTHERN FRONT'S RIGHT WING DURING THE PERIOD 12–30 MAY 1942 Dated: Not earlier than 30 May 1942 (Exact date not available)

To the Supreme High Commander, Comrade Stalin.
... VI. Principal causes of the defeat
1. The offensive on Kharkov was well thought out and organised, but turned out to be not fully protected against enemy attacks along the Barvenkovo axis.
   The weakening of the combat composition and the deterioration of the intended defensive combat formation of 9th Army brought about by the battles for Maiaki and the decrease in its composition by one rifle division (216th RD) deprived that army of the capability of erecting a deeply echeloned defence, backed up by sufficient reserves, and capable of preventing penetration of the front.
   On the first day of the offensive, 9th Army's defence, arrayed in almost a single line, was rather easily penetrated by enemy tank formations. As a result, units of 6th and 57th Armies and Army Group Bobkin were quickly cut off from their bases and were encircled.
   The defeat of 9th Army was, to a considerable degree, the result of the inability of that army command to control its forces in complex combat conditions. All types of 9th Army and Southern Front intelligence failed to detect the prepared attack in timely fashion and thus deprived the command of the ability to undertake additional measures to repel it.
2. It was clear that without the turnabout of the main mass of 6th Army's tank formations to the east, it was impossible to escape the catastrophe. Measures undertaken for the rapid turn around of 21st and 23rd Tank Corps to the east to meet enemy tank units striving to secure crossings over the Northern Donets River in the Savintsy, Petrovskoe sector, were not quick enough. Instead of massing to strike the enemy immediately, at first only 23rd TC was turned and then, one day later, 21st TC and 248th RD.
3. It turned out that the army command and a portion of the divisional and corps commanders, with their staffs, were incapable of controlling forces in complex combat conditions. As a rule, the command leadership of armies, corps and divisions at critical moments during the operation and battles did not direct their forces' formations, but instead travelled around to their subunits. This occurred in Gen Kostenko's Group and in 6th Army during the period of semi-encirclement and encirclement, when the army commanders travelled to one division, the commissars to another and the chiefs of staff to a third.
   The corps and division commanders also followed that procedure. Thus centralised control of whole formations was lost and that disrupted intended actions. One must

Kharkov, 1942

bear in mind that all of this occurred in the most demanding conditions and when the situation required that maximum effort be exerted to direct army units in their escape from encirclement and to organise co-operation between different types of forces on the field of battle.

The general lack of direction and centralised planning finally led to the loss of control of forces and lack of organisation in combat actions on the field of battle. This is one of the principal reasons for the defeat of 9th, 6th and 57th Armies.

4. Enemy aviation played a great role in the defeat of our forces in this operation. From the second day of our offensive, the enemy achieved air superiority and, by means of continuous strikes by a large quantity of aircraft, our forces were deprived of freedom of manoeuvre on the battlefield.

The action of enemy aviation turned out to be especially harmful to our forces once encircled. Continuous enemy air attacks hindered the regrouping of forces for the attack to the east, disrupted the chain of command and threw combat formations into confusion.

Our air forces, despite wanting to concentrate their efforts on the most important targets, could not do so because of the numerical superiority of the enemy and therefore could not support the actions of their own forces.

From:
Commander-in-chief of Southwestern Direction Forces, Marshal of the Soviet Union S. K. Timoshenko
Member of the Military Soviet Southwestern Direction N. S. Khrushchev
Chief of Staff Southwestern Direction Lt-Gen I. Kh. Bagramian[9]

The report was an exercise in disingenuousness. Avoiding all self-criticism and candour, they laid blame for the disaster at the feet of Generals Malinovsky and Kharitonov, the Southern Front and 9th Army commanders, who, they said, permitted a weakening of their forces and the 9th Army defences. They also heaped criticism on 9th Army's staff and subordinate divisional and regimental commanders, who, they claimed, had proved incapable of controlling their forces in complex combat conditions. The charges against Southern Front were hollow, since Bagramian himself had personally ordered the Front to reduce 9th and 57th Armies' strength to nine divisions (from 12) in order to create reserves along the Voroshilov axis, and 18th Army had to be reinforced before the launch of the operation. Moreover, command and control problems had plagued the Soviets throughout the offensive, and not just in the Southern Front sector.

In their turn, Malinovsky, the Southern Front commander, and his chief of staff, Gen Antonov, would have their say in the debate over responsibility for the disaster. On 7 June, at the Stavka's request, they sent their account of the events preceding the operation to Stalin. It read as follows:

FROM THE REPORT OF THE SOUTHERN FRONT COMMAND TO THE CHIEF OF THE RED ARMY GENERAL STAFF, COL-GEN A. M. VASILEVSKY, ABOUT THE ENEMY'S PENETRATION OF THE DEFENSIVE SECTOR OF THE SOUTHERN FRONT'S 9TH ARMY 17–20 MAY 1942
Dated: 7 June 1942

6 Costs and Consequences

MISSION OF THE SOUTHERN FRONT'S ARMIES
During a personal phone call on 6 April 1942 by the Front Military Council (Lt-Gen Malinovsky, Member of the Military Council T. Korniitsa, Maj-Gen Vershinin and the Front chief of staff, Lt-Gen Antonov) to the Commander-in-Chief of the Southwestern Direction, Marshal Comrade Timoshenko, the following order was received from the Commander-in-Chief: the Southern Front will firmly fortify itself in occupied positions and, while protecting the Southwestern Front's offensive on Kharkov with its right flank, will firmly cover the Voroshilovgrad and Rostov axes with its left flank.

From 14 April a new boundary line was established between Southwestern and Southern Fronts, in accordance with which the Southern Front's right flank was extended to Tsaredarovka (7km southwest of Lozovaia).

Eight artillery regiments, three tank brigades and one rifle brigade were allocated from Southern Front's right flank to reinforce Southwestern Front, and one rifle brigade was taken for the Commander-in-Chief's reserve.

By personal order of the chief of staff of the Southwestern Direction, Lt-Gen Bagramian, we had to leave nine rifle divisions in 57th and 9th Armies and create strong reserves on the Voroshilovgrad axis.

GROUPING OF RIGHT WING ARMIES AND FRONT RESERVES
In accordance with assigned missions, a regrouping was conducted according to Front directive No 00177 of 6 April, and 12 RDs and one rifle brigade were left in 57th and 9th Armies to cover the Izium-Barvenkovo axis.

57th Army, consisting of 99th, 317th, 150th and 351st RDs, 14th Gds RD, one separate tank battalion, 476th HA Regt, and 558th and 754th LA Regts with two battalions of anti-tank rifles had the task of defending the line Tsaredarovka, Krishtopovka, Novo-Pavlovka and Mal. Razdol, having allocated one RD to army reserve.

The overall width of the army's front was 80km and the average density for one RD was 6-20 km.

At this time the numerical strength of a division averaged from 6,000-7,000 men.

9th Army, consisting of 341th, 106th, 216th, 349th, 51st and 333rd RDs, 78th RB, 121st and 15th Tk Bdes, 4th Gds HA Regt, 437th and 229th HA Regts, 186th and 685th LA Regts, plus two battalions of anti-tank rifles, had the mission of defending the line Novo-Bakhmetevo, Gromovaia Balka, Novo-Iakovlevka, Kantemirovka, Krasnoarmeisk, Glubokaia Makatykha, Shchurovo and Brusovka, while covering the Barvenkovo region and the axes from Slaviansk to Izium and Krasnyi Liman. One RD and two Tk Bdes were in army reserve in the Barvenkovo region. Subsequently, an additional RD was committed into army reserves in the Ivanovskii region.

The overall width of the army's front was 90km and the average density for one RD was 15-18km.

At this time the numerical strength of a division averaged from 5,000 to 6,000 men.

FRONT RESERVES
5th CC and 12th Tk Bde, in the Brazhovka, Kurulka and Golaia Dolina region; 255th RD and 2nd Tk Bde, Voroshilovgrad; 347th RD and 4th Gds Tk Bde, Rovenka.

It was required that all army and division commanders create dense defences, developed in depth, with well-prepared systems of ATk defences, including defensive earthworks, anti-tank and anti-personnel obstacles and extensive use of defensively prepared civilian dwellings.

Kharkov, 1942

To 17 April in 9th Army, 216th RD was allocated to army reserve in the area east of Barvenkovo.

At that time, by order of the Stavka, 15th Gds RD of 18th Army was sent to the MVO [Moscow Military District] for its deployment as a corps.

As a result, only three reduced-strength rifle divisions remained in 18th Army along an 80km front.

255th RD, detached to the Voroshilovgrad region, still had not been brought up to strength and numbered only 5,434 men.

It was requested that 18th Army be rapidly strengthened to achieve the firm protection of the Voroshilovgrad axis. For that purpose, 216th RD was transferred from 9th Army to reinforce 18th Army.

From:
Front Commander, Lt-Gen Malinovsky
Member of the Military Soviet, Division Commissar Larin.
Chief of Staff, Southern Front Lt-Gen Antonov[10]

Stalin clearly read and understood Malinovsky's report. Moreover, the fate of Soviet commanders involved in the Kharkov operation during the ensuing months indicated whose report Stalin believed. It is also obvious that Stalin knew who had most strenuously urged him to conduct the ill-fated offensive. Absolving himself of guilt, as he accorded blame for the failures, Stalin weighed the military competence of his subordinate commanders against the quality of loyalty to the 'Generalissimo' himself. Heads rolled, but those that did rolled very gently indeed.

On 26 June 1942, Stalin penned a politely scathing directive letter to the Southwestern Front Military Council, the contents of which speaks for itself. It read:

DIRECTIVE LETTER OF I. V. STALIN TO THE SOUTHWESTERN FRONT MILITARY COUNCIL WITH AN EVALUATION OF THE FRONT COMMANDER REGARDING THE RESULTS OF THE KHARKOV OPERATION AND ABOUT SUBSEQUENT MISSIONS OF FRONT FORCES
Dated: 26 June 1942

We members of the Defence Committee and General Staff personnel here in Moscow have decided to relieve Comrade Bagramian from his post as Southwestern Front chief of staff. Comrade Bagramian dissatisfied the Stavka not only as chief of staff, but also as a simple information conduit, responsible for clearly and correctly reporting to the Stavka about the situation at the front. Moreover, Comrade Bagramian turned out to be unable to derive lessons from that catastrophe which engulfed the Southwestern Front. During the course of only three weeks, the Southwestern Front, thanks to his shortsightedness, not only lost the half-won Kharkov operation, but also succeeded in giving 18-20 divisions to the enemy.

This catastrophe, measured by its adverse results, is comparable to Rennenkampf's and Samsonov's catastrophe in East Prussia. After all that has occurred, one would have hoped Comrade Bagramian would have derived lessons and learned something. Unfortunately, this is not apparent. Now, just as before the catastrophe, headquarters communications with the armies remains unsatisfactory, information is of poor quality, orders are given to armies too late and withdrawal of units is also late. As a result, our regiments and divisions are being encircled today, just as they were two weeks ago.

6 Costs and Consequences

I think that I must stop here. True, you very much sympathise with and highly value Comrade Bagramian. I think, however, that here you are mistaken, as in so many other things.

Temporarily I am dispatching to you as chief of staff, the assistant chief of the General Staff, Comrade Bodin, who knows your Front and can provide it great assistance.

Comrade Bagramian is appointed chief of staff of 28th Army. If Comrade Bagramian shows his good side as army chief of staff, then I will address the question of later providing him the opportunity to advance further.

It is clear that this matter does not involve just Comrade Bagramian. There is also discussion of the mistakes of all members of the Military Council, and first and foremost of Comrade Timoshenko and Comrade Khrushchev. If we had reported to the country fully about the catastrophe — with the loss of 18-20 divisions, which the front lived through and continues to live through — then I fear that they would deal with you very sternly. Therefore, you must take stock of the committed errors and undertake all measures to ensure they do not reoccur in the future.

The Front's principal mission at present is to hold onto the eastern bank of the Oskol River and the northern bank of the Northern Donets River firmly, and to hold them at all cost. All of you members of the Military Council will answer with your heads for the security of all of our positions on the eastern bank of the Oskol, on the northern bank of the Donets and in other front sectors.

We have decided to assist you and to give you six fighter (aviation) brigades (without division command and control), one tank corps, two regiments of RS [ed: meaning of abbreviation 'RS' is obscure], several anti-tank artillery regiments and 800 anti-tank rifles.

I cannot provide rifle divisions since we have none ready for battle.
I wish you success.

I. Stalin[11]

Within hours, Bagramian, the immediate scapegoat for the Kharkov disaster, was *en route* to his new assignment. Stalin could not, however, easily dispense with the services of the intensely loyal Timoshenko, who, after all, had been Stalin's accomplice in planning for the Kharkov operation. For years it was assumed, incorrectly, that Timoshenko remained with the Southwestern Direction until July, when he took command of the newly formed Stalingrad Front. New information now indicates that Stalin may have removed Timoshenko from command of the Southwestern Direction on 21 May 1942, day after he made a report in person to the Stavka on the ill-fated operation. Zhukov was reported to have been asked why Timoshenko got off so lightly; he apparently responded, 'I think Stalin limited himself just to taking his job away because the idea of the warning strike had been his own originally.'[12] By 25 July Timoshenko was on his way to command the Northwestern Front, where, in February 1943, he planned and conducted an offensive to liquidate the German Demiansk salient. When that operation failed to destroy the encircled Germans, Timoshenko was removed from his post and would never again command a Front.

The first, and only, detailed classified official assessment by the Red Army General Staff of the causes, nature and consequences of the abortive Kharkov offensive was the 1951 study which forms the nucleus of this book. Although marked by its candour and general accuracy, it addresses only military issues, and, since it was written while

Kharkov, 1942

Stalin still ruled, it neither mentioned personalities nor rendered judgements regarding Stavka responsibility for the offensive. Although the study fixed blame for military blunders and mistakes, it left the thorny question of political responsibility for the failed operation to post-Stalinist generations. The study's military conclusions are, in the main, sound and valid, and they appear here without editorial comment.

Brief Results and Conclusions

The combat operations which unfolded in May 1942 on the southern wing of the Soviet-German front are an example of the acute struggle to improve our forces' operational situation and to capture the initiative for expanded large-scale offensive operations during the summer campaign (see Map 36).

The treacherous delay by the Anglo-Americans in opening a second front in Western Europe during the summer of 1942 created a tense situation for the Soviet Army, which alone continued to bear the entire burden of the struggle against German-Fascist armies.

The intentional Anglo-American avoidance of executing the obligations which they had taken upon themselves created an opportunity for the German-Fascist command to transfer forces from Western Europe to the Soviet-German front freely and safely, while counting on developing an offensive southward in summer 1942 and recapturing the initiative which they had lost in the winter campaign.

In these circumstances, the Soviet Army's execution of the mission of defeating the German-Fascist hordes which had invaded Soviet territory was an extremely complex and serious matter, requiring maximum intensity of effort.

While considering the seriousness of the situation which had unfolded in the south, the Stavka of the Supreme High Command promptly transferred reserves to the Southwestern Direction and demanded the Southwestern Direction command defeat the German Kharkov grouping, thereby forestalling the enemy in developing a summer offensive. The interests of the entire summer campaign of 1942 required that this operation be conducted successfully.

To this end, the Stavka placed considerable assets at the disposition of the Commander-in-Chief of the Southwestern Direction, which ensured force superiority over the enemy for Southwestern Direction forces.

The decision made by the Commander-in-Chief of the Southwestern Direction concerning the delivery of two blows by Southwestern Front, which would envelop the German Kharkov grouping, was appropriate for the missions assigned to the forces, while their favourable operational situation with respect to the objectives of the offensive facilitated the execution of the missions. Thus, the basic conditions favoured successful conduct of the offensive. However, despite this, the missions assigned by the Stavka were not executed. In the northern sector, Front forces were unable to overcome the enemy defences to the necessary depth and, encountering powerful counterattacks by German Panzer divisions, withdrew to their initial positions, holding the somewhat widened Staryi Saltov bridgehead on the right bank of the Northern Donets River. By 28 May, this bridgehead had a front of 70km, a depth of 12km and an overall area of 500 sq km.

In the southern sector, Southwestern Front forces failed to complete the operational penetration and, as a result of sharp changes in the situation in the southern sector of the Barvenkovo bridgehead, ceased their offensive operations. After regrouping forces, 6th Army troops, co-operating with Southern Front's 9th and 57th Armies,

6 Costs and Consequences

went over to the defence to repel the enemy counter-stroke on the southern face of the Barvenkovo salient.

As a result of combat from 17 to 28 May along the Southwestern axis, an important operational bridgehead in the Barvenkovo region was lost. Only a small bridgehead on the right bank of the Northern Donets River in the Savintsy region remained in our forces' hands.

Southwestern Direction forces were compelled to make the transition to the defence in unfavourable conditions, while at the same time the Germans, as a result of their capture of the Barvenkovo salient, provided a stable position for their Donbas grouping and improved their initial position for an offensive by all of Army Group 'South'.

Soviet forces exhibited steadfastness, exceptional bravery and courage during the offensive and in difficult defensive battles, while striving to execute their assigned missions and inflicting heavy losses on the enemy.

In the engagement in the Barvenkovo salient, German attempts to force the Northern Donets River and penetrate within the bounds of the northeastern part of the Donbas were repelled. However, in circumstances when the correlation of forces had changed in favour of the enemy, the threat of the German offensive remained very real. Reinforced during the engagement by divisions which had arrived from deep in the rear, the German shock group was a serious threat to the entire southern wing of Soviet forces.

Careful study of the course of combat operations by Southwestern Direction forces, which led to such a situation, demonstrates that poor troop control and especially poor organisation of co-operation between the Southwestern and Southern Fronts were among the principal reasons for the overall lack of success of these Fronts' operations in May 1942. This is reflected both in the matter of overall planning of force co-operation when preparing for the Kharkov offensive operation and in matters of conducting the offensive, as well as in the direction of the defensive engagement in the Barvenkovo salient. In addition, the unsuccessful outcome of combat operations by each of the Southwestern Direction's Fronts was also a result of those shortcomings which were inherent to the Fronts themselves. These shortcomings should be examined separately.

Organisation of Co-operation between the Southwestern and Southern Fronts
The chief shortcoming in the overall planning of the Southwestern Direction's offensive was the absence of reliable operational protection from the south by Southern Front forces for Southwestern Front's shock group. The Front's northern shock group (28th Army and 3rd Guards Cavalry Corps) was solidly supported by 21st and 38th Armies' operations. However, the advancing left flank of the Southern Shock Group was only protected by operations of Army Group Bobkin.

The front configuration and the presence of uncommitted enemy operational reserves demanded greater initiative in resolving the issue of operational security. Southern Front forces should have received active missions for protecting the offensive of their neighbour to the right against the inevitable enemy counter-stroke.

Active operations by the Southern Front across a wide frontage would not only have pinned down large enemy reserves, but could also have created the threat of capturing the entire German Donbas grouping, which would have been the best solution to the task of protecting the Voroshilovgrad and Rostov axes. Taking into account the presence on these axes of large reserves (12 rifle divisions, six rifle brigades and one tank corps), by 11 May Southern Front had an overall superiority of forces over the enemy

Kharkov, 1942

on the Rostov and Voroshilovgrad axes. The execution of the mission of protecting the Southwestern Front's offensive by active operations was completely within the power of Southern Front.

However, in his Directive No 00241, dated 6 April, the commander-in-chief of the direction assigned Southern Front forces a very limited and essentially passive mission — to consolidate firmly along the occupied lines for the purpose of protecting Southwestern Front's offensive, to assist the latter using its right wing and to cover the Voroshilovgrad and Rostov directions using its centre and left flank. The Southern Front commander did not receive other concrete instructions during the entire preparatory period of the operation right up until 8 May, when the commander-in-chief informed him about the start of Southwestern Front's offensive and gave general instructions about increasing vigilance, conducting reconnaissance along the entire front and developing the depth of the Front's defences.

As a result, not only was no active operational protection of the offensive organised along the Kharkov axis on the part of Southern Front, but there was not even a solid defence of the southern face of the Barvenkovo salient in 9th and 57th Armies' sectors, where a German counter-offensive was most probable. All of this was in direct violation of a number of direct instructions from the Stavka of the Supreme High Command, addressed to all Southwestern Direction Fronts and armies — No 170367, dated 9 May, required the construction of defensive field fortifications to a depth of 10-12km.

The decision by the Southern Front commander, five days before Southwestern Front's offensive, to conduct an operation to improve the operational situation of 9th Army forces in the Maiaki region, did not correspond to the general plan of the Commander-in-Chief of the Southwestern Direction. This operation, which was conducted 7–15 May, diverted 9th Army forces from defensive missions and led to the exhaustion of army and Front reserves in the Barvenkovo bridgehead. Consequently, at the moment of the enemy counter-stroke, the combat formation of Southern Front forces in the Barvenkovo bridgehead was completely inappropriate for defensive requirements.

Among the most important shortcomings in the overall planning of the operation were the under-assessment of the capabilities for massed employment of Southwestern and Southern Front's air assets to assist advancing ground forces, and the absence of daily co-operation between the aviation of these Fronts in their combat work. An attempt to use Southern Front's air assets for support of operations by the Southwestern Front's Southern Shock Group was unsuccessful. Each Front's aviation operated only in the interests of its own Front during the duration of the offensive.

Mistakes in the overall planning of the operation, permitted by Southwestern Direction headquarters, were exacerbated by poor knowledge of the opposing enemy's order of battle and an under-assessment of his ability to manoeuvre forces by rapidly drawing in strategic reserves along a threatened axis, and by transferring them from other sectors of the front, especially from the Donbas region. The mistake in determining the quantity of enemy forces located in front of the Southwestern Front on 1 April 1942 amounted to two infantry and one tank division (23rd Panzer, 454th Security and 4th Infantry Divisions and a Romanian division were not taken into account). By the time the offensive commenced, the difference between the assumed and actual number of German forces in front of Southwestern Front increased by two infantry divisions (71st and 305th), of which the staff of the Southwestern Direction knew nothing.

6 Costs and Consequences

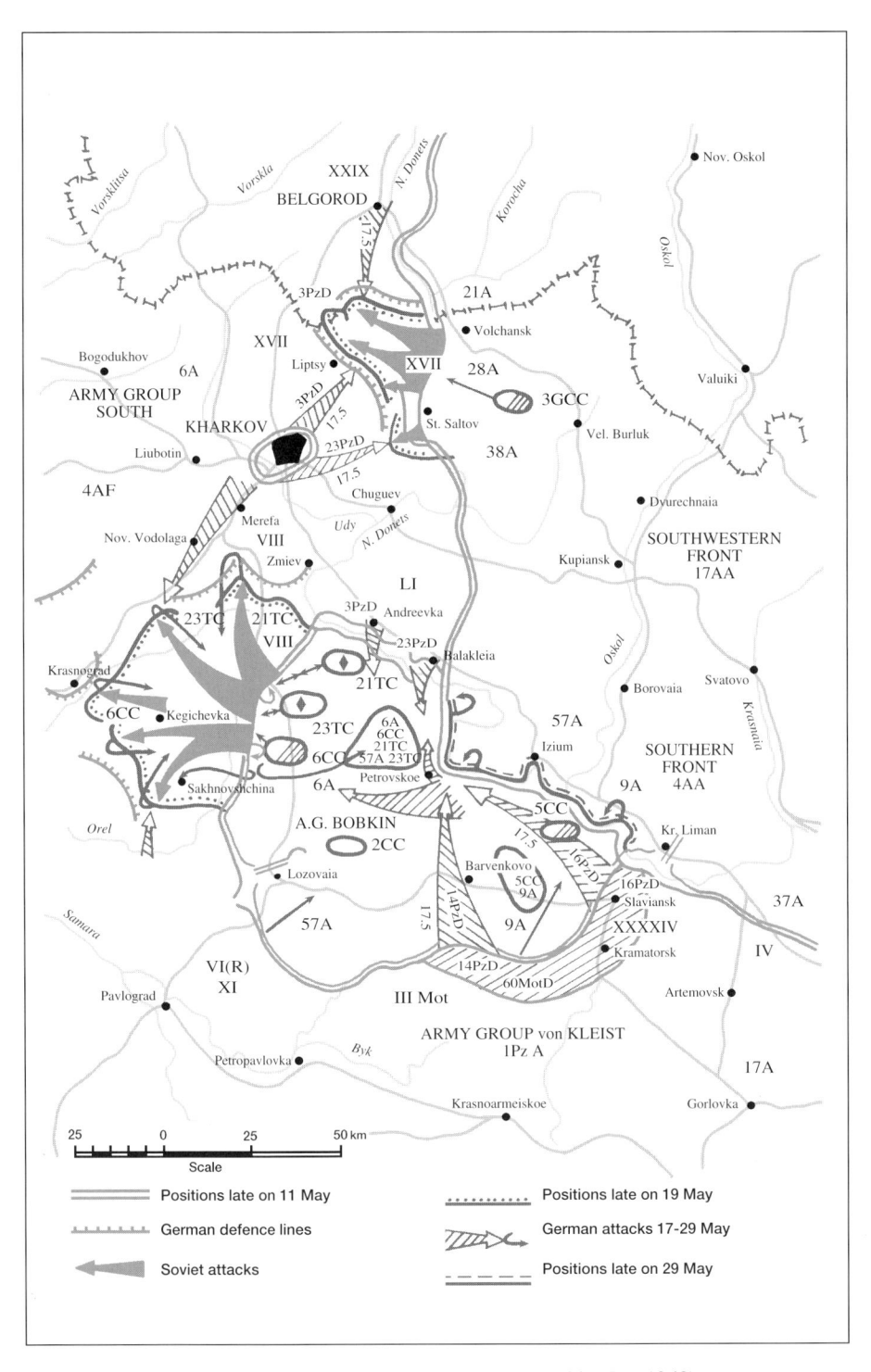

Map 36 — Summary map of the Kharkov Operation (12–29 May 1942)

Kharkov, 1942

The Southwestern Front's offensive plan envisaged the possibility of the enemy transferring — on the fifth or sixth day of the operation — five or six divisions from reserve positions. In fact, enemy reserves began to arrive at the penetration sectors on the second day of our offensive. From 12 to 19 May, the Germans transferred more than four infantry divisions to the Northern Shock Group's offensive sector, and around three infantry divisions to that of the Southern Shock Group.

The possibility of the appearance of large enemy forces on the southern face of the Barvenkovo salient, and the probability of their delivering a counter-stroke against the flank of Southwestern Front's southern group, was not considered at all. In reality, by 17 May the Germans had concentrated one panzer and five infantry divisions to deliver a counter-stroke against the front of Southern Front's 9th Army. Thus, during our offensive the enemy concentrated and committed into battle one Panzer and 12 infantry divisions from his reserve.

The above-mentioned miscalculations in organising Front co-operation and the incorrect assessment by the Commander-in-Chief of the Southwestern Direction and his staff concerning enemy capabilities and intentions played its own negative role, as subsequent events demonstrated, on the scale of the entire Southwestern Direction.

Planning and Preparation of the Southwestern Front Offensive
As was the case in the entire Southwestern Direction, both the planning and preparation of the offensive by Southwestern Front staff were executed with great errors.

Despite having at its disposal a large force which provided the Southwestern Front with a more than 2:1 superiority over the enemy in infantry and tanks and almost a 3:2 superiority in artillery across a wide front, the Front commander, with the exception of tanks in 6th Army's sector, was unable to create a decisive force superiority over the enemy either in the northern or southern active sectors. Maximum superiority over the enemy was achieved in the sector of 28th Army's penetration, reaching 2.8:1 in infantry and 2.1:1 in artillery, which only to an insignificant degree exceeded the overall superiority over the enemy on the entire front of the Northern Shock Group.

Failure to observe secrecy in force concentration and the extraordinary delays in regrouping the shock groups (up to 30 days) led to the fact that the enemy discovered the Southwestern Front commander's plan and was able beforehand to conduct counter-manoeuvres by units of German Sixth Army and introduce reserves in the threatened sectors. Consequently, the German command achieved an increase in the operational density of its forces in threatened sectors and succeeded in creating strong operational reserves in the depth of the defence.

Analysis of the correlation of enemy forces with the troops located in the sectors of our Northern and Southern Shock Groups on 11 May, shows that the enemy, having regrouped his forces, achieved a significant reduction in the force superiority of Southwestern Front's shock groups (see Table 12).

Additionally, decisive superiority in artillery over the enemy was not achieved in the southern sector of the offensive because of mistakes in the plan for regrouping artillery units and the delayed arrival of reinforcing artillery in its region of employment.

For these reasons, despite the relatively high percentage of concentrated forces and means in active sectors (96% of all artillery and 74% of all infantry) and the use of all available tanks on main axes, from the very beginning of the offensive Southwestern Front forces were placed in an unfavourable situation.

6 Costs and Consequences

Table 12 — Comparative Table of Concentration of Forces in the Active Sectors of Southwestern Front on 11 May 1942

	Southwestern Front				German Sixth Army			
	Bns	Guns	Mortars	Tanks	Bns	Guns	Mortars	
Tanks								
On the entire front[a]	156	852	1,305	354[b]	60	578	590	330
In the active sector[c]	115	800	1,040	354	42	418	440	320
% of overall Front forces	73.7	93.9	79.7	100	70	72.3	74.6	97
On the entire Front[d]	90	505	674	425	45	294	434	—
In the active sector[e]	66	485	666	475	40	232	344	—
% of overall Front forces	73.3	96	98.8	100	88.8	78.9	79	—

[a] Of 21st, 28th and 38th Armies (130km)
[b] The overall figure does not include 96 tanks of the three separate tank battalions comprising the Southwestern Front commander's reserve
[c] 55km
[d] Of 6th Army and Army Group Bobkin (145km)
[e] 36km

Despite the fact that the operational plan considered the Southern Shock Group's attack to be fundamental, the distribution of forces and means between both Front shock groups accorded no preference to the southern group. The following shows that operational densities per kilometre of front in penetration sectors were almost identical for both groups:

Shock Group	Inf Bns	Arty/Mor	Tanks
Southern	1.8	30.6 pieces	6
Northern	2	28 pieces	5.9

The inappropriate distribution of artillery and tank assets between main and secondary axes becomes even more obvious when comparing the outfitting of penetration sectors with artillery assets in the Northern and Southern Shock Groups.

While carrying out the most crucial role in the Northern Shock Group, 28th Army with 3rd Guards Cavalry Corps was reinforced with nine artillery regiments, and the artillery density in this army's sector was brought up to 59.5 guns and mortars per kilometre of penetration front; at the same time, 6th Army with 21st and 23rd Tank Corps was reinforced with 11 artillery regiments, which provided a density in this army's sector of no more than 32 guns and mortars per kilometre of penetration front.

Thus, the tactical density achieved in the southern penetration sector, which was considered the main one, was inadequate. The Supreme High Command order concerning the necessity of concentrating up to 50-60 tubes per kilometre of penetration front remained unfulfilled.

The artillery of reserve Front formations and mobile groups was not brought up to participate in the artillery preparation, and the Front commander had no artillery reserves at his own disposal.

All of Southwestern Front's aviation was distributed among the armies making up the shock group, and massing it under these conditions was extremely difficult. As was the case with artillery, there was no aviation reserve in the hands of the Front commander.

The planned tempos for penetrating the enemy defence and developing success were not high, did not correspond with the operational plan and did not stimulate decisive force operations. Thus, the average daily tempo of the force advance was planned at

Kharkov, 1942

5-6km, the depth of the immediate mission for the forces during the first three days was planned at 18km, and the depth of the subsequent mission was planned at 30-35km. Mobile mechanised cavalry and tank groups, in accordance with the operational plan, were to be committed into the penetration on the second or third day after the infantry had accomplished its immediate missions.

A no less substantive error in the planned offensive was the great extension of Front shock groups into the rear. The distance of army second echelons from jumping-off positions in the front line was 15-20km, the distance of the tank corps from the front lines reached 25-28km and that of the cavalry corps was 12-30km. Army reserves were up to 34km distant from the front.

The slow tempos anticipated by the plan for the advance of first-echelon forces, given the great extension of the shock group into the rear, deprived the forces of necessary flexibility and forced them to develop the offensive slowly and indecisively.

Essentially, co-operation among the combat arms had not been organised by the start of the offensive. Although planning tables for combat and co-operation were compiled in the armies, there was no concrete co-ordination of actions among the combat arms on the ground.

Combat training in Southwestern Front forces during the preparatory period was poorly organised. Despite a number of directives from the Stavka of the Supreme High Command, the massed employment of tanks and aircraft were not worked out in the forces, and joint exercises for the combat arms were not conducted on the ground. In exercises, unit and formation commanders were not inculcated with the skills of bold and decisive manoeuvre when penetrating fortified enemy positions and when fighting in the rear of his defences.

It was a mistake to assign to the command and staff of newly-formed 28th Army, who still had no experience in troop control, the most crucial task of directing operations on the main axis of the Northern Shock Group.

The principal shortcoming in the matter of preparing in staffs at all levels communications and command and control of forces in offensive operation was the over-assessment of the reliability of wire communications, and under-assessment of radio communications, coupled with the inability to use them. Staffs failed to pay requisite attention to increasing the flexibility of command and control. The real threat of a loss of communications and troop control was created from the very beginning of the offensive because of the considerable distance from force command posts (army forces — up to 70km; division — up to 8km).

Conduct of the Offensive Operation

From the very beginning of the Southwestern Front offensive, guidance of combat operations took place in an extraordinarily complex and tense situation.

Errors in planning the operation were not promptly revealed. The incorrect notion about enemy forces and capabilities on the part of the Front commander and his staff continued for a long time to dominate the assessment of the situation, created a false impression of the success of his own forces and kept the Front commander from taking measures which could have corrected the situation in timely fashion. The erroneous assessment of the situation, the miscalculation of their own shock groups' capabilities for developing rapid offensive tempos in the operational depth, and the overall under-assessment of the significance of timely commencement of force operations along secondary axes all contributed to the essence of operational blunders, which resulted in the failure of Southwestern Front operations already in the first stage of the operation.

6 Costs and Consequences

The 38th and 162nd Rifle Divisions, which made up 28th Army's second echelon, serve as an example of the erroneous use of second echelons. During the whole of the first day of the offensive, these divisions remained in concentration areas on the left bank of the Northern Donets River. Subsequently, after they crossed to the right bank on 14 May, 162nd Rifle Division remained in the army reserve, while 38th Rifle Division was used to eliminate the German garrison in Ternovaia.

In the southern sector, during the course of the offensive the army second echelon (103rd and 248th Rifle Divisions and 37th Tank Brigade) were located 10-12 km from first-echelon forces. In fact, 6th Army's second-echelon units were not committed to battle until the end of the offensive.

From the very beginning of Southwestern Front's offensive, the distance from the front line of mobile groups was also excessive, something that precluded the possibility of their timely commitment into battle to complete and develop the penetration of the enemy defence.

At the beginning of the offensive, the distance behind the advance of the Northern and Southern Shock Groups' mobile groups was 30km During the first two days they remained in their former regions, and by the close of 13 May, this distance had increased to 38km in the northern group's sector, and 45km in the southern group's sector. Such a posture for mobile groups did not correspond to existing conditions and precluded the possibility of their timely commitment into battle. The indecisiveness of the mobile groups' advance to the front line had no justification.

On 13–14 May, the Southwestern Front command, by failing to introduce the mobile groups into battle, did not exploit a favourable moment for developing the offensive. The introduction of the cavalry corps into the penetration in the Northern Shock Group's offensive sector and the tank corps into the Southern Shock Group's sector during the day on 13 May or on the morning of 14 May would have ensured the rapid arrival of both shock groups into action, the piecemeal defeat from the march of approaching enemy operational reserves and the successful execution of the mission assigned to Front forces to encircle the German Kharkov grouping.

When Southwestern Front's commander-in-chief shifted to the Berestovaia River (15-16km to the northwest) the line of tank corps' commitment into the penetration, the result was that the tank corps was committed into the penetration only after the rifle formations had occupied a bridgehead on the western bank of the river, something that took two extra days. The enemy took advantage of this time to reinforce his first echelon using operational reserves (113th and 305th Infantry Division units), forcing the tank corps to overcome organised enemy resistance not only along the line of its commitment into the penetration, but also on successive intermediate lines.

In the Northern Shock Group, the mobile group (3rd Guards Cavalry Corps) remained in its initial concentration area, was not committed to combat on 13 or 14 May, and on 15 May was used to carry out local missions. 32nd Cavalry Division occupied defences south of Ternovaia, 6th Guards Cavalry Division assisted 38th Rifle Division in destroying the garrison in Ternovaia, and 5th Guards Cavalry Division with 34th Motorised Rifle Brigade covered the gap between 169th and 162nd Rifle Divisions.

Thus, in both the northern and southern groups, first-echelon forces were not supported by second echelons; they weakened the offensive tempo and made it possible for the enemy to bring up reserves from the rear, remove part of his forces from passive front sectors, have them occupy rear defensive lines, and fortify his positions.

Already, by 16 May, the premature exhaustion of the northern group's main shock

Kharkov, 1942

forces during the penetration of the enemy's main defensive belt and during the repulsion of his counter-attacks made a further offensive by this group hopeless. Accomplishing the mission of destroying the enemy's Kharkov grouping fully fell upon the southern group. However, the southern group did not possess sufficient forces and means to resolve this mission, and all Southwestern Front reserves and aviation were concentrated on the northern axis.

Intelligence operated poorly during the entire offensive. It did not detect in time the regrouping of the enemy's forces and the arrival of his operational reserves in areas of combat operations. Staffs did not attach necessary importance to information received concerning the shift of enemy units from passive front sectors. The appearance of new enemy units in front of the shock groups was discovered, in the majority of cases, only during battle against them. In cases where their concentration was detected beforehand, enormous miscalculations were made in determining the quantity of enemy forces. Thus, in the Northern Shock Group's offensive sector, a mistake was made on 12–13 May in determining the composition of the enemy concentrating in front of 38th Army. Reconnaissance noted the appearance of Panzer divisions, but the transfer of four infantry regiments to this axis went undetected. Reconnaissance also detected neither the transfer of 168th Infantry Division and four regiments of 57th and 75th Infantry Divisions from the Kursk and Belgorod axes, nor their deployment in front of 21st and 28th Armies.

The enemy's removal of units from the Chuguev bridgehead was also not detected. From start to finish of the operation, it was thought that the enemy forces around Chuguev remained unchanged. In fact, on 12–13 May four infantry regiments were removed from there; thus, in total, up to 23 May there were only up to 10 infantry battalions defending on a wide frontage opposite 38th Army. Neither the army commander nor the Southwestern Front commander took advantage of this circumstance. Excessive importance was attached to captured German documents which spoke of an offensive being prepared from the Chuguev bridgehead.

In the Southern Shock Group's offensive sector, the location of 113th Infantry Division in the operational reserve was established only on the third day of the offensive. The advance of the reserve regiment of Hungarian 108th Light Infantry Division from the Zmiev region and 305th Infantry Division units from the rear into the area of combat operations was detected only as a result of a direct battle against them on intermediate defensive lines.

The entire regrouping of enemy forces, which took place from 13 to 16 May on a 110km front, was undetected by Southern Front. 16th Panzer Division, which the enemy transferred to the designated penetration sector, and approaching deep reserves (384th and 389th Infantry Divisions) were detected only during the course of combat on 17–19 May.

Poor reconnaissance made it impossible for Soviet forces to draw correct conclusions about the enemy's operations and, as a result, a number of favourable opportunities for developing the offensive were not exploited.

The Southwestern Front commander's refusal to widen the offensive front by beginning an offensive by 38th Army's left-flank units against the German's Chuguev salient on 16 and 17 May must be considered a great operational blunder. The refusal to widen the offensive front made it possible for the enemy to concentrate the efforts of his tank forces and aviation against the narrow penetration sector of Southwestern Front's northern group and to hold the initiative here until the end of the counterstroke.

6 Costs and Consequences

Troop Control in Defensive Battles in the Barvenkovo Bridgehead

The German counter-stroke found Southern Front forces unprepared to conduct defensive battles. The main defensive sectors of 9th and 57th Armies had a total depth of 3-4km; in fact, they had no operational reserves. From the moment the Germans went over to the offensive, Southern Front communications with these armies' headquarters was lost, and troop control on the part of 9th Army headquarters was completely forfeited. On 17 May, the principal portion of 9th Army's operational reserves was still in the midst of regrouping, while 57th Army's reserves (14th Guards Rifle Division) were designated for commitment into battle on the army's right flank. 5th Cavalry Corps with 12th Tank Brigade, which was in the Front reserve, was operating in 9th Army's sector and by 17 May had still not completely regrouped. This situation made it easy for the enemy to penetrate the entire tactical depth of 9th Army's defence rapidly and made it possible to draw Southern Front's operational reserves into an unfavourable position. All these circumstances, as well as the untimely commitment of 2nd Cavalry Corps (the commander-in-chief's reserve) into battle and the inadequate dynamism of Southern Front forces in the defence, had dire consequences, since the initiative at the beginning of the offensive was not snatched from the hands of the enemy.

After it was established on 17–18 May that the enemy had delivered a blow of great force against the southern face of the Barvenkovo salient to isolate Southwestern Front's southern group from the Northern Donets, the Commander-in-Chief of the Southwestern Direction decided to halt this group's offensive and turn its main forces toward the destruction of German forces which had penetrated into the depth of the defence of Southern Front's 9th and 57th Armies. This decision was correct and appropriate for the situation. However, the extraordinarily prolonged period for withdrawing the southern group's shock forces — 21st and 23rd Tank Corps — from battle made implementation of the commander-in-chief's decision extremely difficult.

During the crucial period when the tank corps were turned into Southern Front's sector, 6th Army headquarters did not exhibit sufficient energy in swiftly transmitting the commander-in-chief's order to the troops. The concentration of the tank corps along the line of the Bereka River was delayed 10-12 hours. The mission for a counter-stroke was not clearly assigned. All of this was a major reason why the commander-in-chief's decision concerning rapid defeat of the penetrating enemy group was not executed, and it also led to further complications in the situation.

During the defensive battles in the Barvenkovo salient, staffs of units and subunits did not cope with the troop control problem. Forces were disorganised in their conduct of combat operations. Attempts by the commander-in-chief to co-ordinate force operations were unsuccessful. Communications in general and radio communications in particular were the weakest area of troop control. Poor organisation of communications had a particularly negative effect on the course of battles in encirclement. Operations by encircled forces were disorganised and there was no support for them at the required time from the outside.

The work of rear service organs during the period of the offensive operation and defensive battles exhibited a number of substantive shortcomings. In conditions of the spring thaw, motor and animal-drawn transport could not cope with the tasks of delivering material to the forces and, as a result, attacking forces, on the fourth or fifth day of the operation, were already experiencing acute shortages of munitions and fuel. During the defensive battles, the small number of crossings over the Northern Donets

Kharkov, 1942

River and the poor organisation for their exploitation represented the worst bottlenecks in the work of rear service organisations.

Use of Combat Arms
Despite the fact that massed use of combat equipment on decisive axes was the fundamental concept of the Southwestern Front's offensive, the Southwestern Front command and staff paid insufficient attention to its implementation.

From start to finish of the operation, aviation was used in a decentralised fashion, despite the need during the offensive for the concentration of air operations against particular axes. Decentralised use of aviation did not provide for co-ordinated operations by different aviation groups and hindered their massed employment.

During the operation, there was a complete lack of cooperation between Southwestern and Southern Front's air forces. Southern Front's air assets were not enlisted to support the penetration of the enemy defence by the forces of Southwestern Front's Southern Shock Group, although this was envisaged by the plan. As a result of its poor use, the aviation of both Fronts took practically no part in repelling the enemy counter-stroke in 9th Army's sector on 17 and 18 May.

Tank brigades were used primarily for direct infantry support against enemy tactical defences. This principle for using tanks was not altered until the end of the operation. Of 19 tank brigades, 10 were subordinate to rifle division commanders, three were in the reserve of the army commanders, and only six, combined into two tank corps, were used as an independent shock force.

During the offensive, tank brigades often operated without cooperation from infantry and without adequate artillery support or air cover. This resulted from the fact that co-operation with other combat arms on the battlefield had not been organised beforehand.

Basically, tank brigades were used during the defensive battles in the Barvenkovo salient to fight against enemy tank groups, just as they had been used during the Northern Shock Group's offensive. Artillery and engineer units were not used adequately to repel tank attacks, and their actions were indecisive.

In fact, the artillery grouping was not altered during the operation and extensive manoeuvres of artillery assets were not executed. Army artillery groups were scattered throughout the operation and were in no way a powerful artillery asset for the army commander; this also meant that mobile groups were committed into battle with only weak artillery support.

Artillery assets began to manoeuvre on a wide front only during the defensive battles in the Barvenkovo salient. A large artillery grouping was concentrated in the Savintsy region by 25–26 May. However, by this time it could no longer be used to assist in the penetration by encircled forces.

Engineer forces were not used at all in either attack or defence. Available engineer assets were used in rare instances on the battlefield. Neither in armies nor in divisions were anti-tank reserves or obstacle detachments created, both of which could have been manoeuvred and could have promptly and reliably covered axes favourable for tanks. Engineer forces operated without co-operating with artillery or, crucially, tanks. Their principal mission was to organise and construct river crossings and repair and maintain roads.

In rare cases individual combat-engineer subunits were used to create engineer obstacles. In repelling counter-strokes by enemy tanks in the Northern Shock Group's

6 Costs and Consequences

sector and in conducting defensive battles in the Barvenkovo salient, engineer forces had no substantive influence on the outcome.

The study of Southwestern Front's offensive operation and the defensive battles of Southwestern and Southern Fronts in the Barvenkovo bridgehead demonstrates that, had there been skilful leadership, Southwestern Front's offensive could have been successful, since this Front had adequate forces and means.

Solid and decisive implementation of the basic measures envisaged by the operational plan of attack and Stavka instructions were required to execute the mission assigned by the Stavka of the Supreme High Command to Southwestern Front forces. Deviations from the plan which were permitted, and a number of operational blunders, led to the failure of Southwestern Front's offensive operation. Had there been a timely and decisive execution of the operational plan, the enemy would not have been able to block Southwestern Front's offensive and our forces would have been able to repel his counter-stroke. Under such conditions, Southwestern Front's offensive operation would have concluded successfully.

Air Operations
While referring to air operations in general terms, including planning considerations, periodic comparative sortie rates and overall combat impact, the Soviet General Staff Study understated the importance of air operations in the outcome of the Kharkov operation. In short, the number of Soviet aircraft available and committed, the relatively low quality of many of the aircraft, the inexperience of Soviet pilots, and poor command, control, communications and tactics plagued Soviet efforts to deny the German one lethal element of their Blitzkrieg tactics and accorded the Germans air superiority over the battlefield by 15 May.

Decentralised control of Soviet aircraft and their limited if not totally non-existent night-time capability soon negated initial Soviet surprise and by 15 May Luftwaffe units operated with impunity over the battlefield with lethal effect, despite fierce air battles raging to the south over the Crimean peninsula where German forces were reducing the soviet fortress at Sevastopol' and defending against Soviet relief efforts launched from the Kerch peninsula. Effective control enabled the German command to shift required aircraft into the Kharkov region and practised Blitzkrieg tactics permitted effective engagement of advancing Soviet forces, interdiction of deploying Soviet reserves and logistics and efficient close air support of counter-attacking German panzer formations. Increasing German and decreasing Soviet daily air sorties vividly underlined this sad reality.

Although German ground forces would probably have achieved victory without dominant air support, German air operations crippled the Soviet's ability to respond effectively to the German counter-stroke. The air dimension only multiplied Soviet pain and the scale of the ensuing disaster.

Although concluding that the Southwestern Direction's plan was sound, and the Stavka had provided adequate resources with which to conduct the offensive, the study faulted the Direction and its subordinate Fronts with poor control and co-ordination of the operation. In particular, it blamed Timoshenko and his Military Council for violating strict Stavka directives to ensure that Southern Front protection of the offensive was sound. Among the other numerous shortcomings attributed to the Southwestern Direction Command during the planning phase of the operation were the failure to organise sufficient fire support, weak intelligence collection and pro-

Kharkov, 1942

cessing, poor force concentration, inaccurate assessment of the correlation of forces, clumsy employment of mobile forces, ineffective co-operation between units, lax combat training and poor use of communications. Once the operation commenced, these faults were exacerbated by weak control of forces in battle, poor and untimely decision-making, and a host of lesser tactical errors. Although these criticisms were no doubt accurate, they still begged the main questions, which were, 'Should the operation have been conducted in the first place?' and, if the answer to that question was 'No', then 'Who else should share the blame for failure?' Political realities in 1951, at the time the study was prepared, dictated that blame for the failure be assigned to senior and junior officers in the Southwestern Direction command.

7
CONCLUSIONS

The conclusions of the General Staff study woefully understated the strategic and operational significance of the Kharkov disaster. Regardless of whether the Stavka had conducted the Kharkov operation in May 1942, the German High Command would have begun its summer campaign sooner or later. Even if Soviet forces had been more successful in the operation as they had hoped, in the end German forces would probably have prevailed. At the worst, from the German standpoint Operation 'Blau' and its precursor 'Friderikus' might have been delayed for a matter of days or several weeks. Whenever the Germans were finally able to launch 'Friderikus', the operation would have proceeded generally as planned, and German forces would undoubtedly have cleared Soviet forces from the Barvenkovo bridgehead. Thereafter, the Germans would have launched 'Blau', and it is difficult to imagine the Red Army would have been able to deny German forces initial operational success. It is also likely, however, that, had the Kharkov offensive not occurred, the scale of the ensuing Soviet defeat around Kharkov would have been appreciably less catastrophic. None-the-less, it is also unlikely that the Red Army would have been able to thwart Operation 'Blau', the subsequent German eastward advance toward the Don River and Stalingrad.

By misassessing German intent and underestimating German capabilities, however, Stalin, the Stavka, Marshal Timoshenko, Commissar Khrushchev and Gen Bagramian made the situation worse by walking into an operational trap. Over a quarter of a million Soviet soldiers paid the price for their collective misjudgement. Even after Operation 'Blau' commenced on 28 June 1942, the Stavka was able to withdraw the bulk of its forces in the south, albeit haphazardly, to new defence lines along the Don and along the approaches to Stalingrad. While doing so, they avoided the large-scale encirclements and losses they had suffered in 1941. The speed of the German advance toward the Don and the ultimate depth of German operations resulted, in part, from a scarcity of Soviet forces in the region. That shortage of forces, in turn, was a direct consequence of the immense Soviet losses at Kharkov.

In the end, by November 1942 the Soviets brought the German advance to a halt along the foothills of the Caucasus Mountains, the banks of the Volga and the ruins of Stalingrad (see Map 37). By that time the Soviets had amassed sufficient strategic reserves to strike back in a major counter-offensive. The presence in the Red Army of November 1942 of the quarter of a million Soviet soldiers lost at Kharkov would not have changed the course of the ensuing campaign, but it certainly would have made the Stavka's job an easier one.

The staff study also failed to underline the most important impact of the Kharkov operation: the psychological and practical impact it had on the Soviet senior political and military leadership. The defeat at Kharkov pricked the bubble of Soviet optimism, which had prevailed since the beginning of winter. All exhortations for the achievement of victory were rendered hollow and inflated Soviet expectations were dashed. Henceforth, Stalin, the Stavka and senior Soviet command leadership listened more closely to the advice of the General Staff. For the most part, greater caution and more modest expectations would rule, and it is no coincidence that, after summer 1942, two

Kharkov, 1942

key General Staff figures, Vasilevsky and Zhukov, would play a greater role in planning and supervising the conduct of strategic operations. In short, the Kharkov defeat prompted the Soviet military leadership to take a more realistic and cautious approach to the conduct of war.

The Kharkov defeat also had clear international ramifications. The staff study limited itself to noting that 'the treacherous delay by the Anglo-Americans in opening a second front in Western Europe during the summer of 1942 created a tense situation in the Soviet Army'. The fact is that Allied concern over Soviet military fortunes had abated somewhat in the wake of the Red Army's winter victories around Moscow. In May and June, however, the staggering Soviet defeat at Kharkov and the subsequent precipitous German summer advance across southern Russia rekindled Allied concerns and, at the same time, lent a more urgent tone to Soviet entreaties to the Allies to open a second front in western Europe. During late May and early June, in the immediate wake of the Kharkov defeat, Soviet Foreign Minister Molotov visited England and the US. Haunted by the Kharkov and Kerch débiâcles, he argued strongly for creation of the second front as soon as possible 'by sending 35 divisions across the Channel'.[1] Although the joint communiqué, issued on 11 June 1942 at the end of Molotov's trip, announced 'full understanding' of the issue, nothing was really resolved. To Molotov, 35 divisions was a mere pittance, comparable with the force the Stavka had squandered at Kharkov. To Roosevelt and Churchill, commitment of so large a force in a European landing was impossible. Therefore, Churchill recorded his reservations and doubts about a second front in 1942 in an *aide-mémoire* to Molotov.[2] This exchange underlined not only the vast difference between the war in the Soviet Union and the war elsewhere but also the comparative 'war psychologies' of the respective national leaders.

Changing political circumstances within the Soviet Union after the death of Stalin permitted closer scrutiny of the Kharkov operation, in particular since N. S. Khrushchev rose to power during the years after Stalin's death. As member of the Southwestern Command's Military Council in May 1942, Khrushchev shared blame for the disaster, in as much as any Politburo member could, with Marshal Timoshenko and General Bagramian. This would not do for a rising star in the Soviet political firmament. Hence, as Khrushchev rose to power in the late 1950s, the Kharkov disaster was resurrected as a blot on Stalin's record and a fragment of the de-Stalinisation programme. After Khrushchev was ousted in 1964, his enemies once again exposed the operation to sully Khrushchev's reputation. The historiographical somersaults which paralleled political power struggles thoroughly muddied the waters of blame in the operation. Three general cases are representative of the muddle over blame.

Volume two of the mammoth six-volume *History of the Great Patriotic War*, written when Khrushchev was Party First Secretary and head of the Soviet Union, states the following:

'The Southwestern Direction's Military Council made the decision to cut short a further offensive on Kharkov and, quickly regrouping its forces, to create a strong group to repel the counter-stroke of Group "Kleist". The Stavka did not approve that appropriate decision and demanded that Southwestern Front continued the offensive on Kharkov with their forces and repel the enemy's counter-stroke with Southern Front's 9th and 57th Armies and with reserves along that axis.'[3]

Further on in this work, Khrushchev recalls:

7 Conclusions

'I did not agree with the Stavka decision ... and immediately returned to the Stavka with a proposal to halt the offensive on Kharkov rapidly and concentrate the main forces of the Southwestern Front to repel the enemy counter-attack. The Stavka, however, insisted on the fulfilment of the earlier assigned mission.'[4]

An account of the dispute by the contemporary historian and Stalin critic, Dmitri Volkogonov, explains Khrushchev's view further, writing:

'Later, at the Twentieth Party Congress, Khrushchev blamed Stalin directly for the catastrophe at Kharkov. He recalled that he had called the Kremlin from the front, Malenkov picked up the phone and Khrushchev demanded to speak to Stalin, who, standing only a few paces away, told Malenkov to take the call. Khrushchev told him to ask Stalin to call off the offensive, to which Stalin replied, "Leave things as they are!"'[5]

Marshal Zhukov, writing in his memoirs in 1969 after the removal of Khrushchev from power, contradicted this condemnation of Stalin, writing:

'That day [18 May] I was present at the Stavka during a conversation Stalin had with the Commander of the Southwestern Front. I clearly remember that the Supreme Commander made it quite plain to Timoshenko that he was deeply disturbed by the enemy's success in the Kramatorsk area. Towards evening on May 18, he discussed the problem with Khrushchev, the Southwestern Front's Military Council member, who expressed the same ideas as the Front Command: the threat from the enemy's Kramatorsk group had been greatly exaggerated, and there was no reason to halt the operation. On the basis of these reports from the Military Council of the Southwestern Front on the need to continue the offensive, the Supreme Commander rejected the arguments of the General Staff. The existing version that the Military Councils of the Southern and Southwestern Front sent warnings to the Stavka does not correspond to the facts. I can testify to this because I was present during the Supreme Commander's conversation.'[6]

In 1975 the officially prepared *History of the Second World War* supported Zhukov's view, emphasising the reluctance of the General Staff to continued the operation and the adamant position of the Southwestern Direction Military Council to continue the operation:

'The General Staff once again proposed that the Stavka cease the offensive operation at Kharkov, turn the main force of the Barvenkovo shock group, liquidate the enemy penetration and restore the situation of Southern Front's 9th Army, However, the Southwestern Front's Military Council was able to convince Stalin that the danger from the enemy Kramatorsk group was strongly exaggerated, and there was no basis for cutting the operation short.'[7]

Thus, the first of these three contradictory sources place the blame for the failure to reorient the Southwestern Front's shock force southward to deal with the new threat at the feet of Stalin and the Stavka. The latter two redirect the blame to the Southwestern Front's Military Council. Recently released documents, in particular the Southwestern Direction Military Council's report of 18 May, seem to support the latter.

Kharkov, 1942

Participants in the operation, in particular Bagramian, whose reputation had been sullied, and Moskalenko, whose army had failed to rescue the encircled Soviet Barvenkovo force, were able to wade into the dispute by means of their memoirs. Writing in 1969, Moskalenko distributed blame for the operation equally, stating, 'There is no doubt that the Stavka committed a mistake in agreeing to the conduct of the operation. But, as I already mentioned, it did this based on the insistence of the Southwestern Direction Military Council.'[8] Moskalenko searched for reasons why the Military Council insisted on conducting such an ambitious operation in the spring and thought he found the answer in the excessive enthusiasm of the Front and Direction command to capitalise on the victories achieved during the winter. He cites an essentially political report prepared by the Assistant Chief of Staff of the Southwestern Front, Col I. N. Rukhle, entitled 'Missions of Staff Party Organizations in Guaranteeing Front Force Operations in Spring 1942'. When describing conditions at the front, the report said:

'The winter period was distinguished by the fact that the initiative was seized from the Germans and passed into the hands of the Red Army. The Red Army passed from the defence to the offensive, removed the immediate threat to Moscow and threw the enemy back to the west. It follows that, from the beginning of winter, the war entered a new stage of dynamics with the Red Army with all of its advantages as the attacking side.'

The report finished with the following exhortation:

'In the end, Fascist Germany expended its advantage of strategic surprise (a temporary factor). The superiority of the Red Army's material and moral strength (a constantly operating factor) secured our success during the course of the winter. We have still before us in the spring campaign a great army, technically well equipped, but with a broken belief in victory, and, having lost the best of its cadre and mass of equipment, the Fascist Army will not succeed in re-establishing its former size in the course of war.'[9]

Moskalenko believed that this mood and the related fear that, if the advantage was not exploited, the Germans would regain the initiative, drove Soviet staffs and commands into offensive action and imbued them with an inordinate and unrealistic optimism over what they could achieve in the spring. Moskalenko added, however, that this view 'did not correspond to the situation'. He went on to say that the Southwestern Direction Command underestimated the threat of Kleist's group, reacted too slowly to the developing German counter-stroke and committed many of the errors mentioned by the General Staff critique. In his view, the Kharkov operation was 'a bold and decisive action'. 'Unfortunately,' he wrote, '... the decisiveness of the Front's, command's and staff's actions were somehow identified with unwarranted risks. That led to the fact that almost everywhere we lagged behind.'[10] As evidence that they had come close to achieving victory, Moskalenko cited a passage from the German military historian, Wilhelm Adam's book, *Difficult Decisions*, which read:

'We found ourselves in a threatening situation. The strikes of Soviet forces penetrated our defences in a series of sectors. Soviet tanks stood only 20km from Kharkov ... In the battles for Kharkov, Sixth Army suffered very appreciable casualties, having lost 20,000 men killed and wounded.'[11]

7 Conclusions

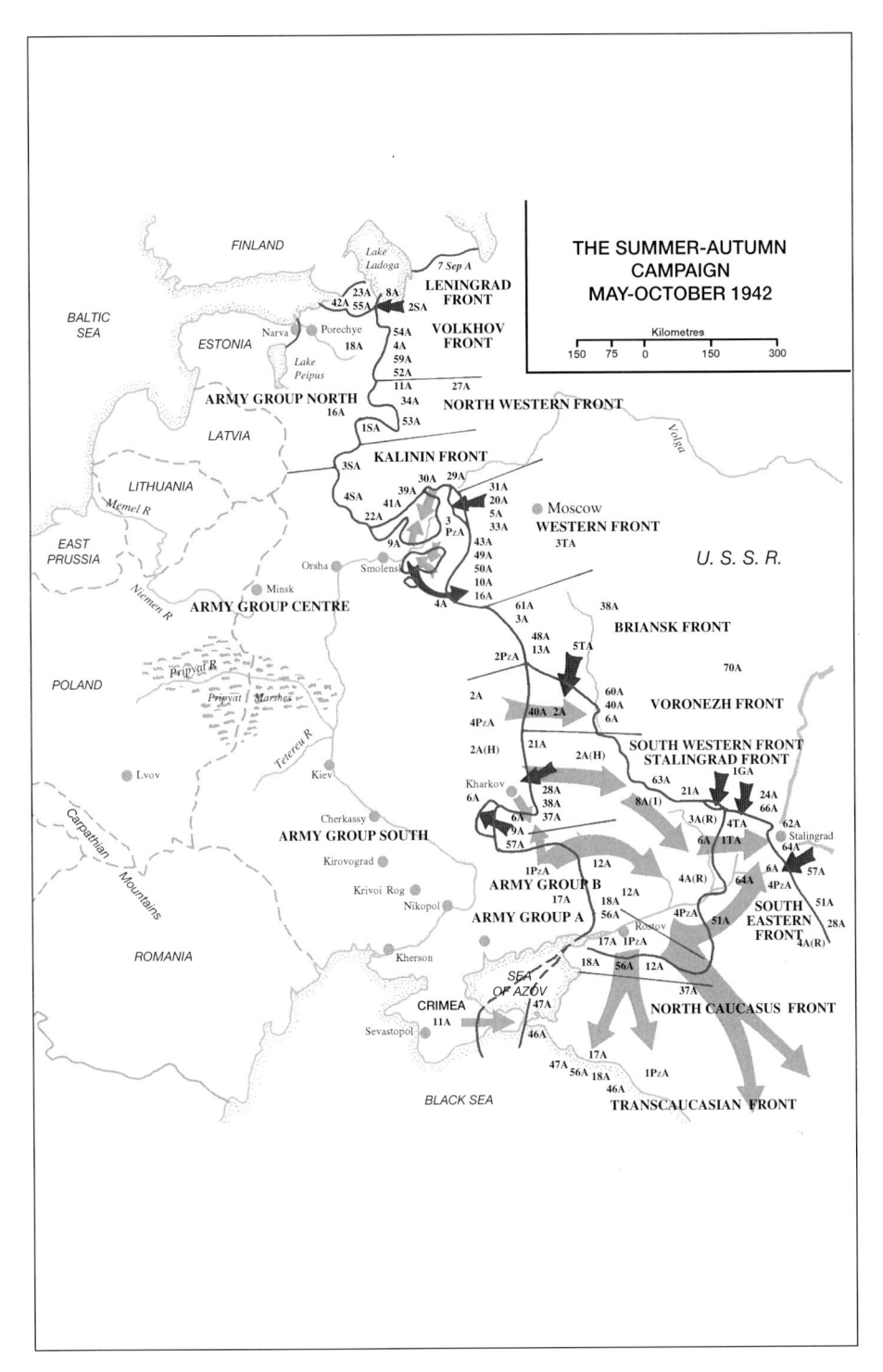

Map 37 — The Summer-Autumn Campaign, 1942

Kharkov, 1942

In the end, Moskalenko rationalised the experience, writing:

'Combat operations in the Kharkov region were characterised by a keen struggle for the initiative in the development of large-scale offensive operations and in the improvement of the operational formations of the contending sides. Having lost the battle in May, Soviet forces lost an important operational bridgehead and were forced to shift to the defence in unfavourable conditions. This served as a severe lesson. The most important aspect of this was that we renounced exaggerated notions about our success in accumulating experience in the conduct of modern war.'[12]

In 1977 Bagramian, then a Marshal of the Soviet Union, reflected on the operation in his memoirs. Asking himself how an operation which had begun with such success could have ended with such a 'large-scale failure', he admitted that, 'During the war I endured [the failure] with great bitterness and mental anguish, and it disturbed me in the postwar years.'[13] Bagramian admitted that both the Stavka and the Southwestern Direction Command misassessed German strategic intentions during the spring and that, in light of this incorrect assumption, Southwestern Direction force strength was inadequate for the task. Citing and agreeing with Vasilevsky's judgement that the Stavka tried to do too much in spring 1942, he repeated Vasilevsky's comment, 'Errors permitted by the Stavka and General Staff in planning combat operations in summer 1942 were instructive in the future, especially in summer 1943, when decisions were made regarding the nature of combat actions in the Kursk bulge.'[14]

Bagramian went on to admit that Southwestern Direction forces were not sufficiently strong and argued that an absence of strategic and operational reserves in the region exacerbated the problem:

'On the Red Army's entire huge southern strategic wing, behind the front lines for an overall distance of more that 800km, at the beginning of the summer campaign of 1942 the Stavka had neither a single combined arms army nor a tank army in its reserve. Here its reserve consisted of only four rifle divisions, which were in the process of disbanding or refilling their personnel and equipment. Because of this limitation in forces, the Southwestern Direction had no capability for creating appropriate reserves.'[15]

To underline the importance of this deficiency, Bagramian cited Zhukov's judgements regarding the root cause for the Kharkov disaster, to the effect that:

'While analysing the causes of failures in the Kharkov operation, it is not difficult to understand that the basic reason for the defeat of Southwestern Direction forces lay in the underestimation of the serious threat posed by the Southwestern Strategic Direction, where the necessary Stavka reserves had not been concentrated.'[16]

Moreover, the Stavka, wrote Bagramian, failed to fill out Southwestern Direction formations with requisite manpower and materiel prior to the offensive. Finally, Bagramian criticised the Stavka for refusing to launch a companion supporting offensive by the Briansk Front, whose conduct, in his view, would have deflected German reserves away from the Kharkov region.

Having heaped blame on the Stavka for many errors, Bagramian then criticised his own command. Included in this list of shortcomings were the Southwestern

7 Conclusions

Direction's failure to create adequate flank security for its attacking shock group, poor Front intelligence collection and processing, underestimation of enemy force strength and manoeuvre capabilities, and the slow and untimely Front reaction to the German counter-stroke.

Bagramian reserved special criticism for the Southern Front Command and staff, which he accused of conducting faulty threat estimates and neglecting its critical flank security responsibilities. He admitted, however, that part of this was due to faulty control over the Front by the Southwestern Direction headquarters.

Bagramian also pointed out structural weaknesses of the Red Army, which contributed materially to the 1942 defeat. These included the absence of mobile armoured forces and air forces which could compete successfully with the more experienced and better organised Germans.

Bagramian's final judgement on the Kharkov operation was a philosophical 'shrug of the shoulders' on his part, as he wrote:

'The mistakes permitted both during the preparation for the Kharkov operation and during its conduct aggravated still more the exceptionally unfavourable strategic situation in which the Soviet forces of the Southwestern Direction found themselves on the eve of the summer campaign. Regarding the latter, it often seems as if the outcome of the struggle at Kharkov and the failures befalling the Red Army during the entire 1942 summer campaign depended exclusively on the mistakes and shortcomings permitted by the command and staff of Southwestern Direction forces in planning and conducting the Kharkov operation. In reality, as is apparent, the problem about which I speak was very complex and is far beyond the limits of these subjective notions.'[17]

During the last years of the Gorbachev government, in particular after 1987 and since the dissolution of the Soviet Union, the debate over blame for the Kharkov disaster has intensified. It is as if the last word on Kharkov is required before these historians can move on to reveal and discuss other, even more tragic, previously forbidden topics related to the course of the war. This new debate has been better informed by archival materials, although the Russian government still has not released documents concerning Stavka wartime decision-making, the most important category of missing materials.

The most recent Russian assessments of the Kharkov operation reiterate those shortcomings detailed in the 1951 General Staff Study and tend to distribute blame for the operation among all the chief participants. The most common general conclusion is that Soviet forces in May 1942 were insufficiently strong to accomplish the ambitious offensive task. In this sense, they argue that the General Staff was correct to recommend against the conduct of the operation. These new studies challenge the correlation of forces provided in the 1951 study and, instead, argue that German forces outnumbered their Soviet counterparts in the Southwestern Direction sector. Specifically, while tank forces were equal, the Germans outnumbered the Soviet by a factor of 1.1:1 in manpower, 1.3:1 in guns and mortars, and 1.6:1 in aircraft. Moreover, they argue that the Germans outnumbered the Southern Front by an even greater margin and, along the southern face of the Barvenkovo bridgehead, the German superiority reached 1.3:1 in manpower, 4.4:1 in tanks, and 1.7:1 in artillery. The same source accepts the 1951 study's figures for Soviet superiority in the Southwestern Front's penetration sector.[18]

Kharkov, 1942

These figures are disingenuous and contradict the correct conclusions of the 1951 General Staff Study. German and Soviet strength along the German-Soviet front in May 1942 was approximately 3,580,000 Germans (including 950,000 Allies) and 5,449,898 Soviets (in operating Fronts and armies).[19] Strength returns for the Soviet Southwestern and Southern Fronts were 614,073 and 578,313 men, respectively, plus an additional 331,548 men in the Crimean Front, for a total of over 1.5 million men opposing German Army Group 'South'.[20] These figures generally agree with the recent Soviet figure of 765,300 men recorded to have taken part in the Kharkov operation. On the other side, German Army Group 'South' on 1 May 1942 had 50% of its required infantry strength, and the total strength of the Army Group, including Allied forces, did not exceed 1.3 million men.[21] The force the German command brought to bear on the Barvenkovo bridgehead did not exceed 500,000 men (including Allies). German victory at Kharkov was achieved not by numbers but, rather, by superior tactical skill and concentrated use of armour and aircraft.

Other criticisms levelled at the Soviet commands involved in the operation are more understandable. These include weak Soviet intelligence collection and processing, Timoshenko's ineptitude in controlling operations once they had begun, and his inability to move quickly enough to counter German counter-attacks. In Timoshenko's defence, it must be noted that German dominance in the air destroyed effective Soviet command and control of operations very early on and prevented Soviet decisions from being carried out. Soviet loss of command and control also had other unforeseen consequences. The appallingly high command losses at regimental and divisional level were a product, in part, of the necessity for these commanders to travel into battle to see that their commands carried out required missions.

One particularly acute assessment of Timoshenko's leadership capabilities stands out for its candour and accuracy. Made by the distinguished Russian military historian, F. D. Sverdlov, it read:

'It is surprising for many how I. V. Stalin and the Stavka VGK, during the course of operations, could be guided by the assessments and decisions of S. K. Timoshenko — a man whose strategic horizons were limited. It is clear, the false assessment of the situation and the desire to pass off wishes as realities played a role here.'[22]

Sverdlov went on to enunciate the harsh truth of the Kharkov battle:

'But the main reason [for Soviet failure], in my opinion, was that during the operation S. K. Timoshenko was not able to evaluate properly new information on the situation and did not possess the talent of operational-strategic foresight. His command of the Front and reports to the Stavka recall to a large degree the actions of a brave cavalry leader, as he was in 1st Cavalry Army during the Civil War, but not the Supreme High Commander of Direction and Front forces. The commanders of armies and divisions also made mistakes. Furthermore, their combat experience in no way compared with the experience which German generals and officers had obtained in France, Poland, Yugoslavia and Ukraine. One must not forget about the qualifications of commanders. From 1937 until 1941, 40,000 men, principally from higher commands, were repressed, including 90% of army commanders, 80% of corps commanders, and more than 70% of divisional commanders. On the whole, the armies of the Southwestern, Southern and other Fronts were commanded by former division commanders, and divisions by former regimental commanders. Certainly they made mistakes, but their

7 Conclusions

blunders in no way compared with the errors of the senior leadership of the country and the Armed Forces, which led to catastrophes.'[23]

The scale of the ensuing catastrophe was clear to Sverdlov:

'So it was on the Southwestern Front in September 1941, when Stalin forbade the timely withdrawal of forces from Kiev. That decision led to the encirclement east of Kharkov of 600,000 Red Army troops and the rapid advance of Fascist forces to the east. So it was at Kharkov. As a result of this defeat, the situation on the southern wing of the Soviet-German front sharply changed to the advantage of the enemy. The Southwestern and Southern Fronts suffered immense losses and were considerably weakened. By the middle of June 1942, the enemy threw Southwestern Front forces back to the east to the Oskol River, which to a considerable degree facilitated the further advance of Fascist forces to the Volga and into the northern Caucasus.'[24]

While essentially correct, Sverdlov was also more than kind to Stalin and his favourites in high command positions. Both Stalin and Timoshenko, and, to a lesser extent, other army commanders, were carried away by their winter success and optimism over what could be achieved in the spring. Moskalenko's lament that psychological, and even ideological conditioning, had inspired Stalin and senior Soviet commanders to reach too far, was correct. Sadly, Soviet soldiers paid the price.

Notes to Chapters

Notes to the Preface
1 'Opisanie operatsii voisk iugo-zapadnom fronta na khar'kovskom napravlenii v mae 1942 goda' (Account of operations by Southwestern Front forces on the Kharkov axis in May 1942); *Sbornik voenno-istoricheskikh materialov Velikoi Otechestvennoi voiny. Vypusk 5* (Collection of military-historical materials of the Great Patriotic War, Issue 5);Voenizdat, Moscow, 1951. Classified secret. Declassified 1964.

Notes to Introduction
1. Stalin, I. V.; *Voprosy Leninisma* (Problems of Leninism); 11th edition, Politizdat, Moscow, 1950, p323.

Notes to Chapter 1
1. For details on the Zhukov proposal, see Glantz, David M.; *The Military Strategy of the Soviet Union; A History*; Frank Cass, London, 1992, pp87-91.
2. Details on the Barvenkovo-Lozovaia operation in Saviny, M., ed.; *Barvenkovo-Lozovaia operatsiia (18-31 ianvaria 1942 g.): Kratkii operativno-takticheskii ocherk* (The Barvenkovo-Lozovaia operation [18-31 January 1942]): A short operational-tactical study); Voenizdat, Moscow, 1943. Prepared by the military-historical section of the Red Army General Staff. Classified secret. Declassified 1964.
3. Among others, see Zhukov, G.; *Reminiscences and Reflections, Vol 2*; Progress, Moscow, 1985, pp71-72.
4. See Losik, O. A.; *Stroitel'stvo i boevoe primenenie sovetskikh tankovikh voisk v gody Velikoi Otechestvennoi voiny* (Formation and combat use of Soviet tank forces in the Great Patriotic War); Voenizdat, Moscow, 1979, pp50-52.

Notes to Chapter 2
1. For an excellent description of German strategic and operational planning in spring 1942, see pp286-290, Ziemke, Earle F. and Bauer, Magna E.; *Moscow to Stalingrad: Decision in the East*; Center of Military History, United States Army, Washington, D. C., 1987.
2. See pp364-365, Zhukov, G. K.; *The Memoirs of Marshal Zhukov*; Delacorte Press, New York, 1971.
3. See p183, Vasilevsky, A. M.; *Delo vsei zhizni* (Life's work); Politizdat, Moscow, 1983.
4. Ibid, p185.
5. See pp159-163, Moskalenko, K. S.; *Na iugo-zapadnom napravlenii*, T.1 (On the southwestern axis, v.1); 'Nauka', Moscow, 1969.
6. See pp48-49, I. Kh. Bagramian, *Tak shli my k pobeda* (As we went on to victory); Voenizdat, Moscow, 1977.
7. Vasilevsky, p186.
8. Ibid.
9. Ibid.
10. Moskalenko, pp173-174.
11. Ibid.
12. Ibid, p174.
13. Bagramian, p52.
14. Moskalenko, pp176-177.
15. Ibid, p177.
16. Begunov, S. F., Litvinchuk, A. V., Sutulov, V. A.; 'Agde pravda, Nikita Sergeevich!' (What then is the truth, Nikita Sergeevich!); *Voenno-istoricheskii zhurnal*, (military-historical journal), No 12 December 1989. 12-16 contains the entire document. Hereafter cited as *VIZh*, with appropriate number and date.
17. Bagramian, p67.
18. Ibid, p54.
19. Ibid, p60.
20. Ibid, pp61-62.
21. Ibid, p65. See Appendix 2 for full text of the request for reinforcements.
22. Ibid.
23. Ibid, p66.
24. For a good survey of overall Stavka strategic intentions in spring 1942, see A. N. Grilev, 'Nekotorye osobennosti planirovaniia letne-osennei kampanii 1942 goda' (Some peculiarities of planning for the 1942 summer-autumn campaign), *VIZh*, No 8 August 1987, pp20-25.
25. Bagramian, p68.
26. Begunov, et al, 'Vot gde pravda' (What then is the truth), *VIZh*, No 12 December 1989, 19. See the entire Operational Plan of Southwestern Front Forces to Secure the Kharkov Regions and Subsequently Attack Along the Dvepropetrovsk-Sinelnikovo Axes in Appendix 3.
27. Vasilevsky, p186.
28. Moskalenko, pp178-179.
29. Begunov, et al, 'Vot gde pravda' (What then is the truth), *VIZh*, No 1 January 1990, pp9-11. See Appendix 4 for full text of Directive No 00275.
30. Bagramian, pp71-72.
31. Begunov, et al, 'Vot ge pravda' (What then is the truth), *VIZh*, No 1 (January 1990), p12. See Appendix 5 for full text of Southern Front Operational Directive No 99177.
32. Ibid, p13.
33. Bagramian, p72.
34. Ibid, p76.
35. Ibid, p74.
36. Ibid, p75.
37. Moskalenko, p186.
38. Ibid, pp186-189.
39. Bagramian, p82.
40. Ibid, pp80-81.
41. Ziemke and Bauer, p272.
42. Halder, Franz; *War Journal of Franz Halder*, VII; typescript translated copy, US Army War College, Carlisle, PA., undated, p1433.
43. Ibid, p1435-1437.
44. Ibid, p1439, Goerlitz, W.; *Paulus and Stalingrad*; The Citadel Press, New York, 1963, pp176-178.
45. Ziemke and Bauer, p273.
46. Grilev, pp23-24.
47. Stalin, I. V.; *O Velikoi Otechestvennoi voine Sovetskogo Soiuza* (On the Great Patriotic War of the Soviet Union); 5th edition; Politizdat, Moscow, 1946, pp43-44.
48. In calculating the operational density, all rifle divisions and brigades were taken into account. Two brigades were counted as one division.
49. Operation Directive No 00275 of the Southwestern Direction, dated 28 April 1942. During preparations for the operation a number of local changes were made in the army's make-up and mission.
50. 21st Tank Corps consisted of 64th, 198th and 199th Tank and 4th Motorised Rifle Brigades; 23rd Tank Corps consisted of 6th, 130th and 131st Tank and 23rd Motorised Rifle Brigades.
51. Tank corps were formed by the Southwestern Direction Commander-in-Chief in accordance with a directive from the Stavka of the Supreme High Command, dated 17 April 1942. Three tank corps (21st, 23rd and 24th) were formed, each consisting of three tank and one motorised rifle brigade. The formation of a fourth tank corps (22nd) was, in fact, never completed. Two of the three tank brigades planned for this tank corps were allocated to reinforce rifle divisions in the penetration sectors, and the third was left in the reserve of the 38th Army commander. After its formation, 24th Tank Corps comprised the reserve of the Southern Front commander.
52. RAG-5 was part of Southern Front and was attached to the Army Group.

Notes

Notes to Chapter 3
1. For a full discussion of these axes, see Glantz, David M.; *The Strategic and Operational Impact of Terrain on Military Operations in Central and Eastern Europe*; Foreign Military Studies Office, Fort Leavenworth, KS, 1991.

Notes to Chapter 4
1. For more details on evolving Soviet force structure, see Losik, Babich, Iu P., Baier, A. G.; *Razvitie vooruzheniia i organizatsii Sovetskikh sukhoputnykh voisk v gody Velikoi Otechestvennoi voiny* (The development of weaponry and Soviet ground force organisation during the Great Patriotic War); Akademii, Moscow, 1990. Prepared by the Order of Lenin and October Revolution, Red Banner, Order of Suvorov Frunze Academy history department; P. A. Kurochkin, ed.; *Obshchevoiskovaia armiia v nastuplenii* (The combined arms army in the offensive); Voenizdat, Moscow, 1966; and Radziyevsky, A. I.ed.; *Armeiskie operatsii* (Army operations); Voenizdat, Moscow, 1977.
2. For more detail on the nature and evolution of Strategic Directions, see pp54-59, Savushkin, R. A.; *Razvitie sovetskikh vooruzhennykh sil i voennogo isskustva v Velikoi Otechestvennoi voine 1941-1945 gg* (The development of the Soviet Armed Forces and military art in the Great Patriotic War 1941-1945); VPA, Moscow, 1988.
3. For more details on the organisation and function of Fronts, see pp31-33 Kirian, M. M.; *Fronty nastupali* (The Fronts attack); 'Nauka', Moscow, 1987.
4. Babich and Baier, pp37-38.
5. Ibid., pp34-37. Details on the penal battalions in Khomenko, S.; 'Disciplinary Battalion Joins Battle', *Soviet Soldier*, No 11 November 1990, pp36-38. Each battalion of 800 men was made up of mid and high ranking commanders who were guilty of 'violating discipline through cowardice or instability'. Convicted privates and sergeants manned five to ten companies (of 150-200 men each) subordinated to armies.
6. Babich and Baier, pp37-38.
7. The best description of a Soviet rifle brigade is found in German Foreign Armies East records. See, for example, 'Russ. Schutz-Brig. vom 17.4.42'. *Kriegsgliederungen der Sowjetunion* (Order of battle of the Soviet Union); FHO (Fremde Heere Ost). NAM-T-78, Roll 550. NAM refers to National Archives Microfilm series, in this case T-78. Hereafter referred to as FHO, with appropriate microfilm series and roll.
8. Ibid., Babich and Baier, pp40-42.
9. 'Kriegsgliederung einer sow-russ. mot. Schutz-Brigade', *FHO*, T-78, Roll 550.
10. See pp195-199, Soshnikov, A. Ia. ed.; *Sovetskaia kavaleriia* (Soviet cavalry); Voenizdat, Moscow, 1984. Also Babich and Baier, pp61-62.
11. 'Kriegsgliederung einer Kavallerie-Div Dezember 1941'; *FHO*, T-78, Roll 550.
12. Ibid.
13. Babich and Baier, pp50-56.
14. Ibid., p51. See also pp54-80, Degtiarev, P. A., Ionov, P. P.; *Katiushi' na pole boia* (Katiushas on the field of battle); Voenizdat, Moscow, 1991.
15. See pp13-14, Peredel'sky, G.; 'Artileriskoe nastuplenie v armeiskikh operatsiiakh' (The artillery offensive in army operations); *VIZh*, No 11 November 1976.
16. See Vol 7, pp511-12, Sbytov, N. A.; 'Stavka verkhovnogo glavnokomandovaniia' (The Stavka of the High Command); *Sovetskaia voennaia entsiklopediia* (Soviet military encyclopedia); 8 vols, Voenizdat, Moscow, 1976-1980. Hereafter cited as SVE with appropriate volume and page.
17. See p51, Savushkin; *Razvitie, 1941-1945 gg*.
18. 'Anfilov, V.; Semen Konstantinovich Timoshenko', in H. Shukman, ed., *Stalin's Generals*, Weidenfeld and Nicolson, London, 1993, p 241. See also pp66-68., 'Marshal Sovetskogo Soiuza S. K. Timoshenko', (Marshal of the Soviet Union S. K. Timoshenko); *VIZh* No 2 February 1986,
19. See pp253.Anfilov, ibid

20. 'Khrushchev, Nikita Sergeevich'. *SVE*, Vol 8, pp393-394.
21. In addition to his memoir already cited, see Bagramian, I. Kh.; *Tak nachinalas' voine* (How war began); Dnipro, Kiev, 1975. Also Jukes, G.; 'Ivan Khristoforovich Bagramian,' *Stalin's Generals*, pp25-32; and numerous short biographies in VIZh.
22. Zhukov, I.; pp207-208.
23. Nekhanov, G.; 'General-leitenant F. Ia. Kostenko'. (Lt-Gen F. Ia. Kostenko); *VIZh*, No 5 May 1967, pp97-100.
24. For this and other army histories as well as the short histories of corps, divisions, and brigades of various types, see Poirier, Robert G., Conner, Albert Z.; *Red Army Order of Battle in the Great Patriotic War*; second edition, unpublished manuscript, chapter 4, pp70-71. Hereafter cited as *Red Army OB*. See also specific Soviet unit histories and the voluminous FMO document, 'Truppen-Ubersicht und Kriegsgliederungen Rote Armee, Stand: August 1944' (Troop-List and Order of Battle of the Red Army in August 1944), *FHO Ic.-Unterlagen Ost, Merkblatt geh.11/6 Pruf-Nr: 0157* in NAM, T-78, Roll 459. Hereafter cited as 'Truppen'. See also 'Dvadtsat' vos'maia armiia' (28th Army); *SVE*, Vol 3, pp104-105.
25. 'Riabyshev, Dmitrii Ivanovich'; *SVE*, Vol 7, pp207.
26. Abyzov,V.; *Aleksandr Rodimtsev*; Political Literature, Moscow, 1981. Also Samchuk, I. A.; *Trinadtsataia gvardeiskaia* (13th Guards); Voenizdat, Moscow, 1971.
27. *Red Army OB*; chapter 12, pp48-49; *73-ia gvardeiskaia* (73rd Guards); Kazakhstan, Alma Ata, 1986. The 73rd Guards was originally the 38th Rifle Division.
28. *Red Army OB*; chapter 12, pp194-195; Kachur, V. P., Nikol'sky, V. V.; *Pod znamenem sivashtsev* (Under the banner Sivash); Voenizdat, Moscow, 1989. The latter is a history of the 169th Rifle Division.
29. *Red Army OB*; chapter 12, pp201-202.
30. Ibid., chapter 12, p269.
31. 'Truppen'; pp326, 342, 348.
32. *Red Army OB*; chapter 6, p11, chapter 7 pp18-19. Also Soshnikov, pp197-198.
33. 'Kriuchenkin, Vasilii Dmitrievich'; *SVE*, Vol 4, pp498.
34. *Red Army OB*; chapter 10, p3, chapter 11, pp19-20. Also Soshnikov, p198.
35. *Red Army OB*; chapter 10, pp10-11, chapter 11, p23. Also Soshnikov, p198.
36. 'Truppen'; p206.
37. Vyrodov, I. Ia., ed.; *V srazheniiakh za Pobedu: boevoi put' 38-i armii v gody Velikoi Otechestvennoi voiny 1941-1945* (In battles for victory: the combat path of 38th Army in the Great Patriotic War 1941-1945); 'Nauka', Moscow, 1974.
38. In addition to Moskalenko's memoirs, see pp137-153, Erickson, John; 'Kirill Semenovich Moskalenko', *Stalin's Generals*.
39. 'Truppen'; 28. Also *Red Army OB*; chapter 12, pp94-95.
40. *Red Army OB*; chapter 12, pp141-142.
41. 'Gorbatov, Aleksandr Vasilevich'; *SVE*,Vol 2, p605. Also Gorbatov, A. V.; *Gody i voiny* (Years and wars); Voenizdat, Moscow, 1980.
42. *Red Army OB*; chapter 12, pp317, 321. Also Strength from Vyrodov, p79.
43. 'Truppen'; pp330, 336, 356.
44. 'Dvadtsat' pervaia armiia' (21st Army); *SVE*, Vol 3, pp106-107.
45. Gordov, Vasilii Nikolaevich; *SVE*, Vol 2, p606.
46. *Red Army OB*; chapter 12, pp89-90. Also Strength from Vyrodov, p79.
47. *Red Army OB*; chapter 12, pp251-252.
48. Ibid., chapter 12, p311. Also Strength from Vyrodov, p79.
49. 'Truppen'; p328.
50. 'Shestaia armiia' (6th Army); *SVE*, Vol 8, pp508-509.
51. 'Gorodniansky, Avksentii Mikhailovich'; *Velikaia Otechestvennaia voina 1941-1945*; *Entsiklopediia* (The Great Patriotic War 1941-1945: An Encyclopedia); Sovetskaia entsiklopediia, Moscow, 1985, p214.
52. *Red Army OB*; chapter 12, pp51-52.
53. Ibid., chapter 12, p59.

Kharkov, 1942

54. Ibid., chapter 12, pp119-120.
55. Ibid., chapter 12, pp273-274.
56. Ibid., chapter 12, pp. 278-279.
57. Ibid., chapter 12, p289.
58. Ibid., chapter 12, p398.
59. 'Truppen'; pp336, 338, 358.
60. *Red Army OB*; chapter 7, p64 Also 'Truppen'; pp342, 368-369, 168.
61. *Red Army OB*; chapter 7, p66. Also 'Truppen'; pp200, 328, 356.
62. Bagramian, p88.
63. Moskalenko, p212. Although Moskalenko urged Bobkin to leave his son with 38th Army's Military Council, Bobkin refused, and his son shared Bobkin's fate.
64. *Red Army OB*; chapter 12, pp293-294.
65. Ibid., chapter 12, p391.
66. Ibid., chapter 7, p23; Soshnikov, pp165-167, 198.
67. *Red Army OB*; chapter 10, pp15-16, 22.
68. 'Truppen'; p328.
69. *Red Army OB*; chapter 7. Also Soshnikov, p198.
70. Soshnikov, pp198-200.
71. *Red Army OB*; chapter 10, p20.
72. Ibid., chapter 10, pp25-26, 27-28. Also Soshnikov, p182.
73. *Red Army OB*; chapter 12, pp298-299.
74. Ibid., pp353-354. Also Naumenko, Iu. A.; *Shagai pekhota!* (Infantry marches on); Voenizdat, Moscow, 1989. Also Samchuk, I. A.; *Gvardeiskaia poltavskaia* (Poltava guards); Voenizdat, Moscow, 1965. Both are histories of the 343rd Rifle Division.
75. Golubovich, V. S.; *Marshal R. Ia. Malinovskiy*; Voenizdat, Moscow, 1984. Erickson, John; 'Rodion Yakovlevich Malinovsky', *Stalin's Generals*, pp117-124. Also Malinovsky, R. Ia.; *Budapesht-Vena-Praga* (Budapest-Vienna-Prague); 'Nauka', Moscow, 1965.
76. Gaglov, I. I.; General Antonov; Voenizdat, Moscow, 1978. Also Woff, Richard; 'Alexei Innokentievich Antonov', *Stalin's Generals*.; pp11-23.
77. Konashenko,N. T.; 'Piat'desiat sed'maia armiia' (57th Army); *SVE*, Vol 6, pp655, 656. Also 'Kuzma Petrovich Podlas'; *SVE*, Vol 6, p387.
78. *Red Army OB*; chapter 11, pp44-45.
79. Cherniavsky, K. I.; *Vsegda s boitsami* (Always with the soldiers); Voenizdat, Moscow, 1979. Also *Red Army OB*; chapter 12, pp114-116.
80. *Red Army OB*; chapter 12, pp173-174.
81. Ibid., chapter 12, pp332-333.
82. Ibid., chapter 12, pp360-361.
83. ' Deviatiia armiia'; *SVE* Vol 3, pp121-122. Also Oreshkin, A. K.; *Oboronitel'naia operatsiia 9-i armii (oktiabr'-noiabr' 1941g)* (The defensive operation of 9th Army [October-November 1941]); Voenizdat, Moscow, 1960.
84. 'Fedor Mikhailovich Kharitonov'; *SVE*, Vol 8, p359.
85. *Red Army OB*; chapter 12, pp63-64.
86. Ibid., chapter 12, pp121-122.
87. Ibid., chapter 12, pp240-241.
88. Ibid., chapter 12, pp346-347.
89. Ibid., chapter 12, pp348, 353.
90. 'Truppen'; p220.
91. Ibid., pp340, 354.
92. *Red Army OB*; chapter 7, pp18-19. Also Soshnikov, p198.
93. 'Pliev, Issa Aleksandrovich'; *SVE*, Vol 6, pp356-357. Also Pliev, I. A.; *Pod gvardeiskim znamenem* (Under the guards banner); 'IR', Ordzhonikidze, 1976.
94. Pliev, pp25-49.
95. *Red Army OB*; chapter 10, p17.
96. Ibid., chapter 10, p19.
97. Ibid., chapter 10, p25.
98. 'Truppen'; p330.
99. For details on German force structure see pp15-26, Mitcham, Samuel W.Jr.; *Hitler's Legion: The German Army Order of Battle, World War II*; Stein and Day, New York, 1985,
100. According to Directive No 99275, dated 28 April 1942, from the Southwestern Front commander.

Notes to Chapter 5

1. Samchuk, p81.
2. Ibid., pp81-82.
3. Kachur, Nikol'sky, pp51-53.
4. Morozov, A. K.; 'V mae-iule sorok vtorogo' (In May-July 1942); *73-ia gvardeiskaia*, p23. Morozov commanded the division's 2nd Battalion, 48th Rifle Regiment.
5. Moskalenko, p191.
6. Vyrodov, pp113-114.
7. Oleinikov, A.; *Rozhdennaia na zemlikah zaporozhskikh* (Born on the land of Zaporozh'e); Ukrainian political literature, Kiev, 1974, p48. Quoting from Rodimtsev's memoir, Rodimtsev, A. I.; *Tvoi, otechestvo, syny* (You, your fatherland, and sons); p295. A history of 226th Rifle Division.
8. Moskalenko, pp191-192.
9. Ibid., p193.
10. Vyrodov, pp113-115.
11. Moskalenko, pp193-195.
12. Bechtelzheim, Anton Freiherr, von; 'The Battle of Kharkov 1942', *MS# L-023*, Historical Division, Headquarters United States Army, Europe, 1956, pp16-17. Based on a lecture.
13. Ibid., p18.
14. Bagramian, pp90-91.
15. Ziemke and Bauer, p273.
16. Bechtelzheim, p19.
17. Kachur, Niklo'sky, p54.
18. Samchuk, pp83-84.
19. In all, German 3rd and 23rd Panzer Divisions numbered 370 tanks.
20. Bagramian, p92.
21. Vyrodov, pp115-116. All Soviet open sources exaggerate the tank strength of 3rd and 23rd Panzer Divisions, which was about 200.
22. Moskalenko, p115; Bagramian, pp93-94.
23. Kachur, Nikol'sky, pp54-55.
24. Morozov, p24.
25. Samchuk, pp85-86.
26. Ibid., pp86-87.
27. Bagramian, p96.
28. Subsequently, 6th Army's aviation covered the Army Group.
29. Bagramian, p89.
30. Bechtelzheim, p20.
31. For full text, see pp14-15, Begunov, et al, 'Vot gde pravda' (What then is the truth); *VIZh*, No 1 January 1990.
32. Vasilevsky, p192.
33. At 15.00 on 14 May, the supply situation was as follows: for 82mm mortars—0.6 loads; for regimental and divisional 76mm guns—0.6 loads; for 45mm guns—0.2 loads; for 122mm guns—0.2 loads.
34. Ziemke and Bauer, p276.
35. Bechtelzheim, pp21-22.
36. Bagramian, p99.
37. Samchuk, p87.
38. Ibid., pp88-91.
39. Kachur, Nikol'sky, p55.
40. Morozov, p25.
41. Kachur, Nikol'sky, pp55-57.
42. Bagramian, p107.
43. The numerical size of divisions ranged from 8,000-9,000 men.
44. The overall number of guns and mortars included 76mm divisional guns, 122mm and 152mm guns, and 120mm and 82mm mortars.
45. In the calculation, a two-regiment light infantry division was counted as two-thirds of a division, and Barbo's combat group and the punishment battalions were counted as one-third of a division each.
46. Bagramian, p108.
47. Ibid., pp108-110.
48. Ibid., p110.
49. Carrell, Paul; *Hitler Moves East*; 1941-1943; Ballantine, New York, 1973, p488. Translated from the German original. Writing under the pen name of Paul Carrell, Paul

Notes

Schmidt employed a staff of veterans and experts to construct this appealing journalistic account. While journalistic, its facts are accurate and its portrayal of the mood of combat is moving.
50. Kuznetsov, I. I., Maslov, A. A.; 'The Soviet General Officer Corps, 1941-1942: Losses in Combat'; *The Journal of Slavic Military Studies*, Vol. 7, No 3, September 1994, pp548-566. This ground-breaking article provides a definitive roster of perished commanders and considerable information on the circumstances of their deaths.
51. Bagramian, p114. The General Staff study omits mention of the 333rd Rifle Division and the 3 tank brigades.
52. Carrell, p494.
53. Order No 00317, dated 16 May.
54. Begunov, et al; 'Vot gde pravda' (What then is the truth); *VIZh*, No 1 January 1990, p16. Full text in Appendix 7.
55. Ibid., pp16-17. Full text in Appendix 8.
56. Bagramian, p115.
57. Ibid., p116.
58. Ibid.
59. Ibid.
60. Ibid., p117.
61. Ibid.
62. Vasilev'sky, pp192-193.
63. Begunov, et al; 'Vot gde pravda' (What then is the truth); *VIZh*, No 1 January 1990, p18. Full text in appendix 9.
64. Begunov, et al; 'Vot gde pravda' (What then is the truth); *VIZh*, No 2 February 1990, pp35-36. Full text in Appendix 10.
65. Carrell, pp494-495.
66. Kuznetsov, Maslov, pp559-560.
67. Directive No 170395 from the Stavka of the Supreme High Command, dated 18 May 1942.
68. Bagramian, p117.
69. Moskalenko, p205.
70. Begunov, et al;'Vot gde pravda' (What then is the truth); *VIZh*, No 2 February 1990, pp36-37. Full text in Appendix 11.
71. Ibid., p36.
72. Ibid., p37. Full text in Appendix 12.
73. Ibid., pp37-38. Full text in Appendix 13.
74. An operational group, under the command of the deputy commander of 38th Army, Maj-Gen Sherstiuk, was organised for this purpose. The group consisted of the 242nd, 278th, 304th, and 199th Rifle Divisions and the 156th and 168th Tank Brigades.
75. Begunov, et al; 'Vot gde pravda' (What then is the truth); *VIZh*, No 2 February 1990, p38. Full text in appendix 14.
76. Ziemke and Bauer, p281.
77. Ibid., p282.
78. Begunov, et al; 'Vot gde pravda' (What then is the truth); *VIZh*, No 2 February 1990, pp38-39. Full text in Appendix 15.
79. Moskalenko, p209.
80. Ibid., pp208-209. Full text in appendix 16.
81. Carrell, p495.
82. Moskalenko, p210.
83. Carrell, pp495-496.
84. Ibid., p496.
85. Ibid.
86. Ziemke and Bauer, p282.
87. Moskalenko, pp210-211.
88. Ibid., p211.
89. Carrell, pp496-497.
90. Moskalenko, p212.

Notes to Chapter 6
1. Carrell, p497.
2. Begunov, et al; 'Vot gde pravda' (What then is the truth); *VIZh*, No 2 February 1990, p40. Full text in Appendix 17.
3. Krivosheev, G. F., ed.; *Grif sekretnosti sniat: poteri vooruzhennykh sil SSSR v voinakh, boevykh deistviiakh i voennykh konfliktakh* (The classification secret is removed: Soviet Armed Forces losses in wars, combat actions, and military conflicts); Voenizdat, Moscow, 1993, p225.
4. Kuznetsov, Maslov, p559. Maslov, Alexander A.; 'The Unbroken: Soviet Generals/Defenders of the Ukraine Who Perished in Fascist Captivity'; *The Journal of Slavic Military Studies*, Vol. 7, No 2 June 1994, p297.
5. Ibid., p296.
6. Kuznetsov, Maslov, pp559-560.
7. I. E. Krupchenko, ed.; *Sovetskie tankovye voisk 1941-1945* (Soviet tank forces 1941-1945); Voenizdat, Moscow, 1973, p60.
8. *TsAMO*, op.12479, d.1188, ll.5,7 (translated from German) as found in Begunov, et al, 'Vot gde pravda' op. cit., pp41-42.
9. *TsAMO*, f.251, op.646, d.145, ll.238, 266-269. Copy. Ibid., p42.
10. *TsAMO*, f.251, op.646, d.189, ll.2-4, 23. Original. Ibid., pp43-44.
11. Ibid., pp45-46.
12. 'Anfilov'; *Stalin's Generals*, p252.

Notes to Chapter 7
1. Stoler, Mark A.; 'The Soviet Union and the Second Front in American Strategic Planning, 1941-1943', *Soviet-US Relations 1933-1942*; Progress, Moscow, 1989, p93. See the remainder of this important volume for fresh views on the second front issue.
2. Ibid., p94.
3. *Velikai Otechestvennaia voina Sovetskogo Soiuza*, T. 2 (The Great Patriotic War of the Soviet Union, Vol. 2); Voenizdat, Moscow, 1961, p414.
4. Ibid.
5. Volkogonov, Dmitri; *Stalin: Triumph and Tragedy*; Weidenfeld and Nicolson, London, 1991, p432.
6. Zhukov, II, pp76-77.
7. *Istoriia vtoroi mirovoi voiny 1939-1945* T. 5 (A History of the Second World War 1939-1945, Vol. 5); Voenizdat, Moscow, 1975, p130.
8. Moskalenko, p213.
9. Ibid., pp214-215.
10. Ibid., pp215-217. Original: *TsAMO*, f. 251, op.646, d.189, 11. 2-4, 23.
11. Ibid., p218. Copy: *TsAMO*, f.3, op.11556, d.8, ll.212-214.
12. Ibid.
13. Bagramian, p122.
14. Ibid., p124.
15. Ibid., p125.
16. Zhukov, II, p77.
17. Bagramian, p127.
18. Begunov; 'Chto proizoshlo pod Khar'kovom v mae 1942 goda' (What occurred at Kharkov in May 1942); *VIZh*, No 10 October 1987, p47.
19. House, Jonathan and Glantz, David M.; *Clash of Titans: The Red Army and the Wehrmacht, 1941-1945*; Lawrence, KS, University of Kansas Press, 1995, appendixes.
20. 'Postanovlenie: GKO ot 5 maia 1942 g' (State Defence Committee Decree of 5 May 1942); *TsPA*, UML, f.644, op.1, g.33. Copy of original from the Central Party Archives. Briansk Front would have added another 426,778 soldiers.
21. Ziemke and Bauer, p324. German strength in the south numbered 65 divisions (45 infantry, 5 light infantry, 4 motorised and 11 Panzer, plus 25 allied divisions). Of the 1.3 million, about 1 million troops were German.
22. Sverdlov, F. D.; 'Katastrofa pod Khar'kovom' (The catastrophe at Kharkov); *VIZh*, No 6-7 June-July 1992, p58.
23. Ibid.
24. Ibid.

Appendices

Appendix 1

From Report No 00137/op of the Southwestern Direction High Command to the Stavka VGK (Headquarters, Supreme High Command) concerning the situation in mid-March 1942 of Southwestern Direction Fronts and proposals on prospective military operations by Direction forces during the spring-summer period of 1942.

Dated: 22 March 1942

Missions assigned for the winter period of 1942 have not yet been fully executed by Southwestern Direction forces.

As a result of a series of operations involving attacks on important and vital enemy axes, Southwestern Direction Fronts have seized the initiative, inflicted severe losses on the enemy and liberated significant territory from German-Fascist occupiers.

Operations were especially effective at the junction of the Southwestern and Southern Fronts, where our forces succeeded in penetrating the enemy fortified belt, inflicting heavy losses on him and having secured the Alekseevka, Lozovaia and Barvenkovo region, deprived the enemy of the important Kharkov-Donbas rail line and threatened the deep rear of his main group, operating in the Donbas and Taganrog regions.

At the same time, our forces occupied a rather favourable position for developing an attack on Kharkov. Only insufficient numbers and means prevented us from fully exploiting our achieved success to finally defeat the main enemy group in the south and secure Kharkov.

1 Evaluation of the enemy and his probable intentions

As a consequence of completed and ongoing offensive operations, we have succeeded in disrupting enemy forces' normal operational formations, forced him to expend not only all of his operational reserves, but also to fragment his divisions in the first line of defence, right down to separate battalions, in order to localise our success.

Our forces' active operations have led the enemy into such a situation that, without allocating large strategic reserves and significantly strengthening his forces and equipment, he will not be able to undertake operations with decisive aims.

According to agent reports and prisoner-of-war debriefings, the enemy has concentrated large reserves with a significant number of tanks east of Gomel and in the Kremenchug, Kirovograd and Dnepropetrovsk regions, clearly with the aim of making the transition during spring to decisive operations. Today it is difficult to predict the scale of that offensive. One can only suggest the likely operational axes and the enemy's operational-strategic aspirations.

We think that in the spring, in spite of his large-scale failure in the autumn offensive against Moscow, the enemy will again attempt to seize our capital. To that end, his main grouping stubbornly strives to hold on to its positions along the Moscow axis, and his reserves are concentrated against the Western Front's left wing (east of Gomel and in the Briansk region). It is more probable that, together with frontal attacks against the Western Front, the enemy will attempt to envelop Moscow from the south and southeast with large motor-mechanised formations attacking from the Briansk and Gomel regions, reach the Volga River in the Gorki region and isolate Moscow from the most vital industrial and economic centres in the Volga and Ural regions.

In the south we can expect an offensive by large enemy forces between the Northern Donets River and Taganrog Gulf to secure the lower Don and, subsequently, the Caucasus oil fields. This attack will probably be accompanied by an offensive against Stalingrad by a secondary force grouping and by amphibious operations from Crimea against the Caucasian coast of the Black Sea.

To protect his main shock group operations against Moscow and in the Caucasus, the enemy will undoubtedly attempt to deliver a secondary blow from the Kursk region toward Voronezh. When these enemy groups reach the Voronezh, Liski and Valiuki regions, we would lose the important railroad link between Moscow, the Donbas and the Caucasus.

Appendices

Hydro-meterological conditions permit the development of extensive military operations in the south in mid-April and in the north during the first part of May.

But, considering the advantages of a simultaneous transition to the offensive of large forces on all fronts, one can presume that the enemy will begin decisive operations in mid-May of this year.

At the present time, enemy forces opposing the Southwestern Direction are estimated as follows:

Table 1: Estimation of Enemy Forces

Front	Inf Div	Mot Div	SS Div	Pz Div	Total Div	Total Tanks	Total Guns	Av Operational Density (Km/Division)
Briansk	6	2	1	2	11	50-80	14	21
Southwestern	19	1	—	2	22	150-170	473	25
Southern	23	3	2	3	31	250-300	703	3
Total	48	6	3	7	64	450-550	1290	17

While characterising the enemy's combat composition on the basis of agent and prisoner reports, one can conclude that his infantry has suffered losses, and few replacements have been received. Thanks to this, he has large shortages. The 48 infantry divisions identified in front of the Southwestern Direction have the following strength: 14 infantry divisions at 2-4,000 men (30%), 15 infantry divisions at 4-6,000 men (40%), 13 infantry divisions at 6-8,000 men (50%), and 6 infantry divisions at 8,000 or higher (70-80%). The personnel shortages of these divisions amount to approximately 430,000 men.

Our intelligence has not detected receipt of such a quantity of replacements, but reinforcement has begun opposite Briansk and Southern Front forces.

Enemy tank divisions engaged us in combat with only motorised units and a limited quantity of remaining serviceable and repaired tanks. The principal part of tank crews remained in the rear expecting to receive new combat machines. According to an agent report, 3,500 tankers — or crews for 1,000-1,200 tanks — are concentrated in Poltava.

If one presumes that all tank and motorised divisions now located opposite the Southwestern Direction will be manned to the level of the beginning of the war, then we could have opposite the Southwestern Direction the following [enemy forces]:

Table 2: Enemy Forces Opposing Southwestern Direction

Front	Opposing Divs	Variant 1 Tks/Div	Variant 1 Tks in Divs	Variant 1 Total Tks	Variant 2 Tks/Div	Variant 2 Tks in Divs	Variant 2 Total Tks
Briansk	17th, 18th TDs	500	1,000	1,500	250	500	600
	Two MDs	250	500	250	50	100	
Southwestern	3rd, 9th TDs	500	1,000	1,250	250	500	550
	One MDs	250	250	2,250	50	50	
Southern	13th, 14th, 16th TDs	500	1,500	5,000	250	750	900
	Two MDs	250	750	2,250	50	150	
SW Direction	Seven TDs						
	Six MDs						

Considering the decline in the offensive spirit of infantry, one must expect that, to support its combat operations, the enemy must have up to 30 separate tank battalions of 30 tanks each, 900 tanks in all, in the 64 infantry divisions expected to be available in spring. Furthermore, we do not exclude the possibility of the appearance against Southwestern Direction forces of up to three new tank divisions with a total of 750-1,500 tanks.

As a result, one can reckon that, in total, the enemy will have opposite Southwestern Direction forces at the beginning of the spring campaign, 2,400 tanks in the first variant, and 3,700 tanks in the second. However, considering the considerable enemy losses during the duration of the war, it is more probable that he will have more than the number of tanks in the second variant against us, that is up to 3,700.

While examining the question of increasing the quantity of infantry divisions against Southwestern Direction forces, we must reckon that the enemy can direct against the USSR up to 45 infantry divisions, forces billeted in Germany and occupied countries, of which not less than one third (15 divisions) he would hurl against Southwestern Direction forces.

It is also necessary to take into account that the enemy, evidently, will receive up to 20 Romanian,

Kharkov, 1942

Slovakian and Hungarian infantry divisions and, in favourable conditions, can replace his 7 infantry divisions in Crimea with Romanian/Hungarian infantry divisions and also send them to the Southwestern Direction's fronts.

As a result, the enemy will increase his forces opposite the Southwestern Direction by 22 German infantry divisions and 13 Romanian/Hungarian infantry divisions.

Table 3: Average density of divisions per Front (in km)

Front	Inf Divs	Mot Divs	SS Divs	Tk Divs	Total	Tanks	Guns	Div Density
Briansk	10	3	1	4	18	1,105	422	11.5
Southwestern [1]	30	1	—	2	33	800	863	5.5
Southern [2]	43	3	2	3	51	1,200	160	7
Southwestern Direction	83	7	3	9	102	3,105	2,888	10.5

[1] Includes 8 Romanian/Hungarian Divs
[2] Includes 3 Italian and 5 Hungarian/Romanian Divs

Considering his aims, one can assume that his reserve divisions opposite Southwestern Direction forces can be used as follows: in the Briansk Front sector — 4 infantry divisions; in the Southwestern Front sector — 3 German infantry divisions and 8 Romanian/Hungarian infantry divisions; and in the Southern Front sector — 15 German infantry divisions and five Romanian/Hungarian infantry divisions.

The introduction of that quantity of divisions will not especially increase the enemy's operational densities along the entire front, but we cannot expect the enemy to be evenly disposed along the front.

We must be prepared for the enemy to try again to shift to operations along decisive axes by massed, mobile groupings and to employ his reserve divisions fully on those axes.

Summing up, we need to consider that the enemy at the beginning of the offensive operation will have the forces and equipment shown in Table 3.

To achieve decisive successes or when forces are not sufficient to secure them, the enemy will not hesitate to use means of chemical war. Indicative of this is information about the transport and creation of reserves of chemical weapons in the Stalino region, the systematic conduct of chemical training in his forces, and the filling out of chemical service positions in his units.

2. Immediate strategic aims of Southwestern Direction force operations

According to all indicators, spring should be characterised by a renewal of extensive enemy offensive actions.

Irrespective of this, during the period of the spring-summer campaign, Southwestern Direction forces must strive to achieve the principal strategic aim — to defeat the opposing enemy forces and reach the middle Dnepr River (Gomel, Kiev and Cherkassy) and further to a front from Cherkassy through Pervomaisk to Nikolaev.

Depending on concrete conditions and, first and foremost, the real correlation of forces which exists at the beginning of main operations, this principal strategic aim will be resolved on each front of the Southwestern Direction by various means.

To create favourable conditions for the entry of Southwestern Direction forces into the spring-summer campaign, it is necessary to use the remaining time before the spring *razputitsa* (thaw) to maximum effectiveness, in order to:

a) successfully complete a series of local operations and place our forces in a more favourable operational position by the beginning of the spring campaign;

b) reinforce forces with personnel and equipment, bring up necessary reserves and, having adopted a suitable operational formation, to be ready to join the first operation of the spring campaign in organised fashion;

c) reveal, in timely fashion, the concentration regions of large enemy operational groupings designated to make the transition to the offensive and, by all available measures (conduct of local operations, aviation actions and partisan detachment actions) hinder and, where possible, frustrate enemy preparations and his transition to the offensive.

Appendices

3. Combat Composition of Southwestern Direction Forces

The overall length of the front of Southwestern Direction forces is 1,073km.

Southwestern Direction forces consist of: 70 rifle divisions, 10 rifle brigades, 18 cavalry divisions, 2 motorised rifle brigades, 22 tank brigades, 2 separate tank battalions, 32 artillery regiments RGK, 11 AT [anti-tank] artillery regiments, 3 guards mortar regiments [*Katiusha* multiple rocket launchers], 3 guards mortar battalions and 26 ski battalions. In total: 74 rifle divisions (including 10 rifle brigades and two motorised rifle brigades counted as four divisions), 2,451 field guns, and 1,003 tanks. Of the latter, 327 are in capital repair, 195 are in unit repair, and 481 are operational.

The overall condition of Southwestern Direction forces is characterised by the following basic data:

a) personnel shortages in rifle formations alone has reached 370,888 men, which equals 46% of the establishment (TOE) strength;

b) among the 70 rifle divisions, only 3 divisions have up to 75% of establishment strength, and the remaining have 50% or less. 30 divisions have less than 5,500 men each and from 1,000-1,200 active riflemen;

c) the average provision of these forces with weapons amounts to (in percentages): 51.2 of rifles, 22.5 of mounted machine guns, 24.3 of hand-carried machine guns and machine pistols, 46.4 of mortars, 67.0 of field artillery pieces, 26 of anti-tank guns, 46.0 of anti-tank rifles, 63.3 of tanks, 52.5 of vehicles and 61.8 of tractors.

Average monthly personnel losses amount to 110-130,000 men. Appointed replacements hardly cover these losses and forces continue to remain in short supply.

To overcome this extremely abnormal phenomenon, it would be appropriate to cover the existing shortage — 427,000 men before the beginning of the spring-summer campaign — and, subsequently, provide a normal monthly influx of reinforcements of 130,000-150,000 men.

Signed:
Higher Commander of Southwestern Direction Forces, Marshal of the Soviet Union, Timoshenko
Member of the Southwestern Direction Military Council Khrushchev
Chief of the Southwestern Direction's Operational Group Lt-Gen Bagramian

TsAMO, SSSR, f.251, op.646, d.145 ll.34-60. Copy.

Appendix 2

From a report of the Southwestern Direction High Command to the Supreme High Command and I. V. Stalin.

Dated: 30 March 1942

In accordance with your personal order, we have worked out an operational plan for operations by Southwestern Direction forces in April-May 1942.

1. The principal aim of Southwestern Direction forces in the indicated period is to seize Kharkov, then to conduct a regrouping of forces and secure Dnepropetrovsk and Sinel'nikovo by a blow from the northeast, in order to deprive the enemy of important crossings over the Dnepr River and the rail head at Sinel'nikovo.

Southwestern Direction forces must firmly defend currently occupied positions along the remaining extent of the front.

2. To secure the Kharkov region, according to our calculations, it is necessary to have:
Rifle divisions — 27
Cavalry divisions — 9
Rifle brigades — 1
Motorised rifle brigades — 3
Tank brigades — 26
Artillery regiments RGK — 25
Total: tanks — 200; field guns — 1,200-1,300; aircraft — 620 (of these 30 — U-2) . . .

Kharkov, 1942

3. The basic concept of the operation for the Kharkov offensive is: while delivering the main blow to envelop Kharkov from the south and southwest and a secondary blow to envelop the city from the north, encircle and destroy the enemy Kharkov grouping, secure Kharkov and reach the line: Sazhnoe, Tomarovka, Graivoron, Ekaterinovka, Vodianaia St., Orchinovka-Chernetkina, Aleksandrovka and Krishtopovka.

Signed:
Timoshenko
Khrushchev
Bagramian

Appendix 3
Operational plan of Southwestern Direction forces for the occupation of the Kharkov region and a further offensive toward Dnepropetrovsk and Sinel'nikovo.

'Confirmed'
Commander in Chief S.W. Direction Forces
Marshal of the Soviet Union S. Timoshenko
Dated: 10 April 1942

1. In accordance with directives of the Stavka of the Supreme High Command for forestalling enemy development of offensive operations and preserving the initiative in the hands of our forces on the southwestern axis during the April-May period, I establish for ourselves the following principal aim: to secure the Kharkov region, to conduct a force regrouping and, by a subsequent attack in the direction of Dnepropetrovsk and Sinelnikovo Station, deprive the enemy of important crossing sites over the Dnepr.
    Particular Front objectives are as follows: for Southwestern Front — destruction of the enemy Kharkov grouping and arrival on the line Nikitovka, Karlovka and Buzovka to protect subsequent operations by Southern Front forces toward Dnepropetrovsk; for Southern Front — firm defence of occupied positions (lines) and covering of the Rostov and Voroshilovgrad axes, and the Barvenkovo, Slaviansk and Izium regions.

2. To achieve the established objectives, the basic concept of Southwestern Front operations is as follows: encircle and destroy the enemy Kharkov grouping by enveloping attacks by 6th A from the south and 28th A from the north, reach the designated positions and create favourable jumping-off positions for regrouping for the next attack on Dnepropetrovsk and Sinel'nikovo Station.
    The basic concept of Southern Front operations consists of creating a deeply echeloned defence along the most important axes and conducting an active defence to tie down the opposing enemy forces.
    To carry out the projected concept, I plan the following Front operations:

I Stage (Preparatory)
During the course of the first stage, the Southwestern Front regroups its forces, deploys 28th Army formations and replenishes material-technical means for the forthcoming operation. The Southern Front, having detailed part of its forces to the Southwestern Front, continues to fortify occupied defensive positions.
    Air Force missions: the destruction of enemy aviation at airfields and in the air; the destruction of industrial objectives in Taganrog and Mariupol'; the destruction of material units of military equipment in concentration areas; and the destruction of communications hubs and lines of communications.

II Stage (6-7 days: Penetration of the enemy defence)
The Southwestern Front penetrates the enemy defence and, on the 6th-7th day of the offensive, its rifle formations reach the following lines: on the right flank — Kleida, Tolokonnoe, Liptsy and Nepokrytaia; on the left flank — Dudkovka, Taranovka, Vlasovka, Eremeevka, Kokhanovka and Pokrovskoe. By the end of the second stage, mobile formations will reach:

Appendices

3 GdsCC —the Kazachia Lopan, Zolochev and Stalino region
2 MC —Cheremyshnaia, Znamenka and Rakitnoe
3 MC —Snezhnoe, Rozhdenstvenskoe and Minkovka
2 CC —Stanichnyi, Kirillovka and Karavanskoe
6 CC —the Krasnograd region
  Southern Front — [mission absent in original]
  Air Force Missions: co-operate with attacking forces in suppressing enemy ground defences, cover forces from aviation attacks and operate against enemy reserves approaching the front.
  The depth of this stage of operations is 30-35km. The average tempo of advance is 5-6km per day. The duration of this stage is 6-7 days.

III Stage (7-8 days. Completion of the encirclement and destruction of the enemy Kharkov grouping)
The Southwestern Front completes the encirclement of the enemy and, with its forward units, reaches the line: Sazhnoe, Tomarovka, Bogodukhov, Koviagi, Chutovo, Popovka, Skalonovka and southeast along the northern bank of the Orel River.
  Southern Front — [mission absent in original]
  Air Force Missions: operations against enemy reserves to prevent the flow of new enemy forces into the Kharkov region. Protection of one's own forces from enemy aviation strikes. Suppression of enemy resistance in the Kharkov region.
  The depth of this stage of operations is 40-45km. The average tempo of advance is 7-8km per day. The duration of this stage of the operation is 7-8 days.

3. The following grouping of forces and forces' missions are established to achieve these operational aims:

Southwestern Front:
21 A (consisting of 8 MRD, 293, 297, 226 and 76 RDs, 21 MRB, 10 TB, 8 Sep TBn, 338 and 105 LARs (RGK), 110 HAR (RGK) and 156 AAR (2nd type) is deployed along the front: Marino, Shakhovo, Shebekino (105km) with the following groups of forces: the 8 MRD and 293 RD with two LARs RGK defends along the front Marino, Shakhovo, Miasoedovo (80km); the 297, 226 and 76 RDs with 10 TB, one HAR RGK and 156 AAR, 2nd type, are deployed along the front Miasoedovo, Shebekino (23km) to attack to protect the right flank of 28 A. The 21 A reserve is the 21 MRB and 8 Sep TBn in the Kashcheevo, Korocha and Kazanka region.
  The army missions are: while attacking from the left flank, by the end of the sixth day, reach the line: Kreida, Nelidovka and Tolokonnoe, using forward units sever the Belgorod-Kharkov road, and secure the right flank of 28 A. By the end of the fourteenth day of the offensive, secure the Belgorod region and, with the four left flank divisions, reach the line: Zadelnoe, Tomarovka, Borisovka and Kazachek Station, consolidate their positions and cover 28 A operations from enemy attacks from the north and northwest.
28 A consisting of 13 Gds, 244, 175, 227, 169, 300, 162 and 38 RDs, 3 Gds CC (5 and 6 Gds and 32 CD, 34 MRB); 6 Gds and three additional TBs; 764 ATAR, 651 and one additional LAR, RGK; 7 Gds and 870 HAR RGK; 594 and 266 GAR RGK, 5 Gds, 51 and 233 AAR (2nd type), is deployed along the front Titovka, Rubezhnoe, Khotomlia and Bogorodichnoe (75km) with the following grouping of forces:
  In first echelon along the front Titovka and Oktiabr'skoe (20km) — 244 RD, 13 Gds and 162 RDs with 6 Gds and one additional TB, one LAR RGK, 266 GAR RGK, 7 Gds and 870 HAR RGK, 5 Gds, 51 and 233 AARs, 2nd type. In second echelon in the Malo-Mikhailovka and Baikovo regions — 175 and 38 RDs. In third echelon in the Efremovka, Blagodatnaia and Reznikovo region — 3 Gds CC (5 and 6 Gds, and 32 CD) with 34 MRB and one TB.
  On the left flank — the 227, 169, and 300 RDs, with one TB and 764 AT AR, 651 LAR and 594 HAR RGK attack along the front Oktiabr'skoe, Rubezhnoe, Khotomlia and Bogorodichnoe (50km).
  The army missions are: while attacking from the right flank, penetrate the enemy defence, and commit 3 Gds CC with 34 MRB and one TB into the penetration, and by the end of the sixth day of the offensive reach the front Tolokonnoe, Zhuravlevka, Lipts and Nepokrytaia. Subsequently, while developing the offensive toward Peresechnaia, by the end of the fourteenth day reach the line: Repki, Peresechnaia and Kharkov to complete, together with 6 A, the encirclement of the enemy Kharkov grouping and to continue its destruction.

Kharkov, 1942

38 A consisting of 199, 304, 337 and 47 RDs, is deployed along the front: Bazaleevka, Brigadirovka, Shurovka, Melovaia and Nizhne-Russkii Bishkin (100km), with 81 RD and one TB in army reserve in the Alekseevka and Novo-Nikolaevka region.

The army's missions are: to defend occupied lines firmly and, especially, the Chuguev, Kupiansk and Balakleia, Izium axes. With the commencement of 28 A and 6 A's offensive, activate the defence to tie down opposing enemy forces.

6 A consisting of 253, 266, 103, 411, 393, 270, 248 and 41 RDs; 5 Gds and three additional TBs; 582 and 591 ATRs, one LAR, seven HARs, one AAR, 1st type RGK and three AARs, 2nd type RGK; 2 CC (38, 62, 70 CDs and one TB), 6 CC (20, 28, 49 CDs and 7 TB), 2 MC (two TBs), and 3 MC (6, 130, 131 TBs and 23 MRB) is deployed on the front Kiseli, Alekseevka, Novo-Vladimirovka (incl) and Paniutino (65km) in the following grouping: the 253, 266, 103 and 411 RDs with four TBs, two ATARs, five HARs, and three AARs, 2nd type RGK are deployed in first echelon in the Front main attack sector from Kiseli to Grushino (20km). The 248 and 41 RDs are deployed in second echelon in the Kaminka Farm, Mikhailovka and Liubitskie Farm region. Concentrated in third echelon to develop the army's offensive success are: 2 MC in the Mikhailovka, Lozovenko and Popovka region; 3 MC in the Novobunakovo, Razdole and Novo-Ivanovka region; 2 CC in the Lozovskii, Dmitrievka and Krasnaia Balka region; and 6 CC in the Krasnopavlovka, Kniazevo and Privoe region.

The 393 and 270 RDs with one LAR, two HARs, and one AAR, 1st type RGK are deployed along the front Timchenko Farm, Novo-Vladimirovka (incl) and Paniutino (43km) to conduct secondary operations and protect Southern Front's 57 A.

The army's missions are: while delivering the main attack from the right flank in the direction of Vodolaga and Merchik, penetrate the enemy defence, introduce mobile formations into the penetration and, by the end of the sixth day of the offensive, reach, with rifle formations, the line: Dudkovka, Viasovka, Kokhanovka and Pokrovskoe and, with mobile formations, the line: [mission absent in original]. Subsequently, together with 28 A, complete the encirclement of the enemy Kharkov grouping, secure the Krasnograd region, and, by the end of the fourteenth day, consolidate positions along the front Kolomak, Chutovo, Popovka, Skalonovka, Mazharovo and Pokrovskoe with forward units of mobile formations and left flank divisions.

4. In accordance with force operations, the grouping of Front reserves is established as follows: the field headquarters of Op Group Grechko — in Izium; 343 RD with one TB — in the Aleksandrovka, Kune and Zhovtneva region; 124 RD with one TB — in the Brigadirovka, Nikolaevka and Radkovka region; 277 RD — in the Svatovo region; 130 MRB — in Starobelsk; and 102 RB — in Rostov.

5. Command and control for the period April-May is established as follows:
Operational Group, SW Direction — Svatovo
HQ, SW Front — Voronezh, Alternate Command Post (VPU) — Valiuki (from the beginning of the operations HQ, SW Front — Valiuki).
HQ, Southern Front — Starobelsk; Alternate Command Post (VPU) — Rubezhnoe and Kamensk.

Signed:
Chief of Staff, SW Direction and SW Front, I. Bagramian
Military Commissar, SW Front HQs, Brigade Commissar Bordovsky
Assistant Chief of Staff, SW Front, Col Rukhle

TsAMO, f.251, op.646, d.145., ll.181-188.

Appendix 4

From Operational Directive No 00275 of the Southwestern Direction High Command to Southwestern Front forces concerning the conduct of an operation to encircle and destroy the enemy Kharkov grouping.

Dated: 28 April 1942

Appendices

1. The enemy, while taking stock of his occupied defensive positions, continues to accumulate operational reserves in the Kharkov region. Up to four infantry divisions have been noticed in the Akhtyrka, Kremenchug, Krasnograd and Poltava regions. With the onset of dry weather, it is possible that the enemy will attempt to liquidate the Barvenkovo-Lozovaia bridgehead and, simultaneously, undertake an offensive in the direction of Kharkov and Kupiansk to reach the main communications lines of our armies operating on the internal wings of the Southwestern Direction's Fronts (38, 6, 57 and 9 As).

2. On the right Briansk Front's 40 A is defending the line: Nov. Saviny, Stanovoe and Semitsa, covering the Kursk, Voronezh axis.
   On the left the Southern Front's 57 A is attacking the enemy with its right flank and has reached the line: Sosi-Petropol, Novo-Uplatnoe Farm and Krishtopovka. On its remaining front, it is defending along the existing line: Blagodatnoe and Novo-Kavkaz, covering the Southwestern Front's left wing.

3. To secure the Kharkov region, the Southwestern Front will go over to the offensive with the mission of penetrating the enemy defence and, by the concentrated blows of 6 and 28 As, encircle and destroy his Kharkov grouping in the Kharkov, Zmiev, Balaklaia and Pechenegi region. On the fifteenth to eighteenth day of the operation shift to the defence along the line: Zolochev, B. Tsapovka, Skovorodinovka and Staraia Vodolaga.
   Be ready to attack at the end of 4.5.42.

4. **21 A** consisting of 538 LAR, 8 MRD, 293, 297, 76, 301 and 227 RDs, 1 MRB, 10 TB, 8 Sep TBn, 338 LAR, 135 AR and 156 AR (2nd type), and with three divisions firmly hold on to the line: Spartak, Malo-Iablonovo, Shliakhovo, Miasoedovo, Titovka and Gatishche No 2. Shift to the offensive with two divisions and a tank brigade and artillery reinforcements with the main effort south of Staritsy, along the front from Zavody 1-e, Prilipka and Hill 163.2 with the mission of penetrating the enemy defence, securing the Murom region and, by the end of the third day of the offensive, reach the line Murom, Hill 219.5. Subsequently, while advancing in the direction of Cheremoshnoe, reach the front Pristen, Nedostupovka, Petrovka and hill 205.8 and dig in to protect the right flank of 28 A from enemy attacks from the north and northwest.
   The army reserves are — 1 MRB concentrated in the Chuevo, Krivye Balki and Kholodnoe region and 301 RD —in the Ivitsa, Protopopovka and Krasnaia Poliana region.
   Army headquarters — Korocha, Alternate Command Post — Volchanskie Farm, KIM State Farm.

5. **28 A** consisting of 13 Gds, 244, 175, 169, 162 and 38 RDs, 3 Gds CC (5 and 6 Gds, 32 CD and 34 MRB), 6 Gds, 84, 90 and 57 TBs, 764 ATAR, 651 and 612 LARs, 7 Gds and 870 HARs, 594 and 266 GARs, 5 Gds and 233 ARs, 2nd type RGK, 1 and 2/4 Gds MRs and 110 Sep Gds MBn — shift to the offensive along the front Izbitskoe and Fedorovka, penetrate the enemy defence and, having seized the Ternovaia region, by the end of the third day of the offensive main forces will reach the line: Vysokii, Veseloe, Petrovskoe and Hill 219.1. Subsequently, decisively develop the attack from the right flank along the axis Borshchevoe, northwestern outskirts of Kharkov and, by the end of the sixth day of the offensive, reach the front: Cherkasskoe-Lozovoe, Bolshaia Danilovka and Zaikin farm. Upon seizure of the Liptsy region, commit one rifle division from army reserve in the Borisovka, Neskuchnoe and Sereda region. With the arrival of first echelon divisions along the Sereda, Veseloe line, commit 3 Gds CC into the penetration with the mission of reaching the Dementevka, NKVD State Farm, Liptsy, Vysokaia Iaruga region and protect the seizure by army main forces of the line: Cherkasskoe-Lozovoe, Bolshaia Danilovka and Brazhniki Farm. Subsequently, having replaced 3 GdsCC with infantry, use it for an attack to envelop Kharkov along the axis Dergachi, Gavrilovka.
   Army headquarters — Petropavlovka.

6. **38 A** consisting of 226, 300, 199, 124 and 81 RDs, 22 TC (36 and 13 TBs), 738 ATAR, 468 and 507 LARs, 574 HAR, 51 and 648 ARs (2nd type RGK) and 3/5 and 3/4 Gds MRs, while firmly holding onto the line Bazaleevka, Bogodarovka, Borshchevoe and Olkhovatka, will shift to the offensive with its main forces (four rifle divisions and 22 TC) along the front Hill 199.8, Art. Selianin, Piatnitskoe and Martovaia and, striking a blow along the Molodovoe, Rogan axis, will pen-

Kharkov, 1942

etrate the enemy defence in the Peschanoe and Bolshaia Babka sector and, by the end of the third day of the offensive, will reach the line Lebedinka, Hill 208.7, Zarozhnoe and Piatnitskoe. Subsequently, while developing the offensive along the Rogan and Ternovoe axis, secure river crossings in the Vvedenskoe, Chuguev sector with part of the force, and complete the encirclement of the enemy Chuguev-Balakleia grouping with 6 A units. At the same time, attack the city of Kharkov from the east with the forces of two rifle divisions and two tank brigades in co-operation with 28 and 6 As.

Army headquarters — Kupiansk; Alternate command post — Borshchevoe (northern).

7. **6A** consisting of 253, 266, 103, 411, 47, 337, 248 and 41 RDs, 5 Gds, 37, 38 and 48 TBs, 21 TC (198, 199 and 64 TBs, and 4 MRB), 23 TC (6, 130, 131 TBs and 23 MRB), 582 and 591 ATARs, 8, 116, 375, 209, 399, 435 and 269 GARs, 3 Gds and 671 ARs (2nd type RGK), 1 and 2/5 Gds MRs, and 206 Sep. Gds MBn . . . covered by two rifle divisions along the southern bank of the Northern Donets River, will shift to the offensive with its main forces along the front Nizhne-Russkii Bishkin, Alekseevka and Hill 178.5, to penetrate the enemy defence and secure the Bereka and Efremovka regions, and, by the end of the fourth day of the offensive, reach the line: Zmiev, Taranovka, Vasilevskii Farm, Hill 195 and Berestovaia.

Subsequently, while the main force advances along the Merefa-Kharkov axis and two to three reinforced rifle regiments advance from the Zmiev region to Krasnaia Poliana, by the end of the seventh day, the offensive will reach the line: Butovka, Trasnoi Farm, Merefa and Rakitnoe. When you arrive at the indicated line, withdraw one rifle division into army reserve in the Riabukhino, Kniazhnevo and Melikhovka region. When first echelon divisions reach the line: Bereka, Efremovka be ready to commit army mobile formations into the penetration with the following missions:

21 TC, while developing the attack of the first echelon, by the end of the fifth day of the offensive will seize crossings over the Mzha River and reach the Komarovka, Rakitnoe, Golubov Farm and Ostroverkhovka region and will cut the rail line linking Kharkov with the west. Subsequently, in co-operation with infantry, attack Kharkov from the southwest and west.

23 TC, while developing the attack of the first echelon, by the end of the third day of the offensive will reach the Staraia Vodolaga, Karavanskoe, Stulepovka and Novaia Vodolaga region and, depending on conditions, will be ready to deliver attacks on Liubotin or Valki and Koviagi.

Army headquarters — Fedorovka . . .

8. **Army Group Bobkin** consisting of 393 and 270 RDs, 6 CC (26, 29 and 49 CDs and 7TB), 872 CAR, 29 and 236 HARs, RGK will shift to the offensive, drive the enemy to the west, and, by the end of the third day, the main force of the rifle divisions will reach the line: Sofievka, Tarasovka, Veselaia, Iur'evka and Lukashevka. Subsequently, while continuing the offensive, secure the Kegichevka and Sakhnovshchina region and, by the end of the seventh day, reach the front: 393 RD — Kegichevka, Chervonoarmeiskii and Dar Nadezhdy; 270 RD — Grishevka, Gladkovka, Andreevka and Lukashevka. When units of 393 RD reach the line: Dmitrovka, Mikhailovka, introduce 6 CC into the penetration with the missions of striking a blow in the direction of Kazachi Maidan and, by the end of the fifth day of the offensive, secure the Krasnograd region.

Subsequently, while firmly holding on to the Krasnograd, Petrovk, and Kirillovka regions, secure 6 A's left flank against enemy attacks from the west.

Army headquarters — Petrovka, Army Group headquarters— Krasnopavlovka (western) . . .

9. **Front air forces**
Army aviation:
21 A — 43 FAR, 135 SRBAR and 596 FBAR (20 fighters, 15 night bombers and 12 day bombers)
28 A — RAG-4 (46 fighters, 20 assault aircraft, and 17 bombers)
38 A — 164 and 182 FARs and 598 FAR (40 fighters and 14 night bombers)
6 A — 23, 296 and 181 FARs, 92 AAR, 13 Gds SRBAR, 623 and 633 FBARs (47 fighters, 12 assault aircraft and 14 day and 28 night bombers)
Army Group Bobkin —RAG-5
Front aviation:
Group Riazanov and Group Gorbatsevich (117 fighters, 60 assault aircraft, 20 day and 121 night bombers and 15 DB-3)
Missions of Front aviation:
a) during the course of the preparatory period of the operation neutralise enemy aviation at airfields

Appendices

and prevent transport to the Kharkov area from the Belgorod, Gotnia, Akhtyrka, Poltava and Krasnograd regions; cover the approach and concentration of 28 A's and 6 A's shock forces, while paying particular attention to providing cover for mobile formations;
b) from the beginning of the offensive, be prepared to enlist all aviation forces for continuous co-operation with 28 A and 6 A shock groups on the field of battle. Maintain observation over the Poltava, Kremenchug, Krasnograd, Dnepropetrovsk and Sinel'nikovo axes; and
c) destroy crossings over the Dnepr River at Kremenchug and Dnepropetrovsk by systematic strikes.

10. Front reserves
277 RD in the Novonikolaevko, Volosskaia Balakleika and Blagodatnoe regions. Division headquarters — Staroverovka.
Prepare to defend the line: Arkadievka, Ivanovka, Hill 182.4 and Volosskaia Balakleika, and be prepared to deliver a counter-attack along the Arkadievka, Pechenegi, Poltava and Balakleia axes.
343 RD — in the Sukhoi Iar, Aleksandrovka, Kun and Bugaevka regions. Division headquarters — Bugaevka.
Prepare to defend the line: Nurovo, Hill 191.0, Kun'e, and Krasnaia Poliana.
Be prepared to deliver a counter-attack along the Nurovo, Bogodarovka, Aleksandrovka, Balakleia; and Kun'e, Izium axes.
2 CC — in the Novobunakovo, Gorokhovka, Miroliubovka, Privol'e, Katerinovka and Krasnaia Balka region. Corps headquarters — Gorokhovka.
Be ready to deliver a counter-attack along the Lozoven'ka, Shebelinka; Kniazevo, Lozovaia; and Mechibilovka, Barvenkovo axes.

11. Front headquarters from 2.5.42 — Valuiki
Alternate command post — Svatovo

Signed:
Commander-in-Chief, Southwestern Direction, Commander of Southwestern Front, Marshal of the Soviet Union, S. Timoshenko
Member of the Military Council of the Southwestern Direction, N. Khrushchev
Chief-of-Staff of the Southwestern Direction and Southwestern Front, Lt-Gen I. Bagramian
Assistant Chief of Staff, I. Rukhle

TsAMO SSSR, f.251, op.646, d.145, ll.189-196. (Copy).

Appendix 5
From Operational Directive No 00177 of the Southern Front command concerning a defence aimed at protecting, with its right-flank, the Southwestern Front forces offensive on the Kharkov axis.

Dated: 6 April 1942

1. The enemy is continuing to defend along the entire front, while strengthening his grouping on the Krasnoarmeisk and Slaviansk-Kramatorsk axes by transporting reinforcements from the rear and by transferring part of his forces from the Taganrog and Makeevka axes. His reserves are in the Pavlograd, Krasnoarmeisk, Kramatorsk, Artemovsk, Makeevka and Mariupol regions. The approach of reserves from the depth has been noticed along the line Dnepropetrovsk-Zaparozhe. Active enemy operations are possible along the Barvenkovo, Lisichansk and Voroshilovgrad axes.

2. Armies of the Front are firmly digging in along occupied lines, while protecting the Southwestern Front offensive along the Kharkov axis with their right flank and covering the Voroshilovgrad and Rostov axes with their left flank. The right boundary is (inclusive): Veshenskaia, Starobelsk, Izium (used with SW Front), Vel. Kamyshevakha, Paniutino and Pavlovka. The left boundary is as before.

3. **57 A** consisting of 99, 317, 150 and 351 RDs, 14 Gds RD, one Sep TBn, 476 GAR, 558 and 754 ATARs with two separate AT rifle bns, are defending the line Tsaredarovka, Krishtopovka, Novo-Pavlovka and Mal. Razdol, having replaced units of 370 RD and Group Komkov on the morning of

Kharkov, 1942

14.4. Firmly cover the Lozovaia region and protect the junction with Southwestern Front. Keep one RD in army reserve in the Bliznetsy region. Army headquarters — Bol. Andreevka, Alternate Command Post — Bliznetsy. The left boundary is — Pervomaiskoe, Studenok (incl), Dolgen'kaia (incl), Barvenkovo, Bogdanovka (incl), Novo-Bakhmet'evo, and Mar'ianka.

4. **9 A** consisting of 341, 106, 216, 349, 335, 51 and 333 RDs, 78 RB, 121 and 151 TBs, 4 Gds, 437, 229 HARs, and 186 and 665 ATRs with two battalions of anti-tank rifles, is defending the line Novo-Bakhmet'evo, Gromovaia Balka, Novo-Iakovlevka, Kantemirovka, Krasnoarmeisk, Glubokaia Makatykha, Shchurovo and Brusovka. Firmly cover the Barvenkovo region and axes from Slaviansk to Izium and Krasnyi Liman. Protect the junction with 57 A. Place one RD and two TBs in army reserve in the Barvenkovo region. Subsequently, commit an additional rifle division to army reserve in the Ivanovskii region. Army headquarters — Bogorodichnoe, Alternate Command Post — Propol'e. The left boundary is as before . . .

11. **Front reserves** from 12.4 are:
a) 5 CC with 12 TB in the Brazhovka, Kurulka and Golaia Dolina region
b) 255 RD and 2 TB — Voroshilovgrad
c) 347 RD and 4 Gds TB — Rovenki and Dzerzhinsky village
d) 102 RB — Rostov

12. Require all army and rifle division commanders to create firm defences, well-developed in depth, with well-thought-out systems of fire and AT guns, with defensive outfitting, anti-tank and anti-infantry obstacles developed to a maximum and with extensive fortification of population points

13. **Air Forces**
1) determine the enemy grouping and his reserves by systematic reconnaissance in the depth up to the Dnepr River
2) hinder enemy regrouping
3) deliver strikes against enemy concentrated reserves
4) disrupt rail traffic by destruction of rail centres and staging points
5) destroy repair factories in Mariupol', Taganrog and Kramatorsk

14. Front headquarters — Rubezhnaia, Reserve C. P. — Starobelsk and Kamensk

Signed:
Commander of the Southern Front, Malinovsky.
Member of Southern Front Military Council, Korniets
Chief of Staff, Antonov

TsAMO, f.251, op.646, d.265, ll.119-120, 122-123. Original.

Appendix 6

Report of the Southwestern Direction High Command to the Stavka VGK concerning the transition of Southwestern Front forces to the offensive on the Kharkov axis and about the subsequent conduct of combat operations.

Dated: 15 May 1942

Fulfilling your directives, on the morning of 12 May, after carefully and secretly conducted preparations, the Southwestern Front's armies commenced their offensive on the Kharkov axis. The shift of our forces to the offensive surprised the enemy. Our offensive was planned and undertaken along the entire front and during the first day of the offensive our forces succeeded in penetrating strongly fortified lines and wedged deeply into the enemy's dispositions.

On the Front's right wing attacking Kharkov from the east, our forces destroyed units of 79, 294, 297 and 71 IDs, inflicted significant losses on the enemy 3 and 23 TDs and, by the end of 15 May, reached the front: Maslova Pristan', Murom, Pyl'naia, Veseloe, Petrovskoe, Oktiabr'skii and the

Appendices

Babka River.

The total penetration frontage of the enemy defence reached a width of 50km and the depth of our penetration is from 18 to 25km.

In sum, the Front's left flank armies destroyed up to three enemy divisions and, while successfully developing the offensive on Kharkov from the south and in the direction of Krasnograd, by the end of 15 May, they reached the front: Korobov Farm, Bolshaia Gomolha, Okhochae, Diachkovka, Popovka, Kegichovka, Sakhnovshchina and Iurevka.

The total penetration frontage of the enemy defence reached a width of 50km and the depth of our penetration is from 25-50km.

On the eve of the offensive, Front air forces delivered a series of surprise strikes against enemy aviation at airfields in Kharkov, Krasnograd and Poltava and by virtue of these strikes secured the initiative.

The successful penetration of the enemy defence on such a wide front (100km) is explained, chiefly, by clear-cut organisation of co-operation between infantry, artillery, tanks and aviation on the field of battle.

To parry our offensive on Kharkov from the east, the enemy brought up from Kharkov to the Chuguev, Zarozhnoe and Kamennaia Iaruga regions up to two tank divisions (more than 400 tanks), drove 38th Army's shock group back to its jumping-off positions by attacks in the direction of Zaporozhe, Peschanoe and Nepokrytaia, and at the present time is attempting to develop his success from the Nepokrytaia area into the flank and rear of 28th Army. In two days of the severest combat, the enemy tank divisions lost more than 150 tanks. Our losses in tanks on this front sector were up to 100 tanks.

In other Front sectors, our offensive did not meet great opposition and developed successfully.

Judging from this information, we have reached the conclusion that up to this time the enemy has not divined the concept of our operation, and he directed his principal shock striking force at a secondary front sector, and he has been deprived of his freedom of action by our shock group.

It is now completely clear to us that the two full-blooded enemy tank divisions concentrated in Kharkov were probably preparing to attack in the direction of Kupiansk so that we have succeeded in disrupting his offensive in the midst of its preparation.

It is also clear now that the enemy in the Kharkov region does not possess sufficient forces to develop a meeting battle against us.

Our actions on the Kharkov axis are creating rather favourable conditions for the planned offensive by Golikov [Lt-Gen F. I. Golikov was commander of the Briansk Front].

Assessing the existing conditions, we are reaching the conclusion that, despite the great losses inflicted by us on the enemy tank group, the latter represents a serious obstacle for the development of the offensive on Kharkov by the armies on our Front's right flank., Without rapid and decisive destruction of the main forces of the enemy tank divisions, our operation can be delayed sufficiently to permit the enemy, by the influx of reserves, to strengthen his resistance on the Kharkov axis.

We will undertake all possible measures to secure successful fulfilment of the principal Front missions.

We have insufficient quantity of tanks, aviation and rifle divisions to destroy the tank groups and to continue the development of the operation. To complete the operation successfully, we request the following from you:
- in the near future allocate four tank brigades and two rifle divisions to strengthen the Front right wing and two rifle divisions to strengthen the left wing
- order Golikov to shift to the offensive
- favourably treat our requests for aircraft, ammunition and fuel

Signed:
S. Timoshenko
I. Bagramian
N. Khrushchev

TsAMO, ff.220, op.226, ll.1-6. Original.

Kharkov, 1942

Appendix 7
Combat Order No 0140/op of the Southwestern Direction headquarters to the Commander, Southern Front, regarding measures to repel the enemy offensive in the 9th Army sector.

Dated: 17 May 1942 16.00hrs

With a view to repelling the enemy offensive against our 9th Army's sector, the commander in chief orders:

1. Operationally subordinate 2nd Cavalry Corps (38, 62 and 70 CDs), located in the Rozhdestvenskoe, Shatovo, Gorodnaia, Mechivilovka and Nadizhdovka region, to the Southern Front Commander.

2. To destroy the enemy group attacking Barvenkovo from the south, organise and deliver at first light on 18.5 a counter-attack with the forces of 2 CC and 14 Gds RD, and with reinforcements from the Sukhoi Torets River line (Barbalatovo, Ivanovka) into the flank and rear of the penetrating enemy group. Move up to the Sukhoi Torets River, as swiftly as possible, separate detachments from 2 CC to hold on to river crossings in the sector excluding Barvenkovo and Ivanovka. At the same time, a rifle regiment of 333 RD, reinforced, is holding firmly in Barvenkovo, to prevent enemy tanks and infantry from penetrating to the north.

3. Organise the destruction of the enemy groups attacking from the Slaviansk region against 9th Army's left flank with the forces of 5 CC, 12 and 121 TBs, and 333 RD (minus one regiment).

4. Maintain not less than one CD in the Front commander's reserve in the Barvenkovo region. Simultaneously, quickly begin the transfer to the Barvenkovo region of one RD and one TB from 37th Army.

5. The Commander in Chief's reserve — 343 RD, one bn of anti-tank rifles, and 92 separate Tbn concentrated at the disposal of Southwestern Front in the Izium region, will prepare and occupy a firm defence along the line: Semenovka, Mal. Kamyshevka, Sukhaia Kamenka and Senicheno. The division will prepare to deliver a counter-attack along the Barvenkovo and Slaviansk axes: 343 RD with attached reinforcements will be subordinate to the Southwestern Front commander when it arrives in the Izium region. Its use will be in accordance with the wishes of the Commander-in-Chief.

6. To the Southern Front Commander-in-Chief: Undertake measures to prevent the enemy from expanding his dispositions on the northern bank of the Northern Donets at the junction of 78 RB and 51 RD.

7. Reinforce the operations of 9th Army's shock group with two regiments of (assault bridging

8. Report the receipt of these orders and counter-attack plans.

Signed:
Chief of Staff of the Southwestern Direction, Lt-Gen I. Bagramian
Military Commissar, Headquarters Southwestern Direction, Brigade Commissar Z. Ivanchenko
Chief of the Operations Directorate Maj-Gen Vetoshnikov

TsAMO, f.220, op.226, d.17, ll.8-10. Original.

Appendix 8
Report of the Southwestern Direction High Command to the Stavka VGK concerning the transition of the enemy to the offensive against the Southern Front's 9th Army and measures to strengthen that Front's right wing.

Dated: 17 May 1942 17.30hrs

Appendices

Stavka, To the Supreme High Commander, Comrade Stalin.
From first light on 17.5, the enemy shifted to the offensive against both flanks of Southern Front's 9th Army. The probable aim of enemy action — to secure the Barvenkovo, Izium region and attempt to cut off our offensive on Kharkov from the south.

Units of 9th Army could not withstand the first enemy attack, delivered with the support of aviation and more than 100-120 tanks, and, by 10.00hrs the enemy had succeeded in penetrating through our dispositions to a depth of 5-8km in separate Front sectors.

In order to repel the enemy offensive and subsequently defeat him, in addition to the measures outlined in our Combat Directive No 0140/op, we will reinforce the Southern Front's right wing with 80 recently received tanks, including 57 T-34s and 23 T-60s.

Understanding the exceptional importance of maintaining the integrity of the defences on the Southern Front's right wing for protecting our offensive against Kharkov, we request you provide as reinforcements for the Southern Front's right wing 2 rifle divisions, 2 tank brigades and 1 aviation division, consisting of 2 FARs and 2 regiments of IL-2, and direct them now to the Izium region.

Signed:
Timoshenko
Bagramian
Khrushchev

TsAMO, d.220, op.226, ll. 11-11. Original.

Appendix 9
Combat Report No 0119 of the Southwestern Front Commander to the Stavka VGK concerning combat operations of Front forces on 18 May 1942.

Dated: 19 May 1942 00.30hrs

To the Stavka of the Supreme High Command, Comrade Stalin.
1. From the morning of 18.5, Southwestern Front forces were continuing their offensive, while meeting strong resistance from the enemy, who are shifting to the counter-attack in separate Front sectors. The enemy has halted our units' offensive by means of infantry and tank counter-attacks and strengthened aviation activity. Enemy tank and motorised infantry units, having penetrated Southern Front's 9th Army sector, advanced to Izium and threatened 6th Army's communications.

2. **21st Army** — having defended existing positions on its right and left flanks, went over to the offensive from 12.00hrs 18.5. Having met with heavy opposing fire and strong enemy counter-attacks in up to infantry regimental strength supported by groups of tanks, it conducted combat in its former defensive positions. Eight enemy tanks were destroyed in combat in the Hill 214.6 region.

3. **28th Army** — is defending occupied positions on its right flank, and from the morning of 18.5 shifted to the offensive on its left flank and by day's end was fighting along the line: eastern slope of height 205.4, eastern slope of the heights 3km west of Peremoga and the northern grove 2km east of height 214.3, height 194.5 and Martynovka. During the course of the day, enemy aviation groups conducted periodic raids on the army's combat formations.

4. **38th Army** — having attacked on the right flank, on the morning of 18.5, it battled along the line: eastern slopes of height 199.0, 172.0 and 'K' (1km southeast of Peschanoe), unnamed height 2km east of height 203.1, marker 196.3, and the northern part of Bolshaia Babka. On the left flank it defended its earlier occupied positions. The enemy is displaying strong fire resistance to units attacking from the Nepokrytaia, Peschanoe and the grove southwest of Peschanoe region.

5. **6th Army** — shifted to the offensive during the second half of 18.5 and by day's end, while repelling enemy opposition, it battled along the line: northern outskirts of Gaidary, markers 173.2 and 126.8, Pozharnyi Farm, Krasnyi Gigant State Farm, southern limits of Riabukhino, eastern limits of Kniazhnoe and Stulepovka. The main force of 23 TC has been withdrawn from battle and is moving to Mechebilovka. The enemy, by means of a strong anti-tank defence, counter-attacks and aviation actions, is rendering strong opposition to attacking units.

Kharkov, 1942

6. **Group Maj-Gen Bobkin** — on its right flank continued to fight for Krasnograd and was defending along earlier achieved lines in remaining Front sectors.

7. **Front air forces** — conducted 322 aircraft sorties on 18.5. As a result of air operations, up to 20 tanks, 26 vehicles, six loads of cargo and 8 enemy guns were destroyed. 7 enemy aircraft were destroyed in air combat. 3 of our planes did not return to their aerodromes.

Signed:
S. Timoshenko
I. Bagramian
N. Khrushchev

TsAMO, f.229, op.161, d.842, ll.243-245. Original.

Appendix 10
Report of the member of the Military Council of the Southwestern Direction to the Stavka VGK concerning combat operations of Direction forces on 18 May 1942.

Moscow — To Comrade Stalin

Dated: 19 May 1942 02.00hrs

SOUTHWESTERN FRONT
Southwestern Front forces continued the offensive from the morning of 18.5, and met strong resistance of the enemy, who, in separate sectors, shifted over to counter-attacks.

Having brought reserves forward, the enemy stopped our units' offensive by counter-attacks with infantry and tanks supported by aviation. 21st Army defended occupied positions on its right flank and went over to the attack on its left flank, and having met strong resistance by fire and counter-attacks in up to regimental strength supported by tank groups, it waged battle in occupied positions. Eight tanks were destroyed in battle. 28th Army went over to the offensive on its left flank. During the course of the day, enemy aviation periodically carried out raids against our units' combat formations. 38th Army went over to the offensive on its right flank. The advance was insignificant during the day. Its left flank occupied existing positions.

6th Army went over to the offensive during the second half of the day and by day's end seized Krasnyi Gigant [Red Giant] State Farm and Stulepovka. The army repelled enemy counter-attacks by infantry with tank support. Group Bobkin's right flank continued fighting for Krasnograd. 7th Tank Brigade cut the Krasnograd-Poltava road. In remaining sectors (forces occupied) existing lines. Front air forces carried out 322 aircraft sorties. Up to 150 infantrymen were killed, 20 tanks were put out of action, 24 vehicles, 7 supply transports and 8 combat guns were destroyed. On the Kharkov-Dergachi rail line one train (50 cars) was struck.

Shot down 7 enemy aircraft in air battles.

SOUTHERN FRONT
During the first half of 18.5, the enemy in front of 9th Army continued the offensive in two directions:
1) the Barvenkovo axis — where 1st Mountain-Rifle Division, 100th Infantry Division and 14th Tank Division forces (up to 70 tanks) pushed 9th Army to the north. At 11.00hrs enemy infantry and tanks (30-40) secured Barvenkovo, and its forward units reached the Ilichevka State Farm region (7km northeast of Barvenkovo);
2) the Slaviansk-Izium axis — where 101st Infantry Division with 50 tanks (16th Tank Division), automatic weapons groups and separate tank groups at 14.30hrs seized the southern part of Izium (on the right bank of the Northern Donets River), Shpakovka and Semenovka, and continued the offensive in a northwestern direction to Bel. Kamyshevakha (20km from Izium) using separate groups of tank and automatic weapons troops.

During the day 9th Army units battled for the northeastern outskirts of Barvenkovo.

According to information from reconnaissance aviation, on the morning of 18.5 the movement of 200 tanks and 200 vehicles was detected from the Andreevka region to Barvenkovo.

In 9th Army's sector, during the night and from the morning of 18.5 up to 50 enemy aircraft bombed crossing sites over the Northern Donets River, roads to the crossings and lines of communications in the Izium region.

9th Army units conducted an organised withdrawal from battle to new positions.

Sent by V Ch (special encoded communications means) by order of:
Comrade Khrushchev
Gapochka

TsAMO SSSR, f.28, op.11627, d.1162, ll.114-16. Machine copy.

Appendix 11

Notes of a conversation by direct line of the Chief of the Red Army General Staff, Lt-Gen A. M. Vasilevsky, with the Commander-in-Chief, Southwestern Direction.

Dated: 19 May 1942 15.35hrs

TIMOSHENKO, KHRUSHCHEV on the phone: Hello.

VASILEVSKY on the phone: Hello, I can hear.

TIMOSHENKO, KHRUSHCHEV: On the morning of 19.5, in light of the sharply worsening situation on the front of Southern Front's 9th Army and the rapid advance of the enemy in the general direction of Izium in a strength of five infantry divisions and two tank divisions (14th and 16th) and, with the presence of reserve groupings in the Stalino and Kramatorsk regions (according to intelligence information), including 13 TD, we decided, without wasting time, to assemble all that it is possible, depending on our capabilities, for a blow to destroy the enemy grouping deployed around Izium.

1. We have decided to leave three RDs, two tank brigades and four reinforcing artillery regiments on the Zmiev-Staroverevka front. Group Bobkin remains at full complement in occupied positions, having in mind that, having occupied Krasnograd, the cavalry corps and tank brigades' main forces will be pulled back into reserve (and deployed) at the junction between Group Bobkin and Gorodniansky's three RDs remaining along the front.

2. Command and control of these forces will be conferred on Lt-Gen Comrade Kostenko, and Bobkin's command will be subordinated to him for that purpose.

3. Take the headquarters of 6th Army under command of Gorodniansky and subordinate to it the commands of Pushkin and Kuzmin [E. G. Pushkin, Maj-Gen of tank forces, was commander of 23 TC, and G. I. Kuzmin, Maj-Gen of tank forces, was commander of 21 TC], who already entered the region known to you, and there subordinate to it the three RDs and two TBs of 6th Army and 5 CC, which remains in Gorodniansky's area, and 106 RD of 9th Army, already subordinate to 5 CC. Thus, Gorodniansky will have four RDs, seven TBs, one motorised brigade and six reinforcing artillery regiments. Subordinate to Comrade Podlas's 2 CC, located in our reserve, one TB from 6th Army and 341 RD of 9th Army, which is withdrawing on Podlas's left flank. Create a group on Podlas' left flank for a secondary blow to the right of Gorodniansky.

4. In Malinovsky's Senicheno-Studenok sector gather together under 9th Army, six RDs, four TBs and the 30 CD from 5 CC. This group, operating to the left of Gorodniansky, will deliver a secondary blow.

5. We decided to subordinate Comrade Podlas to me, since Malinovsky did not think it possible to control and support him materially in as much as all of this (force) will be going to Gorodniansky.

Kharkov, 1942

6. Concentrate your newly arrived two RDs and two TBs on the Volokhov Iar-Balakeia axis where we have already concentrated one TB. This group is intended for a strike westward in cooperation with 38 A pressure on Rubezhnoe-Chuguev and Group Kostenko pressure from Zmiev on crossings over the Northern Donets River. Continue fulfilling existing missions in Riabyshev's and Moskalenko's sectors. Group Kostenko is defending along lines reached at the end of the day. All forces and means will fall upon the enemy's southern grouping and destroy it. Advance the left wing of 38th Army with an attack from Kupiansk toward Volokhov Iar-Andreevka-Zmiev to the line of the Northern Donets, having joined the flank of Group Kostenko in the Zmiev region. By virtue of this attack free up up to five RDs and three TBs from Group Kostenko on the Merefa axis. Please report our decision quickly and please confirm it. We will begin working a suitable plan and will send it forth later. Need an answer quickly so that we can issue orders to our forces. That's all from us.

VASILEVSKY: How do you plan on fulfilling that decision in terms of time?

TIMOSHENKO, KHRUSHCHEV: To say now is very difficult, because much depends on the enemy's actions. It is possible that we can thrust Pushkin and Kuzmin into battle today, but tentatively, if conditions permit, then it will begin at the end of 21.5 or on the morning of 22.5. That's all.

VASILEVSKY: When do you think you can begin the withdrawal of Gorodniansky?

TIMOSHENKO, KHRUSHCHEV: It all depends on your decision, but conditions require that it be rapid.

VASILEVSKY: Good. Now I will report. It is likely that your questions were already discussed in the Stavka this morning.

TsAMO, f.229, op.161, d.809a, ll.528-530. Telegraph tape.

Appendix 12
Notes of a conversation by direct line of the Chief of the Red Army General Staff, Lt-Gen A. M. Vasilevsky, with the Commander-in Chief, Southwestern Direction.

Dated: 19 May 1942 15.50hrs

Timoshenko and Khrushchev on the telephone
Vasilevsky on the telephone.

VASILEVSKY: The Stavka approves your decision and proposes that you quickly begin its fulfilment. I request you send your worked out plan in code. That's all. Goodbye.

TIMOSHENKO, KHRUSHCHEV: All is understood. We will turn to its fulfilment. The plan will be sent in code. Goodbye.

TsAMO. F.28, op.11627, p.950, l.159. Telegraph tape.

Appendix 13
Combat order No 00320 of the Southwestern Direction High Command to the Commander of 6th Army forces, Lt-Gen A. M. Gorodniansky, and the Commander of the Army Group, Lt-Gen F Ia. Kostenko, on the conduct of military operations to destroy the enemy on the Izium axis.

Dated: 19 May 1942 19.00hrs

1. The enemy, while containing the offensive of Southwestern Front armies on the Kharkov axis, went over to the offensive on the Izium axis with five IDs and two TDs, and is attempting to reach the rear area and communications lines of 57th and 6th Armies.

Appendices

2. With the aim of destroying this enemy grouping and protecting the subsequent development of the offensive on Kharkov, I ORDER:

Army Group Kostenko, consisting of 253, 41, 266, 393 and 270 RDs, 57 and 48 TBs, 6 CC, four ARs RGK and two ATARs, from the morning of 20.5, will shift to the defence along achieved lines and while firmly holding them, will protect 6th and 57th Armies against attacks from the Kharkov, Krasnograd and Pavlograd axes. Withdraw the main forces of 6 CC (two CDs and two TBs) into Army Group reserve in the Efremovka, Shliakhovaia, Nizh. and Orel region, and prepare for a counter-attack in the indicated direction. Detail a strong detachment to secure the Zmiev region and seize crossings over the Northern Donets and Cheremushnaia Rivers. Right boundary — Korobov Farm, Verkhnii Bishkin, and (incl) Kiseli. Left boundary with 57 A — as before.

For command and control subordinate to yourself the headquarters of Group Bobkin and part of 6th Army headquarters, while not disturbing the command and control of 253, 266 and 41 RDs.

6 Army, consisting of 337, 47, 103, 248 and 411 RDs, 21 and 23 TCs, 37 TB and six ARs RGK, while continuing to hold onto crossings over the Bereka River with units of 23 TC and the southern bank of the Northern Donets with 337 and 47 RDs, by morning on 21.5 will secretly deploy the army's main forces to the line Bol. Andreevka, Petrovskaia, and, while delivering the main attack from the right flank toward Novo-Dmitrovka, will destroy the enemy Barvenkovo grouping in co-operation with 9 and 57 Armies. To the right of 57 Army, deliver a blow with three RDs, 2 CC and one TB from the front Novo-Prigozhaia, Federovka to envelop Barvenkovo from the south. Boundary line with 57 A — Chervonyi Shpil Barvenkovo and (incl) Ocheretino. On 9 A left, while holding back the enemy at crossings over the Northern Donets in the sector from the mouth of the Bereka River to Izium, deliver an attack from the Studenok region toward Kurulki 1-i. Boundary line with 9 A — Starobelsk, Izium, mouth of Bereka River and Barabashevka.

North of 6th Army, Group Sherstiuk, consisting of four RDs and three TBs, shifts to the offensive on the morning of 22.5 in the direction of Volokhov Iar and Chuguev. Boundary line with 6 A — Northern Donets River.

4. Material support of Group Kostenko is the responsibility of 6 A. Bear in mind that the supply and evacuation of 57th army will occur in the sector of 6 A.

Signed:
Commander in Chief of the Southwestern Direction and Commander of Southwestern Front, Marshal of the Soviet Union, S. Timoshenko
Member of the Military Council of the Southwestern Direction and Southwestern Front, N. Khrushchev
Chief of Staff of the Southwestern Direction and Southwestern Front, Lt-Gen I. Bagramian

TsAMO, f.220, op.226, d.17, ll.22-24. Original.

Appendix 14

Combat Order No 0143/op of the Southwestern Direction High Command to the Commander of Southern Front and 57th Army forces concerning an offensive to encircle and destroy the enemy Barvenkovo grouping.

Dated: 19 May 1942 19.00hrs

The enemy, having contained the offensive of Southwestern Front armies on the Kharkov axis, shifted to the offensive on the Izium axis with the forces of five IDs and two TDs and is trying to reach the rear area and communications lines of 57th and 6th Armies.

With the aim of destroying this enemy grouping and protecting the subsequent development of the offensive on Kharkov, I ORDER:

57th Army, consisting of 150, 99, 351, 317 and 341 RDs, 14 Gds RD, one regiment of 333 RD, 2nd Cavalry Corps (62, 38 and 70 CDs), 38 TB and three reinforcing artillery regiments, while holding firmly to occupied positions, will prepare an attack using the forces of not less than three RDs, two CC (three CDs), three reinforcing artillery regiments and one TB from the line Novo-Prigozhaia, Fedorovka to envelop Barvenkovo from the south in the general direction of Viknino. Mission: in co-operation with 6th and 9th Armies, surround and destroy the enemy Barvenkovo grouping. Subsequently, think of reaching the Samara River on the front Nikolkoe, Bezzabotovka

Kharkov, 1942

and Ocheretino with units of the shock group.

Be prepared to attack from the morning 21 May 1942.

From 12.00hrs 20 May 1942, 57th Army will become subordinate to me.

On the right — from the morning of 20.5.42, the Army Group of Lt-Gen Kostenko, with Group Bobkin subordinate to it, will shift to the defence along achieved lines and hold firmly to them, while protecting 6th and 57th Armies against attacks from the Kharkov and Krasnograd axes. Boundary line with it as before.

On the left — From the morning of 21.5.42, 6th Army is prepared to shift to the offensive from the line Bol. Andreevka, Petrovskaia to deliver its main attack from the right flank in the general direction of Novo-Dmitrovka.

Boundary line with 6th Army — (incl) Chervonyi Shpol, (incl) Barvenkovo, Viknino and Ocheretino.

Organise material support across river crossings in 6th Army's operational sector from bases and means of the Southern Front.

Signed:
Commander of Southwestern Direction forces, Marshal of the Soviet Union, Timoshenko
Member of the Military Council of the Southwestern Direction, Khrushchev
Chief of Staff of the Southwestern Direction, Lt-Gen Bagramian

TsAMO, f.220, op.226, d.17, ll.27-29. Original.

Appendix 15

Combat Report No 00323/op of the Southwestern Direction High Command to the Stavka VGK concerning the offensive operations of Front forces since 12 May 1942, the situation to the morning of 21 May 1942, and the plan for subsequent operations.

Dated: 21 May 1942

The offensive of Southwestern Front armies on Kharkov corresponded in time with the German preparation of a large-scale offensive on the Chuguev-Izium and Barvenkovo axes. Our offensive on Kharkov from the northeast forced the enemy to turn away from his offensive on the Chuguev and Izium axes and redeploy his principal forces — the tank formations and aviation — against the Front's right wing.

The offensive of Southwestern Front's 6th Army against Kharkov from the south developed successfully, but since Southern Front's 9th Army was unable to repel the enemy's attack on the Barvenkovo axis, the enemy succeeded in reaching the deep rear areas of 6th and 57th Army and forced us to halt this army's offensive on Kharkov and, in light of the unfinished regrouping, to join in a meeting engagement along the Bereka River and Britai River with large enemy motor-mechanised formations (two-three TDs) attacking from Barvenkovo to the northwest. Conditions were as follows on the morning of 21.5:

1. Units of 21st, 28th and 38th Armies are conducting fierce battles from occupied positions, repelling local enemy tank attacks supported by strong aviation. From the morning of 21.5 an enemy force concentration has been established in the Balakleia region.

2. Heavily battered units of 9th Army, which withdrew across the Northern Donets River, are defending its northern bank on the front Protopopovka, Izium and Studenok. With part of its force, the army forced the river and seized bridgeheads at Izium and Studenok in readiness to expand these bridgeheads.

3. On 20.5 57th Army repelled an offensive by five-six enemy IDs along its entire occupied front. On the left flank, it was subjected to an attack by 120-150 tanks and was forced to withdraw hastily behind the Bretan River along the front Star. Bliznetsy, Blagoveshchenskii and Rozhdestvenskoe with scattered groups of 2 CC and 14 Gds RD. The army has the mission of attacking from the north and northeast to unite with 6th Army.

4. 6th Army, using its main forces — 21 and 23 TCs, 103 and 248 RDs — will deploy by the morn-

Appendices

ing of 21.5 to the line: Krasnopavlovka, Bereka River and conduct an offensive eastward from its left flank to clear the enemy from the Protopopovka, Volvenkovo, Markevka and Petrovskoe regions. Remaining forces are on the march.

5. Army Group Kostenko, hard-pressed by local counter-attacks, has held on to its occupied lines firmly, has the mission of withdrawing to the line Terinovka, Efremovka, Orel River, Ligovka and Veselaia.

6. Front air forces: will direct its main efforts to destroy enemy tanks and motorised infantry in the Petrovskaia, Grushevakha and Mechebelovka regions and to the northeast of Lozovaia.

7. Simultaneously, we are preparing an attack from the east on the enemy Chuguev-Balakleia grouping with the forces of approaching reserves.
The offensive will tentatively begin on the morning of 23.5.

Signed:
S. Timoshenko
I. Bagramian
N. Khrushchev

TsAMO, f.229, op.161, d.809a, ll.521-524. Original.

Appendix 16
Extract from a Southwestern Front Military Council Order to 38th Army.

Dated: 22 May 1942

1. The enemy, while holding on to the front from Pechenegi to Balakleia, is continuing to threaten 6 A's communication lines. This Front sector is especially important in connection with the enemy offensive on the Izium axis.

2. On the right 28 A is continuing to fulfill its former mission. The boundary line with 28th Army remains as before. To the left 6 A is waging stubborn battles along the entire front with the attacking enemy, who are attempting to sever its communications.

3. In order to free 6 A from its half encirclement and insure its continued resupply, on the morning of 24.5.42, 38 A's left flank, consisting of 199, 304, 242 and 277, and 278 RDs, 114 and 156 TBs, and 22 TC (13, 36 and 168 TBs and 51 Motorcycle Battalion) will go over to the offensive along the front Pechenegi, Balakleia and, while delivering its main attack in the Vasilenkovo and Semenovka sector, it has the mission of: penetrating the enemy defence and by the decisive attacks of 199, 277 and 278 RDs, 156 TB, 22 TC and other reinforcing units in the direction of Grakovo and reaching the line 133.8, 129.2, Grakovo, 148.8, 150.3, 149.8 and Verbovka by the end of the first day. Subsequently, while developing the offensive to the west and southwest, by the end of the third day the shock group's right flank will reach the Northern Donets River along the front Annovka, Chuguev, and Mokhnachi. The left flank divisions (304, 242, RDs and 114 TB) co-operating with 337 and 47 RDs of 6 A, will encircle and destroy the enemy on the northern bank of the Northern Donets River.

4. By the end of 23.5.42, 22 Tank Corps (13, 36 and 160 TBs, 51 Motorcycle Battalion and a battalion of infantry) will occupy a jumping-off position in the Getmanovka, Sumskoe and Shevchenkovo region with the [following] missions: with the arrival of attacking infantry along the line Nikolaevka Farm, 162.0 and 163.0, enter the penetration in the Nikolaevka Farm and Mikhailovka sector. With one bound seize Malinovka and destroy crossings over the Northern Donets River at Chuguev. Subsequently, having turned to the south, crush the resisting enemy's combat formations in the Liman, Andreevka and Volochii Iar regions and destroy crossings over the Northern Donets River east of Zmiev.

5. The Army headquarters during the period of operations will be located in Volosskaia Balakleia.

Kharkov, 1942

6. The 242 RD and 114 TB will remain in reserve in occupied positions ready to attack to the west and will not be introduced into battle without permission of the High Command.

Signed:
S. Timoshenko
N. Khrushchev
I. Bagramian

Arkhiv MO, SSSR, f.220, op.220, d.1, ll.351-353.

Appendix 17

Information about the losses of Southwestern Direction forces during the period of battle on the Kharkov axis.

Dated: 10–31 May 1942[1]

Formations & units	Personnel	Rifles	Automatics	MGs	Tanks	Guns	Mortars	Horses
6th Army and Army Group Gen Bobkin	148,325	92,963	4,349	2,463	468	1,000	1,632	32,248
57th and 9th Armies, 2nd and 5th Cavalry Corps	60,695	50,263	4,704	1,196	84	564	1,646	25,378
21st Army	12,190	—	—	—	—	62	—	—
28th Army	24,507	—	—	—	100[2]	—	—	—
38th Army	17,727	—	—	—	—	20	—	—
Front units	3,212							
TOTAL	266,927	143,226	9,053	3,659	652	1,646	3,278	57,626

NOTE: The number of overall personnel losses includes 46,314 wounded and sick, who were evacuated to hospitals, and also 13,556 killed, who were buried on unoccupied territory. The remaining 207,057 persons fell into encirclement.

[1] TsAMO, f.251, 90.646, d.390. ll.166-169, 218-220, 224-225; d.273, l. 1081; and f.229, op.209, d.43, l.505.
[2] TsAMO, f.220, op.226, d.17, l.2.

Appendices

Appendix 18

Soviet Order of Battle (participating formations)

SOUTHWESTERN DIRECTION
Commander, Marshal S. K. Timoshenko
Commissar, Commissar N. S. Khrushchev
Chief of Staff, Col-Gen I. Kh. Bagramian

1. Southwestern Front
Commander, Marshal S. K. Timoshenko
Assistant Commander, Lt-Gen F. Ia. Kostenko
Commissar, Division Commissar K. A. Gurov
Chief of Staff, Col-Gen I. Kh. Bagramian

21st Army
Commander, Lt-Gen V. N. Gordov
Chief of Staff, Maj-Gen A. I. Davilov

76th Rifle Division: Col G. G. Voronin
227th Rifle Division: Col G. A. Ter-Gasparian
293rd Rifle Division: Maj-Gen P. F. Lagutin
10th Tank Brigade
135th Artillery Regiment
156th Artillery Regiment
338th Light Artillery Regiment
538th Artillery Regiment

28th Army
Commander, Lt-Gen D. I. Riabyshev

13th Guards Rifle Division: Maj-Gen A. I. Rodimtsev
38th Rifle Division: Col N. P. Dotsenko
162nd Rifle Division: Col M. I. Matveev
169th Rifle Division: Maj-Gen S. M. Rogachevsky
175th Rifle Division: Maj-Gen A. D. Kuleshchev
244th Rifle Division: Col [?] Afansiev
6th Guards Tank Brigade: Lt-Col M. K. Skuba
57th Tank Brigade: Maj-Gen V. M. Alekseev
84th Tank Brigade
90th Tank Brigade: Lt-Col M. I. Malyshev
4th Guards Mortar Regiment
 (1st and 2d Battalions)
5th Guards Artillery Regiment
7th Guards Howitzer Artillery Regiment
233rd Artillery Regiment
266th Gun Artillery Regiment
594th Gun Artillery Regiment
612th Light Artillery Regiment
651st Light Artillery Regiment
764th Anti-tank Artillery Regiment
870th Howitzer Artillery Regiment
110th Separate Guards Mortar Battalion
3rd Guards Cavalry Corps:
 Maj-Gen V. D. Kriuchenkin

5th Guards Cavalry Division:
 Maj-Gen M. F. Maleev
6th Guards Cavalry Division:
 Col A. I. Belogorsky
32nd Cavalry Division
34th Motorised Rifle Brigade

38th Army
Commander, Lt-Gen K. S. Moskalenko
Assistant Commander, Maj-Gen G. I. Sherstiuk
Commissar, Division Commissar N. G. Kudinov
Chief of Staff, Col S. I. Ivanov

81st Rifle Division: Col F. A. Pimenov
124th Rifle Division: Col A. K. Berestov
199th Rifle Division
226th Rifle Division: Maj-Gen A. V. Gorbatov
300th Rifle Division
304th Rifle Division
13th Tank Brigade: Lt-Col I. T. Klimenchuk
36th Tank Brigade: Col T. I. Tanaschishin
133rd Tank Brigade: Lt-Col N. M. Bubnov
4th Guards Mortar Regiment (3rd Battalion)
5th Guards Mortar Regiment (93rd Battalion)
51st Artillery Regiment
468th Light Artillery Regiment
507th Artillery Regiment
574th Howitzer Artillery Regiment
648th Artillery Regiment
738th Anti-tank Artillery Regiment

6th Army
Commander, Lt-Gen A. M. Gorodniansky
Commissar, Brigade Commissar A. I. Vlasov
Chief of Staff, Maj-Gen A. G. Batiunia

41st Rifle Division: Col V. G. Baersky
47th Rifle Division: Maj-Gen F. P. Matykin
103rd Rifle Division: Col Ia. D. Chanyshev
248th Rifle Division: Col A. A. Mishchenko
253rd Rifle Division: Lt-Col M. G. Grigorev
266th Rifle Division: Col A. A. Tavantsev
337th Rifle Division: Maj-Gen I. V. Vasilev
411th Rifle Division: Col M. A. Pesochin
5th Guards Tank Brigade
37th Tank Brigade
38th Tank Brigade
48th Tank Brigade: Col A. P. Silnov
3rd Guards Artillery Regiment
5th Guards Mortar Regiment
 (1st and 2nd Battalions)
8th Gun Artillery Regiment
116th Gun Artillery Regiment
209th Gun Artillery Regiment

Kharkov, 1942

269th Gun Artillery Regiment
375th Gun Artillery Regiment
399th Gun Artillery Regiment
435th Gun Artillery Regiment
582nd Anti-tank Artillery Regiment
591st Anti-tank Artillery Regiment
671st Howitzer Artillery Regiment
206th Separate Guards Mortar Battalion
21st Tank Corps: Maj-Gen G. I. Kuzmin
  64th Tank Brigade
  198th Tank Brigade
  199th Tank Brigade
  4th Motorised Rifle Brigade
23rd Tank Corps: Maj-Gen E. G. Pushkin
  6th Tank Brigade
  130th Tank Brigade
  131st Tank Brigade
  23d Motorised Rifle Brigade

Army Group
Commander, Maj-Gen L. V. Bobkin

270th Rifle Division: Maj-Gen Z. Iu. Kutlin
393rd Rifle Division
29th Howitzer Artillery Regiment
236th Howitzer Artillery Regiment
872nd Cannon Artillery Regiment
6th Cavalry Corps: Maj-Gen A. A. Noskov
  26th Cavalry Division
  28th Cavalry Division: Col L. N. Sakovich
  49th Cavalry Division: Col T. V. Dedeogly
  7th Tank Brigade: Col I. A. Iurchenko

Front reserves
277th Rifle Division: Col V. G. Chernov
343rd Rifle Division: Maj-Gen Iu. A. Naumenko
2nd Cavalry Corps: Col G. A. Kovalev
  38th Cavalry Division
  62rd Cavalry Division
  70th Cavalry Division
71st Separate Tank Battalion
92nd Separate Tank Battalion
132rd Separate Tank Battalion

2. Southern Front
Commander, Col-Gen R. Ia. Malinovsky
Assistant Commander, Maj-Gen L. V. Vetoshnikov
Commissar, Division Commissar L. P. Korniets
Chief of Staff, Maj-Gen A. I. Antonov

9th Army
Commander, Maj-Gen F. M. Kharitonov
Commissar, Division Commissar, K. V. Krainiukov
Chief of Staff, Maj-Gen E. K. Korzhenevich
51st Rifle Division: Lt-Col B. K. Aliev

106th Rifle Division
216th Rifle Division
333rd Rifle Division: Maj-Gen Ia. S. Dashevsky
335th Rifle Division
341st Rifle Division: Col A. I. Shagin
349th Rifle Division
78th Rifle Brigade
51st Tank Brigade
121st Tank Brigade
4th Guards Heavy Artillery Regiment
186th Anti-tank Artillery Regiment
229th Heavy Artillery Regiment
437th Heavy Artillery Regiment
665th Anti-tank Artillery Regiment

57th Army
Commander, Lt-Gen K. P. Podlas
Commissar, Brigade Commissar A. I. Popenko
Chief of Staff, Maj-Gen A. F. Anisov

14th Guards Rifle Division:
  Maj-Gen I. M. Shepétov
99th Rifle Division: Col Lopatin
150th Rifle Division: Maj-Gen D. G. Egorov
317th Rifle Division: Col D. A. Iakovlev
351st Rifle Division: Col N. U. Gursky
92nd Separate Tank Battalion

Front reserves
5th Cavalry Corps: Maj-Gen I. A. Pliev
  30th Cavalry Division: Col V. S. Golovsky
  34th Cavalry Division: Col A. N. Inauri
  60th Cavalry Division
12th Tank Brigade

From other Front sectors
278th Rifle Division
296th Rifle Division
3rd Tank Brigade
15th Tank Brigade

From RVK reserves
242nd Rifle Division: Col A. M. Koshkin
114th Tank Brigade: Lt-Col. V. Kurilenko

Abbreviated German Order of Battle (initial)
Army Group South
Commander, Field Marshal Fedor von Bock

Sixth Army
Commander, Col-Gen Friedrich Paulus

XXIX Army Corps
  57th Infantry Division
  168th Infantry Division
  75th Infantry Division
  102nd Infantry Brigade (Hungarian),
    (disbanding)

Appendices

XVII Army Corps
 79th Infantry Division
 294th Infantry Division

LI Army Corps
 297th Infantry Division
 44th Infantry Division

VIII Army Corps
 108th Light Infantry Division (Hungarian)
 62nd Infantry Division
 454th Security Division

Reserves
3rd Panzer Division
23rd Panzer Division
113th Infantry Division
71st Infantry Division (one regiment supporting 294th Infantry Division)
305th Infantry Division (approaching Kharkov from the west)

Army Group von Kleist
Seventeenth Army
Commander, Col-Gen Richard Ruoff
(Fourth Army [Romanian] subordinate)

First Panzer Army (elements)
Field Marshal Ewald von Kleist

Group von Kortzfleisch

XI Army Corps
 Gen von Kortzfleisch
VI Army Corps (R)
 298th Infantry Division
 1 Regt, 68th Infantry Division
 4th Infantry Division (R)
 1st Infantry Division (R)
 2nd Infantry Division (R)

III Motorised (Panzer) Corps
 Col-Gen Eberhard von Mackensen

 1st Mountain Division
 14th Panzer Division
 100th Light (Jaeger) Division
 60th Motorised Division

XXXXIV Army Corps:
 97th Light (Jaeger) Division
 68th Infantry Division (-)
 257th Infantry Division
 295th Infantry Division

Reserves
389th Infantry Division
384th Infantry Division
101st Light (Jaeger) Division
16th Panzer Division
20th Infantry Division (R)

Appendix 19
Postscript: The Fate of the Survivors

Although, as a result of the Kharkov operation, an appalling number of senior and mid-level Soviet officers perished or fell into captivity along with tens of thousands of soldiers, many survived to fight in future battles. Only the most fortunate witnessed final Soviet victory in 1945.

Soon after the Kharkov disaster, Stalin assigned Marshal S. K. Timoshenko to command the Northwestern Front. In February and March 1943, Timoshenko planned and conducted the Demiansk operation against German Army Group Centre, but failed to destroy the German Army Group. This was Timoshenko's last Front command. Thereafter, he served as Stavka representative and coordinated operations by the Leningrad and Volkhov Fronts from March to June 1942, the North Caucasus Front and Black Sea Fleet from June to November 1943, and 2nd and 3rd Baltic Fronts from February to June 1944, and the 3rd and 4th Ukrainian Fronts from August 1944 to May 1945. Not coincidentally, all of these Fronts operated along secondary axes.

After the war ended, Timoshenko commanded forces in the Baranovichi (1945–1946), Southern Ural (1946–1949) and Belorussian (1946, 1949-1960) Military Districts. In April 1960 he was appointed to the Ministry of Defence Inspectorate, a literal 'old folks' home' for veteran senior officers and, from 1962, also served as head of the Soviet War Veterans Committee. Timoshenko died in 1970.

Commissar N. S. Khrushchev weathered the Kharkov storm and served through 1944 as Military Council Member (Commissar) of the Southwestern, Stalingrad, Southeastern, Southern, Voronezh

Kharkov, 1942

and 1st Ukrainian Fronts. Politically, from 1944 to 1947 he was chairman of the Ukrainian Council of Ministers and from 1947 to 1949 1st Secretary of the Ukrainian Communist Party Central Committee. Brought back to Moscow by Stalin in 1949, he served until Stalin's death in 1953 as Secretary of the Central Committee and 1st Secretary of the Moscow Party Committee. On Stalin's death he became 1st Secretary of the Communist Party Central Committee and engaged in a struggle for power which, in 1958, elevated him to pre-eminent position as Chairman of the USSR Council of Ministers. During and after the power struggle, he surrounded himself with wartime military comrades who had served with him in the Ukraine. Ousted from power on 14 October 1964 by the Brezhnev faction, Khrushchev became the first Soviet leader to retire, albeit in relative seclusion. He died in 1971.

After his relief by Stalin in July, Col-Gen Bagramian took command of 16th Army (later 11th Guards) and commanded that army through the Orel operation (during the Kursk counter-offensive) in summer 1943. From November 1943 to February 1945 he commanded the 1st Baltic Front and participated in the Belorussian, Riga, Memel and East Prussian operations. From February 1945 until war's end, he commanded the Samland Group of forces and the 3rd Belorussian Front and cleared German forces from the Koenigsberg region.

After the war Bagramian served as commander of the Baltic Military District (1945–1954), Chief Inspector of the Ministry of Defence (1954–1955), Deputy Minister of Defence and a Marshal of the Soviet Union (1955–1956), Director of the General Staff Academy (1956), and Deputy Minister of Defence and Chief of Rear Services of the Soviet Armed Forces (1958–1968). In 1968 he retired as Ministry of Defence inspector and engaged in intense historical writing. A twice Hero of the Soviet Union (1944 and 1977), Bagramian was the only non-Slavic Soviet Front commander.

Despite the Kharkov disaster, Southern Front commander Col-Gen R. Ia. Malinovsky survived Stalin's suspicions about his loyalty and competence, ultimately rising to become one of the Soviet Army's premier and most competent Front commanders and a key figure in the postwar Soviet Army. After May 1942 he commanded Southern Front through the disastrous summer and, in August, led the Don Operational Group covering the approaches to the Caucasus, with Khrushchev 'monitoring his reliability' at Stalin's direction. Malinovsky weathered the storm and, in late August, was given command of 66th Army defending the approaches to Stalingrad. After serving as Deputy Commander of the Voronezh Front (October–November), he took command of the new and powerful 2nd Guards Army and led it to victory against German forces attempting to relieve Stalingrad. For his superb performance, in February 1943 he was appointed to command Southern Front and, in March, the Southwestern Front. He commanded this Front (renamed 3rd Ukrainian in October 1943) until March 1944, when he took command of 2nd Ukrainian Front. He led 2nd Ukrainian Front until war's end, played a leading role in the Iassy-Kishinev, Budapest, Balaton and Vienna operations and was elevated to the rank of Marshal of the Soviet Union. After the war in the West had ended, in August 1945 Malinovsky led the Trans-Baikal Front to victory over the Japanese Kwantung Army in Manchuria.

After the war Malinovsky remained in the East commanding the Trans-Baikal-Amur Military District from 1945 to 1947, serving as Supreme Commander in the Far East from 1947 to 1953, and as Commander of the Far Eastern Military District from 1953 to 1956. Soon after Stalin's death, and reflective of Khrushchev's rise to power, in 1956 Malinovsky became 1st Deputy Minister of Defence (under Zhukov) and Commander of the Soviet Armed Forces. In 1957 he succeeded Zhukov as Minister of Defence, signalling Khrushchev's full rise to power. However, caught between contending political factions and a debate in the armed forces over strategy and the size of the Soviet Army, Malinovsky's support of Khrushchev weakened. In 1964, when Khrushchev was removed from power, Malinovsky did little to help his former patron. Malinovsky went on to serve as Minister of Defence under the Brezhnev-Kosygin regime until his death in 1967.

Southern Front's Chief of Staff, Maj-Gen A. I. Antonov, continued to serve after the disaster and, in July, after dissolution of the Front, he became chief of staff of Marshal Budenny's North Caucasus Front and, in November, Trans-Caucasus Front chief of staff. Vasilevsky noted Antonov's superb performance during the fighting in the Caucasus and, in December 1942, he nominated Antonov to be Chief of the General Staff's Operational Directorate. Stalin accepted Vasilevsky's recommendation and the strategic planning team that would govern Red Army operations to the war's end was born. Antonov became 1st Deputy Chief of the General Staff (and an Army General) in March 1943 and Chief of the General Staff and Stavka member in February 1945. During this period he was instrumental in planning most significant Soviet strategic operations, including the Kursk, Belorussian and Berlin operations, and he attended both the Yalta and Potsdam Conferences.

Appendices

After the war ended, in 1946 Antonov reverted to 1st Deputy Chief of Staff when Vasilevsky returned to his former post as Chief. He then commanded the Trans-Caucasus Military District from 1950 to 1954, at a time when the increasingly paranoid Stalin 'exiled' from Moscow the most distinguished Soviet wartime leaders. After Stalin's death, in April 1954 Khrushchev brought Antonov back from exile to become 1st Deputy Chief of the General Staff and, in May 1955, Chief of Staff of the newly-formed Warsaw Pact forces. He was instrumental in keeping the Pact together during and after the Polish and Hungarian uprisings in 1956, and he established a solid basis for future Pact military doctrine. After suffering a heart attack in 1945, Antonov's health deteriorated and he died in 1962.

The 21st Army commander, Lt-Gen V. N. Gordov, continued as army commander until July 1942, when he was appointed to command the Stalingrad Front. His apparent failure to blunt the German advance on Stalingrad resulted in his removal as Front commander in August and his October 1942 reassignment to command the Western Front's 33rd Army. He commanded 33rd Army throughout the Smolensk operation in summer 1943 and in April 1943, as colonel-general, took command of 3rd Guards Army, which he commanded until war's end. After the war Gordov commanded the Volga Military District and died at the age of 56 years in 1951.

Lt-Gen D. I. Riabyshev of 28th Army remained in command of his army until July 1942 when he was demoted to deputy commander of 3rd Guards Army. Thereafter, he commanded 34th Guards Rifle Corps and served briefly as commander and deputy commander of 3rd Guards Army. From April 1944 until May 1945, he commanded 3rd Guards and 114th Rifle Corps and, in 1945 and 1946, a rifle corps. From 1946 to 1950, he was assistant commander of Eastern Siberian Military District forces. As his record indicated, after the Kharkov disaster, Stalin never again regained confidence in Riabyshev's limited military talents. He remained a lieutenant-general and was retired in 1950.

Lt-Gen K. S. Moskalenko, commander of 38th Army, fared better than Riabyshev. Although, during the war he never rose above army command, he played a significant role in the postwar years, was appointed a Marshal of the Soviet Union in 1955, and lived to write extensively about his experiences. During wartime Moskalenko commanded 38th Army (May–July 1942 and October 1943–May 1945), 1st Tank Army (July–August 1942), 1st Guards Army (August–October 1942) and 40th Army (October 1942–October 1943). His armies played significant roles in the Stalingrad, Kursk, Kiev, Lvov-Sandomiersz and Carpathian operations. For his service along the Dnepr River in 1943, Moskalenko was made a Hero of the Soviet Union.

After the war, in 1946 Moskalenko commanded the key Moscow Air Defence Region. In 1953, after the death of Stalin, he was instrumental in the removal and execution of NKVD head Beria, at Khrushchev's behest. For his role in forestalling an NKVD coup, Moskalenko became commander of the Moscow Military District. The 'Southwestern Direction Group' of Khrushchev, Bagramian, Moskalenko and others had emerged supreme. In 1960 Moskalenko became Chief of Soviet Strategic Rocket Forces and Deputy Minister of Defence. He held the former position until 1962, when he was removed apparently because he disagreed with Khrushchev over Soviet policy during the Cuban Missile Crisis. Late in 1962 Moskalenko became Ministry of Defence Chief Inspector and, again, Vice Minister of Defence. Although abandoned by his patron, Moskalenko would still have the final say, and in writing. His memoirs remain one of the finest and most accurate accounts of Soviet wartime operations. Moskalenko finally retired in 1983 and died in 1985.

Maj-Gen F. M. Kharitonov, commander of ill-fated 9th Army, commanded at army level until his death in 1943. In June 1942, after appointment as lieutenant-general, he received command of 6th Army. He led that army during the Stalingrad operations and the rapid subsequent Soviet advance into the Donbas in February 1943. Fate again caught up with Kharitonov, when, in February 1943, an army under his command was again encircled and destroyed, this time by von Manstein's counter-stroke in the Donba. Apparently wounded in the chaotic retreat, Kharitonov died from his wounds in late May 1943.

9th Army Commissar, Division Commissar K. V. Krainiukov, went on to serve in that capacity for 40th Army and, from October 1943 to war's end, for 1st Ukrainian Front, where he developed a lasting relationship with Khrushchev. After the war he was Commissar for the Central Group of Forces (1945–1947), the Carpathian Military District (1947–1948) and the Baltic Military District (1955–1960); Chief of the Lenin Political Military Academy (1948–1949); 1st Deputy Chief and Chief of the Main Political Administration of the Soviet Army (1949–1950) and Deputy Political Chief of the General Staff's Military-Scientific Directorate (1960–1969). After his retirement in 1969, he wrote two extensive memoirs about his wartime service.

Kharkov, 1942

Many of the corps, divisional and brigade commanders survived to fight on. The commander of 5th Cavalry Corps, Maj-Gen I. A. Pliev, rose to prominance, commanding a cavalry-mechanised group in operations in the Ukraine and Hungary and a Soviet-Mongolian Cavalry-Mechanised Group in the Manchurian operation of August 1945. After the war he commanded an army and, from 1955 to 1968, was deputy commander and commander of the North Caucasus Military District and a candidate member of the Communist Party Central Committee. Pliev retired in 1968, wrote numerous memoirs and died an Army General in 1979.

In June 1942 Maj-Gen V. D. Kriuchenkin, commander of 3rd Guards Cavalry Corps, was selected by the Stavka to command first, 28th and then 4th Tank Army, one of the first Soviet armies of that type. He led 4th Tank during the failed and somewhat clumsy attempts to halt the German advance on Stalingrad. Replaced by Gen Batov in October 1942, Kriuchenkin attended a short course at the General Staff Academy and then commanded 69th Army and 33rd Army throughout the remainder of 1943 and to July 1944. Thereafter, he served as deputy commander of 61st Army and the 2nd Belorussian Front. After the war Kriuchenkin commanded the Don Military District (1945–1946). Apparently retained in command by Stalin because of his affinity with former 1st Cavalry Army cavalrymen, Kriuchenkin disappeared into retirement in 1946, wrote his memoirs in 1958, and died in 1976.

Maj-Gen A. I. Rodimtsev was one of the few division commanders to rise above future obscurity. After commanding the 13th Guards Rifle Division through bitter fighting at Stalingrad, he rose to command the 32nd Guards Rifle Corps (5th Guards Army) until war's end and saw action at Kursk, in the Ukraine and during the Berlin operation. The twice Hero of the Soviet Union commanded at various levels after the war, was promoted to colonel-general in 1961, retired in 1966, and died in 1977 after writing his memoirs. One of his wartime commanders, Lt-Col I. A. Samchuk of 39th Guards Rifle Regiment, lived to write a history of Rodimtsev's 13th Guards Rifle Division. Maj-Gen A. V. Gorbatov, commander of the 226th Rifle Division, also fared well, rising to command 20th Rifle Corps (April–June 1943) and 3rd Army (June 1943–May 1945). After the war he commanded an army, Soviet airborne forces (1950–1954) and, as an army general, the Baltic Military District (1954–1958). He retired in 1958 and died in 1973. Maj-Gen Iu. A. Naumenko commanded his 343rd Rifle Division (later the 97th Guards) throughout the entire war. The author had the honour of interviewing him concerning his division's role in the 1945 Vistula-Oder operation.

Still other commanders survived the Kharkov operation only to perish later in the war Maj-Gen E. G. Pushkin, commander of 23rd Tank Corps, escaped from the Barvenkovo encirclement and was soon given command of a newly-formed 23rd Tank Corps, which he led through the entire summer-autumn campaign and the battle of Stalingrad. Pushkin led the corps through the Donbas in September 1943 and spearheaded Gen Chuikov's 8th Guards Army's seizure of Zaporozhe in October 1943. He died in a German air attack on 11 March 1944 while his corps was struggling along the lower Dnepr River. Col V. G. Chernov, commander of 277th Rifle Division, went on to command 60th Rifle Division throughout 1943 and 1944. He was killed on 17 March 1945 while commanding his division during the Vistula-Oder operation.

Col T. I. Tanaschishin, commander of 36th Tank Brigade, took command of 13th Tank Corps in July 1942 as a major-general and fought under Gen Moskalenko's 1st Tank Army on the approaches to Stalingrad. Ironically, his corps later played a critical role in the encirclement of German Sixth Army, the force which had mauled his 36th Tank Brigade only six months before. For its distinguished service, Tanaschishin's tank corps received the new designation, 4th Guards Mechanised Corps. The corps fought in the September 1943 Donbas operation and was instrumental in the Soviet victory in the Nikopol-Krivoi Rog operation in January and February 1944. Tanaschishin was killed in a German air attack on 31 March 1944 during the successful Soviet operation to seize southern Ukraine.

Another tank brigade commander at Kharkov rose to prominence, only later to die in battle. Maj-Gen V. M. Alekseev, commander of 57th Tank Brigade at Kharkov, took command of 10th Tank Corps in July, and as a lieutenant general he commanded the corps at Kursk in 1943 and during the subsequent Soviet advance to the Dnepr River. The corps was redesignated 5th Guards Tank Corps and, as part of 6th Tank Army, fought with distinction during the Korsun-Shevchenkovsky operation and across the Ukraine. In late August 1944, while 6th Tank Army was marching victoriously into Romania during the later stages of the Iassy-Kishinev operation, Gen Alekseev was killed by enemy fire in the city of Tekuch. For personal bravery, Alekseev was posthumously made a Hero of the Soviet Union.

Appendices

Among the others who perished later in the war was Lt-Col I. T. Klimenchuk, commander of 13th Tank Brigade. Klimenchuk, still a brigade commander in 13th Tank Corps, died on 29 August 1942 during a German counter-attack in the early stages of the Stalingrad operation. Maj-Gen A. D. Kuleshchev, commander of 175th Rifle Division at Kharkov, in late May became 38th Army chief of rear services. He was captured by the Germans in late June 1942 during the initial stages of Operation 'Blau' and died in captivity in 1944.

Moskalenko has described the harrowing escape of Lt-Gen K. A. Gurov, the Southwestern Front commissar, from the Barvenkovo encirclement. Gurov served as Southern Front commissar throughout 1942 and into 1943 only to die in September 1943 during heavy fighting for the city of Donetsk.

Tragically, this roll call of senior Soviet officers who died at Kharkov and thereafter in the war is not complete. Those who can be easily identified amount to almost 50% of those who served at and above brigade and regimental level at Kharkov. Countless other officers, whose fates cannot be precisely identified, also perished before victory was achieved. These staggering numbers, together with the appalling human losses among common Soviet soldiers, vividly underline the horrors and tragedy of the war in the East.

SELECT BIBLIOGRAPHY

BOOKS

Artemenko, I. T.; *Ot pervogo do poslednego dnia: zapiski frontovika* (From the first to the last day: notes from the front); Prapor, Kharkov, 1987.

Babich, Iu. P., Baier, A. G.; *Razvitie vooruzheniia i organizatsii Sovetskikh sukhoputnykh voisk v gody Velikoi Otechestvennoi voiny* (The development of weaponry and Soviet ground force organisation during the Great Patriotic War); Akademii, Moscow, 1990.

Bagramian, I. Kh.; *Tak shli my k pobeda* (As we went on to victory); Voenizdat, Moscow, 1977.

Bechtelzheim, Anton Freiherr, von.; 'The Battle of Kharkov 1942'; *MS# L-023*. Headquarters United States Army, Historical Division, Europe; 1956.

Carrell, Paul.; *Hitler Moves East, 1941-1943*; Ballantine, New York, 1973.

Cherniavsky, K. I.; *Vsegda s boitsami* (Always with the soldiers); Voenizdat, Moscow, 1979.

Degtiarov, P. A., Ionov, P. P.; *Katuishi' na pole boia* (Katuishas on the field of battle); Voenizdat, Moscow, 1991.

Erickson, John.; *The Road to Stalingrad*; Harper and Row, New York, 1976.

'Feindlagenkarten, PzAOK, 1c.' *PzOK* 1,24906/22, NAM T-313, Roll 37, 1–30 May 1942.

' "Friderikus 1", Anlagenmappe 1 zum KTB Nr. 8, PzAOK 1, 1a.' *PzAOK 1, 25179/3*, NM T-313, Roll 5.27 Mar–16 May 1942.

Gaglov, I. I.; *General Antonov*; Voenizdat, Moscow, 1978.

Glantz, David M.; *Soviet Military Deception in the Second World War*; Frank Cass, London, 1990.

Glantz, David M.; *Soviet Military Intelligence in War*; Frank Cass, London, 1990.

Goerlitz, W.; *Paulus and Stalingrad*; The Citadel Press, New York, 1963.

Golubovich, V. S.; *Marshal R. Ia. Malinovsky*; Voenizdat, Moscow, 1984.

Gorbatov, A. V.; *Gody i voiny*. (Years and war); Voenizdat, Moscow, 1980.

Halder, Franz.; *War Journal of Franz Halder*, VII; U.S. Army War College, Typescript translated copy, Carlisle, PA, undated.

Istoriia vtoroi mirovoi voiny 1939-1945, T. 5 (A History of the Second World War, Vol. 5); Voenizdat, Moscow, 1975.

Kachur, V. P., Nikol'sky, V. V.; *Pod znamenem sivashtsev* (Under the banner Sivash); Voenizdat, Moscow, 1989.

Kazakov, K. P.; *Vsegda s pekhotoi, vsegda s tankami* (Always with the infantry, always with the tanks); Voenzidat, Moscow, 1989.

Kir'ian, M. M.; *Fronty nastupali* (The fronts attack); 'Nauka', Moscow, 1987.

Kriegsgliederungen des Sowjetunion (Order of battle of the Soviet Union); Fremde Heere Ost, 1944. National Archives Microfilm [NAM] series T-78, Roll 550.

Krivosheev, G. F., ed.; *Grif sekretnosti sniat: poteri vooruzhennykh sil SSSR v voinakh, boevykh deistviiakh i voennykh konfliktakh* (The classification secret is removed. Soviet Armed Forces losses in wars, combat actions, and military conflicts); Voenizdat, Moscow, 1993.

Krupchenko, I. E., ed.; *Sovetskie tankovye voisk 1941-1945*; Voenizdat,Moscow, 1973.

Kurochkin, P. A., ed.; *Obshchevoiskovaia armiia v nastuplenii* (The combined arms army in the offensive); Voenizdat, Moscow, 1966.

'Lagenkartenmappe zum, Kriegstagebuch No. 11, 1.3.1942-22.5.1042.' *AOK 6, 23758/8*, Mar–May 1942. NAM T-312, Roll 1446.

Losik, O. A.; *Stroitel'stvo i boevoe primenenie sovetskikh tankovikh voisk v gody Velikoi Otechestvennoi voiny* (Formation and combat use of Soviet tank forces in the Great Patriotic War); Voenizdat, Moscow, 1979.

Mackensen, Eberhard von.; 'Zum Kaukasas. Das III Panzer-Korps im Feldzug 1942 gegen Sowjetrussland'. *Pz AOK 3, Ia*. (To the Caucasus. The III Panzer Corps in 1942 Operations against the Soviet Union. Third Panzer Army, Ia.); *PzAOK 3, 34218/1*. NAM T-313, Roll 268.

Malinovsky, R. Ia.; *Budapesht-Vena-Praga* (Budapest-Vienna-Prague); 'Nauka', Moscow, 1965.

Maramzin, V. A.; *Nastupatel'naia operatsiia voisk iugo-zapadnogo fronta na khar'kovskom napravlenii*

Bibliography

v mae 1942 (The offensive operations by Southwestern Front forces on the Kharkov axis in May 1942); The Voroshikov Academy of the General Staff, Moscow, 1955. Classified secret. Declassified 1964.
Moskalenko, K. S.; *Na iugo-zapadnom napravlenii* T. 1 (On the southwestern axis, Vol. 1); 'Nauka', Moscow, 1969.
Naumenko, Iu. A.; *Shagai pekhota!* (The infantry marches on); Voenizdat, Moscow, 1989.
Navysev, I. S.; *Na sluzhbe shtabnoi* (In staff service); Lissma, Riga, 1972.
Oleinikov, A.; *Rozhdennaia na zemlikah zaporozhskikh* (Born on the land of Zaporozh'e); Ukrainian Political Literature, Kiev, 1974.
'Opisanie operatsii voisk iugo-zapadnom fronta na khar'kovskom napravlenii v mae 1942 god' (An account of operations by Southwestern Front forces on the Kharkov axis in May 1942), *Sbornik voenno-istoricheskikh materialov Velikoi Otechestvennoi voiny, Vypusk 5.* (Collection of military-historical materials of the Great Patriotic War, Issue 5.); Voenizdat, Moscow, 1951. Classified secret. Declassified in 1964.
Pliev, I. A.; *Pod gvardeiskim znamenem* (Under the guards banner); 'IR', Ordzhonikidze, 1976.
Poirier, Robers G., Conner Albert Z; *Red Army Order of Battle in the Great Patriotic War*; second edition, unpublished manuscript.
Radzievksy, A. I.; *Proryv (Po opytu Velikoi Otechestvennoi voiny 1941-1945 gg.)* Penetration (Based upon Great Patriotic War experience). Voenzidat, Moscow, 1979.
Rodimtsev, A. I.; *Tvoi, otechestvo, syny* (You, your fatherland, and sons); Politizdat, Kiev, 1974.
Samchuk, I. A.; *Trinadtsataia gvardeiskaia* (13th Guards); Voenizdat, Moscow, 1971.
Samchuk, I. A.; *Gvardeiskaia poltavskaia* (Poltava guards); Voenizdat, Moscow, 1965.
Safronov, I. V.; *Za frontom-tozhe front* (There is also a front behind the front); Voenizdat, Moscow, 1986.
Saviny, M., ed.; *Barvenkovo-Lozovaia operatsiia (18-31 ianvaria 1942 g): Kratkii operativno-takicheskii ocherk* (The Barvenkovo-Lozovaia operation [18-31 January 1942] A short operational-tactical study); Voenzidat, Moscow, 1943. Prepared by the Military-historical Section of the Red Army General Staff. Classified secret. Declassified in 1964.
Savushkin, R. A.; *Razvitie sovetskikh vooruzhennykh sil i voennogo isskustva v Velikoi Otechestvennoi voine 1941-1945 gg.* (The development of the Soviet Armed Forces and military art during the Great Patriotic War 1941-1945); VPA, Moscow, 1988.
Shtemenko, S. M.; *The Soviet General Staff at War 1941-1945*, Book 1.; Progress, Moscow, 1981.
Shukman, Harold, ed.; *Stalin's Generals*; Weidenfeld and Nicolson, London, 1993.
Soshnikov, A. Ia., ed.; *Sovetskaia kavaleriia* (Soviet cavalry) Voenizdat, Moscow, 1984.
Truppen-Ubersicht und Kriegsgliederungen Rote Armee, Stand: August 1944 (Troop List and Order of Battle of the Red Army in August 1944). *FHO Ic-Unterlagen Ost, Merkblatt geh. 11/6 Pruf-Nr. 0157* in NAM T-78, Roll 459.
Vasilevsky, A. M.; *Delo vsei zhizni* (Life's work); Political Literature, Moscow, 1971.
Velikaia Otechestvennaia voina Sovetskovo Soiuza T. 2 (A History of the Great Patriotic War, Vol. 2); Voenizdat,Moscow, 1961.
Volkogonov, D.; *Stalin: Triumph and Tragedy*; Weidenfeld and Nicolson, London, 1991.
Vyrodov, I. Ia., ed.; *V srazheniiakh za Podedu: boevoi put' 38-i armii v gody Velikoi Otechestvennoi voiny 1941-1945* (In battles for victory: the combat path of 38th Army in the Great Patriotic War 1941-1945); 'Nauka', Moscow, 1974.
Ziemke, Earle L., Bauer, Magna E.; *Moscow to Stalingrad: Decision in the East*; Center of Military History, United States Army, Washington, D.C., 1987.
Zhukov, G. K.; *The Memoirs of Marshal Zhukov*; Delacorte Press, New York, 1971.
Zhukov, G.; *Reminiscences and Reflections*, Vol. 2; Progress, Moscow, 1985.
'Ia, Lagenkarten zum KTB 12.' *AOK 6,22856/1a*, May-July 1942. NAM T-312, Roll 1446.
73-ia gvardeiskaia (73rd Guards); Kazakhstan, Alma Ata, 1986.

ARTICLES

Begunov, S. F.; 'Chto proizoshol pod Khar'kovom v mae 1942 goda' (What occurred at Kharkov in May 1942); *Voenno-istoricheskii zhurnal* (military-historical journal), No 12 December 1989, pp12-21; No 1 January 1990, pp9-18; No 2 February 1990, pp35-46.
Begunov, S. F., Litvinchuk, A. V., Sutulov, V. A.; 'A gde pravda, Nikita Sergeevich!' (What then is the truth, Nikita Sergeevich!); *Voenno-istoricheskii zhurnal* (military-historical journal) No 12

Kharkov, 1942

December 1989, pp12-21; No 1 January 1990, pp9-18; No 2 February 1990, pp35-46.

Grilev, A. N.; 'Nekotorye osobennosti planirovaniia letne-osennei kampanii 1942 goda (Some peculiarities of planning for the 1942 summer-autumn campaign)'; *Voenno-istoricheskii zhurnal*, No 8 August 1987, pp20-25.

Khokhlov, P.; 'Atakoi s fronta i flanga' (Attack from the front and flank); *Voennyi vestnik* (Military herald). No 7 July 1987, pp16-18.

Kuznetsov, I. I., Maslov, A. A.; 'The Soviet General Officer Corps, 1941-1942: Losses in Combat'; *The Journal of Slavic Military Studies*. Vol 7, No 3 September 1994, pp548-566.

Maslov, A. A.; 'The Unbroken: Soviet Generals/Defenders of the Ukraine Who Perished in Fascist Captivity'; *The Journal of Slavic Military Studies*. Vol. 7 No 2 June 1994, pp292-298.

Peredel'sky, G.; 'Artilleriskoe nastuplenie v armeiskikh operatsiiakh' (The artillery offensive in army operations); *Voenno-istoricheskii zhurnal*. No 11 November 1976, pp11-22.

Sverdlov, F. D.; 'Katastrofa pod Kharkovom' (Catastrophe at Kharkov); *Voennaia mysl'* (Military thought) No 6-7, June-July 1992, pp54-59.

Index

Adam, Wilhelm, 242
Afansiev, Col, 81-82, 117, 124, 129, 153, 154, 175, 177
Air Fleets, German
    Fourth, 122-123, 127
Akhtyrka, 53
Aleksandropol, 167
Aleksandrov, Maj M. M., 154
Aleksandrovka, 40, 48, 106
Alekseev, Maj-Gen V. M., 82, 124, 129, 146, 278
Alekseevka, 136
Alekseevskoe, 41, 132, 201, 209-210
Aleshki, 66
Aliev, Lt-Col B. K., 99, 181
Alisovka, 66, 167
Alma Ata, 81
Andreevka, 48, 105, 136, 160, 166-167, 169, 191, 197, 201-202, 204-205, 207
Anisov, Maj-Gen A. I., 150, 180, 183, 219
Annovka, 158
Antonov, Lt-Gen A. I., 32-33, 96, 168-169, 222-224, 262, 276-277
Arapovka-Ploskoe, 175, 177-178, 192
Arkadievka, 48
Arkhangelsk, 88
Arkhangelskoe, 121
Arko (artillery commands), German, 108
Armenia, 78, 87
Armies, German
    general, 108
    First Panzer, 43, 95, 110, 141-142, 169, 219-220
    Second Panzer, 59
    Sixth, 25, 35-36, 42, 104-105, 109, 111, 121, 123, 134, 139-142, 160, 166, 179, 192, 194, 202, 218, 220, 230-231, 242
    Tenth, 109
    Eleventh, 40
    Sixteenth, 38
    Seventeenth, 42-43, 104-105, 140, 142, 160, 169, 220
Armies, Soviet
    rifle, general, 71
    1st Cavalry, 76, 83-84, 93, 246
    2nd Cavalry, 93
    1st Guards, 277
    2nd Guards, 276
    3rd Guards, 277
    11th Guards, 276
    7th Separate, 37, 98
    2nd Shock, 29
    1st Tank, 277
    5th, 97
    6th, 18, 24, 30-32, 34, 40-41, 44, 46-55, 57-58, 65, 81-82, 84-95, 101, 111, 113, 120, 128, 132, 134, 136-137, 140-141, 143, 148, 158, 163, 174, 178-180, 183-185, 188, 190-191, 197-198, 201-202, 204-205, 207, 209, 214, 216, 219, 221-222, 226, 230-231, 233, 235, 256, 258-259, 265-272, 277
    9th, 18, 33, 41, 66, 69, 94-96, 98-100, 104, 111-113, 149, 161, 164-169, 171-173, 178-181, 183-185, 187-188, 190-191, 197-198, 201, 207, 219, 221-224, 226, 228, 230-231, 235-236, 240-241, 262-264, 266-267, 269-270, 277
    10th, 83, 90, 92-94, 100
    12th, 41, 69, 78, 82, 84, 92-93, 97, 101
    13th, 79, 86, 89, 98
    16th 89, 276
    18th, 33, 41, 69, 81, 94-95, 101, 222, 224
    19th, 85, 89
    21st, 30, 32, 40-41, 44, 46, 49-55, 57, 65, 81, 85-88, 111, 114, 116, 120, 123, 130,132, 143, 146, 155-156, 177, 192, 194, 227, 231, 234, 257, 259, 265-266, 270, 272, 277
    22nd, 101
    26th, 79, 87, 98-99
    28th, 30-32, 34, 38, 44, 46-47, 49-55, 57, 65, 80-83, 90, 97, 111, 114, 116-120, 122-124, 126-128, 130, 137, 140, 143, 146, 153-156, 158, 164, 175, 177-179, 185, 187, 192, 194, 225, 227, 230-234, 256-257, 259-260, 265-266, 270-272, 277
    33rd, 277
    37th, 41, 69, 86, 90, 97-99, 165
    38th, 13, 24, 31-32, 34, 40-41, 44, 46-47, 49-55, 57, 65, 80-88, 92-93, 98, 111, 114, 118, 120-124, 126-130, 137, 140, 143, 147, 153, 155, 158, 164, 175, 177-179, 185, 187, 191-192, 194, 201-202, 204-205, 207, 212, 214, 216, 227, 231, 233-234, 258-259, 265-266, 270-272, 277
    40th, 30, 81, 87-88, 97, 132, 259, 277
    46th 89
    48th 132
    56th, 41, 69, 94, 98
    57th, 18, 33, 41, 65, 69, 80, 90-91, 96-101, 104, 112-113, 150, 160-161, 163-167, 169, 171, 173, 175, 178, 180-181, 183, 185, 187-188, 190-191, 197-198, 201, 204-205, 207, 209-210, 219, 221-223, 226, 228, 235, 240, 259, 261, 268-270
    66th, 276
Coastal, 40
Turkestan, 82
Army Groups, German
    general, 108
    'A', 59
    'B', 59, 109
    Center, 35, 59, 61, 109, 275
    North, 59
    South, 15, 35-36, 59, 109-110, 139, 220, 227, 246
    Von Kleist, 36, 40, 43, 104-105, 140, 160-161, 165, 167, 169, 181, 188, 192, 198, 201-202, 207, 218, 220, 240, 242
Army Groups, Soviet
    Bobkin, 32, 44, 48-49, 51-53, 58, 88, 92-93, 96, 111, 113, 134-137, 147, 158, 160-161, 163, 174, 180, 184, 190-191, 219, 221, 227, 231, 260, 266-267, 272
    Kostenko, 190-191, 197, 201, 204, 207, 209-210, 212, 214, 221, 268-269, 271
    Vinnitsa, 83
    Zhitomir, 84, 93
Army High Command (OKH), 18, 21, 35, 59, 109, 139, 239
Artelnoe, 204
Artemovsk, 156
Artillery, Soviet, 73-75
Aseevka, 202, 207
Astrakhan, 90
Azov, Sea of, 26, 33, 43, 105

Baersky, Col V. G., 89, 132, 209
Bairak, 116-118, 155, 202
Baklaia, Maj G. G., 156
Baksharovka, 210
Baku, 98
Balakeia, 24, 40-41, 43-44, 46-48, 61, 90, 105, 122, 142, 177, 179, 191-192, 198, 201, 202, 220
Balck, General Hermann, 11
Baltic Sea, 24-25
Bagramian, Lt-Gen I. Kh., 13, 24-30, 32-35, 37, 78-79, 92, 96, 122, 126, 132, 136, 143, 145, 164, 168-169, 177-181, 221-225, 239-240, 242, 244-245, 255-256, 258, 260, 262-263, 265-266, 269-272, 276
Bannovskii, 172, 183-184
Barbaletovo, 198
Barvenkovo, 15, 30-33, 35-36, 40-43, 48, 51, 55-56, 58, 61, 64, 66, 69, 76, 79, 89-90, 94, 96, 99-100, 106, 112-113, 139-140, 142, 160-161, 164-169, 171-173, 178-181, 184-185, 188, 190-192, 194, 197-198, 201-202, 204-205, 207, 209, 216, 218-219, 221, 223-224, 226-228, 230, 235-237, 239, 241-242, 245-246
Barvenkovo-Lozovaia operation (January-February 1942), 18, 79-80, 83-84, 86, 89-100
Batiunia, Maj-Gen A. G., 148, 216
Batov, Lt-Gen P. I., 11
Battalions, German,
    213th Engineer, 174
Battalions, Soviet
    134th Anti-tank, 118
    11th Captured Equipment (Trophy), 134
    16th Captured Equipment (Trophy), 134
    3rd Guards Separate Guards Mortar, 91
    24th Separate Guards Mortar, 116
    206th Separate Guards Mortar, 91
    160th Separate Mortar, 118
    500th Penal, 167
    8th Guards Separate Sapper, 116
    8th Separate Tank, 46, 51, 65
    71st Separate Tank, 48, 93
    92nd Separate Tank, 48, 93, 97, 178
    132nd Separate Tank, 48, 93
Bauer, Magna E., 198
Bazaleevka, 47
Bechtelzheim, Col Anton Freiherr von, 121, 123, 137, 142
Bednyi, 156
Belgorod, 44, 53, 61, 64, 87, 105, 121, 123, 132
Beliaevka, 66
Belogorsky, Col A. I., 83, 177
Belyi Kholodez, 57
Bereka River, 178, 184-185, 188, 191, 197-198, 201-202, 212, 235
Berestov, Col A. K., 85, 118-119, 127, 179, 185
Berestovaia, 47, 105, 161, 174
Berestovaia River, 42, 44, 64, 136-137, 158, 160-161, 163, 174, 233
Beria, L., 13
Bessarabia, 81-82, 84, 94
Bezbozhnyi, 128, 177
Bezeka State Farm, 175
Bezliudovka, 65, 116, 121
Bezugly, Maj J. F., 119
Bialystok, 93
Bichek, Lt-Col S. M., 117
Black Sea, 24-25, 59, 98
Bladoveshchenskii, 207
Blagodatnoe, 66
Blagodatnyi, 210
Blau (Blue), Operation (Fuehrer Directive 41, 5 April 1942), 21, 35, 38, 59, 239
Bobkin, Maj-Gen L. V., 92-93, 134, 137, 147, 219
Bochkovka, 143
Bock, Field Marshal Fedor von, 36, 109, 123, 139, 142, 150, 192, 198, 212, 220
Bodin, Lt-Gen P. I., 24-25, 30, 225
Bogataia River, 44, 64, 136
Bogdanovka, 66, 184
Bogodorovka, 47-48
Bogorodichnoe, 165, 172-173, 183-184, 197
Boldin, Lt-Gen I. V., 93
Bolshaia, 46
Bolshaia Andreevka, 171, 191, 197
Bolshaia Babka, 44, 47, 64, 118, 120-121, 126, 128, 158, 179,
Bolshaia Babka River, 64, 119-120, 127, 130, 153, 177, 194
Bolshaia Danilovka, 46
Bolshaia Gomolsha, 158, 161
Bondari, 105
Borisov, Maj-Gen A. V., 219
Borki, 184
Borodaevka, 48
Borshchevoe, 46, 143, 154
Bratoliubovka, 197
Brazhkovka, 223
Briansk, 26
Briansk encirclement (October 1941), 89
Brigades, Hungarian
    102nd Infantry, 105

283

Kharkov, 1942

Brigades, Soviet
  International, 95
  motorised rifle, general, 73
  rifle, general, 70-72
  tank, general, 70, 72
  5th Airborne, 80
  1st Anti-tank, 84
  68th Guards Rifle, 69
  4th Guards Tank, 69, 223
  5th Guards Tank, 47, 52, 65, 89, 91, 191, 201, 209
  6th Guards Tank, 46, 65, 80, 82, 127, 140, 158, 175
  23rd Mechanised, 84
  133rd Mechanised, 84
  1st Motorised Rifle, 65
  4th Motorised Rifle, 91
  24th Motorised Rifle, 69
  23d Motorised Rifle, 69, 91, 128
  34th Motorised Rifle, 46, 65, 82-83, 192, 194, 233
  6th Rifle, 69
  76th Rifle, 69
  78th Rifle, 66, 99-100, 165, 223
  81st Rifle, 69
  102nd Rifle, 69
  1st Tank, 82
  2nd Tank, 69, 223
  3rd Tank, 173, 185, 188, 204, 207, 216
  6th Tank, 41, 51-52, 91, 197
  7th Tank, 41, 48, 51-52, 58, 66, 92-93, 134, 184, 201, 209
  10th Tank, 46, 51, 65, 87-88
  12th Tank, 41, 69, 100-102, 165, 173, 181, 223, 235
  13th Tank, 41, 47, 65, 84, 86, 118-119, 122, 126, 140, 179, 185, 279
  15th Tank, 66, 173, 181, 204, 216, 223
  36th Tank, 47, 65, 84, 86, 118-119, 122, 126, 140, 179, 187, 278
  37th Tank, 47, 52, 66, 89, 91, 174, 191, 209, 233
  38th Tank, 47, 52, 65, 89, 91, 191, 209
  48th Tank, 47, 52, 65, 89, 91, 132, 191
  51st Tank, 99-100
  54th Tank, 69
  57th Tank, 46, 65, 80, 82, 124, 128-129, 140, 146, 175, 278
  58th Tank, 158, 179, 187, 192
  63d Tank, 69
  64th Tank, 51, 52, 91, 204, 207
  84th Tank, 46, 65, 80, 82, 117, 129, 140, 175
  90th Tank, 46, 65, 80, 82, 116, 124, 130, 140
  114th Tank, 158, 204, 207
  121st Tank, 41, 66, 99-100, 173, 181, 223
  130th Tank, 41, 52, 91
  131th Tank, 41, 51-52, 91, 197
  133d, 41, 47, 65, 84, 86, 122, 126-127, 140
  139th, 51
  142nd Tank, 91
  156th Tank, 178
  168th Tank, 178
  198th Tank, 41, 51-52, 91, 209
  199th Tank, 41, 51-52, 91
Brusovka, 66, 165, 173, 188, 197, 223
Bubnov, Lt-Col N. M., 86, 127
Budenny, Marshal S. M., 76, 79, 83-84, 96
Bugaevka, 66
Bugrovatka, 116
Bukitselovka, 209, 212
Bunakovo, 66
Bykov, Sen-Lt I. M., 154
Bylbasovka, 167

Caucasus region, 21, 40, 59, 84, 110, 239, 247
Chamov, Maj A. P., 118
Chanyshev, Col Ia. D., 89, 136, 185, 209, 214
Chapaevsk, 89
Chasov Iar, 167
Cheliabinsk, 81
Chepel, 202, 204-205, 207, 209, 212, 214, 216-217
Cheremoshnoe, 44, 46, 143, 191
Cherkasskie Tishki, 143
Cherkasskii, Bishkin, 43, 47, 105
Cherkasskoe-Lozovaia, 46-47
Cherkassy, 27, 97
Chernigov, 84, 87
Chernokamenka, 212
Chernov, Col V. G., 94, 149, 179, 187, 278
Chernovtsy, 97
Chervona Roganka, 121, 126-127
Chervonyi, 167

Chervonyi Donets, 201, 204
Chervonyi Shakhter, 61
Chuevo, 65
Chugeev, 24, 31, 42, 44, 47, 61, 64, 86, 90, 105, 120, 122, 143, 158, 166-167, 178-179, 187, 191, 194, 201-202, 217, 234
Churchill, Winston, 240
Communist Party, 57, 78, 95, 172
Corps, German
  infantry, general, 108
  motorised, general, 108
  IV Air, 169, 210
  II Army, 29
  IV Army, 43, 105
  VIII Army, 42, 105, 132, 134
  XI Army, 220
  XIV Motorised, 105
  XVII Army, 42, 105
  XXIX Army, 42, 105, 121, 132
  XXXXIV Army, 43
  LI Army, 42, 105, 121-122
  LII Army, 43, 105-106, 132, 167
  III Motorised (Panzer), 43, 106, 167, 169, 181, 198, 220
  XIV Motorised, 43
  XXXXI Army, 105-106, 167
  XXXXIX Mountain, 43, 105
  XX Panzer, 110
Corps, Rumanian
  VI Army, 42-43, 105-106
Corps, Soviet
  cavalry, general, 70, 73-74
  mechanised, general, 20, 30, 70, 72
  tank, general, 20, 70, 72-73, 248, n51
  3rd Airborne, 80
  1st Cavalry, 80
  2nd Cavalry, 41, 48, 66, 83, 93-94, 166, 173, 179, 181, 184-185, 188, 191, 197, 205, 209-210, 235
  3rd Cavalry, 76, 95, 100
  4th Cavalry, 80, 83
  5th Cavalry, 41, 66, 69, 79, 82-83, 100-102, 164-165, 169, 171-174, 181, 183, 185, 187, 223, 235, 278
  6th Cavalry, 41, 48, 58, 66, 84, 91-93, 134, 136-137, 158, 160-161, 163, 174, 184, 190-191, 201, 209-210, 212, 219
  1st Guards Cavalry, 94
  2nd Guards Cavalry, 101
  3rd Guards Cavalry, 30, 32, 46, 52, 65, 73, 82-83, 100, 130, 140, 146, 155, 227, 231, 233, 278
  3rd Guards Rifle, 69
  2nd Mechanised, 30, 84
  3rd Mechanised, 30
  4th Mechanised, 85
  5th Mechanised, 86
  8th Mechanised, 80, 84
  9th Mechanised, 82
  24th Mechanised, 99
  3d Rifle, 89, 98
  8th Rifle, 98
  14th Rifle, 98
  15th Rifle, 84
  17th Rifle, 97
  25th Rifle, 85
  35th Rifle, 84
  48th Rifle, 88, 95
  50th Rifle, 98
  55th Rifle, 81
  57th Rifle, 99
  21st Tank, 47, 52, 66, 86, 89, 91, 136-137, 140, 161, 174, 180, 184-185, 188, 190, 191, 204, 209, 219, 221, 231, 235, 248, n 50, 260
  22nd Tank, 86, 122, 201, 248, 251
  23rd Tank, 47, 52, 66, 86, 89, 91, 136-137, 141, 161, 174, 178, 184-185, 188, 191, 197, 209, 214, 219, 221, 231, 235, 260, 278
  24th Tank, 69, 248, n 51
Crimea, 24, 29, 37-38, 79, 84, 93, 122-123, 142, 156, 237

Danilovka, 47, 197
Dar Nadezhdy, 48, 160, 175
Dashevsky, Maj-Gen Ia. S, 99, 172, 181, 188
Debaltsevo, 43, 105
Dedeogly, Col T. V., 93, 184
Demedov, Col I. D., 219
Dementevka, 46
Demiansk, 24, 29, 37-38, 225, 275
Dergachi, 46-47

Direction (strategic headquarters), Soviet
  general, 70, 75-76
  Northwestern, 76
  Southwestern, 24-25, 27-35, 37, 41-42, 44, 48-49, 57, 66, 69, 75-80, 89, 94-95, 104, 112, 122, 139, 145, 161, 166-168, 172, 178, 180, 185, 209, 218, 221-223, 225-228, 230, 235, 237-238, 241-242, 244-245, 252-256, 258, 262-264, 266-270, 272
  Western, 76-77, 85
Directives, German
  Directive 41 (5 April 1942), See Blau (Blue), operation
Directives (Orders), Soviet
  Directive No 00137/op (22 March 1942), Southwestern Direction, 252-255
  Directive No 00177 (6 April 1942), Southern Front, 33, 48, 261-262
  Directive No 00241 (6 April 1942), Southwestern Direction), 228
  Directive No 00251 (10 April 1942), Southwestern Direction, 44, 256-258
  Directive No 00241, Southern Front, 48
  Directive No 00275 (28 April 1942), Southwestern Direction, 32, 54, 258-261
  Directive No 00317 (16 May 1942), Southwestern Front, 156
  Directive No 00320 (19 May 1942), Southwestern Direction, 190-191, 268-269
  Directive No 00323/op (21 May 1942), Southwestern Direction, 202, 270-271
  Directive No 00330 (24 May 1942), Southwestern Direction, 207
  Directive No 0140/op (17 May 1942), Southwestern Direction, 264
  Directive No 0141 (19 May 1942), Southwestern Direction, 191
  Directive No 0142 (19 May 1942), Southwestern Direction, 191
  Directive No 0143 (19 May 1942), Southwestern Direction, 191, 269-270
  Directive 0188 (27 February 1942), Southwestern Front, 54
Divisions, German
  infantry, general, 106-107
  motorised infantry, general, 107-108
  mountain, general, 108
  panzer, general, 107-108
  9th Infantry, 43, 105
  44th (Infantry) Hock und Deutschmeister), 40, 42, 105, 122, 126, 141, 143, 166, 202, 207
  57th Infantry, 42, 105, 132, 194, 234
  62nd Infantry, 42, 105, 132, 136, 141, 160-161
  68th Infantry, 43, 105-106, 167
  71st Infantry, 40, 42, 105, 116, 118, 120-123, 126, 141, 143, 166, 175, 177, 179, 194, 228
  73rd Infantry, 43, 105
  75th Infantry, 42, 105, 127, 132, 234
  76th Infantry, 43, 105
  79th Infantry, 42, 105, 121, 127, 141
  88th Infantry, 155, 194
  94th Infantry, 43, 105
  111th Infantry, 43, 105
  113th Infantry, 42, 105, 123, 134, 136-137, 141, 158, 160-161, 163, 209, 233-234
  125th Infantry, 43, 105
  168th Infantry, 42, 105, 132, 143, 155, 175, 177, 193, 234
  198th Infantry, 43, 105
  257th Infantry, 43, 105, 167, 173, 181, 197
  294th Infantry, 42, 105, 116-118, 120-121, 127, 129, 141
  295th Infantry, 43, 105, 167
  297th Infantry, 43, 105, 121
  298th Infantry, 42, 106, 160
  305th Infantry, 40, 42, 105, 134, 158, 160-161, 163, 166, 209, 228, 233-234
  384th Infantry, 43, 106, 167, 188, 197, 201, 205, 210, 216, 234
  389th Infantry, 43, 106, 167, 183, 188, 201, 205, 210, 234
  97th Light (Jaeger), 43, 105, 167, 197
  100th Light (Jaeger), 43, 105, 167, 181, 197, 205
  101st Light (Jaeger), 43, 106, 167, 169, 174, 181, 197
  60th Motorised, 43, 105, 167, 188, 197-198, 201, 205, 210, 220
  'Adolf Hitler' SS Motorised, 43, 105
  'Viking' SS Motorised, 43, 105

Index

1st Mountain, 43, 106, 167-169, 181, 197-198, 205, 210, 212, 220
4th Mountain, 43, 105
3rd Panzer, 42, 105, 121, 123, 126-127, 129-130, 139, 141, 143, 153, 155-156, 166, 175, 177-179, 187, 194, 198, 201-202, 204, 207
13th Panzer, 43, 105
14th Panzer, 43, 105-106, 167, 171, 181, 188, 198, 201, 205, 216, 220
16th Panzer, 43, 106, 167, 169, 181, 188, 197-198, 201, 205, 220, 234
23rd Panzer, 40, 42, 105, 121, 123, 127, 130, 139, 141, 143, 166, 175, 177-179, 187, 194, 198, 201-202, 204, 207, 212, 228
454th Security, 42, 105, 132, 134, 137, 141, 160, 209, 228
Divisions, Hungarian
  108th Light Infantry, 42, 105, 134, 136, 141, 234
Divisions, Italian
  Celere Infantry, 43, 105
  Pasubio Infantry, 43, 105
  Torino Infantry, 43,105
Divisions, Rumanian
  5th Cavalry, 43, 105
  6th Cavalry, 105
  1st Infantry, 106, 209
  2nd Infantry, 42-43, 106
  4th Infantry, 105-106, 160, 228
  20th Infantry, 106, 167
Divisions, Slovak
  Motorised, 43, 105
Divisions, Soviet
  cavalry, general, 70, 73
  rifle, general, 71
  3rd Cavalry (Bessarabian), 82-83
  4th Cavalry, 76, 79
  5th Cavalry, 94
  6th Cavalry (Chongar), 84
  9th Cavalry, 94
  10th Cavalry, 95
  14th Cavalry, 82, 83
  26th Cavalry, 41, 48, 92-93, 209
  28th Cavalry, 41, 48, 92-93, 209-210
  30th Cavalry, 41, 69, 100-101, 165, 181, 183, 188
  32d Cavalry, 41, 46, 65, 82-83, 179, 193, 233
  34th Cavalry, 41, 69, 100-101, 165, 169, 171-172, 191
  38th Cavalry, 41, 94, 166
  49th Cavalry, 41, 48, 92-93, 184, 191, 209
  50th Separate Cavalry, 101
  53d Cavalry, 101
  60th Cavalry, 41, 69, 100-101, 165, 181, 183, 191
  62d Cavalry, 41, 94, 166
  64th Cavalry, 41, 94
  70th Cavalry, 41, 94, 166
  220th Fighter Aviation, 156
  5th Guards Cavalry, 41, 46, 65, 82, 177, 233
  6th Guards Cavalry, 41, 46, 65, 82-83, 177, 233
  1st Guards Rifle, 41, 46, 57
  2nd Guards Rifle, 69
  13th Guards Rifle, 41, 46, 57, 65, 80-81, 116-120, 124, 128-130, 146, 153-156, 158, 177, 278
  14th Guards Rifle, 41, 66, 97, 165, 173, 181, 184, 185, 209, 212, 219, 223, 235
  15th Guards Rifle, 69, 224
  8th Motorised Rifle, 41, 46, 65
  81st Motorised Rifle, 84
  109th Motorised, 86
  17th Rifle, 99
  27th Rifle, 95
  38th Rifle, 41, 46, 57, 65, 80-81, 117, 124, 128-130, 155-156, 158, 175, 179, 187, 192, 233
  41st Rifle, 41, 47, 57-58, 65, 89, 191, 209-210
  46th Rifle, 96
  47th Rifle, 41, 47, 65, 89, 132, 158, 191, 204, 207, 209-210, 219
  51st Rifle (Perekop), 41, 66, 84, 99, 165, 167, 171-172, 181, 183, 188, 191, 233
  73d Rifle, 41, 46, 69
  76th Rifle, 41, 65, 87, 116, 123, 130
  81st Rifle, 41, 46, 57, 65, 84, 118-119, 127, 179, 187
  87th Rifle, 81
  96th Rifle, 97-98
  99th Rifle, 41, 66, 97-98, 165, 191, 197, 201, 209, 212, 223
  100th Rifle, 85
  102nd Rifle, 41, 69

103rd Rifle, 41, 47, 57, 66, 89-90, 136-137, 141, 185, 190-191, 201, 209, 214, 233
106th Rifle, 41, 66, 99, 165, 167, 171-172, 183, 191, 223
124th Rifle, 41, 46, 57, 65, 84-85, 118-120, 127, 143, 179, 185, 187
129th Rifle, 89
150th Rifle, 41, 66, 97-98, 164-165, 175, 191, 197, 204, 209, 214, 219, 223
162nd Rifle, 41, 46, 57, 65, 80-81, 122, 127-128, 155, 158, 175, 177, 179, 187, 233
169th Rifle, 41, 46, 57, 65, 80-81, 88, 117-118, 124, 128, 146, 154-156, 175, 177, 179, 187, 194, 233
175th Rifle, 41, 46, 57, 65, 80-81, 117, 124, 128, 153-154, 156, 177, 192, 194, 278
176th Rifle, 69
199th Rifle, 41, 46, 65, 84, 158, 187
216th Rifle, 41, 69, 99, 221, 223-224
226th Rifle, 41, 46, 57, 65, 84-85, 116, 118-120, 130, 143, 179, 185, 187, 278
227th Rifle, 41, 46, 57, 65, 88, 116, 123, 130, 146, 156, 194
228th Rifle, 41
242nd Rifle, 41, 69, 178, 204
244th Rifle, 42, 46, 65, 80-82, 116-117, 124, 126, 129, 153-156, 158, 175, 192
248th Rifle, 41, 47, 57, 66, 89-90, 136-137, 141, 180, 184, 191, 201, 209, 212, 221, 233
253rd Rifle, 41, 47, 65, 89-90, 132, 158, 174, 191, 209-210
255th Rifle, 41, 69, 223-224
266th Rifle, 42, 47, 57-58, 65, 89-90, 126-127, 134, 136, 158, 161, 184, 191, 209, 214
270th Rifle, 41, 48, 66, 92, 137, 160, 163, 184, 204-205, 209, 219
277th Rifle, 42, 48, 66, 87, 93-94, 128, 158, 179, 187, 193, 278
278th Rifle, 178
282d Rifle, 69
293rd Rifle, 41, 46, 57, 65, 87-88, 116, 123, 130, 177, 192
296th Rifle, 69, 173, 185, 188, 191, 198
297th Rifle, 41, 46, 65
300th Rifle, 41, 46, 57, 65, 84-86, 88, 120, 179, 187
301st Rifle, 46, 65, 132
304th Rifle, 41, 46, 65, 84-86, 88, 158
310th Rifle, 41
317th Rifle, 41, 66, 97-98, 165, 191, 201, 209, 214, 223
333rd Rifle, 41, 66, 69, 99-100, 165, 171-172, 181, 188, 191, 223
335th Rifle, 41, 66, 100, 165, 167, 171, 183, 191
337th Rifle, 41, 47, 65, 85-89, 191, 204, 207, 210, 219
341st Rifle, 41, 66, 100, 165, 167, 171-173, 188, 191, 210, 223
343rd Rifle, 41, 48, 66, 93-94, 158, 178, 181, 185, 188, 191, 197, 278
347th Rifle, 69
349th Rifle, 41, 66, 100, 165, 183, 191, 223
351st Rifle, 41, 66, 97-98, 165, 173, 191, 201, 209, 212, 223
393rd Rifle, 41, 48, 66, 92, 137, 160, 163, 184, 201, 209-210, 219
411th Rifle, 41, 47, 65, 89-90, 92, 136, 158, 160-161, 191, 201, 209, 212
447th Rifle, 90
468th Rifle, 94
469th Rifle, 82
Dmitrievka, 48, 183-184, 188, 201, 210
Dneprodzerzhinsk, 61
Dnepropetrovsk, 26-27, 30, 42, 53, 59, 61, 85, 90, 142, 160, 220
Dnepr River, 27, 30-32, 59, 64, 77, 81, 84, 86-87, 90, 96-97, 99
Dobropol, 209
Dolgenkaia, 165-166, 169, 171-172, 181, 185, 191
Don River, 21, 217, 239
Donbas (Donets Basin) region, 18, 21, 24, 27, 59, 61, 70, 76, 78, 84, 94-95, 101, 227-228
Donetskii, 181
Donskoi, 83, 198
Dotsenko, Col N. P., 81, 118, 124, 128-130, 155, 175, 179, 187
Dragunovka, 46-47, 65, 116, 130, 153
Drozdov, Col P. D., 219
Dubno, 80, 82
Dubrovka, 172
Dudkovka, 174, 184

Dushatino, 97
Dzherzhinsk, 91
Dzherzhinsky (NKVD) Academy, 84
Dzhgun, 184

Efremovka, 46-47, 52, 65, 136-137, 140, 161, 201
Egorov, Maj-Gen D. G., 98, 150, 163, 214, 219
Egorovka, 197, 210
Elin, Col I. P., 129, 153
Elets operation (January 1942), 79, 82-84, 89
Eremenko, Gen A. I. 92-93

Falaleev, Gen F. Ia., 128
Fedorovka, 128, 130,188, 197-198, 210, 212
Finnish War (1939-1940), 98
Fleets, Soviet
  Black Sea, 275
Flossenburg, 219
'Friderikus', operation, 35-36, 40, 123, 141-142, 181, 192, 198, 239
France, 95
Frolov, 94
Fronts, Soviet
  general, 70
  1st Baltic, 276
  2nd Baltic, 276
  3rd Baltic, 275
  3rd Belorussian, 276
  1st Ukrainian, 276-277
  2nd Ukrainian, 276
  3rd Ukrainian, 275-276
  4th Ukrainian, 275
  Belorussian, 93
  Briansk, 27-30, 37, 132, 244, 253-254, 259
  Crimean, 29, 37, 246
  Kalinin, 37
  Karelian, 29, 37
  Leningrad, 29, 37, 275
  North Caucasus, 275
  Northwestern, 29, 37, 75, 77, 225, 275
  Reserve, 80
  Southeastern, 276
  Southwestern, 13, 15, 18, 24-25, 27, 30, 33-34, 37-38, 40-42, 44, 48-50, 52-58, 61, 65, 75-77, 80, 82-89, 91-98, 104-106, 111-114-142, 145, 149, 153, 156, 160, 163-164, 166, 169, 174-175, 178-180, 184-185, 190, 192, 194, 205, 217, 219, 221, 223-224, 226-228, 230-234, 236-237, 240-242, 246-247, 252-254, 256-259, 261-262, 265-266, 268-271, 276
  Southern, 15, 18, 27, 32-33, 37, 40-44, 48, 50, 52-53, 55-57, 61, 66, 69, 75-76, 80, 90, 94-101, 104-106, 111-113, 132, 134, 133-140, 149, 160-161, 163-166, 168-169, 171-174, 178-179, 183, 190-191, 205, 217, 219, 221-223, 226-228, 230, 234-237, 240-241, 246, 252-254, 256-259, 261, 263-264, 266, 269-270, 276
  Stalingrad, 225, 276-277
  Trans-Baikal, 276
  Trans-Caucasus, 275
  Ukrainian, 82-84
  Volkhov, 29, 275
  Voronezh, 276
  Western, 26, 29, 37, 75, 77, 85, 252, 277
Frunze Academy, 78, 80, 82, 85, 95-97, 100

Gaidar, 209
Garkushino, 163
Gavrilovka, 43, 46-47
General Staff, Soviet, 13-14, 17, 24-25, 27, 29-31, 139, 145, 218, 237, 239, 241-242, 244
Glazunovka, 204, 207
Glinishche, 158, 209
Glubokaia Makatykha, 223
Golaia Dolina, 165, 171-172, 223
Golovsky, Col V. S., 181
Golubovka, 167
Gomel, 26-27, 42, 61, 87
Gorbachev, Party First Secretary M. S., 13-14, 245
Gorbatov, Maj-Gen A. V., 85, 118-119, 130, 147, 185, 278
Gordienko, 46, 116, 126, 128, 130, 153
Gordov, Lt-Gen V. N., 86-88, 114, 123, 130, 132, 143, 146, 155-156, 177, 192, 194, 277
Gorki, 86, 91
Gorlovka, 43, 167

Kharkov, 1942

Gorodniansky, Lt-Gen A. M., 88-89, 91-92, 132, 137, 140-141, 148, 158, 161, 174, 178, 180, 184-185, 188, 190-191, 197, 201, 205, 207, 209, 214, 219, 268
Gorokhovka, 47-48
Gorshkov, Col P. D., 219
Gotnia, 53
Grafovka, 43-44, 123-124, 130, 177
Graivoron, 46
Grechko, Maj-Gen A. A., 100
Grigorev, Lt-Col M. G., 90, 132, 158, 174
Grigorevka, 137, 172
Grishino, 84
Grodno, 93
Gromovaia Balka, 167, 223
Groups, German
   First Panzer, 18, 59, 76, 80, 82, 84, 110
   Second Panzer, 80, 86-87, 89, 109
   Third Panzer, 109
   Barbo, 167
   Friedrich, 42
   Gollwitzer, 194
   Koch, 42
   von Sieckenius, 202
   Witte, 143
Groups, Romanian
   Georgesceu, 209
Groups, Soviet
   Belov, 29
   Luiban, 29
   Samland, 276
   South, 207, 209, 212, 214, 217, 219
   Sherstiuk, 204-205, 207, 212, 269
Grushevakha, 188, 191
Grushevatskii, 188
Grushino, 43, 47-48, 65, 105, 132, 134, 137
Guderian, General Heinz, 11, 59, 61, 80, 86-87, 89
Gurov, Division Commissar K. A., 145, 216, 278
Gursky, Col N. U., 98
Gusarovka, 202

Halder, Gen Franz, 36, 109, 123
Hitler, Adolf, 21, 27, 35-36, 38, 40, 109, 141-142, 193
Hube, Lt-Gen Hans V., 181

Iakovenkovo, 158
Iakovlev, Col D. A., 98, 214
Iakovlevka, 165
Ianovichivka, 197
Iaroslavl, 99
Iartsevo, 85
Iavlenskaia, 167
Ilichevka, 172
Iurchenko, Col I. A., 93, 134
Iurchenko, Col N. M., 94
Ivanov, Col S. I., 143, 147
Ivanovka, 48, 197, 216-217
Ivanovskii, 223
Izbitskoe, 43, 46, 65, 121
Izium, 18, 35-36, 40, 48, 55-56, 92, 112, 140-142, 164, 166, 169, 171-172, 177-181, 183, 185, 187-188, 190-191, 198, 202, 207, 217, 223

Kabane, 41, 57
Kachalov, Lt-Gen V. Ia., 80
Kagarmanov, Col M. V., 219
Kaliuzhnoe, 136
Kamenets-Podolsk, 81
Kamenka, 165, 171, 181
Kaminka, 136, 209
Kamyshevakha, 209
Kamyshin, 99
Kantemirovka, 41, 165, 223
Karavan, 184, 191
Karavanskaia Vershina, 174
Kartamysh, 209
Kasenivka, 160
Kasienovka, 184
Katchalinskaia, 91
Katerinovka, 201
Katukov, Col-Gen M. E., 11
Kazachia Lopan, 46-47
Kazachii Maidan, 48, 105, 134, 137
Kazakhstan, 11
Kegichevka, 48, 160
Kerch Peninsula, 29, 37, 40, 99, 122, 237, 240
Kharitonov, Maj-Gen F. M., 99, 149, 164-165, 171, 173, 175, 181, 187-188, 191, 197, 207, 222, 277

Kharkov, 17-18, 24-33, 36, 38, 42, 44, 46-47, 52, 59, 61, 64, 76-77, 79-89, 91-94, 97, 99,101-102, 105, 111, 120-123, 126-129, 132, 134, 139, 141, 143, 154-155, 160, 164, 169, 174, 179-181, 190-191, 201, 218, 220-221, 223-224, 227, 233-234, 237, 240-242, 244-245-247, 275
Kharkov River, 64, 117, 128, 154, 156
Kharziia, Sen-Lt V. K., 156
Kherson, 81
Kholodnoe, 65
Khomenko, Gen V. A., 101
Khoroshee, 167
Khrushchev, N. S., 12-13, 24, 27-28, 78, 168, 180-181, 190, 221-222, 225, 239-241, 255, 256, 260, 262, 265-272, 276-277
Kiev, 27, 42, 59, 77, 82, 84-85, 88, 97, 99, 109, 247
Kiev manoeuvres, (1935), 96-97, 101
Kiev operation (September 1941), 76, 79-81, 84-90, 94-95
Kiptivka, 48, 66
Kirichenko, Maj-Gen N. A., 94
Kirillovka, 48, 184
Kirovograd, 26-27
Kirponis, Col-Gen M. P., 77-79
Kiseli, 207, 209
Kleist, Field Marshal Ewald von, 18, 59, 76, 80, 95, 110, 139, 141, 160, 174, 180, 198, 205
Kliagin, Maj, 130
Klimenchuk, Lt-Col I. T., 86, 118-119, 179, 185, 278
Kniazevo, 210
Kniazhnoe,184
Kokhanovka, 137
Kolchak, Admiral A. V., 82, 95
Komarovka, 47, 52
Komsomol, 57, 114, 172
Konev, Marshal I. S., 12, 85
Konotop, 59, 61, 87-88
Konstantinovka, 156, 167
Kopanki, 171, 183-184
Korniets, Division Commissar L. P., 32
Kornitsa, T., 223
Korobochkino, 44
Korobov, 158
Korosten, 97
Korostovka, 165, 173
Korovino, 121
Korzhenovich, Maj-Gen E. K., 171, 219
Koshkin, Col A. M., 178, 204
Koshparovka, 48, 66
Kostenko, Lt-General F. Ia., 30, 78-79, 82-83, 89, 145, 190-191, 204, 209, 214, 219, 268
Kovalev, Col G. A., 93-94, 166, 173, 184, 187, 197, 205, 210
Kozlov, 177
Krainiukov, Division Commissar K. V., 149, 277
Kramatorsk, 167, 241
Krasnaia Alekseevka, 177
Krasnaia Balka, 202
Krasnaia Gusarovka, 204
Krasnaia Poliana, 41, 65
Krasnoarmeisk, 66, 165, 167, 223
Krasnoarmeiskaia 1-oe, 46
Krasnodar, 99-100
Krasnograd, 32, 42, 44, 48, 53, 64, 85, 92, 105, 136-137, 139, 160, 163, 174, 184, 190, 191
Krasnopavlovka, 201, 209-210
Krasnozorevka, 172
Krasnyi, 116, 124, 126, 130, 137, 153, 177
Krasnyi Gigant, 184
Krasnyi Liman, 41, 188, 197-198, 201, 217, 223
Kremenchug, 26-27, 53, 61, 84
Kremlin (Kreml), deception operation (June 1942), 35
Krikly, Capt I. I., 153-154
Krishtopovka, 66, 165, 223
Kriuchenkin, Maj-Gen V. D., 82, 130, 146, 278
Krivye Balki, 65
Krivoi Rog, 90
Krutoiarka, 66, 207, 209-210
Kuibyshevo (Kuibyshev), 43, 86
Kuimov, Sen-Lt P. D., 129
Kuleshchev, Maj-Gen A. D., 81, 117, 124, 128, 153, 278
Kune, 48, 66
Kupevskaia, 116
Kupiansk, 25, 41, 55, 89, 94, 99, 139, 158, 217
Kurilenko, Lt-Col I. V., 204
Kursk, 24, 27, 29, 37-38, 59, 61, 78, 82, 86, 88, 121, 132, 155, 244
Kurulka 1-aia, 172, 223
Kurulka 2-aia, 165
Kutaisi, 89

Kutlin, Maj-Gen Z. Iu., 92, 147, 163, 219
Kutso Gabebne, 137
Kuzmin, Maj-Gen G. I., 91, 136-137, 140, 148, 161, 174, 184, 188, 191, 197, 204, 219

Ladytskoe, 121, 155
Lagutin, Maj-Gen P. F., 88, 116, 123, 177
Laiok, Brigade Commissar V. M., 204
Lanz, Maj-Gen, 205
Lebedinka, 47
Leningrad, 17, 21, 29, 38, 59, 92, 100
Lepel, 86
Lgov, 24, 132
Ligovka, 136, 201, 204, 209
Likhachev, Maj V. M., 119
Lipets River, 154, 156
Liptsy (Liptsi), 42, 44, 117, 121, 127, 129, 154, 194
Lisichansk, 173
Liuban, 29, 37
Livny, 89
Logovoi, 167
Lomza, 93
Lopan River, 64
Lozavskii, 184, 209-210
Lozovaia, 18, 40, 48, 66, 92, 160, 165, 169, 171, 197-198, 205, 207, 223
Lozovenka, 184, 205, 207, 209-210, 212, 214, 216
Lubny, 84
Luftwaffe, See Air Force, German
Lukashevka, 48
Lvov, 59, 79, 85, 88, 93

Mackensen, Col-Gen Eberhard von, 169, 181, 205, 210, 220
Madrid, 95
Maiaki, 61, 66, 105, 142, 164-165, 167-168, 221, 228
Maisoedovo (Miasoedovo), 61, 65, 132
Makeevka, 167
Malaia Eremovka, 188
Malaia Kamyshevakha, 181, 183
Maleev, Maj-Gen M. F., 82, 177
Malenkov, G. M., 180, 241
Malinovka, 197-198
Malinovsky, Lt-Gen R. Ia., 32-33, 95-96, 164, 168, 171, 173, 179, 222-224, 262, 276
Maloe Prohkody, 117
Malo-Iablonovo, 44
Malyi Razdol, 173, 223
Malyshev, Lt-Col M. I., 82, 116, 124, 130
Mamontov, Maj V. A., 127
Manchuria, 101
Mankovo, 47
Manstein, Field Marshal Erich von, 11
Marevka, 134, 197, 201-202, 205
Margaritovka, 184-185
Marianov, Gen F. G., 183, 219
Marino, 41
Mariupol, 99
Martovaia, 47, 217
Maslovo Pristan, 44, 61, 105, 124, 143
Matveev, Col M. I., 81, 127, 155, 158, 175, 179, 187
Matveevka, 87
Matykin, Maj-Gen F. P., 89, 132, 148, 158, 204, 219
Mechebilovka, 48, 66, 166, 173, 197
Medvedovka, 44, 136, 161
Melitopol, 92, 98
Mellenthin, Maj-Gen F. W., 11
Merefa, 47, 64, 134, 142, 161, 185, 190
Mikhailovka, 136, 184, 198, 204-205, 209-210, 212
Mikhailovka 1-aia, 47, 126, 130
Military District, Soviet
   Arkhangelsk, 80
   Baltic, 276-278
   Baltic Special, 75
   Baranovichi, 275
   Belorussian, 76, 93, 95, 275
   Carpathian, 277
   Central Asian, 89, 101
   Don, 278
   Eastern Siberia, 277
   Far Eastern, 276
   Kalinin, 87
   Kharkov, 84, 87-88, 90, 92, 96, 101
   Kiev Special, 75-79, 81, 84, 93, 95-97, 99
   Moscow, 13, 82, 86-87, 91, 95-96, 99-100, 224, 277
   North Caucasus, 77, 82, 90-91, 94-96, 98-101, 278
   Odessa, 85, 92-94-95, 98-99, 101
   Orel, 82-83, 85-86

Index

Southern Ural, 275
Stalingrad, 90, 94
Trans-Baikal-Amur, 276
Transcaucasian, 82, 87, 89, 98, 277
Ukrainian, 81, 93
Ural, 81
Volga, 86-89, 277
Western Special, 75, 98
White Sea, 88
Minsk, 59
Miroliubovka, 165, 173, 212
Mironovka, 43-44, 105, 132, 134, 209-210
Mishchenko, Col A. A., 90, 136, 184
Mishin, Col I. P., 117, 154
Mitschurinsk, 86
Mius River, 18, 38, 43, 76, 94-97, 105, 220
Mobile group, concept of, 52
Molochnyi, 197
Molodovoe, 65
Molotov, V. I., 240
Mongolia, 101
Morokhovets, 156, 177, 194
Moscow, 17-19, 22, 24-28, 30-31, 35, 40, 59, 61, 77, 79, 85, 89, 93-95, 101, 109, 190, 224, 240, 242, 276
Moscow operation (December 1941-April 1942), 17, 37, 70
Moskalenko, Lt-Gen K. S., 13, 24-28, 31, 34-36, 83-85, 92, 114, 118, 120, 122-123, 126-127, 130, 143, 147, 155, 158, 175, 177-179, 185, 187, 191-192, 201-202, 204-205, 207, 212, 216, 242, 244, 247, 277-278
Mozharka, 163
Murmansk, 88
Murom, 44, 46, 123-124, 128, 130, 143, 175, 177, 192, 194
Murom River, 128, 130, 154, 156
Muzychenko, Lt-Gen I. N., 88
Mzha River, 64, 184-185

Nadezhdino, 198
Nadezhdovka, 166, 173, 201, 205
Nakichevan, 87
Naumenko, Maj-Gen Iu. A., 94, 149, 158, 178, 181, 185, 188, 197, 278
Nechaevka, 143, 175, 177
Nedostupovka, 46
Nekhoteevka, 124
Nepoktytaia, 44, 117, 119, 121, 126, 128, 130, 143, 153, 158, 175, 179, 185
Neskuchnoe, 128, 155-156, 194
Nezhegol, 46
Nikolaev, 27, 81, 98-99
Nikolaevka, 158, 204
Nikolskoe, 165
Nikopol, 90, 97, 165
Nizhne-Russkii Bishkin, 41, 61, 65, 94
Nizhniaia Plesovaia, 66, 209
Nizhnii Olshanets, 130
Nizhnii Orel, 134
NKVD (Peoples' Commissariat of Internal Affairs), 13, 90, 103, 277
Northern Donets River, 15, 18, 24, 26, 32-33, 36, 38, 40, 43-44, 46-47, 55-56, 58, 61, 64-65, 76, 78, 88-90, 95, 116, 122-123, 128, 158, 165-166, 171-172, 174, 178, 181, 183-184,187-188, 191-192, 198, 201-202, 204-205, 207, 212, 214, 216-217, 219-221, 225-226-227, 233, 235
Noskov, Maj-Gen A. A., 92-93, 134, 136-137, 158, 161, 174, 184-185, 191, 209-210, 212
Novaia Derevnia, 155, 192
Novaia Tavolzhanka, 116, 217
Novaia Vodolaga, 47, 174
Novgorod, 38
Novo-Aleksanderovka, 126
Novo-Bakhmetevo, 223
Novo-Beretskii, 137, 161
Novocherkassk, 42, 57
Novo-Dmitrovka, 185
Novo-Iakovlevka, 223
Novokamyshevakha, 183
Novolvovka, 137
Novo-Nikolaevka (Novonikolaevka), 66, 188, 197, 201
Novopavlovka, 66, 165, 202, 223
Novo-Prigozhaia, 173, 184, 191
Novorossiisk, 100
Novo-Semenovka, 134, 137, 161, 197
Novo-Ukrainka, 210
Novo-Vladimirovka, 41
Novopavlovka, 66, 223
Novo-Uplatnoe, 204

Nurov, 48
Nurovo, 48

Oboian, 155
Odanetskii, 198
Odessa, 76, 95
Ogievka, 184
Ogurtsovo, 116, 121
Okhochae, 158, 160-161, 201, 209
Oktiabrskoe, 46
Olkhovatka, 47
Orel, 37-38
Orel River, 44, 64, 134, 136, 207
Orenburg, 80
Osintsev, Maj P. F., 119
Osipenko, 105
Oskol River, 58, 217, 225, 247
Oskol Station, 217
Ostrogoshzk, 83
Ostroverkhovka, 47, 52

Panteleeva Balka, 205, 209
Paraskovaia, 161, 174, 204
Paraskoveevka, 209
Par-Shliakovaia, 136
Paulus, Col-Gen Friedrich, 108, 121, 123, 142, 150, 160, 198
Pavlograd, 93
Pavlov, Lt-Gen D. G., 77
Pavlovka, 44, 48, 136, 184, 210
Pechenegi, 24, 43, 46-48, 105, 201
Peremysl, 98
Peremoga, 105, 116-117, 121-122, 124, 126, 128, 130, 143, 155, 177
Pervomaisk, 27
Peschanoe, 43, 65, 105, 118-121, 127-128, 130, 153, 158, 179
Peski, 171
Pesochin, Col M. A., 90, 132-133, 136, 158, 209
Petrenko, Maj V. A., 117
Petrograd, 96
Petropavlovka, 167
Petropole, 188, 197
Petrovka, 42, 46, 66, 106, 165, 167
Petrovskaia, 166, 183, 188, 191, 197, 201, 217
Petrovskii, 66
Petrovskoe, 44, 46, 124, 126, 128-129, 143, 155, 175, 179, 193, 221
Piatitskoe, 47, 57, 65, 120
Piatnitsa, 124, 193
Pimenov, Col F. A., 84-85, 118-120, 127, 179
Pisarevka, 56, 204, 209
Pliev, Maj-Gen I. A., 100-101, 149, 165, 172-173, 181, 183, 185, 187, 278
Podlas, Lt-Gen K. P., 96-97, 150, 164-165, 171, 173, 178, 183, 185, 219
Pokrovskoe, 105
Polish War (1920), 97
Poltava, 27, 42, 48, 53, 61, 77, 85, 87-88, 142, 160
Popenko, Brigade Commissar A. I., 183, 219
Poserednoe, 46
Prigozhnaia, 184
Priutovka, 121, 124
Priluki, 101
Pripiat River, 59
Prishib, 172, 188, 197
Pristan (Pristen), 46, 65
Privole, 48, 121-122, 126, 209
Proletarskii, 205
Proskurov, 83, 99
Protopopovka, 188, 191, 193, 198, 201-202, 207
Prut River, 95, 98
Pselets, 105
Pukhov, Lt-Gen N. P., 89
Pushkin, Maj-Gen E. G., 91, 136-137, 141, 148, 161, 174, 178, 184, 188, 191, 209, 214, 278
Pylnaia, 130, 177

Radkovskie Peski, 173, 178
Raigorodok, 167
Rakitnoe, 47, 52, 209
Razdole, 212
Regiments, German
  infantry, general, 106
  motorised infantry, 107
  panzer, 107
  131st Infantry, 122, 126
  172nd Infantry, 127

191st Infantry, 122, 126, 175
194th Infantry, 122
208th Infantry, 134
211th Infantry, 116-117, 122, 126
260th Infantry, 136-137
268th Infantry, 137
375th Infantry, 134
429th Infantry, 117, 128
477th Infantry, 173
513th Infantry, 116-117
522nd Infantry, 121
610th Infantry, 134
126th Motorized, 116
2nd Panzer, 181
Regiments, Hungarian
  38th Infantry (Light), 134
Regiments, Soviet
  artillery, 74-75
  heavy artillery, 75
  light artillery, 75
  rocket artillery (katiushas), 75
  582d Anti-tank Artillery, 91
  591st Anti-tank Artillery, 91
  738th Anti-tank Artillery, 86
  764th Anti-tank Artillery, 83
  46th Artillery, 127
  51st Artillery, 86
  135th Artillery, 88
  156th Artillery, 88
  214th Artillery, 118
  233rd Artillery, 116
  307th Artillery, 156
  648th Artillery, 86
  879th Artillery, 172
  872nd Cannon Artillery, 93
  19th Cavalry (Manych), 79
  138th Cavalry, 183
  7th Guards Artillery, 116
  32nd Guards Artillery, 130, 154
  4th Guards Heavy Artillery, 223
  4th Guards Mortar, 86
  5th Guards Mortar, 86, 91
  51st Guards Mortar, 116
  34th Guards Rifle, 116-117, 124, 126, 129
  39th Guards Rifle, 116-117, 124, 126, 130, 278
  42nd Guards Rifle, 116, 124, 126, 129, 153-154
  8th Gun Artillery, 91
  116th Gun Artillery, 91
  209th Gun Artillery, 91
  266th Gun Artillery, 83
  269th Gun Artillery, 91
  375th Gun Artillery, 91
  399th Gun Artillery, 91
  435th Gun Artillery, 91
  29th Heavy Artillery, 93
  229th Heavy artillery, 223
  236th Heavy Artillery, 93
  437th Heavy Artillery, 223
  476th Heavy Artillery, 223
  538th Heavy Artillery, 88
  574th Heavy Artillery, 86
  671st Howitzer Artillery, 91
  870th Howitzer Artillery, 83
  186th Light Artillery, 223
  338th Light Artillery, 88
  468th Light Artillery, 86
  507th Light Artillery, 86
  558th Light Artillery, 223
  685th Light Artillery, 223
  754th Light Artillery, 223
  29th Rifle, 129, 155
  48th Rifle, 129, 155
  240th Rifle (Tver), 95
  246th Rifle, 95
  252d Rifle, 198
  343rd Rifle, 118, 124
  348th Rifle, 183
  434th Rifle, 117, 154, 156
  442nd Rifle, 171
  556th Rifle, 117-118, 124, 129, 154
  622nd Rifle, 127
  680th Rifle, 117-118, 124, 128, 154
  781st Rifle, 119, 127
  985th Rifle, 119
  1116th Rifle, 119
  1118th Rifle, 165, 171-172
  1120th Rifle, 165

287

Reichenau, Gen Walther, 109
Reserve of the High Command (RVK), 41-42, 47, 50-51, 57-58, 74, 87, 90, 92-93, 111, 158, 165, 179, 191
Riabyshev, Lt-Gen D. I., 80, 84, 116-118, 120, 123-124, 126, 128, 143, 146, 155, 175, 177-179, 185, 192, 277
Riadnovka, 116, 184
Riadukhino, 184
Richtofen, Gen Wolfram Freiherr von, 128
Rodimtsev, Maj-Gen A. I., 80-81, 116-120, 124, 126, 128-130, 146, 153-154, 278
Rogachev, 87
Rogachevka, 116
Rogachevsky, Maj-Gen S. M., 81, 117-118, 124, 128, 146, 154, 156, 175, 187
Rogan, 47
Rokossovsky, Marshal K. K., 76, 82-83, 92, 149
Roosevelt, Franklin, D., 240
Roslavl, 80
Rosokhovatoe, 137
Rostov, 59, 137
Rostov (on the Don), 17-18, 21, 24, 33, 43-44, 61, 70, 76-80, 83, 90, 94-99, 101, 104, 110, 166, 223, 227-228
Rovenka, 223
Rozhdestvenskoe, 48, 66, 197-198
Rubezhnoe, 55, 117, 128
Rudaevka, 201, 205
Rukhle, Col I. N., 242
Russkie Tishki, 42
Rybakova, 197
Rybkhoz, 165
Rzhavets, 121
Rzhev, 38

Sabinino, 44
Sakhnovshchina, 48, 106, 160, 163, 191
Sakovich, Col L.N., 93
Samara River, 64
Samarkand, 89
Samchuk, Lt-Col I. A., 278
Samoilovka, 41
Saratov, 88, 100
Savintsy, 48, 56, 177-178, 204-205, 207, 209, 212, 216, 221, 227, 236
School for Red Army Commanders, 84
Semenovka, 137, 197-198
Sereda, 46-47
Seredovka, 46, 48
Serefimovka, 198
Sevastopol, 29, 37, 40, 237
Shagin, Col A. I., 172, 188, 210
Shakhty, 42, 57
Shakovo, 41
Shandrovka, 42
Shaposhnikov, Gen B. M., 22, 24-25, 27-28, 31, 76, 145
Shatovo, 166, 173
Shchegrenev, Sen-Lt I. G., 154
Shchurovo, 223
Shchurovka, 65, 204, 217
Shebekino, 41
Shebelinka, 48, 204, 207
Shepetov, Maj-Gen I. M., 97, 150, 219
Sherstiuk, Maj-Gen G. I., 147, 204, 210, 212
Shestakov, Capt M. D., 119
Shevchenki, 46
Shevchenko, 134
Shevchenkovo 1-oe, 55
Shevelevka, 202
Shliakovaia, 136
Shliakovo, 46
Shurino, 174, 184
Silnov, Col A. P., 132
Sinelnikovo, 30
Skuba, Lt-Col M.K., 82, 127, 175
Slaviansk, 32, 36, 40, 43, 64, 66, 87, 93, 97-98, 121, 141-142, 166-167, 169, 171, 223
Smirnov, Col N. P., 94
Smirnov, Col V. S., 85
Smirnovka, 198, 201
Smolensk, 24-25, 59, 77, 80, 85-86, 89, 101, 109
Sobolevka, 167
Sofievka, 48, 66, 165
Solenyi, 172
Solotnoshcha, 86
Sovetskii, 209
Spanish Civil War, 80, 95-96
Spartak, 44, 46, 65
Squadrons, German

55th Bomber, 156
76th Bomber, 156
3rd Fighter, 156
Srednyi, 197
Stalin, I. V., 13, 15, 17-18, 21-22, 24-29, 31, 35, 37-38, 56, 61, 75-78, 114, 139, 180-181, 190, 221-222, 224-226, 239-241, 246-247, 255, 264-266, 275-277
Stalingrad, 21, 59, 82, 86, 90-91, 96, 217, 239
Stalino, 167, 220
Staraia, Bliznitsy, 171
Staritsa, 43, 61, 81, 116, 120
Starobelsk, 41, 48, 57, 69
Staro Konstantinov, 99
Staroverovka, 174
Starye Bliznetsy, 66, 165, 173
Staryi Oskol, 55, 82, 88
Staryi Saltov, 24, 30-32, 47, 56, 58, 61, 64, 81-82, 84-85, 88, 92, 120, 122, 126-127, 129, 130, 226
State Defence Committee (GKO), 76
Stavka, See Supreme High Command
Stavka Order No 03 (10 January 1942), 75
Stavropol, 94
Stepanovka, 167, 172, 181
Studenok, 181, 183-185, 188, 191, 197-198, 207
Sukhaia Gomolsha River, 158
Sukhoi Iar, 66
Sukhoi Torets River, 172, 181, 185
Sumy, 88, 97
Supreme High Command (Stavka Verkhovnogo Glavnokomandovaniia or Stavka VGK), 15, 17-19, 22, 24-35, 37-38, 44, 49-51-52, 69-70, 75-78, 80, 85-87, 89, 91, 95-96, 102, 132, 139, 178-180, 185, 190, 202, 204, 221-222, 224-226, 228, 231-232, 237, 239-242, 244, 246, 252, 255, 262, 264-266, 270, 276
Svatovo, 41, 57
Sverdlov, Col F D., 246
Sverdlovsk, 42
Sverkhniaia Ilichevka, 172
Sverkhn. Shamino, 130, 177
Sverkhnyi Kommunist, 175, 204
Sviatogorsk (Sviatogorskaia), 92, 185
Sviatushino, 210
Svir River, 29

Taganrog, 26, 41, 43, 98, 105
Tamaschishin, Col T. I., 86, 118-119, 126, 147, 179, 187, 278
Taranovka, 42, 44, 47, 64, 121, 123, 137, 160-161, 174, 201
Tarasovka, 48
Tashkent, 101
Tavantsev, Col A. A., 90, 126-127, 134, 136, 161, 179, 184, 209, 214
Ter-Gasparion, Col G. A., 87, 116, 123, 130, 146
Ternovaia, 43, 117, 120, 123-124, 128-130, 140, 143, 153, 155-156, 175, 177-179, 187, 192, 194, 233
Ternovoe, 46-47, 118, 143
Tichoresk, 94
Tikhopole, 205
Timoshenko, Marshal S. K., 24-34, 44, 61, 66, 75-80, 85, 87, 91-94, 96-97, 120-123, 126-128, 132, 139-141, 143, 145, 155, 158, 161, 164, 168, 173, 175, 177-181, 184-185, 187-188, 190-194, 198, 201-202, 204-205, 207, 209, 212, 216-217, 221-223, 225, 237, 239, 241, 246-247, 255-256, 261-262, 265-272, 275
Tiraspol, 98
Titovka, 46
Tiuman, 81
Trochatyi Station, 136
Trofimenko, Battalion Commissar A. I., 129
Tsaritsyn, 76
Tsaroderovka (Tsaredorovka) (Tseredarovka), 48, 66, 165, 204-205, 223
'Typhoon', Operation (November-December 1941), 109

Udarnik, 204
Udy River, 64, 143
Ukraine, 59, 76, 78-80, 83, 87, 93-95, 97, 101, 110, 121
Ulan Bator, 101
Ulianovka, 134, 137
Uman Operation (September 1941), 76, 82, 84-85, 88, 95, 97-99, 101
Uplatnoe, 205
Ural Mountains, 40
Ustinka, 156

Valuiki, 55
Varvarovka, 105-106, 116, 121, 124
Vasilev, Maj-Gen I. V., 90, 148, 204, 219

Vasilevsky, Army-Gen A. M., 22, 24-25, 27-29, 31, 139, 145, 180, 183, 190, 222, 240, 244, 267-268, 276-277
Velikaia Bereka, 44, 47, 134, 136-137
Velikaia Kamyshevakha, 48, 181, 188, 197
Veliki Burlik, 46
Veliki Luki, 101
Velikoe Pole, 167
Vergolevka, 130, 177, 194
Verkhniaia Bereka, 52, 132, 140
Verkhniaia Plesovaia, 209
Verkhnyi Bishkin (Verkhnii Bishkin), 44, 47, 65, 90, 105, 132, 134, 136-137, 209
Verkhnyi Saltov, 122, 128, 179
Vernopole, 197
Vero-Nikolaevka, 207
Vershinin, Maj-Gen, 223
Veselaia, 205
Veseloe, 44, 46-47, 127-130, 153-156, 175, 177-179, 187, 192, 201
Veshenskaia, 48
Vetoshnikov, Maj-Gen L. V., 168
Vetrovka, 217
Viazma, 29, 38, 81, 85
Viazma operation (October 1941), 81-82, 89-90, 98-99
Vikhrovka, 44, 217
Vikino, 171, 191
Viktorovka, 167
Vinnitsa, 97, 99
Vishnevyi, 106
Vitebsk, 85, 101
Vladimirov, Col V. Ia., 77
Vladivostok, 95
Vlasov, Maj-Gen A. A., 97
Vlasovka, 174
Vodianoi, 167
Volchansk, 36, 41, 44, 55, 90, 122, 198
Volga River, 40, 59, 239, 247
Volkhov Iar, 43, 158, 191, 204
Volkogonov, D., 241
Volobuevka, 202, 214, 216
Volokhovka, 65
Volokonovka, 46
Voloskaia Balakleika, 66, 128
Volvenkovo, 214, 216
Voronezh, 32, 48, 51, 59, 85, 97
Voronin, Col G. G., 87, 116, 123
Voroshilov, Marshal K. E., 77
Voroshilov Academy of the General Staff, 78-79, 96, 99, 276
Voroshilovgrad, 33, 42-43-44, 94, 104, 166, 178, 222-224, 227-228
Voroshilovka, 137
Voroshilovsk, 94
Vvedenskoe, 47
Vysokaia Iaruga, 46
Vysokii Poselok, 209
Vysokii, 46, 124, 165, 184
Vystrel School, 89, 96, 99

Weissenburg, 219

Zagorodnoe, 191, 197-198, 201-202
Zagryzova, 47
Zaitsev, Col G. M., 130, 156
Zakharovka, 46
Zapadenka, 137, 161
Zapolnyi, 202
Zaporozhe, 85, 92, 156
Zarozhnoe, 44, 47, 121-122, 126
Zavodskaia, 188
Zavodskoi, 197
Zelenyi Gai, 209
Zelenyi Ugolok, 174
Zheltye Zori, 205
Zhitomir, 87
Zhmerinka, 97
Zhukov, Marshal G. K., 12, 17, 22, 24, 27, 29, 31, 76, 78-79, 92-93, 145, 225, 240-241, 244, 276
Zhukovka, 217
Zhuravlevka, 46
Ziborovka, 143, 175, 177
Ziemke, Earle, 36, 142, 198
Zmiev, 42, 44, 46-47, 64, 134, 174, 184, 188, 191, 204, 234
Zolotivka, 188
Zusmanovich, Maj-Gen A. G., 148, 219